Ancient Spirit Rising is the recipient of a 2017 Next Generation Indie Book Award in the Current Events/Social Change category! The awards are issued by the Independent Book Publishing Professionals Group (IBPPG), an exciting and prestigious book awards program open to independent publishers and authors worldwide. Next Generation awards are given to the "most exceptional" independently published books. A complete list of the 2017 winners is available on the Next Generation Indie Book Awards website at www.indiebookawards.com.

Praise For
Ancient Spirit Rising: Reclaiming
Your Roots & Restoring Earth Community

Ancient Spirit Rising is an excellent example of the generative and life-affirming possibilities that are created when Indigenous peoples of reputable practice are sincerely listened to, and when Settlers are genuinely oriented towards developing their own earth-based spiritual practices on Turtle Island. It is a timely and much-needed articulation of critical Settler thought, and I hope it contributes in positive ways for generating good life for all humans and the natural world, and encourages a commitment to engaging in reparations with Indigenous peoples in spheres beyond the spiritual.

Waaseyaa'sin Christine Sy (Anishnaabe), Assistant Professor,
Gender Studies, University of Victoria ~ https://giizismoon.wordpress.com

If humans are to survive on Earth, we urgently need to reconnect with the earth-friendly lifeways of our ancestors and become "indigenous" again to our bioregions. Especially for those of us long separated from ancestral homelands and planet-friendly spiritual guidance, Pegi's marvelous new book Ancient Spirit Rising is the practical guide we've been waiting for.

Linda Buzzell-Saltzman, MA, LMFT, Psychotherapist, Ecotherapist, Author, Educator,
Co-editor of "Ecotherapy: Healing with Nature in Mind" ~ Sierra Club Books

Ancient Spirit Rising kick-starts the conversation that First Nations and Settlers need to be having........

Linda Post (Odawa), Filmmaker, Author of "Ojibway Drive from Crumpled Sheets"
Enaajmotaaged Publishing

Pegi's voice is fundamental to understanding what it means to find your ancestral connection. Ancient Spirit Rising is changing my understanding of so many things. A must read! Thank you Pegi, for all the research you have done and your sharing of so many truths.

Barb Phillips, Thanadoula and Educator
Whispering Pines Studios ~ www.barbphillips.ca

In a globalized society predicated on forgetting and displacement, **Ancient Spirit Rising** is a bold reminder that our modern lives are still a chapter of an old, enchanting story whose final pages are yet to be written. Pegi Eyers does not flinch in facing down the complexities of our current global crises of identity, ecology, and essential meaning. Rooted in a deep respect for the many threads woven into the realities of 21st century planet Earth, this book fearlessly strikes a chord and bursts into a song that is willing to guide even the utterly lost through a night whose day is long overdue.

C.B. Ó Corcráin, Producer of the film "Occupied Cascadia"
https://milegaiscioch.wordpress.com ~ https://thegoldrust.bandcamp.com

Ancient Spirit Rising is a fearless and radical call to action. In this bold work, author Pegi Eyers challenges us to approach, with deep humility and respect, the complex issues of cultural identity, privilege, and ecology. Her book is a valuable contribution to some difficult, but necessary, conversations, ultimately aimed at fostering positive social change, equity, and peace.

Chloé McFeters, Director of the film "You Look a Lot Like Me"
www.youlookalotlikeme.com

When so many of us are looking for ways to be in right-sized relationship with the land, right relationship with the First Peoples who have been here forever, and to do right by our own Ancestors, Pegi's book offers us much insight on how we can lovingly move forward. **Ancient Spirit Rising** offers righteous critique of the dominant-Empire-culture and pathways through and beyond, toward an inter-connected cosmology, re-enchanting to our own ancestral visions. I am deeply grateful for Pegi and her work.

byron ~ writer, musician, radio producer and host of
"To Know the Land" CFRU 93.3FM Guelph ~ www.cfru.ca

I am so very appreciative that I have read **Ancient Spirit Rising**. Many times as I moved through the book, I kept saying to myself - this is another good section! I wish that all non-native people who are lost and confused about their spirituality (through no fault of their own) could read and reflect on what Pegi is saying. There is a way for non-native people to heal and connect to our Mother Earth and Creation, without having to appropriate from First Nations ways and teachings.

Alice Olsen Williams (Anishnaabe), Pimaatisiwin Quilts ~ www.pimaatisiwin-quilts.com

I found **Ancient Spirit Rising** to be a fascinating read with a volume of information, including amazing footnotes and quotations. Pegi Eyers reminds us that becoming aware of First Nations traditions brings us closer to the earth spirituality that was lost in our own white culture, and opens the door to learning about our own European Indigenous Knowledge.

Kris Steinnes, Founder and Co-leader at Women of Wisdom (WOW) Foundation,
Host of "Voices of Women" radio show, and Owner of Krysalis Leadership
www.womenofwisdom.org

Can we be honest about our ancestral past? Can we have a truthful conversation about the stolen treasures and cultures of virtually every Indigenous society as a result of a small minority group that has thrived on exploitation, violence, and greed? Pegi Eyers presents these conversations and personal observations with a clarity and depth that allows the reader to see the truth not found in traditional history. Once we acknowledge the past for what is truly was, we can begin to rebuild an authentic society based on our own Indigenous values - not someone else's.

Dawn James, Educator, Author of "Raise Your Vibration, Transform Your Life"
www.raisethevibration.ca

CBC Radio

THE NEXT CHAPTER

Ancient Spirit Rising: Reclaiming Your Roots & Restoring Earth Community by award-winning author Pegi Eyers is an amazing read. This book makes me want to be a better human being, and to answer the question, "Am I who my Ancestors worked so hard for me to be?" with a resounding YES! *Ancient Spirit Rising* is a fine guide for this process, a book for our troubled times, and a balm for the reader. Thank you Pegi Eyers for *Ancient Spirit Rising* - hands raised to you!

Shelagh Rogers, Broadcast-Journalist, "The Next Chapter" CBC Radio, TRC Honorary Witness, Officer of the Order of Canada, Chancellor of the University of Victoria

Ancient Spirit Rising is a very significant book for our time. It challenges current trends toward borrowing Indigenous Knowledge, a tendency that further precipitates intrusion on Indigenous people. Pegi Eyers lays out her case against colonial thinking, and given the numbers of white people re-creating sweat lodges etc. she challenges these behaviors, and asks why people are not cultivating their own Indigenous roots. Why not learn more about the European IK (EIK) traditions of Nordic and Celtic paganism, as well as a host of others from Nordic, Russian or Siberian lands? Eyers discusses the current quest toward ancient ways of reverencing, ancestral practices and re-connecting with the Earth, and asks readers to replace colonial thinking with practices related to one's own history. *Ancient Spirit Rising* is an important and timely read, and I recommend keeping it as a resource for further exploration. Pegi Eyers has gone to great depths to present her thesis, and it is well thought out, well-written and referenced. And most importantly, *Ancient Spirit Rising* presents significant issues for the era in which we are living - a time in which all of humanity is confronted by tremendous change.

Sharon G. Mijares, PhD, Educator, Author, Editor of "Modern Psychology and Ancient Wisdom: Psychological Healing Practices from the World's Religious Traditions" www.psychospiritual.org

Ancient Spirit Rising is a powerful and well-researched voice that advocates ending the erasure of Indigenous peoples through cultural appropriation. Indeed, Pegi Eyers encourages all who are non-native to explore their own Indigenous roots, be they Celtic, Nordic, or other. The end goal is to recover a close and essential connection to Mother Earth, and Eyers offers strategies for rewilding our thinking to create a sustainable future and re-land local community in peaceful co-existence. *Ancient Spirit Rising* is an important contribution to our discussion on racism and ethnic identity. Much can be done to rectify injustices - both past and, shockingly, present - and with the alternatives as offered by *Ancient Spirit Rising*, Pegi Eyers gives us much to contemplate.

Diane Taylor, Educator, Author of "The Gift of Memoir: Show Up, Open Up, Write" https://dianemtaylor.com

Ancient Spirit Rising is a timely Canadian contribution to the growing field of critical white theory, which is dominated by the American experience of race, racism, and white privilege. I believe that many white Canadians are looking for a deeper understanding of their own complex histories and identities, and Pegi's extensive research and urgent call to action provides us with much to think about. A very rewarding read for anyone concerned about justice, and our ability to live in harmony with our environment!

Debbie Harrison, Human Rights Educator, Coordinator of Diversity, Accessibility & International Student Support, Fleming College http://ruralantiracistwhite.blogspot.ca

Ancient Spirit Rising helps begin the conversation on how to heal the European North American soul. Pegi Eyers bravely challenges some Neo-Pagan "orthodoxies" but highlights as well the path toward regaining our own ancestral traditions, to live accordingly in this world.

Daniel J. Miess, Professor, English Department,
Chapman University ~ Poet, Author and Editor

Pegi Eyers is an organic intellectual. Her wide reading and first-hand experience in First Nations community for which she is an articulate advocate, makes her work original, accessible and important at this time in Canadian history. No more borrowing of cultural identity! **Ancient Spirit Rising** *is an excellent guide for discovering our own ancestral roots.*

Rosemary Ganley, Journalist, Activist, Founder of Jamaican Self-Help
www.yellowdragonflypress.ca

Ancient Spirit Rising *is a monumental work addressing the ever-evolving cultural relationship between the traditional Indigenous people of Turtle Island and their Eurocentric political dominators, a situation which demands immediate redress.*

Suzanne Stratton ~ Homestead Publishing

For white women in the Americas who are drawn to the Goddess Path, few boundaries exist in our search for spiritual expression. But we need to acknowledge that our adoption of indigenous or shamanic identities and the practice of "Native Spirituality" may in fact harm and demean the very groups we profess to admire. In **Ancient Spirit Rising**, *Pegi Eyers lays out clearly the difference between cultural appropriation and cultural exchange, and how we can do better. In fact, our pursuit of authentic practice rooted in our own ancient pre-colonial heritage(s) may be an effective way to undo the internalized imperialism and patriarchal homogenization in ourselves and others.* **Ancient Spirit Rising** *is an in-depth guide to reclaiming our root cultures (including Old Europe), and rejuvenating an earth-connected worldview that reflects our interconnectivity with all life.*

Karen Tate, Author of "Walking An Ancient Path: Rebirthing Goddess on Planet Earth"
www.karentate.net

A deeply considered and broadly researched collection of inspirations, **Ancient Spirit Rising** *is a definitive statement on the social, spiritual and ecological havoc colonialism and the appropriation of Indigenous cultures has wreaked. Pegi Eyers "Unsettles the Settler Mentality" and brings us into the light of what consumptive "progress and frontierism at all costs" has done to affect our psycho-social and planetary environments. She reminds us that we are all Indigenous to the Earth, and shares soulful and centered ways to live a life of Earth-honoring, eco-spiritual activism and deep ecology - if only we will. Thank you Pegi Eyers.*

Marcie Telander, Founding Director, Earth Wisdom Institute Mystery School
www.marcietelander.com

Ancient Spirit Rising *is a work of genius, uncompromising in its presentation of many viewpoints and supported by extensive documentation. The book is both encyclopedic in scope and focused on the central theme of earth-grounded spirituality, its multi-various roots, and how they manifest today. These studies form an essential part of the emerging consciousness that will sustain us in the predicament-resolving that we face. The book is valuable in helping us think through a viable and well-mannered approach to the Indigenous Knowledge of living successfully on the Earth. It also makes clear the need to support Indigenous people opposing the threats to their lands that are endangered by the imperial economy of exploitation.*

Philip Kienholz, Author of "Display: Poems" ~ New Roots Press

ANCIENT SPIRIT RISING

ABOUT THE AUTHOR

Artist, author and cultural visionary Pegi Eyers is occupied with challenging worldviews, contributing to the paradigm shift and working with the uncolonization process in herself and others. A Celtic Animist who sees the world through a spiritual lens, she is a devotee of nature-based culture and all that is sacred to the Earth. Pegi Eyers is an advocate for our interconnection with Earth Community and the recovery of authentic ancestral wisdom and traditions for all people. She lives in the countryside on the outskirts of Nogojiwanong in Michi Saagiig Nishnaabeg territory (Peterborough, Ontario, Canada) on a hilltop with views reaching for miles in all directions.

  www.facebook.com/pegi.eyers
www.facebook.com/AncientSpiritRising

See the author's BLOG for updates **www.stonecirclepress.com**
Pegi loves hearing from her readers! pegi-eyers@hotmail.com

Ancient Spirit Rising

Reclaiming Your Roots & Restoring Earth Community

PEGI EYERS

STONE CIRCLE PRESS

Otonabee, Ontario, Canada
www.stonecirclepress.com
stonecirclepress@zoho.com

Cover Design: Pegi Eyers
Interior Design: Pegi Eyers
Illustrations: Pegi Eyers & Robert Hood

Disclaimer: All statements are products of the author's imagination and are used in a fictitious
manner. Any resemblance to actual events or persons, living or deceased, is purely coincidental.

In accordance with the *Allyship* framework, wherever possible and by the extensive use of
references and quotations, I have made sure that First Nations activists, freedom fighters,
academics, authors, artists, journalists, cultural workers, feminists, thought leaders,
community leaders, community peoples, mentors, wisdom keepers and Elders speak first and
take priority. At the interface between First Nations and the Settler Society (and beyond my
central themes) any errors and shortcomings in this discourse are my own.

Library and Archives Canada Cataloguing in Publication

Eyers, Pegi
Ancient Spirit Rising: Reclaiming Your Roots & Restoring Earth Community

Includes Bibliographical References
Also issued in electronic format
First Published 2015
ISBN 978-0-9938345-1-6

In solidarity with the First Nations of Turtle Island, who continue to resist the genocide, colonization and oppression forced upon them by the flawed mega-experiment of Eurocentric Empire in the Americas. And dedicated to true human beings everywhere, who seek to bond with the land and practice their authentic Ancestral Wisdom.

 With love to my partner Robert "Green Man" Hood, who has made the writing of this book possible. My life with you is one of profound contentment and happiness, and I thank you more than words can say.

Ancient Spirit Rising

Reclaiming Your Roots & Restoring Earth Community

CONTENTS
∞

Part Two - Authentic Treasure

SOURCES CONSULTED

RESOURCES

The image on the cover of **Ancient Spirit Rising** honors the archaic tradition of lighting great beacon bonfires across the landscape or along the coast at festival times, to signal the gathering of the clans, to announce attack, or to mark other monumental happenings. Inherent to Celtic society and other European Indigenous traditions, a chain of great blazing fires speaks to our most primal need for celebration, community and connection. As the ancients would marvel at the passing of the great torch through space and time, carrying their hopes, dreams and sacred cultural markers, we can continue with the same sparks of wisdom today. May the rejuvenation of our spiritual ecology in *Earth Community* be the beacon that we light for all to follow!

PREFACE

Among other important messages, the First Nation Elders, academics, intellectuals, activists and freedom fighters of Turtle Island have come forth in our time to tell modern spiritual seekers that we need "to return to our own European ancestral wisdom and earth-rooted indigenity." This simple statement has massive ramifications, and exposes years of ingrained white privilege that has led to the cultural appropriation of native spirituality on a colossal scale. First Nations have endured genocide, colonial oppression, displacement and assimilation for centuries, and the least we can do as the white descendants of the Settler Society (or those more recently arrived to Turtle Island) is to listen deeply to this directive coming from Indian Country and all that it implies. We are being asked to examine what our own Indigenous Knowledge would look like to those of us of European descent who have been displaced from our traditional homelands for generations, and who have been accustomed to accessing any spiritual belief system we choose. "Ancient Spirit Rising" will identify the paradoxical need for critical thinking in spiritual practice, the requirement for an ethical code, and why it is important to stand tall in our own European ancestral traditions. Where and how will those of European descent find re-indigenized roots and a true eco-consciousness in our adopted landscape of Turtle Island? I will also examine the restoration of our ancestral traditions as a revolutionary act that defies the materialism and capitalism of hegemonic Empire. As diverse Indigenous societies and spiritual traditions are telling us, true knowledge is gained by thinking with both the head and the heart - a journey of emotion as informed by the mind - and my research and "Ancient Spirit Rising" reflections will be tempered by my true heart's knowing, and the personal agency of that expression. Please join me on this exciting journey of personal and collective revitalization!

INTRODUCTION

"Everyone needs to get back to their own IK."
Onaubinisay (Walks Above the Ground) / James Dumont
Anishnaabe Elder and Traditional Teacher,
5th Degree - Three Fires Midewiwin Lodge

Why is it that for the modern non-native spiritual practitioner who aspires to connect with nature the symbols of the sacred automatically become the smudge, the dreamcatcher, the headdress, the bone choker, the talking stick and the tipi? Who gave us permission to use these objects and symbols, and where are our own sacred expressions and tools as European people? I would suggest that a truly radical act in defiance to the hegemony that Empire[1] has created, is to let go of our polyglot approach and focus on our own ancestral-sourced indigenity. In the process of becoming the most dominant society on earth, as Eurocentric people we traded away our place in the web of life, abandoned our eco-ethics, and surrendered our bond to the Earth and the sanity that it brings. Today, in an era of massive change, the highest denunciation of patriarchal Empire and colonial values would be to recover a tribal worldview connected to the Earth, followed by developing a sense of the sacred specific to the roots of our ethnicity. As earth-connected peoples secure in our own Indigenous Knowledge (IK[2] ~ or possibly said European Indigenous Knowledge ~ EIK) we could better contribute to the rebalancing of society, and the active "12th hour" shift in worldview that needs to happen for our species to survive.

The benefits, amenities and instant gratifications of industrial civilization have acted as a soothing soporific that has put us all to sleep. No one questions the vacuity of our modern homogenous culture or our disconnected heritage as displaced Europeans, and after ten or more generations of denying earth-connected life in favor of ecocide and industry on Turtle Island, we are certain that our own Euro-Indigenous Knowledge (EIK) as i.e. Gaelic, Baltic or Nordic people does not exist, cannot be accessed, and cannot be recovered. Any suggestion that as the descendants of the European colonial project (or diaspora) we would have to remount our own ancestral earth-centered worldview(s), is met with ridicule, disdain and utter disbelief. We have been coming in droves to the Americas since the landfall of Columbus in 1492, and there has been too much chaos, war, famine, ethnic cleansing, diaspora, emigration, inverted identity, regeneration, civilization building, nationalism, hierarchy, economic growth, spiritual reductionism, technology, Hollywood blockbusters and pop culture for us ever to imagine that we were once tribal peoples. The trail has grown very cold, but the good news is that ancient fragments and contemporary reconstructions of our own tribal societies do exist, and with time, focus, scholarly inquiry, dream archaeology, soul retrieval (or whatever it takes) there is much potential to reconvene our ancestral earth-wise wisdom and join those at the leading edge.

We are entitled through white privilege to imitate, assume or borrow the spiritual traditions of any culture, without asking if those people would approve or give us permission for that enjoyment, and our personal growth, or "liberation," comes at their expense. White privilege bestows on us total access, and to all appearances we have been thriving on a cultural and spiritual banquet of multi-ethnic practices, symbols, objects and belief systems, unrestrained in their exotic diversity and extravagance. Yet, we have to wonder if our dilettante attraction to the "other" and our indulgence at the spiritual feast can ever completely ring true, satisfy us, or fill the void, as evidenced by the diverse and endless outpouring of self-help practitioners, ideologies, books, courses, workshops, conferences, oracles and esoteric tools. The unrestrained consumption of diversified spiritual products made possible by *New Age Capitalism* has taken away our critical thinking process and our ability to focus, which is the only way one can master a specific cultural or spiritual practice.

aoibhneas!

We are the generation that has been told we can "have it all," and for the first time in human history via travel, the internet and other resources, we have full access to the Indigenous Knowledge of any culture, including our own. Then why must we take bits and pieces from the IK systems of Turtle Island[3] when we have our own EIK and ancestral belief systems,[4] sacred objects and ceremonies that are bursting with earth-connected wisdom, beauty and power?

1. "Empire" is an excellent term for any or all of these constructs - *"Civilization, Hierarchy, Domination, Exploitation, Patriarchy, Capitalism, Fascism, Racism, Sexism, Genocide, Ethnocide, Ecocide, and ultimately, Disconnection."* Jeriah Bowser, "The Age of Fever," *The Hampton Institute*, March 20, 2014. (www.hamptoninstitution.org) I would also add white supremacy, imperialism, colonialism, mercantilism, manifest destiny, progress, patriotism, nationalism, scientific reductionism, Cartesian dualism, objectification, positivism, anthropocentrism, technoculture, technoscientific mono-culture, industrial growth culture, eco-fascism, terracide, biocide, unlimited growth, corporatism, globalization, global plutocracy, petro-economy, big media, bureaucracy, oligarchy, technocracy, corporatocracy, monotheistic religion and the military complex.

2. The term "indigenous" coupled with "knowledge" and used as the acronym "IK" is in widespread and popular use among Turtle Island First Nation leaders, academics, authors, cultural creatives, activists, wisdom keepers and community people. "IK" has been found to be the perfect descriptor for a specific Turtle Island First Nations' cosmology, worldview, spiritual traditions and lifeways, as in Anishnaabe IK, Haudenosaunee IK or Hopi IK. I use "European Indigenous Knowledge" or "EIK" to describe ancestral earth-connected cultures that originated elsewhere than Turtle Island. Please see *Chapter 17,* Page 155 "On the Use of the Term 'Indigenous' and Enlarging Settler Self-Indigenization" for the controversy regarding these terms, and my clarification on my use of the terms "indigenous," "IK," "Euro-indigenous" and "EIK."

3. Turtle Island is the ancient Haudenosaunee and Anishnaabe term locating present-day North America from Baffin Island in the north to the tip of Central America in the south. It is an effective way to describe one land mass instead of the many artificial nation-states and current divisions. I use 'Turtle Island" throughout in respect to the original peoples. *"Referring to North America as Turtle Island suggests a view of North America not merely as a land 'discovered' and colonized by Europeans, but as a land inhabited and stewarded by a collection of rich and diverse peoples, a collection that may have room for both Indigenous and colonizer cultures. The re-framing of the continent's identity is intended to bring about a better cohabitation of these two groups of people. Finally, the term suggests a more holistic relationship between the continent's ecology and its human inhabitants, visualizing Turtle Island as an amalgamation of bioregions."* (Wikipedia, 2012)

4. If you are still practicing the earth-connected spiritual traditions of your ancestors, kudos to you! However, if like the vast majority of diasporans transferred to the Americas you have been separated from your ancestral EIK, the challenge is to reclaim your own specific heritage and legacy, such as *Sinnsreachd* (Irish and Scottish Polytheistic Folk Religion), *Senistrognata* ("ancestral customs" in reconstructed Old Celtic), Gaelic Polytheism, Celtic Reconstructionism (CR), Druidry, Scottish Paganism, Nordic Traditions, Ásatrú, or Germanic Paganism (for example). If your EIK has been lost to the mists of time, the renaissance of eclectic belief systems such as Neo-Paganism, Wicca and Goddess Spirituality is good news indeed, and contemporary nature-based spiritualities such as Animism and Ecomysticism hold elements of both ancient and modern practice.

Drawing on cultural studies and contemporary social justice,
Part One *examines the loss of our vital ethnocultural*
connection to tribe and place, and why there is a trend to
borrow identities from other cultures. Discovering alternatives
to common misconceptions can be extremely empowering, as
well as learning intercultural competency skills for healing
our relationships with Turtle Island First Nations. Using
Indigenous values as our model, ***Part Two*** *will examine*
alternatives to Empire as located in old/new earth-centered
societies, and discuss where an authentic self-identity can be
found. A weaving of analysis, evocation and promptings of
the heart, ***Ancient Spirit Rising*** *offers strategies for*
rewilding, restoring our ecocentric worldview, creating a
sustainable future and reclaiming peaceful co-existence in
Earth Community.

Part One - Stolen Treasure

1. Taking Our Direction from Indian Country

"Know Thyself" (Delphic Oracle)

The First Nations of Turtle Island, the survivors and thrivers of Empire, their voices once silenced and seemingly muted, have not only been resisting the juggernaut of Euro-colonization in both ideology and action, but are also engaged in the full restoration of their sovereignty, IK, heritage, and cultural practices. The emphasis today is on the reclaiming and resurgence of the traditions and worldviews of specific communities or groups, i.e. the Michi Saagiig Nishnaabeg are reviving the traditions of the Michi Saagiig Nishnaabeg exclusively. This new-found strength, solidarity and contemporary self-determination has given rise to community cohesion, social activism, and organizations that monitor cultural appropriation and establish boundaries to protect cultural knowledge, IK and intellectual property, as well as compelling documents⁵ such as the *"Declaration of War Against Exploiters of Lakota Spirituality,"* *"A Community Guide to Protecting IK"* and the United Nations *"Declaration on the Rights of Indigenous Peoples."*

Highly-esteemed Anishnaabe Elder, Traditional Teacher and Professor James Dumont is telling us right now that **"everyone needs to get back to their own IK."**⁶ And I for one, am listening. The mandate to recover one's authentic pre-colonial roots is being reinforced by elders and erudite Indigenous activists, scholars and visionaries all over Turtle Island. In 2012, Chief Arvol Looking Horse, Keeper of the Sacred White Buffalo Calf Pipe (Lakota) stated that *"the effort to protect Mother Earth is all of humanity's responsibility, not just aboriginal people. Every human being has Ancestors in their lineage that understood their umbilical cord to the Earth, and to always protect and thank*

Her. Therefore, all humanity has to re-connect to the indigenous Roots of their own lineage - to heal their connection and responsibility to Mother Earth."[7] As early as 1998 Simon Brascoupe summed up the cultural recovery movement vividly when he said that *"the world will have to change its basic value system to save the planet. This is not to say that westerners should become like aboriginal people. But Western society needs to learn from Indigenous people about respecting and living harmoniously with Mother Earth, and return to their own religious and spiritual teachings, their own ancient systems of knowledge, and their customs and practices that respect Mother Earth.*"[8]

After more than fifty years of New Age and Neo-Pagan inroads into the appropriation of First Nation cultures, the directive has finally come from Indian Country. We are hearing that non-natives need to stay away from taking on IK that is not their own, especially if that practice is for material gain. Appropriation of IK and spirituality is a continuation of the cultural genocide perpetuated by the original Settler Society, and charging money for spiritual services makes the non-native practitioner especially complicit. The feeling right now is that non-native people need to **back off** from practices of cultural theft that have been normalized and sanctioned by white privilege.[9] I don't know about you, but I would not presume to go against the wishes of First Nations, or position myself in Indigenous Knowledge spaces that do not reflect the truth of my own heritage and culture.

---

5. First Nations across the world have issued statements and declarations on cultural and intellectual property rights, and the protection of cultural knowledge, spiritual traditions, histories, philosophies, epistemologies and customary laws. Co-written by 500 represent-atives from 40 different tribes and bands of the Lakota, Dakota and Nakota Nations, the *Declaration of War Against Exploiters of Lakota Spirituality* was issued on June 10, 1993 (www.aics.org/war.html). Simon Brascoupe and Howard Mann issued *A Community Guide to Protecting Indigenous Knowledge* in 2001 (www.publications.gc.ca), and the monumental United Nations *Declaration on the Rights of Indigenous Peoples* was adopted on September 13, 2007 by the General Assembly. You can view or download the full *Declaration* at the United Nations *Permanent Forum on Indigenous Issues* website. (http://undesadspd.org)
6. James Dumont (Anishnaabe), "Introductory Remarks," *Elders and Traditional Peoples Gathering*, Trent University, Peterborough, Ontario, February 12-14, 2010.
7. Statement in solidarity with the Idle No More movement by Chief Arvol Looking Horse, *NDN News - Daily Headlines in Indian Country*, December 31, 2012. *"I would like to send out support for Chief Theresa Spence of the Attawapiskat First Nation for giving of herself through fasting and prayers for the protection of Mother Earth."* (http://ndnnews.com)
8. Simon Brascoupe (Algonquin/Mohawk), "Aboriginal Peoples' Vision of the Future: Interweaving Traditional Knowledge and New Technologies," *Visions of the Heart: Canadian Aboriginal Issues*, David Long and Olive Patricia Dickason (editors), Thomson-Nelson, 1998.
9. Those unfamiliar with white privilege may want to explore the "belly of the beast" in *Chapter 16* "White Privilege" on Page 141 before resuming. Also in *Chapter 16*, an overview (if such a thing is possible) of the genocide perpetuated on Indigenous people in the Americas since 1492.

2. *"I Am" Interloper*

My own experiences over many years of growing close to the Anishnaabe - the Odawa, Algonquin and Michi Saagiig Nishnaabeg cultures of my homeland in southern Ontario, Canada - has led to a valuable familiarity with their epic and enriching worldviews, all-encompassing and equivalent to any religious[10] system in the world. As a cultural treasure, the sacred knowledge of the Anishnaabe is an irreplaceable part of the ethnosphere,[11] the collective human legacy and the monumental web of Indigenous and cultural diversity on planet Earth. Through reading, dialogue, cultural events, ceremonies and personal relationships, I learned of Anishnaabe history, spirituality, colonization, resistance, political struggle, protocol, decolonization and contemporary resurgence. And as part of my academic training in Fine Arts and as a prequel to my career as a visual artist, independent curator and writer, I took college courses in Anishnaabe Indigenous Knowledge (IK) and *Contemporary Issues in the Native World.*

During the years that I participated in First Nations ceremonies and events as an invited guest, it was understandable that at other times my white presence was tenuous to the bridge-building dynamic. Although I mixed in at ceremonies, pow wows and cultural events, it never felt right for me to assume any kind of ownership over Anishnaabe tribal expressions. In my own developing sense and knowledge of the sacred, and in collaboration with both native and non-native people, I will admit to wearing Indigenous jewellery, collecting native art from First Nations artists, and making tobacco ties, medicine bags and a ceremonial drum. But ultimately, without a true connection to the communities from which they sprang, these forms or containers for cultural expression naturally and eventually fell away in favor of a syncretisation of Celtic Animism and ecomystic practices[12] more authentic to me. Tobacco at the ready, and as much as the native person seemed to appreciate my offering, it was always an uneasy exchange. And rightly so. My blonde hair, blue eyes and pale skin placed me squarely in another knowledge system, hidden within the homogeneity of Canadian identity, and this remained a mystery both to myself and others for many years.

I will be eternally grateful to the traditional Anishnaabe for the knowledge that they graciously shared with me, and for the many gifts of insight and "good mind." Teachings from the Elders, Indigenous artists, books, film, theatre, music, and my First Nation friends sparked my artistic and spiritual life for two decades. And as much as I developed a great deal of cultural sensitivity, I would like to make apologies here and now, to all the First Nations people who were probably offended by my unbounded enthusiasm for the beauty of their earth-connected traditions. In retrospect, I now see that learning about the Indigenous cultures of Turtle Island enabled a wider opening of my own pre-colonial heart and soul, providing fertile ground for my own EIK to flourish. I have had numerous metaphysical experiences prompted by my closeness to Turtle Island IK, but if the capacity for mysticism did not already exist within me, these inexplicable events, dreams, synchronicities and visions would not have occurred. Turtle Island Indigenous scholars claim that their IK is not transferable, and that it is impossible for a non-native person to experience or carry any knowledge directly connected to their traditions,[13] so I will not presume to detail any of those magical experiences here.

My 20-year path spiralling through the periphery of the Anishnaabe world led to a significant kinship within the Curve Lake First Nation near Peterborough, Ontario, where I resided for three years. Like all quests having a beginning, middle and abrupt end, my personal journey of enthusiasm, tolerance and questionable loyalties came full circle in 2012. At the same time that I was experiencing the rewards of friendship and intercultural sharing, I was also feeling like an interloper, and that my First Nation friends and neighbours were entitled to a dedicated space free of colonial presence (me) for the much-needed revitalization of their cultural expressions. Right on cue (it seemed) I deepened my learning about critical race theory, white privilege and allyship. This new information enlarged my picture of the Settler/First Nations interface dramatically, and shifted my journey of heart and mind to a more neoteric alignment. These days I do not presume to be welcome in First Nations spaces unless invited, and my only desire is to attend First Nations cultural events strong in my own ancestral traditions. First Nations individuals constantly have to navigate through the dominant society that surrounds them, and I have come to understand that the practice of respectful non-interference is the best approach to take. It is interesting how this new cycle in my life coincided with the recent directive coming from Indian Country, that *"everyone needs to get back to their own IK."*

---

10. Even though I use it here, "religious" is not an accurate description of the all-encompassing and holistic nature of IK. Traditional Indigenous cultures do not delineate the spiritual life with categories such as "religion," as the sacred and the secular are indistinguishable.

11. The term "ethnosphere" was coined by renowned anthropologist and author Wade Davis to define the "*sum total of all thoughts and intuitions, myths and beliefs, ideas and inspirations brought into being by the human imagination since the dawn of consciousness. Just as there is a biosphere, a biological web of life, there is an ethnosphere, a cultural web of life, that is humanity's great legacy, the product of our dreams, the embodiment of our hopes, the symbol of all that we are and all that we have created as a wildly inquisitive and astonishingly adaptive species.*" Wade Davis, *The Wayfinders: Why Ancient Wisdom Matters in the Modern World,* House of Anansi Press, 2009.

12. Having Scottish and English heritage, my EIK practice is a blend of animism, ecomysticism and Celtic Reconstructionism, woven with threads of the Old Ways from Gaelic tradition and Druidic spirituality.

"I leave behind the person I once was, who cared so deeply for so many wonderful people, places and things, finding it was all dust.

Then, moving down the trail I am met by everyday magic, as I stir my solitary dust into the sacred cauldron we call life. Newly awakened, or waeccan,[14] to my Celtic roots, kissed by the sun and blessed by the moon, I am infused with an inexplicable desire to SPEAK OUT ~ on behalf of our Mother the Earth, and all those who would live in harmony with Her."

The coming together of my experiences, formal studies, relationships with First Nations individuals, knowledge gained on the sidelines of First Nations community, and my new-found awareness in regard to white privilege and the destructive effects of cultural appropriation have compelled me to examine the ideas in this book. Hearing James Dumont say that *"everyone needs to get back to their own IK"* for the first time was the lightning bolt that activated a monumental set of questions about my own life, and issues in the wider society - questions about denial, obfuscation, entitlement, white supremacy, power, identity, boundaries and Settler Colonialism - issues that I was duty-bound to investigate, and in some cases track down to a final conclusion. For those of us with European heritage, these core questions continue to arise in discourse on locating our ancestral traditions, *Rejecting Empire* (uncolonization), and reclaiming authentic roots in Earth Community, and the themes in this book are an attempt to add to this critical conversation. There is nothing more personal than one's identity, and in response to the white entitlement of cultural appropriation, I offer alternatives and insights on this sensitive subject to all readers currently drawn to, or engaged in, "Native Spirituality." As this book makes its way into the world, it is not my intention to follow it by assuming the

---

13. Overwhelming evidence does exist for the cross-cultural transfer of IK in our shared dreamspace. In *Dreamways of the Iroquois: Honoring the Secret Wishes of the Soul* Robert Moss had extensive dreams about the life and teachings of "Island Woman," a Mohawk Clan Mother (early 18th century), that later became substantiated by the historical record and members of her present-day community. So clear were his dreams that the archaic Haudenosaunee dialect spoken to him by Island Woman was perfectly translated into the contemporary Mohawk language. Also in *Dreaming: Anthropological and Psychological Interpretations,* Barbara Tedlock has collected dream narratives and reports from anthropologists who interact with non-western dreamers, and organically share cross-cultural experiences. In this collaborative process, dreams are reported, shared, interpreted, responded to, and acted upon with the intercultural participation of the entire group. Many dreamwork practitioners and Indigenous societies such as the Haudenosaunee believe that the ancestral spirits and the spirits of the land are seeking to communicate with us in the dreamspace, where there are no cultural boundaries.

role of "cultural appropriation cop." Many angry people, both native and non-native, have made it their business (and rightly so) to uncover the "IK usurpers," "wannabees," "feelabees," "frauds," "twinkies," "culture vultures," "culture thieves," "cultural rapists," "cultural trespassers," "cultural fraudsters," "cultural pirates," "cultural strip-miners," "instant elders," "fly-by-night elders," "popcorn elders," "bubblegum shamans," "shame-ons," "plastic shamans," "candy bar shame men," "shake-and-bake shamans," "self-styled shamans," "chicken shamans," "cybershamans," "Las Vegas Shamans," "plastic medicine men," "Indianthusiasts," "Indian hobbyists," "Indian role-players," "pseudo-Indian charlatans," "fake Indians," "fake-baked natives," "shysters," "fraudulent operators," "commercial profiteers," "ceremony-sellers," "elaborate liars," "thrill seekers," "New Age imposters," "Nuage profiteers," "spiritual vampires," "spiritual phonies," "spiritual voyeurs," "cultists," "spiritual colonists" and "pretendians" (!) and try to induce change with attack, insult, ridicule, threats, cajoling or legal action. My approach will be somewhat different, as I believe that many proponents of "shamanic healing" and "native spirituality" are simply unaware that their ideology and practices are in direct opposition to the First Nations of Turtle Island. I also believe that for many, their overall goals are honourable and come from a place of heart, with a true desire to return to eco-values, to care for humanity, and to support the healing of the Earth. As I have discovered, it is never too late to return to one's own ancestral earth-based knowledge, for that is where our truest spiritual expression is found.

Every situation is unique and special, and many native and non-native people have strong bonds to family and community that enable their IK circles to be fluid and inclusive. Strangely enough, many native people have returned to their own cultural traditions, spirituality and IK hand-in-hand with their white friends and family members. There are also many "blue-eyed blonde Indians" now, some with status registration and all the "benefits" that entails, and many non-native spiritual practitioners have obtained permission and support from First Nations community to express themselves with elements of Turtle Island IK. With the blurred boundaries created by personal allegiances, and centuries of intermixing between First Nation and Settler[15] culture, judging who is and who is not entitled to practice Turtle Island IK is problematic indeed. Many are so far along on the path of mutual co-existence and collaboration that concepts in this book may seem like a step backward, and remind them of divisions they have already transcended. I do not wish to re-politicize the many beautiful interactions and alliances of the human heart and mind that are already functioning between First Nation/Settler individuals and communities, and so I ask that in the reading one "*keep what is worth keeping, and with a breath of kindness, blow the rest away.*"[16] The world of Indigenous cultural practices is a complicated labyrinth having many variations, yet ultimately it is about honoring the wishes of the First

Peoples of Turtle Island, and stopping the inappropriate assault on their nations that they have endured for so long. As Settlers, we need to challenge the "me-me-me" hyperindividualism that has been thoroughly instilled in us by capitalist society, to examine the unrestricted choices in lifestyle and spirituality we take for granted, and to adopt a much-needed code of ethics instead.

Even though many of the subjects in this book are difficult and controversial, have the potential to shake up personal belief systems and highlight the need for major social change, I still wish to inform people in a kind way. To be honest, I remain conflicted about this, as it seems absurd to be wary of hurt feelings and discomfort when unmasking cultural genocide and the racist agenda of knowledge domination and identity theft. Activists everywhere must struggle with the same dilemma, which is how to remain true to one's pacifist ideals in the face of horrific violence, ignorance and inequality. To the depths of my heart, mind and soul I thoroughly despise the Eurocentric racist practices of dominance, hate and discrimination that have been directed at First Nations and people of colour. Yet in my work as an anti-racist activist, I refuse to perpetuate the same weapons of hate and discrimination, or to continue the practices of "divide and conquer" that we have all internalized from Empire. Our challenge must be to show others the same respect that we wish to receive, no matter how vehemently we oppose or despise their beliefs, and to follow the principle of directing anger at the ignorance or social injustice rather than at the person. At the very least, opening up a dialogue about personal and difficult issues such as cultural appropriation may engage us in mutual uncolonization and change-making, instead of continuing with our habitual mindsets and misconceptions.

Moving past the justified moral fury and rage of oppressed groups everywhere, and the anger as expressed by social change activists and allies, we need to hold the hopeful vision of a massive-scale culture of peace. It probably takes more courage to choose restorative justice, forgiveness and reconciliation over violent revenge, and fortunately the growing peace movement is testament to all those who align with the core values of non-retaliation. By assisting all who are oppressed in their fight for equity and justice, and attempting to counteract the destructive practices of cultural appropriation, I will not forfeit the basic compassion and respect that is due all peoples. Having white privilege this is easy for me to say, but I truly believe that at some point we need to rise above the rhetoric and hate, choose to take the high road, and above all, to value the dignity and divinity that lies within each human being.

"As I walked out the door toward my freedom, I knew that if I did not leave all the anger, hatred and bitterness behind, I would still be in prison."[17] (Nelson Mandala)

One thing is clear, is that in whatever form or design our eco-cultural practices take, we are all working toward harmony and peace within ourselves and the world, and to love indigenity with all our heart, mind and soul. May all those who read these pages come to the realization that owning our white privilege, taking responsibility and activating our moral code needs to be our compass as we navigate through the joys of spiritual ecology, and reclaim our original and authentic selves. I offer a diversity of course-corrections for the contemporary spiritual seeker to contemplate, and new ways to embody a genuine earth-connected path. For it is those of us that celebrate and practice indigenity in ourselves and others, in however authentic form that may take, that are the best hope for humanity. There is no predicting what shape this new-found collective will take in future, as it has been suggested by many, both native and non-native, that the First Nations of Turtle Island are the true leaders of the Americas. When we hear Ellen Gabriel say *"First Nations should assimilate the white culture into ours, and we will be a lot gentler when we do"*[18] can we consider this statement both metaphorically and realistically? Or at the very least, would it not be possible to meet the First Nations of Turtle Island halfway, to be strong in our own i.e. Gaelic, Baltic or Nordic beliefs and practices? For if we do not believe that we have common ground in our mutual love for the land and our own IK/EIK, and that it is possible to embody cultural tolerance, peaceful co-existence, compassion and respect, then we perpetuate the Great Forgetting. By returning to our earth-rooted belief systems, and *"reintegrating ourselves with our indigenous selves, we simultaneously reintegrate ourselves with the rest of humanity."*[19] (Ward Churchill) We all have a place in the Indigenous circle, and the ability to love all people as we love ourselves, as we value our "Unity in Diversity." The Earth is a sacred magical place, all beings are a perfect manifestation of the Creatrix[20] or Creator principle of the universe, and each human life is a miracle and a mystery.

My passion for Anishnaabe culture is evident in my intricate drawing of a Dreamcatcher (2001). (*"I Am" Interloper*)

---

14. "Waeccan" or "to be awake" in Old English simply means to be in tune with the presence of the mystery in nature, and I use it to align with my earth-wise Ancestors. When we are *waeccan*, our heart, mind and soul are open to the beauty in ourselves and all of creation. The term "waeccan" may be the root for "wicca" or "witch," but I do not

practice wicca or witchcraft. Drifting far from respectable roots in Old English and Germanic paganism, the etymology of "wicca," "wiccan" and "witch" became progressively dire as a result of Christian oppression. Today, the brave tradition established by feminist foremothers Starhawk, Z Budapest and others to reclaim and embody the term "witch" as a valid, empowering and positive contemporary identity is admirable, and many have been able to disconnect the identity markers "wicca," "wiccan" and "witch" from their negative associations.

15. Referring to the various diasporans and descendants of the original colonizers as "Settler" is gaining wide usage, and is an appropriate reminder of our status as seen through the lens of Empire-building. *"The term Settler is used to denaturalize our status on this land, to force colonialism into the forefront of our consciousness, to cause discomfort and force a reckoning with our inherited colonial status, to create the understanding and desire to embrace, demand and effect change."* Corey Snelgrove and Klara Woldenga, "Why the Term 'Settler' Needs to Stick," *The Martlet*, University of Victoria, March 28, 2013. (www.martlet.ca) Many in the dominant white society object to being called "Settler" as it probably goes against the immigrant impulse, which is to discard and discount the past. However, the denial in this egocentric response is inconceivable to First Nations, as activist, journalist, radio host and publisher of *Native Pride* blog John Kane (Mohawk) explains. *"It is amazing that in the context of protecting land, water and preventing the genocide of our people, we have to address someone's feelings being hurt by being called a Settler."* (www.letstalknativepride.blogspot.ca)

16. Dinah Maria Craik, *A Life for a Life*, 1859, Amazon Digital Services, reprint, 2012.

17. Danny Schechter, *Madiba A to Z: The Many Faces of Nelson Mandela*, Seven Stories Press, 2013

18. Ellen Gabriel (Mohawk), *Nation 2 Nation Now - the Conversations*, OISE Auditorium, Toronto, ON, Spreecast, March 23, 2013. (www.youtube.com)

19. Ward Churchill, *Indians are Us?* Between the Lines, 1984.

20. "Creatrix" refers to the Divine Feminine principle that births all life from a cosmic womb or chalice - the spark that eternally renews the life cycle in all forms and manifestations. The Creatrix, or Mother Goddess, was actualized and revered in ancient matriarchal societies as the personification of fertility, and She presided over the mysteries of birth, nourishment and regeneration.

3. Intersections

As far as miracles go, not too long ago I was stunned to find my own Ancestor mentioned in a book on the history of small-town Ontario that interlaced new threads of paradox, gratitude and wonder into my personal mythology.

"The first white child to arrive in the village came in the arms of the Chippewas."[21] (Randy Richmond)

During the time of the settlement of Orillia by Europeans in 1832, a newborn baby of Scottish parents (my third great-grandmother) was on a boat that capsized in the waters known today as "The Narrows" at Lake Couchiching. She was rescued from the channel and brought safely to shore by a kind member of the Chippewa (Ojibway) Nation. As part of the immigrant wave that engulfed a pristine wilderness, the flourishing of Eliza Emily Bailey and her family has given me the haunting legacy of her miraculous rescue, and my deep roots in the Orillia landscape. Her story reminds us that the first contact Settler Society were welcomed, integrated and dependent upon First Nations everywhere, who freely gave us gifts of land, food, medicine and our very lives. Their generosity and kindness is woven into the heritage fabric of our families and communities. Even the structure of Canada owes a great collective debt to the first peaceful treaty agreements between native and non-native leaders, and to the partnership model of Indigenous diplomacy that contributed to our first constitutions and laws.[22]

The ongoing agenda of white supremacy has given us permission to deny, forget about or gloss over the early contributions to Anglophone Empire by Canada's First Nations. So thorough were the racist policies of genocide and apartheid that growing up in Orillia, my contemporaries and I were completely oblivious to Mnjikaning, the oppressed and decimated Anishnaabe community across the lake. Whatever relationships had been successful in the past were un-acknowledged, and new relationships were not encouraged. The only reference I ever heard to our First Nations neighbours in my entire 15-year childhood in Orillia was my grandmother's casual mention of a finely-wrought birchbark basket that she had purchased from a door-to-door Ojibway vendor. No one in my family ever mentioned the significance of Eliza Bailey's rescue, or kept it alive as an incredibly important part of our oral tradition. It speaks volumes about the racially imperious attitude of Euro-Canadians, that it fell to a modern historian to include it as an interesting footnote in his survey. Would the generations of Vick/Woods/Trill/Lightfoot and Eyers families even exist I wonder, had Eliza perished in the waters of Lake Couchiching? Would musical icon Gordon Lightfoot (my uncle and direct descendant of Eliza Bailey) have been born, to go on and write a canon of songs that defined the Settler narratives of Canadian nationalism and celebrated Canadian identity? Alternating between pride and sorrow, my response to the inexplicable story of Eliza Bailey is bittersweet, and its deeper meaning still unfolding within the continuum of my personal journey. What I do know is that the antique plaque commemorating Eliza Bailey found in St. James Anglican Church in Orillia, is disturbing in its overt proclamation of whiteness, as if to announce that no other ethnicity was worthy, or even existed, before - or after - her arrival in Canada.

Eliza Emily Bailey
"Orillia's First White Child"
Photo by Robert Hood
St. James Anglican Church
Orillia, Ontario, March 2013

The presence of this plaque in St. James Anglican Church is not surprising, coming from a town that hosted a *Settler Re-enactment*[23] in 1925 celebrating the unveiling of the Champlain Monument, and thematic of native-newcomer relations.

Taking place in Couchiching Park, the newly-created jewel of the Orillia waterfront, the all-white gathering featured a group in period dress performing the epic landing of the "explorer" Samuel de Champlain on the shores of "Terra Nullius."[24] Champlain was welcomed with open arms by over 250 townsfolk painted, dressed and feathered as Indigenous Hurons wielding "tomahawks" and bows and arrows, who demonstrated great joy and gratitude to be "discovered" and "rescued" from their state of "primitivism" and "savagery." A jolly time was had by all next to the Champlain Monument, a towering edifice to manifest destiny, religious superiority and white supremacy if there ever was one. Of course, nothing in this celebratory re-enactment portrayed the disease, displacement, land grab or genocide that befell the Huron and Chippewa post-contact. The mock "welcome of the conquerer" was followed by the jovial enjoyment of social mingling, and refreshments such as lemonade, tea biscuits and jam.

The Champlain Monument in Orillia, Ontario, is topped by the magnificence of Samuel de Champlain wielding his weapons and insignias, flanked by a Jesuit priest menacingly holding a raised cross, and a haughty fur-trader carrying the carcasses of animals that have been converted into mercantile "products." This triumvirate of soldier, priest and merchant represents the Eurocentric ideology and overall colonial agenda ("glory, god and gold") that was forced upon Indigenous people everywhere with military might, religion, and capitalist commerce. Hunched at the feet of the European patriarchs are two sets of semi-nude Wendat/Huron "braves" in a "tabula rasa" attitude of "primitive" innocence, submission and awe.

*"Navigation has always seemed to me to occupy the first place. By this art we obtain knowledge of different countries, regions and realms. By this we attract and bring to our own land all kinds of riches, by it the idolatry of paganism is overthrown, and Christianity proclaimed throughout all the regions of the earth. This is the art.....which led me to explore the coasts of a portion of America, especially those of New France, where I have always desired to see the Lily flourish, together with the **only** religion Catholic, Apostolic and Roman."*

Samuel de Champlain, Founder of Quebec and Father of New France,
Les voyages du Sieur de Champlain, Pt. V, Paris, 1613

Peaceful co-existence and tolerance for cultural diversity was never the policy of the Eurocentric colonizer. Sanctioned by the corporation that is the Roman Catholic Church, this elaborate sculpture glorifies white superiority and the "Divine Right of Kings & Conquerers" to subjugate Indigenous people and the land, and it celebrates the commerce and religiosity of Empire in the new colony of Canada. Today, the grandiose Champlain Monument needs to be dismantled (or put into storage) in alignment with human rights advancements in general, and in accordance with the anti-racist and anti-colonial principles of decolonization for both First Nation and Settler societies.

To fully understand our own Euro-colonial history and transform our relationships with First Nations today, we need to face the inconvenient truth of our paradoxical past and shake off the complacency that comes with white entitlement, privilege and power. As John Milloy says, *"there are actually two Canada's - aboriginal and non-aboriginal Canada."*[25] The uncolonization process, what many are now referring to as "unsettling the settler within," requires us to identify our unconscious privileges as well as the invisible ways in which we comply with the dominant hegemony. Our struggle, as the descendants of the original Settler Society, is to shift from unconsciousness, racism, denial and guilt about our colonial legacy to the righteous anger of critical thinking, reflection and social activism. As we come to an authentic recognition of our shared history with First Nations and explore the myths and misconceptions we have had about each other, we can become empowered to use our new-found awareness in building solidarity, and as a catalyst for change. Each one of us who is descended from a Euro-Settler is directly or indirectly living on stolen land, and is benefitting from the genocide of the original inhabitants of Turtle Island. This baseline would imply a totally new and different set of ethics, and with this in mind, there is much that we can do to eliminate institutional racism and contribute as allies to the anti-oppression, human rights and land claims struggles of our First Nations neighbours. Learning about and respecting Indigenous cultures and lifeways, attending anti-racist training, and understanding white privilege from reading and videos is our first step (see "What Can We Do?" on Page 134).

Today, we see that the white supremacist drivers of manifest destiny (whites only!) and the myth of progress that founded the Americas has created an illogical, unsustainable quagmire, destructive to all beings and ecosystems that share the planet. The history of my own family leads me to believe that as we shake free of our colonial past, it is essential that we **all** become protectors of Turtle Island, to stop the destruction and plunder of what has become our ancestral lands as well. By virtue of our rootedness in our communities, our buried Ancestors, and our mutual love of the land, for better or worse both native and non-native people now share Turtle Island. And as much as First Nations (or Settlers) would wish it so, it is simply not feasible for those of us in the diaspora to return to our places of origin. Regardless of the current controversy, attempting to define those of European descent as re-landed within Turtle Island by virtue of our buried Ancestors[26] is a positionality to which I will return in *Chapter 17*, and as I explore further in *Chapter 29,* it may not be too late to establish the peaceful co-existence that the colonial powers denied us all.

My niece Jessie Vick, namesake of Gordon Lightfoot's mother and my grandmother, Jessie Vick Lightfoot, balanced on railway tracks near Barrie, Ontario in 2012. The heyday of industry is long over, the resources are rapidly being depleted, and the unsustainable paradigm of Empire-building is coming to a close. How are we preparing the youth of today to deal with the coming storm? Will they be able to voluntarily move away from the destructive simulacrum of a humancentric civilization? What kind of world will Jessie's generation be leaving to her descendants?

21. Randy Richmond, *The Orillia Spirit: An Illustrated History of Orillia*, Dundurn Press, 1996.

22. Canada's first constitutional document, the *1763 Royal Proclamation*, was ratified at the Treaty of Niagara in 1764 between the British and 2000 leaders from the First Nations surrounding the Great Lakes - the Nipissing, Anishnaabe, Algonquin, Odawa, Huron and Haudeneshanee. At this event, the British accepted a nation-to-nation relationship rooted in a policy of non-interference, and codified by the symbology of covenant chains and wampum belts in a sacred ceremony, all parties agreed to benefit equally from the bounty of the land. The ongoing legitimacy of Canada, and our Canadian identity stem from these original constitutional relationships between the Settler Society and the First Nations. Rooted in the philosophy and practice of non-interference, peaceful co-existence and respect, the founding agreements make us **all** treaty people, and the legacy of Indigenous diplomacy, law and peacemaking benefit **all** Canadians. The ensuing years of oppression, archaic legislation such as the Indian Act, de facto apartheid, and Euro-domination over Canada's First Nations does not detract from the foundational status of the treaties.

23. I kid you not. See Randy Richmond, *The Orillia Spirit: An Illustrated History of Orillia*, Dundurn Press, 1996, page 65, for a description of this municipal travesty. The immorality, ignorance and injustice of this genocidal re-enactment, the "ignorant natives joyfully welcoming their new masters" scenario, is beyond belief.

24. Among other insidious concepts brought to the "New World" by the Settler Society was the idea of "Terra Nullius," that the land was empty and devoid of life, requiring a European presence and sensibility to make it bona fide. In reality, most locations where Euro-Empire was established were once someone's beloved homelands.

25. John Milloy, Historian and Professor, Department of Indigenous Studies, Trent University, Peterborough, ON, *National Day of Prayer, Honour the Apology*, July 25, 2013.

26. The burial of our motherlines and fatherlines in Turtle Island automatically creates sacred space and generational bonding with the land, which is an empowering way for the Settler Society to adopt earth-centered values.

The Canadian Railroad Trilogy ~ Gordon Lightfoot

There was a time in this fair land when the railroad did not run
When the wild majestic mountains stood alone against the sun
Long before the white man and long before the wheel
When the green dark forest was too silent to be real.
But time has no beginnings and history has no bounds
As to this verdant country they came from all around
They sailed upon her waterways and they walked the forests tall
And they built the mines, the mills, and the factories for the good of us all.
For they looked in the future and what did they see
They saw an iron road running from sea to sea..........

Lyrics ©Warner/Chappell Music/Moose Music/Early Morning Music, 1967

The writing of Canada's powerful "national anthem" *The Canadian Railroad Trilogy* by Gordon Lightfoot in 1967 was a celebration of the prevailing meta-narrative, which promoted parochial empire building, industry, technology, and the paradigm of limitless progress; undisputed principles that went on to fuel the "good life" and the realization of the American-Canadian dream. During the boom years that followed the great world wars, who would have believed that the same paradigm of wealth and technological innovation so full of promise and benefit in 1967, would bring us to the brink of economic and environmental collapse today? In just a few short decades, as societal problems worsen and environment degradation intensifies, we can see that the dominant paradigm is unsustainable, and millions of us are waking up to the impossibility of continuing to believe in the imperialist lies of Empire. Our system of capitalism and endless growth is not compatible with the life-generating design and natural systems of the planet, and the sooner we come to terms with this undeniable fact the better. The time has come to challenge the colonial legacy of domination, resource extraction, eco-fascism, industrial "progress" and corporatism, and to take responsibility for the fact that the Americas were created with an agenda of slavery, genocide, ethnic cleansing and stolen land.

As we actively move away from and *Reject Empire*, the original voices of Turtle Island First Nations, their history, narratives and experiences on the land are of primary importance to all Canadians. Beyond our urban cocoon we learn that this beautiful country is a four-season paradise, and that there are cultural groups who have lived here happily for millennia, and have survived and thrived and flourished. But more importantly, we learn that human beings are meant to honour the Earth in all we think, say and do, and that there is a better, more harmonious way for us to live, interconnected with nature, the other-than-human world, and *Earth Community*.

4. Don't Go Where You Are Not Wanted

"Many traditions that have been appropriated from Native people (such as sweat lodges and medicine wheel ceremonies) are performed by white people allegedly in the name of such lofty goals as world peace, spiritual mending, and mutual understanding. One of the things needed for world peace, spiritual mending, and mutual understanding to occur is an end to racism. But cultural appropriation is a form of racism, and as long as racism exists, there can be no world peace, spiritual mending, or mutual understanding. It is unacceptable for white people's healing to come at the expense of the cultural survival of People of Color."[27] (Natán Rebelde)

As challenging as it may sound, I urge my kindred spirits to stop borrowing from the First Nations cultures of Turtle Island and assume the work of reclaiming their own EIK. The difficulty in the lexicon has been that when we hear the words "Indigenous Knowledge" we automatically assume that it applies to the First Nations of Turtle Island and elsewhere, and not to us as i.e. Gaelic, Baltic or Nordic people. The actual dictionary definition of "Indigenous" is *"belonging to place, originating in and naturally living in a region or country."* (Encarta 2012) However transplanted as we may be, reclaiming our original eco-wisdom is an important and powerful first step. We need to take a truthful sightline back down the path of our own ancestry, to learn and practice the spiritual traditions of our foremothers and forefathers. As lost to time and impossible as it may seem, to be in alignment with one's own ancestral roots, to stand tall in one's own Indigenous Knowledge, is to find empowerment and actualization as an authentic human being.

If we have been incorporating elements of Turtle Island IK into our spiritual practice, it may be time to deconstruct our belief systems and tools in favor of those more authentic to us. We are needed at the table of worldwide IK, but to gain the respect of other Indigenous people we need to be empowered and strong in our own specific EIK traditions. For example, when we look at the worldwide phenomenon that is the *Thirteen Indigenous Grandmothers*, we see that a Grandmother from an EIK tradition is not included. At first glance it may seem ludicrous to suggest that the oppressor claim space with the oppressed, but these are the kind of inversions that may occur in the uncolonization process of Settlers and other recent immigrants to Turtle Island. Asking why the Ban-Draoi, Awenyddion, Gallicenae or Seiðkona are not found within the *Sacred Circle* of earth connection begins to take on validity, and their absence may suggest that people of European descent have a lot of catching up to do. The glaring question is how did "white" and "European" become synonymous with "non-indigenous," with urbanity,

rootlessness and all that is estranged from the land? Can it be that as
we recover indigenous mind and evolve as spiritual beings, our purpose
is to become truly aligned with our own ancestral knowledge, and the
sacred earth that gives rise to this wisdom?

The uninformed "leaning in" that happens when non-native people
without a specific EIK draw close to native spirituality can have dire
consequences for all. At powwows and other gatherings over the years I
have become acutely aware that if a "wannabee" white woman turns her
back for a moment, the besieged Anishnaabe women may ridicule,
demean and laugh at her, or determine how she can be used in some
way. I have also observed that the non-native women, in starry-eyed
proximity to the Anishnaabe, see only what they want to see, and are
oblivious to this covert yet justifiable behavior across the cultural divide.
Among other delusional activities, I have also seen that the desperate
need for IK has led white women to fabricate elaborate and detailed
personal relationships with First Nation "wisdom keepers" after only
the briefest and most superficial of contact, and to indulge in the more
patronizing aspects of "Elder Essentialism."[28]

Before anyone cries "*how dare Indigenous women insult white women
- that is racism!*" it has become cohesively clear through the anti-
oppression methodologies of both native and non-native activists and
intellectuals that "reverse racism"[29] does not exist, and that the
negative (so-called) actions of people of colour are simply a "response
to racism." Understandably, the "response to racism" will continue
until all First Nations are healed from genocide, residential schools and
oppression, and not a moment longer. Colonization has fractured First
Nations' collective identity and spirit, and has caused intergenerational
trauma, anguish and emptiness. Like the Borg in Star Trek, the dominant society is a faceless nameless enemy that is hated entire, and
white people may be detested both individually and collectively. To feel
offended or victimized by this is ludicrous. It is Euro-Settlers who are
accountable to First Nations for the catastrophic effects of racial
stratification, dispossession and oppression, not the other way around!
To fully understand the arising of this "response to racism" we need to
turn the tables and imagine *ourselves* the targets of devastating cultural
and individual genocide. What would our lived reality be like?

How anyone in the dominant society could expect that those who have
been murdered, marginalized, criminalized, driven off the land,
experimented on,[30] ignored and oppressed not to harbour anger[31] and
negative feelings toward the oppressor is complete nonsense, and the
repudiation of these honest feelings, (called "blaming the victim"[32])
continues to perpetuate the racist agenda of the overculture and the
invisibility of whiteness. In actual fact, the eternal patience, equanimity
and kindness that we often see as embodied by many First Nations
people in the face of genocide is beyond belief. Subordinated through

imperialism and Eurocentric pedagogy, they have been engaged in the monumental work of resisting the Settler State for centuries now, and have employed all the means and methods possible to keep their beautiful cultures alive, in whole or in part, each one a priceless link in the global ethnosphere. In these postcolonial times, it is the white majority, **not** people of colour, who need to take responsibility for the disaster created by the white supremacist founding and maintenance of the Americas, to eliminate racism and the intersectional oppressions, and to create the conditions in which equality is the outcome of equity, and tolerance can unfold for all.

It is not my place to speak for native people who are engaged in the decolonization process and healing from personal and historic trauma, yet I have observed that great comfort and healing can be found in the holistic principles of traditional teachings, ceremony and medicine, and by renewing one's sacred connection to the community and the land. But many Anishnaabe argue that the soul loss, "generational grief"[33] and pain are insurmountable, and that they cannot forgive and forget while the colonial process is still ongoing and part of their daily lived experience. How does one "move on" exactly, and erase from memory one's oppression and that of their Ancestors? How does one even begin to forget that one's culture was criminalized until recent times? Like an embedded genetic code, the ancestral memories from those lost to genocide are still emanating from the spiritual realm to their descendants today. As painter Dazaungee/Paul Shilling (Anishnaabe, Mnjikaning First Nation) once explained to me, every one of the portraits that manifests on his canvas is an Ancestor coming through from the no-time and no-space of the spirit world, one of his people who were brutalized, raped, stolen, starved, massacred or killed by pandemics in the years of white supremacist colonial expansion.

"Ancestors"
by Dazaungee,
(oil on canvas)
collection of the author

27. Natán Rebelde, "Cultural Appreciation or Cultural Appropriation?" *Unsettling America: Decolonization in Theory & Practice*, September 16, 2011. (https://bit.ly/3BtAlWc)
28. See *Chapter 9* "Who Are Your 'Elders?' " on Page 66.
29. In *Chapter 15, see* "The Impossibility of Reverse Racism" on Page 133.

In the process of building empire on Turtle Island we have created a racially homogenous world, and within the insularity and ignorant bubble of white privilege, the PTSD, disenfranchised grief, and suffering of Canada's First Nations has long been invisible. The practice of perspectivism,[34] which is the elevation of the dominant perspective to become the unquestioned truth and "norm" for the entire society, has allowed us to deny any form of non-white reality. Since the crimes against humanity carried out in the founding and development of Anglo-Canada have gone virtually unpunished[35] to date, I wonder if the unresolved karma, or fallout from these genocidal actions is somehow being played out in the ongoing psychological dysfunction, delusions and viciousness of the dominant white society. As they say, what goes around comes around!

It is only since the late 1980s that a renaissance of healing, collaborating, rebuilding, and re-visioning has occurred within Turtle Island First Nations, and the future looks very positive for the continued resurgence and reclamation of their self-recognition, self-determination and traditional IK. Through decolonization, the bond to the land and the holistic aspects of traditional teachings that are evoked from IK hold the key to restoring the hearts and minds of the individual and the community, and Turtle Island First Nations have much to celebrate as they take renewed pride in their spiritual worldviews and traditional values such as kindness, respect, balance and inter-connection. A benefit of the healing process for all those affected by the intersectional oppressions is that one can slowly reawaken the heart, optimally recovering the lost parts of the soul, and restore the ability to feel empathy for one's self and others again. *"Perhaps it is time to make our way back through our oral traditions, written words and deeper sorrows. Then, Indigenous people can collectively create new understandings and go willingly through the painful memories once again, in order to resolve and release the historic trauma and free ourselves from its tyranny."*[36] (Aboriginal Healing Foundation)

---

30. Scientific experiments carried out in residential schools were uncovered in a comprehensive study made widely available by Ian Mosby, PhD in 2013. "Administering Colonial Science: Nutrition Research and Human Biomedical Experimentation in Aboriginal Communities and Residential Schools, 1942–1952," *Histoire sociale/Social history*, Volume 46, Number 91, May 2013.

31. I have come under fire from the anger of First Nations individuals a few times in my social interactions, and my response has varied from being in correct alignment with Ally Theory, to failing spectacularly. I discuss the difficulties and ethics of handling confrontation and anger in my blog post "Speaking Truth to Anger" at www.stonecircle press.com.

32. "Blaming the victim" and denying the reality of the oppressed is similar to the abuser/abused relationship, in which the dysfunction is for the abuser to gaslight and/or scapegoat the victim and deny their own accountability.

33. The study of epigenetics has identified "generational grief" as the continuous passing on of unresolved and deep-seated emotions, such as grief and chronic sadness, to successive descendants. "Report on Historic Trauma and Aboriginal Healing," *Aboriginal Healing Foundation*, 2004.

In reconciliation work of all kinds, it is recognized that forgiveness can be an expansive practice that often has nothing to do with the abuser, yet can free and heal the self. Native people are in charge of their own recovery and I do not presume to speak for them, but based on my own warm friendships with First Nations women I envision a multitude of safe spaces where encounters can take place between native and non-native community members, and social relationships can be healed. This aspect of the reconciliation continuum would require an expansion of intimate heart-knowing for all participants, and we would be encouraged to acknowledge the residual pain of historic and contemporary injustice. *"One can forgive but one should never forget."* Modelled after the *Truth and Reconciliation* (TRC) process in Canada to hear First Nations testimony, create awareness, make recommendations, work toward justice and support reconciliation, these gatherings or small groups could continue to take place in diverse communities. If it is something we truly want, perhaps we can navigate the emotional waters together, seeking an opportunity to have "risky conversations," while edging toward shared acceptance and reconciliation. I think that together we could become agents of unconditional love by mutually recognizing the devastation of the past, mapping out an understanding of our common future, and working toward the goal of peaceful co-existence. Perhaps the timely directive to re-land ourselves, to reclaim our own IK or EIK is a parallel objective, and that our mutual responsibility, as native or non-native, is to coexist as green seers, wisewomen and *Keepers of the Earth*. (It's a jump I know, to go from colonization to mutual co-arising, but considering the *Seven Generations* code,[37] where else can we be going?)

It is my habit to use the dominance of the patriarchy as a lens through which to view history, and to describe our own liberated and recently-reclaimed history as white women in broad strokes, we lost our best European wise women, keepers of the *Old Ways*, "waeccan," "wycces" or wicca practitioners and healers in the 1450 to 1700 genocide of the Burning Times (otherwise known as the "Women's Holocaust"). In the

---

34. Also known as "universalizing the particular," white privilege allows those in the dominant society to define reality for everybody else, with the expectation that this position will be fully backed by the power of the media, institutions and the dominant hegemony. Perspectivism means that those with white privilege are allowed to think that their own experiences apply to everyone else.

35. Unlike other countries where genocide has occurred, there has not been any actual results in Canada (as yet), from the movement toward the persecution of church and government officials and their predecessors for *Crimes Against Humanity*.

36. "Report on Historic Trauma and Aboriginal Healing," *Aboriginal Healing Foundation*, 2004.

37. It is an important teaching of both the Anishnaabe and Haudenosaunee to consider the well-being of the *Seven Generations* yet to come in all endeavors, and this responsibility requires the ethics of sustainability and care. Ultimately, the tribal landbase, well-being, collective identity and cultural traditions in the past, present and future are all enhanced and protected by this directive.

total supremacy of a "man's world," white women have long been the passive and suffering victims of Empire, or the supporting cast and game players who internalized the values of the patriarchy and were complicit with the colonial directive. Until the flowering of first-wave feminism with the suffragettes in the late 19th century, European women were owned, dominated, controlled, and victimized by the patriarchy for millennia. And as much as we have achieved emancipation and empowerment today, we need to realize that the benefits and privileges we experience as white women are the result of Euro-supremacy. The gifts and amenities we take for granted have come at the high cost of human suffering, and the near-annihilation of both Indigenous cultures and the land.

"There needs to be struggle in order to lay out a path to co-existence, and that the process of being uncomfortable is essential for non-indigenous people to move from being enemy to adversary to ally."[38] (Taiaiake Alfred)

Once lost in the hegemonic agenda to stomp out EIK and IK all over the world, white women and men are now waking up in unprecedented numbers from the patriarchal mass delusion that equally dominates women, the Earth, and tribal peoples that live in connection to Her. It has taken us a couple of millennia to finally rebel against the horrors and inequalities of male supremacy (!) and our liberation is well underway. We are working hard within a vast coalition of women and men to "set things right," to shift our society to the non-patriarchal values that embody cooperation and inclusion instead of hierarchy and control. There is evidence everywhere of a collective movement toward the *Divine Feminine* paradigm which promotes biophilia,[39] personal and planetary healing, community cohesiveness, earth-connected sustainability and peaceful co-existence. We are also being asked at this monumental time to choose between collaborating with, or resisting racial injustice.

Any kind of racism perpetuates the division between women, and sabotages the potential for us to work together as allies and "Sisters in Spirit." Unfortunately there is not a lot of common ground in feminist ideology, as feminism has failed to acknowledge the historic differences between white identity and that of native women, and white feminists have incorrectly assumed that non-native and native women are working through the same liberation process. Yet, our oppressions are not interchangeable, as white women seek to reject or overthrow the patriarchy, while native women are primarily working toward the recovery of their own traditional culture, sovereignty and self-determination. It does not seem to occur to white feminists that the struggle in the dominant society for women's rights has no equivalent in Indigenous resistance efforts that seek decolonization, as Poesia explains. *"There is a difference between fighting for 'rights' and fighting against ending occupation, imperialism, and femicide. When we seek 'rights,' we are asking to be integrated into a system that aims to destroy our entire existence.*"[40] To make things even more complicated, patriarchal oppression did not exist in Indigenous societies and is a colonial overlay, the racist agenda being to devalue both genders and set up false hierarchies where none existed before. Traditional Indigenous societies were egalitarian and based on the model of the consensus circle, with the emphasis on gender harmony rather than gender equality. *"The Indigenous Circle of Life philosophy more appropriately embodies Aboriginal women's conceptions of human nature, their political philosophy and their strategy for social change and liberation."*[41] (Grace J.M.W. Ouellette)

Our trajectories are completely different, yet if there is one thing that both native and non-native women have in common, it must be the countless years of enforced silence whereby our voices were denied, suppressed, criminalized, and unwelcome at the table. For the entire Christian era, white women were expected to be silent, obedient and invisible. The legend is passed down that when learning of the status of white women at the time of European contact, First Nations often wondered - what kind of demented people would marginalize, enslave, denounce and abuse their own women?

The majority of Turtle Island Indigenous women continue to deny the universalist notions of a *Global Sisterhood* and reject the principles of modern feminism by situating it as a movement directed entirely by white privilege. Indigenous women and women of colour may also object to the idea perpetuated by the overculture, that we share identity or experience simply by virtue of being women, and possessing the same reproductive and nurturing female anatomy. But many would agree that the EIK-based tenets of Celtic Reconstructionist Paganism, Druidry, or Goddess Spirituality (an offshoot of feminism) would be comparable to their own IK. Recovery from colonialism has no timeline, yet it may be possible to embody at some point the heart-knowing that all women, both native and non-native, are the frequency holders for the global recovery of IK/EIK and the paradigm shift to earth-wise feminine values. The ancient matriarchal cultures of *Old Europe* provide models for their descendants today, and many Indigenous societies have never relinquished their traditional matriarchal, matrifocal or matrilineal structures. In the pre-colonial Haudenosaunee world, the Clan Mothers held the highest authority as the earth-keepers and life-givers, and were highly skilled at making decisions affecting the well-being of the entire tribe. In our mutual decolonization, there is much to suggest that the empowerment of women in our time and the resurgence of women in governance and spiritual life is either culturally inclusive or transcends ethnicity altogether. The prominence of women in key leadership roles continues to rise in Turtle Island First Nations community, and in diverse ethnic and cultural groups worldwide, as well as in the dominant society.

Meanwhile, our task as white women is to become re-rooted in our own EIK and recover the sacred essence that perpetually spirals us back to a deep connection to the land. Call me a dreamer, but could our love for Mother Earth be the force that unites us all?

Non-native sisters take care - don't voluntarily position yourself in the spaces of any aspect of Turtle Island cultural practice or IK. (Alternatively said, don't go where you are not wanted.) Become strong in your own earth-connected heritage instead, and help to create a true coming-together of hearts and minds in emotional integrity, equality and right relationship. In building a bridge between cultures, white women need to remain aware of the legacy of colonialism (which is our own history), and to value First Nations counter-narratives as fully equal to our own. There is no level ground in this coming together, no "automatic harmony," and to expect otherwise is to dismiss native identity and impose yet another form of assimilation. *"There is a reductionism inherent in liberalist conceptions of Unity, and from the Aboriginal perspective, the best laid plans for native/non-native partnership may always have the feel of homogenization."*[42] (Sam Grey) We need to be aware that in all sectors of society and culture (feminism, Neo-Paganism, Neotribalism and New Age Spirituality included) neo-liberalism can claim a universalist, humanist approach while having an effect on oppressed peoples that is the exact opposite.

White men and women need to stop their highly offensive appropriation and romanticization of native cultures, and become accountable for their white privilege in a realistic way. As I explore in the chapter "Allyship" there is an acceptable process unfolding that allows white people to draw close and give back to First Nations as activists in the struggle for racial justice. So, except for certain Elders who enjoy being patronized or may be receiving financial benefit in some way, the majority of Turtle Island First Nations knowledge keepers have had enough of non-native inroads into their spirituality, and we are being told to cease and desist from cultural theft. To ignore these directives coming from Indian Country, and to continue the appropriation of any element of First Nations material or spiritual culture just because it appeals to us, is an act of arrogance and cultural imperialism.

"Cultural exploitation is the appropriation of elements from a subordinated culture by a dominant culture without substantive reciprocity, permission, and/or compensation."[43] (Richard A. Rogers)

---

38. Taiaiake Alfred (Kahnawake Mohawk), Introduction, *Unsettling the Settler Within: Indian Residential Schools, Truth Telling and Reconciliation in Canada* by Paulette Regan, UBC Press, 2010.
39. The term *"biophilia"* describes our innate affinity for all living things, as popularized by biologist E.O. Wilson's famous essay of the same name. As the organizing principles

that guide people into closer connection with the systems of Earth, biophilia also refers to our primeval roots that can be re-awakened at any time. In opposition to biophilia, Wilson identified a "selfish gene" which stresses individual gain over collaboration, and the competition for wealth and power that is linked to resource extraction and environmental destruction.

40. Poesia, "Death of Empire: Decolonizing Feminism(s)," *Shades of Silence (SOS) Colors of Revolt*, June 5, 2013. (http://shadesofsilence.org)

41. Grace J.M.W. Ouellette. *The Fourth World: An Indigenous Perspective on Feminism and Aboriginal Women's Activism*, Fernwood Publishing, 2004.

42. Sam Grey, "Decolonising Feminism," *Enweyin*, Vol. VIII, 2003-2004. (www.academia.edu)

43. Richard A. Rogers, *From Cultural Exchange to Transculturation: A Review and Reconceptualization of Cultural Appropriation*, School of Communication, Northern Arizona University, 2006.

5. Poetics

The progressive concept of "inclusivity" is linked to neo-liberalism, white privilege and power, and I am aware that it is only the dominant white society that argues in the name of the universal, but regardless of blowback (and without pretending we are all the same) I continue to hold the vision for a thriving collective of diverse *Earth Sisters* bonded to the *Ancient Spirit* of the land.

Liminal Zone

I know I have no right to speak -
As the shadows gather
your tears continue to flow
my care - yet another burden
another misguided platitude
that doesn't quite fit the healing pattern.
Nothing tangible is accomplished
yet, with or without your blessing
this is what I have to say.

That if it was in my power to take the pain away,
        the weight of history, I would.

The heart-wounding of generations
you embody, the diaspora you carry
from the dawn to dusk of every waking day,
the rape of the women, the butchering of the children,
the almost complete annihilation from genocide, forced relocation,
        residential schools,
assimilation strategies born from racist colonial policies,
the sacrifice of your best warriors -
the severing of your people from traditional knowledge
        and ancient wisdom
and the surrender of your soul-connection to the land.

So many losses -
massive damage beyond comprehension
barely a context left from your original life to hold on to,
        to treasure
mere whispers from the Ancestors,
a sovereign truth compared to this bleak new world.

Who would have predicted that the wild rice would be gone?
That the land would be controlled and the rites of passage forbidden?
That the devouring monsters would come right to your front door?

You stand before me - the enemy -
with icy demeanor
you call me "privileged white woman"
in this your voice is strong
you assume that I do not know of isolation, trauma or despair
and you need to tell me that you hate me.

What is it I can do?

If it was in my power to take the pain away,
the burden of history, I would.

But the only real power I have is the power of One,
the power of my own heart-speak.

I cannot demean you further.
I cannot change the past.
I cannot ask your forgiveness.
To do so would align me with the most destructive force
        the world has ever known,
Criminals that have lost their place in the circle of creation
The soulless ones that worship Empire, those that dominate and
        destroy.

The only real power I have is the power of One,
And with this I can fight for the rights of Anishnaabe women
        and the Earth
As writer, as ally, as friend -
And if you know anything about my whiteness, know this:
That my life's work is to honour the Earth in all I think, say and do.
And above all, to reject the patriarchal ethics that dominate
        our humanity and the land.

My only power is that of my own true heart's knowing.

And so ~ with or without your blessing,
what I choose
is to love you as Soul-Sister.

Threshold to Sisterhood

And in this fledgling love
A small fire in the darkness
The spirit luminous in every woman
Before time and before place
There is something we all share
Each a spark of the Great Mystery
In our natural divinity we are whole
Nothing has ever been broken
Knowing our true heart's home
We hold ourselves gently
In perfect love and perfect trust

Daughters of the Earth!
We remember our connection to Gaia
We align ourselves with Her
We embrace Her as we embrace Ourselves

We ~ eternal reflections of the Great Mother
Red, yellow, black, brown, or white
Our roots ever-spiralling from ancient motherlines
Seeds that burst forth in flowering beauty!
All of us ~ Daughters of the Goddess!
Intimates of the blood mysteries
The nurturers of the living
Sacred vessels for spirit
Ever perfect, ever loving, always blessed

We are strong in our bones as the earth is strong!

Daughters of the Earth!
We remember our connection to Gaia
We know ourselves in Her
We embrace Her as we embrace Ourselves

We reclaim our true power
As the mystics, seers and saviors
As the steady hands that rock the cradle

Our circles form in bonds of protection
We speak for the green realm, for all beings
We are the Wise Women and Warriors
The Keepers of the Water
We align ourselves with natural law
And we express the Divine Feminine
In all we think, say and do

Daughters of the Earth!
We remember our connection to Gaia
We bind ourselves to Her
We embrace Her as we embrace Ourselves

We are Luminaries rising
We are Sisters in Spirit rising
We are Wild Women rising
We are Grandmothers rising
We are the Old Ones rising

Maiden, Mother, Crone
Rooted to Mother Earth
Healing ourselves and all beings
Our *Divine Feminine* dancing
Our thriving sisterhood in Her

We are eternal reflections
Of the Great Mother
And in the sacred circle of life
SHE will guide us all back home

6. We All Have IK

"Blessed are those who hunger and thirst for the survival of Indigenous cultures, for they shall preserve a legacy of wisdom accumulated from the beginning of time."[44] (Daniel Quinn)

With his epic anti-appropriation statement *"Everyone needs to get back to their own IK,"* James Dumont has given us a great blessing by implying that IK is the collective birthright of all humanity, and that we all have original IK. Before the rise of patriarchal warlords and the hegemony of organized religion, science and economic power, all cultural groups (including the Gaelic, Baltic or Nordic, for example) were indigenous, often matriarchal, and came from societies deeply connected to the land and the cycles of all life. At one time we **all** lived in tribal groups that acknowledged the sacred in every activity and emphasized the bonds of the community over the cult of the individual. Our indigenous world was perceived through our history, traditions and kinship groups, and experienced through our relationships with the animals and the wild. We were comfortable in the natural world and were in unity with the spirits, elementals, Ancestors and spiritual forces with whom we shared our lives. As Daniel Quinn outlines in *The Story of B*, all humans were once "Leavers" as opposed to the "Takers" that eventually built our civilization.[45] At some point in everyone's history, the technological warlords took hold and decimated our traditional, earth-connected, pagan way of life.

Beginning in Europe, the colonization of white folk through religious and economic dominance went on for centuries before the creation of homogenous Empire in the "new world." As we fast forward past the witch-burnings of the Inquisition(s), the arrival of scientific reductionism with its further attempt to abolish natural mystery and magic, past the diabolical practices of the nuclear age to our own era of toxic hypermodernity, it is finally declared that transplanted modern North Americans come from a culture void of spirituality. To look back to the most common and typical baby boomer childhood in suburbia this is absolutely true. If those of us developed a sense of the sacred or followed a spiritual path it was probably of our own making, and came later in life when we were able to consciously reject the church, the cultural bias on left-brain thinking, and the rise of materialistic consumerism. Like a volcano lying dormant for eons, the explosion of spiritual choices in our own time (today's "spiritual smorgasbord") is the polarized response to a painful lack of spiritual life taken to the extreme.

The term "spirituality" can imply infinite personal variations, but sadly, those in the mainstream automatically make a default association with organized religion and the church. Monotheistic religions such as Christianity seem to be more about dogma, control and convenience than an authentic spiritual life that arises from independent thought, mystical experience, and a personal connection to the divine or Mother Earth (which indigenity sees as the source of all that is sacred). As Deepak Chopra says, *"religion is a belief in someone else's experience, and spirituality is having your own experience."* Aside from political-religious fanaticism, paying lip service, and the convenient "fallback" death-bed mechanism that Christianity provides, the hold of the church over the educated, critical-thinking population is definitely on the wane.

Yet, as stripped of our ancestral myths and knowledge as we Settlers seem to be, we defy the position of patriarchal dominance and undermine the notion of cultural superiority when we reclaim the roots of our authentic indigenity. It is our birthright as human beings to declare our true status as *People of the Earth* (as it is for all cultural groups), and if we collectively reject the delusional separation from nature that Empire has forced upon us, we move back into right relationship with the Earth and all beings. Anchoring ourselves deeply into our earth-honoring culture and reclaiming our EIK is a powerful blow against the monolith of cultural imperialism.

*"The Settler Society were **all** displaced - they **all** left something behind, and that must be why they are attracted to Native Spirituality."*[46] (Lee Maracle)

---

44. Daniel Quinn, *The Story of B: An Adventure of the Mind and Spirit*, Bantam, 1997.
45. Ibid.
46. Lee Maracle (Stó:lō), "Idle No More: Looking Back, Moving Ahead," panel discussion, *Lakefield Literary Festival*, 2013.

The entire era of the patriarchal rise and maintenance of Christianity as a dominant ruling force (from the first century to the present) marks the constant wearing away and fragmenting of IK all over the planet. And as we come to understand colonization over millennia and the historical impact it has had on **all** people, including us as Europeans, we become aware of how and when our eco-values were stolen from us, and how many of our own people lost their lives as a result of the structural violence endemic to establishing Empire. As we were forced to assimilate into the monocultural white mainstream in the Americas we had to leave behind the traditional elements we still held from our EIK - our European languages, foods, music, games, rituals and spiritual expressions. Military invasion, war, the socio-economic class system, food shortages and poverty (as a result of hegemonic policies and patriarchal greed) drove us to abandon our deep-rooted EIK traditions in the frenzy of expulsion and relocation. During the collective dementia of economic, religious and forced immigration, we sacrificed our European histories and spirituality, our love of place, our deep connections to our Ancestors, and our most important cultural keystones. In exile, our survival mechanism kicked in, and our EIK was traded away and our cultural loss forgotten for the promise of a new land and a new life.

"We white Americans of European ancestry had our indigenous cultures stolen from us, and had our lands, lifestyles and lives destroyed, just as we have gone on to steal and destroy around the globe. It happened long ago, of course, so we barely remember it......the land remembers it......it's all there, still reverberating through our bodies, like gongs still sounding centuries after they were struck with the mallet......and that pain shapes us, and hurts us still, and that, of course, is the deep reason we do what we do now to the planet. If we don't seek to understand that, how can we ever expect to change our behavior?"[47] (Tim Bennett)

Today, as the descendants of the Settler Society, we need to examine how this immense cultural soul loss has led to our collective and personal dysfunction, and how the stories of our disconnect must be at the root of our ongoing spiritual hunger and our yearning for holistic earth-connected community. Clearly the loss of cultural diversity and the exile from our own EIK is the contributing factor to our romanticization and appropriation from the vibrancy of other cultures. Important elements of our own EIK, such as song, dance and games, have been insidiously replaced with expressions of manifest destiny, progress, patriotism and nationalism that only reinforce the hegemonic dominance of religion, the military complex and the capitalist economy. Today no one questions that the emotional responses we naturally feel and express for these homogenous state-sanctioned EIK substitutions

---

47. Writer/Director Timothy S. Bennett, *What a Way to Go: Life at the End of Empire*, Producer Sally Erickson, VisionQuest Pictures, 2007. (www.whatawaytogomovie.com)

could be better directed to celebrations of earth-connected culture, sustainability and a reverence for all life. Empire is the great leveler of all cultural diversity, and "*anthropologist Margaret Mead spoke of her concern that, as we drift toward a more homogenous world, we are laying the foundations of a blandly amorphous and singularly generic modern culture that ultimately will have no rivals. The entire imagination of humanity, she feared, might be confined within the limits of a single intellectual and spiritual modality. Her nightmare was the possibility that we might wake up one day and not even remember what had been lost.*"[48] (Wade Davis)

In the grand scheme of things, the Euro-invasion of the so-called "new world" and the building of the North American civilization is relatively new. Here on Turtle Island, we have internalized the oppression of the dominating stratum and white hegemony, and our hearts and minds have been colonized. Whatever we call it, most activists, social critics, feminists and spiritually-awake people are engaged in uncolonization, and the work of deconstructing the colonialism in themselves and others. Uncolonization remembers and rebuilds IK/EIK, and good work is going on today within the many components of culture such as governance, environmental sustainability, nutrition, medicine and spirituality. For all of our alliances and relationships, uncolonization insists that we understand ourselves as pre-colonial people, and that by implementing ancient themes and ideals we can adopt holistic solutions and build earth-connected community once again.

IK systems found all over the world are irreplaceable members of the global ethnosphere, and need to be rejuvenated and protected. IK embodies the wisdom and understanding that is accumulated over thousands of years, and provides alternative models to Empire and domination. There are no universal laws governing the diverse forms of IK found worldwide, but earth-honoring cultures do share common tenets and lifeways. Alternative definitions or terms for IK may include "indigenous roots," "traditional knowledge (TK)," "traditional ecological knowledge (TEK)," "indigenous ways of living in nature (IWLN)," "traditional cultural expressions (TCEs)," "animist folk traditions," "indigenous spiritual ways," Original Instructions, "indigenous science," "ecological science," "land-emergent knowledge," ancestral wisdom, ancestral wisdom teachings, ancestral knowledge, ancestral thinking, ancestral pathways, "folk knowledge" or local wisdom. Informed by my own personal land-based knowledge, here is a comprehensive collection of *IK/EIK Tenets and Lifeways* drawn from ancient origins, including those that most certainly were (and still are) found in the wide range of EIK and pagan traditions of *Old Europe*, plus Celtic Reconstructionism (CR), Nordic Paganism, Druidry and Matriarchal Studies.

---

48. Wade Davis, *Light at the Edge of the World: A Journey through the Realm of Vanishing Cultures,* Douglas & McIntyre, 2007.

A Compilation of IK/EIK Tenets & Lifeways

- The Earth is the Sacred Mother of All, the source of all life and joy. We honour our blessed Gaia and support the interconnected web of life that sustains us all.

- The world is a place of sacred mystery, and our relationship with the world is rooted in a profound respect for the land and all life. Humans are not above creation but part of it, and we flourish within the boundaries of the *Sacred Circle.*

- Expressions of cosmic order are apparent in all things, material or divine, and we acknowledge the great *Turning Wheel* of macrocosm and microcosm in the physical, emotional, mental and spiritual aspects of all beings. We are not separate from the whole, but are an essential part of the collective of all life, and with our wisdom-in-action we seek to maintain the interconnectivity, balance and harmony that is intrinsic to Creation. *"As above so below."*

- From the cyclical patterns of the natural world we learn that all things are constantly in motion, shifting and changing, and we embrace these ephemeral conditions of existence, embodying the principles of spontaneity and transformation in our own lives.

- All things in nature are alive and intelligent, with their own purpose and evolution. All life is equal, and the presence of animation, the life spark, implies a degree of consciousness whether it is in human or more-than-human life. We recognize that the patterns in nature, elements, geoforms, plants, animals and humanity are all kindred spirits, and that our common destinies are linked together.

- When we fully recognize the interconnectivity of all creation, we acknowledge that it is the responsibility of human beings to use our agency to enrich and protect the sacred web, especially the life-giving elements of water, earth and air. We have a love and reverence for all life, and a balanced and harmonious relationship with the Earth.

- *"The earth is not just here for human consumption, as all species have a right to exist for their own sake, and we live in balance with the needs of nature instead of trying to mold nature to fit the needs of humans"* (see the definition of "biocentrism" on Page 270). We consider our actions in relationship to the *Seven Generations* yet to come and the long-term effects on all life, not just on short-term expediency or the comfort of the human community. This does not mean that we cannot use the elements, species and plants respectfully, but that our use has limitations, and when we respect these boundaries with full care and consideration, our human communities also thrive as a result.

- At the heart of the epistemology of all IK systems is the recognition that human beings need the water, plants and animals to live, and that the water supply, food forest, and predator/prey relationship is essential to all life. This fundamental sacred dynamic is approached with great propriety, humility, gratitude, respect, protocol, care and ceremony. The ability to stay within natural limits and in a symbiotic relationship with the ecosystems of the planet represents the height of human intelligence and sophistication, and there is absolutely nothing in the belief systems, achievements, or technologies of misguided humancentric western civilization that even comes close to this pre-eminence.

- Collected over time, we communally hold a wealth of information on the appropriate use of plants, animals and elements as food, medicine and material culture, and the transfer of this IK within the community is properly authenticated.

- All human culture arises or is informed by the land, from our bond to a particular landscape, and we are connected to the climate, beings, deities and spirits that dwell there. Our very blood and DNA is tied to our ancestral lands, and we are rooted in place, inseparable from our homelands, deeply linked to the sacred places that are the source of our origin stories, folklore and myths. The love of the land and our tribal group is the only true wealth we have - we are part of the Earth and the Earth is part of us.

- Our IK/EIK is an ancient, communal, holistic and spiritual wisdom that encompasses every aspect of human existence. Gathered over many eons, our oral tradition covers a canon of themes rich in mystery and power, in which complex interactions are encouraged between humans, animals, greenery, spirit beings, ancient energies, deities and the elementals in the natural world. Our origin, creation and migration stories are deeply embedded in the land, follow natural law, and hold the keystones to our traditions and cultural meanings. At the heart of our worldviews are narratives of emergence that outline our arising from the weave of nature, our interconnectivity with the sacred elements of earth, water, fire and air, and the beings that populate the more-than-human world.

- Our stories and storytelling are sacred practices in indigenous societies, as traditional narratives and songs compiled over time in our own unique language link us to our Ancestors and the sacred ecology of the land. Myths, poetic sagas and folklore are passed from storyteller to storyteller and bard to bard for countless generations, and our most valuable origin stories, histories, memories, beliefs, insights, cultural keystones, prophecies, guiding forces and magical happenings are embedded within our dynamic oral tradition. Sets of stories or story "bundles" serve as valuable teaching aids for understanding different aspects of tribal life such as governance, hunting, harvesting of wild foods, healing, medicine, women's mysteries, ceremony, pilgrimage, and guidance for our children as they grow.

- In our intrinsic knowing and experience with the structures and beauty of the Earth, IK/EIK societies worldwide gravitate toward the sacred geometry that is at the heart of the natural world, and our cultural, ceremonial and artistic expressions are based on symbols such as the concentric circle, quadrated circle, four directions or quarters, zigzag, spiral, diamond shape, meander, line in the landscape, sacred passage, world tree, labyrinth and nautilus shell; and systems such as the golden ratio and the fibonacci sequence. These archetypal forms appear over and over, suggesting that the "building blocks of life" are connected to our identity and have great meaning, as we experience our lives in a fundamentally sacred way.

- Human beings are gifted to have a unique interface with the Earth through our senses and sensibilities, and our ceremonies, rituals, songs, dances, performances, art, craft, prophecies and dreams are interconnected intellectual, artistic and spiritual expressions of our unique culture and IK/EIK. The empowerment of both the individual and the community is tied to creative practice and artisanal work, as using our hands to produce functional and decorative objects with natural materials such as wood, stone, clay, bone, feathers, shells, hide, plant fibre and pigment allows us to enter the "timeless time" of creative flow. Similarly, giving voice to our souls through music and dance connects us to the natural rhythms of our bodies, the earth and the entire cosmos.

- The natural energies, animals, creatures, plants, stones, elements of earth/fire/water/air, and the very Earth itself - any or all aspects of the natural world can have deep personal significance and meaning for any person who is attuned to the wonder, magic and mystery of creation. We are in sync with the cycles of the seasons and the rhythm of our days, and are comfortable in non-linear time and space. Our interaction with the plants, animals, elementals, spirits of the land, sacred fire, and other primordial forces can give rise to awe-filled and luminous encounters. We acknowledge the sacred in every activity and emphasize the bonds of the community over the cult of the individual. We have no interest in denying natural law or penetrating the *Great Mystery*, but are content to know our place within creation.

- Local experience is key to IK as it is developed and lived in connection to a specific place and environment within a 50-kilometer radius (excluding trade routes). As we experience the land, learning directly from the wild and formulating our knowledge as connected to a specific locality, we naturally define IK as "*our extensive knowledge systems of the land, our interaction with the complex, energetic local environment, our knowledge gained through observation and introspection, and our understanding of our connectedness to Creation. This knowledge base, or 'Original Instructions' is our local adaptation, acquisition of knowledge, and the union of perception, symbolism, social reinforcement, belief and understanding.*"[49] (Robert Lovelace)

- Our existence is sustained by expressions of gratitude such as prayer, ceremony, meditation and fasting, as we unconditionally give thanks for all life and the elements that make life possible. We are in a symbiotic relationship with the Earth, as everything we need to live a *Good Life* comes from the land, and our activities are intertwined with the cycles and seasons of nature. When we embody these principles and have respect for all beings through ceremony and prayer, the cosmic balance is upheld and restored, and the survival of the community ongoing.

- The reciprocity of maintaining good relationships with each other and all beings is a shared collective value, and our elders, bards and mentors teach us and model to us the virtues of wisdom, bravery, generosity and selflessness that guide us in these interactions. It is our responsibility to hold the role of our teachers in the highest regard, and to ensure that the generations following also become *Wise Elders*, and continue to pass on our collective values, history and IK/EIK.

- In marked contrast to the competitive "possessive individualism" of western-centric capitalist systems, we as indigenous or re-indigenized people are not indoctrinated by the selfish goals of material acquisition or ego advancement. Our focus is community-based, and we support the unique strengths of each person to contribute to the whole. We practice kindness and loyalty, cooperate with each other, take pride in our connectivity, work toward common goals, share responsibility to create material and spiritual culture(s), take turns at leadership, gently critique or unconditionally praise in equal share, be good hosts to those from other territories, and realize strength from our disciplined collectivity - all in service to the well-being and unity of the community.

- Our personal goal in life (and that of all the individuals in our kinship group) is to become whole and true human beings, to value who we are from infant to elder, to fulfill the potential of our personal mythology, and to harmonize and integrate all aspects of our being equally - our physical, mental, emotional and spiritual awareness – all culminating in the agency of personal sovereignty.

- Even with the best of care and preparation, members of traditional societies will face the harsher seasons of nature and experience loss, hardship, and times of hunger, and we must depend on the ethics of communal sharing to survive. In times of scarcity, we are able to call on our reserves of equanimity, personal resolve and willpower, and to practice a discipline of "mind over matter." Earth-connected peoples are trained to let our minds and spirits take over when the physical body is weak, and extraordinary achievements of stamina, strength and endurance are entirely possible. In times of crisis and adversity, the metaphysical world takes prominence over the physical world, and spiritual experiences such as dreams, visions, natural phenomena and visitations become our guiding forces. The vagaries and inconsistencies of life are a reality, and however dire, are not entirely unexpected in societies that do not adhere to binary thinking or false dilemmas.

- Certain individuals in indigenous societies[50] will be called to seek wisdom, guidance and oracular assistance from the worlds of non-ordinary reality on a regular basis, exploring eternal themes such as living and dying, spiritual connectivity, and healing practices that are accessible through illness, fasting, trance, drumming, chanting, dancing, dreaming, intake of psychotropic plants and other visionary experiences. *"The task is to dwell in the land of the spirits - and then to return to the Earth world, bringing back the information and wisdom learned. The task of a sacred undertaking is to inform, guide, and inspire the people."*[51] (Chellis Glendinning) Constant change is the magical fabric of life, Earth is the source of all enchantment and spiritual power, and potent transformational experiences in conjunction with the elements, forces and spirits in nature are equally available to all people.

- We honour the life-creating power of the *Sacred Feminine* and the women in our culture as an extension of the miraculous divinity of creation. Women are revered, and their fertility, procreative and nurturing abilities are known to be exactly the same as the Creatrix, chalice, crucible or cosmic womb that exists at the center of the universe. The inviolate nature and wholeness of women allows them to be exempt from tribal methods of spiritual seeking, petitions, initiations such as the "vision quest," or sweatlodge renewal. In traditional and modern matriarchies or egalitarian societies, our IK teaches us to embrace the naturalness of physical contact in raising our children, and in expressions of familial, friendly or passionate love. We are well aware that human beings are designed in every way for the enhanced physical, spiritual and emotional wellness that comes from physical contact. We are at one with the mysteries and capabilities of our bodies, with nudity, with touching, with closeness, with intimacy, with sexual expression, with movement, with posture, with exercise, with pain, with illness, with aging, with dying, and all the natural manifestations and expressions of our physical bodies, the ground of our being. *Women's Mysteries* are a sacred and respected part of the IK/EIK held communally by the tribe.

- We revere and honour our Ancestors, the trustees of the Earth, and our offerings and altars enable us to feel their presence, connect us to our original culture and place of origin, and preserve our heritage. Those who have gone before have established the traditions that guide us, and their bloodlines and genetic material have created us. There is no greater continuity to our IK/EIK memory and oral tradition, both individually and collectively, than communing with the ancient wisdom of our *Ancestral Spirits*. With gratitude we call upon them to teach us and show us the way, and we understand that in the greater continuum of time we are the Ancestors of the future.

- Humans are born pre-wired with indigenous attributes that are either eroded through imperialistic western knowledge systems or supported by earth-connected community. Suggested from the IK of diverse traditional societies, indicators of personal health, holism and interconnectivity can appear as:

> *"Quiet mind,*
> *happiness like that of a child,*
> *vitality - an abundance of energy and creativity in the body,*
> *a commitment to mentoring others,*
> *empathy and a deep connection to all beings,*
> *proactive cooperation, with the initiative to help others,*
> *being fully alive and giving one hundred percent to every endeavor,*
> *embodying the natural law of impermanence,*
> *and having a loving heart and compassion for all life."* [52] (Jon Young)

- Our IK is not frozen in time, but has proven to be highly adaptive to many influences and conditions, such as displacement and urban environments. Our journey of discovery and revitalization is to recover, re-learn, embody, thrive with, and preserve our traditional IK/EIK in the places we are living, for all land is sacred land!

Presenting the most optimal and earth-connected traditional IK/EIK tenets, this compilation may appear at first glance to be far removed from contemporary life. Yet taken individually or as a whole, this in-depth collection of IK/EIK principles can give us a firm foundation and guide us toward our own EIK recovery project. Considering the eroded condition of the environment today and our restricted access to wild nature, it may be impossible to fully re-create the vibrancy and inclusivity of an earth-wise culture. Our challenge then, is to reclaim or enhance for ourselves the aspects of a foundational bond to the land that will give rise to our own EIK, and find our kindred spirits and community links.

For those living in urban areas either by choice or necessity, there are many ways to practice our ancestral wisdom, reclaim "indigenous mind" and bring the wonder of nature back to the city streets. In our exploration of the green commons, public parks, planted spaces, borders, cemeteries, quiet corners, abandoned lands and so-called "wastelands," we can revere urban space just as much as wild or semi-wild ecosystems. And as we get to know the landforms and ancient cultures that were there before urbanization, we will find that the magic of the earth is ever-present in the older landscape beneath the surface of the city. As they always have, the ancestral spirits and "genius loci"[53] (spirits of place) are willing to communicate with us, and we need only to be open to their messages. Taking strength from earth energy, practicing "earthing,"[54] paying attention to the tree people, stones or birds, and bringing elements and natural objects from the wild into our urban interiors, are all ways to stay connected to the land. Marking the seasons and cycles of the moon, celebrating the quarters and solstices, and coming together with like-minded community in ceremony and ritual are ancient practices that express our earth-rooted beliefs in urban spaces. Rewilding, re-greening the commons, urban herbcraft, natural medicine and community farming are all ways to create deep connections to the actual and spiritual gifts of the soil.

As we travel along our newly-found spiritual path and reconnect deeply with our eco-selves and the land, doesn't it make more sense to reawaken our own specific ancestral wisdom and EIK? Surely this will please both our Ancestors and the Divine, not to mention the worldwide network of earth-honoring cultures to which we belong. If we desire to anchor into our own EIK, to alternate between the heart and mind of authentic theory and practice, each of us will find our place in the Indigenous circle. To love the land completely, with our entire heart and soul, is to protect and sustain the sacred ground of our collective being for the generations yet to come. There are many hopeful and exciting examples and suggestions for uncolonizing ourselves, reanimating our ecological worldview and practicing our authentic ancestral knowledge, either in full or in part (and to the best of our ability) in *Part Two*.

---

49. Robert Lovelace (Tslagi/Algonquin), Presentation, *Lakes Commons Gathering*, October 22, 2012. (www.youtube.com)

50. In Indigenous societies the mystics, seers, medicine people, conjurers, curanderas and shamans were indispensable to the health and welfare of both the individual and the collective. A heightened focus on these practitioners by Western knowledge systems such as anthropology and ethnology has led to the New Age, Neo-Pagan and Neotribal emphasis on the "shamanic journey," which has been appropriated and lifted out of context from the originating IK system(s). The fabricated contemporary "spiritual practice" of "shamanism" continues to grow, but reflective of consumerism it is a free-for-all compiled from a multitude of belief and practices, and does not include the essential holistic connection to wild nature, the other-than-human world, and the specificity of sacred homelands.

51. Chellis Glendinning, *My Name is Chellis and I'm in Recovery from Western Civilization*, Shambhala, 1994.

52. Wilderness guide and author Jon Young (http://jonyoung.org) has summarized eight indicators of indigenity and initiated a collaborative global movement across cultural lines to reconnect people deeply to nature and their ancestral knowledge. Along with his associates he offers support and mentoring in the hypermodern world, repairing and reclaiming life-enhancing cultural practices that renew our connection to nature, peaceful community and the web of all life. *"Deep nature connection changes us. It rewires us and enables us to make much more of our human potential. Deep in all of our roots, there are stories of our Ancestors living in healthy, regenerative communities, villages where people of all ages were in deep relationship with the land, each other, and themselves."* (Jon Young) The regeneration process, including building the tools for sustainable business and permaculture, takes about two years to achieve. Experiential, nature-based programs such as "The Art of Mentoring" help us to remember the *Old Ways* and apply them to our modern communities. (www.regenerativedesign.org)

53. All land is sacred, but places that embody "genius loci" can be said to be more highly charged with spiritual energy or healing power from natural formations such as ley lines, songlines, wellsprings, forest groves or mountains. Known as "numina" to the ancient Romans, these special places are home to the "numen" - ancient earth spirits, intelligent entities, orbs or deities - or are sites that still resonate with culturally-significant historical events and pilgrimages (psychogeography). Sacred sites with "genius loci" and living spirit presence are often marked with unique human creations such as megalithic stone circles, mounds, petroforms, petroglyphs, medicine wheels, spirit roads, labyrinths, earthworks, temples and shrines. See more on *Sacred Sites* on Page 249.

54. See more on *Earthing* on Page 225.

7. Lifting IK and Inventing Identity

"Native people do NOT use the label 'Shaman.'"[55]
(NAFPS/New Age Frauds and Plastic Shamans)

The challenge today certainly, for those of us of European descent, is to turn back or move forward to more sustainable eco-ethics, and to take on the work of uncolonizing our hearts, minds and opulent lifestyles. We need to re-enchant and rebalance the world with a massive injection of earth-connected and holistic principles promoting biophilia, rewilding, personal and planetary healing, peace-making, social justice, earth-connected sustainability and peaceful co-existence. This resurgence is happening everywhere, in all sectors of society, and the various knowledge systems and their disseminators are doing a wonderful job at bending the curve.[56] But what is often missing in these practices are the spiritual expressions that would arise from a strong, grounded connection to the land itself, from the recovery of our own ancestral traditions, and from *"getting back to our own IK."*

Unfortunately, statements of eco-consciousness that are present in esoteric usage and holistic ventures are often token injections of some aspect of blended philosophy (i.e. Lakota or Hopi), lifted from an earth-connected culture worlds away from the place and natural landscape where one is actually living. These fantasies and fabrications follow the lead of the countless native-identified New Age or Neo-Pagan spiritual practitioners and authors who have been offering their appropriated versions of "tribal wisdom" since the rise of the 1960's counterculture. Brand-new spiritual practices and ceremonies have been created by borrowing aspects of initiation rites, vision quests, healing modalities or purification rituals from groups as diverse as the Lakota, Navajo or Cree, and given newly-created names such as "sweet medicine," "native medicine-ways," "great spirit mandala" or "sacred shields." These days I wince whenever I see a "Twyla Dancing Raven" or a "Susan Moon Feather" who is visibly disconnected from any real ancestral lineage or membership with a First Nations cultural group.

These homogenous quasi-native practices and statements are looking more and more nonsensical, when

a) one is practicing IK without holding themselves accountable to their local First Nations communities,
b) one has the infinite beauty of their own cultural EIK to access,
c) one is not connecting to the highest truth of their self, their own cultural group and their own Ancestors,
d) one is not exhibiting a genuine desire to do the hard work that is required to develop an authentic EIK, to involve oneself in genuine cultural expressions and stewardship of nature, to join the *Circle of all Life* grounded in the truth of one's being.

It is true that human societies have always shared and traded stories, ideas, TEK and articles of commerce, and through a process of syncretism, have created new cultural blends, hybrids, and aesthetic combinations. Cultural exchange and adaptation is a good thing, and knowledge is constantly shifting and changing, but cultural appropriation occurs when a power imbalance is in play from centuries of racism and imperialism, and there is a relationship between a dominant and subordinate culture. When looking at the colonial project closely, fragments of knowledge have been constantly taken from the sacred IK systems of subordinate cultures without any ethical consideration whatsoever. Like precious jewels on a string, the elements of an IK system are built up over millennia, and the sacred keystones and heart of that specific worldview are connected to every other component. Like a house of cards, pieces and parts cannot be taken out and used without serious harm or collapse being done to the whole system. In today's New Age environment, the manipulation and simulation of clothing, objects, story, ritual, image, song or ceremony by non-natives culminates in a newly-packaged identity that enriches the public self these "shamanic practitioners" offer to paying clients.

Any kind of identity theft from Turtle Island First Nations perpetuates the colonial agenda which moves first to seize the land, then the resources, and finally, specific elements of the Indigenous cultural identity that have already been subjected to ethnic cleansing and genocide. More than just the lifting of ideas, practices and physical objects, cultural appropriation and identity theft are direct acts that **dominate** the way oppressed groups present themselves to the world. Not to mention the disempowerment and loss of basic human dignity this suggests, Indigenous people no longer have their own autonomy or control over how they are represented in the public domain, which is a fundamental right for every human being. When white academics, scholars, writers and New Age or Neo-Pagan practitioners (those with advantage and power) write or teach about the cultural and spiritual traditions of Indigenous societies, they are in fact dominating the original IK. Their versions of IK become the valid narratives, fabrications that are sold back to the white majority and even to Indigenous peoples themselves. The white privilege and imperialism of cultural appropriation undermines the efforts of Indigenous groups to preserve their own specific IK, and 168 Nations worldwide have acknowledged these rights by signing the United Nations *Declaration on the Rights of Indigenous Peoples*.[57] A major victory for the Indigenous people who took part in drafting this monumental declaration, September 13, 2007 marks the day when the United Nations and its member states, in collaboration with Indigenous societies worldwide, began the process of reconciling the painful legacy of colonization and moving forward guided by the standards of international human rights.

From Grey Owl to Mary Summer Rain to Little Grandmother,[58] playing around with one's personal identity is clearly an indulgence of the white leisure class, a privilege for those whose own culture is *"not under siege or in danger of annihilation."*[59] Critical responses by First Nations to the white appropriation of their spirituality and culture is now readily available in books, essays, blogs, Facebook groups and pages, and judging from their comments, they are shocked, horrified and insulted by any adoption of native identity in any sphere of popular culture or spiritual life. NDN's[60] stress over and over that there are absolutely no conditions that make it acceptable for a non-native person to assume a native identity and become a "cultural ambassador" of First Nations IK to other white people. Also in these groups and pages, we see that white pseudo-shamans are an object of ridicule and derision by First Nations peoples. If you don't believe this to be true, then I would suggest following the work of Indigenous activists and organizations[61] that monitor cultural appropriation such as *NAFPS: New Age Frauds & Plastic Shamans; Native Appropriations: Examining Representations of Indigenous Peoples;* or *F.A.I.R. MEDIA* for a couple of days.

---

55. Introduction, *NAFPS/New Age Frauds and Plastic Shamans.* (www.newagefraud.org)
56. According to Paul Hawken in *Blessed Unrest: How the Largest Social Movement in History Is Restoring Grace, Justice, and Beauty to the World* (Penguin, 2007) there are over two million organizations working toward ecological sustainability and social justice on the planet (with this number rising exponentially). *"The 'largest social movement in history' stems from a commitment to act for the sake of all life on earth, and having the vision, courage and solidarity to do so."*
57. For more on the United Nations *Declaration on the Rights of Indigenous Peoples* see *Note 5* on Page 22.
58. Jamake Highwater, Evelyn Eaton, Sedonia Cahill, Dhyani Ywahoo, Osheana Fast Wolf, Shequish Ohoho, Robert "Ghostwolf" Franzone, Wolf Moondance, Mary Summer Rain, Brooke Medicine Eagle, Jamie Sams, Lynn Andrews, Harley "Swift Deer" Reagan, Little Grandmother (Kiesha Crowther), White Eagle Medicine Woman (Rachel Holzwarth and her giant "medicine drum") and James Arthur Ray have all been exposed as frauds by First Nations community. Grace Spotted Eagle, Wallace Black Elk, Ed McGaa/Eagle Man and Chief Golden Light Eagle (Star-Knowledge) have been denounced for selling pan-Indian IK to white spiritual seekers by their own Lakota, Dakota and Yankton people.
59. F.A.I.R. MEDIA (For Accurate Indigenous Representation), Facebook comment, 2013.
60. NDN is the American acronym for "North American Indian."
61. For details see *NAFPS: New Age Frauds & Plastic Shamans* (www.newagefraud.org), and *Native Appropriations: Examining Representations of Indigenous Peoples* (http://nativeappropriations.com). Facebook groups and pages that comment on cultural appropriation are readily available, such as *F.A.I.R. MEDIA, Land O Fakes, When White People Go Bad, Global Decolonization Initiative, Eradicating Offensive Native Mascotry (EONM), Not Your Mascots, Unapologetically Indigenous,* and *Native Imagery Appropriation Wall of Shame.* There are watchdog individuals and organizations within Indian Country that will launch legal action to address extreme forms of cultural theft and appropriation in the worlds of fashion, pop culture, sports, fine art and New Age Capitalism, and the illegal activity connected with this kind of commercialization. It is a good idea before using **any** First Nations element in your project, spirituality or marketing to find out what First Nations people actually think about it. If you are unsure, ask your local First Nations community leader or academic, or start a Facebook dialogue!

In the pursuit of spiritual expression, when you have become enchanted by native-themed "shamanic" Neo-Pagan or New Age practices, what you adore is a complete fabrication, a white invention separated out from the original context, a spin-off, a stereotype, and a commodification of authentic IK. And when First Nations people are telling us over and over that cultural appropriation is demeaning and disempowering (as well as a continuation of colonialism), we really need to rearrange our ethical maps and stop our offensive behavior. In grappling for the shiny treasures we lack in our own lives, white people have forgotten basic values like honour and respect.

Sadly, the popular practice of assuming the title of "Shaman" to describe one's quasi-native practice is now so widespread that it would be impossible to send it back to the Pandora's box, or misguided inclusivity, from which it came. (Is it possible to repatriate colonized words back to the originating culture? Not likely.) First coming to light in the 1914 reports of American ethnologists, the origins of the term "shaman" describe the practices of the Evenki-speaking Tungusian and Samoyedic tribes of eastern Siberia, and it can be argued that only practitioners from those specific Indigenous societies have the entitlement to use it. "NeoShaman," "Urban Shaman" or even "Post-Urban Shaman" may be a better choice, as it at least honestly indicates that the shamanism practiced is a modern hybrid, created from disparate and pan-Indian elements of traditional IK. To deal with the problem of nomenclature, when we go back to our ancestral lines and specific EIK (or combination thereof), we may find a culturally-appropriate term that replicates the various roles and responsibilities of a "shaman" in our own original pre-colonial culture. Examples of acceptable alternatives could include Celtic Priestess, Anglo Druidess and Waeccan Green Seer, plus Ban-Filid (Irish Seer), Ban-Draoi (Irish Druidess), Ingheaw Andagha (Irish Priestess and "daughter of fire"), Awenyddion (Welsh oracle and soothsayer), Taibhsear (Scots Gaelic for "vision seeker"), An Dà Shealleadh (Scots Gaelic for "second sight"), Gallicenae (Gaulish Priestess), Senae (Priestess of Brittany and guardian of the sacred cauldron), Seiðkona (Old Norse seer and spirit traveler), Enaree (ancient Scythian Amazon Priestess), Drabarni (Romany or Roma), Curandero (traditional Spanish or Latin American healer), Animist, Sibyl, Spirit-Worker, Wise Woman, Loremistress, or Woodspriestess. It has also been my observation that individuals in Anishnaabe or Haudenosaunee community respond with perplexity or cognitive dissonance when "shaman" is mentioned in the conversation, as the term is not part of their traditional worldview or language.

"Shaman is NOT a North American Indian word......shaman is a word created and stitched together by European anthro-pologists, a Euro-colonial code word for spiritual and cultural appropriation."[62] (N. Jostein Hetland)

The contemporary over-use of the term "shaman" (or "shamanic") to describe a wide array of practices, attitudes and mystical experiences has rendered it almost meaningless, and if modern "shamanic practitioners" actually took the time to find out, they would learn that the vast majority of Turtle Island First Nation individuals are strongly opposed to the use of the term "shaman" by any white person. "Shaman" is never used in genuine Turtle Island community to describe wisdom keepers, medicine holders, healers or other Elders, and anyone self-identifying as a "shaman" is immediately perceived to be lacking in any form of authentic cultural connection. First Nations also view the promotion or marketing of "shamanic healing" or "wisdom services" in any context to be extremely egotistic, a hubristic gesture of elitism and a sign of disrespect to the genuine knowledge keepers. As a highly-charged identity marker, the use of "shaman" is becoming more and more problematic, yet the good news is that there are many well-respected non-native authors, mystics, visionaries and practitioners who have the good sense NOT to use it. *"I do not use the term 'shaman' because, in the current of my own soul, I experience the word as an invocation that holds too much magic of a culture that is not my own."*[63] (Emma Restall Orr)

The major flaw in the contemporary and rapidly expanding "shamanic" movement is that most practitioners are completely disconnected from the Earth, and situate their services in artificially-created urban spaces, some even denying indigenity altogether. Inseparable from the aspects, elements, wild nature and other-than-human world of the home landscape, pre-colonial shamanism has always been rooted in place, and the work of the shaman is impossible without a genuine earth-spirit connection, as David Abram explains. *"Anthropology's inability to discern the shaman's allegiance to nonhuman nature has led to a curious circumstance whereby many persons in search of spiritual understanding are enrolling in workshops concerned with 'shamanic healing techniques.' Shamanism has come to connote an alternative form of therapy; the emphasis, among these new practitioners of popular shamanism, on personal insight and curing. These are noble aims, to be sure, yet they are secondary to, and derivative from, the primary role of the indigenous shaman, a role that cannot be fulfilled without long and sustained exposure to wild nature, to its patterns and vicissitudes. Mimicking the indigenous shaman's curative methods without his intimate knowledge of the wider natural community cannot do anything more than trade certain symptoms for others, or shift the locus of dis-ease from place to place within the human community. For the source of stress lies in the relation between the human community and the natural landscape."*[64]

Even more troubling is the claim by practitioners that they teach "core shamanism" or "universal shamanism." This is a perfect storm of pan-Indianism, whereby different IK systems are misinterpreted & blended together, perpetuating the falsehood that all IK is the same, and giving license to perform and sell any kind of IK or ceremony. In today's hopeful climate of Turtle Island Indigenous resurgence, it is considered an act of racism, aggression and domination when a New Age "shaman" refutes or ignores the requests or demands from First Nations to stop with their cultural appropriation. Even if the false "shamanic" identity has been perpetuated for years and the practitioner has an established business, they need to stop aligning with the racist policies of colonialism and white knowledge domination. Shifting to the authentic earth-connected wisdom traditions of one's own ancestors and offering that EIK to one's cultural group is not such a difficult thing, and would be a blessing to all involved. So-called "shamans" and "shaman-priestesses" have re-created themselves once, and can do it again (!) this time using their own true identity and ethnicity, and their followers will love them for it. In fact, with the millions of spiritually-starved and culturally-alienated diasporans in the Americas, it is inconceivable that those focused on spiritual and cultural renewal would not see the value in offering their own authentic EIK teachings to others!

As "exotic" as these self-created novice "shamans" are, paradoxically they fulfill (for a price) the yearning arising from non-native people today for a simpler life, a connection to nature and community, and a return to earth-based values. In actuality, the contemporary yearning for IK and ecological civilization is a healthy, valuable consciousness that will hopefully culminate in the "tipping point" required to halt the destructive practices of Eurocentric empire and lead to the healing of ourselves and the planet. Keeping in mind however, that the first European Settlers were transplanted in massive population movements and diasporas to Turtle Island, we who are their descendants need to respect the Ancestors and traditional IK of Turtle Island First Nation cultures, and practice the EIK that is authentic to us.

62. N. Jostein Hetland, Facebook comment, *When White People Go Bad*, 2013.
63. Emma Restall Orr, "Animism, Anarchy and Living Druidry," *Sacred Hoop: A Quarterly Magazine for Shamanism, Sacred Wisdom and Earth Spirituality*, 2004. (www.sacredhoop.org)
64. David Abram, "The Ecology of Magic," *The Spell of the Sensuous: Perception and Language in a More-Than-Human World*, Vintage Books, 1997.

8. Who Gave You Permission?

"*It is a belief shared by Native Americans that all cultures were given certain gifts and a certain place by the Great Mystery. That they differ from one another is not a theological contradiction or even a problem. What makes the Whiteshaman feel compelled to go outside of his or her own culture for spiritual and creative nourishment? And, further, to disregard accuracy?*"[65]
(Wendy Rose)

The practice of cultural appropriation has a long and uneasy history. Since white Europeans are the dominant race with all the privilege, the automatic assumption (theft) of an oppressed people's ideas, spirituality, artifacts and worldview has taken place without question. A thread of justification since colonial times has been the anthropological and artistic efforts such as the "recovery project" photography of Edward Curtis, and the "documentary" paintings of artists such as Paul Kane, Edmund Morris, Frederick Arthur Verner and Emily Carr. The culturally-sanctioned popular notion in the colonial era was to document the tribe-as-subject and add these portraits to the historical record, since those groups were dying out anyway. This despicable legacy, the genocide that accompanied the Eurocentric white supremacist founding of the Americas, has yet to be fully addressed with sufficient apology, justice, true reconciliation, or any kind of reasonable compensation whatsoever. Early colonial depictions of Indigenous people in photography, painting and advertising were fabrications of the love/hate Euro-conqueror mentality toward First Nations, and the creation of the "Imaginary Indian"[66] has continued to the present day with the proliferation of stereotypical New Age posters, memes and messages. Yet, it is with amazing resiliency, pride, and power that First Nations everywhere are recovering, thriving and restoring their IK on a massive scale, in communities, academia and urban centres. A huge renaissance has been underway, and has revived their spiritual life, connection to source, connection to the land and connection to each other.

A phenomenon that has had negative consequences for sovereign First Nations is "pan-Indianism" (just as misleading as "core shamanism"), whereby partial traditions from different groups are blended together to create so-called knowledge systems and cultures that never existed in the first place. This artificial combining of cultural elements using the "white gaze," reinforces false ideologies and romanticized stereotypes, and does nothing to strengthen specific First Nation communities and their recovery of nationhood, ancestral lands and cultural traditions. You can see the evidence of pan-Indianism everywhere, in publishing, fashion, trends and movements, and in the commodification and marketing of so-called "First Nations" products. Across the New Age and Neo-Pagan spectrum, elements of cultural and spiritual property that have been lifted from Turtle Island First Nations are found in pseudo-rituals for creating sacred space, four directions petitioning, smudging, talking stick circles, drumming, "featherwork," vision quests, sweatlodge recreations, sacred fire gatherings, initiation rites, and the aesthetic delights of Indigenous material culture such as headdresses, wardrobe, jewellery and décor. The ongoing popularity of native-themed creations, symbols and fabrications in the worlds of fashion, fine art and entertainment suggest that First Nations are a thing of the past or "frozen in time," and these stereotypes negate the reality that Indigenous people are part of contemporary, living cultures struggling to overcome oppression. In many cases Indigenous people are erased in the concepts of the overculture, such as the immoral practice of using derogatory racist slurs for team names or "mascots" in sports, or using Indigenous people as dehumanized decorative props to sell goods, ideas and services. The genuine voices, cultural markers and IK of First Nations people themselves are negated in this hodgepodge and *Indians who are trying to find their way back to the old ways become hopelessly lost in the morass of consumerist spirituality.*[67] (Andrea Smith) Even more alarming are the cult-like intertribal communities or "societies" that have come into being, usually led by a charismatic or bombastic non-native with fake native credentials.[68] Unfortunately today, most people's knowledge of First Nations is erroneous information based on various elements of synthetic pan-Indianism.

A commonly-held stereotype that came out of early New Age activity was the belief that wise medicine men and mystical elders were just waiting around on Indian reservations for the non-native spiritual seeker to show up. They took the white man or woman under their wing, performed some magical rite, dispensed cryptic wisdom, gave them their native name with an eagle feather, and bestowing on them the blessings of their newly-adopted IK, set them off on an itinerant journey down the Red Road. It would take some delving to uncover the exact source of this *New Age Myth* (Carlos Castaneda, Lynn Andrews and Ed McGaa/Eagle Man come to mind) and what role native people themselves played in perpetuating it. Desperate for the means to survive on Indian reserves, providing spiritual services may have been one way of putting food on the table, and this kind of income may have led to the beginning of spiritual tourism and the "Indigenous Industry."[69] In another twist that continues to privilege New Agers, First Nations were forced into poverty by white imperialism in the first place, and by purchasing their spiritual property today, white spiritual seekers are taking advantage of colonization and forging yet another link in the chain of cultural genocide.

Many spiritual practitioners are surprised to learn that what they have been doing is a form of cultural appropriation. Without being told otherwise, they have made the assumption that fabricating a tribal identity for themselves is socially acceptable. Being blessed with white privilege, those adopting native identities don't seem to know or care about the racialized histories of their actions. Seeing themselves as rebels, and feeling good about identifying as tribal in opposition to the non-tribal industrial civilization, white shamanic practitioners are unaware that their appropriation of IK can *"stereotype, homogenise, objectify, commodify, distort and invalidate"*[70] Indigenous cultures. In the belief that their shamanic practice somehow "celebrates other cultures" they are in denial that their privilege is a direct benefit from the "*power dynamics that have been in place from centuries of imperialism, racism, exoticism, capitalism and colonialism. They may choose to believe they are disconnected from any form of oppression, but even their sense of entitlement to have an experience of the 'other' is symptomatic of white privilege.*"[71] (harshbrowns)

For those who have fabricated native identities or are considering doing so, Celeste McCaw gives a clear guideline:

"*Because cultural appropriation often entails a financial gain on the part of the appropriator, I would argue that it is akin to identity theft. However, unlike the crime of identity theft, there is no remedial recourse for the group of people whose culture has been appropriated. Thus, those individuals who own the appropriated culture continue to endure the countless hardships and setbacks that their culture oftentimes face while the appropriators profit from those sufferings. Maybe cultural appropriation is a crime, and we just haven't given a punishment to it yet.*"[72]

When your own culture is void of spirituality, and the church holds no interest, where is one supposed to turn for modern tribalism or earth-wise spirituality? It is heart-breaking that in many cases our first stirrings of spiritual life, or spiritual awakening in this aspiritual materialistic society, is linked to an intermittent experience with a Turtle Island First Nations ceremony or pseudo-ceremony, in some kind of default position. Why should a spiritual life be something that is approached haphazardly, purchased in a consumer marketplace, or taken from the cultural markers of oppressed people? Where is our own EIK, sacred ceremonies, earth-honoring rituals and rites of passage? Since we have been assuming that the roots of Gaelic, Baltic or Nordic EIK are lost to the mists of time, it has been much easier to access knowledge from the Anishnaabe or Lakota, and two hundred years of history is much easier to delve into than two thousand. Unfortunately, it has become painfully clear that the "pretend Indians" are more interested in appropriating the material culture, iconography and tools of "native spirituality" than to acknowledge the ongoing oppression and social justice struggles of real Turtle Island First Nations, who are the original creators and holders of the IK traditions. Cultural appropriation is so widespread that a complete axiology would be impossible, but we know for sure that white privilege has allowed this activity to carry on without permission or an ethical code, or any kind of critical thinking whatsoever.

---

65. Wendy Rose, "Just What's All This Fuss About Whiteshamanism Anyway," *Coyote Was Here: Essays on Contemporary Native American Literary and Political Mobilization*, Bo Schöler (editor), The Dolphin, No. 9, April 1984.

66. Reflective of white culture and attitudes, early Euro-colonizers manufactured a wide range of false ideologies about First Nations, such as the thematic wild and free "primitive barbarian," "heathen," "superstitious pagan," "human wolf," "brave," "wicked savage," "noble savage," "backward savage," "hostile savage," "incorrigible savage," "ignoble savage," "bloodthirsty red-skin," "warrior," "exotic curiosity," "pristine environmentalist," "Indian princess," "strange race," "timeless Indian," "natural man," "wise elder," "mystic shaman," "forest philosopher," "blessed innocent" and "indigene." None of these racist stereotypes, caricatures, distortions, or exotic romanticized fantasies of the "textbook Indian" had anything to do with the reality of First Nation culture(s), and the fabricated image of "the other" was integral to the invention of Canadian identity. *The Other came to stand for everything the Euro-Canadian was not.* Daniel Francis, *The Imaginary Indian: the Image of the Indian in Canadian Culture*, Arsenal Pulp Press, 1992; and *National Dreams: Myth, Memory and Canadian History*, Arsenal Pulp Press, 2002.

67. Andrea Smith, "For All Those Who Were Indian in a Former Life," *Cultural Survival Quarterly*, 1994.

68. There are many, but the most extreme cases would have to be Harley "Swift Deer" Reagan of the "Deer Tribe Metis Medicine Society/Red Lodge Longhouse/Sweet Medicine SunDance Path." "*Quodoushka (the sex-ceremonial practice of the DTMMS) is a direct affront to all Native Americans. These people are not authentically native in any sense, shape or form. Harley Reagan, a racist and survivalist gun nut, is one of the most despised people in Indian Country.*" Al Carroll, American Indian Movement (www.phoenixnewtimes.com). Also, while not exactly presenting himself as a neo-shaman, New Age Guru James Arthur Ray incorporated First Nations sweatlodge pseudo-ceremonies into his highly-priced empowerment program without any permission, or understanding of the original IK. He misused the form and sacred teachings of the sweatlodge ceremony and people died as a result, for which he has claimed no responsibility. It is no wonder Turtle Island First Nations are opposed to white spiritual seekers learning about, or participating in Indigenous ceremony! See "The Red Road is Not For Sale" by Wambli Sina Win (Lakota), *The Native Times*, March 2011. (www.nativetimes.com)

69. There are dual meanings for "Indigenous Industry." One refers to the many-tentacled institutional and funding bureaucracies that are the result of the paternalistic relationship of governments to First Nation communities. My use here is different, as the "Indigenous Industry" can also said to be the First Nations teachers, elders and pseudo-native practitioners who collect fees to offer bits and pieces of white-approved and whitewashed versions of IK. It is not possible to make a complete generalization, but it can be noted that many genuine wisdom keepers are primarily occupied with the recovery and resurgence of IK in their **own** communities, not by getting on board with white-led IK interpretations or New Age ideologies.

70. "The Kreayshawn Complex: Cultural Appropriation as Counter-Cultural Expression," *harshbrowns*, (blog), March 7, 2012. (http://harshbrowns.wordpress.com)

71. Ibid.

72. Celeste McCaw, "The New Identity Theft: Cultural Appropriation and Redefining Identity in America," *Race & Social Justice Law Review*, September 21, 2015. (https://race-and-social-justice-review.law.miami.edu/identity-theft-cultural-appropriation-redefining-identity-america)

9. Who Are "Your Elders?"

Non-native spiritual seekers need to take a step back and re-examine their present or future relationships with Indigenous Elders, much of which is based on incoherent thinking and erroneous assumptions. "Elder Essentialism" is the belief that **all** elders are keepers of IK, the "more-than-human" holders of the keys to the mysteries, and as our profound teachers and mystics are deserving of our worship and devotion. To indulge in this veneration is considered to be interference, as it is only the members of a specific First Nations community who are entitled to name their own Elders. Without knowing the community consensus, white spiritual seekers are not qualified to label any native person as "Elder." Nor do governments, institutions, or any outsiders have the right to label anyone an "Elder" without being privy to the community-based naming process. In step with New Age practices, colonized and lost Indigenous identity mixed in with pan-Indianism has given rise to brand-new coalitions and societies where none existed before. White spiritual seekers may fall prey to aligning themselves with the many dubious native or non-native "shamanic" practitioners presenting themselves as "Elders," who are claiming to represent an IK system or "tribe." Even those in Indigenous communities fall prey to these "snake-oil sellers" and *the young ones who are vulnerable and unknowing, believe in the myth of who these people are.*[73] (Jessica Jones)

To make matters worse, the white spiritual seeker who happens to be accommodated in their quest by a community member (or so-called "Elder") will always make the assumption that "their Elder" acts as the representative of the entire community, and that the community is in agreement with the elder's actions. The idea that one individual can represent an entire Indigenous community, or speak on behalf of all Indigenous people, or is an expert on IK, is called "tokenism." When white spiritual seekers latch on to a token, it creates the appearance of inclusiveness or tribal consensus in matters such as IK activity, which may not be the actual reality. In most cultural groups today, complete agreement, unanimity or accord is extremely rare, and why should it be any different for First Nations? The legacy of colonialism and the brutal tactics of "divide and conquer" have scattered Indigenous communities far and wide, and community members are often divisive and fragmented instead of united. Today, decolonizing awareness and healing is underway in *Indian Country* to address this infighting and lack of consensus.

Hostility, intense competition, and lateral violence can take place in any marginalized person, group or culture. Documented as the "crabs in the bucket" phenomenon, crabs in boiling water will claw at the ones trying to escape, pushing them back down into the pot and ensuring their collective demise. Best described by the expression *"if I can't have it neither can you"* this analogy in human behavior negates and diminishes the achievements of successful individuals out of envy and spite. The "crabs in the bucket" syndrome can be used as a metaphor to describe social situations in which members of the disenfranchised group will pull down those who are trying to improve themselves and their lives. Overall, lateral violence can stem from internalized oppression, or an internal lack of self-value that corresponds to external oppression. In our mutual decolonization process, we begin to see that this type of short-sighted and non-constructive behavior is exactly what Empire and the ruling elite want, to keep people fighting each other instead of the true source of the oppression!

The defining qualities of a genuine Elder are not all that complicated, and in native community it is obvious who the "go-to" people are for healing, guidance, prayer and ceremony. An Elder is one who has the wisdom and experience to focus on the important things in life, and who "walks the talk" by embodying this knowledge in their daily lives. An Elder gains authority and leadership in the community as members begin to rely more and more on the accuracy of their counsel. Usually the Elder's discourse is based on values and ways of thinking that transcend confusion and discord, with the emphasis on "good mind" and peace-oriented models for positive and holistic living. As documented in Alanis Obomsawin's film on the Oka crisis, *Kanehsatake: 270 Years of Resistance*, the Mohawks recognized the leadership qualities of an 8-year old boy who basically became an Elder due to his excellent guidance in conflict strategy. Being regarded as an elder, knowledge keeper, wisdom keeper, teacher or mentor is not so much related to age as it is to teachings of wisdom and insight, and *"the community knows who their elders are."*[74] (Roger Speilmann)

An article in the *Canadian Journal of Native Studies* differentiates between an "Honorable Elder" and a "Spiritual Elder,"[75] and outlines their different (yet often interchangeable) functions in Cree community as counseling, teaching, advising, mediating, conflict resolution, conducting ceremonies, healing, storytelling, group problem-solving and role modeling. It has been suggested that the word Elder, since it is established in-situ, is a meaningless designation outside of the originating community, and that it is highly problematic to consider who is actually qualified or authorized to label one's self or another as "Elder." Regardless of the controversy in *Indian Country*, the use of the term "Elder" is currently expanding into non-native culture, as exemplified by the recent use of "Earth Elder" by environmentalists and other cultural creatives to describe the mentoring movement (Earth Elderevolution[76]), and new ventures such as "The Elders,"[77] an independent group of multi-ethnic global leaders established by Nelson Mandala in support of human rights and peace work.

If you are practicing IK that is not your own under the guidance of an Indigenous Elder, you would do well to examine their underlying motives closely. Just because an Elder is willing to share their spiritual knowledge does not mean it is ethical for you to participate, or delve into their IK. If a native "Elder" (or non-native "pseudo-shaman") charges exorbitant fees for workshops, ceremonies, or one-on-one sessions, this is usually an indicator that they have latched onto the pan-Indian New Age circuit, as a genuine community Elder would probably not be participating in these lucrative "pay to pray" arrangements. It takes years to learn the traditions and spirituality unique to a specific culture, and beyond an honorarium, energy exchange or fee to cover expenses, authentic teachers are not in the habit of charging high prices for their IK teachings. And when the memes in the "teachings" of Indigenous elders seem to be derived from the IK-influenced New Age rhetoric that has been fabricated by white authors, academics and spiritual seekers, it may be a reflection of James Dumont's cautionary statement that *Indigenous concepts are appropriated by the dominant culture, 'painted up' and handed back.*[78] We cannot speak for every Indigenous Elder, and every case is unique and different, but we can detect a New Age "guru to the desperate" overlay with some of the jet-setting pay-to-pray wisdom keepers, who consciously or unconsciously buttress the fragmented spiritual life of privileged white people by making them feel better or more "indigenous" for a couple of hours. In defence of this phenomenon, introducing white people to Peruvian, Hawaiian or Mexican myth, story and IK can work as a device to open hearts and minds to the possibility of one's own indigenity, but we would hope the favor is returned in a way that actually addresses the many oppressive challenges faced by the First Nations community member presenting. For all those involved in cross-cultural sharing, it needs to be emphasized that learning about First Nations IK can enhance our overall understanding of earth-connected culture and spirituality, but our main concern is to take on the hard work of reconstructing our own ancestral knowledge and bonding with the land. As those of European descent focus on reviving our own EIK, the practice of bringing in expensive "tokenized" Indigenous speakers and ceremonialists from places like Peru, Mexico, Hawaii or the Amazon may eventually cease.

It can be said that certain elders and "pseudo-shamans" who travel the world offering New-Age influenced spiritual teachings and the universalist "flavour of the moment" experiences to white audiences for a fee, are participating in the "Indigenous Industry" to some extent. It is also true that due to the barrage of New Age spiritual seekers, First Nations Elders have been forced to rethink and redefine themselves and their roles, and to set parameters for sharing important and valuable cultural knowledge. The majority of Indigenous leaders have been called to respond to the environmental crisis with clear directives coming from tribal prophecy, personal vision or the spirit world, and their mandate is to offer Indigenous guidance rooted in their own IK to the world, expecially to those in western society who have lost their way. The consensus among the most prominent leaders is that **all** people need to return to a recognition of the sacred, a spiritual way of life in harmony with natural law and *Earth Community*, and sustainable practices for the generations yet to come. We must deeply admire those who "walk in both worlds" and maintain the balancing act of presenting their vital message to the world, while at the same time remaining focused on cultural survivance, localized resurgence, the spiritual needs of their own communities, and the protection of their own IK, which is probably under threat in some way. In a rapidly-changing world, First Nations are also evolving, and Indigenous scholarship, traditional knowledge, and/or guidelines for sacred space, ritual, ceremony and cultural expressions can also shift and adapt to new ideas, new methods and new places.

If you come across an Elder that approves of you practicing their IK or enables you to do so, it may be that they are desperate for affection, prestige or recognition, or are using you in the millennia-old role of helper or "oshkabaywis" (Anishnaabe). Long ago in traditional communities, assisting the work of the Elders was not the result of a hierarchal structure, but was considered an honour and a privilege. However, in contemporary times this relationship can be insidious in some cases, akin to a dysfunctional co-dependency. Often, relationships between non-native and native individuals play out on a shifting ground of suspicion, indifference and the ever-present barriers of white perspectivism, implicit racism, and the response to racism. Some native people will enable the demands of the non-native spiritual seeker to enact some sort of revenge on the oppressor. And who can blame them?

---

73. Jessica Jones, "Concern Raised about Self-Proclaimed Elders," *Alberta Sweetgrass,* Volume 20, Issue 1, 2012, The Aboriginal Multi-Media Society (AMMSA). (www.ammsa.com) For a survey of the contemporary definition of "Elder" and how the perception of "Elders" has been formed and influenced by the dominant society since the late 1960's, see "The Role of Native Elders: Emergent Issues" by Joseph E. Couture in *Visions of the Heart: Canadian Aboriginal Issues, 2nd Ed*, edited by David Long and Olive Patricia Dickason, Thomson-Nelson, 1998.
74. Roger Spielmann, *Anishnaabe World: A Survival Guide for Building Bridges Between Canada and First Nations*, Your Scrivener Press, 2009.
75. Andrew Hatala and Michel Desjardins, "The Spirit Messenger and the Traditional Exemplar: Two Figures of the Elder among Plains Cree Communities," *The Canadian Journal of Native Studies*, Volume XXX, No. 1, 2010.
76. "Earth Elderevolution," *Center for Human-Earth Restoration* (www.centerforhuman-earthrestoration.com) and Fred Lanphear, "A Movement of Earth Elders: Learning, Living and Empowering Others to Live," *Center for Ecozoic Studies: Seeking Integral Community in an Ecological Age*, 2009. (www.ecozoicstudies.org)
77. *The Elders: an independent group of global leaders working together for peace and human rights* was initiated by Nelson Mandela in 2007. The organization defines Elders as those who no longer hold public office; are independent of any government or vested interest; have earned international trust, demonstrate integrity, and have a reputation for inclusive, progressive leadership; share a common commitment to peace and universal human rights; and bring with them a wealth of expertise and experience. Categories of Elders include *peace makers*, with decades of experience mediating and resolving conflicts around the world, *peace builders* who have helped post-conflict societies to heal and rebuild, *social revolutionaries* who transformed their own countries by reducing poverty, improving the status of women or championing nonviolent struggle, and *pioneering women* who have governed their countries, led international institutions and spearheaded movements to empower other women. An Elder is also a *changemaker* - someone who can lead by example, creating positive social change, and inspiring others to do the same. (www.theelders.org)

78. James Dumont, "Issues in the Native World: The Native Perspective," Class Lecture, *Aboriginal Studies*, Georgian College of Applied Arts & Technology, Barrie, ON, October, 1996. "Painting up" is akin to the process of "whitewashing," whereby an ethnicity, cultural identity or concept is adopted from a subordinate culture by a member of the dominant society, modified with a white face or white ideology, and proclaimed to be the same or better than the original. Clearly these efforts are ridiculous caricatures, and racist attempts to uphold white superiority in political and cultural life. Whitewashing also refers to the process whereby the presence of people of colour (POC) are erased (or glossed over) in reconstituted narratives from historical or contemporary events. It seems that "white" is always the default, and the term "whitesplaining" refers to the entitled, condescending and colorblind tendency to define issues of race and racism for the benefit of people of colour (while exhibiting one's own racism in the process). POC do not need paternalistic "white translators" or "white saviors" to speak for them, or to be expected to answer questions on behalf of their entire ethnic group (which is tokenizing). Whitesplaining reflects the dominant white perspective and the white gaze, and usually involves unsubstantiated "facts," oversimplification, obfuscation, derailment, grasping at straws, outright errors, and a focus on personal details instead of discussing the systemic roots of racism, racial bias or oppression. The new term "Columbusing" refers to the white tendency to "discover" a traditional cultural practice, object or idea from any subordinate group or society, disregard its true origins, appropriate it, strip it from the original meaning, and claim ownership.

10. The Rainbow Tribe & Visioning "The One"

A driving force for the creation and convenient use of pan-Indianism came from the modern myth of a "Rainbow Tribe" that arose in the earliest days of *New Age Spirituality*, hippie culture and the back-to-the-land movement. A remarkable and timely yearning in young white people to reclaim tribalism and develop some kind of a spiritual life was at the heart of the 1960 - 1980 counterculture, and it is not surprising that many Elders and holders of Turtle Island IK became their "gurus" and spiritual "guides." Apparently found in the oral and later written traditions of the Hopi, the "Warriors of the Rainbow," or "Rainbow Tribe" legend tells of people coming together from the four sacred directions of the globe, united in their desire to save Mother Earth from the greed and eco-destruction of western civilization. The origins of the "Rainbow Warrior" tale are nebulous, and the work usually referred to as the primary source for the story - *The Book of the Hopi* by Frank Waters (1963) - actually makes no reference to it. Also attributed to *Black Elk Speaks*[79] by John G. Neihardt (1932), Black Elk's wonderful visions do have some elements of multicultural inclusivity and reference rainbows as having meaning specific to the Lakota people, but there is no actual "Rainbow Warrior" story. To address this strange lack of provenance, over time the myth[80] became described with pan-Indian terminology as a "Native American Legend." The paradisiacal belief in a "Rainbow Tribe" has been growing steadily for both native and non-native people since the early days of New Age Spirituality, and as positive as this trope would appear to be, it has been a major contributor to the pan-Indianism that has interfered with specific Turtle Island communities attempting to recover their sovereignty, cultural traditions and ancestral IK.

Rebelling against the establishment (otherwise known as "the man," "the system" or "big brother") the mandate of the "peace and love" hippie-freaks was to live in harmonious egalitarian alternative communities, and by 1972 plans were underway for the first ever "Rainbow Gathering." (Now a thriving movement called the "Rainbow Family of the Living Light," 1972 - ongoing.) As the story goes, in 1971 a group of "Rainbow Warriors" found a stone on their property with strange markings that they believed to be one of the lost oracle tablets of the Hopi people - the actual keystones etched with the creation stories, prophecies and worldviews of Hopi IK. Taking it with them, they traveled to the Hopi lands for confirmation, but the Hopi Elders they met could not come to any agreement on the authenticity of the stone. Apparently one Hopi Elder spoke of prophecies but implied that it was not clear to him if this particular group of young people were indeed the fulfillment of a "Rainbow Warrior" legend from Hopi oral tradition (or not). The stone continued to be held as sacred by some, both native and non-native, until one day when a hippie hitchhiker forgot it in a passing vehicle!

Rejecting the dominant culture in droves, the hippies reconnected with nature and experimented with communal living, turning to the IK, material culture, folklore and spiritual tools of Turtle Island First Nations with their use of tipis, native foods, clothing, crafts and natural medicines. The prophecies that came forward at the time from various elders were seemingly "a priori" and spoke of white people who would grow their hair long, wear beads and come to Turtle Island Elders for guidance. *"Many will remember their purpose for being on this earth walk and will learn to develop their gifts to assist the whole of humanity. Truth will shatter the bonds of separation and goodness will prevail."*[81] (Rainbow Woman) In the telling and re-telling, the concept of a "Rainbow Tribe" was sanctioned by a wide range of native elders and pseudo-elders, creating an alternative view of an all-encompassing tribalism and blurring the boundaries for those working toward cultural sovereignty and self-determination. The most interesting collection of comments by First Nations elders[82] in favor of the *Rainbow Tribe* includes remarks made by many considered to be fraudulent elders or shamans by NAFPS (*New Age Frauds and Plastic Shamans*).

---

79. The accuracy of John G. Neihardt's Eurocentric rendition (or is it invention?) of the testimony of Black Elk in *Black Elk Speaks* (1932) is currently under fire. See "Black Elk and the Fabrication of Memory" by Barnaby Thieme, *Mesocosm*, 2012. (http://mesocosm.net/2012/12/11/black-elk)

80. The "Rainbow Tribe" concept fits the category of "urban legend," which is a form of modern folklore that serves the purpose of a social group to perpetuate and preserve it, whether or not the story is true.

81. Moriah Puah, "Rainbow Woman," *The Goddess Projects*, 2013. (www.goddessschool.com)

Since its origins in 1972, the concept of a "Rainbow Tribe" continues to be found in the domain of Neo-Pagan and New Age Spirituality, and has been the ongoing inspiration for many concepts and environmental protection ventures such as Greenpeace's "Rainbow Warrior" eco-activist program. The positive message of a Rainbow Tribe suggests a sacred vision of humanity, a coming together of earth-connected warriors in transformative thought and action to turn the tide on ecological devastation. As the protectors and defenders of Mother Earth for the *Seven Generations* yet to come, it has been said that *"we are the ones we have been waiting for."*[83]   But if we are to participate in the Rainbow Tribe, we would do well to revisit this movement by being firmly anchored in our own EIK, instead of leaning in to the IK of Turtle Island First Nations.   In the years since 1972, teachings have continued to appear from diverse sources (including the prophecy of Indigenous Elders) that emphasize the message of a collective movement toward world peace and harmony - a unified consciousness or "One" - and that the qualities of kindness and compassion will be integral to the survival of our species.

"As we move into the future we will work, laugh, play, study, vote - to renew democracy and renew the lives of all. The new mestizaje is the joyous birth of a new humanity. No more barriers, no more racism. The past will not be forgotten but will be blended into the new bodies and cultures that will emerge out of our coming together not in battle or conquest, as in the days of old, but in Love, which is the only force that can unite us without destroying us. That is the way to world peace and harmony, and we struggle, dream and work for that future."[84]   (Virgilio Elizondo)

Assuming that the "One" refers to a "unified consciousness" either within or without (or both), this meme can be examined from every angle. The great mystery traditions and literary canons worldwide confirm that humanity shares knowledge of the "One," a vibratory field that connects all things, a place of universal love and enlightened rapport with the Divine. Alternatively described as "the cosmic unity of One energy," "cosmic consciousness," "the unmanifested absolute," the Over-soul, Indra's Jewels, "the mind of God," "the word," "the music of

---

82. Dan Vantari (aka Firebird, aka Narada Das), "The Rainbow Bird Tribes," presents comments and testimonials by Elders in support of the rainbow tribe, *Bird Tribes,* 2006. (www.birdtribes.net)

83. Erroneously attributed to "Hopi Elders" by New Agers, this clever phase is originally from a 1978 poem by civil rights activist June Jordan, and was recently popularized by Alice Walker in her book *We are the Ones We Have Been Waiting For: Inner Light in a Time of Darkness*, The New Press, 2006.

84. Virgilio Elizondo, "The Sacred in the Latino Experience," *Americanos: Latino Life in the United States*, by Edward James Olmos, Lea Ybarra, Manuel Monterrey and Carlos Fuentes, Little, Brown and Company, 1999.

the spheres," the Tao, shizen (Japan), the Akashic Records, "the unified field," "the field of compassion," "the universal essence," "the source," "pure being," "the global brain," "the holographic realm," "the conscious universe," "the great chain of being," Gnosis, Logos, Unio Mystica, uBuntu, "embracing all that is," "a unity of being that underlies everything," "the frequency domain," "the power of creativity that supports all life," "zero-point field" or the primordial OM, this field of energy is found in the inner worlds of human awareness and our core being, which aligns with the invisible realms and outer worlds of tangible form. Variations of the "unified consciousness" can be reached by opening the heart, prayer, fasting, visioning, dreaming, drumming, focused intent, magical workings, "in the zone" creative or athletic pursuits, yoga, and meditation practice.   I have experienced the "One" many times myself, in dreams, meditation, reverie, focused creativity and times of intense illness. There is no doubt that this multi-level, multidimensional state exists and is within reach, and has been accessible throughout human existence. Many versions of the Indigenous "shamanic journey" enter this layered space for healing, spiritual guidance and problem-solving on behalf of the tribal group. However, the contemporary use of language is inadequate to describe the "One," and better lexicon choices may be "matrix" or "web." The term "oneness" is also problematic in that it assumes a universality to human experience, whereas there are utterly endless ways to experience, interpret and assign cultural meaning and cosmologies to this network. "Oneness" also implies that accessing the matrix tends to be a communal activity with a group of people (which can happen) but when fully examined, experiences are often of a solitary nature.

"Spirituality started to emerge from within us, rising up in each person like a great tide of love, inspiration and Oneness with the source of our being, activating us by the millions. I felt the great light that the mystics speak of radiating outward from within us all. Then in a flash, I felt all people on Earth, and the Earth itself, being healed spontaneously. In that moment of revelation, I felt waves of unconditional love for the whole planetary body and all Earth-life spreading through millions of us."[85] (Barbara Marx Hubbard)

The contemporary movement toward universal unity, "Oneness," "The Law of One," "One Spirit," "One Mind," "One Vision," "One Energy," "One Blood," "One People," "One World," "One Tribe" or "Unitribe" is emerging from all directions - multifaith theology, perennialism, new age spirituality, noetic philosophy, alternative lifestyles, pop culture and yes, even Turtle Island IK. Manifesting today as the collective impulse toward a global consciousness, the "One" implies an ideal and utopian coming together of humankind in love energy, mutual cooperation, harmony and peace. Contributing to this ideology was the work of scholar and visionary Joseph Campbell, who as a beloved "change agent" created the opening for many contemporary seekers to embrace the spiritual life and "follow their bliss." Campbell promoted the idea that the mythology from any cultural tradition could be seen as an aspect of the universal "One Myth" or "monomyth." Now critiqued as an over-simplification, and the *"profoundest flaw in mythological thinking,"*[86] this kind of reductionism leads to the breaking down of cultural diversity, and also allows for the normalization of cultural appropriation. Being immersed in the ethics of Eurocentric patriarchal scholarship, Joseph Campbell could not see that the specific religious property and/or spiritual practices unique to each cultural group should be preserved, not stripped of ethnographic context. Diversity should be the priority, not universalism, and contrary to the popular "One" meme, *"all religions are not different paths up the same mountain – they're different paths up different mountains."*[87] (John Beckett)

From mythology to the study of the human mind, the new philosophy of Noetics, metaphysic theory and contemporary quantum science have all suggested that the interaction of human thought and the connectivity of our belief systems (known as the "noosphere") can actually impact the biosphere, pointing to a form of shared consciousness. Many visionaries claim that 2012 was the beginning of a new era for humanity, as we evolve into a group consciousness more in alignment with universal law and focused on unconditional love, *"which does not judge, exclude nor adhere to one perception."*[88] (Jan Porter) The ethereal idea of a Golden Age for humanity does seem to have taken root, and many believe that it is possible to emulate the way of the universal mind, the "One" beyond all physical limits. Variations on the "One" meme promote a "new dimensional shift," an "evolutionary transition," a "quantum leap forward," and a "new world dawning" for both humanity and the planet itself. But, as the exalted concept of the "One" continues to find popular usage, we need to bring clarification and examine it from a more grounded perspective.

"One Tribe" or the "One" should not mean coming together in a uniform monoculture or some kind of "global order." All beings are subject to the laws of nature which stress that species diversity works better than homogeneity, and that diversity is essential to a healthy ecosystem.

---

85. Barbara Marx Hubbard claims that the planetary birth epiphany she experienced in 1992 signaled the *"next turn on the spiral of evolution, the planetary shift, the birth of a new Earth and a new universal humanity."* From *Birth 2012 and Beyond: Humanity's Great Shift to the Age of Conscious Evolution*, Shift Books, 2012.
86. According to Robert Ellwood *"a tendency to think in generic terms of people or races is undoubtedly the profoundest flaw in mythological thinking."* *The Politics of Myth: A Study of C.G. Jung, Mircea Eliade and Joseph Campbell*, SUNY Press, 1999.
87. John Beckett, "Unfortunate Effects of Joseph Campbell," *Under the Ancient Oaks: Musings of a Pagan, Druid and Unitarian Universalist* (blog), March 2, 2014. (www.patheos.com)
88. Personal communication, Rev. Jan Porter, author and Spiritualist Minister, 2011. (www.inspiredsoulworks.com)

This principle applies to the human community as well (however much we have distanced ourselves from nature), and diversity is the keystone to healthy, thriving human populations. Traditional Indigenous societies were well aware of this natural law and established the clan system, also putting taboos in place to prohibit marriage within one's extended family. Today, it is extremely important for us to develop an appreciation for cultural diversity, and a tolerance for different peoples, stories and sensibilities. But if in actual fact humanity did come together into "One Tribe," it would spell the end of us. As Daniel Quinn says in "The Story of B," "*a multiplicity of tribes and cultural groups in diversity has worked for millions of years and hopefully it will continue for millions more.*"[89] In the interest of further clarification, those in the spiritual community may want to re-examine their over-use of the meme "We Are One," as it could, on some level, be associated with or linked to secular thinking i.e. the neoliberal globalization that perpetuates the hegemony of Empire, colonization and capitalist control. The current push toward globalization actually promotes inequality between cultures and nation-states by applying unrealistic undemocratic standards of homogenous economic exchange, and denies the importance of locally-rooted culture, which naturally gives rise to a healthy diversity of IK/EIK systems.

It is also troubling when we notice that the neo-liberal concept of "inclusivity" and the contemporary meme of "Oneness" is led by a majority of privileged white people, some very wealthy, suggesting yet another form of white hegemony, or perspectivism. It is mostly the dominant society that promotes universality, and white people are leading the charge, making sense of the interrelations for "One," interpreting it for everyone else, and moving us all forward into a utopian future. Also, as Ward Churchill points out, the overuse of the Lakota expression "mitakuye oyasin" (we are all related) and the "One" meme by New Age capitalism allows for cultural appropriation. "*We are all related, we are all the same, which means we are entitled to anything of yours we want.*"[90] The beautiful illusions that the "love and light crowd" hold dear come from a place of privilege, which makes it easy to ignore their shared history with the disenfranchaised, and to deny any accountability for their white racism. In reality, the "One" concept may work for the privileged, but it is hard to imagine marginalized groups having the agency to pursue the interconnectivity of "Oneness" with the oppressor, while engaged in counter-racism work, resistance, and daily survival. What an insult it must be for people of colour to hear "We Are One" coming from the dominant society that is the source of their unrelenting oppression!

---

89. Daniel Quinn, *The Story of B: An Adventure of the Mind and Spirit*, Bantam, 1997.
90. Ward Churchill, *Indians are Us?* Between the Lines, 1984.

"You asserting to me, especially in the face of me critiquing your privilege and racism, that you consider 'all people equal' and that you 'treat all people the same,' denies my experience, and affirms to me your complicity in white supremacy. We do not have an equal experience of the world, and your supposed equal treatment can never be experienced equally."[91] (harshbrowns)

To reinforce the "One" vision it is easy to find obvious similarities and commonalities between cultural groups, but this is hardly the point. Perhaps it is only people devoid of spirituality that need to find similarities between cultural traditions to buttress their own miniscule understanding and practice of holistic ancestral thinking. Beyond a basic knowledge of and respect for the sacred keystones in other Indigenous groups, I have noticed that First Nations people do not indulge in comparative multifaith theory, and it may be a good idea to examine why. Knowing they already have ancestral alignment with their own traditional knowledge, they embody the tools and treasures of their own specific worldview and IK, or are in the process of unpacking them. Why call yourself a member of the "Rainbow Tribe" when you already belong to a specific First Nation, the Michi Saagiig Nishnaabeg, for example? Fortunately, the more appropriate memes of "Different Yet All One" or "Unity in Diversity" are gaining currency, which is also in accord with the recent phrase "All Nations, All Faiths, One Prayer"[92] as put forth by Chief Arvol Looking Horse.

Perhaps the utopian dream that the world will someday exist in peace and love is just more magical thinking, as there is another aspect of natural law that avows our entire existence to hinge on the balance of opposing forces. Beyond any cultural understanding, interpretation, worldview or philosophy, natural law states that by default, the introduction of any concept automatically summons its opposite. As Pagan leader Selena Fox says, *"harmony is not the absence of conflict, but the balance of forces."*[93] And, despite what New Age philosophy advises, the Americas are not going to mystically "wake up" one fine morning. There is no "Oneness" in the quotidian world right now and no amount of ethereal prayer, visualization or wishful thinking is going to make it so. The way that the concept of the "One" continues to be touted by the spiritual community as a philosophic solution to every problem of human life allows spiritual seekers to disassociate themselves from any type of meaningful activism, resistance or political activity. *"What changes culture is legislation, regardless of how much one pleads for divine intervention."*[94] (Derek Beres) Parroting over and over that "We Are All One" allows the "spiritually enlightened" to imagine that this is already the case, and enables the privileged majority to ignore the activism "in the street," "on the ground" or at the grassroots level that would create the conditions for equality or the metaphysics of unity to actually unfold. The most reprehensible aspect of New Age thinking is spiritual bypassing, or the refusal to look at uncomfortable realities *("only focus on the positive – by examining the negative you add more negative!")* which implies a serious level of solipsistic self-deception, and encourages the indulgent behavior of living in a fantasy world. Overlooking the human rights struggles of our fellow humans is morally wrong, and what spiritual seekers perceive to be a move toward enlightenment in the collectivity of the "One" is actually the position of a coward, who has no interest in confronting injustice, or engaging with the reality of serious social issues beyond their cocoon of privilege.

"What I want to criticize are not New Age practices - some of which strike me as possibly beneficial, others as grossly counterfeit - but the way New Age notions discourage engagement with social problems and political realities."[95] (Michael Parenti)

It can also be argued that members of the Settler Society should clean our own house first, by claiming our ethnic karma and becoming accountable to the oppressed peoples of Turtle Island. Equity comes before equality, and placing ourselves behind First Nations peoples in a subordinate position that propels the most oppressed forward is the only solution. "Equity and equality are not equal!"[96] Working toward real change by being responsible for our white privilege and serving to end racism in the real world are the steps we need to take[97] before we begin to think about such abstract and colorblind concepts as "Oneness."

"There will be no social justice, no anti-racism, no feminist emancipation, no liberation of any kind for anybody on this continent unless aboriginal people win their demand for self-determination."[98] (Sunera Thobani)

"The most misused phrases among self-proclaimed 'allies' of Indigenous peoples are 'we are all related', 'all my relations', and 'we are all one.' Most often it seems to mean 'we are all the same' - a mantra used to sidestep the discomfort of discussing colonialism, and the fact that there are those who suffer from colonialism, and those who benefit."[99] (Barbara Low)

*"I am a little bit tired of all my non-POC friends posting the endless feel-good 'We Are One' memes, while they never lift a finger to change the status quo, which they benefit from every single day. I have a handful of friends who realize the price of their privilege and walk their talk, and are true allies in making change, but literally, it's a **handful**. In my experience, the 'love and light' brigade tend to be very hyper-focused on their own personal growth while rarely extending that effort to the greater community. Only privileged people can afford to be that way. Some of us have to deal with the reality of 'what is' on a daily basis, and no, it's not unicorns and rainbows."*[100] (Juliana K'abal-Xok)

"By denying the spiritual and political autonomy of native people, the New Age rainbow people subvert whatever good intentions they may have about multicultural community. What gets created is multi-cultural white middle class dominance in yet another form."[101] (Myke Johnson)

"I call on white people to admit that the Rainbow Nation is a myth, and until we truly are able to recognise the humanity of all people, we cannot claim to be post-racist."[102] (Gillian Schutte)

As I see it, the true danger in practicing the consciousness of the "One" is to ignore or bypass what is precious and sacred about the specific place and community where we are actually living. At the core of the IK common to all human groups is a revered focus on the environment, plants, creatures, cycles and elements of nature in our homelands, not on gratuitously importing other things that are pleasing. The "One" principle may work on an etheric level, but like angelic visitations, extraterrestrial assistance, starseed messages, galactic guidance, planetary alignments, "ascension" and other lofty New Age beliefs, it reinforces an abstract, vertical spirituality away from and separate from the Earth, instead of promoting a horizontal vision which encompasses the Earth, our one beautiful and precious home. According to eco-visionary David Abram, *New Age Thinking* and scientific reductionism share the same misguided principles that separate us from the land. *"New Age spiritualities abandon nature entirely, inviting their adherents to focus their intuitions upon non-material energies and disincarnate beings assumed to operate in an a-physical dimension, pulling the strings of our reality and arranging earthly events according to an order that lies elsewhere, behind the scenes. Commonly reckoned to be at odds with one another, conventional over-reductive science and New Age spiritualities actually fortify one another in their detachment from the Earth, one of them reducing sensible nature to an object with scant room for sentience and creativity, the other projecting all creativity into a supernatural dimension beyond all bodily ken."*[103]

In a society detached from nature, popular claims such as "the purpose of human life is the pursuit of happiness" can be seen as more liberal navel-gazing, and I also take issue with the New Age concept of "evolving to a higher state," as I feel it to be a hubristic and delusional goal focused entirely on humancentric objectives, with an arrogant disregard for the human place in creation. We don't need a new and more enlightened way to inhabit the earth - Indigenous cultures (including our own in *Old Europe*) existed comfortably and sustainably on the planet for millennia, exactly the way human beings are supposed to be living. We already have an honourable niche **within** the circle of all life, and it is supercilious to suggest that we transcend it, or place ourselves above or beside the interconnected web. It is our responsibility to use our human intelligence in service to that network, and to embody reverence in our relationships with the more-than-human world. It is not about the narrow confines of the self, our shadowplay with other human beings, our imaginary connection to a "divinity" outside the earth's sphere, or our incestuous interactions with our own linear concerns, creations or technological wizardry. Clearly we have lost our respect for other beings and the natural world, the very elements that give rise to life itself, so how can anyone claim that humanity is "evolving to a higher state?" It seems to me that the moment we step outside of the *Sacred Circle*, give up our connection to the Earth and our humility in the face of the *Great Mystery*, and start to dominate and control creation, we immediately lose any potential to actualize a spiritual existence.

*"We have to stop with the idea of creating peace **on** earth and begin with creating peace **with** Mother Earth. We have tried the first alternative for thousands of years and look where that has led us - now is the time of the Original Ways, the Native Ways."*[104]
(Tiokasin Ghosthorse)

As we move away from the alienation that was imposed on us by the scientific paradigm, we become empowered to reconnect to the land and the cycles of life, and to engage in the recovery of our essential eco-self and EIK. An important part of our practice is to reflect on the love and harmony between people, and to honour the unique diversity that is the human experience. All beings are distinctly separate but forever connected in the *Circle of Life* and *Earth Community*, and we would do well to embrace our "unity in diversity." Perhaps there is a groundswell of consciousness that is birthing the next cycle of our collective human journey, but if our communities evolve into tribes, may our spiritual practices reflect our "Oneness" with nature and our beloved landscape, the place we call home.

"What many people – even spiritually alert people – seem to miss is that we are all creatures of this earth, this planet, this biosphere. And there's no escaping this condition. Wisdom is epi-phenomenal to life on the Earth – any claim to wisdom that doesn't make us more cognizant of our relationship to trees, insects, dirt and water, is probably a false claim. This is not to say that there's nothing 'transcendent,' but that whatever 'transcends' our earthly condition must be rooted – like a Great Oak, Ash or Willow Tree – in Air, Fire, Water and Stone."[105] (Montague Whitsel)

---

91. "Good White Person," *harshbrowns*, (blog), September 13, 2011.
(http://harshbrowns.wordpress.com)
92. Statement in solidarity with the Idle No More movement by Chief Arvol Looking Horse, *NDN News - Daily Headlines in Indian Country*, December 31, 2012.
(http://ndnnews.com/2012/12/this-is-about-mother-earth-statement-from-chief-arvol-looking-horse)
93. Selena Fox, transcript, *Pagan Spirit Gathering Press Conference re: Dianic Rituals and Transgender Inclusion*, June 2012. (www.selenafox.com)
94. Derek Beres, "Why Marianne Williamson Needs To Face Reality," *Yoga Brains*, 2012.

95. Michael Parenti, "The New Age Mythology," *Land of Idols: Political Mythology in America*, St. Martin's Press, 1994.
96. Blair Mann, "Equity and Equality Are Not Equal," *The Education Trust*, March 12, 2014. (https://edtrust.org/the-equity-line/equity-and-equality-are-not-equal)
97. See *Chapter 13*, "Allyship" on Page 106 or *Chapter 14* "Ethics Are Us" on Page 118 for suggestions on this process.
98. Sunera Thobani, speech at the conference "Women's Resistance: From Victimization to Criminalization," 2001, *Herizons Magazine*, Winter 2002. (www.herizons.ca)
99. Barbara Low (Mi'kmaq), Facebook comment, 2013.
100. Juliana K'abal-Xok (Mayan), Facebook comment, 2013.
101. Myke Johnson, "Wanting to be Indian: When Spiritual Searching Turns into Cultural Theft," *Unsettling America: Decolonization in Theory and Practice*, 2011. (https://unsettlingamerica.wordpress.com)
102. Gillian Schutte, "Dear White People," *Thought Leader*, Mail & Guardian Online Network, 2013. (www.thoughtleader.co.za)
103. David Abram, *Becoming Animal: An Earthly Cosmology*, Vintage Books, 2011.
104. Tiokasin Ghosthorse (Cheyenne River, Itazipco/Mnicoujou and Oglala Lakota) Facebook comment, January 2013.
105. Montague Whitsel, *Wellsprings of the Deer: A Contemporary Celtic Spirituality*, 1stBooks, 2002.

11. New Age Thinking

"I can remain oblivious to the language and customs of persons of color who constitute the world's majority, without feeling in my culture any penalty for such ignorance."[106] (Peggy McIntosh)

White descendants of the Euro-migration to Turtle Island have been lacking in the elements that give rise to an authentic spiritual life until recent times. To fill the gap left by our postmodern rejection of organized religion, the ideology of consumerism (a major driver for Empire-building) has been adopted in our approach to spirituality as well. To our credit, we have done monumental work in establishing a continuum of spiritual belief systems and practices, a mind-boggling array of different ideologies, all perfectly accessible to the modern spiritual seeker for cherry-picking either in whole or in part. However, when looking at this vast collection of spiritualities closely, it becomes clear that many of the elements that make up our diverse spiritual paths have been made possible by the domination of other cultures, including those who have been destroyed, oppressed and assimilated by Euro-centric supremacy and colonization.

Elements of cultural appropriation in the practices and publications of New Age "neo-shamans" are part of a much wider picture, and white spiritual seekers need to understand how imperialist domination works. For centuries now Indigenous people have been *"talked about and not with, and were not even considered to be entitled to their own knowledge,"*[107] or the knowledge they carried in regard to the natural or man-made world(s). As discussed in the chapter "Lifting IK and Inventing Identity," the study, expertise and practice of Turtle Island IK by non-natives has been made into an academic discipline and/or "*niche industry*"[108] from which the original IK holders have been excluded. Cultural appropriation allows those with political and economic advantage to consider the "open availability" of the "other" as ripe for the plucking, and to generate their own versions of IK, which become "*dominant over those of the subjugated people.*"[109] When people in authority and power create representations of the colonized, they automatically control and influence how the colonized are "*treated, how they represent themselves, how they feel about themselves and how they access resources.*"[110] Understanding the connection between imperial domination and the activities of "pseudo-shamans" practicing their own fabrications of Turtle Island IK should activate the moral code of any thinking human being.

"*I'm not here to burst your bubble of unity and friendship – but I am here to remind you that while you want to be our friends and ignore cultural differences, you can't ignore the history and current-day presence of colonialism and racism. I don't need to list the statistics of health disparities and poverty in Native communities to prove this to you – just consult the facts. I don't want to be the angry Indian, so do me a favor and when you talk about your 'right' to participate in whatever culture you want because we're all human, know that there is such a thing as cultural protocol. Many of us are in crisis on how best to protect our IK.*"[111] (Jessica Yee)

It may be helpful to become aware of the patterns of learning we have assumed from the dominant culture as we take on our ancestral wisdom reconstruction project(s). Since the 1960's our continuous "free-floating" experimentation with spiritual practices has been based on the consumer model, and we have been presented with a steady stream of new information and stimulation. We go to workshops and talks, or read the latest spiritual bestseller which resonates with us on a deep level, or inspires us to adopt new principles for happiness and enlightenment, and we promise ourselves that we will eliminate our blocks and bad habits once and for all. Yet, instead of achieving new heights of "transformation" in just a few days, our spiritual experience has been forgotten, subjected as we are to the fast-paced stimuli of the modern world, new irritations at work and the familiar frustrations and humiliations of daily living. Constantly stimulated by the newest trend, we lack the inner structure or focus that would bring lasting change, growth, or mastery over ourselves or a body of knowledge. The vast array of pick 'n' mix products and tools being offered in the spiritual supermarket suggest that we are lacking something, or that there is a vacuum that needs to be filled. Yet no one acknowledges that we may already have too much to begin with and should be occupied with letting go, not acquiring more! In the end, *New Age Capitalism* means that we come to conflate the passage from one novelty to the next for the spiritual path itself.

"If you want to be trendy with what you wear and what you eat, fine. But don't expect anyone to take you seriously if you do it with your spirituality."[112] (Irasna Rising)

The popularity of the New Age and Neo-Pagan canon and the successful marketing of tribal ideologies and "shamanic training" products to white spiritual seekers has created a devious möbius loop linking superficial pan-Indianism with many genuine fragments of IK, and the newly-emerging themes of earth-connected spirituality. The conflation of native identity with homogenous stereotypes and inaccuracies will persist until the white majority deliberately acquires some knowledge regarding the specific history, worldview, and traditions unique to each First Nation (hopefully the communities in one's own backyard). It is so much easier to believe in the romantic notion of a generous all-knowing quasi-native *Medicine Woman* or "shaman" than to delve into the xenophobic challenges and racist persecutions faced by actual contemporary First Nations communities, who continue to suffer the fall-out from cultural genocide. Critical thinking has not been paramount to spiritual seekers as they take a cruise through the spiritual supermarket, and our obliviousness to the specific histories and traditions of Indigenous cultures has long been the hallmark of white privilege. Taking the path of least resistance shows up over and over in the metaphysical mumbo-jumbo of *New Age Thinking*, and ingrained blind spots are clearly apparent in both the ideological discourse and common vernacular.

Although perfectly acceptable within the modern self-help and spiritual growth movement, our shared responses to the issue of cultural appropriation seem shocking in their implacability, when viewed through the lens of cultural imperialism, white privilege and knowledge domination. A typical response, known as "derailment," reflects our bias and how deeply systemic racism is ingrained into our society as a whole. White privilege gives us total access, and white spiritual seekers do not expect to be denied access to any image, object, geographical location or realm of knowledge. In fact, we have been educated by imperialism to move into any sphere, to compete with everyone, and dominate others in our knowledge production and practice. The central presumption of

---

106. Peggy McIntosh, "Unpacking the Invisible Knapsack," *Beyond Whiteness*, 2014. (www.beyondwhiteness.com)
107. Ardhra, "What is Cultural Appropriation," *The Long Way Home* (blog), February 26, 2012. (https://ardhra.wordpress.com)
108. Ibid.
109. Ibid.
110. Ibid.
111. Jessica Yee, "Feminist Intersection: On hipsters/hippies and Native culture," *Bitch Media*, 2010. (http://bitchmagazine.org)
112. Irasna Rising, "Spiritual Trendiness," *The Shift Has Hit the Fan* (blog), 2013. (http://earthenergyreader.wordpress.com)

cognitive imperialism is the validation of our WK (western knowledge) by academia and publishing, and then to assume automatic authority over all other knowledge systems. In the genre of New Age Spirituality, well-intentioned modern seekers need to be aware that their publications and practices are having a negative impact on the ability of Turtle Island First Nations to reclaim their own specific IK, traditions and sovereignty, and that the Indigenous people they so deeply admire are in complete opposition to the theft of their cultural and spiritual property.

To gain a perspective on the full scope of *New Age Thinking*, and for your amusement and edification, I present an interesting collection of typical *Derailment Responses*.

Typical statements that proclaim the freedom and privilege of white spiritual seekers to have no restrictions of any kind in formulating an identity or personalized spiritual path.

- If it speaks to my soul I can claim it.
- How dare you tell me what I can and cannot believe? I answer to no one. You cannot stop me from believing and practicing what is right for me. I follow my own divine guidance/visions/deities and/or spirit guides. (Otherwise known as unverified personal gnosis or UPG.[113])
- I have total spiritual freedom - I have had many past lives in many different cultures, and this gives me the right to access any knowledge system I choose. How dare you suggest otherwise?
- I have had a dream or a vision or a past-life regression that I was native in my past life, and I am supposed to be practicing *Native Spirituality*.
- My soul is free to claim any lineage or ancestral line from whatever culture I choose - "We Are All One" and I can celebrate and practice any ancestral tradition that moves me and touches my soul.
- I don't need your approval to validate what I believe! I am at peace with my Native American name and shamanic ceremonies, and the manifestation of my own happiness is my highest authority.
- There is no point in protecting or keeping your traditions to yourself, as spirituality cannot be "owned" by anyone!
- Protection of culture is wrong - it is more important that I be allowed to use elements from as many Indigenous tribes as possible in my *Sacred Shamanic Rainbow Medicine Path*© course! (It is $3600 for the weekend if you would like to sign up and learn something.)
- I have a Cherokee ancestor, and at some point I'm going to prove it!
- I have an old photograph of my great-grandmother, and she looks very Native, or Métis, or dark-haired, or something like that, and I feel I am part-Native, so it must be true.
- Why should I have to prove that I have Native blood to anyone? If I feel this connection deep down in my soul, that's good enough for me.

- Your whole argument is flawed - no one in this country is black, white, yellow or Native American - we are all one big tribe, and we are all American!
- Why are you defaming my character? You are the one with the identity problem, not me. It has been spiritually ordained that I am the reincarnation of White Buffalo Calf Woman.
- Please don't say such hurtful things, you are having a negative effect on my chakra balance and depleting my positive energy! Why don't you look in the mirror - you are the racist one!
- I am not offended by my *Über Urban Shaman©* practice - don't you have anything better to do?
- Sorry, but I am more concerned about offending the *Ancient Ones of the Cherokee* who have chosen me to carry on their Indigenous lifeways for them, than the hostility of Native Americans.
- I am not accountable to anyone except my own Gods in my *Native American/Shamanic* spiritual practice, and it is certainly not your place to judge the spiritual path of anyone!
- I have been called to do my shamanic work from the realm of spirit, so the normal rules don't apply. In fact, my spiritual knowledge is so important and sacred, I am going to add another thousand dollars to my fee.
- I am not dealing with actual native people! I am dealing with native energies, native spirits and native dreaming. This is important work, and completely different from the "cultural appropriation" you are talking about. Anyway, there is nothing I can do to help native people.
- I don't practice *Native Spirituality* exclusively, I am also Buddhist, Wiccan, Druidic, Sufi and a member of the Spiritualist Church - I think you missed that part.
- From all the modalities I have tried for my healing and self-development, the *Shamanic Path* is the one that works best. Why would I give that up?
- The Universe is unfolding exactly as it should, and following the *One Tribe Shamanic Power Transformational Path©* of native spiritual healing is exactly where I need to be right now for my highest good.
- No one can stop me from believing and practicing what feels right to me. I go with my intuition, not what narrow-minded (Indigenous) people think.
- I have complete freedom to describe myself as the direct descendant of an ancient Indigenous tribe - who is going to know the difference?
- I am native in my heart so that makes me native too.

---

113. Unverified personal gnosis (UPG) are insights received from spirits, deities, dreams, visions, ancestors and intuition. UPG is a necessary part of spiritual practice, but should be presented as UPG and not fact-based knowledge. From ancient times to the present day, having a community to validate UPG is crucial, as it keeps one grounded and confirms that one is actually receiving information from the spirit realms, and not from the imagination or delusional thinking.

Typical statements that unwittingly reflect habitual and implicit bias, deeply ingrained systemic racism, denial of white privilege, and how the Settler Society benefits from the white domination over people of colour in the Americas. These folks dwell in the realm of cultural amnesia, and need to take another look at the true history of the founding of the Americas, the role of their European ancestors and colonizers in the building of Empire, and how genocide, colonization, racism, oppression, displacement and assimilation continue to be directed toward Turtle Island First Nations.

- Where are you getting your information? Indigenous people do not sit at computers as we do, so how do you know what they think?
- First Nations people have made a conscious choice to live in poverty and third world conditions the way they do, as I have made the choice to live the way I do (in this sparkling clean and tastefully decorated suburban mega-home).
- I had nothing to do with what happened to First Nations, so don't blame me for their problems, we are all in exactly the same place right now!
- I am not responsible for what my people did hundreds of years ago - get a life! It's people like you who are causing problems in this country.
- First Nations need to embrace the many superior opportunities civilization has given them by celebrating the North American lifestyle, and they need to get a job, a house and a car just like everyone else.
- All that bad stuff happened a long time ago - First Nations need to "get over it" and move on!
- First Nations live exactly like white people now - many of the successful ones have forgotten their traditional IK and spirituality, so they need me to carry on their traditions for them.
- The Indigenous Knowledge of many First Nations has stagnated, and I am sure they realize that to keep their cultures healthy and vibrant, they need to bring in new forms of knowledge. My humble contribution is an important part of this process.
- First Nations are influenced too much by the modern white world, and they are doing a terrible job at maintaining their customs and traditions. At least my drums, regalia, Pow Wow dancing and sacred pipe ceremonies are authentic - somebody has to keep the culture alive!
- As a serious student of Native traditions I deserve respect, especially as Native Americans are losing their own heritage.
- Indigenous people should be honored that I am practicing their spirituality!
- There are not a lot of native people in my province (or state), so I am filling in the gap, making sure *Native Spirituality* is available to everyone, that's what it's all about!

- First Nations need to speed up their healing process already - as a registered *New Tribe Lightworker Energy Healer and Shamanic Spiritual Coach©* I can send them love, support and compassion, but I cannot help them heal if they continue to hold on to their anger and pain.
- The spiritual code I live by is that to react to any assault or insult directed toward me is to give away my *Personal Power*, and First Nations really need to adopt this important principle as well. Who cares what (Indigenous) people say or do - it has no effect on me!
- I have made a vow with my transformational coach to eliminate negative people and events from my life, and all this talk about "cultural appropriation" is highly offensive to my love-and-light *Sacred Rainbow Circle Awakening Tribe©* beliefs. Anyway, there is nothing I can do to help native people!
- First Nations use and enjoy many elements of white culture - why is OK for them to appropriate from my culture but it is not OK for me to use anything from theirs? In fact, everyone is always appropriating white culture, and we don't complain!
- Why is it OK for some native people to call themselves "Shaman," but as a European I'm not allowed? That's reverse racism!
- White people also have had sweatlodge ceremonies, bear tooth necklaces, dancing around the sacred fire and dreamcatchers in our own traditions, so what exactly is the problem?
- The First Nations lady who lives down the street (I think she is Métis) doesn't have any objection to my shamanic *Find Your Totem Power Animal Blessings©* workshop, so that settles this ridiculous debate. I just know that all NDN's are supporting me with this important work.
- Racism, white privilege, oppression and cultural appropriation are just someone's opinion, not the facts, so don't tell me what I can and cannot do!
- Your negativity is causing more negativity, as inequality is just a state of mind. Why don't the minority groups realize this - that we already live in a perfect world - and just declare themselves as equal?
- Why are you so fanatical about this? Explain to me please, how my self-created native identity is doing any harm to anyone!
- What is so wrong with white people offering sweatlodge ceremonies anyway? Who cares?? Picky picky.
- It is sad that Indians don't feel honored that I choose to walk the *Red Road* with them. The Christians in my community are always trying to recruit me to join their religion, so I find it confusing when Indians are offended instead of flattered.
- No one "owns" spirituality in this day and age, what a ridiculous thought!
- Who cares what a hate-filled Indigenous person thinks, I am SO tired of this whole debate! If they don't like my *Cosmic Light & Love Shamanic Dreamcatcher Teachings©* it's up to them to tell me what I should be offering instead!

- I have freedom of religion as guaranteed by the *Universal Declaration of Human Rights*, and I am sorry that vindictive people like you have nothing comparable in your life.
- If an Indigenous person has a problem with me using their spirituality, it is their problem, not mine.

Typical statements that reflect white domination over authentic IK in brand-new versions, and the New Age "shamanic" or "tribal" genre that has been in the public domain since the 1970's. Also reflected is the exoticization of First Nations, the re-hashing of old stereotypes, and the belief in an Indigenous utopia.

- But the books and workshops of Lynn Andrews, Jamie Sams, Eagle Man/Ed McGaa, Ted Andrews and Little Grandmother are so popular! How can it be wrong?
- What are you talking about? I have been a practicing Shaman for 20 years, and I have a huge following across eight states! You're just jealous of my success.
- Among other paths that resonate with me, *Native Spirituality* has been a valid spiritual path for many years now, and it has nothing to do with cultural appropriation.
- The teachings of the *Red Road* and the *Medicine Path* come naturally to me. *Native Spirituality* is a lifestyle choice anyone can adopt who is dedicated to the responsible service of healing others.
- You cannot possibly know my complicated history, or my deep love for *Native Wisdom*. Here, come closer, let's create safe space together, and I can pass on my *Chameleon Shapeshifter Medicine Teachings©* with a free one-time gift of a special mood ring, if that will help you "change" your mind.
- It was never my intention to appropriate from First Nations in my smudging, sweatlodge and drum-making workshops - you don't even know me, or the sacred work that I do!
- I am paying First Nations the highest compliment with my drum-making/shamanic healing/sacred circle business!
- Indigenous people are generous and share their rituals and spiritual tools with me - then I can decide how to use these rituals and tools in a way that feels right to me.
- I am a *Registered Shaman* from my weekend workshop with medicine man and ceremony seller Grandfather Knowing Eagle, and nothing you can say will diminish my experience, or my sacred mission as a shamanic healer!
- After going to Pow Wows for years to dance in the sacred circle wearing the most expensive regalia money can buy, one day I was gifted with an eagle feather by the most sacred and wise Elder, a true holy man (Grandfather Knowing Eagle). I did not ask to be honored in this way, but since I now have an eagle feather, I must be a member of Native Community!

- You are wrong about Grandfather Knowing Eagle, he is the real deal! Mitakuye Oyasin, "All My Relations," "Walk In Balance."
- My shamanic practice promotes understanding and good relationships between all cultures.
- I am in shamanic spiritual communion with Indigenous traditions that do not believe in writing down their knowledge, and my practice keeps their oral lineage alive. So when I find an idea or ritual that appeals to me, I make sure that I modify and customize it to suit myself.
- Why are First Nations complaining about cultural appropriation? I thought they were directly connected to the 'One" higher-power-great-divinity-of-true-spirit, and above such petty concerns!
- First Nations culture and spirituality are the product of living on American/Canadian soil, so they are the correct cultural and spiritual beliefs we should all be practicing, whether or not First Nations approve.
- First Nations elders and shamans are true holy people and the embodiment of all that is sacred, and white folks can only aspire to have the kind of enlightened knowledge that they carry! First Nations wisdom keepers are our spiritual guides and gurus on the *Red Road*, and worthy of our unconditional love, trust, devotion and adoration.
- First Nations represent a time when we lived in harmony with Mother Earth and each other, were allowed free expression, and shared our gifts communally in bliss and joy. We need to re-create this *Gathering of the Rainbow Tribes* in our daily lives today, to manifest the "New Age," come together in sacred intention, and re-activate the cosmic power of love and light.
- First Nations once lived in peace and harmony with all of creation, and with the blessings of our spiritual Elders at our upcoming *Gathering of the Tribes* we will re-create this transcendental reality and weave together a new *Era of Enlightenment in Global Unity*.

More statements that reflect a belief in the modern urban myth of the "Rainbow Tribe," the "We Are All One" meme, monism, perennial philosophy and universalism.

- Any group attempting to assert cultural sovereignty can be disregarded – they are part of the old paradigm and are to be pitied, since we are all moving toward a "One Tribe" and the evolution of the human race anyway.
- Right now we are in the process of evolving toward a "Rainbow Tribe," a global consciousness, a unified vision of humanity and "We Are All One," so cultural differences don't matter anymore, we are above all that!
- Since all Indigenous wisdom comes from the same universal source, we need to focus on our similarities instead of cultural distinctions, and come together as "One."

- Indigenous Knowledge comes from the cosmic knowledge that exists beyond time or influence, and as a lightworker my inner mind has access to that space.
- If you go back thousands of years we all came from the same ancestors, so choosing ancestors or traditions from any culture I want is perfectly normal.
- It's too confusing to attach spirituality to a specific culture, and having specific histories, worldviews and symbols just alienates everyone else - spirituality is a universal experience and we should be focused on that!
- Sorry, "We Are All One" and Indigenous people do not get to decide what can be shared and what cannot. Besides, all that bad stuff happened hundreds of years ago!
- Spirituality has no tribe - are we "One" or are we not?!   Stop clutching at straws.
- I take pride in calling myself a "universalist," as sticking to one's own cultural group can lead to conformity, intolerance and misplaced loyalty.
- It's OK to mix and match your spiritual beliefs, as long as you have a full understanding of the history and the ceremonies as they were practiced.
- You are so wrong! White Buffalo Calf Woman and the Celtic Goddess Brigid are just different names for identical energies found in different places.
- My *Rainbow Medicine Man©* shamanic trance tours and events promote cultural exchange, which is an important part of the shift to "One Tribe." Buy tickets here - Respect, y'all.
- I have love in my heart for everyone, and I will continue to be a "frequency holder" for the great vision of unity and "Oneness," until Indigenous people wake up and catch up to me.
- First Nations need to stop complaining and join us (lead us even) into the new Rainbow Tribe!
- Can't we all be nicer to each other?
- It's all Kumbaya, y'all.

Also, ridiculous statements that reflect pan-Indianism, and the lack of research, focus or critical thinking that is endemic to the New Age smorgasbord of eclectic spiritualities.

- I was expecting that medicine man to give me a reading, an oracle, or some kind of guidance from the other side (the spirit world) but he didn't give me any message at all. How disappointing, I should have asked for my money back but he has left town!
- I am the reincarnation of White Buffalo Calf Woman, my great-grandmother was a *Cherokee Princess* (I think) and I offer a fusion of aura cleansing, medicine wheel teachings, chakra therapy, hypnotherapy, "meet your power totem animal" sessions, divination

techniques, reiki, dowsing, fairy card readings, shamanic healing, therapeutic touch, soul coaching, lomi lomi, falan gong and ceremonies for every occasion.

- The world needs my *Instant Medicine Path© Native Spirituality* teachings, and I will sound the drum!
- I have no interest in tribalism, but this shamanism stuff really works!
- Let us smudge, pray to the four directions, go on a shamanic journey to the beat of the drum, but whatever you do, don't look at the elephant in the middle of the room.

Rooted in WK (western knowledge) these New Age statements are unspeakably heinous. There is no excuse for the white supremacy, patriarchal dysfunction and psychosis that has led to systemic racism and genocide. If you subscribe to these statements then you have normalized the violence and domination of Empire as universal human behavior (which is NOT the case). Also, turn the tables and imagine your own cultural group as the subject of these statements.

- As all human beings create their own reality and agree to their "soul contract" before they are born, the rape, violence and ethnic cleansing that the oppressed have encountered is their own chosen fate. For both abuser and abused, there is a higher purpose - either for personal growth or the evolution of humanity.
- Where did all the souls of the Indigenous people that were destroyed by genocide go? They have been reincarnated as white spiritual seekers and neo-shamans.
- I don't know why my Native American spirit guides chose me to have a native soul and be a Shaman, but it must be because native people are dying out, and what better way to influence white society than to become a white person?

Typical statements that deny that if traced back through time, all cultural groups, including Gaelic, Baltic or Nordic, have earth-connected ancestral knowledge.

- I don't want to identify with my own cultural group or Ancestors - they are so boring and rigid!
- I am ashamed of what my white Ancestors did.
- I have no idea what my ancestry is, or where my people came from.
- I have way too many different nationalities in my family tree to select just one (or two) to identify with or reclaim, so I won't bother. I am an American, and that's that!
- There's nothing in our European past of any value, and we need to move forward, not back. Let's create new traditions!
- I hate white people, I don't want to have anything to do with their European culture!
- Sorry, but white culture just doesn't "speak to me" the way Native American and Buddhist Tantra cultures do.

- It is a nice idea, to reclaim my own ancestral knowledge, but it is impossible in today's fast-paced technological world. I'm too busy remodeling the house, taking care of the cottage, doing the accounting for my husband's business, running my metaphysical shoppe and holistic spa, setting up online financial empowerment teleseminars, and teaching *Shamanic Reiki.*
- There is absolutely no way I can recover my own ancestral knowledge, it's way too much work!!

The first thing we notice about these derailment statements is an overwhelming sense of personal entitlement, and that the white spiritual seeker has no problem thinking that the culture, society and spirituality of the oppressed are up for grabs. The reliance on UPG, dreams, visions and delusions to manifest their personality would suggest that white people have actual psychological identity problems, with a bizarre need to identify with (or as) native while at the same time creating their own fantasies of what an Indigenous person is. Of course, this unresolved identity crisis and lack of an earth-connected ethnicity comes from centuries of colonization, but admitting there is a problem is always the first step toward solving it! The most common derailment by far is that the pretendian has native blood from an ancestor (usually Cherokee) from "way way back," and yet it is far too much trouble to accurately trace this link in the ancestral line. The lack of proof or community recognition for these claims demeans and interferes with the very real and critical process of actual First Nations, who are trying to re-formulate their own lost identity due to genocide and colonization, and to claim their own legitimacy and cultural ties through an imposed model of "blood quantum." In the face of residential school horrors, the "lost generation," the abduction of children by foster care (the 60's/70's scoop), and the babies still being forced into white homes today, claiming any tiny element of BQ or questionable native identity is ludicrous, and demeans and disempowers those who have genuine and valid claims to First Nations community.

Many of the derailment statements are explicitly racist, clearly reflecting a colorblind pan-Indian bias and condescendingly speaking for Turtle Island First Nations as one homogenous mass, which reinforces the lack of recognition and respect for specific First Nations, their sovereignty and IK. Also, negating ethnic difference by declaring "we are all American" is more colorblind racism, and clearly out of step with reality, as anti-racism activist Elijah Hamilton explains. *"I'll subscribe to a colorblind approach when everyone else does and when racism is over. Until then, I have an obligation to acknowledge my privilege as a white man, and to use it to fight against white supremacy, rather than ignoring it and saying that 'I'm not white, I'm just American.' That would not be telling the whole story."*[114] It is also clear that New Agers think that "racism just fell from the sky" and are completely oblivious to the monumental work that is required within specific Indigenous communities to heal themselves, and recover and restore their sovereignty and traditional IK. As for the suggestion for "getting over it" and moving on, Winona LaDuke says *"you cannot get over it if you are still in the same circumstance as a consequence of what happened a hundred years ago."*[115] In the face of historic and contemporary destruction of Indigenous cultural autonomy, saying "get over it" to First Nations who are struggling both for survival and the protection of their sacred homelands is pretty much the same as saying *"just die, already."*[116]

The observation that some First Nations individuals are successful in their careers and have material success in the "white world" is only one side of a long continuum of adaptation and excellence, and does not invalidate the overall brutality of colonization and the assimilation process. Conforming to the structure of domination, or giving the hegemony of the Settler State a place in one's value system, is an internal matter for First Nations to discuss and/or unpack in their decolonization process.[117] Other patterns in *New Age Spirituality* are the blatant use of the most sacred tools such as the pipe and sweatlodge (taken out of context from the original IK) which is very disturbing to First Nations, as James Dumont explains. *"That there are so many plastic medicine men 'carrying pipes' is totally out of hand. It devalues the sacred aspects of our IK and diminishes the importance of the pipe in Anishnaabe culture. It should not be so easy to give the pipe away."*[118] And when it is suggested that only one Indigenous person is required to approve the white seeker's "shamanic" activity, and that this person is assumed to represent or speak for all Indigenous people, the pattern of tokenism is again apparent. Another constant thread of confusion in these derailment statements is the lack of understanding regarding the difference between cultural exchange and cultural appropriation. Cultural exchange can only take place between societies and groups that are on equal footing without dominating or oppressing the other, and the sharing or exchange is done in a respectful way under the direction of the sharer. Within the oppressor/oppressed and dominator/ subordinate dynamic that exists on Turtle Island, cultural appropriation of IK by those with privilege and power is performed

114. Elijah Hamilton, Facebook Comment, *Whites Against Racial Inequality*, September, 2014. (www.youtube.com)

115. Winona LaDuke (Anishnaabe), *The Winona LaDuke Reader: A Collection of Essential Writings*, Voyageur Press, 2002.

116. Andrew Gavin Marshall, "A Brief Message for Canadians: Get Over It!" *See the World Through a Different Lens*, 2013. (http://andrewgavinmarshall.com)

117. In the final days of Empire, Settlers are also engaged in deconstructing the embedded values of Empire in our hearts, minds and souls. (See more on the uncolonization process in *Chapter 19* "Rejecting Empire" on Page 174.)

118. James Dumont, "Native Heritage Rites & Ceremonies," Class Lecture, *Aboriginal Studies*, Georgian College of Applied Arts & Technology, Barrie, ON, February, 1997.

without permission, and certainly not according to terms set out by the source culture.

With this choice statement *"racism, white privilege, oppression and cultural appropriation are just someone's opinion, not the facts"* we see a perfect example of the entitlement that allows for the denial of the historical record, while at the same time revealing an appalling ignorance regarding the ongoing consequences of colonization. Overcoming deeply embedded racial bias and illiteracy is crucial, and *"we should never deny facts because we don't like them."*[119] (Jesse Prinz) Being so disconnected from their own root culture and traditions, New Agers have come to believe that "no one owns spirituality," but this is patently untrue, and this kind of rhetoric perpetuates an erroneous "one size fits all" mentality. In fact, the IK and spirituality that each First Nation holds has been acquired over millennia, is specific and unique to them, and like a well-fitting garment, is not transferable or necessarily of use to any other cultural group. As James Dumont reminds us, *"Anishnaabe spirituality is based on centuries of myth connected to the landforms, flora and fauna of a specific place, and non-natives should not pick up what doesn't belong to them."*[120] Another major error made by those conditioned by western thinking and monotheistic religion is that "spirituality" is separate from "culture," whereas in Indigenous and other pre-colonial societies, culture and spirituality constantly flow one into the other and are not distinct endeavors, as culture informs spiritual practice and spiritual practice is informed by culture. And how ironic that New Agers would claim freedom of religion as guaranteed by the *Universal Declaration of Human Rights,* while at the same time denying those same rights to Turtle Island First Nations, and defiling their religion in the process!

Off the scale on "highly amusing" if not tragically ironic, the solipsistic claim that one "gives away their power" by acknowledging the critique of others is highly problematic, when it is the dominant group who already have social power making these claims! Again, how insulting this must sound to people of colour who are still fighting for their basic rights and the freedom to live without oppression or discrimination, let alone being able to thrive and actualize their personal or collective sovereignty (or "power"). When one's perceived "lack of power" comes from **too** much abundance, **too** much choice, **too** much entitlement and **too** much of everything else, it may be time to examine the enigmatic principle of "scaling back" on the deleterious abundance that spoiled modernists enjoy. Also, protesting that the popularity of "native spirituality" products, seminars and books is proof of meaningful

---

119. Jesse Prinz, *Beyond Human Nature: How Culture and Experience Shape Our Lives,* Allen Lane/Penguin Group, 2012.
120. James Dumont, "Issues in the Native World: The Native Perspective," Class Lecture, *Aboriginal Studies,* Georgian College of Applied Arts & Technology, Barrie, ON, 10/96.

exchange is another illusion, and the commercial success that New Age hucksters have achieved is indicative of the "lifestyle choices" trend within the larger context of consumer culture. Linked to the notion that spirituality is something that can be purchased, these fabricated and disposable commodities imply that one can easily find and possess *Native Spirituality* or "shamanism" instantly, just by reading a book or attending a workshop. In reality, it is the work of an entire lifetime to actualize the mystic or healing potentials in traditional Indigenous societies, and the suggestion that a self-absorbed and narcissistic privileged spiritual seeker can achieve the same goal faster and better, is in itself a racist declaration of white supremacy. Real First Nations don't count, and in their privileged fantasy worlds, white shamans portray themselves as "better Indians" than the actual Indians! Also, the short-term online courses pseudo-shamans offer as "training" show a *"cavalier disregard for substance resulting in numerous distortions and half-baked notions floating around the New Age blogosphere, lapped up as fact by spiritual tourists and neophytes."*[121] (Vikram Zutshi) We also see that the derailment of "intent" is a popular one, but protesting that one did not "intend to" indulge in cultural appropriation is not an "exempt pass" from the power differentials in society, as all acts of cultural domination reinforce the oppression of Indigenous people, whether the non-native individual is aware of it or not.

Loosely based on pan-Indian IK, many of the newly-created "shamanic and tribal myths" are fantasies created as escapism from the techno-scientific monoculture - "Rainbow Utopias" that stress individual self-empowerment and loudly proclaim spiritual seekers as "wild and free." The cohort of white folks may feel better, but with their narcissistic cultural appropriation they ignore genuine tribal members, and feel no remorse in never having actually met or talked to a First Nations person! New Age products and fabricated versions of IK are based on distorted images and romanticized ideas of native people, and rely heavily on the many stereotypes and white fantasies that the Settler Society has created. Also, the suggestion that a casual exchange makes one a "member of native community" is ludicrous, as Paula Gunn Allen (Laguna Pueblo) explains. *"You cannot 'do' Indian spirituality without an Indian community – it is physical, social and spiritual, and they are fused together."* One of the most popular stereotypes, or misconceptions, is the automatic assumption that "Indigenous" is synonymous with "spiritual." Those in traditional pre-contact Indigenous societies were just as equally rational/pragmatic and mystical/intuitive as any other human being, and did not live in some sort of timeless "enlightened state of grace" or monumental elevation of bliss. Just because they lived in harmony with the natural world, without taking more than the ecosystem could sustain, this appears "spiritual" to those of us in

---

121. Vikram Zutshi, "On the Bastardization of Yoga, like Indigenous Traditions by Low-Brow Pop Culture," *Yoganonymous*, April 14, 2014. (http://yoganonymous.com)

western society who have forgotten what it is like to respect boundaries and live in balance with the land.

Overall, we need to examine why New Agers and positivity coaches have the egoic impulse to become a guru for others in the first place. Why do they insist on sharing their every thought as a "spiritual awakening" and then proselytize their "teachings" so loudly and obnoxiously? Many "neo-shamans" have the grandiose need to create a following (or an entourage) for themselves, and then assume that other people will be hanging on their every word. The intensity of this bombastic "spirituality" combined with cultural piracy and *New Age Capitalism* is problematic indeed, and in complete opposition to how genuine community Wisdom Keepers share Indigenous Knowledge. In the derailment responses we also see that the concept of "We Are All One" has taken root, and that in their white privilege New Agers have not taken the time or trouble to understand cultural imperialism or listen to Indigenous counter-narratives, or to even find out what Turtle Island First Nations actually think about the appropriation of their spiritual traditions. And why is it that white people are never asked to speak for all white people, yet feel entitled to speak for minority groups and make any number of rules on their behalf? (Also, why is it that white people are not defined by their ethnicity, as is every other racial group?) What also stands out is that there are no references to white cultural cohesion, or the existence or beauty of a specific EIK. The idea that one has their own ancestral wisdom traditions to access doesn't even seem to occur to New Agers. We need to hear more comments along the lines of *"I profoundly support the resurgence of your culture and traditions as an Ally, and I admire your IK, but I am also deeply immersed in the reclamation, embodiment and expression of my own sacred Gaelic/Ásatrú/Hellenismos/Romuva spirituality. May we come together as required to share our holistic understandings on behalf of our Mother the Earth."*

Clearly the modus operandi of New Age and Neo-Pagan spirituality is to de-emphasis critical thinking,[122] and to ignore and erase the fractured histories and contemporary lives of Indigenous people. The horrific belief that those subjected to genocide have somehow chosen their own destiny by virtue of a "soul contract" is parroted by those with no experience of oppression, and if substantiated proof for this myopic statement exists I would like to know about it. What a great way to "blame the victim," normalize the criminal behavior of psychopaths and deny any responsibility for working toward real social change! The human capacity for violence is **not** common to all ethnic groups **nor** is it endemic to the human condition - it is behavior taught by cultures that value territorial expansion, war, destruction and domination over others, such as autocratic imperialist patriarchies. Suggesting that someone would "choose" a violent experience, or that both inflicting and receiving abuse is a normal part of "soul growth" is ludicrous, and there is NO justification in this realm or the next for any crime of senseless brutality. The other absurd and blackly humorous suggestion is that in their past lives white spiritual seekers were the decimated Indigenous peoples of Turtle Island. The evidence that this is magical thinking at its best is that Indigenous people *never* claim to have past lives in Gaelic, Baltic or Nordic societies! Why is it that only European spirits travel freely, and reincarnate[123] outside of their own cultural group? The mind boggles to think that the superiority complex of white entitlement and the endless choices of consumerism must also be an active rubric "beyond the veil!" As for claiming to be "chosen" by "Native American Spirit Guides," it has to be the height of racist arrogance to think that white people are better Indians than the Indians ("what better way to influence white society than to become white?"), or that from their disappeared locations in the spirit world the cultural survival of Indigenous people would depend on locating and enlisting a bunch of "white saviors" as instant neo-shamans!

Overall, the benefits of white privilege that have been sanctioned by *New Age Spirituality* allow for the lifting of bits and pieces of knowledge from sacred IK systems without consideration of the whole, or how all the fragments fit together to form a complete worldview. It must be the very definition of immorality to strip away the IK of an Indigenous tribe, then a few generations later move in and lay claim to those same IK practices, all the while professing to have a better spiritual focus than the original IK holders (certainly with cuter outfits, drums and jewellery[125] anyway). Considering the history of systemic ethnic cleansing in the Americas, the appearance of a white person all decked out in native regalia must appear ghastly, macabre even to an Indigenous person. How can IK theft by a white "shaman," a member of the dominant group who has attempted to eradicate First Nations over and over, be in any way acceptable? Identity theft is just another way of perpetuating the racist practices of the original genocide, by dissolving and destroying the traditional culture the way the first Settlers did. Every act of cultural appropriation "*stereotypes, objectifies, distorts and invalidates*"[126] specific Turtle Island First Nations.

---

122. An intense resistance to critical thinking is noticeable among those immersed in the various New Age modalities such as lightworking, channeling, mediumship, crystal therapy and magical supplements. The agreed-upon "suspension of disbelief" in the rhetoric is defended with magical thinking, and the unpleasantness of intellectual exchange or factual evidence is avoided and denied. As documented in existing and ongoing studies, the New Age phenomenon is linked to a lack of logic and delusion-like experiences, and I have observed that most New Agers are highly delusional in whatever various theories, behaviors or identities they currently adhere to.

123. There is consensus among Indigenous, earth-rooted or spiritual cultures and modern-day mystics, that souls will most often chose to reincarnate within their own ancestral, ethnic and family group. Bonds of love, connection to the home landscape, moral obligations, soul debts, "unfinished business" or collective transformation are all miraculous reasons that come to mind for this sacred mystery.

When being "called out" New Agers and white spiritual seekers will come up with an endless set of derailments and protests to sideline the issue of exploitation, and they will predictably try to make it seem that the anti-racist activist has "anger issues" or is a "bully" with a disruptive agenda. With years of investment in a "shamanic" identity, of course there will be a tendency to make all sorts of outrageous claims to avoid a discussion on the appropriation one is practicing. When critiquing white spiritual seekers on their cultural appropriation, be prepared to encounter denial, resistance, insult, and inventive doublespeak such as *"you are the racist!"* One tidy New Age rejection from the many choice examples is this spiffy statement *"the spiritual law that I follow is that what others say and do is a projection of their own reality, so back off!"* Even though it may feel that way, being called out on cultural appropriation is not a personal attack or a moral judgement concerned with emotions or personal intent, but rather an appeal for education, and to become part of social change. Understanding the centuries-old patterns of oppression, domination, exploitation and appropriation that have occurred from the power imbalances of cultural imperialism is critical to our uncolonization as Settlers, and inherent to our own reclamation of ancestral knowledge and the re-inhabitation of the land.

"The New Age blindly pursues Native solutions to European problems but completely neglects to provide European solutions to Native problems."[124] (Sherman Alexie)

The attraction that contemporary spiritual seekers have to "native spirituality" is in fact a veiled desire to reclaim one's own ancient indigenity, and the process required to seek out, uncover, and re-discover the ways of one's own ancestors is not all that difficult. Yet, most of what passes for so-called spiritual "practices" today are disconnected snippets completely ungrounded in a wider or deeper field of knowledge. This kind of ersatz-spirituality does not carry enough weight for a transporting belief system or true transformation, so clearly what is also needed is to return to the source of all spiritual knowing - an intimate and humble interaction with the land, the ground of our being. In the meantime it would be best for white spiritual seekers, lightworkers and neo-shamans to relinquish ALL claims to the spiritual practices and tools of Indigenous peoples, as these groups continue to engage in "survivance"[127] and their much-needed recovery from social disorganization. Examining the ethos of the New Age subculture and *Self-Help Capitalism* has made it clear that our mission, if we are indeed evolving toward a genuine New Age, is to synthesize our moral code and critical thinking skills with our heartfelt social consciousness. If we are truly shifting to a new spiritual paradigm, can we commit ourselves to the theoretical and practical work it will involve, and take on the responsibility to learn what is truly valuable and worth rekindling in our own ethnic-based earth-wise traditions?

Without exception, the wisdom and cultural traditions of all human beings comes from the land. Not to realize this is to remain disconnected from the Earth, the source of our spiritual ecology and ancestral roots, and to perpetuate the goals of Empire, which is to separate us from our embeddedness in the natural world. To think you have met your soul needs in the law of attraction, angelic advice, mediumship, remote viewing, numerology blueprints, clairvoyance, sound healing, evolutionary re-programming, celestial knowledge, a self-help guru or some other spiritual flavour of the month, is to remain disembodied, lost in a fantasy of how you fit into the circle of creation, and an outcast to your own ecocultural existence. What we need more than anything in these vainglorious times, is to reconstruct top-to-bottom worldviews and lifeways fully integrated with the land.

---

124. Sherman Alexie, "White Men Can't Drum," *New York Times Magazine*, 04/10/1992.
125. As "sybarite shapeshifters," white privilege allows those in the Settler Society to wear the apparel from any culture or ethnic group anywhere in the world, "racialized minority" or otherwise.
126. "The Kreayshawn Complex: Cultural Appropriation as Counter-Cultural Expression," *harshbrowns*, (blog), March 7, 2012. (http://harshbrowns.wordpress.com)
127. "Survivance" a term highly relevant to First Nations experience, was coined by visionary and scholar Gerald Vizenor (Anishnaabe).

12. Taking Without Giving Back

"White women seem determined NOT to look into their own cultures for sources of strength. This is puzzling, since pre-Christian European cultures are also earth-based and contain many of the same elements that white women are ostensibly looking for in Native American cultures. This phenomenon leads me to suspect that there is a more insidious motive for latching onto Indian spirituality. When white 'feminists' see how white people have historically oppressed others and how they are coming very close to destroying the earth, they often want to disassociate themselves from their whiteness. They do this by opting to 'become Indian.' In this way, they can escape responsibility and accountability for white racism. Of course, white 'feminists' want to become only partly Indian. They do not want to be part of our struggles for survival against genocide, and they do not want to fight for treaty rights or an end to substance abuse or sterilization abuse. They do not want to do anything that would tarnish their romanticized notions of what it means to be an Indian. While New Agers may think that they are escaping white racism by becoming 'Indian,' they are in fact continuing the same genocidal practices of their forebears."[128]
(Andrea Smith)

---

128. Andrea Smith, "For All Those Who Were Indian In A Former Life," *Cultural Survival Quarterly*, 1994.

And what about giving back? As Andrea Smith says in this lengthy passage, spiritual seekers do not wish to renounce their "New Age Gaze" or tarnish their romantic notions of Turtle Island indigenity. For many years in the New Age, Neo-Pagan and Goddess Spirituality genres and particularly noticeable in the "Shamanic Healing" movement, philosophies and practices have been lifted and used from the Indigenous groups of one's region (or more likely from another place) without any significant reciprocity, or consideration given to the day-to-day issues faced by Indigenous people as a result of genocide and oppression. For privileged white folks in their bastions of abundance and equanimity (the invisible benefits of white privilege) it has been unseemly to burden themselves with a historical awareness of the horrors perpetuated on Turtle Island First Nations, and the challenges of the day-to-day lives of the disenfranchised and colonized. It is much easier to indulge in the syndrome of spiritual bypassing, which is to have an attitude of detachment and ignore anything "negative," than to cultivate a genuine compassion or awareness by examining the painful cultural, political, economic, social and spiritual consequences of Settler-Colonialism in the Americas. Ask any person Indigenous to Turtle Island and they will tell you how many times their IK systems have been extrapolated, and nothing has changed for the better in their communities. Explicit racism, resource extraction, the land claims process, pollution on native lands, inadequate housing, education and justice reform, poverty, the rape and murder of native women, the disgraceful legacy of the Indian Act in Canada, and unstated paternity leading to the loss of Indian status and benefits, are just a few of the horrendous issues facing native people today.

"When did Lynn Andrews ever use her media platform to stand up for Shoshone land rights? True honor and respect would include using her privilege to support First Nations sovereignty."[129] (Max Dashú)

Circles of non-native women continue to gather (including white feminists who should know better) and call in a pseudo-shaman or actual "Elder" who needs a gig, enjoys being patronized or seeks approval. Complicit with the "Indigenous Industry" this token native then performs a fragmented ceremony, and all the women go about their business seemingly spiritually enlightened yet completely oblivious to the real ways they could be helping First Nations. There needs to be a better mutual understanding among both native and non-native people that white privilege does not give us entitlement or casual random access to the spiritual practices of First Nations on any level. The most important tasks must be our anti-oppression efforts as allies to First Nations, our resistance to Empire in the general and the specific, and the recovery of our own EIK and spiritual practices. One shudders to think of all the money for self-improvement that has gone to "pseudo-shaman" ceremonialists in "pay to pray" workshops and conferences, that could have been better directed to the true holders of those IK practices and their Indigenous communities. Did any of the New Agers travelling to Sedona for workshops and tours to connect with their "native spirit guides" or "past-life Indian selves" give anything back to the Navaho or Hopi communities in a real way, short of a few purchases of tribal art at a roadside stand? Or did any of the thousands of white attendees at the *Symbiosis Gathering Eclipse Festival* metaphysical dance party and neotribal "shamanic ceremony" on the sacred Pyramid Lake lands in Nevada assist the Northern Paiute with their pressing issues, or move the reconciliation process forward? Probably not, but this really needs to be our direction in the future. Claiming responsibility in the First Nation/Settler interface comes first, followed by actions within the allyship or accomplice framework.

There is a trend for neo-liberals to talk about racism and the intersectional models of oppression as a form of atonement, as if by acknowledging the problems they are not obligated to do anything about them. As Andrea Smith says, "*it is a consistent practice among progressives to bemoan the genocide of Native peoples, but in the interest of political expediency, implicitly sanction it by refusing to question the legitimacy of the Settler Nation responsible for the genocide.*"[130] However, there are concrete ways that the modern spiritual seeker can make amends, *Reject Empire* and actively serve the needs of Indigenous community. But prior to becoming an Ally, the best thing is to become knowledgeable about the real history of the Americas, not the master narrative[131] as presented by the dominant society. Why should our First Nations neighbours have to continually explain what has been done to them? That the white majority is in denial has become a huge embarrassment, and it must be the height of cultural arrogance not to understand that every feature of your civilized life, the amenities and privileges that you experience right NOW, where you live in your city or in the country, have been made possible by the genocide and oppression of First Nations people.

---

129. Max Dashú, "Respect and Responsibility," *La Gazette*, Santa Cruz, October 1994. (www.suppressedhistories.net/articles/respect.html)

130. Andrea Smith, *Conquest: Sexual Violence and American Indian Genocide*, South End Press, 2005.

131. Master narratives are the stories or core myths that countries and federal states construct about themselves, forming a foundation for national identity and disseminated in the curriculum of the educational system. For example, the history and folklore inherent in the Canadian master narrative present Canadians as peacemakers - polite, industrious, fair, tolerant, cooperative and equitable. However, like all master narratives this portrayal is a lie, as Canada has a long history of genocide and racist colonial policies that have been conveniently left out of the nationalist worldview. By giving us an illusory identity that ignores the reality of our white supremacist racist past, the master narrative allows us to believe we are something we are not. In addition to the disgraceful amount of explicit racism held by the body politic, Canadians are also skilled at "polite racism" which promotes the idea of a multicultural mosaic offering equal treatment and opportunity for all, yet white dominance in cultural and political life remains the default, and there is considerable oppression and discrimination going on.

Being a member of the dominant white society allows us to ignore how race shapes all of our lives. Racism is not a First Nations problem, it is a white problem (!) and in our insular white bubble we are oblivious to the consequences of racism lived out daily by Indigenous peoples. Collectively, we have a moral responsibility to learn about the social issues, to listen, to respect, and to make decolonizing space for Indigenous history, contemporary voices, and the rich counter-narratives that exist across Turtle Island. We must also challenge the patronizing attitudes of the white hegemonic authorities and all those who think they know what is best for Indigenous people. Also, to assume that we know what is required in our anti-racism work is to often replicate the same colonial practices we are trying to undo - it is best that we take our direction directly from First Nations peoples themselves. With the ultimate grace and kindness, we continue to be invited into First Nations spaces, but instead of datamining their IK or cultural property, our solidarity and activism needs to reflect the entire spectrum of Indigenous reality, as Georgie Horton Baptiste explains. *"Anyone with a good heart is welcome to our ceremonies and cultural events, and no one is turned away. But it takes work, an endless amount of patience and understanding if you want to walk with us. It's hard work being an 'Indian' - spiritually, socially and politically. If you cannot walk with us in all of these areas, then a person has to question their motives when they take only the spiritual aspects of our culture."*[132]

Here are some suggested initiatives for giving back to Turtle Island First Nations.

- Solidarity in general starts with self-education on racism, white privilege, allyship and First Nations issues, mobilizing (which is showing up for rallies and actions), followed by long-term organizing in the community that can lead to successful coalitions.
- Join your local activist community. Protests, marches, rallies, demonstrations, civil disobedience (with proper permits of course), and all types of creative rebellion have the potential to create social change, either incrementally or suddenly. You have a voice! Don't be complicit with Empire by your silence or inactivity, or align with human rights struggles elsewhere in the world without addressing the "third world" conditions right in your own country.
- Select your battle(s). To affect political reform and social change we must have an active participation in electoral politics. Work with the political process to change colonial policies and archaic legislation affecting Indigenous people, such as land claims, resource theft, denial of original treaties and extinguishment of Aboriginal Title. Initiate petitions, call, write and pressure your MP, cabinet ministers or the Prime Minister; write letters to the editors of major newspapers; and lobby and form outreach groups to mobilize at the local, regional or national level. Align with social protest movements

and practice an engaged civic activism - speak up and act! Forms of social media offer spontaneity in direct actions and patterns of political activism. In Canada, First Nations remind us that this country was founded on a treaty relationship between two (or more) sovereign nations for the benefit of all people, and we need to support those attempting to convert unilateral Ottawa-centric decision-making into a true working partnership. *"Indigenous people of Canada are literally some of the most legislated people in the world."*[133] (Cheyanne Turions) Entrenched racism and archaic laws benefiting Canadian imperialism, corporations and industry are blocking change, and First Nations need our help now more than ever. The founding documents and declarations of the Canadian nation-state mean that *"We Are All Treaty People"* and mainstream Canada needs to confront the Canadian government en masse to express our outrage, to protest the refusal to honour treaty rights, and the disgraceful treatment of First Nations.

- Get to know the history and current challenges of the Indigenous community closest to you, and take direction from that community as to what you can do as an ally. *"A good ally would ask us what they can DO for us, not what they can TAKE from us."*[134] (Barbara Low)
- When a First Nations person in your community or nearby asks for help or assistance in person, through an organization or on social media, respond! Debating the issues, agreeing "in theory," or indulging in some kind of casual exchange with those that have been experiencing oppression and racism all their lives highlights your privilege, and is demeaning to the First Nations person. Because of white supremacy, those in the dominant society are used to First Nations people being silent and invisible, and when dialogue is finally happening, the last thing you want to do is assume that "everyone is on the same page." Learn humility, listen, and be willing to get "hands-on" with the real needs of the First Nations person or group.
- Offer your skills as a volunteer for any number of pressing issues, projects or organizations. For example the *Sacred Water Circle* initiative in my own community uses an inclusive circle model for a cross-cultural committee to address water-related issues, awareness and solutions. Assist non-native or native-led wellness, social justice, or environmental NPO/NGO organizations that benefit Indigenous communities with your time, resources and/or money.[135]
- Support native or non-native businesses, partnerships, celebrities, alliances and organizations that actively honour the uniqueness and beauty of First Nations-led education, art, music, entertainment, sports and cultural expressions. In contrast to the mass-produced native-themed consumer kitsch in the marketplace (which should be avoided and objected to), your purchases of First Nations art, craft and décor should be from a vendor who is an authentic member of native community.
- Do practical things in your own community to assist marginalized

First Nations, those who are homeless and require care and protection. For the needs of the shelter, contribute funds, volunteer, raise money for food and other necessities, donate clothing, help with assistance applications, recruit local sponsors, stand up for the civil rights of the homeless, and help to create ways and means for empowerment and new directions.

- Learn all you can about the ethics of landback, repatriation, or the return of cultural property, human remains and sacred objects from archeological projects, land use planning, building development and museums to the originating First Nations. As required, get involved in the protection of ancient Indigenous villages, longhouses, hunting camps, portage areas, burial mounds, sacred sites and artifacts - all precious elements of First Nation heritage.

- If you are a lawyer, offer pro bono legal services for human rights abuses and land claims negotiations.

- If you are in the medical professions forget about sending brigades to other countries for a while - how about "Doctors Within Borders," and restore the wellness of Canadian First Nations first? Why be an ally for disenfranchised groups in other countries (ie. Haiti, Honduras or Zimbabwe) when we have the exact same conditions in Canada? The basic requirements for health that we take for granted such as fundamental nutrition, clean water, and basic sanitation are still pressing issues in many Canadian Indigenous communities.

- If you are a teacher in the mainstream school system, don't teach the master narrative or the dominant white-led view of history; teach racism, white privilege and history from the point of view of the oppressed.[136] Educating children and youth is the first step in transforming our society to one that is free of intersectional oppressions and based on principles of equity. Lobbying to make anti-racist training and white privilege studies mandatory in the education system would be an excellent use of your time.

- Educate others! **Talk to other white people** about racism, white privilege, historical truth and the third world conditions that exist in Canada. Many First Nations live in disgraceful ghetto-like (de facto apartheid) conditions because of racism perpetuated by white Canadians, and it is white Canadians who need to reverse this hegemony.

- Come to the defense of First Nations - speak out and act (!) whenever you see appropriation, IK interference, the use of negative stereotypes, offensive fashion accessories, dehumanizing mascots, stupid jokes, racism and racist attitudes or statements that are directed toward native people. Do this independently, and on principle. It is not necessary to inform a First Nations person every time you speak out on their behalf, but it is necessary to take responsibility for the battle. If you need back-up, call in other Settler-activists, as First Nations people have already seen (and been hurt by) these kinds of incidents countless times.

As we continue to develop our intercultural competency, we also need to be aware of the terrible history of paternalism based on false assumptions and perspectivism coming from churches, non-profits, governments and other coalitions that have robbed First Nations of their dignity, and created a culture of dependence and disempowerment. *"The road to hell can be paved with good intentions."* However, there is much genuine kindness, concern and sensitivity in the non-native community as well, that can be directed in positive directions toward healing the colonizer/colonized divide. But we need to be aware that the heartfelt gifts white people may feel to be suitable do not address the pressing needs of the Indigenous community, and may actually offend instead of being beneficial. The goal is **not** to make the non-native person feel better by giving, but to find out what the Indigenous person or community actually needs. Initiating a toy drive or sending truck-loads of clothing and bed linens to remote Indigenous community may not be the best idea, when their priority is to improve housing and other infrastructure. Contributions of material goods are fine to a point, but focusing on the amenities ignores the underlying systemic issues that caused the problem in the first place. In First Nations community a contemporary movement toward environmentally compatible, self-sustaining projects is on the rise, with alternative and renewable energy; water cleansing; wildlife and fish restocking; greenhouse gardening; building using green technology; and cultural centres designed specifically for IK expressions in ceremony, song, dance, spiritual teaching, arts and other activities.[137] As allies, the potential is there for our contribution to a diversity of ventures as led by First Nations in their own communities, and the success of these alliances will come from an attitude of deep listening, humility, and mutual respect.

---

132. G. Horton Baptiste (Saulteaux Anishinaabe), Facebook comment, 2014.

133. Cheyanne Turions, "Reflecting on Couchiching: Some Thoughts on what it Means to Navigate," *Cheyanne Turions: Dialogue Around Curatorial Practice,* (blog), February 6, 2014. (http://cheyanneturions.wordpress.com)

134. Barbara Low (Mi'kmaq), Facebook comment, *Denial No More*, 2013.

135. It is beyond the scope here to provide a complete directory of organizations focused on Indigenous rights, social issues, resurgence and wellness. For a progressive collection of over 150 native/non-native partnerships, coalitions and bridge-building initiatives in Canada, see (http://transformingrelations.wordpress.com). *Canadian Roots Exchange* at (www.canadianroots.ca) is a great cross-cultural initiative for native and non-native youth to "*break down stereotypes, open dialogue, and build honest relationships between Indigenous and non-Indigenous people living on this land.*" Major Indigenous resistance grassroots movements at this time of writing are Idle No More, Unist'ot'en Camp, Barriere Lake Solidarity, Klabona Keepers, Yinka Dene Alliance, Free Grassy Narrows and Oshkimaadziig Unity Camp; networks or organizations are RAVEN (Respecting Aboriginal Values and Environmental Needs), Defenders of the Land, Indigenous Environmental Network and Families of Sisters in Spirit; and the court challenge Hupacasath First Nations vs Canada-China FIPA agreement.

136. There are many, but good starting points to revisionist history are *An Indigenous Peoples' History of the United States* by Roxanne Dunbar-Ortiz (Beacon Press, 2014), *A People's History of the United States* by Howard Zinn (Harper Perennial Modern Classics, 2010), *A Different Mirror: A History of Multicultural America* by Ronald Takaki (Back

Bay Books, 2008), and *Conquest: Sexual Violence and American Indian Genocide* by Andrea Smith (South End Press, 2005). For a true history of the founding of Canada, *Clearing the Plains: Disease, Politics of Starvation, and the Loss of Aboriginal Life* by James Daschuk (University of Regina Press, 2013) recounts the politics of ethnocide that led to the deaths and subjugation of thousands of aboriginal people in the realization of Sir John A. Macdonald's "National Dream." These books illustrate that master narratives are a smoke-screen disguising the conflict in the Americas between Euro-Empire and people of colour, whom they destroy, enslave, exploit and oppress.

137. Examples of First Nations communities who are modelling holistic values in the creation of infrastructure while preserving the integrity of their rich cultural heritage and IK are the Dene community *Deline* on Great Bear Lake in the Northwest Territories, the Anishnaabe *White Earth Nation* in Minnesota (Winona LaDuke's community), and the Cree community of *Ouje-Bougoumou* in the boreal forest of northern Quebec. With the intersecting goals of environmental, social and economic sustainability, these communities and many others continue to live within the carrying capacity of the land.

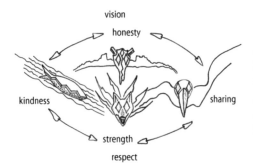

Looking back, I see that my drawings are not authentic depictions of Anishnaabe IK. (1997) How could they be?
("I Am" Interloper)

Traditional Values of the Ojibway Anishnaabe

13. Allyship

"An ally is a member of the dominant group who questions or rejects the dominant ideology and works against oppression through support of and as an advocate for the oppressed population."[138] (Minneapolis Committee on Civil Rights)

As white spiritual seekers go about the business of focusing on their own enlightenment by visioning the "One" and projecting their bliss onto the world, First Nations continue to deal with one imperialist onslaught after another, and real change for them is happening slowly, if at all. For example, in November of 2012 sneaky tactics by the Harper government sought to undo years of fragile negotiations by passing Bill C-45 that would assimilate ("assimilate" being another form of genocide) First Nations into the existing federal and provincial orders of the government of Canada, and dissolve their constitutionally-protected and internationally-recognized treaty rights. The contrast between the non-native and native world(s) in Canada could not be more extreme, and we should be outraged that genocidal policies and colonization are continuing unabated, not to mention that the Harper government's scheme to pass legislation without consulting the parties involved is a disgraceful affront to the democratic process. Clearly, the colonial takeover of the Americas, with its imperialist capitalist agenda and subjugation of First Nations, is still ongoing today.

"First Nations don't want or need 'equal rights.' What we need is to be able to live our own lives in accordance with our own customs and traditions without being physically, mentally, socially, politically and economically assaulted every single day by the Canadian government."[139] (John Ahni Schertow)

The explosion of the *Idle No More* movement in the winter of 2012/13 generated a renewed focus on Indigenous human rights violations in Canada, and it has become apparent that the support and solidarity of non-native allies is needed now more than ever. Worldwide, the impetus for social change and collective resistance to the hegemony of Empire is building, with wave after wave such as the Occupy movement and other global uprisings. People everywhere are standing up and saying "*no more!*" to the ruling elites who dictate the future for us all, who value money over life itself, and who are devoid of any basic respect for human decency or environmental protections.

In the late 1990s, new guidelines giving structure to the *Ally Process* arose from the cross-cultural challenges that native and non-native activists and scholars were encountering in their working relationships. Since then, *Ally Theory* and practice has been gaining momentum, and non-native allies are at work in communities, church groups, social justice organizations and academic institutions across Turtle Island. When we become allies to First Nations and assist them in their anti-racism and anti-oppression efforts, we advance the cross-cultural learning that is integral to social justice struggles, and create radical change in ourselves, the community and the world.

In *Alliances: Re/Envisioning Indigenous-non-Indigenous Relationships*[140] Lynne Davis describes the three types of relations that are possible between Indigenous and non-Indigenous peoples as:

1) *Walking side-by-side as with the two-row wampum, each culture following its own path, laws and customs in peaceful coexistence,*
2) *paternalism, which is the legacy of colonialism whereby non-Indigenous people assume that they know what is best for Indigenous peoples, and*
3) *Indigenous peoples provide leadership and non-Indigenous people (allies) take action in support of the direction that the Indigenous peoples have determined.*

Luckily for us, through the Allyship model outlined in point 3), there is now an ethical, responsible way to build relationships and conduct ourselves in solidarity with First Nations. Contrary to what most mainstream Canadians believe, **there is no level playing field** between non-native and native Canadians. First Nations are not a "special interest group," "stakeholders" or another part of the "multi-cultural mosaic" of Canada. Intrinsically connected to the land for all time, as the *Original Peoples* thriving on Turtle Island for millennia before European arrival, they have traditional cultures and worldviews completely bonded to place, and inherent rights to their homelands through treaties and constitutional agreements. The rest of Canada, the dominant society to which we belong, has not experienced genocide, oppression, and the criminalization of culture (not recently anyway). Yet First Nations are survivors, not victims, and with or without our help are more than capable of decolonizing themselves and working toward their goals of sovereignty, which will protect the environment and benefit all Canadians in the process. It takes much humility to set aside our privilege and bias, to listen to First Nations, and place their needs and worldview at the center. This is what an Ally does, and the reversal of the habitual power relationship is essential to eliminating racism and the intersectional oppressions. It is only by placing ourselves behind the most oppressed and moving them forward will true progress be made.

After years of being entangled in the web of colonialism, settler culture, racism and structural inequality, First Nations are now empowered by *Ally Theory* to set forth tasks for non-native people to perform. From first contact until the present day, Indigenous groups have suffered constant interference in the form of well-intentioned meddling that has served the overculture and not the First Nations themselves. But only First Nations can truly know what is best for them, and they are justified in taking back the personal and collective power that has been denied them for so long. Taking our direction from them as allies, we must first and foremost acknowledge our own white privilege and power, fully understand the machinations of the dominant colonial mindset, and question our unconsciousness sense of entitlement. Through the media and the schools, white people have been trained by the system to be oblivious to injustice or oppression, and to have the luxury of believing in the master narrative. Connected to a self-congratulatory nationalist social structure and having unearned unjust

---

138. Minneapolis Committee on Civil Rights, *Privilege, Allyship and Safe Space*, pamphlet providing information to help dismantle systems of oppression and join the movement for social justice, 2010.
139. John Ahni Schertow (Haudenosaunee/European), article comment, "Harper Launches Major First Nations Termination Plan: As Negotiating Tables Legitimize Canada's Colonialism" by Russell Diabo, *Intercontinental Cry/IC Magazine: Supporting the Indigenous Peoples Movement*, November 9, 2012. (http://intercontinentalcry.org)
140. Lynne Davis, (editor), *Alliances: Re/Envisioning Indigenous-non-Indigenous Relationships*, University of Toronto Press, 2010.

power, we must constantly listen to what Indigenous people are saying, and assist them on their own terms. Engaging as allies is a *"transformative decolonizing pathway toward more just and peaceful relations with Indigenous peoples."*[141] (Paulette Regan)

Our Challenges As Allies

Being an ally is a practice and a process, rather than an identity or a role, and allows us to have accountable, ethical ways of working with marginalized Indigenous groups. The task of forming alliances begins with recognizing that for native people, having a bicultural existence has already given them a thorough understanding of the dominant society, whereas non-native people need to educate themselves about historical and contemporary Indigenous issues and culture(s). Then, by rejecting the oppressive colonial system (uncolonization) and placing the Indigenous worldview at the center, the ways we ordinarily organize and think can be shaped by another way of being. *"Cross-cultural learning is both hopeful and immensely threatening - once it occurs, we can no longer claim that any single culture has a monopoly on the truth."*[142] (Schultz & Lavenda)

According to Lee Maracle *"it's simple - A good ally with indigenous solidarity needs to align with the host laws of Turtle Island. The host laws state that everyone eats, every woman has a house, and everyone has access to the unlimited wealth of the land."*[143] In essence, she is saying that there is no place for capitalism on Turtle Island, and that if Europeans wish to stay they need to learn and abide by the host laws, and respect and honour Indigenous sovereignty. She outlines our Allyship movement by reminding us that *"the world was created by a rapacious predatory dysfunctional people and they are still in charge, and we need to object!"*[144]

The key challenge for allies to address in self and others is the denial of colonial violence, and the endemic lack of awareness regarding racism, white privilege and the kyriarchy of intersectional oppressions. Social activism starts with self-education, *Rejecting Empire*, mobilizing (which is showing up for rallies and actions), followed by long-term and strategic organizing in the community that can lead to successful coalitions. Allies need to perform their solidarity work with humility and responsibility, and to be dedicated and organized if they are to be of service. At the First Nations community level it is better not to approach

---

141. Paulette Regan, *Unsettling the Settler Within: Indian Residential Schools, Truth Telling and Reconciliation in Canada*, UBC Press, 2010.
142. Emily Schultz and Robert Lavenda, *Cultural Anthropology: A Perspective on the Human Condition, 5th Edition*, Mayfield Publishing, 2001.
143. Lee Maracle (Stó:lō), *May Day Assembly on Migrant Justice*, April 4, 2011. (www.youtube.com)
144. Ibid.

with a specific goal in mind, but rather to enquire what the priorities are, and humbly ask what can be done in the spirit of solidarity. Building trust can be difficult and time-consuming, and the complexity of relationships challenging, but we need to be open to learning from each other. Solidarity and allyship work have the potential to build bridges, and renew relationships between native and non-native people, communities and nations.

Experienced activists tell us not to have an expectation of unity, as contradictions are likely to arise, and that it is important neither to avoid conflict nor exacerbate it. The role of the Ally is to try to reconcile the issue(s) and to learn from the conflict. We need to be conscious that elements of our western worldview may be inappropriate to the conversation. As just one example, do not make the mistake of touting the meme "We Are All One" to native community as they find this laughable, "*a mantra used to sidestep the discomfort of discussing colonialism*"[145] (Barbara Low) and a projection of our own idea on how people recover from slavery or genocide. It is not for us to assume we know anything about the recovery process, and in our work as allies we need to stay away from the methods of the colonizer, which include perpetuating stereotypes, patronizing behavior, the use of perspectivism (assuming others share our worldview), or making rules for the disenfranchised group. It is quite possible that Indigenous people hear the solutions, observations, ideas and aspirations as offered by white people as patronizing, arrogant or ill-informed. Assuming you know what Indigenous communities need in terms of western ideology or infrastructure, and imposing these "benefits" on them intentionally (or with subterfuge), is known as the "white savior" complex. White people are not heroes or heroines riding in on a white horse to save everybody (!) we are assisting a group of people who already have a plan in place. Allies cannot presume to know about the experience of Indigenous people, or to speak authoritatively about Indigenous community. Targets of oppression are experts on the totality of their oppression and we need to listen to them. Our task is to be mindful of how power is operating in any given context, to think before speaking (if we must speak), and to let the Indigenous voices be heard. We are cautioned by experienced activists to understand that our anti-oppression work is not about *our* needs, or to feel good about ourselves, but *it is about the needs of the targets not to be oppressed.* So if we make mistakes we can apologize, but we should not expect coddling or forgiveness, as the needs of the Ally are irrelevant. This dynamic will make more sense within the context of the *Six Rules for Allies* (see Page 115, in this chapter).

A textbook example of perspectivism was the projection of the "New Age Gaze" and the white spiritual seeker experience onto the recent *Idle No More* movement. Hundreds of seemingly well-intentioned members of the dominant society, many after joyfully participating in "round dance" actions in malls and other locations, came forward to proclaim INM as the "long-awaited birth of the new era of universal love," or "a new time of enlightenment and peace for all," or "the coming together of all races in peace and harmony," or even "flash-mob round-dancing under the flowering tree of peace as the unified *Rainbow Nations of the Globe*." In actually, INM was **none** of those things, being a resistance movement rising up from the most marginalized and oppressed population in the Americas, and focused exclusively on Indigenous rights, anti-colonial and anti-oppression activism, restoring the claims of specific First Nations to their land and resources, and protecting Mother Earth for the generations yet to come. Members of the so-called "Rainbow Tribe" may chose to ignore or deny marginalized voices in their pursuit of the "One," but to Indigenous freedom fighters, New Age spiritual seekers are just another manifestation of white colonial dominance and white privilege.

"There are too many self-proclaimed allies running around, who have no clue what Idle No More is about, and don't have the respect to really find out - instead, they are just gluing their own agendas and wish lists onto the movement. It's not an environmental movement. It's not a New Age movement. It's an Indigenous rights movement. The treaty relationship must be rebuilt. Canadians are going to have to come to terms with their privilege, and their complicity in colonialism and genocide. And when Indigenous rights are acknowledged and respected - then you will get your clean land and water. So get over your liberal left-wing selves, and stop telling Indigenous people what Idle No More is all about!"[146] (Barbara Low)

Acknowledging our privilege, examining how dominance plays out in our own lives and becoming an ally is a matter of personal choice. *"We cannot become fully human or whole without coming to terms with our relation to the suffering of others."*[147] (Joseph Amato) An ally believes that it is in one's own self-interest to fight oppression, and is driven by this responsibility whether or not the oppressed choose to respond. There is also a definite need for allies to engage in specific and separate work among other allies, as well as supporting the struggles of those we are in alliance with. To truly support and nurture each other across cultural or colour lines, we need to be *"hard on issues and soft on people."*[148] (Jen Margaret) As dismantling colonialism may take a **long** time, we also need to celebrate our successes and value our contributions along the way, and be nurtured by our own spiritual practices and/or EIK.

"Allyship is a state to work toward with the understanding we may never actually reach it."[149] (Wombat Cascadia)

Being an ally means supporting native community directly under their leadership, as well as performing ongoing actions on our own that will undermine and chip away at institutionalized racism. We cannot put the burden entirely on native community alone, as it is the members of the dominant society that need to reverse racism, and whites can effectively make change. Long-term allyship requires that our solidarity relationships are based on the principles of decolonization, and that we are committed to the well-being and sovereignty of the Indigenous community as a whole. However large or small, or intermittent our contributions to the struggles of Indigenous people, as Allies there is a huge amount we can be doing.

Action Points for Allies

- Get to know the history of your region and the Indigenous peoples who have lived there, and who live there now, so that they are not invisible to you. What are their current struggles? What are they thinking? What monumental work are they already doing in survivance, cultural revival, land ethics, intellectual discourse, human rights activism and decolonization? What are their successes and what are their ongoing challenges?   Extending the proper respect to the original inhabitants of Turtle Island in our process as anti-racism ally is key.

- Do not lean into the Indigenous Knowledge of First Nations - it is enough to understand the basics of their IK and how it stems from the land, and then focus on uncovering your own ancestral EIK treasures. It may seem to be at cross-purposes to suggest that whites learn all they can about Turtle Island IK, but that is where a moral code comes in. To respect another culture with full knowledge of their IK, without interfering or appropriating any elements for yourself, is what peaceful co-existence is all about. *"Recognizing native spirituality is honoring, adopting it is stealing."*[150] (Robert Hood)   You are only an authority when it comes to your own ancestral EIK, and avoid patronizing behavior or attitudes.

- Inform yourself and do your own work in reading, research and awareness-raising. Then, **educate others who share your white identity** (!) on colonialism, honoring treaties, respecting the protocols of the land, making governments accountable, mobilizing resources, and taking action on addressing systemic racism and oppression everywhere it is found (in government, the legal system, the media, the commons, and within other social movements such as

145. Barbara Low (Mi'kmaq), Facebook comment, *Denial No More*, 2013.
146. Barbara Low (Mi'kmaq), Facebook comment, *Denial No More*, 2013.
147. Joseph Amato, *From Guilt and Gratitude: A Study of the Origins of Contemporary Conscience*, Greenwood Press, 1982.
148. Jen Margaret, "Working as Allies," *Winston Churchill Fellowship Report*, August 2010. (www.communitymatters.govt.nz)
149. Wombat Cascadia, So You Want to Be An Ally, online zine (re-blogged), *Deep Green Resistance*, 2012. (http://deepgreenresistance.org)
150. Robert Hood, personal communication, 2013.

feminism). You can express your outrage with public demonstrations to demand change, and make sure your protests are known to your inner and outer circles. Lead by example, with effective communication and by sharing resources. It is not necessary to have a "holier than thou" attitude in our anti-oppression work, as *our primary responsibility as allies is to challenge and bring into the fold those who share our identity. Calling people out, with no desire to call them in or to engage them (or others) in dialogue or action toward justice, is just lazy, faux activism. Stop it.*"[151] (Jamie Utt) Activist-Allies believe that change is a process, and that mistakes, anger and hurt feelings are likely to happen, and in addition to "calling out" we need to "call in" by encouraging dialogue, showing patience and compassion, and trusting that difficulties are part of the transformation toward shared values. Ultimately, our role as allies is to engage with other white folks in the educational process, not to sidetrack the discomfort we feel by over-reacting, dismissing each other, or hurling insults. As allies, Indigenous people and people of colour are counting on us to educate and engage other white people, as we are the ones who have the most influence with white people and access to white spaces! It is a balancing act for sure, but the last thing we should do is turn away in frustration or anger from the difficult conversations we need to be having.

- **Speak Up!** Watch for racism and injustice in the things that people say and do, the way organizations are structured, in the schools, how law enforcement takes place, and with job opportunities. Observe as a sociologist would - be on the alert, challenge racist acts directly, and call things out. For example, if you repeatedly confront a customer service person on their habit of racial profiling, they will eventually become embarrassed and change their behavior. Do not just think about injustice when you see it online or in the media, act! We are obligated to use our knowledge and proficiency in social media and internet activism to make things right. When raising awareness, it is helpful to tone down one's provocative position with concrete actions that everyday citizens can take. Unfortunately, being an anti-racism spokesperson will make you a target for hostility, anger, denial, and online opprobrium from other members of the dominant society. As I have, you will find that there are literally thousands of creative and angry rebuttals those in the overculture will come up with to evade responsibility for their hegemony and privilege. Apparently, many deluded white people feel that their "whiteness" is above reproach, and this is just not true. In your condemnation of "whiteness" as the historical colonizer, the dominant culture and the ruling elite, you will be accused of **racism against white**

151. Jamie Utt, "30 Ways to Be a Better Ally in 2014," *Everyday Feminism Magazine,* January 14, 2014. (http://zinelibrary.info/files/allyship.pdf)

people, but do not fall into this trap. It is not more racism to see clearly that the source of racism and racist behavior, both historically and in modern times, is coming from white people, and it is we who are white that need to make change, not any other group. After centuries of unquestioned superiority, we need to challenge our deep sense of entitlement and learn new skills for honest discussion and actions on "race."

As with any other praxis, there are gaps between the theory and practice of Allyship. Much confusion and controversy exists regarding the use of the term "ally," both in *Indian Country* and by non-native people already integrated into native community either by marriage, personal relationship, consulting roles or other assisting capacity. Many folks, both native and non-native, just don't like the term "ally" and are unsure how to use it, or how it applies to them. Some groups or individuals say that it is not up to the white person to self-identify as an Ally, and that it is only First Nations community that can designate anyone as an "Ally." Others say that calling yourself an "Ally" is an important part of the mutual decolonization process. You may also find that the First Nations community in your area is not aware of *Ally Theory* or does not officially recognize the ally process, and that they are not in the habit of reaching out to non-native people as a source of support or solidarity. Some First Nations community members may feel that offers of help coming from earnest white activists are intrusive and alarming. However, regardless of the level of acceptance for the term "ally" or "allyship," or recognition for the help the ally is offering, or the level of inclusion of the ally in First Nations community activism or events, the basic mandate of counter-racism work is that we perform the work on principle. For example, we can say that the anti-racist and anti-oppression work of Tim Wise or Robert Jensen is hugely successful in informing and raising the consciousness of other white people, leading to an acknowledgement of white privilege and the responsibility this entails, regardless of any support for their work or applause coming from people of colour.

"An individual has not started living until he can rise above the narrow confines of his individualistic concerns to the broader concerns of all humanity." (Martin Luther King, Jr.)

There is much that we can discover about allyship from the experiences as shared by successful indigenous/non-indigenous alliances, however they take shape. From Jocelyn Cheechoo we learn that *"the relationship between a non-indigenous group and an indigenous community is most successful when the ally acts as a resource in various capacities such as media writing, media outreach, fundraising, networking, and providing access to a wider skill network. The decision-making must be left up to the indigenous community. The ENGO (environmental non-governmental organization) needs to understand that what an indigenous community wants in resolving their struggle may not align with the ENGO's interests."*[152] Together we can co-create solidarity cultures of love, support and mutuality, find our power in community by sharing our stories, and take action for a long-term vision of equity leading to equality. It is also useful to consult the excellent guidelines that have been put forth for Allyship, such as the *Six Rules for Allies*[153] by African-American feminist and artist Omi Osun Joni L. Jones, PhD.

Six Rules for Allies

- Allies must be **radical** - it is not sufficient to be liberal (liberalism is a hegemonic force of the academy, is numbing, and supports the status quo of the academy; plus oppressions cannot be undone in the academy). Allies as warriors work for freedom (unlike soldiers, who work for the state).
- Be loud and crazy - speak out! Say it - tell authorities and your superiors on behalf of the oppressed. Don't be reckless - strategize. Be willing to relinquish some piece of your privilege in order to create justice - step up and do the work that has left others weary. Be the one to advocate on behalf of the oppressed.
- Do not tell anyone in any oppressed group to be patient. This is a sign of your own privilege, and your absolute disregard for the people to which you are speaking. *"Freedom is never voluntarily given by the oppressor, it must be demanded by the oppressed. And justice too long delayed is justice denied."* (Martin Luther King Jr.) Wait/patience is a delay tactic, a diversionary tactic, a patronizing recommendation made by those who do not believe oppression is killing us all.
- Recognize the new racism and sexism that is institutional and structural. The absence of people of colour in any space is not accidental. The absence of powerful women in any space is not accountable to chance or accident. Racism, sexism and homophobia are **real**. **Listen** to those with the lived experience within multiple oppressions - this is not talked about enough. Do not offer an objection to the sharing coming from the oppressed. Let the knowledge settle, don't react. Spot oppression and support others as they reveal their wounds.
- When you are called out on your racism, sexism or homophobia, don't be embarrassed, don't cry, don't run away or think that the speaker is crazy. Be grateful - we are all racist, and exposure is one more step toward freedom. Recognize and welcome the opportunity to get rid of isolation and fear. Your choices, ideas and words may be erasing those around you. It is not about your intent - whether you mean it or did not mean it - it is about the damaging effect your choices may have on others. We reinforce patriarchy/hegemony by our actions. Allies want to know when they have contributed to the very oppressions they oppose, and allies are not above reproach.

- Allies actively support unconventional possibilities such as alternative publishing choices, poetics, painting, teaching with a loose map, and elliptical styles. *"The master's tools will never dismantle the master's house."* Recognize that the transgressive power of alternative academic strategies have the power to undo white supremacy, patriarchy and the insatiability of capitalism. **We are dreaming ourselves into the world we want to live in.**

"If women of colour were free it would mean that everyone else would have to be free, because our freedom would necessitate the destruction of all the systems of oppression. Allies need to get to know one another as people who are willing to take on racism, sexism and homophobia. We all need to practice these rules, as they are for everyone. Practicing the rules will suggest that we need to do a lot more truth-telling. The oppressed need to speak up and feel the support."[154] (Omi Osun Joni L. Jones, PhD)

As Dr. Jones points out we are **all** allies, and we can elect to support each other interchangeably across the five intersectional oppressions, which have been mutually determined by scholars and activists as ~

- Race (white at the top/people of colour below),
- gender (male at the top/female below),
- class/socioeconomic disparity (rich at the top/ middle-class and poverty below),
- sexual orientation (heterosexual at the top/LGBT community - lesbian, gay, bisexual and transgender below), and
- able-bodied (healthy at the top/disabled below).

These oppressions are interchangeable, overlapping, interlocking and intersecting - unique to each individual - and as the common adage goes, "we all have some nickels in the quarter." The wide range of oppressions and control mechanisms that pass for socialization in western society can be obvious, invisible or even taboo, and become normalized when surrounded by silence. The structural hierarchy of the intersecting oppressions grant individuals and institutions at the top actual rule and "power over" those below, whereas other subjugations are suggested, covert, or implied. When we begin to see the mechanics of oppression clearly, we notice a continuum of even more biases and prejudices in our society, including:

- Christianity at the top/all other religions below;
- young at the top/older below;
- thin at the top/obese below;
- married at the top/single below;
- highly educated (ie. PhD) and "professional" workers at the top/ other levels of education and occupations below;
- able-minded at the top/mentally-challenged below;

- those physically fit and active at the top/those less fit and active below;
- those considered to fulfill the societal ideal of beauty at the top/ everyone else below;
- those who own housing at the top/those who rent below;
- those who subscribe to capitalist meritocracy at the top/those who value the entire spectrum of human physical, mental, emotional and spiritual experience below;
- the political and corporate elite who disseminate the agenda of Empire and have a stake in, or support the values of Empire either consciously or unconsciously at the top/those who resist the imperialist paradigm, the "leftists," "socialists," "pacifists," "tree-huggers," "filthy revolutionaries," "raving environmentalists," "eco-terrorists," "radicals," "crazies" and "free-thinkers" below.

All oppressions stem from the highest value being placed on white male political or corporate power and wealth, and like an indoctrinated worldview, the intersectional oppressions can be perpetuated by anyone, not just the elite rich white male class. Kyriarchy,[155] a term coined by Elisabeth Schüssler Fiorenza, is useful to describe the multiple structural positions that are assigned to each of us at birth, the ruling oppressions and stratifications of gender, race, class and religion. The many unjust inequities, divisions and prejudices in our society are beyond belief - all oppressive, dehumanizing and unfair, and all based on the normative hetero-patriarchal notions of false superiority, elitism, aggression, meritocracy, competition and hierarchy. Including speciesism, the intersectional oppressions are tightly woven together, and our most effective work as social justice activists is to target more than one oppression at a time, i.e. by organizing an action that would challenge both disability and gender oppression. As we become more adept at the Ally process, and continue to speak out against unequal power relations, racism and oppression on principle, we anticipate that our individual and collective acts are contributing to the eventual demise of a white supremacy based on divisive and violent colorlines. *"The only requirement you need to enter allyship is a commitment to justice and human equality."*[156] (Zerlina Maxwell) Allyship enlarges the awareness that those of us with white skin enjoy certain privileges and benefits, and that people of color are still attacked, marginalized and oppressed every day in the Americas.

Becoming aware of white cultural dominance, racism, white privilege, the kyriarchy of oppressions, speciesism and the true history of Empire-building in the Americas means that we naturally come to realize that cultural appropriation is another aspect of racism and oppression, and we steer clear of making that mistake. *"Performing indigenity is a hostile act of colonialism."*[157] (Barbara Low) As the descendants of the original Settler Society, it is our responsibility to promote the principles of compassion, respect, solidarity and cooperation fully into living practice. There is an exciting new movement happening called *The Power of Outrospection*[158] (Roman Krznaric) that promotes the enlargement of our empathic potential by stepping outside of ourselves, discovering the lives of others, and expanding our moral universe. For example, empathy was a major driver for the principles to abolish slavery in 1834, and nurturing this connective power across colorlines, time and space can lead to monumental social change. Forming empathic bonds with First Nations community can make us more compassionate people and *"our instinctive resistance to the unjust treatment of others will make Allyship and solidarity natural and normative behaviors."*[159] (Tim Wise) Allies know that silence is no longer an option, feel empowered to speak out, and believe that at some point in the future a determined collective force will undo racism. According to the original Quaker definition, "speaking truth to power" means communicating first to those in power, then to the citizenry, and finally to the notion of power itself. When we become Allies to Indigenous people who have a long history of survivance and resistance, and who are now engaged in powerful decolonization strategies, we reject the ethics of hierarchy, domination and eco-genocide that harm us all. First Nations worldviews that protect and revere the earth are still in place today, and by assisting them in their struggles for sovereignty, we are ensuring that precious watersheds, lands and ecosystems will be protected for all in *Earth Community*. In collaboration with all those who have resisted injustice in the past, present and future, we are committed to that struggle.

---

152. Jocelyn Cheechoo (Cree, Moose Factory), "Ooshkahneekwayweuk, Living What I Love Most," *Lighting the Eighth Fire: The Liberation, Resurgence, and Protection of Indigenous Nations*, Leanne Simpson, (editor), Arbeiter Ring Publishing, 2008.
153. Omi Osun Joni L. Jones, PhD, "Keynote Speech - 6 Rules for Allies," *Emerging Scholarship in Women's and Gender Studies Conference*, University of Texas at Austin, February 19, 2010. (www.youtube.com)
154. Ibid.
155. Elisabeth Schüssler Fiorenza, *But She Said: Feminist Practices of Biblical Interpretation*, Beacon Press, 1993.
156. Zerlina Maxwell, "Melissa Harris-Perry Teaches Us How to be a Good Ally," *Feministing: an online community for feminists and their allies*, 02/04/2013. (http://feministing.com)
157. Barbara Low (Mi'kmaq), Facebook comment, November 19, 2013.
158. Roman Krznaric, *Outrospection*, a blog dedicated to empathy and the art of living (www.romankrznaric.com) and *The Power of Outrospection*, 2012. (www.youtube.com)
159. Tim Wise, *White Like Me: Reflections on Race from a Privileged Son*, Soft Scull Press, 2011.

14. Ethics Are Us?

"Our white lives are thoroughly racialized, and only when we begin to see that the problem of racism is OURS alone can we begin to take action to solve it."[160] (Tim Wise)

Why does any of this matter, you are asking? What can any of this possibly mean to me and my life? Don't we live in a post-racist multicultural society now where everyone is on a level playing field, and the mistakes of the past are behind us? Unfortunately this is not true, and those misconceptions are white privilege speaking. As members of the dominant society, white privilege has given us the luxury to ignore the social ethics of racism and oppression completely, and for many, conversations about race are out in the open for the first time. The hegemony of white domination is so powerful that even the concept of having an ethnicity has been invisible, and many people are startled and shocked even, to be called "white!" Michelle Alexander, author of *The New Jim Crow: Mass Incarceration in the Age of Colorblindness* has this to say about white people. *"We too have a race, we are not raceless neutral people, we are not objective observers of the American racial drama, we are part of it and we have a responsibility to do more than sit back and watch."*[161] The prohibitive conditions on non-white reality that the overculture devised were firmly in place until recent times, being challenged finally in the 1950's with the civil rights movement, the work of AIM (the American Indian Movement) and the First Nations resistance that arose in the 1970's. And, other than Dr. Martin Luther King and a few others, the revolutionary activism of the main players and their white allies, although not entirely kept secret, are not considered a major cause for celebration in North America society. And why would that be, one wonders? There can be no denying that the fortress of white supremacy is alive and well.

"I call on white people to reflect on what it means to be born into unearned privilege, to excavate our long history of racist exploitation and assumed superiority - to acknowledge that this is what we were taught and then to reject it wholly."[162] (Gillian Schutte)

In terms of personal ethics and a moral code, your positionality depends on whether you are willing to see the Americas through the lens of genocidal empire building, and accept some kind of responsibility for the privilege and high standard of living you enjoy as a result of Empire (or not). As Arthur Manuel says *"why should the Settlers be the only ones benefiting from the original treaty relationships?"*[163]

Why Does Any of This Matter?

BECAUSE IT IS WRONG that Empire was founded a) on a land grab and the genocide of the First Nations who occupied the land and b) with the labour of black slavery that fueled the engine of Empire-building.
BECAUSE IT IS WRONG that the patriarchal founders and robber barons of Empire, the rich, rapacious, entitled, racist, privileged, greedy, misogynist, bloodthirsty, warlord, bible-thumping, immoral, power-mad, dysfunctional white men and their policies have imposed their will on our bodies, minds and souls, and have dictated the destruction of our world. And we need to object!

BECAUSE the white male founders of Empire have monopolized the reality of the ecosphere and our ethnosphere for far too long with manipulation, lies, justifications, fear-mongering, economic traps, silencing, peer pressure, brainwashing and lateral violence. With all the connective and educational tools available to us today, this hegemony is becoming less and less plausible.

BECAUSE directing hatred towards someone because of their ethnicity is the behavior of a sociopath, and we need to challenge all the white folks who are racist bigots and demand that they stop acting like entitled demented psychopaths. Why is this behavior normalized and tolerated?

BECAUSE IT IS WRONG that cultural amnesia and the denial of history in the inviolable bubble of white privilege perpetuates the dominance of a white supremacist society.

BECAUSE IT IS WRONG to dominate and appropriate the knowledge, cultural property and spiritual traditions of Indigenous people through unearned white privilege and white entitlement as an extension of the oppressor/oppressed pathology.

BECAUSE the enforced blanket of silence and the invisibility of First Nations is a disgrace, and the taboo on claiming Turtle Island ancestry and declaring oneself to be Indigenous that has been in place until recent times is depraved and immoral. And why are First Nations still treated like second-class citizens and excluded from the body politic of the Americas? First Nations are everywhere in the Americas, and are healing, recovering and thriving, but the human rights and land claim issues that affect them are still in the dark ages.

BECAUSE the original treaties between the Euro-colonizers and Turtle Island First Nations assigned power and respect between nations and peoples, and defined peaceful co-existence and the sharing of the land. As this did not happen as the original signatories envisioned, this means that as members of the Settler-Society we are compelled to challenge our own ethics and morality.

BECAUSE we are living on stolen land which was taken without compensation or consent from the original peoples, and our neocolonial nation-state and abundant rich lifestyle is fueled by the primary resource extraction of lumber, diamonds, mining and oil from unceded Indigenous land.

BECAUSE Empire was built on deceptive values - the unsustainable economic agenda of resource extraction consolidates wealth and power into the hands of the few, while destroying the Earth and Indigenous societies that live in harmony with the Earth.

BECAUSE our wealth and privilege comes at the expense of human oppression and suffering.

BECAUSE what affects First Nations affects us all. First Nations issues are everyone's issues. Their priority is to protect the land, the water and the resources, and we need to unite with them in solidarity on behalf of *Mother Earth*.

Even if you didn't perform the genocide yourself and if it was enacted by your ancestors long ago (and this is by far the most common derailment) you still benefit from the land grab and subjugation of "the other" that allowed your ancestors to prosper, in turn passing on their assets and privileges to you. As activists in South Africa recently declared on a T-shirt, "*I Benefited from Apartheid,*"[164] the dynamics of this meme can also be applied to Canada, Australia or any number of colonies where Euro-Empire was established. And if you don't express or believe in racism but keep quiet about it, you are complicit with the continuing colonial policy, and your silence indicates that you are in agreement with the original mindset. The fact that Indigenous people continue to suffer from cultural genocide and colonization is immoral and disgraceful, and should not be tolerated for one moment.

How can we make amends in our lifetime? If you respect Indigenous peoples and revere earth-connected culture, then have the human decency to do everything you can to end racist colonial policies wherever they are found. You can balance the spiritual (which is you benefiting from a good life on Turtle Island, enabling your spirituality to flourish) with the material (which is you getting serious about working as an anti-oppression ally to support the struggles of Indigenous peoples). Why not adapt our thinking and behavior to accommodate First Nations? After all, they have had to accommodate the hegemony of the dominant society for centuries in everything they think, say or do.

"Try to reconsider the possibility of the healing potential of apologizing collectively and genuinely for the wrongs our history has perpetrated against the Indigenous people of this land. Instead of defending your privileges by denying them and nursing your guilt through misguided outrage - why not get your hands dirty while helping to restore this country to a space of dignity and respect for all? Be grateful that you are still welcome in a land that was stolen."[165] (Gillian Schutte)

160. Tim Wise, *White Like Me: Reflections on Race from a Privileged Son,* Soft Scull Press, 2011.

161. Michelle Alexander, *White Like Me,* a film about race, racism, and white privilege featuring Tim Wise, Media Education Foundation, 2013. (www.whitelikememovie.org)

162. Gillian Schutte/Settler Sister, "Dear White People," *Thought Leader,* Mail & Guardian Online Network, 2013. (www.thoughtleader.co.za)

163. Arthur Manuel (Ktuanaxa/Secwepemc), *Nation 2 Nation Now ~ the Conversations,* OISE Auditorium, Toronto, ON, Spreecast, March 23, 2013. (www.youtube.com)

164. "*I Benefited from Apartheid*" T-shirts printed by filmmaker Roger Young created controversy and new directions for dialogue in South Africa. *Guardian Africa Network,* November 16, 2012. (www.theguardian.com) Other recent T-shirt memes "*I Benefit from Colonialism*" and "*Got Land? – Thank an Indian!*" have been marketed by First Nations in Canada to both positive and negative response.

165. Gillian Schutte/Settler Sister, "Dear White People," *Thought Leader,* Mail & Guardian Online Network, 2013. (www.thoughtleader.co.za)

15. *"Race" and Racism*

"Race is a historically and socially constructed concept. 'Race' means whatever people decide it means. The people who have the most to say about what it means tend to be people in positions of power in political, economic, and ideological institutions – which continue to be white people."[166] (Robert Jensen)

"Any hatred felt long enough no longer feels like hatred, it feels like economics or religion, or just the way things are."[167] (Derrick Jensen)

"Race" and "racism" impacts every aspect of the First Nation/Settler interface, and a thorough analysis is integral to understanding Empire-building and colonization in the Americas. Most people are surprised to learn that race theory is a relatively modern creation, and that this invented social construct is based on white supremacist bias rather than scientific phenomena. Racial science, or the division of humanity (homo sapiens sapiens) into different biological groups based on skin colour and other characteristics, is a deception that has affected every aspect of our worldview, and racism is deeply embedded into personal and public perception and the institutions and structures of western society.

During the Scientific Revolution and the Enlightenment in the 18th century, the idea of race was invented by European patriarchs – a cadre of anthropologists, ethnologists, scientists, aristocrats, intellectuals and statesmen,[168] who set about busily measuring skulls and other manipulations of human physicality to buttress their ranking of ethnicities along a so-called "evolutionary" line of development. It was decided that intellectual ability could be assessed according to the size of one's scull (!), with the Anglo-Saxon ideal of perfect form and capability at the top of a fabricated hierarchy. This "fixing" of distinct biological races placed so-called "inferior" or "flawed" human beings in a subordinate position to the so-called "superior" qualities and dispositions of the ideal "civilized" white European (preferably Anglophone). That this racial hierarchy was a complete fabrication can be seen by the low placement of Irish, Poles, Jews, Italians and Slavs on the charts of the day, reflecting the prejudice of the ruling elite against white ethnic groups very similar to themselves. In reference to their own Celtic people, the autocratic definition of Anglocentric racial superiority would be amusing if it wasn't so tragic!

As a derailment response, those in the dominant society are fond of proclaiming that racism has always existed in all kinds of cultural groups and societies. However, historians and experts on the subject have found that *"those who assert that racism is universal and can be detected in all societies throughout history are wrong. While we have located considerable evidence of tribalism, ethnocentrism, and anti-Semitism, these do not amount to racism. The us-against-them mentality is universal, but it is often based on differences of religion, culture, tradition and other social features, not biology.*"[169] Examining the attitudes of the ancient Greeks, Romans and early Christians, scholars have discovered that even though they were ethnocentric, they did not view "the other" with racial superiority. In the surviving literature, a bias was employed to distinguish between "civilized and "primitive" people, yet they acknowledged ethnic variations in either flattering, humorous or puzzled ways. Both the Greeks and Romans noted human differences of colour and appearance in their visual art, but attached no particular moral or social significance to these illustrations. In terms of describing themselves, there are no actual mentions of "white people" found in antiquity, as the Greeks referred to themselves in relation to culture, and Roman identity was linked to war, alliances and imperialism. Recognition of "the other" was based on diverse customs and mores, not on a system of prejudice set up along colorlines. In fact, as Frank Snowden says in *Blacks in Antiquity,* "*the Ancients are a model by which we could start to reform our own racially intoxicated society.*"[170]

Early racial science and the later development of eugenics allowed for the rule of Euro-Empire, and the perceived superiority of European ideology within political, military, religious, economic and legal structures. The new model of racial hierarchy was the perfect justification for global imperialism, genocide and slavery, and for the colonization of the "New World." With no ethical or moral reservations whatsoever, entire Indigenous societies were enslaved or simply wiped out in the imperialist project, with the goal being to bring people and their lands under some form of "civilized" control. The prevailing meme of the day was "*we are the superior race of Anglo Saxons. It's only to the benefit of everyone if we people the entire hemisphere.*"[171] (Noam Chomsky)

166. Robert Jensen, *The Heart of Whiteness: Confronting Race, Racism and White Privilege,* City Lights Publishers, 2005.

167. Derrick Jensen, *The Culture of Make Believe,* Chelsea Green Publishing, 2011.

168. Racial science - the drawing of racial lines and the fixing of racial types - was invented by a cadre of German and English white men who were either aristocrats, intellectuals, politicians, religious leaders, pundits, scientists or anthropologists. Josiah Nott, Louis Agassiz, Samuel George Morton, Joseph Arthur de Gobineau and Johann Friedrich Blumenbach were all white supremacists, and all obsessed with the fetishization of tall, pale, blond beautiful Anglo-Saxons. The pinnacle of this racist worldview is methodically outlined in *The Inequality of Human Races* by Gobineau, published in 1853. Hume, Kant and Hegel, the principal philosophers of the Enlightenment, also promoted the idea of white Europeans as the superior race, and in the colonies, Ralph Waldo Emerson was a "genius" of 19th century white race theory. *The History of White People* by Nell Irvin Painter (W.W. Norton & Company, 2010) has got to be the most riveting book on the subject.

169. Dinesh D'Souza, *The End of Racism: Principles for a Multiracial Society*, The Free Press, 1995.

170. Frank M. Snowden, *Blacks in Antiquity: Ethiopians in the Greco-Roman Experience,* Belknap Press, 1970.

This hegemony is also well-defined by Howard Adams when he says that *"Eurocentrism assumes there is only one view of the human race, that of the privileged European"*[172] and that *"Eurocentric history is a political interpretation of the world based on Christianity, exploitation, economic profit and Western Europe's blind faith in its cultural superiority."*[173] Another disturbing fact is that the concept of "white people" was also defined in the same era as racial science, when German physician, naturalist and anthropologist Johann Friedrich Blumenbach devised a flawed classification system that divided human beings into five races - Caucasian (white), Mongolian (yellow), Malayan (brown), Ethiopian (black) and American (red). He named white people "Caucasian" after some female slaves in Georgia (Caucasus region and former Soviet republic) that he found particularity attractive (*"white slavery as beauty ideal"*[174]), and declared the Caucasian to be the most beautiful and most ancient race of humanity - false ideas that supported white supremacy. While Blumenbach's four other racial terms have become obsolete, unfortunately "Caucasian" is still widely used, and there are valid arguments for discontinuing not only the word, but the concept of "whiteness" itself. From Stephen Hui we learn that *"the pseudoscientific term 'Caucasian' reinforces the erroneous notion that there is a scientific basis for racial hierarchies,"*[175] and Tim Wise recommends that *"the concept of 'the white race' is a scientific and cultural fiction created by people of various European descents to subjugate non-European/non-white peoples, and deserves eradication."*[176] And lastly, Noel Ignatiev argues for abolishing the white race, defined as *"white privilege and race identity."*[177] If our goal is to create a just world, the material institutions that keep people of color subordinated need to be challenged, and the concepts of "whiteness" and "blackness" ultimately abandoned, as they make no sense outside of the realities of white supremacy.

Of course, the biological conception of race reached its zenith with the "science" of eugenics, and its conclusion in the Nazi promotion of a so-called "superior Aryan race" and their fascist policies of racial purity

171. Noam Chomsky, *Power Systems: Conversations on Global Democratic Uprisings and the New Challenges to U.S. Empire (Interviews with David Barsamian).* Metropolitan Books, 2013.

172. Howard Adams, PhD (Métis), *Tortured People: The Politics of Colonization*, Theytus Books, 1999.

173. Ibid.

174. Nell Irvin Painter, *The History of White People.* W.W. Norton & Company, 2010.

175. Stephen Hui, "Five Reasons Why We Should Stop Calling White People 'Caucasian,' " (featured blog), *Georgia Straight*, Vancouver's Online Source, November 8, 2013. (www.straight.com)

176. Tim Wise, "No, I Haven't 'Changed My Mind' About Whiteness and Racism," *Tim Wise*, December 23, 2013. *"Please note I said the concept of whiteness deserves eradication, not the people currently called white."* (www.timwise.org)

177. Noel Ignatiev, *How the Irish Became White*, Routledge, 2012.

and domination. *"By progressively eliminating inferior types, the most vital and intellectual strains could be chosen to carry on the white race. Madison Grant and other eugenicists envisioned negative eugenics as the glorious future of evolution. If this sounds Nazi-like, it most certainly is, and Nazis in Germany took lessons from Grant."*[178] (Nell Irvin Painter) Recognizing the pathology of racism as an ideology specific to white people, and as a pattern that can be accurately traced and identified, has finally come forth in the work of contemporary scholars and activists. As early as 1967, Susan Sontag drew criticism for a truth bomb by writing in the *Partisan Review* that *"Mozart, Pascal, Boolean algebra, Shakespeare, parliamentary government, baroque churches, Newton, the emancipation of women, Kant and Balanchine ballets do not redeem what this particular civilization has wrought upon the world. The white race is the cancer of human history."*[179] Sending more shock-waves through the white psyche in 1991, Michael Bradley argued that whites have a historic proclivity for racism which has caused most of the world's problems. *"Racism is a predisposition of but one race of mankind - the white race. Nuclear war, environmental pollution, resource rape.......all are primary threats to our survival and all are the results of peculiarly Caucasoid behavior, Caucasoid values, Caucasoid psychology. There is no way to avoid the truth. The problem with the world is white men."*[180] From the positionality of the enslaved and oppressed this can hardly be argued, and engaging in critiques and deconstructions of white supremacy is vital to our work as anti-racism activists.

To find alternative points of view, we need to go outside of the hegemony of the master narratives found in the "official" historical record. As a witness to the ravages of Empire in the Americas, Afrocentrist and abolitionist Hosea Easton (1799-1837) left us with a grim observation on the violence and brutality of the white race. *"It is not a little remarkable, that in the nineteenth century a remnant of this same barbarous people should boast of their national superiority of intellect, and of wisdom and religion; who in the seventeenth century crossed the Atlantic and practised the same crime their barbarous ancestry had done, bringing with them the same boasted spirit of enterprise, and not unlike their fathers, staining their route with blood, as they have rolled along, as a cloud of locusts towards the West. The late unholy war with the Indians, and the wicked crusade against the peace of Mexico, are striking illustrations of the nobleness of this race of people, and the powers of their mind."*[181] From his point of view, Easton considered the whole of European history a meta-narrative of savage aggression, which is highly ironic considering that 19th century white Europeans and those in the Colonies declared themselves to be the superior civilization! What the white supremacist Empire-builders were busy promoting as the products of a thriving free enterprise system, Easton defines as stolen treasure gained *"by the dint of war,*

*and the destruction of the vanquished, since the founding of London 49
A.D. Their whole career presents a motley mixture of barbarism and
civilization, of fraud and philanthropy, of patriotism and avarice, of
religion and bloodshed.......and instead of their advanced state in
science being attributable to a superior development of intellectual
faculties, it is solely owing to their innate thirst for blood and
plunder.*"[182] The renowned author of *The History of White People*,
Nell Irvin Painter tells us that *"Easton connects civilization to white
people, but only as an outcome of violence rather than of innate
intelligence. White people are not smarter; they are meaner."*[183] Even
Ernest Thompson Seton, although single-handedly responsible for
creating most of the romantic stereotypes and whitewashed fantasies
about Turtle Island First Nations in the first decades of the 20th
century, wrote that *"the civilization of the whiteman is a failure - it is
visibly crumbling around us, and has failed at every crucial test."*[184]

The flawed experiment of Euro-Empire in the Americas is our legacy
today as descendants of the original Settler Society, and the evidence
before us calls into question our customary pride in the so-called
achievements of our nation-states (i.e. Canada and the U.S.A). Equity
and healing between all those who now call Turtle Island home will
never happen until white people acknowledge the colonial project
historically, and discontinue those same Eurocentric practices today.
What is most shocking in the collective amnesia of the dominant society,
is the normalization of racism, colonization and oppression, and the
obliviousness to the experiences of Indigenous people and people of
colour that our conditions of privilege allow. Speaking to the
prevalence of systemic racism that continues in the overculture, Toni
Morrison says that *"white people have a very serious problem and they
should start thinking about what they should do about it! There is
something distorted about the white psyche, and no one examines
racism for what it is. Racism feels crazy and is crazy, and the
corruption of it leaves as much a deleterious effect on white
people as people of colour."*[185] Taking this dysfunction to its logical

---

178. Nell Irvin Painter, *The History of White People*. W.W. Norton & Company, 2010.
179. Susan Sontag, "What's Happening to America? (A Symposium)," *Partisan Review*,
1967.
180. Michael Bradley, *The Iceman Inheritance: Prehistoric Sources of Western Man's
Racism, Sexism and Aggression*, Kayode Publications, 1991.
181. Hosea Easton, *A Treatise on the Civil and Political Condition of the Colored People
of the U.S. States and the Prejudice Exercised Towards Them*, Cornell University Library,
Samuel J. May Anti-Slavery Collection, 1837.
182. Ibid.
183. Nell Irvin Painter, *The History of White People*, W.W. Norton & Company, 2010.
184. Ernest Thompson Seton wrote his treatise in the midst of the Great Depression.
The Gospel of the Red Man: A Way of Life, commemorative edition, World Wisdom, 1965.
185. Toni Morrison, *Toni Morrison Takes White Supremacy To Task*, March 24, 2012.
(www.youtube.com)

conclusion, we clearly see that whites are at the center of the problem, not any other group, and that racism is actually a white problem, NOT a black or brown problem. To deny this is to lay more blame at the feet of the oppressed, and does nothing to further the process of Settler accountability for racism and white privilege.

It may be hard for those of us in the dominant society to hear these essential critiques of "whiteness," or come to terms with the implications. Yet these diatribes are not aimed at white skin, specific white people, or the entire white race in a kind of reverse-racism, but are directed to the **construct** of "whiteness" and the **system** of patriarchal white dominance, and to all those who continue to perpetuate the hegemony of white oppression and racism (however implicit or explicit, conscious or unconscious). Critical to our uncolonization project (*Rejecting Empire*) is an examination of how European dominance has been structured and normalized, and how white supremacy has been, and continues to be, integral to the colonial project. To further our understanding of racial subjugation in the Americas, we need to know that the ruling Eurosupremacists formulated "whiteness" as a construct to create an underclass of working people of colour, and that their white middle-class overseers were poor and previously of "questionable ethnicity" before being allowed to join the "white club." With profit as the ultimate goal, the version of reality we call modern life in the Americas began as a manifest destiny notion between an elite company of rich, rapacious, entitled, chauvinistic, war-crazed, greed-consumed white men. Knowing the truth of this today (!), there is no excuse for not working to right the wrongs of history, and eliminating racism and racist attitudes.

The idea that one group can set themselves up as superior to the rest of the human family by virtue of a pathological so-called "science" of racial biology is a disgrace, and we are still living with this mess today. The consequences of patriarchal white greed and power affect us all, and we have a responsibility to challenge white supremacy and imperialism in all the institutions and spheres of modern society. The ruling elite that initiated Empire-building in the Americas were driven by patriarchal values, and it is worth noting these characteristics in contrast to matriarchal and/or earth-connected Indigenous societies. The work of scholar and visionary Riane Eisler has been key to de-constructing the patriarchy, and the visual aid I have formulated from her methodology[186] will identify, compare and clarify the dominator model of a patriarchy with the relationship model of a matriarchy, values observed by Eisler over a long continuum or timeline.

To describe a "matriarchy" more precisely, it is **not** the simplistic reverse of a patriarchy, with women dominating or abusing men through some kind of "mother-rule," nor is it the Jungian notion of an early and necessary "stage" in the evolutionary development to a higher culture (i.e. patriarchy). The definitive text on the subject, *Societies of Peace: Matriarchies Past Present and Future*[187] is a collection of essays by feminists, scholars, activists and Indigenous women who identify the elements of historic and present-day matriarchies all over the world. Heide Goettner-Abendroth argues that matriarchies are societies that place the highest value on the aspects of nurture, care and generosity usually associated with motherhood. *"Matriarchies do not affirm that only women can be nurturers of life. Quite the opposite, they assert that the highest role for anyone - male or female or other - is to nurture life. This is so far from the way we think, that it is easy to misconstrue."*[188] (Carol Christ) It is hard to imagine, but in matriarchal societies men **do** hold power as brothers and uncles, but in collaboration with mothers and grandmothers through an egalitarian process whereby all voices are heard, and there is no value placed on the ability to dominate. Based on matriarchal partnership models, creating an alternative, life-affirming society today is the logical response to the oppression we have experienced (for over 5000 years) from the military industrial complex and the "civilizing force" revolving around the dominator "Big Man." The contemporary explosion of women's empowerment, advancements in women's rights, and the rise of the *Divine Feminine* in our spiritual life point to the beginning of this transformation.

Resistance to Empire has been a cumulative process over the centuries, and movements such as *"abolitionism, pacifism, anarchism, anti-colonialism and environmentalism describe different manifestations of the same andocratic monster as the totality of the problem, yet they fail to address the fact that at its heart lies a dominator, female-dominated model of the human species."*[189] (Riane Eisler) This is extremely important to recognize as feminists and intersectional change agents everywhere confront and deconstruct the masculinist hegemony that is ingrained in every aspect of western society. The entire narrative of "frontier expansion" in the Americas was modelled on the masculine subduing and "taming" of the feminine (or wild nature), and to make the continent "safe" and free from "barbarism" by plowing the land and delineating urban space for commodity production and capitalism. Chauvinistic values and patriarchal fascism continue to dominate and oppress both women and the land, and the "cult of masculinity" must be resisted until the violence perpetuated by men is no longer normalized or tolerated.

---

186. Riane Eisler, *The Chalice and the Blade: Our History, Our Future*, HarperCollins, 1988.
187. Edited by Heide Goettner-Abendroth, one of the founding mothers of modern matriarchal studies. *Societies of Peace: Matriarchies Past, Present and Future*, Inanna Publications, 2009.
188. Carol P. Christ, "Matriarchy: Daring to Use The 'M' Word," *Feminism and Religion* (blog), February 17, 2014. (http://feminismandreligion.com)

Comparison of Dominator/Partnership Models
As inspired by *The Chalice & the Blade* ~ Riane Eisler

Male
The Blade
Dominator Model
Patriarchy
Phallocentric
Androcracy[190]
Male supremacy.
Authoritarian social
structure.

Female
The Chalice
Partnership Model
Matriarchy
Gynocentric
Gylany[190]
Actualization of all peoples.
Peaceful and egalitarian
social structure.

The Blade	The Chalice
Identification with the father.	Identification with the mother.
Venerate the masculine.	Venerate the feminine.
Worship the God.	Worship the Goddess.
Place higher value on the power to take rather than give life, aligned with killing and destruction.	Place higher value on the nurturing and life-generating powers of the feminine.
Focus on ranking and hierarchy.	Focus on linking.
Power equated with dominance over women and/or ethnic groups.	Power and leadership with love and responsibility to the whole community.
Autocratic, dictatorial, warlord rule.	Wisdom of mother honoured above all.
High degree of male violence and warfare.	Focus on the sacredness and unity of all life.
Values of brutality, oppression.	Values of compassion, non-violence.
Sexually repressive.	Sexually equalitarian.
Separation between sacred and secular.	No separation between sacred and secular.
Social stratification based on private property with male dominance over women.	Lands held and worked communally, both men and women as *Children of the Goddess.*
Acquire material wealth through ever more effective technologies of destruction.	Focus on nurturing, sharing and Gift Economy rather than acquisition by conquest or hoarding.
Worship the power of the blade ~ symbol of masculine power, competition, dominance, control and destruction.	Worship the sacred chalice or grail ~ symbol of the feminine generative powers of the universe in birth, nurture, death and rebirth.
Man the warrior, Man the hunter.	*"The whole of life is pervaded by an ardent faith in the Goddess Nature, the source of all creation and harmony"*
Rigid roles for men, maladaptive, massive regression.	

189. Riane Eisler, *The Chalice and the Blade: Our History, Our Future*, HarperCollins, 1988.
190. New terms created by Riane Eisler - **androcracy** more precisely refers to a system ruled by men than "patriarchy," and **gylany/gynocentric** refers to a system that links both genders, instead of ranking them in a heirarchy. Riane Eisler, *The Chalice and the Blade: Our History, Our Future*, HarperCollins, 1988.

Clearly, feminism is not just "a woman's issue," and anti-sexist men such as activist Jackson Katz are taking up the fight by openly stating that *"one of the key characteristics of power and privilege is that dominant groups maintain and reproduce themselves, and are rarely challenged to think about their dominance. Men have the ability to lack introspection, to go unexamined, and to be rendered invisible in the discourse. In fact, men are largely erased in the conversation about a subject that is centrally about them!"*[191] For both men and women, our imperative must be to challenge the centrality of patriarchal Empire, which has used reductionist science, racial theory and other toxic ideologies to dominate egalitarian societies based on interconnectivity (such as IK and women's knowledge) for far too long. The good news is that monumental cracks are appearing in the patriarchal façade.

"We're all cut from the same genetic cloth, and race is an utter fiction."[192] (Wade Davis)

Finally liberating the human spirit from the parochial tyrannies based on racial divisions that have haunted us for centuries, modern genetics has recently exposed racial theory to be a complete fabrication, a political ruse rather than the result of genuine scientific phenomena. Much to the dismay of white supremacists, bigots and overt racists everywhere (!) this new evidence is the most revolutionary scientific breakthrough of modern times. The amazing fact that modern genetics has uncovered is that the entire human family has a common ancestry in our mitochondrial DNA and genetic connection to Africa from 60,000 years ago, and that from those origins we miraculously migrated in all directions to inhabit the world. According to research provided by the scientific race to decode the human genome,[193] there is an astounding 99% similarity in all human beings, and we are all descended from ONE African woman, our ancestral clan mother, or "Mitochondrial Eve."[194] We are 99% the same, we have more in common than we are different, and in terms of variation, people from the same race can be more dissimilar than people from different races! The corrected theory of humanity's origins shows no sharp genetic

191. Jackson Katz, Ph.D, "Violence Against Women – It's A Men's Issue," *Violence & Silence: at TEDxFiDiWomen*, 2013. (www.youtube.com) (www.jacksonkatz.com)

192. Wade Davis, "The World is Not Dying……It's Changing," Interview with Paul Luke, *The Province*, Pacific Newspaper Group, Vancouver, B.C., January 4, 2014. (www.theprovince.com)

193. Through the developing science of molecular genetics, the "human genome mapping project" was a race between the *National Institutes of Health* (governmental organizations) and *Celera Genomics* (private company), with a tie declared by President Bill Clinton in June 2000.

194. Term coined by Bryan Sykes, author of *The Seven Daughters of Eve: The Science that Reveals Our Genetic Ancestry*, W. W. Norton & Company, 2010. See more on *Oxford Ancestors: Explore Your Genetic Roots* on Page 131 and 284.

differences among populations, only geographic gradients that affect skin pigmentation, and differences in culture such as the way that technologies are used is simply a matter of choice, not as predetermination or because of "superior genes." Another incredibly exciting development is the map of worldwide human migration and evolution made possible by the discoveries of ancient human remains by archaeologists, who have been able to accurately pinpoint the geographic placement of DNA groups through genome studies. The fact that race does not exist must be extremely upsetting to overt white supremacists, and makes the social construction of racial classifications seem ridiculous indeed.

The Seven Daughters of Eve: The Science That Reveals Our Genetic Ancestry by Bryan Sykes is a fascinating study of how all human DNA traces back to one African Ancestor, the "Mother of Us All," the 27 matrilineal clans that evolved from her worldwide, and how the "Seven Daughters of Eve" subcategory formed the family trees for tens of millions of European people. Matching DNA samples from the global archaeological record with modern samples, Sykes has been able to solve historical mysteries and trace the branches of a great diversity of ethnic and cultural trees. His company *Oxford Ancestors* in the UK provides DNA testing for those fascinated with genealogy, and eager to discover links to their own ancestral kinship groups. Human beings have always organized themselves into tribal, clan or kinship groups much like extended family, and along fluid and dynamic cultural lines. We are also physically diverse, and for terminology "ethnicity" continues to be a better substitute for the obsolete term of "race." We now know that "race" and "racism" are **not** a reality and are no longer regarded as biological fact, yet the "white is right" pathology has given Europeans free rein to subjugate and/or assimilate other cultures based on some crackpot notion of civilizational hierarchy and progress. Ideas of racial hierarchy without any reasonable or objective basis became systems of oppression that were violently thrust upon Turtle Island First Nations, as *"many many years ago, there was no term to distinguish race or nationality amongst native people - colonization brought these terms to us."*[195] (Charle-Sherry Peltier) The concept of race was a creation of a powerful elite - and politically, socially and economically, race is, of course, still a brutal reality around the globe today. It may be a pseudo-reality, but race still shapes our interactions, and before we begin building bridges over the racial divide, we need to acknowledge that these divisions still exist.

The crude fabrication of racism seems to have diminished today, yet the construct of "whiteness" continues to operate through the oppressive policies directed to assimilate people of colour into a homogenous (white) neo-liberal democratic society. As Ward Churchill says, *"conceivably American society comprises a racial/cultural 'melting pot' which has produced a wholly new people, even while enforcing racial codes indicating the exact opposite.*"[196] One of the most reprehensible elements of white privilege is the assumption that all other ethnicities wish to be "like us." My own experience has informed me that Turtle Island First Nations are different from the dominant society in countless obvious and ephemeral ways, and are entitled, like any other sovereign people, to full self-actualization and cultural freedom. Peaceful co-existence was never the goal of the colonial powers, and we need to re-examine the immoral and oppressive assimilationist policies that were born in the "promised lands" of the Americas. Coming together in a common "crucible" millions of emigrants were supposed to transcend the religious and ethnic alliances of their homelands and embrace an acculturation program that we now know to be a propaganda cover-up for ingrained racism and white supremacy. A "melting pot" will always fail, as ethnic groups tend to want to hang on to their own languages, traditions and ancestral knowledge, and may chose to remain separate from the mainstream (imagine that). Even though contemporary thinkers have identified multiculturalism, or the "cultural mosaic" as a more accurate description of modern society than a "melting pot," sadly the *American national culture is the most homogeneous culture of any nation in the world, and derives most of its traits and characteristics from the early colonial settlers from Britain, Ireland, and Germany.*"[197] And as Harsha Walia states so well, *"multiculturalism and the industry promoting it, is an effective cloak that continues to situate whiteness as hegemonic in order to maintain racial and colonial hierarchies.*"[198]

The term "multiculturalism" has become a popular catch phrase that implies a cultural fusion or some kind of peaceful co-existence, but is actually a contentious concept, with *"patterns and practices our culture has used in order to envisage, negate or welcome the Other.*"[199] (Kalaga & Kubisz) The multicultural environment assumes that those from other societies will quickly become confident citizens in a competitive world, but the reverse is often true, resulting in alienation and marginalization. The promotion of acculturation to people of colour and new immigrants forces their capitulation to the dominant white society, with its patriarchal values of industrialization, emphasis on individualism instead of cooperation, and perceived benefits of consumerism. Eventually the internalized oppressor within the colonized individual begins to place a higher value on consumer goods and a technological lifestyle than one's own ancestry, cultural keystones or gifts of the Earth. In the face of this assimilation, holding on to one's identity and self-determination agenda as a cultural group is extremely important, as it is actually one's own IK/EIK values that provide strength, identity and a moral compass. Ultimately, cultural differences should be preserved, each group remaining unique and distinct but contributing to the public sphere and shared commons as required. *"Multiculturalism implies a community of communities, or what*

Gandhi once described as an oceanic circle of villages, bound together by mutual self-interest in commerce and defence, sharing only a minimal core of civic values."[200] (Allan Smith)

Recognizing and tolerating difference in peaceful co-existence is not a complicated approach, and is key to our mutual First Nations/Settler decolonization project. But first, we need to act to challenge white supremacy, take up critical race theory and counter-racist work, and instill the values of equity into our private and public lives. It would also help enormously if white people would unhinge themselves from Empire, abandon their warlike ways, stop thinking of themselves as part of a "white is right" pseudo-patriotic nation-state that is "superior" to other forms of social organization, and begin to emulate cultures that revere the land, put the *Earth First* and restore local ecosystems and communities. Then, and only then, can true sharing between equals begin.

---

195. Charle-Sherry Peltier, Facebook comment, *Idle No More*, 2013.

196. Ward Churchill, *Indians are Us?* Between the Lines, 1984.

197. *Wikipedia: The Free Encyclopedia*, Wikimedia Foundation, 2014.

198. Activist and author Harsha Walia, Facebook comment, 2013. (www.nooneisillegal.org)

199. Wojciech Kalaga and Marzena Kubisz (editors), *Multicultural Dilemmas: Identity, Difference, Otherness*, Peter Lang International Academic Publishers, 2008.

200. Allan Smith, *Canada – An American Nation? Essays on Continentalism, Identity and the Canadian Frame of Mind*, McGill-Queen's University Press, 1994.

The Impossibility of Reverse Racism

I have come to learn that there is no such thing as "reverse racism." As already discussed, the classification of humanity into biological and "racial" groups specifically to reinforce white supremacy is entirely a creation of the white male European mind. The psychotic theories of racism toward so-called "inferior races" (people of colour) justified the colonization of the Americas through the religious terrorism of the Papal Bulls, and the genocidal white supremacist ideologies of Terra Nullius, the Doctrine of Discovery, Manifest Destiny and Settler-Colonialism. As the fabricated "science" of racial distinctions has gone on to generate institutionalized, systematic, and historical oppression on the basis of race, we must conclude that only white people can be "racist." Therefore "racism" as expressed by Indigenous cultures and POC (people of colour) is actually hierarchal behavior learned from the European colonial powers, and was never an aspect of their original worldview(s). What may be perceived to be racism coming from a person of color today is not racism, or even reverse racism, but simply a **response to the racism** and bigotry they experience on a daily basis. It is only privileged white people who have never lived with racism or discrimination on a daily basis that complain of "reverse racism" in an effort to uphold and protect their whiteness. Proclaiming "reverse racism" implies that white people think they are inviolable, and that racism cannot be applied to their cultural group, only to those it normally happens to, like First Nations or African Americans. Put another way, racism is backed by the socioeconomic structures of society, and since only white people hold power and privilege from these institutional advantages and social benefits (and BIPOC do not) it is impossible for BIPOC to be racist. Racism is **systemic** oppression, and since there is no systemic power differential affecting white people, reverse racism cannot exist! Racism is structural, not personal, and the cries of "reverse racism" that often come from white folks means they are uncomfortable talking about race or racism, or discussing their own role in the power dynamics. The bottom line is that racism kills people of colour in the Americas, not white people. The reprehensible way that racism has been built into every institution of Empire is beyond belief, but the fact that racism has been normalized is even worse.

What Can We Do?

"Ask yourself - what might a society based on love, mutual aid, and mutual respect look like? Which of my values uphold this? Organize toward that. We all must do our part. The only failure is to stop trying."[201] (T. Thorn Coyle)

In our counter-racist work to fix inequality and deconstruct white supremacy, we can start by being honest about implicit racism and the stereotypes we all carry. The dictionary erroneously describes "racism" as the bigoted acts of individuals, but racism is much more systematic and system-wide, and racist ideologies are at the core of 400 years of policies and practices in the institutions of the Americas. Most of us in the dominant society have been taught to see certain people - because of their ethnicity or class - as inferior, and when we become aware of this deeply rooted prejudice, we can work to rise above it. According to Tim Wise, explicit bias (overt prejudice and racism) is not as common anymore,[202] but we all have implicit bias carried over from our early exposure to racist images and racist programming. Still present in our subconscious, this aversive racism is so subtle and pervasive that even those trained to avoid bias can still be subject to it, like a habitual neural response. We may sincerely hold egalitarian goals, yet at the same time be at risk for perpetuating racism because of our long-term conditioning. Racism has impacted everyone, and the best we can do is acknowledge and be aware of it, challenge our habitual response, and try to see each person as an individual instead of belonging to a category of age, class or race. *"Don't emphasize difference and separation, let us emphasis what we have in common. Don't just sit there and say you are this and I am that – how can we work together?"*[203] (Nell Irvin Painter)

Contemporary research has shown that we have egalitarian tendencies, and the ability to promote the egalitarian mind to build a society in which difference is not stigmatized, but recognized and embraced. In our personal lives, the path to more positive interracial exchanges would be to expand our moral, emotional and social circles to include people different from ourselves. To develop equity in the structures of society, we need to create checks and balances in the judicial system and the job market, and to build in safeguards that make sure people of colour are well represented. Cross-cultural management and diversity training in business, health care, social services and community development requires workers to become aware of the racism that has long been systemic in organizational policies and practices, and to combat both inherent and overt bias in their attitudes and habits. The intercultural competency that is gained from this training generates a better understanding, appreciation and respect for different ethnicities, root cultures, and the diverse socio-economic backgrounds of one's colleagues and clients. In the educational system, we need to promote tolerance and equality, make anti-racism training mandatory, provide anti-racist and anti-bias intervention in the classroom, and include narratives from other cultural traditions to develop a more inclusive curriculum. As Rinku Sen, publisher of Colorlines, tells us *"we may wish that we were finished with the race project, but much remains to be done in education, housing, voting rights, criminal justice and employment. The way to make that progress is not by ignoring racial bias, endorsing a color-blind approach or by focusing on people's intentions. Instead, the path forward lies in understanding fully how such bias works in our public schools, prisons and at the ballot box - and how those systems enable or discourage discriminatory actions."*[204] Building the relationships that will create a post-prejudical society will take time, and by having the patience to build understanding with heartfelt dialogue. We need to really listen to what Indigenous people, people of colour, and marginalized people are saying, without discounting their lives, taking a voyeuristic attitude, or derailing the conversation in the process.

Part of having white privilege is that if we are uncomfortable, we don't have to talk about race or racism at all, and can continue to ignore inequality. And of course, the prevailing obfuscation in the dominant white society does not encourage systemic injustice or racism to be mentioned or pointed out, with the goal being to neutralize and obliterate the identity of the "other." My own experience with this

201. T. Thorn Coyle, "Confronting Racism is Spiritual Work," *T. Thorn Coyle: Know Thyself* (blog), July 14, 2013. (www.thorncoyle.com/blog)

202. Tim Wise, panel discussion, "Are We All Racist?" *The Stream: Al Jazeera*, 2013. (www.youtube.com)

203. Nell Irvin Painter, featured author, *2010 National Book Festival*, Library of Congress, 2010. (www.youtube.com)

204. Rinku Sen, president and executive director of *Race Forward* and the publisher of *colorlines.com*, "Why there will be another Trayvon," *Aljazeera America*, February 26, 2014. (http://america.aljazeera.com)

unspoken taboo, is to be repeatedly accused of being a "racist" for daring to bring any mention of race or racial disparities into the conversation, even though it may be discourse based on critical race theory or anti-racist work! The lack of logic here is astounding, as if anti-racism work is not required to address structural racism, which will be sure to go away as long as we ignore it.

Also, the bad habit of making the conversation about our personal lives and feelings (it's all about me!), instead of the systemic and institutional nature of racism, is never going to lead to change. *Rather than thoughtfully discussing race, Americans love to reduce racial politics to personal feelings and etiquette. It's the personal and dramatic aspects of race that obsess us, not the deeply rooted and currently active political inequalities. That's our predicament: racial debate, in public and private, is trapped in the sinkhole of therapeutics."*[205] (Rich Benjamin) Those in the dominant society need to "get out of their own way" and let go of the privileged ego-driven need to place their own perspectives and emotional needs ahead of the oppressed. Also, seeing the world through a colorblind lens and pretending that racism doesn't exist is yet another form of racism, as it negates the reality of the power differentials in society based on colour. We can't help but notice ethnic differences, and trying to convince ourselves otherwise creates cognitive dissonance, and a denial of the socioeconomic inequities that still persist along racial lines. The ideology of colour blindness causes increased racial bias as well, because the baseline of commonality is then assumed to be white, with the implied intent to "whiten" the other. Ignoring or disregarding ethnicity is always an insult to racial and cultural identity. To quote Bell Hooks, *"the notion that we should forsake attachment to race and/or cultural identity and be 'just humans' within the framework of white supremacy, has usually meant that subordinate groups must surrender their identities, beliefs and values, and assimilate by adopting the values of privileged-class whites, rather than promoting racial harmony."*[206]

Research consistently finds that the only way to overcome deep-seated racial bias is to become consciously aware of the associations we attach to perceived racial differences. For instance, judging skin colour as inferior is socially conditioned, whereas seeing skin colour at all is cognitively inevitable. We can recognize and talk about ethnic difference, while at the same time communicating to others that it is wrong to hold racial prejudice. All people deserve to take pride in their ethnic identity and cultural traditions. A major force that is unbalancing the power dynamics and consequences of "race" and systemic racism today must be the explosion of interracial partners and mixed-race children. No longer a taboo or stigma, "mixies"[207] are becoming the norm all over the world and especially in Toronto, a Canadian urban centre where those of European ancestry and people of colour from diverse places (the so-called "racialized minorities") mingle and thrive.

Taking the fusion even further, the children of multiracial marriages will soon have children of their own, again marrying across ethnic lines and producing a sweet symphony of "mixie" babies. Young people today appear to be postcolonial, post-prejudicial, colormute and colorblind, and united in their desire to be simply "Canadian." However, the millennial generation growing up bicultural and multiracial still experience serious challenges from the legacy of systemic racism and white supremacy. How does one explain one's background? Which parent does one identify with? Does one identify with the "lighter" parent in an effort to blend in? These are not trivial questions to be sure, but it may be better to focus on the egalitarian nature of the human heart, which sees no boundaries or restrictions. As outmoded attitudes shift and change for the better, it will be exciting to see if the old stereotypes dissolve and the ethos of equity finally emerges, at least in places like Toronto. At this point in time however, education, opportunity and employment are still segregated, and these systemic racial gaps will continue until the millennial generation and their predecessors are able to make change. Yet, looking into the future, if a "post-racial" acceptance of ethnicity is based on universal participation in the structures of society as established by white Europeans, true multiculturalism is still a a fiction, and we continue to live in a world where cultural diversity is eroded and white homogeneity is the rule.

"We declare our right on this earth to be a wo/man, to be a human being, to be respected as a human being, to be given the rights of a human being in this society, on this Earth, in this day, which we intend to bring into existence by any means necessary." (Malcolm X)

---

205. Rich Benjamin, *Searching for Whitopia: An Improbable Journey to the Heart of White America*, Hyperion, 2009.
206. Bell Hooks, *Killing Rage: Ending Racism,* Henry Holt and Company, 1995.
207. Nicholas Hune-Brown, "Mixie Me: will Toronto be the world's first post-racial metropolis?" *Toronto Life Magazine*, February 12, 2013.

Ancestral Origins & Cultural Recovery

In terms of recovering our ancestral wisdom, no reasonable person would advocate for a strict adherence to ethnicity in all things - that is far too challenging, if not impossible, in today's polyglot world! Historically, humanity evolved in closely-connected societies that allowed intermingling with other groups, or adaptations to new and different groups, with the boundaries of the "tribe" being somewhat permeable, and focused on kinship and loyalty rather than skin colour, gender or wealth. As the ravages of Empire play out, this may become our goal again in the future (!) as we may find ourselves by choice or necessity living in small localized kinship groups once again, looking to our own ancestral traditions for a template to survival. Many will point out that it is impossible to re-create one's own ancestral wisdom in pure form, that our genealogy is a weaving of diversity, and our bloodlines far too mixed. It certainly cannot be suggested or implied that ethnicity would be the complete determining factor for one's ecocultural recovery or spiritual practice, in some weird new form of spiritual racial profiling, eugenics or "biological determinism!" Multicultural family lines are far more common than not, and it is more about being in alignment with self, making conscious choices, and factoring in the physical make-up of our being and the building blocks of our family tree that point to a complete EIK/IK system, as treasure just waiting to be discovered. Becoming part of a specific ancestral group can give us a firm foundation, and a place to turn for spiritual guidance, cultural values and familial connection. If we are the lucky ones who know the details of our heritage, how beautiful and how honoring of ourselves and our ancestors to re-create our specific traditional roots to the best of our ability. Diversity works best, and to move away from the commercialized New Age expressions that are not connected to any specific EIK or spiritual tradition. Spirituality with a moral code means restraint and discernment, and the integrity of focus. For example, if you have heard the ancestors of the Kogi "calling you," and consider yourself one of the Kogi "people," you really have to wonder if the same deities also informed the Kogi that you are part of their culture? Or if you are convinced that your past life as Lakota, Cherokee or Huichol gives you special insights, or the entitlement to claim ancestors from those traditions, do you really need to "go public?" Perhaps it is a private matter best understood over time, as you continue to explore the continuum of your personal mythology.

In a sad state of affairs, many contemporary Pagans, Neo-Pagans, Druids, Reconstructionists, Ásatrú and Heathens have conflated ancestral alignment and the preservation of cultural values with isolationism, ethnic nationalism, genealogical extremism, "religious apartheid," "racialist affiliation" and/or the perpetuation of racism. However, beyond the white supremacists who continue with their criminal xenophobia and are easily spotted, the modern movement to retrieve and practice specific ancestral traditions makes absolutely no claim to an ethnic hierarchy, separatism, or superiority over others, but rather promotes tolerance, peaceful co-existence and cultural recovery for **all** peoples. This particular conversation would not even be happening if Settlers found the value in restoring what Empire has taken away, or had unbroken connectivity to their ancestors from living in an animist universe, but our identities have been normalized as nationalistic, über rational, hypermodern and consumer-driven pastiches. Instead of celebrating our ethnocultural roots, the separatist notion of "racial pride" has been so warped by Eurocentric white supremacy in recent times, that many modern white folks now consider cultural or ethnic integrity to be taboo (for white folks, anyway). In a new twist deriving from the toxicity of racism, we now have white people attacking other white people (the oppressor) without any people of colour (the oppressed) even entering the conversation! Meanwhile the fear is very real that the perverse "racial purity" agenda of the white nationalists, white supremacists, eugenicists and nazi cults could rise again, and we have to be on guard, but ethnicity aligned with cultural traditions is the way humanity has been self-organized for millennia all over the world, long before the fabrication of "racial science," German occultism, or the invention of white superiority. When we look to the colonizer/colonized power imbalance that is our legacy, and the reality in the Americas today, racist **or** anti-racist white folks who are in no danger of dying out from genocidal attack simply sound ludicrous when making the rules for cultural preservation. The psychoses of *Eurocentrism*, *White Superiority* and *Ethnic Hierarchy* ("racial" stratification) are the **only** issues that need to be called out and addressed, not the reclaiming, celebrating or practicing of specific pre-colonial earth-rooted ethnoculture by any individual or community.

The same policies of the patriarchal Eurocentric elite who created Empire continue to practice "epistemicide"[208] all over the world, and destroy ethnic and cultural cohesion in favor of the default of global capitalism. Harmonizing with our own unique earth-rooted ancestors and ancestral group, and recovering a wide variety of human societies in the process, is a blow against this hegemony. Cultural diversity is natural to the planet, not homogeneity, and you are deluding yourself if you think you can have it both ways, to be a "universalist" while at the same time bemoaning the worldwide loss of human biodiversity and IK/EIK systems. In marked contrast to other cultures around the world, it is only western society that is in complete denial that spiritual practice is usually determined by ethnicity. Displaced Europeans and colonized diasporans who have had their traditions stripped from them now consider homogeneity to be the "norm," and have forgotten what it is like to have one's ethnicity entwined with cultural practice and spiritual expression. Localized ethnic or kinship groups have lost their value, and the white privilege of historical amnesia has given rise to the notion that it is only the exotic "other" who indulges in these kind of antiquations. Additional factors that have led to the fallacy that alignment with ancestry equals "ethnic racism" or "spiritual apartheid," is the prevalence of the generic "monomyth" principle (see Page 75); the many popularized versions of the rainbow nation/one tribe and universalist "we are all one" memes; and conflating the newly-found pan-human 99% identical genome with the idea that cultural diversity is outdated and irrelevant. The cursory New Age understanding of "we are all one tribe" is not true IK or EIK, no matter how much we pretend the traditions are our own, and when we look to Indigenous nations all over the world, we can see that identity is linked to place and kinship group, and Indigenous people know exactly who they are. It is only members of the entitled white majority who have unlimited choices in superficial lifestyle and spiritual practice from any IK/EIK or ancestors they desire from any tradition, that actually reinforce the goal of Empire, which is to normalize "multicultural" globalization with white homogeneity as the default. Those in Pagan, Neo-Pagan, New Age, Reconstructionist, Ásatrú and Heathen circles who critique the practices of cultural recovery as aligned with ancestry should be more concerned with those in their own eclectic communities who openly claim a imaginary or UPG-derived "soul connection" to ancestors in a cultural group or ethnicity not their own, as this unsubstantiated behavior can be interpreted in many cases to be racism perpetuated by a member of the dominant society. And all the time spent perpetuating false views of what racism "is and is not" should be resolved, and instead of ridiculous debates involving "white on white" racism, white spiritual seekers should invest in the actual pro-active deconstruction of white superiority, and dismantling the roots of the genuine racism that continues to be directed at POC in the Americas.

"The world is populated with people who have lost their seeds. They are not bad or useless people, but they are not real until they refind their seeds......in some small, never-looked-at-place in the forgotten wilderness of their souls, their Indigenous seeds of culture and lifeways live."[209] (Martin Prechtel)

White privilege has given us automatic access to the intellectual and spiritual property of any culture we choose, but instead of empowering us, I would argue that in the ignorance of our own cultural practices and the assumption of the "other" we are the most bereft of all. The ethics of reclaiming genuine EIK from our own ancestral tradition(s) will automatically gain respect from those already rooted in ancient earth-honoring culture(s), forming both an actual and metaphysical membership in the circle of worldwide indigenity. Even if you know of only one ethnic group in your composition, you can express elements of that with authentic passion. For those who are aware of their family tree it is incredibly exciting to delve into ancient tribal connections, and unique combinations are going to look quite normal, for instance an Irish and Hawaiian EIK/IK mix! Ultimately, knowledge is always shifting and changing, but each human being worldwide has one or more root culture(s) with earth-connected aspects that can be embraced. Working on your bond with nature in the landscape where you are living will validate your IK or EIK, and more importantly, evoke your eco-activism and protection of the land. If nothing else, listening to what the Earth is telling you in your ethnocultural practice, plus embodying the elements of the ancestral traditions that sing to your soul, is to experience the joy that comes from authentic living. Taking flight across the centuries by visiting the homelands of your ancestors may spark more of a deep connection to place and the flourishing of your eco-identity than you ever imagined. When you are rapt with wonder as you view the mountains on your way to the Isle of Skye and never want to leave that place,[210] or when you thrill to the sight of upright stone circles, or find you are spellbound by the music of the harp, pipes or bodhrán, or have a sense of being "at home" when you study Welsh or Irish mythological cycles, or have been compelled to create a *Green Man* mask without quite knowing why, then you have found your place in creation. When you are touched by the truth of your ancestral soul, you will know!

---

208. Colonial dispossession is known as "epistemicide," or the killing of knowledge systems (epistemologies).
209. Martin Pretchel, *The Unlikely Peace at Cuchumaquic: The Parallel Lives of People as Plants, Keeping the Seeds Alive,* North Atlantic Books, 2012.
210. This was the exact experience of John McLeod, who travelled from his home in America to Scotland, and later found out he had deep ancestral connections to the Isle of Skye. James Hunter, *Scottish Exodus: Travels Among a Worldwide Clan,* Mainstream Publishing, 2007.

16. *White Privilege*

"I benefited from colonialism long before I understood what the word meant."[211] (Erin Wunker)

"White privilege is defined as (a) a right, advantage, or immunity granted to or enjoyed by white persons beyond the common advantage of all others; an exemption in many particular cases from certain burdens or liabilities, and (b) a special advantage or benefit of white persons with reference to divine dispensations, natural advantages, gifts of fortune, genetic endowments, and social relations."[212] (Beyond Whiteness)

"Let me tell you something about privilege - it is so intoxicating that you will fool yourself that you don't have it."[213] (Goldie Taylor)

As much as contemporary spiritual seekers try to deny it, those in the New Age, Neotribal, Neo-Pagan, Druidic, Avalon, Wicca, Celtic Reconstructionism, Ásatrú, Heathen and Goddess Spirituality communities who are descended from the original Settler Society do not exist outside of the rubric of white dominance, and have been entitled through white privilege to appropriate elements of Turtle Island First Nations IK, culture and identity as a normalized and unchallenged practice. The truth is, that unless we are native to the Americas, we are interlopers to this place. And from the point of view of the oppressed, we are either "Imperialist or Ally,"[214] with not a lot of continuum in between. But, as mentioned countless times already, what exactly is "white privilege?" I came to learn about white privilege in recent years, and how the dominant society benefits from whiteness both materially and psychologically, and by a host of other visible and invisible ways. I knew that Anglos pretty much called the shots for everyone else on

Turtle Island, but to actually approach the "belly of the beast" and find out just how much white privilege is embedded into every aspect of our culture is beyond belief. When one learns about the colonial systems of white privilege and the deplorable machinations of institutionalized racism it can be very unsettling – for the first time we have to think about what it means to be white in our time and place. And if you cannot examine and own your white privilege you will never be able to truly look at the oppression of the "other." My own immersion in First Nations culture and my emphasis on historical accuracy, contemporary issues and IK/EIK naturally led to a path of uncolonization and my heartfelt process as an ally, but learning about white privilege, however discombobulating, put all the· pieces of the puzzle together. (But truly, it's not about me.)

"It can be said that America was founded on three major holocausts, perpetuated and made possible by a racist ideology. The first was the genocidal campaign waged against the Indigenous peoples of the Americas, with an extermination rate of 95%. The land base for Empire was secured with war, starvation, disease and exposure, and whites are culpable for it all. The second is that African slavery was essential to the emergence of the USA as an industrial power; and the third is the ongoing domination of the USA as a world power over the third world to consolidate their empire-building, and acquire more power and resources."[215] (Robert Jensen)

Before listing all the features and benefits of white privilege, the most important aspect is to fully comprehend that the founding of the Americas was a white supremacist project, and that this colonial history gives us the privileges we enjoy today. As previously noted in the chapter "Race and Racism" Empire was driven by a racist ideology created by an elite group of European male (primarily Anglo-Saxon and Germanic) philosophers and scientists in the 1700's, generating a false belief in superiority that culminated in the age of imperialism (late 1800s) and the divinely-ordained "manifest destiny" of expansion into the Americas. The concept of *Social Darwinism* was also widely held, whereby the stronger, "superior" cultures (white) would overtake the weaker, "inferior" cultures (people of colour) in the "survival of the fittest." It cannot be overstated that the religious dogma of the church also propelled the exploration of territory and extraction of resources, and white supremacist principles were enshrined in religious

211. Erin Wunker, PhD, Canadian Studies, Dalhousie University, *Idle No More Teach-In at Dalhousie University*, Part 5 of 9, January 10, 2013. (http://halifax.mediacoop.ca)
212. Introduction, *Beyond Whiteness*, internet journal, 2015.
(www.beyondwhiteness.com)
213. Goldie Taylor, *Real Time with Bill Maher*, October 19, 2012. (www.billmaher.com)
214. Mato Woksape (Lakota, Blackfoot and Potawatomi), Facebook comment, 2014.
215. Robert Jensen, *The Heart of Whiteness: Confronting Race, Racism and White Privilege*, City Lights Publishers, 2005.

manifestos such as the Papal Bulls and the "Doctrine of Discovery." These same attitudes were manifest in the actions of the Settlers when they first arrived on the continent and massacred or assimilated essentially the entire "savage" Native American population. At the time of colonial invasion, there were literally millions of people living in the Americas, thousands of unique Indigenous cultures from coast to coast, each with their own specific civilizations, languages, achievements, economies, cultural practices, diplomacy, and IK that had been developed over millennia. What the diverse Indigenous nations "lacked" were mechanical weapons (superior "firepower"), monolithic military tactics, harmful technologies, ethics of capitalism, sole proprietorship and wealth accumulation, and an ideology of dominance, oppression and control over others. As opposed to the constructs of the colonial invader, Indigenous societies had complete cosmological systems that were superior to any western epistemology, science or religion; interconnected worldviews in harmony and reciprocity with the natural world; and the ethics of care and respect for all living beings. Their highly-evolved belief systems rejected self-interest in favor of equitable coalitions that worked together to establish the success and survival of the collective - principles that we would do well to re-establish today.

The white supremacist meme of "primitive versus civilized" allowed for the exponential growth of Empire in the Americas and the formation of the industrial era, killing millions of people and ravaging entire cultures in the process. Black slavery provided the labour that fueled the engine of Empire, and the original Indigenous inhabitants provided the territory. Caught in the modern bubble of perspectivism, it is hard for whites to see that white supremacy - the policies and beliefs of domination - are central to Empire and always have been. American and Canadian economic expansion and imperialist projects are inextricably intertwined with racism, and racism has equalled cultural genocide. In true fact, domination, racism, greed and psychopathic murder are at the heart of Empire-building in the Americas. *"The problem is the depravity of white people, the unjust exercise of power in a white supremacist society, and the unearned privileges that come with whiteness."*[216] (Robert Jensen) The dominance of white supremacy, white entitlement and white privilege were taken for granted as our founding institutions and the heart of our civic life until recently, and it has only been in the last 50 years that this despicable history was even talked about (!) beginning with the whistle-blowers, academics and activists, and then slowly becoming mainstream knowledge. "White privilege" is the reality that those of us in the Settler Society benefit from crimes against humanity and the ongoing theft of Indigenous resources, in the abundance of material culture and the colonial values of land ownership that we enjoy today.

To clarify what we are up against, here are two succinct definitions of white supremacy.

"When I use the term white supremacy......I intend a latitudinarian conception, one that encompasses de facto and de jure white privilege and refers more broadly to the European domination of the planet that has left us with the racialized distributions of economic, political, and cultural power that we have today. We could call it global white supremacy."[217] (Charles W. Mills)

"Racism/white supremacy is a global system of people who classify themselves as white and are dedicated to abusing and/or subjugating everyone in the known universe whom they classify as not white."[218] (Gus T. Renegade)

Within the white supremacy construct, the Settler Society reaps the benefits of the system in countless ways, both mentally and physically, and as we have seen with the New Age movement, in terms of spiritual life as well. The study of this inequality and "white privilege" began in 1986 when Peggy McIntosh noticed that when racism put people of colour at a disadvantage, the same system bestowed huge advantages and privileges on white people, and that there can be no "disadvantaged" groups without "advantaged" groups - the flip side of the coin.

Her keystone text *Unpacking the Invisible Knapsack*[219] is still in wide circulation today; other scholars and activists have furthered the understanding of white privilege over the years, and "Critical White Studies" or "Settler Colonial Studies" has become a new academic discipline.[220] Like any social manifestation, white privilege is incredibly complex, with various benefits conferred on a continuum that also takes into consideration different environments, the variables of identity, the hierarchy of class and wealth, and the intersectional oppressions of gender, sexual orientation and ableism. Peggy MacIntosh established that the benefits of white privilege are unearned, automatic and institutional, and I highly recommend reading her powerful essay, including a listing of the many privileges that white people take for granted. To give you a sense of this dynamic, that Indigenous people or people of colour do not receive the same benefits as white people, here are a few of the "white privileges" from her extensive list.

- I will feel welcomed and "normal" in the usual walks of public life, institutional and social.
- When I am told about our national heritage or about "civilization," I am shown that people of my color made it what it is.
- I can be sure that my children will be given curricular materials that testify to the existence of their race.
- I can watch movies, turn on the television or open to the front page of the paper and see people of my race widely represented.
- I can easily find academic courses and institutions which give attention only to people of my race.

- I can expect figurative language and imagery in all of the arts to testify to experiences of my race.
- I can be pretty sure that if I ask to talk to the "person in charge," I will be facing a person of my race.
- I can do well in a challenging situation without being called a credit to my race.
- I am never asked to speak for all the people of my racial group.
- I can remain oblivious of the language and customs of persons of color who constitute the world's majority without feeling in my culture any penalty for such oblivion.
- My culture gives me little fear about ignoring the perspectives and powers of people of other races.
- If I declare there is a racial issue at hand, or there isn't a racial issue at hand, my race will lend me more credibility for either position than a person of color will have.
- I can criticize our government and talk about how much I fear its policies and behavior without being seen as a cultural outsider.
- If a traffic cop pulls me over or if the IRS audits my tax return, I can be sure I haven't been singled out because of my race.
- I can be sure that if I need legal or medical help, my race will not work against me.
- I can think over many options, social, political, imaginative or professional, without asking whether a person of my race would be accepted or allowed to do what I want to do.
- If I should need to move, I can be pretty sure of renting or purchasing housing in an area which I can afford and in which I would want to live.
- I can be pretty sure that my neighbors in such a location will be neutral or pleasant to me.
- Whether I use checks, credit cards or cash, I can count on my skin color not to work against my appearance of financial reliability.
- I can go shopping alone most of the time, pretty well assured that I will not be followed or harassed.
- I do not have to educate my children to be aware of systemic racism for their own daily physical protection.

---

216. Robert Jensen, *The Heart of Whiteness: Confronting Race, Racism and White Privilege*, City Lights Publishers, 2005.

217. Charles W. Mills, *Blackness Visible: Essays on Philosophy and Race*, Cornell University Press, 1997.

218. Gus T. Renegade, "Interview with Gillian Schutte," *C.O.W.S. (Context of White Supremacy) broadcast*, December, 23, 2013. (http://recordings.talkshoe.com)

219. The ground-breaking must-read essay "Unpacking the Invisible Knapsack" by Peggy McIntosh is widely available on the internet, in anthologies and other publications, and a good reproduction can be found at the online journal *Beyond Whiteness*. (www.beyondwhiteness.com)

220. For introductory texts see the sections "Racism, White Privilege, White Studies," Page 391 and "Alliances, Allyship, Reconciliation and Peace Work," in Resources section, Page 395.

There are more benefits listed in *Unpacking the Invisible Knapsack*, but as we can see from these examples, white people in the Americas automatically enjoy preferential treatment. And depending on one's placement within the hierarchy of class, white people also receive a huge jump-start in life over people of colour due to the advantages of material wealth, education, health care, personal safety and resources. This unearned social power gives white folks better access to job opportunities or loans from financial institutions, and they are less subject to harassment from the authorities through racial profiling. *"White Privilege refers to the legacy of social, economic, political, geographical, and institutional advantages that have been (and in many ways continue to be) reserved exclusively for those with white skin. These advantages were born of white supremacy for the benefit of whites, at the expense and exclusion of people of color. This means the (white) privilege of lower incarceration rates, lower mortality rates, historical and current access to wealth and property, 'nicer' neighborhoods, prolonged political power, and little or no discrimination in employment or education. Government, housing, criminal justice, education and any number of other institutions were designed for a very specific, racially identified part of the public; despite much of the written and spoken appeals to equality, people of color were never part of the original equation."*[221] (Postcards from Factasyland)

All of this social stratification is of course encouraged by the competitiveness of the marketplace, which seeks to divide and separate according to race and class. As Allan Johnson notes, *"capitalism is not an engine that moves us to equity and justice."*[222] Even in the intellectual arena, the supremacy of western empiricism has made white scholars the automatic experts and authorities in all fields, conferring on them the freedom to access and reinterpret the knowledge systems of any culture they choose. White privilege is a direct result of the racial subjugation and epistemic violence that accompanies racism, and these privileges are gained in stark contrast to the experiences of people of colour. Indigenous people and people of colour are denied rights and privileges because of formal or state-sponsored oppression, and endure countless daily microaggressions[223] that reinforce this hegemony. *"In proportion as my racial group was being made confident, comfortable, and oblivious, other groups were*

---

221. Author (anonymous), "Translation(s)," *Postcards from Factasyland: Politics, Whiteness, and Everyday Hegemony* (blog), 2011. (http://factasyland.wordpress.com)
222. Allan Johnson, "Washington State University Interview 1," dialogue based on Allan Johnson's books *Privilege, Power, and Difference* and *The Gender Knot*, 2015. (www.agjohnson.us)
223. Coined in the 1970's by psychiatrist Chester Pierce, microaggressions refer to the *"brief and commonplace daily verbal, behavioral, or environmental indignities, whether intentional or unintentional, that communicate hostile, derogatory, or negative racial slights and insults toward people of color."* (http://en.wikipedia.org)

likely being made unconfident, uncomfortable, and alienated. Whiteness protected me from many kinds of hostility, distress, and violence, which I was being subtly trained to visit, in turn, upon people of color."[224] (Peggy McIntosh)

Of course, privilege can come in many forms, and the combination of race, class, gender, sexual orientation and ability specific to each person determines our intrinsic identity and how we view the world. Even if you happen to be a white, male, wealthy, educated, able-bodied, heterosexual Settler and benefit from every major axis of oppression, it is still important to recognize and own your privilege as part of who you are, and that your social power is not something that can be denied or ignored. The activation of a moral code varies from individual to individual, but we can only hope that more and more people will begin to contribute to counter-racist work and the shift to equity and equality. Once we get over the shock of finding out that we live in a white supremacist society and have white privilege, the next step means becoming aware of the advantages we have been given, and using our privilege in constructive ways to undo the damage of white dominance. *"As allies, our primary work must be with people who share our privileged identity. Thus, the more we can work to bring people who share our identity to understand their identity and privilege and to act for justice, the better."*[225] (Jamie Utt) You cannot relinquish your privilege, but if enough people truly dedicate themselves to the redistribution of social power, change can happen.

"Colonial relations do not stem from individual good will or actions; they exist before your arrival or your birth, and whether you accept or reject them matters little."[226] (Albert Memmi)

Unfortunately, we also need to be aware of the huge backlash coming from the dominant society. Many variations of outrage, hostility and rebuttal are voiced when white people are confronted with embedded racism and the evidence of white supremacist Empire-building on the backs of people of colour. There exists a huge system of denial from every demographic, as to quote Dr. Martin Luther King Jr., *"privileged groups seldom give up their privileges voluntarily."* As the dominant group, we have been afforded the luxury of obliviousness, and we will take the path of least resistance to "fit in" with our peers, rather than talk about, or confront systemic racism. We are trained to **never** discuss the harsh realities of oppression or inequality, which conveniently have become the "problem of the subordinate group."

---

224. Peggy McIntosh, "Unpacking the Invisible Knapsack," *Beyond Whiteness,* 2015. (www.beyondwhiteness.com)
225. Jamie Utt, "30 Ways to Become a Better Ally in 2014," *Everyday Feminism Magazine,* January 14, 2014. (http://everydayfeminism.com)
226. Albert Memmi, *The Colonizer and the Colonized,* Plunkett Lake Press, 2013.

There is no accountability, and white people are under no compunction to do anything about white privilege. When learning about these concepts for the first time, the response is usually an uncomfortable one, as we have been taught all our lives to think that "white is right" and that colonization is a great and noble thing. Whether by natural ignorance or more calculated denial, we have been insulated and protected from examining the harsh realities of the racism and discrimination that surrounds us. In fact, as Olivia Cole says *"you have been trained to see your whiteness as the norm, the default, the center of the world - you think that Other people have a race, but you, are just.....you. Your whiteness has been an invisible tool that you have wielded your entire life, mostly without realizing it, but now that people are criticizing the invisible tool, you are angry, defensive, and maybe even afraid. I would say that's normal. Everything you've been taught is being contradicted, so a little discomfort is expected."*[227]

All the mechanisms and "moves to innocence" that Settlers use to deflect white privilege, the "I haven't had it easy either," "that happened to me too," and "I didn't mean it" arguments, are also actions of white privilege, devices that keep the conversation centered on the white person's identity and experience rather than the reality of implicit or explicit racism. Another smoke-screen is the popular tendency in the face of critique to create a fallacy of aggrieved "white victimhood," with cries of "reverse racism" (which doesn't exist, as explained in *Chapter 15*, "The Impossibility of Reverse Racism" on Page 133). In a crazy reversal of reality, the real narratives coming from Indigenous people or people of colour are diminished or made invisible by these false claims of "white oppression." Having racist attitudes as a building block of one's identity is reprehensible, and if the white supremacist values we have internalized are not benefiting ourselves or anyone else, it is definitely time to let go of these outdated and toxic beliefs.

"Talking about racism does not equal 'attacking you personally!' We desperately need to stop being so insecure every time anyone brings up anything remotely related to race or racism. You don't have to agree, but to immediately jump into 'eyes-closed-and-screaming' mode speaks volumes about you and the kind of world in which you would prefer to live."[228] (Kyle "Guante" Tran Myhre)

The most common "at first glance" objections to white privilege is that many people who come from a place of poverty cannot fathom that they

---

227. Olivia Cole, "Open Letter to the Three White Students Who Filed a Discrimination Complaint Against Their Black Teacher," *BlackVoices: The Huffington Post*, December 3, 2013. (www.huffingtonpost.com)
228. Kyle "Guante" Tran Myhre, "How to Completely Miss the Point in a Conversation About Racism," *Opine Season: Minnesota's co-op op-ed page*, July 22, 2013. (http://opineseason.com)

have any "privilege" at all. But if one examines the intersectionality of multiple systems of oppression, it is obvious that poor white people still have many more advantages than people of colour. For instance, even the most economically-challenged white person in the Americas is a natural-born white citizen, possibly privileged that their first language is also the national language, possibly privileged as an able-bodied person, possibly privileged as a cis-gendered woman, and then possibly privileged that they were born with an intellect or ambition that could pull them up and out of poverty. What we have to understand about privilege and the manifold oppressions, is that these artificial social constructs **harm everyone**, and oppressive class, wealth and gender stratifications are set up within the dominant white society as well.

"White guilt" is another response that often comes up, but this does not lead to motivation or any kind of meaningful action, and as Harsha Walia argues *"is a state of self-absorption that actually upholds privilege."*[229] White guilt turns the focus back to the experience of white people, with the need for others (including people of colour) to provide reassurance and soothe hurt feelings (which is hardly the point). Instead of indulging in guilt, it is much more effective to own our privilege, use this power in constructive ways, and take responsibility to undo the systemic inequalities that still exist in society today. Of course, we did not individually create "race" or "racism," and the ongoing problems of injustice are much bigger than our individual feelings of guilt or innocence. Anger is a better emotional response, and with it, the commitment to counter oppression and dismantle system-wide racism and privilege. As Tim Wise explains, *"you only feel guilt if you actually did something, so this is obviously not the case. Guilt by association is illogical. The only correct response is responsibility - that is, we are left with the mess our Ancestors made and now we have to clean it up, as it is affecting everyone."*[230] White privilege is something we can acknowledge impartially, recognizing that we do live in a white supremacist society, and work to undo this construct. We can support projects aimed at a more democratic distribution of power, and as allies, join with people of colour in their struggles for racial justice. Part of the learning curve is to relinquish the need for a self-centered response, as *"having privilege isn't something you can usually change, but that's okay, because it's not something you should be ashamed of, or feel bad about. Being told you have privilege, or that you're privileged, isn't an insult. It's a reminder! The key to privilege isn't worrying about having it, or trying to deny it, or apologize for it, or get rid of it. It's just paying attention to it, and knowing what it means for you and the people around you. Having privilege is like having big feet. No one hates you for having big feet! They just want you to be careful where you walk."*[231] (Sindelókë)

Another common misconception is that by exposing white dominance and privilege, the activist is attacking or demeaning their own cultural group, as a "white traitor" as it were. In my own case, I can state equivocally that it is not individual white people that I find abhorrent, it is the system of "whiteness" and the construct of white supremacy, white dominance and white power. And I really object to the idea that one group can set themselves up as superior to the rest, just by virtue of a pathological so-called "science" of racial biology that a brotherhood of entitled aristocrats created to justify their urge for domination, plunder and power, and that we are still living with the consequences of this patriarchal white greed today. To further this understanding, if someone interprets the statement "I hate white supremacy" to mean "I hate white people," they are *"exhibiting their unexamined beliefs in white supremacy and white power as a normalized social foundation."*[232] (Ian Ki'laas Caplette) It is not white skin, or white people, that activists critique (often vehemently) - it is the construct of "whiteness" and the hegemony of white supremacy. Being born with white skin is neither positive nor negative, and each member of the human family is an important part of the whole, but we all have the opportunity to make better choices in our emerging or ongoing work for social justice.

Without a doubt, the imperialist agenda has been to create an intentional and universal system of exclusion, yet any social construct that dominates people of colour through racial "science" or racism harms whites as well, by denying them access to their own humanity. How do we "reverse" our privilege? Can we ever fully transcend the white supremacist construct? Learning about the magnificence of other cultures, and the qualities and values we all share, can certainly add to the breakdown of white hegemony. But Indigenous people and people of colour have been engaged in resistance for far too long, and eliminating racism must now beome the responsibility of white people. Fully understanding how white privilege works means *"a shift in consciousness, making choices from a more informed place, taking risks, and often becoming the target by standing up and making statements that make everyone uncomfortable."*[233] (Allan Johnson) As the adage goes, if you are not part of the solution you are part of the problem, and being oblivious or colorblind continues to keep the power in the hands of the ruling elite. In addition, our silence perpetuates the

229. Harsha Walia, "Decolonizing Together," Briarpatch Magazine, January 1, 2012. (http://briarpatchmagazine.com)
230. Tim Wise, *Lecture at Providence College*, February 20, 2013. (www.youtube.com) and Tim Wise, "Guilt or Responsibility," *Michigan Roundtable for Diversity and Inclusion*, November 4, 2010. (www.youtube.com)
231. Sindelókë, *Of Dogs and Lizards: A Parable of Privilege*, (blog), January 13, 2010. (https://sindeloke.wordpress.com)
232. Ian Ki'laas Caplette (Tsimshian First Nation), Facebook comment, July 18, 2013.
233. Allan Johnson, *Washington State University Interview 1*, dialogue focused on Allan Johnson's books *Privilege, Power, and Difference* and *The Gender Knot*, 2015. (www.agjohnson.us)

delusion of a level playing field, and *"maintains the myth of meritocracy, the myth that democratic choice is equally available to all."*[234] (Peggy McIntosh) Developing new awareness and changing individual behavior is great, but systemic change will not happen unless a collective outpouring of white people take on the work of dismantling white supremacy and building a multiracial society. Educating other white people and finding like-minded social justice activists is an integral part of the journey, and support can be found through the flourishing white privilege network and conferences[235] associated with the movement. Discussion and study are the first steps, but our learning will grow exponentially when we are actively working for social justice by attending rallies, demonstrations, actions, meetings and cultural events, and joining committees or organizations. There are no shortage of tools for the highly-relevant learning curve that Allen Johnson calls *"racial reconciliation and cultural competency."*[236] Whether we are approaching anti-racist activism as a new direction or have been working as a change agent for years, it is extremely useful to look at the model of "The 8 White Identities" by Barnor Hesse.[237]

"There is a regime of whiteness that governs society through racial rule and there are socially visible, action-oriented white identities in everyday dialogue with that regime. People (not only white people) may identify with whiteness in one of the following ways." (Barnor Hesse)

The 8 White Identities

1.   *White Supremacist*
A White Supremacist maintains and advocates a clearly marked white society that preserves, names, and values white superiority.
2.   *White Voyeurism*
A White Voyeur would not challenge a white supremacist's stated beliefs. They desire non-whiteness because it is interesting and pleasurable to them, and they seek to control the consumption and appropriation of non-whiteness. They may express a fascination with culture, for example: consuming Black culture without the burden of Blackness; consuming and appropriating Native American cultures, clothing, or spiritualities without the burden of racism or prejudice.
3.   *White Privilege*
A White Privileged person may critique white supremacy, but they maintain a deep investment in questions of "fairness" and "equality" that normalize whiteness and white rule. They may have a sworn goal of "diversity."
4.   *White Benefit*
A White Benefit person is sympathetic to some aspects of anti-racism, but only privately. They will not speak or act in solidarity publicly, because they are benefitting through whiteness in public.

5.   *White Confessional*
A White Confessional person will speak about and point out whiteness to some extent, but only as a way of being accountable to People of Color after the fact. A White Confessional seeks validation from People of Color.

6.   *White Critical*
A White Critical person will take on board critiques of whiteness and invest in exposing and marking the regime of whiteness. They refuse to be complicit with the regime, and might be seen as whiteness speaking back to whiteness.

7.   *White Traitor*
A White Traitor actively refuses complicity in the regime of whiteness, names and speaks about what is going on, and intends to subvert white authority and tell the truth at whatever cost.

8.   *White Abolitionist*
A White Abolitionist changes institutions that are historically based on white rule, dismantles the regime of whiteness, and does not allow the regime or white rule to reassert itself.

Becoming aware of the privilege we have in our own lives, and moving beyond denial, defensiveness or ennui means changing the system of oppression in both small and large ways. Actions speak louder than words, and "checking our privilege" may mean relinquishing the traditional patriarchal "voice of authority," letting others lead the conversation, listening deeply to the experiences of other people, refusing to participate in institutions that favor whiteness and wealth (such as private schools), and making space in your life for relationships across colour and class lines. Whatever we do, we need to point out that racists are wrong, not make allowances for them. Speaking out on racism is how we oppose racism, not by pretending everyone is white and that there is no history of racism, or by ignoring that racism is a contemporary problem in every aspect of society. We all carry implicit or explicit bias, yet our work is the undoing of the pathology that is systemic racism in the Americas, created and perpetuated by the white-dominant overculture to which we belong. There are no allowable "degrees" of racism in either word or deed – even the tiniest bit of racism or bigotry makes both the perpetuator and those who support them dysfunctional, and complicit with the all-white dominant colonial agenda that has destroyed, oppressed, marginalized and attempted to assimilate people of color in the Americas. In the end, it is not about having "white guilt" or demeaning our own cultural group – it is about becoming informed so that we can take responsibility to clean up the mess created by the white supremacist founding of Empire in the Americas.

"White people need to realize we are not the point of reference for everything. White is not the norm, the standard, the best. White is just white."[238] (Robert Jensen)

234. Peggy McIntosh, "Unpacking the Invisible Knapsack," *Beyond Whiteness,* 2015. (www.beyondwhiteness.com)

235. *The White Privilege Conference* (www.whiteprivilegeconference.com) and *Understanding & Dismantling Privilege,* the official journal of the White Privilege Conference, 2015. (www.wpcjournal.com)

236. Allan Johnson, *Washington State University Interview 1,* dialogue focused on Allan Johnson's books *Privilege, Power, and Difference* and *The Gender Knot,* 2015. (www.agjohnson.us)

237. Barnor Hesse, PhD, "The 8 White Identities," widely-circulated lecture notes from his course entitled *Unsettling Whiteness.* Barnor Hesse, Associate Professor of African American Studies, Political Science and Sociology, Northwestern University, Evanston, IL. (http://reverseracism.tumblr.com)

238. Robert Jensen, *The Heart of Whiteness: Confronting Race, Racism and White Privilege,* City Lights Publishers, 2005.

"Everyone needs to get back to their own IK."
Onaubinisay (Walks Above the Ground) / James Dumont
Anishnaabe Elder & Traditional Teacher
5th Degree - Three Fires Midewiwin Lodge

*Using Indigenous values as our model, **Part Two** will examine alternatives to Empire as located in old/new earth-centered societies, and discuss where our authentic self-identity can be found. By reclaiming practices and directions from our own ancestral wisdom traditions, **Ancient Spirit Rising** offers strategies for uncolonization, placing the Earth First, restoring our eco-selves, creating a sustainable future, furthering our solidarity with Turtle Island First Nations, and expressing peaceful co-existence in Earth Community.*

Part Two - Authentic Treasure

17. On the Use of the Term "Indigenous" and Enlarging Settler Re-Indigenization

"The descendants of the tribes of Europe were so successfully and completely colonized and assimilated that we have been conditioned to confuse the narratives of Empire with our own, identifying with the ruling-class elite and confusing their interests with our own, which we in turn work to protect and defend. We were forced off our ancestral lands into the cities and factories of industrialism, shipped around the world to feed the growing industry in newly-colonized areas, and we continue to destroy the Earth that gives us life today, because we think industrial civilization feeds, clothes, and shelters us, rather than the Earth herself. It is therefore both attractive and mutually beneficial for all to aspire and actively work towards once again becoming Indigenous in place, firmly rooted in a landbase with which one's culture has an intimate and deep-rooted connection."[239] (Tlalli Yaotl)

"What makes a people Indigenous? Indigenous people believe they belong to the land, and non-Indigenous people believe the land belongs to them. Can we commit to the land and each other? Let's hope so, because our current civilization is a one-time-only experiment. Once it has failed, we are going to have to re-braid ourselves back into the web of 'all our relations' - plant, animal and human. If there are future civilizations, they will be Indigenous."[240] (Derek Rasmussen)

"We all sat before the sacred fire of life. We all came from the same blood. We are all members of one human family, and therefore, we are all Indigenous to our beloved Mother Earth."[241] (Chief Phil Lane, Jr.)

"Underneath our skin we are all Indigenous people, but how much we choose to rediscover and revitalize this knowledge in our work and everyday life is a decision that has tremendous bearing on the future of us all. The knowledge of the Americas will begin to rise again, not only through the earth, but through the people of the earth. It will feel as if we are waking from a dream."[242] (Apela Colorado)

There has been an expression in common usage for many years by native and non-native artists, scholars, cultural workers and activists alike that *"we are all indigenous to somewhere."* This begs the question of what exactly is the determining factor in being indigenous to place? What makes one indigenous? The actual dictionary definition of "Indigenous" is *"originating in and naturally living in a region or country, belonging to place."* The crux of the matter is that in our rush to colonize the Americas, those of us in the European diaspora gave up our bonds to our places of ethnic origin, and our indigenity as connected to those lands. In the rootlessness and bustle of modern life, the Canadian in us may have forgotten, but our Celtic DNA must yearn to wake in the Cumbrian hills each morning or worship at Stonehenge, but in any case here we are next to dazzling Lake Ontario, in the magnificent Canadian Shield, or perched beside luminous Georgian Bay. All land is sacred land, and when we embrace our connectivity to the Earth we bypass the dominance of modernity and go directly to the source of our eco-being. Yet, our bonds to the landscape into which we have been born and/or are currently living, will always be preceded by the much deeper attachments of the original First Nations. And despite the raging debate on extending the definition or allowing the use of the term "indigenous" for those of European descent, I suggest that cultivating our ecocultural identity is of primary importance in our mutual care for the Earth, and Settler nativization is part of our essential uncolonization process. As members of *Earth Community*, it is the birthright of the entire human family to be indigenous to the Earth, to appreciate and love the natural world, and to find our *"indigenous place within."*[243] We must all face directly our innate need to be at one with wild nature, to enjoy the blessings of Mother Earth and all her creatures, to experience green spaces as an opening to mystery and magic, and to work tirelessly at preserving nature for nature's own sake.

So, what makes us indigenous? However separated by the human-built world, we are gifted at birth with the elements of air, water, earth and fire that are specific to the landscape around us. Inseparable from the archetypal patterns and intricacies of nature, we are imprinted with ions of air, fire in the form of energy from the sun, and especially the life-giving waters of a particular ecosystem. The molecules of the watersheds of our region are virtually found within our bodies, as these life-giving waters make up 60% of our physical being. As children we are drawn to the natural world, and often our earliest memories are of time spent in green spaces with flowers, plants and trees. The same building blocks of organic matter such as carbon, oxygen and nitrogen that form the Earth and all Her creatures, also sculpt the human form. Unique to each individual, human beings also have an innate sensitivity to electrical and electromagnetic fields, and are equipped with a multitude of sensory processes by which to interact with the other-than-human world. The biome is part of us, our bodies resonate with the energies of the earth, and we are indigenous to place from the moment we are born.

Being indigenous has been defined as having deep roots in the landscape that give rise to fully-formed lifeways and IK/EIK. *"The earth remembers us, and the places where we grew up or have lived a long time recognize our patterns, just as we recognize the patterns of those places."*[244] (T. Thorn Coyle) Also, indigenity is often described as "belonging to ancestral land" which means that many generations have come and gone to mark their collective psychic and physical presence on the land. But by virtue of our buried ancestors in the land, and the spirits of our *Beloved Dead* that inhabit our psychogeography, how many generations does it take to establish indigenity? Two generations? Five generations? Ten? According to renowned author Leslie Marmon Silko (Laguna Pueblo), indigenity is quantified by having at least a thousand-year presence in a specific place.[245] It would certainly be a Settler sidestep to suggest a debate on the issue with Turtle Island First Nations, but are Europeans to be "persona non grata" forever? As an example, my motherline in Ontario goes back to 1832. That's seven generations of interlopers being born on Turtle Island. If we define "indigenity" by the number of generations that have been born and reclaimed by the earth, then perhaps by now descendants of the original Settler Society might qualify. Or, *"maybe indigenity is something that eventually just happens to people whose ancestors*

239. Tlalli Yaotl (Recovering Wasi'chu/Wetiko), "Decolonizing Our Hearts and Minds: Part I: Preliminary Thoughts & Explorations," *Unsettling America: Decolonization in Theory and Practice,* January 7, 2011.

240. Derek Rasmussen, "Non-Indigenous Culture: Implications of a Historical Anomaly," *YES! Magazine,* July 11, 2013. (www.yesmagazine.org)

241. Chief Phil Lane, Jr. (Dakota/Chickasaw), *Global Indigenous Wisdom Summit,* The Shift Network, November 18-20, 2014.

242. Apela (Pam) Colorado, "Indigenous Science," *Edges: New Planetary Patterns,* Vol. 4 Number 1, June 1991. Apela Colorado, PhD (Oneida) is Founder and Director of the *Worldwide Indigenous Science Network,* Lahaina, HI. (www.wisn.org) (http://ancestors-speak.blogspot.ca)

243. *Planet IndigenUS: Celebration of Nations,* Harbourfront Centre Toronto, August 2012. (www.harbourfrontcentre.com)

244. T. Thorn Coyle, *Kissing the Limitless: Deep Magic and the Work of Transforming Yourself and the World,* Weiser Books, 2009.

245. Thomas Irmer, *An Interview with Leslie Marmon Silko,* Alt-X Berlin, 1995. (www.altx.com/int2/silko.html)

stayed in one place long enough, or maybe the land itself gets to decide who is indigenous and who is not."[246] (Robert Mathiesen) Once we have successfully healed our disconnect from nature and become caring Earthkeepers and stewards of the land, it naturally follows that dedicating the bones of our Ancestors to the soil of our homeland(s) makes us responsible to that land.

"Within the Celtic Spiritual traditions, the physical spirit and body of one's Ancestors are given back to the land at the time of their death. In this way, the Ancestral energy, the sacred spirit of each person literally lives within the land, waiting to be called upon in ritual and ceremony."[247] (Sirona Knight)

Consciously or not, with the founding of the Americas the sacrifice of our cultural ecology and ancestral knowledge, and the lack of white ethnic or cultural identity has affected our empowerment and psychological well-being. Not totally secure in our sense of belonging to the "new world," we accepted the imperialist paradigm and the expressions of false nationalism that were imposed upon us. The building of modern Anglophone Empire has forced us to become caricatures of ourselves, and we endlessly sift through myriad identities and cultural surrogates while ignoring the treasures and truths in our own authentic ancestral traditions. We have not placed enough importance on the earth-honoring stories connected to place that our Ancestors held or generated as part of the Settler diaspora, and we either have to recover this psychogeography, or re-create our own stories bonded to the land.

Even if we can establish that **all** people are indigenous to place, it must be stressed that using the term "indigenous" to describe *our identity* as Euro-American or Euro-Canadian is *not* appropriate, and ethnic or culturally-specific identity markers such as Gaelic, Ásatrú, Hellenismos, or Romuva are more precise. There is a serious controversy swirling around the use of the term "indigenous" that needs to be addressed, and the complexity of this divisive argument unravelled. To apply the term "indigenous" to those of us in the diaspora, the Euro-descendants of the original Settler Society (or those more recently transplanted to the Americas) is a highly political act, and is being used as a cudgel or a divider in many circles. Word choices vary from place to place, but the consensus is that it is only the original First Nations of Turtle Island who are allowed to be described as "Indigenous."

In the UN *Permanent Forum on Indigenous Issues* and *Declaration on the Rights of Indigenous Peoples* it has been determined that there

---

246. Robert Mathiesen, blog comment, *The Indigeny Debate*, by P. Sufenas Virius Lupus (blog), *Patheos: Pagan*, September 6, 2012. (www.patheos.com)
247. Sirona Knight, *Empowering Your Life with Wicca*, Alpha Books, 2003.

is no universal definition of "Indigenous," but the understanding of the word "Indigenous" has been developed by extensive criteria,[248] including the following:

- *Self- identification as Indigenous peoples at the individual level and accepted by the community as their member.*
- *Historical continuity with pre-colonial and/or pre-settler societies.*
- *Strong link to territories and surrounding natural resources.*
- *Distinct social, economic or political systems.*
- *Distinct language, culture and beliefs.*
- *Resolve to maintain and reproduce their ancestral environments and systems as distinctive peoples and communities.*

The *UN Permanent Forum* recognizes that assigning the term "Indigenous" only to groups that have been colonized is ambiguous, as there are Indigenous peoples in privileged societies who have not been colonized, yet have a long-standing ecological knowledge of their landbase. Instead of offering a full definition, Article 33 of the United Nations *Declaration on the Rights of Indigenous Peoples*[249] highlights the importance of self-identification, and that it is Indigenous peoples themselves who will define their own identity as "Indigenous." Ultimately, each culture and each group of people are self-validating, and their collective name and distinct identity is more important to them than what another culture pins on them.

For the Settler Society, adhering to these identity marker guidelines is extremely important, as there is a trend for non-native spiritual seekers to call themselves "indigenous" while continuing to incorporate the theft of Turtle Island IK and tools into their New Age or Neo-Pagan "shamanic" healing modalities and practices. Even more alarming are the white supremacists, both in Europe and the Americas, who are co-opting the term "indigenous" to connect them to a place of origin in order to perpetuate their metapolitical practices of racism, superiority, and white dominance over people of colour. Being aware of the non-native spiritual seekers and white supremacists who are using the identity marker of "indigenous" while continuing to perpetuate a self-serving agenda means remaining vigilant, calling them out, and confronting them wherever they are found. As part of the expanding

---

248. View or download the full "Indigenous Peoples, Indigenous Voices Fact Sheet," United Nations *Permanent Forum on Indigenous Issues Fifth Session*, United Nations Headquarters, New York, May 15-26, 2006. (http://undesadspd.org/IndigenousPeoples/ UNPFIISessions/ PreviousSessions/Fifth.aspx)

249. View or download the full declaration at the United Nations *Permanent Forum on Indigenous Issues* website (adopted by the General Assembly on Thursday, September 13, 2007). (http://undesadspd.org/IndigenousPeoples/DeclarationontheRightsofIndigenous Peoples.aspx)

anti-racist response to the insidious and genocidal effects of cultural appropriation in the Americas today, my own goal with *Ancient Spirit Rising* is to coax the modern spiritual seeker toward the recovery of their own ancestral-sourced EIK, the reclamation of authentic ethnicity, and identity markers other than "indigenous."

The continuing antithetical use of the term "indigenous" by white people in identity theft and cultural genocide has forced the monitors of cultural appropriation such as *NAFPS* (New Age Frauds and Plastic Shamans) and *CAORANN Council* (Celts Against Oppression, Racism and Neo-Nazism) to label **any** white person who uses the word "indigenous" as an identity marker to be **racist**. However justified, assigning a new category of racism to address all those who use the word "indigenous" may be problematic, as it suggests that the objectivity is in place to clearly differentiate between those who have a valid claim to Turtle Island Indigenous Knowledge (for whatever individual reason) from those who do not. Obviously this is not the case, and screaming "racist" at first meeting does nothing to encourage the education of genuine but uninformed white spiritual seekers. To make the polarization even more complicated, there are many highly-regarded First Nations thought leaders and visionaries engaged in decolonization work that apply the terms "Indigenous" and "re-indigenization" to **all** peoples currently living on Turtle Island. As language is constantly shifting and changing, the fluidity of certain words defy ownership, and there may always be multiple and various meanings ascribed to highly-charged words such as "Indigenous." We could also declare that the word "Indigenous" is a colonial overlay used to describe every First Nation by a pan-Indian device of homogeneity, and that it should not be used by anyone! Anglophone labels such as "native" and "Indian" have also been forced on Turtle Island First Nations as tools for assimilation, and there is an onging struggle with the use of those terms. Taking issue with the offensive use of the word "aboriginal" in Canada, the *Anishinabek of Ontario* and the *Assembly of Manitoba Chiefs* (AMC) have launched a campaign[250] to eliminate it from the lexicon, and in examining the problems with the term "Indigenous" John Ahni Schertow has this to say. *"The term 'indigenous' is fairly contentious as well, but not because of its etymology. Rather, because it seems to be such a subjective term. Sometimes it's used to define a racial identity, other times a political one. And there are people who aren't considered indigenous at all, but are technically indigenous people. In any case, the issue is not so much about a word as it is about reclaiming identity. You see, in a spiritual and cultural sense, these terms deprive us of our own face. And in that deprivation we find ourselves forced to adopt a new one."*[251]

250./251. John Ahni Schertow (Haudenosaunee/European), "Anishinabek Outlaw Term 'Aboriginal,' " *Intercontinental Cry/IC Magazine: Supporting the Indigenous Peoples Movement*, Jun 30, 2008. (http://intercontinentalcry.org)

There is no doubt that many Eurocentric words are highly inappropriate, like the ridiculous misnomer "Indian" that Christopher Columbus (the so-called "Great Navigator") pinned on the Taino People at first contact, thinking he was in the Indies. Yet if one subscribes to the overarching definition of "indigenous," all human beings **are** considered indigenous, Indigenous Knowledge **is** the collective birth-right of humanity, and we most certainly **all** have original IK. Throughout *Ancient Spirit Rising* I use the words "Indigenous" and "Indigenous Knowledge" (IK) in line with the consensual meaning to describe lifeways and worldviews that pre-date industrial civilization - First Nation societies that are living, complex and earth-connected. I do **not** use "indigenous" as a label or identity marker for those of European descent, and I encourage the use of ethnic or culturally-specific identity markers such as Gaelic, Ásatrú, Hellenismos or Romuva (for example) rather than "indigenous."

I decided to use "Euro-Indigenous," "Euro-Indigenous Knowledge" (or EIK) as shorthand to separate out the ancestral traditions of Europe being articulated from those of Turtle Island, and I apologize to any First Nation or Settler individual who takes issue with my use of these terms. "Neo-indigenous" may be a possible solution for those of us in the Euro-diaspora with short ancestral lines in the Americas, to highlight our own love for the land and our connectivity to earth-wise culture. Not widely used, there is no concrete definition of "neo-indigenous" as yet[252] so it may be a useful term for expressing the connection to place from cradle to grave for all peoples, and the ongoing recovery of our eco-selves as important to the process of uncolonization. For Settlers, "Neo-indigenous" is not an identity marker but a possible description of the inevitable activity and **process** of Settler connectivity to Turtle Island. And yet, calling ourselves "neo-indigenous" is probably not a good idea, until Earth Rights, Indigenous Sovereignty and Black Liberation have been achieved, and we have fully dismantled our "whiteness." Certainly other terms are in wide use and are in some cases interchangeable - terms such as indigenous   mind, indigenist,   re-indigenous,   re-indigenization,   self-indigenization, indigenize, indigitize, indigenism, indigenosity, indigination, ingenium, nativization, naturalize, ecocultural identity, ecodigenous, ecoist, eco-wisdom, ancestral, ancestral knowledge, ancestral roots, ancestral-sourced, ethnic-based, DNA-sourced, animist, neoanimist, primal, primeval, archaic, feral, tribal, neotribal, new roots, future primitive, primitivist, anarcho-primitivist, paleo and even "urbindigenous" (I'm not so sure about that one!). Gaining in popularity, general terms for eco-identity and tribe can also include earth-wise, eco-wise, earth-centered, earth-connected, earth-honoring, earth-rooted culture, earth-based spirituality, earth-based philosophy, nature-based spirituality, spiritual ecology, nature mysticism, earth-based worldviews and earth-honoring civilization. If the lexicon to describe the stolen indigenous identity of European diasporians was normative (or available), this conversation - and controversy - would not even be happening. It's not as if Settlers deliberately colonized themselves and then set out to undo the damage millennia later with the intent to enrage others with their lack of terms for self-validation! All sincere efforts and frameworks used to *Reject Empire* and recover indigenity must widen and deepen our essential return, and from the various terms that are available, the acronym EIK (European Indigenous Knowledge) may be the most elegant, unassuming and non-confrontational.

Many diverse peoples now share Turtle Island, and as much as it is the birthright of every person to be indigenous to place, I know that my roots and reverence for the land cannot compare to the familial relationships and all-encompassing bonds to place as held by First Nations. Yet, in this contradictory time and place whereby all people (First Nations included) are enjoying the vibrancy of cultural pluralism, in our hearts we must realize that those who love the land are the true Earthkeepers, regardless of ethnicity. You cannot destroy that which you love! There are Turtle Island Indigenous people who use pesticides on their lawn (no way) or who will not sit outside in the summer because of all the "bugs" (they don't bother me!).253   I am not advocating for competition in such matters, but now is probably a good time to demystify the stereotype of all First Nations people as being the exclusive Earthkeepers and holders of earth-connected knowledge. All contemporary peoples, if they work hard at rejecting the ecocidal values of the modern "megamachine" and uncolonize themselves, if they lose the "cult of the individual" in favor of reclaiming community with the *Web of all Life*, are more than capable of becoming keepers of the Earth, green seers and wise elders.

*"Compared to indigenous ways of knowing, western knowledge systems contain zero knowledge, as they have completely lost their way in the past 500 years, and do not see the abundance in either people or the natural world. All of us are indigenous members of Earth Community equally - there is no higher placement of a master over another - and it is high time for all of us to become indigenous again."*255   (Vandana Shiva)

*"Ordinary people have to have their sense of moral injustice ignited. They have to come to understand that they are being called upon to care about what happens to the peoples and living things of this world. That's a huge job, but that's the spiritual call of the re-indigenization of the world."*254   (John Mohawk)

The Lanark Highlands in Ontario is home to the Purdon Conservation Area,256 a park set aside to protect a special ecosystem where an abundance of pink Lady Slipper orchids are found. A descendant of the original Settler Society, Jo Purdon loved nature and made it his life's work to nurture this grove, which numbered over 16,000 orchid plants at the time of his passing. When his daughter Rhodena Bell visits the park today, she feels her father's presence, and is convinced that his spirit lives on, embedded in the land, watching over his beloved wild gardens. You can be *"sure that indigenity lives,"*[257] and rests deep inside each one of us, waiting for an unfolding to occur with our immersion in our beloved green landscapes. *"A great many native people have a long-standing relationship with the natural world. But that relationship is equally available to non-natives, should they choose to embrace it."*[258] (Thomas King) Without a doubt, enlarging self-indigenization as applicable to those of us in the Settler Society is the great work of our time.

ecoceoceo

252. So far, in academia and popular culture "neo-indigenous" has been used by a small number of dance and visual arts practitioners; to describe multiple subcultures and hybridized communities in large urban centres i.e. "neo-indigenous cosmopolitanism" (*Being, Becoming, and Belonging: Improving Science Fluency During Laboratory Activities in Urban Education* by Wesley Pitts, ProQuest, 2007); by discourse on pluricultural writers and poets in Chile (*Ethnogenesis or Neo Indigenous Intelligentsia: Contemporary Mapuche-Huilliche Poetry* by James Park, Latin American Research Review, Vol. 42, No. 3, 2007); as the local knowledge of a landbase acquired by generational farming (*What is Indigenous Knowledge? Voices from the Academy, Indigenous Knowledge and Schooling* by Ladislaus M. Semali and Joe L. Kincheloe, Routledge, 1999); and as a long-standing, intimate and ecological knowledge of nature held by either indigenous or non-indigenous people (*Bridging Cultures: Indigenous Ways and Scientific Ways of Knowing Nature*, by Glen Aikenhead and Herman Michell, Pearson Canada Inc., 2011). In 2013, United Natures Media and Dir. Peter Charles Downey released the documentary *United Natures: a United Nations of All Species* based on the *Universal Declaration of the Rights of Mother Earth* featuring earth jurisprudence, philosophy, permaculture, spirituality and a *"neo-indigenous future for humanity."* (http://therightsofnature.org/united-natures-movie)
253. Unfortunately, all who share Turtle Island today are regularly complicit with whiteness and Empire in the things they do, both consciously and unconsciously. In various circumstances, this phenomenon can be referred to as "internalized oppression."
254. John Mohawk (Seneca), "Re-Indigenization Defined," *Original Instructions: Indigenous Teachings for a Sustainable Future*, edited by Melissa K. Nelson, Bear & Company, 2008.
255. Vandana Shiva, *Sacred Seeds*, Lecture, KWIC and Trent University, Wenjack Theatre, Peterborough, ON, November 16, 2014.
256. The story of Joe Purdon's love for Lady Slipper orchids and the Purdon Conservation Area is told in the documentary "The Land Between," produced by the *Ontario Visual Heritage Project*, Living History Multimedia Association, 2012. (www.visualheritage.ca)
257. The phrase "be sure that indigenity lives" is inspired by Milton Acorn's classic poem *On Speaking Ojibway*. At the heart of the poem is the idea that human interaction and interconnection with the land is endless and timeless, and that human indigenity is embedded in the land and can be activated at any time. Milton Acorn, *The Island Means Minago*, NC Press, 1975. *"There's no bending or breaking in the wind, no egg hatching, no seed springing that isn't part of Ojibway. Therefore be sure Ojibway lives."*
258. Thomas King, *The Inconvenient Indian: A Curious Account of Native People in North America*, Doubleday Canada, 2012.

I am an ecocultural weaver
Of the old and the new,
Senistrognata in the blood
Nogojiwanong sings to the soul.

I am a creature of Earth
I belong to Her only.
I am a creature of Earth
I belong to Her whole-y.

I have given my heart to the Earth,
She holds the warp and weft of me.

Walking these hills
I meet leaf, rune, stone
Weaving over and under
In, out and through -
Stories in feather and ice.

I have given my heart to the Earth,
She holds the warp and weft of me.

I am a creature of Earth
I belong to her only.
I am a creature of Earth.
I belong to her whole-y.

I am an ecocultural weaver
Of the old and the new,
Senistrognata in the blood
Nogojiwanong sings to the soul.

You Are Ecocultural If ~

- You are truly yourself, truly at peace, truly at home on the land.
- You find yourself either silently or audibly talking to last year's faded ground cover, the trees that were decimated in the ice storm of spring, the first buttercups, white clover and daisies of the season, the plant life in endless diversity and importance, the glowing health or special challenges of the animals either domesticated or wild, the intricacy and knowing of insects, the light that keeps changing, the infinity of wonder in the blue space above, the clouds that keep a record of your days, the green hills that rise and fall for a reason, the heartbeat of the land that you hear in the hushed tones of dawn - and you offer praise and gratitude for the perfect skeleton-bones of a deer.
- You sink tearfully into a bower of long grass and languish there for hours, letting the sun-washed scents and softness caress your skin, and after giving your concerns and contradictions to the Earth you rise refreshed, rejuvenated, informed and restored.
- With gratitude you taste the first offerings and fruits of the garden, the strawberries and miniature tomatoes that nourish your soul and open your heart to the eco-spirits inhabiting the sacred green realms, the kindred spirits with whom you have co-created a food-producing commons for all beings with full reciprocity and care.
- You walk barefoot on the soft sandy beach and when you glance up you see a feminine human form apparent in the shape of a mountainous island across the strait, and you fall in love with this ancient granite being and Her scented atmosphere as much (if not more) than with any living person.
- Walking along the border of the forest at dusk - the sweet and verdant air tastes of deep leafy green - you thrill to the sight of a doe and her fawn crossing the pasturelands at twilight time, and you feel elemental spirits reaching out to you in the magical transition betwixt day and night, when the portal opens wide between the worlds.
- Caressed by the blossom-scented breeze on a warm summer's night, you follow the trail of the fireflies' pulsing to where the ancient seashells embedded in the sand glow in the moonlight, and your profound ecstasy is complete. You are overcome with joy and wonder, and you overflow with praises to the Earth!
- You stare into the verdant forest canopy of swirling branches and lush greenery, the shapes and forms of the leafy hearts endlessly moving and chiming in all directions, and you are awestruck and humbled to be a witness to the layers of energetic messaging going on. An hour passes, another one, and then one more, and the dancing faces and beings that have emerged in the trees - shapeshifters from past, present and future - fill you with their storied presence, each strange and wondrous narrative a unique and sacred part of the whole.

As both observer and participant in their luminous healing power and ultimate green realm joy, you are ensouled with the deep knowing of being intrinsically linked to *Mother Earth*, and the interconnectivity of all creation.

- You savor each hour of the day and the progression of light, warmth, breeze, movement, atmosphere, growth, melt and decay that comes to you from the natural word. The choices that you make revolve around the ever-changing daily conditions of the texture, essence and temperature of the land around you. You are honored by the presence of the creatures, plants, trees, watersheds and beings of the more-than-human world that fill your consciousness with blessings. You are deeply informed and motivated by the waxing and waning of the moon and the stellar progression of the stars and constellations. Your goals, activities and aspirations are in sync with the cosmos and the cycles of the year - new growth, new initiatives and planting in the spring, nurturing, tending and celebrating in the summer, harvesting and taking stock in the fall, and resting and storytelling in the winter. Your soul is in the land and the land is in your soul.

- Everything you encounter is filtered through a default or baseline of knowing and loving the land, and the earth-connected society that manifests from this belonging, and you are constantly asking yourself *"How does this serve my essential eco-self?"* or *"Would this be happening or be an issue in a traditional Indigenous society?"* You are acutely aware of the need to course-correct in everything you think, say and do - steering your one precious life toward the direction of the ecosphere every time.

- Your personal mythology and the stories held by your family and kinship group begin to be deeply rooted to place, embedded in specific locations in the landscape that shape the narrative of your lives. Both the land and the more-than-human world are central to your individual and communal existence.

- Your thoughts and actions go beyond the narrow confines of your individualistic concerns and revolve around *Earth Community* and the welfare of the whole, and you are well on your way to becoming ecocultural, a true human being. In the Druidic tradition, the practice of "peaceful abiding" in nature leads to a heightened appreciation and embodiment of beauty, goodness, abundance and especially peace, extending from the self to the world. These principles are embodied in the character traits of hospitality, justice and truth, that give rise to happiness, prosperity and peaceful co-existence. In the Anishnaabe tradition, *The Seven Grandfather Teachings* are shared for the benefit of all, and encourage us to exhibit and practice 1) love 2) respect 3) bravery 4) honesty 5) humility 6) wisdom and 7) truth toward our human community as well as the other-than-human world. Whenever you practice and exhibit qualities such as these from the Druid or Anishnaabe living traditions, you are contributing to the paradigm shift by reclaiming and embodying the types of behaviors that arise from the core principles of earth-connected culture.

- You hold as truth that First Nations cultures need to be held sacred by all peoples. You also believe that tribal life in close connection with the Earth is the only acceptable way to live on our sacred planet, and that everything else is an aberration.

Mother Earth and all of her creatures are impeccable and perfect, including the wondrous human being that the Creator designed to be in harmony with the sacredness of the land. And how strange that we, the "civilized" human, have forgotten and disregarded our intrinsic bond with the earth, and that every physical fibre of our being is connected to place. With or without modernity *"we are hard-wired to experience everything our 'deep time' Ancestors experienced, and our own wildness."*[259] (Frances Weller) That we should have turned our back on natural law is an indescribable act of arrogance and stupidity. What could possibly be worth it, to situate ourselves outside of our own ecology? What could possibly be the advantage of moving away from our cradled and blessed place in the embrace of holistic perfection matched to the human form? What hubris or terror or dementia provoked us to flee from the Garden? How did we shift from the "we" of the primal matrix to the modern "me-me-me" of the hypertrophied ego? Since time immemorial, our primeval mandate has been to be at one with wild nature, as an interconnected part of the flourishing of life on this rare and wondrous planet.

The sacred magic of the interface between the human and natural world is an unconditional gift from the Creator, visible in how each cultural group carries the essence of the place from which they arose and flourished.[260] Before the rise of Empire, for millennia our ethnic and genetic maps evolved in synchronization with a particular landscape, our human form matched to the terrain of our beloved homelands. *"The word 'indigenous'.....means being so completely identified with a place that you reflect its' very soul."*[261] (Gregory Cajete) Apparent in size, shape and colouring, the Gurung (Tamu) people of the Nepalese Annapurna mountain range have brown almond eyes, dark hair and high cheekbones that echo their craggy and wind-blown territory, the beauty of a Laplander's creamy white skin and long limbs are in harmony with their lands' rocky fells, forests and tundras and could not have happened anywhere else, the petite shapeshifter Dani people of Indonesian New Guinea mirror no other place but their rainforest highlands rich in tropical plant and animal life, the tall forms and deep bronze of the Kenyan Maasai people are perfectly adapted to their semi-nomadic culture in African deserts and scrublands, the characteristics of the Dakota/Lakota/Nakoda are in perfect symbiosis with their plains of flowing grasses, rich waterways, foothill valleys and mountain passes, and the beautiful Anishnaabe are cradled one and the same with their watersheds, wild rice ecosystems and lush deep sacred forests. Before the rise of modernity and the dulling of our senses to magic and mystery, tribal peoples were able to read another person's physique, and intrinsically or intuitively assess the elements of the land and water to which they were bonded. The quintessence of wind, water, rock, root, tree, lake, river, ocean, wildflower meadow, inlet, island, underground cave, towering crag, fertile valley, sacred sand desert, spring, forest, wetland, woods, escarpment, ridge, tundra, rainforest or savannah can animate the spirit and physical form of any human being. These Indigenous physicalities, or at least the observation of them, have diminished over time in the "civilized" world as dominated by the western paradigm. Yet not entirely, as psychologist Robert Sommer observed in a 1996 *Spirit of Place* keynote, as people can become "a voice" for the spirit of a region as much as for a human community or a relationship. *"The Lakota holy man Black Elk was a voice for the Black Hills of South Dakota. John Muir seemed to embody the spirit of Yosemite Valley. Rachel Carson was inspired by Cape Cod to write about 'the sense of wonder' in nature as well as the dangers of pesticides to ecological balance. Becoming a voice for the land creates a psychic anchor that is important to genuine human needs."*[262]

As all living beings embody, contain and mirror the natural world, when you trace it back completely to the source, all Indigenous cultural knowledge is also informed by the land. Every single cultural tradition

---

259. Francis Weller, "Five Gates of Grief," *Robert Bly's Minnesota Men's Conference,* November 4, 2013. (www.youtube.com)

260. The connection of physical human form to landscape is a well-known phenomenon. "*Like many other people in the ancient world, the Greeks typically attributed differences of appearance and of custom to the influence of geography and climate.*" (Dinesh D'Souza, *The End of Racism: Principles for a Multiracial Society,* The Free Press, 1995) In western knowledge traditions the argument over human behavior as a product of genetics or cultural influences (the nature-nurture debate) has been raging in philosophy, anthropology, psychology, sociology, genomics and neuroscience circles for decades. Those who emphasize the biological causes of human behavior employ perspectivism, and incorrectly assume that all human minds function the same way. Considering human psychology to be fixed, or hard-wired, they view any variation in capacity or attitude to be pathological, and biological determinism or "naturism," has been used to justify racism and oppression. On the other hand, new developments in the exciting fields of cultural psychology and cognitive science have found that human beings are the only species that can radically alter their innate biology by cultural and environmental influences. The "nurturists" agree that human behavior is extremely flexible, and that the vast diversity in our perception, intelligence and temperament is a result of cultural influences. Leading-edge philosophers such as Jesse Prinz (*Beyond Human Nature,* Allen Lane, 2012) have determined that our behavior is shaped by *both* genes and environment - our original nature plus the social and environmental forces that affect our lives.

261. Gregory Cajete (Tewa), *Look to the Mountain: An Ecology of Indigenous Education.* Kivaki Press, 1994.

262. Robert Sommer as cited in "Spirit of Place: Seeking the Modern Relevance of Ancient Wisdom," by James A. Swan, Ph.D, *Dialogues With The Living Earth,* anthology based on the *Spirit of Place* presentations, Quest Books, 1996.

or meaning has deep roots and memories in an intimate bonding with the land - the place where we flourish, the place where we are born, our sacred landscape. *"Indigenous cultures are extensive knowledge-based cultures, not material-based cultures. Indigenity is not what's in your blood, although that can be a marker - it is the lifestyle, the culture to which you adapt to and acquire over the course of your life, by gaining knowledge and introspection. IK systems are complex reflections of empirical local experience, rational discovery, symbolic imagery and social reinforcement."*263 (Robert Lovelace) If culture is a set of principles learned from the land, and however adapted, changed, modernized or enhanced, those of the diaspora still hold deep memories of the EIK practices and deities of our ancient traditions. It is possible for those of European descent to model our earth-connected practices after those that align with our own cultural group, to find our own ancestral roots rich with meaning and magic, to rewild our lives, and to perform the ceremonies and rituals that honour the natural cycles, elements, earth spirits, deities and Mother Nature herself. We need to spark our own learning, recover our EIK, and in a new form of syncretism, apply these ancient principles in combination with the natural ecosystems where we are now living. All human beings are designed through our physical and emotional "sensories" and spiritual interfaces to be completely bonded with the natural world, to be a conduit of living knowledge freely given by nature to those who are in complete connection with the Earth. To explore this further, we can say that any human being who lacks the connection to the natural world in favor of an urban life needs to return to that fundamental bond, and this needs to happen in the place which they find themselves, where they are now living. There is no waiting for the perfect time and place, just begin, NOW, where you are. Look at nature, listen to nature, absorb nature, learn about the attributes of the different green growing things in nature, learn about the habits of the animals and all the creatures in nature, and spend huge amounts of time in nature without the distractions of the human-built world. Love nature, defend nature, make nature the largest part of your soul, and soon you will be on your way to being an earth-connected person, which is what must ultimately define "indigenity."

*"Mother Earth is indigenizing all of us – everything we need to know about the future will come from the land - how to live and how to correct our behavior. The land is going to shift our governance and economy, mental and physical health – it is the land that will indigenize us."*264 (Diane Longboat)

---

263. Robert Lovelace (Tslagi/Algonquin), *Great Lakes Commons Gathering*, October 22, 2012. (www.youtube.com)

264. Diane Longboat (Kahontakwas (Mohawk), "Indigenous Wisdom and Prophecies Are Helping Humanity Shift to New Paradigms," *Global Indigenous Wisdom Summit*, The Shift Network, November 18-20, 2014.

Within these pages I urge those of European descent to recover and practice their own indigenous wisdom entirely, **NOT** to appropriate any aspect of the cultural property or spiritual life of the First Nations of Turtle Island. My goal is to bend the curve on bringing diasporans back to their own ancestral earth-connected roots, in *whatever* shape that takes. In this day and age elements of syncretisation are inevitable, yet I would stress that what is acceptable, is the reconstruction, embodiment and practice of pre-colonial IK/EIK combinations *that each person holds as unique.* The directive to claim our ancestral earth-honoring ways as white people in peaceful co-existence is extremely important as we join the circle of earth-connected cultures, and align with the birthright of every human being, which is to be indigenous to the Earth. Self-identifying as Gaelic, Ásatrú, Hellenismos, or Romuva (for example) will enable our own uncolonization process and recovery from the dictatorship of the western paradigm, with its unsustainable economic system, religious dominance, white supremacy, intersectional oppressions, harmful technology and all the philosophies that are killing the planet. By declaring ourselves as earth-centered peoples we are reaffirming a return to sanity, to a respect for all life, to earth-connected culture, to peaceful co-existence and to honoring the Earth in all we think, say and do. What could be more important?

"For all of us, becoming indigenous to a place means living as if your children's future mattered, to take care of the land as if our lives, both material and spiritul, depended on it."[265] (Robin Wall Kimmerer)

"Put your ear to the ground and listen and you will know the ceremonies are all around us. We just have to be patient and listen." (Mohegan Elder, Connecticut)

---

265. Robin Wall Kimmerer, *Braiding Sweetgrass: Indigenous Wisdom, Scientific Knowledge and the Teachings of Plants,* Milkweed Editions, 2015

18. Anishnaabe Prophecy

Beyond a doubt, pre-contact societies in the Americas were highly evolved, and as Wade Davis tells us, early ethnographers were confounded by Amazonian IK as *"an astonishingly complex worldview, a tangle of religious beliefs and myths that informed all of life and gave rise to patterns of social organization Byzantine in their sophistication yet perfectly elegant in their elaboration, representing nothing more than a triumph of the human spirit and imagination."*[266] Similarly, the cosmology embedded within the oral tradition of Anishnaabe society that has accumulated over millennia - the origin stories, myths, parables and prophecies - are encoded with directions for living the "good life" from the cradle to the grave. Their meta-values are held within the collective cultural teachings and spiritual literacy of a living, dynamic IK system. Western society, with its history of dominance, control, separation from nature and convoluted religious practice, can only aspire to the holistic interweaving of sustainable relationships between the individual and the community, the natural world and the cosmos that the Anishnaabe worldview achieves. In contemporary times, keepers of Anishnaabe ancestral wisdom and the oral tradition such as Edward Benton-Banai, James Dumont, William Commanda and many others have been willing to share their teachings with us, as found in *The Prophecies of the Seven Fires.*

SACRED FIRE

"In the time of the Seventh Fire, the light-skinned race will be given a choice between two roads. One road is the road of greed and technology without wisdom or respect for life. This road represents a rush to destruction. The other road is spirituality, a slower path that includes respect for all living things. If we choose the spiritual path, we can light yet another fire, an Eighth Fire, and begin an extended period of peace and healthy growth."[267]
(Edward Benton-Banai)

As we sort out the effects of cultural imperialism and the racialized histories of both native and non-native people on the ground, it is fascinating to learn that the implications of the Euro-colonial takeover of the Americas were already addressed in First Nations prophecy. Speaking of a time when human greed would cause a great eco-catastrophe, *The Seventh Fire Prophecy* is extremely relevant to our current eco-crisis and EIK recovery project. The prophecies outline the mythic migrations of the Anishnaabe across Turtle Island, and the devastating genocide and colonization that occurred post-contact. The *Fourth Fire* tells of the coming of the "white skinned race" and that in the time of the *Seventh Fire* "*there will be a rebirth of the Anishnaabe Nation and a rekindling of old flames, and the sacred fire will again be lit.*"[268] Many traditional leaders believe that we have entered the time of the *Seventh Fire,* and that we must now choose between the two roads of materialism or spirituality. It is said that if the light-skinned Settlers choose the right road, the *Seventh Fire* will light the Eighth and final Fire, the internal fire of peace, love and human harmony. The prophecy also tells of a long-awaited group of Indigenous people who will finally step into their power, and we see this materializing today with a maturing generation fully assuming advocacy, leadership and professional roles in fields such as law, medicine, journalism, education and engineering. The *Seventh Fire* generation is finally breaking free from the hegemony of the colonial mind, and with their governance, the future looks promising for the realization of an Indigenous-led postcolonial cosmovision.

Not only is the message of the *Eighth Fire* of primary importance to our recovery of IK and EIK, we have been blessed with the presence of highly-esteemed Elder William Commanda (Algonquin, 1913-2011), the holder of the wampum belt spiritually encoded with the *Seven Fires Prophecy*. Commanda worked tirelessly as an advocate for indigenous human rights, Algonquin land claims and cultural sovereignty, and by transcending the demands of the quotidian world, became a peace activist and true visionary for all people, as well as his own Algonquin Nation. There are few holy people that walk the earth today, and lost in our dangerous ignorance and the incessant fallout from divisive hegemony, without sacred teachers like William Commanda, James Dumont and Chief Arvol Looking Horse we would never know what tolerance for diversity and unconditional love look like in action. And as much as Commanda's expansive vision brought white spiritual seekers temporarily under the umbrella of Turtle Island IK, we will always be deeply and forever indebted to him for his peerless example. Over the years he spoke about the necessity for ALL nations to come together in peaceful co-existence, to share knowledge freely, to work toward equity, to eliminate racism, and to move forward as an enlightened human collective.

The *Seventh Fire Prophecy* is both a warning and a promise of a better future if we can put aside our egos, our cultural and racial bias, and come together for mutual healing and the healing of Mother Earth. The impulse to reinforce our interconnectivity with nature, and choose the spiritual path over the material, is manifesting everywhere in society today. To select just one example from many, the new documentary *Femme: Women Healing the World*[269] illuminates the current shift away from the hierarchy and domination of the patriarchy to egalitarian life-sustaining feminine values of compassion, caring, sharing, love, peace and harmony. The rise of women's power today, either intellectually, socially or politically, will hopefully lead to a true partnership with men and the much-needed balancing of society. *"The opposite of patriarchy is not matriarchy, but fraternity. And I think it is women who are going to have to break the spiral of power and find the trick of cooperation."*[270] (Germaine Greer) If women step up en masse as they seem to be doing, and continue their work with equality, cooperation, and the nurture of self, family, community and the Earth, the womancentric partnership model could transform the world.

In the different narratives of the *Seventh Fire Prophecy*, the notion was even put forth that it would be the First Nations knowledge keepers and leaders of Turtle Island who would light the way through the apocalyptic darkness. It is said that Indigenous Elders will guide the people who have lost their way, offering teachings and wisdom that will bring them back into balance with the Earth, and help them to recover their place within (not above) the *Circle of all Life*. This is a wonderful vision, but how much better it would be if we meet them halfway, to come to the table to revitalize earth-connected cultures all over the world as Gaelic, Baltic or Nordic Wisdom Keepers (for example) - strong and knowledgeable in our own heritage and EIK, and honorable in our mutual care for Mother Earth.

---

266. Wade Davis, *Light at the Edge of the World: A Journey Through the Realm of Vanishing Cultures*, Douglas & McIntyre, 2009.
267. I chose this passage from many adaptations of the original text. Edward Benton-Banai, *The Mishomis Book: The Voice of the Ojibway*, University of Minnesota Press, 2010. (www.wabanaki.com/seven_fires_prophecy.htm)
268. Ibid.
269. Emmanuel Itier and Amanda Estremera, *Femme: Women Healing the World*, Wonderland Entertainment Group, 2013. (www.wonderlandentgroup.com)
270. Germaine Greer, introduction to "Fire On Babylon" by Sinead O'Connor on her album *Universal Mother*, Ensign/Chrysalis, 1994. (www.sinead-oconnor.com)

Settler Song

We touch the earth through you
You are this land
Your blood, the rivers
Your hands, the rocks we rest upon
Your breath, the sacred flame on distant hills ~
Your life-spark, a warmth the Firekeepers know
Your strawberry heart drums the living earth
Your dance, the survival of us all

Storm-born, new moon, new world rising
We wander west, émigré but free
We swim your sacred waters, woman-blessed

And in the forest, pitiful, we are the "other" you find
You teach us respect
How to conquer with love
Your kind voice, our home
Your arms, the circle

Our animals and trees heal each other
Renewal of life, markers of wampum
Fatherland fades away

Anishnaabe, take us back to common ground
May we find *Mino Bimaadiziwin - the Good Life,* again

In the process of examining our own "whiteness" and our participation in the imperialist hegemony of the European diaspora to the Americas, it may be useful to envision other ways of being. The poem "Settler Song" presents a worldview that is less arrogant, less domineering, less paternalistic, more kind, more humble, more heart-focused, and more aware of being a newcomer to a land already inhabited by a magnificent diversity of sophisticated societies.

19. Rejecting Empire

"A long habit of not thinking a thing wrong gives it a superficial appearance of being right."[271] (Thomas Paine)

"Tribal peoples would retake the Americas; tribal people would retake ancestral land all over the world. This was what Earth's spirits wanted: her indigenous children who loved Her and did not harm Her."[272] (Leslie Marmon Silko)

As the fulfillment of the *Seventh Fire Prophecy*, it is imperative that all people find their way back to ecological awareness, the inner and outer narratives that honour Mother Earth, and to attitudes and practices that are in true symbiosis with the landscapes we call home. Our recovery of authentic ancestral wisdom, if we are to embody our IK/EIK fully into our lives, means rejecting the dominant paradigm and moving away from the values of patriarchal imperialism inherent in governance, religion, economy and culture. The current era of Empire goes back to 1492 and the "Age of Discovery," when the *"colonial imagination went global"*[273] and was imposed dramatically and violently on Indigenous peoples and localized cultures worldwide. Scientific reductionism in the 1700's followed by the industrial revolution changed the whole basis of society, including people's relationship to each other and the land. Christianity taught us that human beings were superior to other life by virtue of having a soul (other beings were "soulless") and science went on to brainwash modern humanity into viewing nature, natural phenomena and the other-than-human world as lifeless "resources." *"While Western culture has in the past been based on an earth-centred and later a God-centred worldview, its current foundations are human-centred, whereby the Earth is seen as primarily for human use."*[274] (Thomas Berry) The heinous theories that separate humanity from the holism of nature have justified the expansion of colonial empire, what Winona LaDuke calls "a *predator society based on conquest*"[275] into the industrial era and beyond, enslaving and killing millions of Indigenous people and ravaging the natural world in the process. *"We live at a time when the living body of our Earth is under attack, and the attacker is not an alien force but our own industrial-growth society."*[276] (Joanna Macy and Chris Johnstone)

Clearly, we need to reject the destructive principles of monotheistic religion that claim humanity to be superior to the earth, in addition to rejecting the fantasies of a utopian existence as extolled by the proponents of a technological, industrial way of life. The values of Euro-Empire that created the hegemony of colonization and guided unchecked progress in the Americas for the past five hundred years are patently untrue. The idea that "evolution equals progress" is an out-dated Victorian notion, and instead of some kind of futuristic utopia, what we have is crime, homelessness, lack of community, harmful technologies, destruction of natural systems, unsustainable growth, environmental breakdown and tremendous inequality. Technological progress has been widely embraced because of its perceived benefits, but the fact *"that millions of people share the same forms of mental pathology does not make those people sane."*[277] (Erich Fromm) Globalization has also forced homogenization onto cultures and entire regions, and *"monocultural perspectives can be dangerous in that they encourage only one way of thinking and looking at the world."*[278] (Roger Spielmann) We have been in a colonized trance, and by addressing the social and ecological crisis we now face, we must reject the values that emphasize growth economics and the accumulation of commodities, and abandon the technologies that are incompatible with sustainability and diversity. *"We live on a continent that thinks man's laws are the highest laws, and we have a 'centric' civilization - it is all about us - ethnocentric and anthropocentric; and greed and public policy make paupers of all our relations. No matter how many times they tell the lies does not make them true. We are subject to the natural laws of sustainability, and we need to live in accordance with Creator's Law."*[279] (Winona LaDuke) At this point in history, it would seem highly rational to also reject the humancentric and hubristic notion that human beings are a "God Species" that rule the world, that more and better technology will solve the problems that technology created in the first place, and that continued "progress" is the only way forward. Our transition, what some are calling the "Great Turning," must be from the doomed economy of industrial growth to a life-sustaining society, committed to the recovery of the natural world and our place within it.

"Uncolonize now, voluntarily, intentionally, with full awareness and the selective use of resources, OR, uncolonize later under duress and hardship, as a dramatic response to traumatic conditions when the current economic paradigm reaches the limits of its sustainability. But uncolonize you must, or fade away with the memories of a lost civilization."

271. Thomas Paine, *Common Sense*, Philadelphia, 1776.

272. Leslie Marmon Silko, *Almanac of the Dead*, Penguin Books, 1992.

273. Eve Tuck and K. Wayne Yang, "Decolonization is Not a Metaphor," *Decolonization: Indigeneity, Education & Society*, Volume 1, No.1, 2012. (http://decolonization.org)

274. Thomas Berry, *The Great Work: Our Way into the Future*, Crown, 2011.

275. Winona LaDuke (Anishnaabe), *The Winona LaDuke Reader: A Collection of Essential Writings*, Voyageur Press, 2002.

276. Joanna Macy and Chris Johnstone, *Active Hope: How to Face the Mess We're In Without Going Crazy*, New World Library, 2012.

277. Erich Fromm, *The Sane Society*, Routledge, 1991.

278. Roger Spielmann, *Anishnaabe World: A Survival Guide for Building Bridges Between Canada and First Nations*, Your Scrivener Press, 2009.

279. Winona LaDuke (Anishnaabe), *Keynote Address at Powershift 2012*, Ottawa, ON, 28/10/2012. (www.youtube.com) *Winona LaDuke at PowerShift 2012*. (http://vimeo.com)

The term "decolonization" has been applied mainly to Indigenous cultures engaged in their recovery from colonization and reclamation of sovereignty as individuals and nations, and by far the majority of scholarship and activity regarding "decolonization" has been by First Nations. Indigenous "decolonization" encompasses healing from genocide and cultural attack, human rights work, anti-oppression and anti-racism efforts, landbase recovery through original land claims, and the return to tribal traditions - the *Original Instructions* and IK/TEK of a specific First Nation, including traditional governance and diplomacy. There is a controversy regarding the use of the term "decolonization" by those of us in the dominant society, as our own rejection of Empire (which is gaining momentum daily) is not the same process as that of Indigenous peoples. And as much as our projects or goals may be similar, the positionality of the oppressor is never the same as the oppressed. It has been noted by Indigenous scholars and activists that using the term "decolonization" in our white theory and practice is actually an appropriation, and can be critiqued as such. Groups in sectors such as education have been co-opting the term "decolonization" in reference to improving our society and our schools, i.e. using the phrase "decolonize student thinking" without any discussion of Indigenous peoples, their struggles for sovereignty, or the contributions of "*indigenous intellectuals and activists to theories and frameworks of decolonization.*"[280] Using "decolonization" as a metaphor without addressing our white presence on stolen land continues to perpetuate the status quo of Settler values, re-centering whiteness and continuing with the colonial process. Many of our social change actions such as the *Occupy* movement also perpetuate white privilege and dominance by subscribing to values incongruent with true decolonization, such as patriotic fervor, private land ownership, and a cash-based capitalism-type economy. From an "Open Letter to Occupy Wall Street" we learn that "*the nationalistic language of phrases like 'take our country back' is something that should be examined in terms of its associations with imperialism and colonialism. The occupy movement should oppose and seek to end colonialism, as much as it opposes and seeks to end unregulated capitalism, imperialism, war, or institutional racism.*"[281] (John Paul Montano)

As Settlers, clearly we need to be careful not to use "decolonization" as a metaphor or combine it with other pre-existing agendas, and to be aware of how we use the term in any ideology or action that leads to the "*resettlement, reoccupation, and reinhabitation that actually furthers settler colonialism.*"[282] I use the term "decolonization" sparingly in

---

280. Eve Tuck and K. Wayne Yang, "Decolonization is Not a Metaphor," *Decolonization: Indigeneity, Education & Society*, Volume 1, No.1, 2012. (http://decolonization.org)
281. John Paul Montano, "An Open Letter to the Occupy Wall Street Activists," *ZASHNAIN @bedlamfury: Outbursts of freedom, self expression, determination and fury* (blog), September 24, 2011. (www.zashnain.com)

favor of "uncolonization" or "Rejecting Empire," and focus on the principles of a paradigm shift to simple, sustainable communities and sacred lifeways for all people. For some Indigenous scholars and visionaries, and rightly so, the true meaning of "decolonization" means the final completion of the *Ghost Dance* movement, the return to a way of life before colonization, "*the native futures, the lives to be lived once the settler nation is gone.*"283 It is true that if we were to truly decolonize the Americas, the Settler Society would have to repatriate all the land back to the original First Nations, relinquish the dominance model of "power over," and give up the privileges and amenities of Empire-building, both in the material and abstract. This may sound like the scenario for a good fantasy novel (!), but who knows what the future may hold? The Setter Society is living on stolen land, and our uncolonization process should support the resurgence of Indigenous sovereignty and lifeways, and the return of decision-making concerning the land to the original peoples. Moving forward, *Rejecting Empire* will involve working toward sustainable local community partnerships, Indigenous rights, cultural reclamation, ecological restoration and peaceful co-existence - values all people can share.

For the majority of the Settler Society, as kings and queens of our own domains, we are the first generation **ever** to have the material wealth and luxury comparable to individual fiefdoms, and we may be the last to have such incredible privilege. Our attraction to the newest trend and our total choice in escapism, fantasy, luxury, travel, food, health, wellness, wardrobe, entertainment, sports, hobbies, arts, literature, technology, toys, gadgets, conveniences and spiritual life are the direct result of capitalist consumerism, and this excess (or surplus) in the western world has led to a very real change in the human condition. Never before in history has our unlimited choice in accouterments, lifestyle or opportunity outpaced our ability to manage this barrage, or to make the right decisions based on an infinity of possibilities. Both a blessing and a curse, the modern lifestyle that we take for granted (which fosters no loyalty to our neighbours or dependence on community whatsoever) is an unsustainable construct and doomed to expire. As Robert Jensen says in *We Are All Apocalyptic Now: Moral Responsibilities in Crisis Times,* it is essential to stand up to power, and to speak the truth that almost no one wants to hear. "*Life as we know it is almost over. This high-energy high-technology life that we in the affluent societies live, is a dead end, and we are closer to that end than ever before. A large-scale human presence on the planet at this level of consumption is impossible. We can't predict when this party will end, but make no mistake folks, the party is over.*"284 Being both the best and worst of times, these last days of Empire are the most luxurious, most innovative, most clever, most diverting, most exciting, most amusing, most extravagant, most titillating, most laissez-faire, most contradictory, most discombobulating, most disturbing, most toxic, most deceitful, most immoral, most decadent, most wasteful, most rapacious, most criminal, most destructive, most precarious, most chaotic, and most tragic times ever.

If we face the future realistically, we can see that in this era of *The Long Emergency*[285] industrial civilization is headed for a brick wall, and that the time to make change is long overdue. Rejecting the hegemonic lies of a false and unsustainable economic paradigm, uncolonizing ourselves in heart-mind-body-soul, and moving toward an "ecological civilization" is the great work of our time. Whether we realize it or not, we have all been colonized, and by extension, the same hetero-patriarchal values that have oppressed people along a continuum of racial, economic, gender, ability and sexual orientation lines has also oppressed the natural world. Known as "speciesism," the creatures and elements of Mother Earth are living things with intrinsic rights, and they too have been oppressed, colonized and abused. The trees, plants, rocks, soil, minerals, water, animals, birds, insects and fish have been extracted, mined, cut down, harvested, dug up, or slaughtered to feed the engine of civilization. The economic paradigm has done enough damage, and it is time to preserve our life-support systems – the earth, watersheds and other elements that make up the diverse ecotones of our unique homelands. *"The universe is a presence to be **communed with** and **instructed by**, not a collection of natural resources to be used for utilitarian purposes."*[286] (Bill Plotkin) Wild nature needs to be safeguarded against further exploitation, and we need to protect our local biodiversity, topsoil, forests, water and clean air for future generations. *Rejecting Empire* means addressing the environmental, social and health impacts of industrial growth, and recognizing that our first priority is to care for ravaged communities and ecosystems. In this regard, one of the most powerful contemporary movements is the action to legislate *Ecocide Law*[287] by 2020, which would change the course of history.

"We must all consciously and continuously challenge every model, every program and every process that the West tries to force upon us......the people who are living on this planet need to break with the narrow concept of human liberation, and begin to see liberation as

---

282./283. Eve Tuck and K. Wayne Yang, "Decolonization is Not a Metaphor," *Decolonization: Indigeneity, Education & Society*, Volume 1, No.1, 2012.
284. Robert Jensen, *We Are All Apocalyptic Now: Moral Responsibilities in Crisis Times*, KDP, 2013.
285. Author James Howard Kunstler coined the phrase "the long emergency" to describe the general state of the world in the 21st century. James Howard Kunstler, *The Long Emergency: Surviving the End of Oil, Climate Change, and Other Converging Catastrophes of the Twenty-First Century*, Grove Press, 2006.
286. Bill Plotkin, *Soulcraft: Crossing into the Mysteries of Nature and Psyche*, New World Library, 2010.
287. Please see *Earth Rights* on Page 269 for more information on *Ecocide Law*.

something that needs to be extended to the whole of the Natural World. What is needed is the liberation of all things that support Life - the air, the waters, the trees - all the things that support the sacred web of Life.[288] (Jerry Mander)

As stated previously, there is a contemporary movement toward sustainable eco-ethics already happening, a huge renaissance engaged in the work of uncolonization (both within the decolonial framework and beyond). Whatever we call it, rejecting Eurocentric Empire is paramount as we replace external authority with community, transcend the colonial identity that is our legacy, and begin to live as earth-centered peoples once again.

"Before the white man could colonize anyone else, he had to colonize himself. And so, before he can truly stand beside anyone else to confront the tasks of decolonization and resurgence, within, against, or outside of the dominant order, he must attend to his own decolonization at the level of both the individual and the community."[289] (Richard J.F. Day) Taking the long view, there are many questions we need to be asking ourselves at this juncture in history. How deep is the colonization in our souls? In our minds? What is delusional and what is real? As we move away from Empire, what is our level of commitment? This is the white conversation. To completely uncolonize can we truly reject all that does not serve the earth, like exploitative economies and resource extraction, and to fully understand that capitalism is a brutal, fascistic system that kills millions of beings physically and millions more spiritually? And as we have normalized it for centuries, does "white" have to equal the juggernaut of Empire and modernity? The answer, emphatically, must be NO. As Tim Wise articulates, *"white is to dream of different ways to live in this skin"*[290] and Winona DaDuke reminds us that *"you can have a worldview that is not based on Empire."*[291] As I see it, the most important activity of uncolonization is **rejection**, a refusal to participate in Empire any longer, and this rejection needs to happen at the core of our being and as the basis of our resistance.

Reprogramming ourselves and realizing our true potential (known as "entelechy"[292]) leads to an interconnection with the evolving processes

---

288. Jerry Mander, *In the Absence of the Sacred: The Failure of Technology and the Survival of the Indian Nations*, Sierra Club Books, 1992.

289. Richard J.F. Day, "Angry Indians, Settler Guilt, and the Challenges of Decolonization and Resurgence," *This is an Honour Song: Twenty Years Since the Blockades*, Leanne Simpson and Kiera L. Ladner (editors), Arbeiter Ring Publishing, 2010.

290. Tim Wise, *White Like Me: Reflections on Race from a Privileged Son*, Soft Scull Press, 2011.

291. Winona LaDuke (Anishnaabe), *Keynote Address at Powershift 2012*, Ottawa, ON, October 28, 2012. (www.youtube.com)

292. Analogous to the unfolding of our personal mythology, entelechy (en-'te-le-kē) is the revealing of our inherent potential(s) hidden within, manifesting as lived reality, true purpose and wisdom at various phases of life, or over an entire lifetime.

of all life, and brings us back to our essential bio-lineage. Recovering our specific ethnic and culturally-based indigenity is key, as suggested by Zainab Amadahy. *"If the aim of decolonization is to rid ourselves of colonial mindsets why not centralize our own wisdom traditions when they enable us to think and act in ways that support our communities, including Mother Earth, Our Relations and the Great Spirit?"*[293] Decolonization insists that we understand ourselves as we existed before modern civilization, and that implementing holistic solutions and traditional earth-connected ways of life are vital to the survival of the human race.

"By any measure The Great Turning will not be an easy transition. The adjustment can play out in the mode of Empire, as a violent, self-destructive, last-man-standing competition for individual advantage. Or it can play out in the mode of Earth Community, as a cooperative effort to rebuild community; to learn the arts of sufficiency, sharing and peaceful conflict resolution; and to marshal our human creativity to grow the generative potential of the whole. The process depends on whether we find the courage and vision to embrace this transition as a moment of opportunity."[294] (David Korten)

Rejecting Empire may mean encountering a monumental process of grieving and an overwhelming sadness for all living things that have been sacrificed on the altar of progress and to feed the engine of economy. Do the means justify the ends? Also, we can see that all those who embrace, justify, or keep silent about the western paradigm are buying into the immoral principles of unsustainability. Unfortunately *"we are living on a planet with finite resources and infinite human greed."*[295] (Sheelah McLean) And finally, we come to realize that the rapacious values of an old boys network of conquerors, religious zealots and misguided masters of industry - **all white and all male** - have dominated the rest of us and dictated and monopolized our reality for far too long. The use of "resources" has been their way, food production and distribution their way, the legal system their way, law enforcement their way, medical care their way, social mores their way, "mutuality" their way and "inclusivity" their way! It is hard to accept that we have been manipulated and steered away from the fact that the natural world is our highest value, but engaging with the paradigm shift can create a profound change in one's perception. *"That's the great torment - because our way of life is so compellingly victorious (on the surface*

---

293. Zainab Amadahy, "Why Indigenous and Racialized Struggles will Always be Appendixed by the Left," *Unsettling Settlers: Where We Talk about Unsettling Our Settler Selves*, August 1, 2012. (http://unsettlingsettlers.wordpress.com)
294. David C. Korten, *The Great Turning: From Empire to Earth Community*, Berrett-Koehler Publishers/Kumarian Press, 2006.
295. Sheelah McLean (one of the four founders of *Idle No More*), Facebook status, June 2013.

*of it), it takes enormous insight to recognize that it is actually a
calamity that has not collapsed in upon itself yet."*[296]
(Stephen Jenkinson)

For those of us in the Euro-diaspora moving toward uncolonization in
the Americas, there is a renaissance of guiding lights, truth-tellers,
teachers, authors and activists actively engaged in *Rejecting Empire* and
its toxic hegemonies (see "Resources," Page 393) , and leading the shift
toward localized ecologically-based communities. There is a good
gender balance of those working in decolonization, activism and
"apocalyptic studies," with karmic justice at play in the efforts of the
influencers who are working hard to undo the destructive legacy of their
white supremacist forefathers. A good meme to address this dynamic
may be that *"white men created Empire and it is up to white men to
undo it!"*[297] I highly recommend pursuing the ideas and actions of these
visionaries in your own lives and communities.

---

296. Stephen Jenkinson, "Interview with Ian MacKenzie," *Orphan Wisdom*, January 2013.
297. See my blog post "White Men Created Empire and it is Up to White Men to Undo It!"
at (www.stonecirclepress.com).

Rejecting Empire ~ Re-centering Indigenous Values

*"Decolonization is not a process which solely entails the Indigenous
nations of this continent. All people living in Canada have been
distorted by Colonialism. It affects us all, not only those whom it
most severely oppresses."*[298] (Nora Butler Burke)

In addition to learning all we can about First Nations history, challenges
and contemporary narratives, we can turn to the work of Indigenous
scholars and activists, the *"best of the new generation's anti, non, de
and un colonial thinking"*[299] for inspirational frameworks in our own
process of *Rejecting Empire*. Wisdom is readily available from First
Nation intellectuals, leaders, visionaries and public figures who excel in
every location of society, making their mark with distinction after
epochs of mistreatment and exclusion. In *What is Indigenous
Knowledge?* Semali & Kincheloe suggest three goals for studying
Indigenous Knowledge. *"1) To help western peoples relate to their
habitat in ways that are more harmonious, 2) to liberate peoples who
have been conquered by a modernist nation state system, and 3) to
provide a perspective on human experience that differs from western
empirical science."*[300] Enlarging our own community transitions, social
justice movements and First Nations solidarity work with the
knowledge of local IK is a valid approach, and it is also to our benefit to
learn about *"Indigenous solutions to the problems continued
colonialism creates."*[301] (Leanne Simpson) Re-centering Indigenous

ethics does not give us permission to appropriate the spiritual or cultural property of First Nations, but is a recommendation to embrace Indigenous **values** such as reciprocity, balance, and respect for natural law. Without romanticizing, misinterpreting or denying the holocaust that occurred in the Americas, it has been suggested that we can look to the original peoples to learn how to thrive, survive and flourish on Turtle Island, interconnected with the land and all life. After all, as outlined by Gustavo Esteva in *Chapter 22* "Earth First" (Page 223) everything we need for the paradigm shift is *"already in place as it has been for millennia, being lived by Indigenous Knowledge and Indigenous people."*[302] Decolonization is most certainly the challenge faced by all those who call Turtle Island home, and many Indigenous scholars such as Taiaike Alfred, John Mohawk and Robert Lovelace agree. *"Indigenous peoples and Settlers have our own histories, where those histories have led us, and where the possible futures might lie for us together. Because guess what, we are here and now, we're not going to change that fact, but what we can do is change the possible futures that we face."*[303] (Robert Lovelace) As we take on the work of becoming deeply bonded to the land in our uncolonization process, we are being invited to learn from the First Peoples in whose territories we are now living (in my case, the Michi Saagiig Nishnaabeg). Those of us in the dominant society need to understand the First Nations IK of our home landscapes, in order to practice sustainability and relate to the environment properly. As an example, Winona LaDuke tells us that the ability of the Seminole Nation to preserve and practice their IK benefits the wider society in turn, as *"the presence of these traditions in the Native community provides a yardstick against which to measure your own values, your own way of life, and your own choices."*[304] Being guided to access the vast storehouse of knowledge held by local First Nations for millennia would seem highly apropos, as Anishnaabe educator and activist Christine Sy explains. *"Given that Anishinaabe knowledge about how to live in Anishinaabegogamig is grounded on*

---

298. Nora Butler Burke, "Building a 'Canadian' Decolonization Movement: Fighting the Occupation at 'Home,'" *The Anarchist Library*, 2004. (http://theanarchistlibrary.org)

299. Taiaiake Alfred, "Opening Words," *Lighting the Eighth Fire: The Liberation, Resurgence and Protection of Indigenous Nations*, Leanne Simpson (editor), Arbeiter Ring Publishing, 2008.

300. Ladislaus M. Semali and Joe L. Kincheloe, *What is Indigenous Knowledge? Voices from the Academy*, Routledge, 1999.

301. Leanne Betasamosake Simpson, "Oshkimaadiziig, The New People," *Lighting the Eighth Fire: The Liberation, Resurgence and Protection of Indigenous Nations*, Leanne Simpson (editor), Arbeiter Ring Publishing, 2008.

302. Gustavo Esteva, Lecture, *2013 Elders Conference*, Indigenous Studies Department, Trent University, Peterborough, ON, January 28, 2013.

303. Robert Lovelace (Tslagi/Algonquin), *The Architecture of a Decolonized Society: Reindigenizing the Self, Community and Environment*, lecture, Kawartha World Issues Centre (KWIC), Trent University, Peterborough, ON, January 18, 2013.

304. Winona LaDuke (Anishnaabe), *All Our Relations: Native Struggles for Land and Life*, South End Press, 1999.

thousands of years of knowledge generation built on the shoulders of Anishinaabeg giants, it seems logical that non-Anishinaabeg would consult with our Elders on how to live in Anishinaabegogamig. Our knowledge comes directly from the land in which we live. This knowledge is undisrupted, sustainable and holistic; provides an education that maintains human and natural life; flourishes this life, and is both ancient and relevant."[305]

It is essential that we locate descriptions of Indigenous cultures in the "first person" by those who actually live in them, not by "objective" outsiders from the disciplines of ethnology or anthropology (however revisionist). From First Nation narratives such as *Following Nimishoomis: The Trout Lake History of Dedibaayaanimanook Sarah Keesick Olsen*,[306] I have discovered that my own landscape of Ontario, Canada is a four-season paradise rich in game, fishing harvests, wild rice, berries and healing plants, with the human and other-than-human interaction and practicalities of life on the land giving rise to *Mino Bimaadiziwin*,[307] "The Good Life." By gathering and preserving the oral traditions of her culture, author Helen Agger illuminates traditional Anishnaabe lifeways, values, customs, myths and cultural keystones in a format that becomes a living treasure for all. We learn how their deep bonds to the Earth and generations of connection to place are interwoven into Anishnaabe experiences with each other, their good manners, their care for all beings with gentleness, kindness and respect, and their appropriate protocol in all things. Ancestral knowledge and the consciousness of Indigenous people lie embedded in the features of the land, and recovering the cultural meaning this provides is essential to individual and collective identity and well-being. *"The basic premise of Indigenist and decolonizing theories is that we bring the knowledge of the ancient ones back into contemporary relevance, by capturing the revolutionary nature of those teachings."*[308] (Leanne Betasamosake Simpson)

---

305. Christine Sy/waaseyaa'sin (Anishnaabe), "From Decolonizing Education to Traditional Anishnaabe University: A Photo-Essay," *anishinaabewiziwin: all the elements that make up anishinaabe life* (blog), December 16, 2012. (http://giizismoon.wordpress.com)

306. Helen Agger (Anishnaabe), *Nimishoomis: The Trout Lake History of Dedibaayaanimanook Sarah Keesick Olsen*, Theytus Books, 2008.

307. The Anishnaabe concept of *Mino Bimaadiziwin*, or "The Good Life" is a perpetual guidance system that promotes positive personal, family and community relationships in education, economy, politics and governance. Focused on accountability and reciprocity, this set of IK teachings gives direction for individuals to interact with each other, the children, the community, other nations and the land. *"It was the quality of their relationships - not how much they had, not how much they consumed - that was the basis of my ancestors' happiness."* Leanne Simpson as cited in "Dancing the World into Being: A Conversation with Idle No More's Leanne Simpson," by Naomi Klein, *YES! Magazine*, 2013.

308. Leanne Betasamosake Simpson, "Our Elder Brothers: The Lifeblood of Resurgence," *Lighting the Eighth Fire: The Liberation, Resurgence, and Protection of Indigenous Nations*, Leanne Simpson, (editor), Arbeiter Ring Publishing, 2008.

The relational frameworks and *Original Instructions* that served Turtle Island First Nations for millennia prior to colonization are alive and thriving, perfectly intermeshed with localized landscapes and sustainable in today's world. In fact, pre-colonial IK may *"be crucial to getting the human species out of the mess we now find ourselves in on Mother Earth."*[309] (Zainab Amadahy) Both native and non-native communities now share Turtle Island, and as we change our attitudes, alter our frameworks and revise our activities, we may find common ground in the recovery of our own ethnoculture(s) and earth-wise spiritualities. Our decolonization processes are not the same, but *"we are all in this together, impacting each other in a web of life processes that inter-relate,"*[310] (Zainab Amadahy) and *"decolonization should involve **all** Nations on this land looking after the land, water, plants, animals and people together, equally."*[311] (Beth Newell) The earth wisdom teachings in our own ancestral traditions allow us to reclaim our true nature, and to re-inhabit what was taken away - our unity with nature. To fall in love again with the spirit in all things, is to recover an earth-centered worldview that blends the wisdom of spirituality with deep ecology, and the love of the land should inform our new ventures in sustainable community and organic democracy. *"Decolonization is as much a process as a goal. It requires a profound re-centring of indigenous worldviews in our movements for political liberation, social transformation, renewed cultural kinships, and the development of an economic system that serves rather than threatens our collective life on this planet."*[312] (Nick Montgomery)

Tslagi/Algonquin activist and scholar Robert Lovelace, in conjunction with the *Great Lakes Commons Initiative,*[313] has developed an excellent decolonization framework situated within the landscapes of the Great Lakes, with the mandate to move into an ecological-based society that is in symbiotic interaction with dynamic, living ecosystems. At the beginning of his presentation *The Architecture of a Decolonized Society: Reindigenizing the Self, Community and Environment,*[314] Lovelace identifies the embedded racism and unsustainability of corporate capitalism. Locke, Kant and the other early designers of capitalist theory failed to see any limitations, failed to see the fragility of nature, failed to see that the land and all beings have intrinsic rights, failed to see the consequences of the domestication of labour, and certainly failed to see the side effects of pollution in the economic paradigm they promoted. Our current political boundaries were created to serve a system of colonial settlement, resource extraction and industrial manufacture, and in the decolonization process Lovelace counsels us to pay attention to our local watersheds and biomes above all, and to reconfigure our governance systems to restore ecological balance. Obviously, we have had enough of capitalism (!) and in these times of challenge and change, we need to study how the language, governance and social relations of Indigenous Knowledge fit perfectly into local ecosystems. Recognizing that a diversity of Indigenous societies are the "norm" within the landscapes of Turtle Island, it is possible to emulate the health and holism of the Indigenous worldview today, and also moving forward into the future. All the aspects of life we need to consider in our rejection of Empire are determined by, or reinforced by, our interaction with the local environment, and the use of energy, food security, diplomacy, trade, defensive boundaries, *customary law*[315] and the checks and balances of population levels are all physically defined by the existing watersheds and ecotones of our territory. Adopting the Indigenous worldview means living lighter on the land, and building a society in which the ideal is to "*never consume more than can be replenished in a particular ecosystem, and don't expend more energy than what can be replaced by what is consumed.*"[316] Setting these physical boundaries in place will naturally give rise to our own unique cultural expressions, rituals, ceremonies, dances, songs, poetry, stories and art, in short, a thriving earth-emergent tradition incorporating elements from our own ancestral traditions as appropriate, and in syncretisation with the local landbase. With our love for the Earth as our common ground anything is possible, and as Robert Lovelace suggests, being indigenous to place is achieved "*when the human and ecosystem activity support and enhance one another.*"[317]

The most interesting aspect of Lovelace's decolonization framework in my opinion, is that he sees the paradigm shift rising from within the social-cultural realm, not from the worlds of politics or technology. In fact, except for recognizing their essential humanity (however hidden), he advises us to give up on railing against or trying to change the ruling

---

309. Zainab Amadahy, "Why Indigenous and Racialized Struggles will Always be Appendixed by the Left," *Unsettling Settlers: Where We Talk about Unsettling Our Settler Selves*, 2012. (http://unsettlingsettlers.wordpress.com)

310. Ibid.

311. Beth Newell, "A Few Words About Consultation, Decolonization, Self-determination and Assimilation" (blog), *Idle No More Kingston*, 2013.
(http://idlenomorekingston.wordpress.com)

312. Nick Montgomery, "Monstrous Settlers: Zombies, Demons, and Angels," *Cultivating Alternatives to the Dominant Order* (blog), 17/01/2013.
(http://cultivatingalternatives.com)

313. The *Great Lakes Commons Initiative* is "*an effort to declare and live the Great Lakes as a commons, a protected bioregion and a public trust.*"
On the Commons, (www.onthecommons.org).

314. Robert Lovelace (Tslagi/Algonquin), *The Architecture of a Decolonized Society: Reindigenizing the Self, Community and Environment*, presentation, Kawartha World Issues Centre (KWIC), Trent University, Peterborough, ON, January 18, 2013.

315. *Customary Law* is the cornerstone of Indigenous culture(s) and human rights, and legal approaches for the protection of IK should be grounded in customary laws and practices. Ideally, customary law should exist next to national legal systems, and the recognition of customary law is key to regulating the use and protection of traditional knowledge.

316./317. Robert Lovelace (Tslagi/Algonquin), *The Architecture of a Decolonized Society: Reindigenizing the Self, Community and Environment*, presentation, Kawartha World Issues Centre (KWIC), Trent University, Peterborough, ON, January 18, 2013.

elite. Synthesized cultures of neocolonialism are not sustainable, and Lovelace says there are three possible pathways to the "tipping point" scenario, which may occur in our lifetime. 1) **Fortress Capitalism**, a fragmented world of local imperial fiefdoms ruling over oppressed communities (a perfect example being the movie *The Hunger Games*), or more hopefully, islands or oases of holism and earth-based community here and there among the ongoing bastions of Empire. 2) **Bending the Curve**, or the millions of organizations, coalitions of resistance, and visionary individuals and communities that are working right now to physically manifest the paradigm shift to earth-honoring civilization. 3) **Societal Breakdown,** the erosion or collapse of natural or human systems, a massive dieback in the human population, and/or further speculations on drastic change in the face of uncertainty.

No one really knows what the future will hold, and we already live in a time of great cataclysms. If you ask the people who were in Thailand, Japan or New Orleans when the great wall of ocean arrived, or in California or Australia when the fire breached the neighbourhood gates, or in Pilger, Angus or Moore when the tornado touched down, or in Calgary, Colorado or Croatia when the water rose, they will tell you that the apocalypse has already come and gone.

It is clear that modelling our future after Indigenous values is key to our rejection of Empire, and ancient knowledge combined with modern IK in the revitalization of local community will enable us to survive the fast-approaching climate change crossroads. *"Coming from a culture of domination, Settlers now want a different relationship with the land, and the first thing we need to do to re-envision the world is to change ourselves."*[318] (Robert Lovelace) Of course, changing ourselves does not mean replicating the mistakes of liberal pluralism, which forces Indigenous identities to fit into Settler groups and narratives. Instead, Settlers need to take a personal inventory, stop acting on our privileges of race or gender, and *"surrender our preconceptions and privileges to the process of indigenization."*[319] (Joyce Green & Michael Burton) The best scenario would be for Settlers to become informed by First Nations values and models in our re-landing process, and to honour the primary cultural signifiers that reflect the original inhabitants of Turtle Island and the territory they hold.

The principles of hospitality have always been found on Turtle Island, as exemplified by the Mnjikaning First Nation (Ojibway) *Keepers of the Fish Fence,* next to my hometown of Orillia, Ontario. As my ancestor Eliza Emily Bailey was so graciously received and cared for in 1832, the

---

318. Robert Lovelace (Tslagi/Algonquin), *The Architecture of a Decolonized Society: Reindigenizing the Self, Community and Environment*, presentation, Kawartha World Issues Centre (KWIC), Trent University, Peterborough, ON, January 18, 2013.
319. Joyce Green and Michael Burton, "A Twelve-Step Program for a Post-Colonial Future," *Canadian Dimension*, December 6, 2013. (https://canadiandimension.com)

Mnjikaning people have hosted gatherings of tribes and travellers for millennia at the ancient fish weirs of The Narrows at Lake Couchiching (Chippewa for *Lake of Many Winds*). In accordance with Anishnaabe values that are embedded in familial relationships with the land, the wild beauty of the commons and the vitality of all people are sustained and nurtured. As modelled to us by the Mnjikaning people, the powerful ability to build bridges for mutual healing and "unity in diversity," and to ensure the well-being of *Earth Community* within the complex ecosystems of forests, deep water lakes, abundant fish, plants and animals, are the *Original Instructions* that we need to emulate today.

First Nations are beginning to notice that many in the dominant society are already unlearning the practices of Empire, moving toward a new epistemic template and embracing the move to bioregionalism and ecological civilization, as Algonquin activist, artist and scholar Paula Sherman describes. *"Our neighbours have begun to decolonize themselves and to also contemplate their relationships and responsibilities within the Natural World. We welcome this direction and respect it as a sign that it is possible to achieve existence within our homeland, wherein the rights of the Natural World and those of human beings are considered together when contemplating resource development and exploitation."*[320] For both native and non-native people, a massive decolonization will mean rejecting capitalism and the resource extraction model in favor of a regained intimacy with the land, and the renewal of sustainable community. Place-based practices may include decentralized, regional governance structures based on participatory, consensus decision-making; local economies revolving around renewable resources such as planting, harvesting, gathering, hunting and fishing; cultural production activities for the requirements of life such as clothing or tools; and ceremonial activities honoring the many sacred qualities of our unique bio-cultural landscape(s). Taking the first steps toward decolonization in both theory and practice is the way forward for all those who call Turtle Island home, and *"taking good care of ourselves, our localized communities and the land is a life-long learning process."*[321] (Robert Lovelace) Coming together in the common crucible of *Rejecting Empire* is an entirely new venture, and hopefully the results will resemble a fusion of the best from both Indigenous and Settler Society.

 Today we are more connected than ever before, and yet we still fail to communicate. Many groups don't have visibility, and when they are finally recognized there is a barrier of stereotypes and stigma which makes connecting with them even harder. In the midst of all this there is a simple solution that has often been overlooked - respect. Respect for oneself, others, and most importantly, Nature.[322] (Daisy Komujuni)

> *"To decolonize means to honour your own roots,*
> *culture and philosophies.*
> *And it's open to everyone regardless of race, colour or creed.*
> *This is how we break the harmful patterns and ideologies*
> *into which we were born.*
> *We are the people of the hoop. We can stop the cycle. Redirect it.*
> *We can honour All Our Relations.*
> *We can be the warriors this world needs."*[323]
> (Aaron Paquette)

320. Paula Sherman, *Dishonour of the Crown: The Ontario Resource Regime in the Valley of the Kiji Sibi*, Arbeiter Ring Publishing, 2008.
321. Robert Lovelace (Tslagi/Algonquin), *The Architecture of a Decolonized Society: Reindigenizing the Self, Community and Environment*, presentation, Kawartha World Issues Centre (KWIC), Trent University, Peterborough, ON, January 18, 2013.
322. Daisy Komujuni, "Looking to the Past to Heal the Problems of the Future," review of *Wisakedjak*, based on Dr. Paula Sherman's 2007 PhD dissertation, chapter entitled "Wisakedjak and the Explorer/Colonizer," Market Hall Performing Centre, Peterborough, ON, *Arthur: The Peterborough and Trent University Independent Press*, October 28, 2013. (http://trentarthur.ca)
323. Aaron Paquette, "The Validity of Conflict in Resistance," *Aaron Paquette Network*, November 19, 2013. (www.aaronpaquette.net)

Rejecting Empire ~ The Psyche & Myth-Busting

In the process of *Rejecting Empire*, we come to realize that preserving the neocolonial corporate paradigm is not a rational choice, and it is only by stepping outside of the imperialist power-program that we will develop a mind and soul free of offensive conditioning. Uncolonization is a personal choice made by dismantling the western mind, and as a response to the dangers of modernity, our goal is to achieve a re-balancing in ourselves and the other spheres of human activity. Deeply embedded in our psyches, the core memes of Empire have been created, spread, upheld and perpetuated over time, yet it is patently untrue (and another lie of Empire) that somehow the very structure of the human mind has pre-determined these choices. All of us hold the power and have the agency to challenge our habitual thinking and belief systems, and like the "myth-busting" suggestions below, to make the essential changes in attitude that are required for the recovery of an ecocentric worldview. Once we have decided to locate the conditioning that Empire has inculcated in our hearts, minds and souls, we can work to eliminate this programming, and then go on to resist the ongoing conditioning that Empire continues to push at us. Far from the rainbow-shaman "heal yourself first and the world will follow" superficial self-seeking project as touted by the *New Age Industry*, we need to dig much deeper to see that the systemic ego-driven insatiability of capitalism we have internalized is the real enemy. The new trend toward essentialism, downshifting and saying "no" doesn't even begin to cover the extreme amount of rejecting and relinquishing we need to master, with "NO," "NO" and "NO" becoming our daily mantra. Decolonization must be the most difficult challenge we face individually and as a species, to unplug from the false paradigm of Empire and unlimited progress, and to dismantle the systems of hierarchy and humancentric entitlement that make it possible.

"We only become what we are by the radical and deep-seated refusal of that which others have made of us." (Jean-Paul Sartre)

"You can best serve civilization by being against what usually passes for it." (Wendell Berry)

"Decolonizing is not just the recovery of the memory traces of indigenous identities in all of us, but a creative psycho-spiritual, moral, political and activist endeavor. First and foremost, decolonization must turn its gaze to the center of colonial processes, Europe, and interrupt the process of our self-colonization."[324]
(Jürgen Werner Kremer and R. Jackson-Paton)

By no means a comprehensive list, this initial foray into revealing our colonized habits will hopefully lead to a fuller inventory of unlearning, and to new thinking, gestures and actions that will reflect our responsibilities to *Earth Community*. Uncolonization starts off as an individual practice, but it is important to quickly move forward in solidarity with our communities and/or chosen kinship groups. As more and more people answer the call to change our thinking patterns and ways of living, we will begin to insist on system-wide transformation, and the shift to an ecocentric paradigm and peaceful co-existence will become an unstoppable movement.

Reject consumer capitalism. How much do we really need to live a comfortable life? The Settler Society has strayed far beyond the boundaries of natural law that keep us in balance with the natural world, and it is likely that in the near future we will pay the price for this miscalculation in countless drastic ways. The current levels of consumption cannot be maintained, and it is far better to begin our uncolonization process now, to give up our expectation of material wealth and endless accumulation, and to see our privileges and benefits as the illusions that they are. We have been conditioned to view ourselves in the mirror of fabulous lavish luxury and ostentatious wealth, and to think that the best backdrop for our happiness is the exquisitely high-appointed lifestyles of the high-rolling jet-setters. This colonial dream is an unsustainable fantasy, the planet cannot sustain all of us living like kings and queens, and anyone that indulges in the major acquisition of luxury goods and services is stealing the future

---

324. Jürgen Werner Kremer and R. Jackson-Paton, *Ethnoautobiography: Stories and Practices for Unlearning Whiteness, Decolonization, Uncovering Ethnicities*, ReVision Publishing, 2013. (http://ethnoautobiography.net)

from the *Seven Generations* yet to come. Capitalism and consumerism have infiltrated every aspect of our lives, and it will take much examination to discern between the things we need, and the things we think we need. Beyond the necessities for a comfortable life, we must give up the "greed to possess" and the desire for extraneous and superficial materialism. True uncolonization means we have an obligation to view the collecting of beautiful expensive "things" or "experiences" as morally reprehensible, and to actively protest this consumer behavior. Forget about the compulsion to acquire the perfect partner, the perfect vehicle, the perfect home, the perfect décor, the perfect furniture, the perfect appliances, the perfect internet device, the perfect HD surround sound, the perfect giant screen, the perfect set of friends, the perfect job, the perfect restaurant, the perfect travel destination, the perfect wedding in paradise, the perfect spot to picnic, the perfect place to canoe, the perfect tools, gadgets or sports equipment, the perfect skin care products and the perfect wardrobe. You are morally bankrupt if you think that these non-essential superfluous things are achievable goals in the present and will continue to be in the future. Reject the notion that industrial civilization is the only way to live, or that those of us in the western world will continue to live this way for decades to come. Be content with the simple things, find valuable meaning in slowing down, going for a walk, riding a bike, basic unadorned food choices, a few good pieces of clothing, the beauty of the ecosystem, exploring your community and landbase, tending the gardens, the company of friends and the more-than-human world, and the pleasures of your own making in art, craft, music and text. There are countless alternatives to the opiates and distractions of shopping therapy, the accumulation of "stuff," and being defined by what you buy, use and wear. Stop chasing after the latest trend, and learn to be a creator instead of a consumer! Accumulate only what you require to fulfill your purpose, and focus on what you can give back to the world, not what you can consume. Our liberation from Empire comes from having gratitude for what we already have, not from wanting more, and true happiness is realized from creativity, spiritual pursuits, and being of service to others and the land. Replace the shopping malls with employee-owned essential businesses, solar grids, greenhouses, gardens, art studios, gratitude cafes, comidas and community activity spaces! Learning to live well within the boundaries of natural law means giving up the artificial and erroneous notions of entitlement and privilege, being content with the principles of wabi-sabi (the beauty of imperfection), giving thanks, and working on true cultural cohesion - economic alternatives, localization, sustainable patterns and building community.

Reject the impact of commercialism on your identity formation by resisting the brainwashing coming from the worlds of entertainment, movies, sports and fashion. Above and beyond a healthy sharing of creative ideas, the marketing machines in these mega-industries exist to make you think you need something that you do not, or that you are someone you are not. The notion that the excitement and indulgence of shopping is a necessary part of our emotional life, or that the acquisition of material goods makes us feel safe and secure, or that specific "brands" in sports or fashion define who we are, are all powerful illusions that amount to a web of capitalist lies. As consumers we are conditioned to invest our identify in the hubristic fantasies of mass-produced movies, music, fashion and sports, all products designed to extract wealth from the masses to fund the money managers and palatial lifestyles of the megalomaniacal rich and famous, financing the so-called "creative" (or more apt) glitzy side of the capitalist paradigm. Haven't you wondered why the success of non-business people like guitarists, writers, performance artists and hockey players are still gauged by how much money they make? From the capitalist paradigm we have internalized the key principle that wealth and fame equals worth, and are measures of that worth, but this is a grievous delusion resulting from the absence of true connection and the sacred in our lives. It can be said that the degree to which you buy into celebrity worship and the idolization of others (who are simply people, just like you) is the exact same degree of what you lack in self-knowledge, self-love, maturity, adulthood and your own enlivement of the sacred. Also, the impulses generated by pop culture and the toys and gadgets of the lavish cult of consumerism indicate a complete alienation from natural law and the organic processes of the Earth. When you pursue the most "hip" or "cool" or "trendy" surroundings, wardrobe and articulations for years and years (and years) in narcissistic bliss as the boomer generation has done, Empire has found full expression through your parasitic existence, and neither you nor your wasteful lifestyle has done anything to maintain the ecological integrity of the planet.

Reject the impact of commercialism on your spiritual life. The blueprint of capitalist consumerism and endless innovation runs deep, and it is a peculiar delusion endemic to North Americans to think that spiritual enlightenment can also be obtained in the marketplace. Spiritual products, conferences and workshops have become commodities, and careers in self-help, spirituality and self-empowerment have become big business. Clearly, any society that needs to constantly revise or re-create a spiritual practice, or "pay to pray," has blended their priorities into a strange new world. In the same way that we strive to keep the sacred (religious bias) separate from the secular (political sphere), perhaps we also need to realize that the economic paradigm has no business in our spiritual lives, and adopt other structures of energy exchange for spiritual sharing like community sessions, barter, or the gift economy. We could use much Indigenous ingenuity in this area, or "injunuity"[325] and look to the integration between the sacred and profane as achieved in Indigenous societies.

Reject artificial values that are not your own. Instead of a direct experience of the natural world and the processes in nature that affect our well-being in every aspect of our lives, Empire has surrounded us with synthetic ideas and infrastructures that cushion us from reality. Instead of genuine connection and participation in living communities, both human and other-than-human, we are conditioned to conform to societies that are artificially created to suit fabricated notions of politesse and prosperity. Instead of participating in the natural flow of life, we are held back by a static fixation on an ideal set of circumstances that will never be fulfilled. The maintenance of the capitalist consumer society is unsustainable both physically and mentally, and we need to reject the artificial values of Empire in favor of models such as rewilding, reindigenization, and regaining our place within *Earth Community*. Our conditioning can be broken, and our belief systems can be changed.

Reject the success = happiness myth. One of the great memes of Empire is the idea that true happiness can only be achieved when we have reached the pinnacle of financial achievement, success in the workplace, or the leadership (domination) of others. Only a market-based society would perpetuate the fallacy that being a high achiever is the only worthy goal, and this false myth teaches us that our physical, emotional and spiritual well-being is dependent on wealth, power, and the ongoing accumulation of property, objects and experiences. The dichotomy of the "haves" and the "have-nots," the "winners" and the "losers" accentuates difference, creates false hierarchies between the rich and the poor, and does nothing to bring people together. "Success" is only achievable with hyperindividualism (or stand-alone corporatism) that promotes the values of self-interest and competition above all, and in many cases, puts enormous pressure on the individual psyche to live up to impossible goals. The commodification of human skills is built on a toxic system of evaluation, judgement and qualification that is objectifying, demeaning, depersonalizing, infantalizing and alien-ating, and there is no compunction to value community or share knowledge or expertise with others. And even though western society is engineered around the theme of meritocracy, many at the top are there only because of inherited wealth, bullying, illegal activity or other sociopathic skills, instead of superior vision or leadership ability. Hyperstructured work environments can be authoritarian, bureaucratic places of control, and surveillance and rules are applied to increase

---

325. *Injunuity* TV Series, Dir. Adrian Baker, animated documentaries and ongoing multimedia projects at (www.injunuity.org, 2015). *"Injunuity is a collage of reflections on the Native American world, our shared past, our turbulent present, and our undiscovered future. From Columbus to the western expansion to tribal casinos, we are taught that the Native way, while at times glorious, is something of the past, something that needed to be replaced by a manifest destiny from across the ocean. But in a world increasingly short of real answers, it is time we looked to Native wisdom for guidance. It is time for some Injunuity."*

production and further the goals of the corporation and the ideology of Empire. In marked contrast, the individual in IK/EIK societies is accountable to the well-being of their own kinship group, who in turn are accountable to the well-being of the individual - and at the root of these values of respect and reciprocity, everyone is accountable to the land, the other-than-human-world, and the entire *Earth Community*. Claiming our true freedom means choosing to live outside of the established narrative of "success." We need to get back to ecocentric values as the source of our happiness, and the dictates of corporate-capitalism are not the answer.

Reject hierarchy and privilege. Empire has inculcated us with the toxic structures of patriarchal hierarchies that are ultimately damaging to ourselves and the planet. Beyond the necessary leadership that tends to emerge organically in any human collective, ranking, stratification, "othering" and oppression have no place in the new paradigm. Uncolonization means being aware of how and when we perpetuate racism, classism, speciesism, ableism or genderism, and working to rid ourselves of this conditioning. Judge people for their actions on behalf of the living earth and their kind compassion for all beings, not by their gender, age, colour, wealth (or lack thereof), culture, sexual orientation or ability! Once you see that the various intersectional hierarchies of Empire and your place within them are an illusion, it becomes impossible to maintain or benefit from the privileges of ethnicity, gender, wealth, ableism or heteronormativity.

Reject domination. *"The arrogant doomed principle upon which our civilization is based is that the world was made for man, and man was made to conquer and rule it."*[326] (Daniel Quinn) Of course, to live in a society that prizes dominance is to have dominance in our souls. Watch how you monopolize any situation, sphere of activity or ecosystem, and be mindful of how your speech and actions directly or indirectly convey that unmistakable sense of racial, economic, cultural, or even human, superiority. In direct opposition to what we have been taught by the business model of capitalist consumerism that promotes competition, individualism and the cult of narcissism, the world does not revolve around you, your hypertrophied ego or your petty ambitions and concerns. Collectively, and as a species, we need to re-learn our humble place within natural law and the natural cycles of life, which brings us to our next point - humility.

Reject self-importance. A huge driver in the building of Euro-Empire has been our delusional separation from the natural world, and humanity's place within the circle of all life. Our humancentric bias has convinced us that it is only our admiration for ourselves, and the obsession with our own creations and technological achievements that

---

326. Daniel Quinn, *The Story of B: An Adventure of the Mind and Spirit*, Bantam, 1997.

is important. Our own inflated egos and self-obsessions are a microcosm of the system-wide imperialist **EGO** that puts the needs of human beings before anything or anyone else. Some day we will pay the price for this huge and hubristic mistake. On this gorgeous paradise of a planet, surrounded by natural wonders and the manifestations of mysteries we will never fully understand, our best response would be to cultivate an attitude of humility, gratitude and grace.

Reject the notion that human beings have some kind of special "entitlement." The so-called "perfect" conditions of weather that provide us with beautiful sunny days are not just the backdrop to a textbook set of activities that further your appearance, your ego, your need for acquisition, or the diligent daily machinations of capitalism you enact to perpetuate the goals of Empire. The phenomena and elements of nature that make themselves apparent to us as humans are a blessing and our highest authority, not something to take for granted, ignore, put in a cage, or complain about when the conditions don't suit us. Forget about the perfect weather, the perfect car, the perfect outfit and the perfect pet to showcase the perfect you - the natural world is not there to be enslaved and endlessly provide for your egocentric wants and needs. Our only status is to stay respectfully within the boundaries set out in natural law, and the notion of human entitlement is a tragic delusion.

Reject adolescence (unless you are an adolescent). Have you ever wondered why pop stars in their 50's and 60's act exactly the same as someone who is 18, or a man in his 60's drives around in a flashy sports car hoping to impress someone? This highly visible behavior is a reflection of the entire egocentric value system of the western world, that disavows the wisdom and responsibility associated with true elderhood, promoting instead an arrested adolescence "forever young" mentality. Our difficult transition through adolescence (the passage of puberty) has never been fully supported in western society, and therefore the immature patterns from this stage of life continue on in the insecurity, identity confusion, self-gratification, displaced aggression, jealousy, relentless greed and power obsessions that are endemic to world leaders, celebrities and citizens alike. The structures of Empire (i.e. the workplace) treat adults like children incapable of thinking independently, and this infantalization has given rise to all sorts of pathologies and behaviors, such as narcissism, living in a fantasy world, hero (or heroine) worship, hostile competition, racism, ageism, violence, lack of moral development, and the inability to have intimate relationships. The worst part of this infantalization is that we lack any sense of boundaries or limits, which explains the conspicuous consumption and unchecked materialism of the industrial growth model that is now threatening the Earth. Our egocentric entitlement and privilege even blinds us to the fact that the massive energy footprint we have created with our self-absorbed participation in capitalism has jeopardized the well-being of the *Seven Generations* yet to come. Both individually and as a species, we need to develop the maturity to know that we are **not** above natural law, that boundaries and restrictions **do** apply to us, that we need to uncolonize and simplify our lifestyles, and that passing a secure world on to our children is our top priority. Making the long-delayed passage to reach true adulthood means learning the skills of empathy instead of focusing on our own selfish needs, shifting to ecocentric thoughts and actions that protect the intrinsic rights of all species, rooting our lives in the cycles and wisdom of nature, and taking responsibility to make conscious decisions that enable the well-being of the entire *Earth Community*.

Reject self-indulgence. Don't get caught in the self-absorbed emotional traps of fatalism, escapism, alienation, apathy, numbness or ennui – there is work to be done! You are part of a living ecosystem, and your gratitude for the natural world that sustains you, should ennoble and empower you to hold the vision for a return to earth-centered culture and spiritual ecology. To please the Divine is to treat yourself scrupulously with total love, respect and positive energy, and to know that you are the perfect manifestation of beautiful exalted glowing divinity. *"Love yourself. Then forget it. Then, love the world."*[327] (Mary Oliver) It is essential to be rooted in your own goodness, then to seek healthy expressions in acts of generosity, empathy and kindness toward all beings. We have to have the collective will, and each one of us doing what we can to honour, protect and restore Mother Earth for all life and the generations yet to come. Of course the attractions and amenities of Empire are hard to shake, but one is either caught up in the mutual delusional fantasy or one is not, and the *Earth Community* movement is the only one that counts. Detoxify your life by eliminating activities that do not align with your true values, and negative pastimes that emit a low vibration, such as gossip, personal drama or consumer entertainment.

Embrace Critical Thinking Skills. Instead of encouraging a good intellectual workout, exchange or dialogue, Empire sustains its hierarchy of command by not emphasizing critical thinking, or offering much in the way of CT training in the educational system. There is a pitiful lack of critical thinking in society today, and perceived as a threat, taboos are even in place to deny, devalue, disparage and shun those who employ critical thinking skills in their daily discourse. Mainstream neo-liberal society spends the majority of its time in emotional territory, a middle-class morass of emotive values that alternately inspire, provoke or stimulate us to new heights and directions, or manipulate us with wish fulfillments, memes and material objects, all clamouring for our attention and competing for our heartstrings. Consumer capitalism is successful precisely because it

---

327. Mary Oliver, *Evidence: Poems*, Beacon Press, 2010.

appeals to our emotional lives, and addresses our perceived inadequacies, lacks, and longings with products and services that will ostensibly and miraculously make things better. We can certainly apply critical thinking to every feature of western society, but examining the ways that we are deceived and manipulated by consumer capitalism would be a great place to start. Critical thinking and deep analysis may be the most important qualities for surviving and thriving in these tumultuous times. Developing good critical thinking skills is the ultimate empowerment, and may literally save your life.

Embrace your True Self. It is essential to continue the process of uncolonizing the fabricated identities we have assumed from our conditioning and what we do for a living, and to reclaim our authentic self. Solitude, deep introspection, time spent in nature, dreamwork, and other spaces and places outside of Empire allow us to explore who we really are, and to claim the ideas and pursuits that make us feel most vibrant and alive. As mature adults with the responsibility to care for the interwoven relationships we are blessed to have with each other and the other-than-human world, each one of us has an important purpose and valuable skill to contribute to the whole. A wonderful resource for discovering our true ecocentric identity, soul purpose and vocation as rooted in the cycles of wild nature is Bill Plotkin's *Nature and the Human Soul: Cultivating Wholeness and Community in a Fragmented World*. Actualizing our true identity as embedded in *Earth Community* will lead to the cultural transformation of both the individual and the collective.

Embrace Community. Don't buy into the myth of social isolation-ism that Empire has perpetuated to keep us working like cogs in the modern wheel of endless industry and disconnected from one another. The toxic cult of individualism, the sterility of our institutions, the competition in the workplace, and the endless entertainments and distractions of the man-made world do not lead to the happiness, security and connectivity that we crave. Like all networks in the natural world, human societies are also mutually empowered by the gifts of sharing, and by the care of one another. Our survival is dependent on supporting the collective and the collective supporting us, and western industrialized capitalist societies seem to have forgotten this essential fact. *Rejecting Empire* in this case means putting an effort into sustaining our current relationships, nurturing new connections, building healthy social networks, and linking people together in authentic ways for community building, healing, soul nourishment and celebration. Children, youth, marginalized groups and the elderly are especially affected by the dehumanizing pathologies of Empire. Creating new forms of authentic human connection, finding meaning once again in our bonds with the natural world, and re-engaging with our friends, neighbours and local community is essential for making the shift from "I" to "We," and the elusive *Beloved Community* that humanitarian Martin Luther King envisioned. Having compassion for one another, making decisions together, and sharing our basic needs such as housing, food, alternative healthcare and healing modalities, will go far in acknowledging our interdependence, and materializing the inevitable post-Empire ecological (and re-indigenized) world.

Embrace the Sacred. For millennia now, the nonspiritual society that modern civilization has created can be located by the glaring lack of spiritual values at the root of the systems, structures and relationships we now take for granted. For some bewildering reason human beings have adapted well to materialistic life, and like *Wonder Woman* without her superpowers, the vast majority of us are accustomed to the dysfunction of the profane, which is far from our natural way of being. Bizarre practices that are substitutes for drawing close to the divine begin to be normalized. An example of what can happen in a non-spiritual society is the "cult of celebrity" and the excessive godlike worship of actors, musicians, artists and writers. Everyday creative practices - one's "bliss" - become a commodified elitist activity instead of the artistic expressions that are authentic to us all. As a result of materialism, we have lost the ability to realize the world through a spiritual lens or to see life in a sacred manner among all sacred beings, and this disconnect means we are constantly seeking to understand the meaning of life over and over again. Human beings are first and foremost spiritual beings, an integral part of the interconnected web of life, and we need personal and communal expressions of our essential "unity of being" such as ritual, myth, ceremony, song, dance and tribal art as much as we need food and drink. Experiencing the natural world simply and directly connects us to wisdom long buried under the illusions of civilization, and our connection to "natura," the soul of nature, is essential for true happiness. Our task is to regain our awe and reverence for nature, to celebrate magic, earth spirits and mystic forms or tools as conduits to aliveness and mythical modes, and to return to the collective soul beyond rationalism, materialism, positivism, scientism, mechanism, empiricism and secularism. "*It is not easy to overcome or heal thousands of years of patriarchal conditioning and its influence and manifestations in our own psyches, lives or world. But if we are to do this, we must integrate with the living Earth, the Gaia-field.*"[328] (Leila Castle) The Earth is alive, the helping spirits are active, the elemental forces are already in place ready to mix and blend with our activities, and ancient places and wild creatures continue to roam the plains of vision, myth and imagination. Accessing dreams and primal memory through creative expressions in earth-wise ritual, rites of passage, art, music, literature or outdoor theatre reveals ancient forms of consciousness, the mysterious realms, the manifestation of inter-relatedness, and our co-creation with nature. Embracing the sacred

---

328. Leila Castle, "Dragon Priestesses of the Earth," *Earthwalking Sky Dancers: Women's Pilgrimages to Sacred Places*, Frog Ltd. Books, 1996.

through an active soul connection to the land and the stewardship of *Earth Community* naturally creates a deeply grounded and authentic spiritual life, the same enchanted and holistic world that our tribal ancestors experienced, and to which we must return. As we rewild our lives and embrace Gaia once again, reclaiming ourselves as spiritual beings is integral to the re-enchantment of the world.

Embrace Massive Change. There is no doubt that the years ahead will challenge our fundamental belief systems, and both natural and man-made events may force us to change our entire way of life. Our civilization and our worldview are not eternal or unassailable, and contrary to what the green-veneered neo-liberals believe, our high-consumption lifestyle cannot be maintained with a few simple adjustments to energy resources or the shift to a so-called "knowledge economy." The more that we remain in denial about peak oil and massive change, the more painful it will be. All actions have consequences, and when an Empire is built on principles that go beyond the boundaries of natural law, it will fall. It's just a matter of time. We were born to be witnesses to this turbulent time, and instead of getting all traumatized about it, we can be joyful that such a toxic civilization may be ending. In an uncertain world, the best response would be to ground our souls in overwhelming gratitude for the gift of life, and to be thankful that we have the agency to make choices that lead to the healing of ourselves, and the remediation of *Earth Community*.

Modalities and philosophies for *Rejecting Empire* can be applied to both personal and collective transformation, and once we have addressed the "neurodecolonization" (term © Michael Yellow Bird, PhD) of our psyches, we can turn to the practicalities that make a good life possible in ecological communities. Experiencing enduring, caring relationships with kindred spirits and the natural world by embracing the *Old Ways* in new configurations is our sacred task and responsibility. There is power in cooperation, and the most important activity is to love the land, know the trees, work with the soil, celebrate sacred cycles through art and song, and rewild our lives with natural foods, natural medicines and sustainable energy. By living within our ecological means, embracing non-linear timelines, and focusing on small localized communities, we can *Occupy Earth* (!) with new delight, respect and reverence. Are we willing to trade western knowledge, western civilization and its amenities for a return to the garden and right relationship with the land? Activating indigenous mind and remembering the wholeness of tribal reality is the timeless paradigm we venture into, and the following compilation of means and methods provide guideposts on the journey. There are diverse and exciting uncolonizing options available right now in every sphere of human existence, and as we build a new world we must also step up our work as social activists in challenging the old paradigms of hierarchy and stratification.

Rejecting Empire ~ Practicalities, Movements & Tools

"It takes vision, courage and stamina to break away from the pack, to carve out a niche where you can sustain yourself and your family without being consumed by commercialism and technology, and without inflicting more damage on an already wounded world. All that's missing is the blueprint."[329] (Tilda Truchan)

"To change the world we need to hand out real tools, rugged, free, collaborative tools for understanding the world and our role in it, for seeing the systems in which we are trapped - tools for learning how to work together to either transform those systems or destroy them completely and bioremediate the rubble. Tools that help us as people make meaningful changes in both our own lives and the world. We need to make people participants, not consumers."[330]
(Gina Colamarino)

Voluntary Simplicity, Simple Living, Downshifting, and the Slow Movement. Giving up the unsustainable ethics, corporatism, materialism and fast pace of the capitalist paradigm means downshifting, and slowing down to the rhythms and cycles of the natural world. The impulse to decelerate and choose a life connected to nature and community is becoming a major movement today, and rejects the technological premise that ongoing "progress" and innovation is normal, that life has to continuously speed up, or that we have to "keep up." The voluntary simplicity and simple living movements are gaining ground, with subcultures thriving that emphasize "quality over quantity" in regard to our basic needs of food, shelter, creativity, community and ultimately, connection. The growing "less is more" anti-consumerism movement allows us to concentrate on the things that really make us happy, like self-expression, family, friends, community, locally-sourced food, and EIK traditions connected to the land. These cultural movements interweave beautifully with green living, the forming of intentional and collaborative communities, rewilding, permaculture, ecological restoration, and the reclaiming of our eco-selves. Slowing down and stepping ouside of the chaos of modern life will automatically give us a perspective more in harmony with our agrarian and indigenous ancestors.

Duane Elgin – Voluntary Simplicity (http://duaneelgin.com)
The Simplicity Collective (http://simplicitycollective.com)
Happy Simple Living (www.happysimpleliving.com)
Slow Movement (www.slowmovement.com)
Slow Food (www.slowfood.com)
The World Institute of Slowness
(www.theworldinstituteofslowness.com)
Center for a New American Dream   (www.newdream.org) *"We seek to cultivate a new American dream—one that emphasizes community, ecological sustainability, and the celebration of non-material values."*

"Life really is better when you get off the technological/industrial wheel and conceive of some other way. It makes people happier. It may not make them more money, but getting more money hasn't worked out. Filling life with commodities doesn't turn out to be satisfying, and most people know that."[331] (Jerry Mander)

Localvore, Slow Food & CSA. For our optimum health, and break the stranglehold the capitalist fossil fuel-burning food industry has on our food supply, nothing is more important than reconnecting with our local food sources and establishing local food security. Enjoying exotic foods that are transported thousands of miles to reach our plate may soon be a thing of the past, and the unsustainable global distribution model that is "high in greenhouse debt" has no place in post-peak living. At the same time that we are recovering our ancient earth-honoring EIK traditions and reinhabiting the land, we also need to sink our roots deeply in the food systems of our ecoregion, grow our own food, and build relationships with local farmers and food producers. To have healthy, thriving, sustainable community we need nutrient-rich, fresh food that has been grown in healthy, nutrient-rich soil, and farming that supports the "field to fork" or "garden to table" model leads to improved soil health, species diversity and environmental sustainability. More than a passing trend, the "localvore" movement means acquiring food in season and all year-round in a 50 to 75-kilometer radius from home, a "foodshed" ideally aligned with the watershed and natural features of our local bioregion. In agriculture today, there is a major shift happening toward the green principles of local, organic, seasonal, sustainable and fair trade produce, and counting our food miles means knowing and supporting the progressive farmers who are actualizing these ideals. Eating local, and re-situating our food production, processing and distribution network within our own bioregion enhances the overall economic, environmental and social vibrancy of our communities. Like a revival of the timeless "village square," farmer's markets and other community events based on food and food production are rapidly becoming the focus for our social life, with offerings of healing modalities, seasonal celebrations, café culture, expressions in art, craft, music or theatre, and alternative economies.

Farmer-to-consumer markets are challenging corporate agriculture and reducing the carbon footprint, and even better are the pre-arranged CSA ("Community Shared Agriculture") distribution ventures that unite

329. Tilda Truchan, "The Vision," *A Resource Guide for Green and Alternative Enterprises in the Haliburton Highlands Bioregion*, Haliburton County Community Co-operative, 2000.
330. Gina Colamarino, Facebook Comment, 2013.
331. Jerry Mander as cited in an interview on his book "In the Absence of the Sacred: The Failure of Technology and the Survival of the Indian Nations," *The Sun, A Magazine of Ideas*, Issue 192, November 1991.

farmer and consumer during the growing cycle. Providing much-needed capital, the consumer invests in the farm at the beginning of the season and receives high-quality delicious and nutritious food each week, like fresh seasonal fruits, vegetables, greens, herbs, eggs, poultry or maple syrup. The concept of food hubs is also on the rise, and these regional food system solutions show great promise for strengthening sustainability, and offering fresh, whole and locally-grown food directly to consumers. Since 1986, the *Slow Food Movement* continues to celebrate local culinary traditions and foods worldwide, and encourages the growth of plants, seeds and livestock that are indigenous to local ecosystem(s). In addition to lobbying against GMO's, protesting pesticide use, and encouraging ethical buying, the objectives of slow food and agroecology include maintaining seed diversity banks to preserve heirloom varieties, preserving and promoting local and traditional food products, and organizing small-scale food processing in the community. The *Slow Food Movement* emphasizes the centrality of growing, preparing and enjoying food to all ethnocultural traditions, and the importance of returning to these traditional values in our cultural recovery. Eating locally and with the seasonal cycles is an important aspect of the *Old Ways*, and these practices can renew the ancient patterns of sustenance that build strength and the overall health of both self and community.

Of course, growing our own food allows us to spend quality time in the outdoor spaces we have created, and reverses "nature deficit disorder" while at the same time providing us with beautiful fruits, vegetables, flowers and herbs. Building greenhouses, saving seeds, companion planting, learning permaculture methods and eco-friendly gardening with old-fashioned rain barrels and hand tools are all connective ways to grow organic food for yourself and your community. Permaculture transforms the consumer model into a co-creation partnership with the patterns of the natural world, and sharing tasks and tools, hosting a seed exchange, protecting heirloom varieties and participating in community-supported agriculture further these holistic principles at the local level. With a brilliant new movement known as "foodscaping," urban neighbourhoods are blossoming, each yard transformed into an organic garden. The planting of specific fruits, vegetables, herbs and flowers are agreed on ahead of time by all involved, so that produce can be traded and shared. Acquiring fresh healthy food from the yards in our neighbourhood instead of supermarkets is certainly an idea whose time has come, and hopefully foodscaping will begin to happen all over the world! We may not all take up farming in the years ahead, but the choices we make in food purchasing and advocating for legislation as related to localvore and slow food will have a major impact on replacing the wasteful and unsustainable global food industry.

If done sustainably and with respect, harvesting natural foods in the wild can also contribute to our own health and the well-being of the community. The most important rule for foraging and wild-crafting is to take only what you need, leaving enough of the species to propagate itself and nourish the other plants in the food forest. To return to our sacred relationship in reciprocity with *Earth Community*, planting trees, forest farming, and helping to restore the well-adapted native plants that were part of a region's biodiversity before Empire will stabilize the soil and rewild the land. Eating lower on the food chain by reducing meat, cooking in bulk, turning meals into rituals, composting, and reducing throw-away packaging are all *Slow Food* essentials. At the very least, our earth-wise cultural recovery means rejecting "big food" corporate agriculture that has a massive carbon footprint, and turning our support instead to our friends and neighbours, and local field or forest farmers committed to regenerative practices.

Post-Peak Living & the Transition Movement. The post-peak living movement is focused on present-day preparations for the inevitability of the "global contraction" financial crisis and low-energy society of the future, as oil begins to run out and goods and services become more expensive. It is likely that we will not be living with the same luxuries, amenities, opportunities and expectations in the future that we have now, and adapting to this new reality will mean a heightened reliance on establishing food security, localization, community rights and relationships, living simply, being content with less, sharing, exchanging, and building resilience. For those called to leadership, the goal will be to empower others to let go of the trappings of civilization to which they have become accustomed, and to survive and thrive in chaotic times.

(www.postpeakliving.com)
(www.peakprosperity.com)
(www.collapsenet.com)
(www.postcarbon.org)

In response to the key issues facing humanity today such as peak oil, global warming, rapid change and economic instability, the *Transition Town* movement is a *"quiet revolution unfolding around the world,"* and the first Transition Town to be initiated in Canada was my home community of Peterborough, Ontario! Founded in the UK by Rob Hopkins, the *Transition Network* challenges the idea that relentless economic expansion is a good thing (or even possible on a finite planet) and that we need to grow local community instead, focusing on social justice, well-being and resilience (which is the ability to respond and adapt to the unexpected). Establishing a collective sustainable vision for our community or neighbourhood with local economies, alternative currencies, peer-to-peer businesses, wealth-sharing, alternative livelihoods, community foodshares, community gardens, localvore, permaculture, greenspace protection, ecologic restoration, grassroots activism and community-owned renewable energy are all initiatives that reduce the ecological footprint and contribute to a low-carbon future. Positive local action is the way to change the world, and *Transition* provides the map and the tools for supportive, nurturing, healthy communities. *"Localize, Reskill, Resilience - Sustainable Relationships, not Sustainable Development!"* There are thousands of *Transition Town* communities in 40 countries around the world - you can become a transitionist in your own community or establish your own. (www.transitionnetwork.org)

The New Economy and Alternative Currencies. Movements such as social justice, Indigenous rights and earth democracy are deeply intertwined, and the current economic paradigm is the primary source of inequality, oppression and violence toward human societies and *Earth Community*. In these times of growing economic instability, it has become increasingly clear that alternatives must be found to replace the dysfunction of the current monetary system with other means of exchange based on equity and sustainability. In her far-reaching work on anti-capitalism, Naomi Klein has identified that *"endless growth doesn't deliver well-being or economic stability, and is leading to widening inequality."*[333] With the objective to decentralize, reconstruct or replace capitalism, theories and movements such as Degrowth, the New Economy, Deep Economy, Cooperative Economy, Gift Economy, Generosity Economy, Sacred Economy, Caring Economy, Shareconomy, Slow Money, Solidarity Economy, Solution Economy, Regenerative Economy, Moneyless Society, and Community Resilience are emerging worldwide. The more individuals and collectives that can participate and shift over to these new economies, the more smoothly and effective the transition will be, as a critical mass, from Empire to *Earth Community*.

"The economy is a wholly owned subsidiary of the environment, not the reverse."[332] (Herman E. Daly)

For centuries now, control and dominance have characterized the humancentric attitude toward the natural world, and culminating in today's economic dysfunction, *"capitalism has the dubious honor of being the first civilization lacking in a cosmovision."*[334] (Chris Gilbert) Our greed, attachment to money, and the illusory promise of more money to come, has led to the outer limits of what the natural world can sustain in terms of exploitation and destruction. Clearly, moving forward to an equitable and ecologically-balanced world will mean

---

332. Herman E. Daly, *Steady-State Economics: 2nd Edition with New Essays*, Island Press, 1991.
333. *The Big Issue*, "Naomi Klein Interview: A 3-Day Week Will Help to Save Life on Earth," December 14, 2014. (www.bigissue.com)
334. Chris Gilbert, "Needed: An Ecosocialist Cosmovision," *Climate & Capitalism*, May 10, 2013. (http://climateandcapitalism.com)

readjusting our attitudes to money, releasing ourselves from the tyranny of money, and creating alternatives to the hegemony of capitalism. By necessity or personal choice, the priority to localize and respect natural boundaries is reflected in modern movements that seek to replace overshoot and excess with new economies and resilient communities. Without losing any of the quality of life that we already have, *Degrowth* is an excellent framework for understanding and living within our biophysical limits, for shrinking the economic system to a level the Earth can sustain, and for transitioning to sustainable forms of technology, production and consumption. It is impossible to provide high-end affluence for every person on the planet anyway, and the consumer-driven lifestyle and accumulation of material goods must decline in favor of community cohesion, social justice, nature connection, voluntary simplicity, personal well-being and planetary health. Aspects of the *Deep Economy* model as promoted by Bill McGibbon[335] include re-thinking the nonsensical notion of "endless progress," rejecting strict "economic theory" in favor of realistic possibilities at the local and ecological level, switching to the reliance on community instead of the stand-alone "capitalist self," and identifying what truly makes us happy.

Responding to the systemic challenges of our time, the *Cooperative Economy* advocates for worker-owned companies and cooperatives at the local grassroots level, resulting in the decentralization of corporate and governmental power. The communal values of municipal enterprise, employee ownership plans, and community land trusts are excellent alternatives to capitalism, and provide local jobs and economic stability. Economic growth (which may or may not occur) is not the objective, and with the *Cooperative Economy* model, community nonprofits can provide essentials such as solar installations for renewable energy, property ownership to support low-income housing, or mega-greenhouse and agricultural operations that supply food to the community and beyond. Health care, childcare, charities and cultural organizations all fit neatly into the *Cooperative Economy* vision, and with the collective values of mutual ownership, consensual decision-making and sustainability, a collaborative approach between human society and *Earth Community* is possible.

Embracing collaborative models and re-inhabiting the commons can create social (as opposed to monetary) capital that infuses community exchange systems as well as the steadily-growing *Gift Economy, Generosity Economy* or *Shareconomy*. The guiding light for the *Gift Economy* movement, Genevieve Vaughan discovered that the practice of "freebies" such as housework, childcare and other "random acts of

---

335. Bill McKibben, *Deep Economy: The Wealth of Communities and the Durable Future*, Henry Holt and Company, 2007.

kindness" have always existed in society, and have long been unrecognized and unappreciated by the dominant patriarchy. In Vaughan's matriarchal model of a *Gift Economy*, Mother Earth meets all human needs, and is realized as the source of all abundance and joy. Indigenous societies have always known that the most important things - the natural world, the cycle of predator and prey, the elements and the life force itself – are gifts offered freely by the *Great Mystery*, the Creator-Creatrix and/or *Earth Community*, and are far beyond any price or monetary value. It is this unconditional sharing, or the giving and receiving without compensation, that has ensured our continuation as a species! Within matriarchal societies, modes of distribution are based on the principles of nurture, and needs are met directly, resulting in a more functional community than that of a market economy based on self-interest, profit and greed. It is also understood that unconditional giving is more important than receiving, and celebrating the generous gifts of life with the freedom of everyday sharing, feasts and ritual gatherings are integral to community bonding. Gift-giving creates positive relationships, justice and solidarity, and with radical change, the gift paradigm has great potential as an alternative to capitalism. Starting with small gifts and progressing to caregiving, blocks of time, professional services or large bequests, the process of networking and sharing to lift each other up is an amazing confirmation of our care and connectivity in *Earth Community*.

The principles of the *Gift Economy* and *Generosity Economy* are being integrated into viewpoints and practices worldwide, and the *Sacred Economy*[336] as promoted by Charles Eisenstein traces the history of money from ancient gifting systems to the modern paradigm, revealing how capitalism has created scarcity, competition and a lack of community. Capitalism is not working anymore, for anyone, and waking up to the toxicity of Empire is our sacred opportunity to align with the truth, and create an economy that embodies the values of gift-giving at this moment in time. *"The gift economy is not about competition - it is about sharing your abundance with someone else, having the inherent gratitude and grace to give back - and this reciprocity will create security and status for yourself. Gift-giving builds a true community and a true society."*[337] (Charles Eisenstein) The relocalization of economic functions, peer-to-peer financing, sharing in the wealth of the commons, celebrating our cultural heritage and falling in love with the Earth again, are a few of the many ideas and practices in Eisenstein's extensive body of work.

Responding to the lack of imagination and vision in the mainstream discourse on economic reform, Riane Eisler (*The Chalice and the Blade* Page 127-129) has identified that the functions of care-giving have been

---

336, 337. *Sacred Economics with Charles Eisenstein - A Short Film,* Dir. Ian MacKenzie, Fierce Love Films, March 1, 2012. (www.youtube.com)

undervalued, underpaid and ignored by both capitalism and socialism. Calling for a different framework to support sustainable growth and development, Eisler proposes that moving forward will mean examining the type of economy that leads to a fuller realization of human potential, and that new economic policies and practices are required to support the care of people and the environment. To the old economic map that supports the triad of market economy, government economy and illegal economy, Eisler adds three life-sustaining sectors with a much higher value - household economy, natural economy and volunteer economy – new categories that have the greatest potential for addressing the monumental social, economic and environmental challenges we now face. Patriarchal hierarchy, gender superiority, racism, oppression and exploitation are designed to consolidate wealth and power into the hands of the 1%, and to rebalance this domination, Eisler's partnership model offers an egalitarian structure with praxis placing a higher value on mutual respect and caring relations for both family and community. As a major contributor to the public good, it is high time that the caregivers of the children, the sick, the disabled and the elderly are compensated by society or the state, leading to a new definition of "productivity," and an open declaration on what is most important to our happiness and well-being. Embracing the partnership model of the *Caring Economy* would create an abundant, more caring and equitable economic system, and ecological sustainability in *Earth Community*. The mission of the *Center for Partnership Studies (CPS)*[338] as established by Riane Eisler, "*is to accelerate the movement to partnership systems of human rights and nonviolence, gender and racial equity, economic prosperity, and a sustainable environment through research, education, grassroots empowerment, and policy initiatives that promote:*

- *human development,*
- *social well-being, and*
- *long-term economic success, with special emphasis on valuing the work of caring and caregiving still primarily done by women.*"

Building on the possibilities of the *Gift Economy*, different forms of the *Sharing Economy* (i.e. peer-to-peer economy, mesh economy, collaborative economy or collaborative consumption) are growing rapidly throughout the world in response to the ongoing economic crisis, and the movement has a definite role to play in shifting away from the

---

338. You can support this flourishing movement at the *Center for Partnership Studies (CPS): Building Our Future Together* at (www.partnershipway.org) and the *Caring Economy Campaign* (http://caringeconomy.org), or access training to bring the *Caring Economy* to your own community through the *Caring Economy Leadership Program.* CPS is a growing international collective working toward a saner, more practical economic system "*that acknowledges the work of caring for people and the planet as the essential foundation of economic success.*"

dominant paradigm. At the local level and beyond, sharing, exchanging or renting goods, services, transportation, housing, tools, health care and resources has exciting implications for decentralizing capitalism and cultural transformation. *Sharing Economy* structures can be non-profit, for-profit, barter or co-operative, with talents and assets made available to the wider market through networks, online platforms, social media and community exchange systems. Without having to own things outright, peer-to-peer users can rent or share occasional necessities such as transportation or tools, and by boosting the common practice of "reduce, reuse, recycle and repair," items that used to be thrown away are redistributed to others who need them. Goods are absolutely free in markets and local stores such as *The Freecycle Network* (www.freecycle.org) and *Transition Town Media Free Store* (www.mediafreestore.com), or traded through various swap websites. Networks are also growing that offer people with similar interests the ability to share and exchange intangibles such as time, space, expertise, skills and money.

Based on the ideas of Charles Eisenstein plus precepts found in traditional IK, *The Buy Nothing Project* (http://buynothingproject.org) is a worldwide network of local gift economies offering ways and means to give, lend, receive and share, with the emphasis on expressing gratitude, making neighbourhood connections and building community. *Impossible.com* is another popular social network that allows people with similar interests to fulfill their "wishes" freely, and to share services, resources and items at no cost, with "thank you as the currency that is earned but never spent." Registering online with worldwide exchanges such as *NeighborGoods* at (http://neighbor goods.net/) or the *Community Exchange System* at (www.community-exchange.org) provides users with the option to offer something of value that is exchanged (bartered, swapped, gifted or shared) with goods and services of equal value. In terms of the crowdfunding phenomena, financing via *Kickstarter* and *Indiegogo* is a revolutionary way to launch programs and products, and through the *Open Cooperativism* model, *Fair Coop: the Earth Cooperative for a Fair Economy/ FairFunds* focuses on financing projects that add to "people empowerment" and the common good. In the true spirit of generosity, *The Pollination Project* has the mandate to promote anti-oppression, equity and "compassion consciousness," and offers seed grants to social change agents who seek to extend compassion toward all life, both human and other-than-human. In efforts focused on transition and localvore, *Slow Money* is an extension of the *Slow Food* movement, with investors funding small food enterprises, local food systems and organic farms. Overall, the "social consciousness and sustainability economy" is on the rise, and as alternatives to capitalism, the free flow of information and transparent exchange of learning opportunities is also flourishing, with trust as the key requisite between those who give and those who receive.

To make the *Gift Economy* and *Shareconomy* a reality, the challenge is to shift our value systems from personal benefit and financial gain to that which sustains the commons and the public good, and to focus on issues that affect everyone, such as world poverty and climate change. In an exciting reversal attitudes are changing, as people begin to recognize the value in accumulating experiences instead of "stuff," to change their spending habits to reflect quality over quantity, and to ask *"why own when you can borrow?"* The consumer-orientated mindset is hopefully declining in favor of collaboration and social exchange, and sharing resources instead of personal ownership. In conjunction with social justice movements to restore equity and sustainability, the *Sharing Economy* is an excellent framework for addressing root causes and affecting real change. As networks expand and grow worldwide, the *Sharing Economy* has the potential to make the "endless growth" principle of capitalism redundant, and to become a greater political force for addressing poverty, reconciliation, peace-building, rewilding and environmental protection.

Of course, learning to live without money is the ultimate way to *Reject Empire* and reverse the dominant paradigm, and change agents in the *Moneyless Society* movement are leading the way. Making the decision to live without money, *The Moneyless Man* (Mark Boyle)[339] developed a leading-edge philosophy for escaping the hegemony of money in every area of our lives, and what it truly means to be "sustainable." Challenging the prevailing economic theory, his book *The Moneyless Manifesto* is a radical new perspective that reveals our illusory attitudes toward money, and shows how liberating, simple and enjoyable it can be to live with less. As Boyle discovers, surviving by interacting with the natural world and thriving through the *Gift Economy* is at the heart of our transition from the current economic paradigm to a world of resilience and genuine sustainability. Sharing, caring, living within our means, creating and sustaining a local all-inclusive *Gift Economy*, reconnecting our hearts with the natural world, and forming sustainable villages or permaculture cooperatives are all links in the process. With creative strategies, new tools and practical solutions for living more with less, Mark's work is great inspiration for making important changes as we uncolonize and deal with massive change. As a movement on the rise, the *Moneyless Society* and the *Gift Economy* connect us to what is real and most important in our lives, and confirm our reciprocity with *Earth Community* as the source of all true wealth, and the pathway to personal freedom.

"Decolonization is a dramatic re-imagining of relationships with land, people and the state. Much of this requires study. It requires conversation. It is a practice; it is an unlearning."[340] (Syed Hussan)

In response to the new era of transition and localization, the alternative currency movement is also thriving, with complementary means of exchange being created worldwide, such as the Bristol Pound, Brixton Pound and Lewes Pound (England), German Cheimgauer, Bernal Bucks (San Francisco), Sand Dollars (Santa Cruz), Sonoma Go Local, Corvallis HOUR (Oregon), Equal Dollar (Philadelphia), Ithaca Hour, Massachusetts Berkshare, Salt Spring Dollar, Tetla Tsetsuwatil (Coast Salish), Powell River Dollar, Calgary Dollar and the Peterborough Loon. The *Transition Town* movement is a major advocate for local currency systems that boost local food production and a "buy local" attitude, and that reward nonprofits, businesses and members who are invested in community. As a complement to conventional money (for now), alternative currencies, electronic bartner networks, LETS exchange (*Local Economic Trading System*), and swapmeets keep the money flowing in the community, while registering with a *Skillshares* timebank allows participants to earn time dollars by exchanging services and skills (things they love to do) with services and skills received in return. With good vision, leadership and ethical practice, communities can regain control of their flow of money and credit, and the local economy begins to serve the collective instead of being subject to the dictates of outside forces. With the debt crisis looming, pre-adapting to a local currency ecosystem is an excellent plan, and will result in a strong interconnected community, a resilient economy, and self-sustaining interdependence.

In terms of the *Green Economy* that has developed from the world of environmental activism, thousands of new organizations, companies and ideas have been created to fulfill the demands of society, but in many cases, this brand of environmentalism has morphed into *Greenwashing* or *Green Neocolonialism* and replicated the capitalist goals of Empire. "Green" corporations, products, services and technologies pretend to support the paradigm shift to *Earth Community*, yet continue to place environmental protection secondary to economic activity, the dominance of the profit principle and the scenario of endless growth. There are transnational companies who have put on a "green face" yet continue with exploitative and unethical practices that destroy biodiversity and expand the market structures of capitalism. Many "Big Green" NGO's are working hand-in-hand with bioprospecting, forestry, traditional mining, monoculture and resource extraction companies. Greenwashing projects such as the advancement of agribusiness in Mato Grosso to deforest the lands of the Xavante (Brazil), or pushing large-scale wind power parks onto Zapotec and Ikoot lands (Mexico), continue to dispossess Indigenous people and perpetuate the root structures of an expansionist capitalist economy. There may be certain products, ventures or aspects of the *Green Economy* we can adapt to localization and the reduction of our carbon footprint as we align with decolonial values, but we must be discerning, and continuing with destructive technologies such as agribusiness, biotechnology or massive resource extraction is not the answer.

The ideology of capitalism has always been synonymous with self-sufficiency and the freedom of the individual, and this deeply-held conditioning will be the hardest to unlearn. *"To be in need of no one is supposedly to be more developed and liberated. Thus are the unfortunate necessities of modern-day isolation transformed into virtuous accomplishments."*[341] (Michael Parenti) However, our truest liberties will only be realized when we are free from our dependence on the corporatocracy and the unsustainable and destructive notions of endless growth. Freedom means being empowered by interexistence instead of acquisition, and as the quotation printed on the *Lewes Pound* tells us, *"we have it in our power to build the world anew,"*[342] and to shift to a completely different set of values that promote giving instead of taking. In line with the goals of the *Transition Town* movement, we can be resourceful, develop a frugality mentality, and embrace the *"less is more"* and *"reduce, reuse and recycle"* memes as a way of life. Engaging with new and exciting opportunities for collaborative movement-building and creative strategies can re-create a world that places the highest value on holistic relationships. Whether it is small-scale community-owned renewable energy projects in Indigenous communities that create self-sufficiency; purchasing carbon offsets or contributing them to ethically-sound and Kyoto-compliant renewables or greening projects; pooling money for peer-to-peer lending; more authentic marketing; business initiatives that donate to social causes; cryptocurrencies[343] and socially-responsible online payment systems; or certified *B Corporations* that use the power of business to solve environmental problems, a new paradigm in economic thinking is well underway, and the manifold niches of a regenerative economy are rapidly being filled. With a *Global Transition to a New Economy,* visioning non-monetary abundance and practicing healthy means of exchange can lead to our recovery of a sustainable world. *"When we must pay the true price for the depletion of nature's gifts, materials will become more precious to us, and economic logic will reinforce, and not contradict, our heart's desire to treat the world with reverence and, when we receive nature's gifts, to use them well."* (Charles Eisenstein, *Sacred Economics*, Evolver Editions, 2011)

---

339. Mark Boyle, *The Moneyless Manifesto: Live Well, Live Rich, Live Free*, Permanent Publications, 2013 and *The Moneyless Man: A Year of Freeconomic Living*, Oneworld Publications, 2010. (www.moneylessmanifesto.org)

340. Toronto activist Syed Hussan as cited in "Decolonizing Together" by Harsha Walia, *Briarpatch Magazine*, January 1, 2012. (http://briarpatchmagazine.com)

341. Michael Parenti, "The New Age Mythology," *Land of Idols: Political Mythology in America*, St. Martin's Press, 1994.

342. As an alternative currency, the *Lewes Pound* was introduced by town council in 2008 by *Transition Town Lewes* as a response to the challenges of climate change and peak oil. English and American political activist, philosopher, political theorist and revolutionary Thomas Paine was a resident of Lewes from 1768-1774. (www.thelewespound.org)

343. For a full list of cryptocurrencies such as *Bitcoin* and *The Ripple Network* see (http://altcoins.com).

Rejecting Empire ~ Conclusions

"In a time of ecological crisis, we need to mobilize the deeper reaches of our capacity to nurture. I would go so far as to say that Mother Universe is calling to every human person to become a powerful nurturer and protector of life."[344] (Dennis Rivers)

It has become clear that resisting the flawed mega-experiment of Eurocentric Empire in the Americas means going up against the "windigo" spirit of rapacious destruction as described so eloquently in the oral traditions of the Anishnaabe, Cree and other Turtle Island First Nations. The industrial-dominator model trashes people and the planet alike, and as neo-liberalism and the paramount rule of market continue to prop up the *Old Order*, the final colonial pillage of resources is underway in the most pristine natural places i.e. the Canadian wilderness, the Australian outback and the northern reaches of the Arctic. Yet worldwide resistance to non-democratic government, environmental degradation, and the whole range of toxic dysfunctional attitudes upheld by Empire is rapidly growing, and the shift to lateral power continues. We can step up our activism and boycott behaviors and products, lend our strength to campaigns, petitions, rallies and legal proceedings, and join with other coalitions to protest the practices that are threatening our world. Holding direct actions is essential, and success can occur through determined and sustained activism, such as the victorious campaign to stop shale gas drilling by Royal Dutch Shell and protect the old-growth forest of the Sacred Headwaters[345] in northern B.C. Collaborative activism between native and non-native communities and organizations can save lives, ecosystems, and the gene pool for successive generations, but it is not enough as more damage keeps occurring. Creating environmental and social awareness is great, but we need to strategize against Empire, and form horizontal alliances among disparate groups to replace or transform the systems causing harm. *"As Settlers, we must assert our own autonomy within our respective communities, and resist our governments' attempts to further consolidate its control over all communities, indigenous and non-indigenous alike."*[346] (Nora Butler Burke) If we continue with the disgraceful paradigm of relinquishing our irreplaceable green spaces for more progress and development, people in the future are going to think that we were the most destructive generation that ever lived!

By *Rejecting Empire* we are supporting the many emerging strands of a sustainable-equitable-resilient culture, and becoming full participants in the paradigm shift to *Earth Community*. As the ideas and actions of the leading visionaries, elders and changemakers become contagious, the inspiring perspectives of those who embrace eco-values, environmental stewardship and spiritual practice are passed on, and at a certain point the balance will shift and we will reach critical mass. As we re-discover better ways to live that bring benefit instead of harm, we become motivated to replace and transform toxic systems with practices that are life-sustaining. Rethinking our habitual patterns, plus the creative redesign of the structures and systems that make up our local communities, will develop and deepen our sense of belonging in the world. And as a solid bridge between spiritual practice and environmental activism, adopting insights and practices that resonate with our ancestral traditions can renew our connection to nature and effect true environmental healing. First taking place in the heart and mind, the shift from dominator culture to collaborative culture empowers us to contribute our unique gifts in service to our community and the land. *"All boundaries fall away with love."*[347] (Joan Halifax) It cannot be stressed enough that our essential bond to nature provides us with the complete nurture of body/mind/heart/soul, and our love for the Earth provides the momentum for our life purpose. To that end, let's explore re-landing, earthing, animism, ecomysticism and other exciting elements of *Earth First* on our revitalization journey!

"As we claim to be the stewards of the earth, we take it upon ourselves to state that we are here to protect, prevent, preserve - and restore the very essence of all that remains to the natural laws of this land."[348] (Deanna Harrison)

344. Dennis Rivers, "Companions in the Storm, Companions in Blessing: the Role of Friendship in Mending the World," *Ecobodhi Interfaith Meditation Prayer/Study/Action Community*, April 9, 2012. (http://ecobodhi.org/guide/companions-in-blessing)
345. Skeena Watershed Conservation Coalition, *Sacred Headwaters: Safeguarding the Shared Source of British Columbia's Skeena, Nass and Stikine Rivers*, online activism, news, initiatives, projects and scholarship. At the time of this writing, the Sacred Headwaters are still under threat from *Fortune Minerals* and their plan to turn Mount Klappan into an open pit coal mine. (http://skeenawatershed.com) (http://www.sacredheadwaters.com)
346. Nora Butler Burke, "Building a 'Canadian' Decolonization Movement: Fighting the Occupation at 'Home,'" *The Anarchist Library*, 2004. (http://theanarchistlibrary.org)
347. Joan Halifax as cited in *Occupy Love: Revolution of the Heart*, Dir. Velcrow Ripper, Fierce Love Films, 2013. (www.occupylove.org)
348. Deanna Harrison (Anishnaabe), *Sacred Water*, poem by Deanna Harrison, presented at the *Gchi-Nbi Sacred Water Circle*, Peterborough, ON, 2013. (www.sacredwatercircle.ca)

20. Where Are You Located?

"The soul of a landscape, the spirits of the elements, the genius of every place will be revealed to a loving view of nature."[349] (Karl Jaspers)

"The best thing we can do for the environment is to stay put." (Gary Snyder)

The need to connect deeply with the land, to love and respect the natural place we call home, is the starting point for reclaiming our EIK. Beyond the structures, complexity and toxicity of human civilization, and the patriarchal oppression of people and the land, we find our true selves in community with wild nature. The land welcomes the entire human family, and earth-based cultures have lived successfully for millennia deeply connected to place. *"It is this place that holds our memories and the bones of our people......this is the place that made us."* (Pueblo Elder) Throughout time, human societies have been shaped by our interconnectivity with the sacred elements, landforms, waters, creatures and plants of our homelands, and there is much to suggest that this can continue, that the places where we live today can give rise again to our IK or EIK. The greatest challenge then is to bond with nature, to let the land inform us as to what stewardship, reciprocity, cultural practices, ceremonial expressions and prayers are needed, and then to bring in elements of our own ancestral knowledge in whatever form and practice that may take. *"When we rekindle our deep respect for the Earth, we will stop destroying it."*[350] (Trish Tuley) Biophilia means to love the land with one's entire heart and soul - to revere and protect - and the myriad forces, powers and beings will return that love and care in both obvious and mysterious ways.

As descendants of the original Settler Society we need to understand the true history of the land we occupy, and what agreements were in place before the building of Empire. What treaty area do we live in? Whose land are we on? In the process of answering these questions we may discover that our title to the land is questionable, and begin to see the contradictions in the foundational myth of Canada's master narrative. *"Except for those dead set on being racist white supremacists, the disconnect between the mythology and the reality of Canadian land acquisition should propel Settler-Allies to decolonize, advocate for change within the system and build alliances with First Nations."*[351] (Taiaiake Alfred) The immorality of being on stolen land suggests the need for dialogue between the dominant culture and First Nations on the responsibility to honour existing treaties, table new ones and acknowledge the right to self-determination (which has never been withdrawn). It is time to become an honourable partner with First Nations and return to the original values of sharing the bounty of the land. As we transition to an ecological-based society instead of an economic one, our mutual concerns should focus on ethical land use, and actions that oppose and protest the desecration of all lands and waterways. Green technologies are in place that do not impact the land in destructive ways, and the time is long overdue to embrace and implement these sustainable means and methods.

"Each of us has the ability to act powerfully for change. Together we can regain that ancient and sustaining harmony, in which human needs and the needs of our companions on the planet are held in balance with the sacred, self-renewing processes of Earth."[352] (David Suzuki)

The concept of land ownership was established globally at the onset of the Neolithic revolution (10,000 BCE), putting into place the first boundaries between the wild and the human-built worlds. By clearing the land alongside nature to grow crops, wall enclosure systems were eventually built for farming and animal husbandry, and protected by hilltop fortresses that laid claim to the surrounding landscape, the world slowly became more "safe," domesticated and controllable. The practice of delineating the land into territories and agricultural parcels is not going to fade anytime soon, but there are still many things we can do to contribute to the "ancient wisdom rising" of respecting the Earth and the IK/EIK systems that develop from our connection to place. If we respect the land, love the land, steward the land, protect the land and nurture every living thing on the land, we can re-establish the true bond and interconnectivity that is at the core of all IK and EIK systems. There are many modes of land ownership and tenure, but converting the intrinsic sacredness of the land into a commodity is an illusion, and places human beings in a false position of dominance and separation. Our eco-identity informs us that we do not **own** the land, rather that the land holds us in its embrace, and as we fulfill the directives of balance and right relationship with place (which are the goals of uncolonization) we realize the highest value for all people. The change-makers among us see the concept of the commons spreading far and wide, the creation and nurture of inner-city and rural green spaces, and the land itself liberated from the tyranny of oppression. Many urban greening projects such as *Open Spaces Sacred Places* are being initiated to support the creation of public green spaces that bring beauty to our lives, nourish the soul, and renew community. *"These sacred places reawaken and reaffirm the powerful connection between nature, spirit and human well-being."*[353] Like a set of shared gifts, the air, water, ecosystems, watersheds, parks, urban green zones and wild lands that make up our green commons, are spaces that can be enjoyed, celebrated and protected as priceless community assets. No one has a right to destroy any aspect of the commons, and each of us has a sacred duty to protect these spaces from privatization (unless the lands are of hybrid ownership), and to pass them on in pristine condition to the *Seven Generations* yet to come.

---

349. Karl Jaspers (1883-1969), *Philosophy of Existence* published as *Existenzphilosophie* in 1938 and *Philosophy of Existence (Works in Continental Philosophy)*, University of Pennsylvania Press, 1971.

350. Trish Tuley and Myra Dutton, *Healing Ground: A Visionary Union of Earth and Spirit*, Celestial Arts, 2003.

351. Interview with educator and activist Taiaiake Alfred (Kahnawake Mohawk), "Idle No More movement and Bill C-45," *Acimowin Radio*, December 20, 2012. (www.youtube.com)

352. David Suzuki, *The Sacred Balance: Rediscovering Our Place in Nature*, Greystone Books, 2007.

353. *Open Spaces Sacred Places*, established by TKF Foundation and based in Annapolis, MD, is a non-profit organization that funds publicly-accessible urban green spaces. *"We believe that nature both heals and unifies us, and we partner with organizations to create 'Open Spaces Sacred Places' to increase a sense of community and contribute to the deepening of human connections."* (www.openspacessacredplaces.org)

"We often forget that WE ARE NATURE. Nature is not something separate from us. So when we say that we have lost our connection to nature, we've lost our connection to ourselves."[354]
(Andy Goldsworthy)

The emphasis on the importance of the human-built, monolithic, techno-political, money-centric world by the dominant culture, and our incestuous interaction with the technologies and systems of our own making, has created a parasitical existence that demeans both humanity and the Earth. In our colonized trance we believe the deceptive propaganda in movies and advertising that tell us wild nature is threatening and hostile to humanity. Certainly natural law influences all living things with necessary checks-and-balances, but these fearful deceits keep us separated and alienated from our essential bio-lineage and true intra-connection with *Earth Community*. For millennia Christian dominance has perpetuated the expulsion from Eden as the operating myth of Western civilization, and it is high time to reject this fallacy and return to the Garden. Never before has there been a time when human beings have been so disconnected from the web of life - the bedrock of our being - and the elements in the natural world that sustain our very lives. This hubristic unsustainable worldview has naturally led Indigenous people to believe that Settlers are incapable of bonding with the Earth, and we need to prove them wrong.

"It is impossible for non-natives to feel the sorts of emotions that are called upon when Indigenous peoples speak about ancestors, about Earth, about the symbiosis that exists between human and animal. Non-natives come from another psychic and physical place, and we have been here for centuries."[355] (Beth Brant)

"They may see it as beautiful, or exploited, or crowded, or expensive, or hostile, or even as a haven for racism, but they cannot ever see our land as familial. That is to say, non-Natives can never know what we know, or feel what we feel, about our Mother, the land."[356] (Haunani-Kay Trask)

"Settlers suffer from alienation from this land, and fundamentally, their own selves; Settlers have not yet rooted themselves and been transformed into real peoples of this homeland."[357] (Taiaiake Alfred)

"Settlers cannot have the same deep connection that First Nations have to the land that is tied to language and cyclical ceremonies, an understanding of the whole ecology and a feeling of deep responsibility."[358] (Ethan Baptiste)

"As a society North America does not have the sense of land that Native people do. North American societies simply see land as a

*commodity - what you can take from it and what you can do with it. Certain individuals may have a different perspective on land and I am happy that is true, but in terms of provincial, state or national policy land is a commodity."*359 (Thomas King)

How disheartening to find that our First Nations neighbours think that members of the Settler Society have absolutely no respect or affection, let alone biophilia, for the land! There are many who honour the earth in all we think, say and do, yet there needs to be a groundswell not only of nature lovers, but a major paradigm shift to bonding with the land in rural areas, towns and cities, and to placing *Earth Community* at the center of our lives. Ironically, the agrarian era of our grandparents when Settlers were busily clearing the land and farming gave new immigrants of all ethnic backgrounds a rootedness and love of place. As farming was phased out by the mega-agricultural complex, technology-based industries and urbanization, the earth-connected rural mindset of our recent ancestors rapidly diminished in my own lifetime. I once heard an older Canadian woman of German descent, originally from a farming community and now living in a high-rise condo, say *"all I want to do is go back to the Holland Marsh and walk barefoot on the earth again, and hold that soil in my hands before I die."* I truly believe that **all** people have the capacity for a deep and abiding love and connection to the Earth, and re-awakening this primal need is our best future.

*"The land is sacred, and we should learn again to walk gently for we tread on holy ground."*360 (Martin Palmer and Nigel Palmer)

*"Only by immersing ourselves in the world of nature, recognizing our complete interdependence with it, and accepting our role as active cultivators, observers and celebrants of its richness, can we hope to ensure the survival of our own species, of our humanity and of our most treasured cultural values."*361 (Peter Bane)

---

354. Landform artist Andy Goldsworthy, "25 Quotes By Sculptor/Photographer Andy Goldsworthy," *John Paul Caponigro: Illuminating Creativity* (blog), April 11, 2014. (www.johnpaulcaponigro.com/blog)

355. Beth Brant (Mohawk), "Anodynes and Amulets," *Writing as Witness: Essay and Talk,* Three O'Clock Press, 1995.

356. Haunani-Kay Trask (Hawaiian), "Feminism and Indigenous Hawaiian Nationalism," *Journal of Women in Culture and Society*, 1996.

357. Taiaiake Alfred (Kahnawake Mohawk), *Wasase: Indigenous Pathways of Action and Freedom*, Broadview Press, 2005.

358. Ethan Baptiste (Syilx/Okanagan), Review of the book *We Are All Treaty People* by Roger Epp, *Canadian Journal of Native Studies*, Volume XXX, No. 1, 2010.

359. "Shelagh's extended conversation with Thomas King," *The Next Chapter* with *Shelagh Rogers*, CBC Books, February 4, 2013. (www.cbc.ca)

360. Martin Palmer and Nigel Palmer, *Sacred Britain: A Guide to the Sacred Sites and Pilgrim Routes of England, Scotland and Wales*, Piatkus, 1997.

361. Peter Bane, *The Permaculture Handbook: Garden Farming for Town and Country*, New Society Publishers, 2012.

In the migrations and diasporas to the so-called "new world" our ancestors *"carried the economic plague known as capitalism, and before long they turned around and reproduced the same anti-social arrangements in their new homelands that had existed in the Europe that evicted them. Thus, the enclosure of Europe led to the enclosure of the Americas. French philosopher and activist Simone Weil once warned that what had undermined Europe was 'the disease of uprootedness.' Once uprooted, one 'uproots others,' and everywhere this new civilization goes, it ostracizes folks from the land."*[362] (Derek Rasmussen) Constantly in motion, the mandate of empirical expansion to head West and occupy the "frontier" has been a constant in the Euro-founding of the Americas, culminating in our massive propensity for travel and innovation. As promoted by the conquest agenda of "manifest destiny," the entitlement to be in motion for business or pleasure is one of our greatest freedoms. The impulse to move around the continent instead of staying in one place is a foundational myth of the Americas, and these massive movements of "globalsapiens"[363] have created a society without roots, or any notion of rootedness. If somewhere or something doesn't suit us, there is always somewhere or something else that does. (Hopefully! Or if not, keep moving.) The emphasis on mobility and consumption does not promote sustainability, reciprocity, respect or gratitude for the land, and this neophile[364] dysfunction has been accurately described by various Indigenous scholars as a "predator and prey" relationship. Also, the entire system called "globalization" attacks our localized bonds to the land, and should be rejected in favor of reclaiming a sacred relationship with place, food, soil and community. To restore our world, we need to stay in one place, sink our roots deep, learn about local history, plants and animals, and support healthy, living food systems, local food markets and local farmers committed to ecological practices. We can all play a part in honouring and creating these new systems for our *Settler Re-landing*. The following list of inquiries and action points can strengthen our local connection to the land, and in turn give rise to our own EIK.

"Most people would like to find their one true place, their ecological niche, their island of belonging."[365] (Richard Louv)

Strengthen your Local Connection to Place - Action Points

- What great cataclysms formed the land? Glaciers left behind, ancient watercourses, gorges, cliffs, or networks of caves - examine the geological epochs that have created variance in the ecosystem(s).
- What artifacts and evidence have been found of ancient peoples i.e. arrowheads, pottery, whole villages uncovered by archaeology - on what plants and animals did they depend? Imagine the lushness of the forests and waterways before colonization.
- Identify local geography, landforms, watersheds, wetlands, eco-systems, native plants, trees and animals - what was here before the

Settler Society? Go on a "bioblitz" to discover the unique species, trees, plant, animal and insect life of this region, to gain a new understanding of your own environment.

- Who were the original First Nations of the territory where you live? What were the first treaty relationships, and what are the intricacies of those agreements? What would be the nation-to-nation obligations required to honour those treaties today?

- Find out if a map or mapping project is available of your region that identifies the place names in the language of the original inhabitants of the land. First Nations created maps that expressed an earth-connected worldview and a respect for sacred sites and the bounty of the land. Becoming aware of the intimate knowledge of the land embedded in the deeper meaning of the original place names is extremely important to our localization.

- What are the local stories, legends, folklore and myths of the original peoples, and of the early Settler Society that connected with the land?

- What types of soil and rock comprise the foundation of the land? What is the nearest body of water – stream, river, lake, ocean - and how does its presence affect the landscape? What is the highest place i.e. hill or mountain, and what is the view from the top?

- What wild creatures call this place home? Become familiar with the animals, birds, insects, reptiles, fishes and amphibians, and their shared ecosystems.

- What are the trees and plants that thrive in the area? Learn the names, characteristics and green gifts of all the trees within a 30-kilometer radius of your home. What wild plants, grasses, herbs, fruits and flowers bless you with food, medicine and fragrance? Where is the oldest tree? Imagine all the generations that have passed beneath its shade and beauty.

- What are the nearest sacred sites in the natural landscape or the human-built world, and what are the deep meanings inherent for both ancient and contemporary people?

- Where are the nearest cemeteries and burial places, and what deeds of the dead still influence the living? How did our Ancestors and the Ancestors of other people honour this place?

- Where is agriculture being practiced and local food produced, and what is your relationship to these crops?

- What natural places or parklands are special to you, and why? How do they make you think, feel, or enliven your sensate animal body? Where did you spend your childhood, and what are your earliest memories of the land?

- What elementals, nature spirits, devas, ancestors or other-than-human presences have informed your bliss and allowed the deep mystery, or the "green fuse" that animates all life, to flow through you?

Honoring the Earth aligns us with what is truly sacred, and including your home ecosystem, every part of the earth is *"a paradise, and wherever you set your feet is holy ground."*[367] (Pelletier and Poole) For the past 500 years under the domination of Empire, Settlers have been abysmal stewards of the land, and we must now re-learn earth literacy and an obedience to natural law, and reinhabit the places we call home. Knowing that ecological balance is integral to our freedom and our survival on Turtle Island, a new paradigm of governance and co-existence as connected to the web of life is paramount. As James Conlon so eloquently describes, *"Earth literacy is an intimate bond with the natural world that perceives the Earth not as **mine**, but **me**, and enables us to contemplate our world and our place in it. To practice earth literacy we need to draw on the resources of ancient wisdom to transform our hearts and minds, and in turn, the region of Earth we call home."*[368] If we are mindful of our privileges and grateful to be living on Turtle Island, a spiritual connection to the land can perhaps be shared by both native and non-native community. As we collectively move toward decolonization, our earth literacy and interdependence with the land and each other can make us aware that we have obligations to First Nations, to empower their sovereignty and create the conditions that make peaceful co-existence possible.

I pledge allegiance to the soil
of Turtle Island
one ecosystem
in diversity
under the sun -
with joyful interpenetration for all.[369]
(Gary Snyder)

---

362. Derek Rasmussen, "Qallunology 101: A Lesson Plan for the Non-Indigenous," *Dhamma, The Buddhist Peace Fellowship: Turning Wheel Media*, April 4, 2013. (www.buddhistpeacefellowship.org)

363. The term "globalsapiens" was coined by David de Rothchild, *The Live Earth Global Warming Survival Handbook: 77 Essential Skills to Stop Climate Change - or Live Through It,* Live Earth/ Rodale, 2007.

364. A neophile is one who rejects tradition and routine in favor of extreme change and the endless attraction of novelty - the "new" in people, experiences, technology, ideas, material objects and even spirituality. A product of market/state and modernity, a neophile is a new type of person who dovetails perfectly with the aims of consumer capitalism.

365. Richard Louv, *The Web of Life: Weaving the Values That Sustain Us*, Conari Press, 1996.

366. A brilliant example of this work is *Mapping Roots: Perspectives of Land and Water in Ontario* by visual artist Christi Belcourt (Métis), that explore Métis and Anishnaabe perspectives of land and water. This series of paintings express an Indigenous worldview by melding together contemporary road maps with research on original native place names, along with other motifs. (www.christibelcourt.com)

367. Wilfred Pelletier and Ted Poole, "A Sacred Place," *Earth Prayers From Around the World: 365 Prayers, Poems, and Invocations for Honoring the Earth,* edited by Elizabeth Roberts and Elias Amidon, Harper Collins Publishers, 1991.

368. James Conlon, *Lyrics for Re-Creation: Language for the Music of the Universe,* Continuum Publishing, 1997.

369. Gary Snyder, "A Sacred Place," *Earth Prayers From Around the World: 365 Prayers, Poems, and Invocations for Honoring the Earth,* Elizabeth Roberts and Elias Amidon (editors), Harper Collins Publishers, 1991.

21. Eco-Soul (Manifesto)

How deeply are human beings entwined with the natural world? Bespoke wisdom, a vision, or an offering from my ancient *Celtic Clan Mothers*, an epiphany came to me one evening, in the trance state between sleeping and waking. This fantastical manifesto, an ontology inspired by our most ancient beginnings, extends past the far reaches of modern environmental theory, and gives us much to contemplate as we continue to be humbled by the *Great Mystery*.

What if it was proven beyond the shadow of a doubt that your soul is eternal? That your soul is a unique and sacred spark, a blessed part of the Divine Mystery that animates your inner life from birth to death and beyond? And what if it was established that your soul is on a continuous forward journey? And what if proof exists that between lifetimes your soul resides in the landscape and in the various features, elements and creatures of the natural world? And if in fact, the natural environment serves as a cauldron, vessel or holding place for your spirit? In truth, the trees, plants, wetlands, grasslands, wildflower meadows, sand dunes, mounds, rocky escarpments, underground tunnels, caverns, ponds, lakes, rivers, elements and animals – any of these numinous and holy places and creatures can serve as a temporary dwelling-place for your soul.

And knowing this to be true, believing beyond a shadow of a doubt that the continuum of our soul depends on this eco-resting place, how can we allow the destruction of the natural world to continue? The contamination created by our conveniences and technologies; the pollution dumped into the water systems, air and earth; the forests logged; the animals harvested; the earth's body stripped by mining; the replacement of the wild with highways, fences, factories and cities, all pose a very real and terrible danger to our personal destiny. After your physical death, where the Great Mystery will place your spirit cannot be predicted. (Unless one has had exceptional training and has willed it so. Making personal decisions affecting the process of being born into death are a given in certain Indigenous societies).

*Therefore the reckless and thoughtless damage to the environment on every level **must be stopped!** It goes far beyond the meme of "we are all connected" to see that we are dependent on the life support systems of water, air and earth to survive and thrive. We now know that without access to the undisturbed natural places on this beautiful planet that have been provided for our souls' rest and return, our spirits will surely and completely disappear. Contrary to the worldview of the Industrial Growth complex, humans are not meant to exist in close proximity to concrete cities, technology and built environments, but thrive in the truest sense **only** in the embrace of the green and natural world. The farther away we push nature, the smaller our souls become – this is not a metaphor but fact, as experienced by the millions who feel a vacuum and something missing in their lives. Endless void-fillers, distractions and therapies exist to address this emptiness, but most of the practices and theories bypass the simple truth that would address the foundational requirements of our eco-soul. The contemporary endemic shrinking of the spirit is a reality, and healing is possible when we return to our ancestral and earth-connected roots, reclaim our enchantment with the world, embrace the wild for our "ensouling," and re-establish the connection to Mother Earth so vital to our well-being.*

As we co-existed peacefully with the Earth for millennia, we must expand once again into our true nature and potential as fully-realized human beings. To survive as beings of both body and spirit, we must acknowledge our vital reciprocal relationship with nature and embrace our true human role as keepers and protectors of Earth Community.

ECO-SOUL

OUR SOULS LIVE IN THE EARTH AND THE EARTH LIVES IN OUR SOULS

Examples of the *Eco-Soul* dynamic can be found in earth-connected and Indigenous societies worldwide, in oral tradition, myth, and even contemporary filmmaking. Based on *Yolngu Matha* IK and filmed in the Ganalbingu language, the Australian award-winning film *Ten Canoes*[370] recreates a pre-contact hunter-gatherer society in Arnhem Land, Northern Territory. In between lifetimes, the souls of the members of the tribe live in a luxuriant green wetland, and pregnant women go there in reverence to coax a soul into their belly. Sourced from the ancient folklore of Europe and elsewhere, James Frazer states in *The Golden Bough*[371] that the spirits of the dead reside in the trees, awaiting rebirth. The Indigenous peoples of Lithuania, Greece, Italy, Germany, Sweden, Britain, Africa, Indonesia and the Americas worshipped the trees as sacred beings with in-dwelling souls, and protected them from harm. Depending on the culture, trees can be the abode of spirits, gods, ancestors, or souls waiting to be born. One of the ancient megalithic structures found in Malta, the Hypogeum in Ħal-Saflieni, is the oldest intact underground temple in the world, and is thought to have been sacred space for rituals of birth, death and regeneration. Both above and below ground, the temple complex of this ancient matriarchal society (3800 to 3600 BCE) reveals construction and symbols that celebrate fertility and the female form. Having amazing acoustic properties, the subterranean chambers and structures enabled powerful communication with the spirit realm, and were places for worship, divination and healing. From tomb to womb, the Hypogeum in Ħal-Saflieni was also the burial place for thousands of community members, and the *Chamber of All Souls* held the spirits of the collective between lives as crucible, vessel and cauldron. The highly-evolved wisdom held by this society allowed for the successful migration between disembodied and incarnate spirits, in a dance of *Sacred Mystery* that embraced the perennial cycles of life.

---

370.   *Ten Canoes,* Dir. Rolf de Heer in collaboration with the Yolgnu people of Ramingining, Palace Films, 2006. (www.palacefilms.com.au/tencanoes)
371. James Frazer, "The Worship of Trees," "Tree-spirits," and "Beneficent Powers of Tree-spirits," *The Golden Bough: A Study in Magic and Religion*, MacMillan Press, 1974.

22. Earth First

"The majority of the world does not find its roots in western culture or tradition. The majority of the world finds its roots in the natural world, and it is the natural world, and the traditions of the natural world, which must prevail."[372] (Haudenosaunee Address)

"The land is our greatest strength – if we look to Her we will survive."[373] (*Wisakedjak*)

In the magnificent journey to reclaim our own Ancestral Knowledge, our essential bond to the land and our own form of ecocultural identity on Turtle Island, there are diverse paths and modalities that can lead our hearts and minds back to the natural world. From the minute they rolled out the pavement, my sense is that the human race has been devolving (!), and that every technological advance and infrastructure development is another act of self-destruction when compared to the infinity of sacred treasures found in Indigenous life. Situated at the core of western civilization is the master narrative of Christianity encoded in our expulsion from the Garden of Eden, and this scenario has been reenacted over and over for millennia. Reinforced by the isolationist perception that nature is a hostile force, cultural groups worldwide have hidden themselves away from the dangers of wild animals "red in tooth and claw" and the vagaries of weather, and better to make your stronghold fast. Over time, the culmination of this vast separation from the natural world has become a huge embarrassment to the artists, mystics, visionaries, and practitioners of our European-based *Old Ways*, who have tried from time to time to amalgamate bits and pieces of nature worship and earth connection into the public sphere, keeping indigenity alive in a covert way and adding a much-needed eco-awareness to the western canon. For centuries religion, philosophy and science developed elaborate theories to justify and cloak our separation from the natural world, inevitably coming full circle in contemporary times to spiritual ecology, the "greening of religion" and a scientific backtrack to the original cosmology of *Indigenous Science* (found all along in living IK systems).

Already in place as they have for millennia, it is the IK/EIK in every domain of human activity that hold the key to our mutual decolonization process and survival into post-industrial society. The popular meme that a *"new view of reality is emerging in which spiritual insight and scientific discovery **both** contribute to an understanding of ourselves as intimately interwoven with our world"*[374] (Macy and Johnstone) implies that we need to conjure up a brand new paradigm, a cutting-edge convergence of modern technology with spiritual enlightenment. The truth is, everything we could possibly need is already waiting to be found in earth-connected IK/EIK systems, and this actuality is expressed by renowned Mexican scholar Gustavo Esteva.

*"The system is not working, and everyone is realizing it. People are looking everywhere, imagining and theorizing the possibilities, grasping at more creations of their own making in the built infrastructure, seeking the paradigm shift in science, technology, medicine, the Occupy movement and so on that needs to happen, whereas it is already in place as it has been for millennia, being lived by Indigenous Knowledge and Indigenous people. Any course-correction discipline to decolonize ourselves is already in practice by Indigenous peoples, from astronomy to ethnobotany to medicine to food sources to community living, to intimate knowledge of the land base. You name it, it is already being lived and practiced. The only thing that the dominant society needs to access this storehouse, held by the people for the people, is **humility**. The paradigm shift is already being lived by millions of earth-connected cultures and Indigenous people worldwide, and the time has come to let the slowest set the pace."*[375]

In the throes of Euro-civilization building in the Americas, vital aspects of sustaining our eco-identity while existing under the blanket of colonialism seems to have fallen to the green thinkers, the herbalists, the naturalists, the wilderness guides, the artists (yet again!), the outcasts, the discontents, the malcontents, the cultural creatives and the introverts. An interesting contemporary phenomena is the anomie of certain people visiting the cities who experience great discomfort and have to leave, sensitive souls who cannot abide the noise, pollution, and grey-on-grey tangle of the urban jungle. This almost begs the question that there must be two distinct types of humans, those that have evolved in the artificiality of cities - the thriving urban dwellers who love their metropolises - and those to whom concrete urban spaces are anathema, the ones who are out-of-step with the values of Empire and need to maintain their kinship to the natural world at all costs. Some have even gone so far as to say that *"the souls who are more comfortable in the cities are no longer comfortable on this planet, and should travel to another planet!"* [376] (Krow Fischer) Then there are the folks who exist in a kind of liminal space or twilight zone, a little bit urban while their hearts continue to resonate with the natural world, forced to live in small cities yet not fully embracing the rural life or countryside either. Wherever one is situated, to heal our rift from nature and reclaim our ecological self, we need to put the highest value on loving and experiencing the land, for this is how our EIK will emerge. To this end, I offer the following collection of diverse paths, both ancient in origin and modern in voice, that place the *Earth First*.

"Nature gives birth to your soul – and that of all other animals and plants on the planet. You can count on wild nature to reflect your soul, because soul is your most wild and natural dimension." [377] (Bill Plotkin)

372. Jerry Mander, "A Basic Call to Consciousness, the Haudenosaunee Address to the Western World," *In the Absence of the Sacred: The Failure of Technology and the Survival of the Indian Nations.* Sierra Club Books, 1992.
373. Public Energy, *Wisakedjak/Mazinaw Rocks,* dance theatre performance, Market Hall, Peterborough, ON, 10/31/2013.
374. Joanna Macy and Chris Johnstone, *Active Hope: How to Face the Mess We're In Without Going Crazy,* New World Library, 2012.
375. Mexican activist, "deprofessionalized intellectual" and nomadic storyteller Gustavo Esteva, *Traditional Elders Conference 2013,* Lecture, Indigenous Studies Department, Trent University, Peterborough, Ontario, January 28, 2013.
376. Krow Fischer, *Weavers of Light: A Channelled Book of Knowledge for Our Changing Times,* Here On Earth, 2008.
377. Bill Plotkin, *Soulcraft: Crossing into the Mysteries of Nature and Psyche,* New World Library, 2010.

EARTH FIRST ~ *Go Outside*

"Nature is not simply a collection of objects and energy, but rather a dynamic, ever-flowing river of creation inseparable from our own perceptions. Nature is the creative center from which we and every-thing else have come and to which we will always return." [378] (Gregory Cajete)

In order to embrace an earth-rooted spiritual path and lifestyle, it is essential to go outside, to go wild (!) and open the door to a familiar landscape or a whole new world of discovery, and to take ourselves home to the *Green Mysteries* where we will find the timeless source of all being, including our own life purpose and peace of mind. To spend time in green space and wild nature is to surrender to the intricacy of the world, to learn how the elements and beings influence each other (how the leaves of the silver maple embrace the wind, or small seeds sprout in time with the migrating swallows' return) as an interplay of forces and the dance of mutuality to which we all belong. In nature our feelings of physical well-being that arise inform us that we are interconnected with all creation, as *"the epidermis of our skin is ecologically like a pond surface or a forest soil, not a shell so much as delicate interpenetration. It reveals the self extended as part of the ecosystem, because the beauty and complexity of nature are continuous with ourselves, and we affirm that the world is a being, a part of our own body."*[379] (Paul Shepard)

Our bodies, senses, inner vision and heart are the gifts we have been given, portals that allow us to see, hear and feel the sacred in nature, to act on this knowledge, and to shape communities that honour and respect the complex latticework of both human and nonhuman life. Just as the wild egalitarian souls of our ancestors moved in synchronicity with wild nature, we have the same capacity today to evoke and celebrate our "connectigence"[380] and the harmony of the cosmos. Wherever you are, come back to the *Sacred Circle*! May your heart-connected exploration of urban parks, gardens, rural landscapes, forests, wetlands, wilderness, waterways and borderland spaces prompt the emergence of your inner ecomystic, and activate your role as *Earth Keeper* and protector of Gaia for the generations yet to come.

───────────────

378. Gregory Cajete, PhD (Tewa), "Western Science and the Loss of Natural Creativity," *Unlearning the Language of Conquest: Scholars Expose Anti-Indianism in America* by Four Arrows (Don Trent Jacobs), University of Texas Press, 2010.

379. Paul Shepard, "Introduction: Ecology of Man - a View Point," *The Subversive Science: Essays Toward an Ecology of Man*, Paul Shepard and Daniel McKinley (editors), Houghton Mifflin, 1969.

380. *Connectigence: Performances Celebrating the Harmony of the Universe*, Open Secret Bookstore, Gallery & Cultural Center, San Rafael, CA, July 19, 2013.

EARTH FIRST ~ *Earthing*

"We are Children of the Earth. Yet we have been hoisted away from Her by the hypertrophy of the rational intellect, and we have strayed far from our own sensate groundedness and presence. To come fully to rest on the ordinary Earth is to rest in the present moment. The tyranny of time dissipates, and we find that we are simply here, belonging to the place our senses have newly discovered."[381]
(Philip Shepherd)

As children we instinctually know that physically connecting our body to the Earth, stretching out under the trees on a hot summer day, rolling in the grass, thrusting our hands into the soil of the garden, or digging our toes in the sand makes us feel wonderful, alive and free. Called "earthing" and touted as some "new" kind of discovery in recent times, earth-connected Indigenous cultures have always embodied the miraculous energy and well-being gained from physical contact to the land. For all ethnocultural groups that flourished on the planet prior to Empire (and in non-Western cultures today) humankind has been intimately connected to the ground for all of our activities, including walking and sleeping. Made from natural materials, rammed earth dwellings, stone, shell, clay or timber walls; wooden lodges, caves and other forms of shelter have been built in close proximity to the earth. In their daily lives, earth-rooted and Indigenous people continue to be merged with the healing and energizing properties of the earth, which has been identified by modern science as the transfer of electrons (the earth's natural, subtle energy) into our bodies. This physical bond of the body to the Earth is embedded in complete IK/EIK worldviews, and enacted through a panoply of cultural wisdom practices, such as healing or oracle work, reciprocity ceremonies, and growing crops in collaboration with the green world. One example of this essential dynamic is the Mesoamerican empowerment ritual of recapitulation, whereby individuals are covered in layers of rich living earth for many days, until one is completely free from the negativity of past conditioning.

As long as I remember I have wanted to be in natural spaces. I instinctually began a conscious "earthing" practice for solace and healing in the early 1990s, spending hours whenever I could on the floor of the Simcoe County forest or on the banks of the Otonabee River gazing at the blue sky, flowing green leaves, interlace of branches, small plants, shrubbery, and rushing water for hours, breathing in the scents and sounds of nature's perfection in harmony with the "ground" of my being. By staying in one place and just be-ing, I discovered the holistic benefits of bodily contact to the Earth on the emotional, physical, intellectual and spiritual levels of existence simultaneously. Even if the effects were not immediately apparent, after a "timeless time" I was firing on all cylinders and ready to face the man-made world again.

Both the philosophy and material culture of our high-tech post-industrial society conspire to keep us from connecting to the Earth and its boundless storehouse of healing and energizing electrons. Walking on concrete with rubber or plastic-soled shoes, living indoors buttressed with insulative materials, travelling by vehicle from place to

---

381. Philip Shepherd, *New Self New World: Recovering Our Senses in the 21st Century*, North Atlantic Books, 2010. Exceptional work on helping us relinquish the burden of our head-centric culture's self-absorption and the pull of its fantasies with earthing, grounding ourselves, reclaiming our root chakra, and experiencing the natural intelligence of the body.

place, working under artificial lights, and spending hours on electronic gadgets all take their toll on our physical and spiritual health and well-being. Studies on the disruptive and negative effects of synthetic environments on human vitality such as "sick building syndrome" point to a reduction in our health and overall malaise. It has been determined that even the viewing of pictures showing natural landscapes has a stronger and more positive effect on our health than looking at city-scapes and urban scenes! Without a doubt, it is our immersion in green spaces and our bodily contact with the Earth that promotes tranquility, reflection and restoration for the human spirit. Personally, I am grateful to modern science for pointing out ("discovering") the holistic benefits of connecting with the Earth, as the next time an over-urbanized city dweller asks if I am "not feeling well" because I'm reclining on the ground in a public park, I can say, *"Oh I'm fine, thank you, I'm just Earthing."* The most amazing thing about the soothing, strengthening, grounding and cleansing practice of "earthing" is the simplicity and access – our backyards are perfect, and in many urban areas of Turtle Island, parks, green space and wilderness lands are all nearby.

---

the land heals me

loamy soil somewhat dry
bower of trees and leaves
nesting or cave-like
long grass caressing
body cleaves to packed earth

wind or breeze
dappled sunshine
birdsong

Just Stay There

let the land bring me to perfect health

I am body
I am Earth
We are one.

The more we engage with re-connecting to our essential eco-selves, the more apparent it becomes that the Earth is the ultimate source of all wellness and invigoration. In our time and place, the flow of healing and energizing power from nature that interacts with the intricate mechanisms of our physical body is another major reason for reconnecting to the land. Being outside, absorbing nature's limitless conducive energy systems and "getting grounded" can reverse chronic health conditions, enhance our immune system and keep us young. In addition to enhanced health and wellbeing, our sensate animal body experiences a pure joy and happiness when we are physically connected to the Earth, and we can access this miracle at any time. *"We give ourselves precious little chance to taste the nourishment that springs up into us whenever we touch the ground, and it's hardly surprising that we've forgotten the erotic nature of gravity and the enlivening pleasure of earthly contact."*[382] (David Abram) Walking in natural places or out on the land everyday is the perfect way to refocus our thoughts, uplift our spirit, open our intuitive channels, enhance our physical endurance, and revive our connectivity to the rhythm and energy of the Earth. And let's not forget about the universality and sacredness of the dance! With shells, bells or natural decoration on our ankles to express our ancestral knowledge and to honour ourselves and the land, strong women, wise women, and "daughters of the green realm" throughout time have known that *"the Earth loves to feel dancing feet on her body."*[383] (Le'ema Kathleen Graham) Rituals of release, play, spontaneity, walking barefoot, dancing, picnicking, and making love are just a few of the many joyful ways we can recover our intimate connection to the healing and energizing powers of the Earth.

"The soil is the great connector of lives, the source and destination of all. It is the healer and restorer and resurrector, by which disease passes into health, age into youth, death into life. Without proper care for it we can have no community, because without proper care for it we can have no life."[384] (Wendell Berry)

Re-visioning our reciprocity with the natural world requires the ethics of genuine care, and as every good gardener knows, the soil itself needs to be nurtured and tended. Age-old practices in subsistence communities worldwide honour the Earth under our feet as alive and divine, a sacred and life-giving force that can be enhanced and nourished for greater yields and for the vitality of all beings. Indigenous societies know the soil to *"have human form, and we hint at the same spiritual insight when we speak of rich soil as humus – a word having the same etymological root as human – for when we care for the soil we care for ourselves."*[385] (Patricia Monaghan) Composting methods, vermiculture, and transferring lawn clippings back to the Earth instead of sending them to the landfill, are a few of the soil-building practices we can adopt right away. Part of the "new story" for our transitional society are the many prayers and gratitude rituals that can express reciprocity for the infinity of gifts we receive from the soil - the

Earth and ground of our being. It has become my practice to place special containers of sacred soil or sand on my household altars and decorative spaces, to honour the centrality and importance of the Earth from birth to our final resting place. *From our mother we are born and to our mother we return.* In addition to finding great comfort and healing out on the land at times of loss and grieving, the green burial movement is rapidly expanding, with the use of sustainable organic materials and simple earth-connected crossing-over ceremonies. The liturgical expression *"earth to earth, ashes to ashes, dust to dust"* must certainly be a carry-over from an ancient EIK tradition!

"If you will think of yourself as coming out of the earth, rather than having been thrown in here from somewhere else, you see that we are the earth, we are the consciousness of the earth. These are the eyes of the earth. And this is the voice of the earth."[386]
(Joseph Campbell)

Certainly our lack of healthy bodily contact to the Earth's surface is the physical manifestation of a culture that promotes the activity of the rational mind above all, celebrating all that is left-brain, logical, conceptual and cerebral. A true human being moves effortlessly between the four facets of mind, body, heart and soul equally, yet the Hellenistic Order and western knowledge systems that created urban life have denied our access to the land, and the grounding that makes this holism possible. The lack of connection to the land creates the corresponding lack of connection to our own psyche and true essence. In marked contrast, many narratives and post-contact photographs show how Indigenous people literally love the soil, and sit or rest on the Earth with a feeling of being close to a nurturing power. The Earth Herself is the source of all health and wellness, and for the *Sahtu Dene* people of the Délı̨nę First Nation in the Northwest Territories, Elder Charlie Neyelle tells us that it is imperative for those who are sick to go out on the land to sleep on the surface of the Earth for a number of days, knowing in advance that "this will change their entire system"[387] for the better. Modelled to us by both pre-colonial and contemporary IK, today all people have the ability to realize their potential by fully occupying our human niche in physical connection to the ever-welcoming embrace of the Earth Mother, and to become energetic in mind, body, heart and soul, charged with positive elements and forces.

---

382. David Abram, *Becoming Animal: An Earthly Cosmology*, Vintage Books, 2011.

383. Le'ema Kathleen Graham, author of *Dancing the Inner Serpent: Memoirs of a Suburban Snake Priestess* (GoddessWork, 2009), Facebook comment, 2013.

384. Wendell Berry, *The Unsettling of America: Culture and Agriculture,* Sierra Club Books, 1996.

385. Patricia Monaghan, *Magical Gardens: Cultivating Soil and Spirit*, Llewellyn Worldwide, 2012.

386. Joseph Campbell and Bill Moyers, *The Power of Myth,* Anchor, 1991.

387. Charlie Neyelle, "Sacred Water Circle Gathering," *Gchi-Nbi Sacred Water Circle*, Peter Gzowski College, Trent University, May 2-4, 2014. (www.sacredwatercircle.ca)

For me, nothing conveys the vitality of earth-bonded indigenity more than this poignant photograph of Geronimo and his people resting on their beloved desert soil, sitting and squatting beside the train they are travelling on to be "relocated" to Florida as political prisoners.

see how easy it is
see how they do it
contact with the bedrock of being
true and whole human beings

Photo sourced from U.S. National Archives and Records Administration, Wikimedia Commons. The caption reads: *"Band of Apache Indian prisoners at rest stop beside Southern Pacific Railway, near Nueces River, Texas, September 10, 1886. Among those on their way to exile in Florida are Natchez (center front) and, to the right, Geronimo and his son in matching shirts."* (http://commons.wikimedia.org)

I apologize for using this moment in time (circa 1886) that the fierce and unrelenting resistance of Geronimo and the *Bedonkohe Apache* are finally overcome by Euro-Empire as an illustration of "earthing." My intent is not to simplify, derail, essentialize, romanticize, glamourize, adore, misinterpret, trivialize, whitewash, move to innocence, make a colonial alibi or perform a *Settler Sidestep*, but rather, that I continue to be forever haunted and moved to tears by the multiple layers of meaning in this photograph, and the full implications of the Euro-colonial takeover of the Americas. The unerring truth is that the photograph depicts human beings fully bonded to the land, exhibiting the familiarity and reliance of this connection in every aspect of their being.

EARTH FIRST ~ *Animism*

"Animism, because it seeks to relate and converse with the world, rather than to define and control it, always renews itself. It wakes up every morning fresh and alive, and every evening it tucks itself to bed to dream again for the very first time. Since animism involves a relationship with the world, a living being that exists in the now, the present moment, what more relevant perspective could you find?"[388] (Willem Larsen)

"Nature is alive and talking to us. This is not a metaphor." (Terence McKenna)

Before the rise of totalitarian agriculture and its culmination in a globalized hegemony, tribal societies all over the world lived within an "animistic" reality in which everything, inanimate or animate, was possessed of life, energy and spirit. By respecting the Earth as a living entity and acknowledging all forms of consciousness in the natural world and the cosmos, Indigenous people were masters of "holism" long before the invention of the word. Hardly relinquished and on the rise again today, *Animism* is the worldview that works best for humanity when we take our appropriate place within (not above) the circle of all life. Signs of the life force in nature such as the movement of waters and stars, or the growth of plants and animals, imply the presence of indwelling spirits, and stones, trees and other aspects of the natural world are self-aware, autonomous and willful beings who possess their own traits and dispositions. A spiritual force pervades all of nature, and the other-than-human world embraces a host of endlessly expressive and individualistic living entities whose actions we may adore, emulate, decipher, predict and even influence. *"Sympathy binds human beings to plants, animals, rocks and stars. Therefore they become beings rather than objects, fellows rather than things, and members in a circle of social relations."*[389] (Peter Nabokov) The Earth is totally sentient and aware, and a mountain or an entire territory can be the outward form of spiritual presence, or an abode of elemental forces inhabited by sentient beings and creatures. On a smaller scale the land holds myriad earth spirits, or even the ghosts of our beloved Ancestors.

The world is alive with purpose, energy and divine life, as environmental writer Theodore Roszak explains. *"In tribal societies, there is so much to see and hear. The bear speaks, the river speaks, the rainbow signifies, the eclipse is a sign. The animistic personification of natural objects may be difficult for us to accept in any 'literal' way. Yet, judged solely on intellectual grounds, animism can be credited with a more sophisticated perception of physicality than Western knowledge. Far from regarding matter as dead stuff, tribal societies perceive it as infused with mind, will, and intention."*[390] In constant interaction with the ecosystem, IK societies worldwide are in agreement that everything has a spiritual aspect or soul, and that our dependency and reciprocity binds us to the earth, air, fire, water, plants, animals, rocks and stars with whom we share experience. Immersed in the spiritual universe by virtue of being connected to the land, monotheism is not a principle recognized by the animist perspectives of Indigenous people, who evoke, honour and obey a multiplicity of spirits, deities, elements and powers. By extension, our collective responsibility to all life applies to our human clans and kinship groups as well, with the all-inclusive community practices of sharing, care and support. In the Anishnaabe tradition, the intrinsic cooperation and communication between humans, animals, birds, insects, plants and spirit beings is known as the "Council of Life." Also, in the traditional language of the Anishnaabe, most nouns are animate, indicating that in this Indigenous conceptual framework "things" are alive, and have autonomous standing and spirit. The animist perspective is also apparent in the cosmology of the Haudenosaunee, as *"the world around and all its features – rivers, trees, clouds, springs and mountains are regarded as alive, endowed with spirit and sensibility every bit as real as those of humans, and in fact of exactly the same type and quality as a human's. Among the Iroquois this was called Orenda, the invisible force inherent in all parts of the universe."*391 (Kirkpatrick Sale)

Animism is the way humanity has been deeply connected to the land and its seasonal cycles for millennia, in rapport and conversation with the animals, plants, living spirits, Ancestors and spiritual forces, and *"indigenous animism looks to the wholeness of nature for its principal teachings."*392 (Emma Restall Orr) As Indigenous societies were well aware, and western knowledge has recently "discovered" from deep ecology393 and studies such as *The Secret Life of Plants* and *The Gaia Hypothesis*, the elements, sentient beings and creatures in nature are awake and aware, albeit in slightly different form than how we perceive consciousness as humans. The affiliation between all beings, whether spiritual or physical, indicates an acceptance of multiple realities within the natural world. Deeply related and interactive in our mutual admiration, kinship and needs, the cycles and manifestations of growth that occur in self and nature correspond both materially and spiritually. We have never been separate from the life-affirming power of the natural world, and as it was in ancient times, the magical and mysterious presences and spirit beings in forests, shorelines, caves, mounds, springs, meadows and cliffs continue to present themselves to us, and communicate great insight, awareness, numinosity and enlightenment. The elementals, earth spirits, plant allies, faeries and "devas" can have identifiable personalities or other characteristics such as gender, and mythic narratives and story cycles from the oral traditions of IK/EIK systems worldwide portray these

388. Willem Larsen, "Becoming Traditional: Animism, Culture, and the Newly Born," *The College of Mythic Cartography*, March 6, 2007. (www.mythic-cartography.org)
389. Peter Nabokov, *Where the Lightning Strikes: The Lives of American Indian Sacred Places*, Viking Penguin, 2006.
390. Theodore Roszak, "The Greening of Psychology: Exploring the Ecological Unconscious," *The Gestalt Journal*, Volume 18, Number 1, Spring, 1995.
391. Kirkpatrick Sale, *Dwellers in the Land: The Bioregional Vision*, University of Georgia Press, 2000.
392. Emma Restall Orr, *The Wakeful World: Animism, the Mind and the Self in Nature*, Moon Books, 2011.
393. *"The Deep Ecology movement rejects the idea of human supremacy within nature, the anthropocentric view, in favor of an egalitarian relationship with the biosphere, deeply experiencing nature and our embeddedness within creation."* Paul Devereux, *Revisioning the Earth: A Guide to Opening the Healing Channels Between Mind and Nature*, Simon & Schuster, 1996.

other-than-human beings as neutral, lovable, exuberant, terrifying and even mischievous!

If we are open to sharing through our heart, mind, dreaming body and other senses, the stones, trees, plants, animals, birds, insects and sacred creatures with whom we share this wondrous planet have an infinity of healing, guardianship, and learning experiences to offer. By stilling our inner dialogue, focusing on positive intent and emotions, and listening deeply with our ears plus our entire range of senses, we have the ability to initiate conversations with earth spirits, creatures or energetic beings, and the results can be surprising and awe-inspiring. Some people hear actual voices, for others it is a waking dream, powerful vision or spontaneous experience, while others receive messages through night-time visitations, intuitions or strong feelings. Interpretations can either come easily with an undeniable "knowing," or become clear over time and distance. There are an infinity of examples found worldwide that reflect interactive success between the human and nonhuman world, and in the western tradition we can turn to the recent "miraculous" communications within the Findhorn community in the UK.[394] By opening up their heightened consciousness and wider sensory abilities, and developing empathy skills, Eileen Caddy, Peter Caddy and Dorothy MacLean were able to hear the wisdom and tutelage as expressed by the overarching nature spirits, or "Devas" of the plant realm. In a state of heightened awareness - a space of great joy, freedom and unconditional love - they found that the Devas were thrilled to be noticed by humans, and with ongoing interaction they became close companions in cooperative gardening and spiritual co-evolution. All forms of life start with energies that are materialized into specific physical form by the overarching soul essences of each being, the "Kingdom of Devas" who hold the archtypal patterns. As recommended by Findhorn's Dorothy MacLean, feeling and harmonizing one's self with the soul essence of a plant can evoke a response from a Deva, such as this cooperative communication received from the *Flowering Gentian* plant.

"We bring breaths of open spaces and hills, of sunshine, showers, and breezes. All of these are part of your being. Even if you live in the midst of a busy city, these natural things are home to you. They are part of the atmosphere of this Earth, part of the surroundings in which you live and grow. Even if your life and thinking are completely enmeshed in the human world, still you are part of our deva world, which works for the perfect flowering of all life. This is your birthright. You may turn your back on it, but someday you will learn the truth and live in connection with all life on this planet. Only then will you tap your highest potential."[395]   (Gentian Deva)

At the very moment that we are uplifted by the beauty of the earth, or in touch with the harmony of the green world, we are in contact with the

Devic realms. Our ancestral soul also remembers and responds to our personal sacred plant teachers, the plant spirits or Devas that function as doorways to sacred realms of healing, knowledge and wisdom. The same way curanderas or traditional and modern healers practice "plant spirit medicine" by approaching their plant allies, we find that the plants are willing to give information to us directly or through dreams and visions. With love and respect as our guiding forces as we enter the green web, we discover that the plants themselves are the ultimate authority on their medicinal and nutritional uses, which may or may not correspond with standard allopathic treatments. In collaboration with the green world, miraculous work continues to be done today in homeopathy, herbalism, alchemy, aromatherapy, flower essences and the heirloom seed movement. By incorporating elements of animistic communication with nature intelligences into modern paths of green wisdom, deep ecology, biomimicry, co-creative gardening, eco-feminism, eco-art, earth literacy and spiritual adventures in nature; earth-based culture is thriving as we re-awaken to our biophilia, our connection to our primeval roots, and our innate affinity with all life.

For the practicing Animist, deeply personal messages and affinities are all around us, and the appearance and timing of phenomena like a rainbow, the cawing of a raven, the patterns etched in sand or the visitation of a snake can have great individual purpose and meaning. In my own case I have always held an Animist knowing and companionship with wild nature, as I continue to see, feel, sense, observe, know and communicate with other presences out on the land - creatures, beings, elements, earth spirits, deities, plant allies or the archetypal animal spirits. In just one of many awe-inspiring visitations I have been blessed to receive, as I was looking up from a wilderness meadow one beautiful warm summer day at the clouds billowing overhead they coalesced into the exact shape and archetypal configuration of the "Venus of Willendorf," the well-known carved-stone figurine from an ancient matriarchal culture in *Old Europe*.

Digital re-creation of the Venus of Willendorf floating in the clouds!

Humbled before the powerful consciousness of the natural world, I will never know the how or why of the *Great Mystery*, but will treasure this moment in my soul forever. Honoring the life force in creation and knowing that all beings are sacred are the core beliefs of Animism, and it is our collective responsibility to support this interexistence and our connectivity of all life with the highest respect and generosity of spirit.

A wonderful contemporary example of honoring and engaging with the spirits of the land is the work of the earth-wise Pagan troupe the *Dragon Ritual Drummers*, who reached out and "woke up" the mythical dragon spirit who resides in an ethereal cave on the brink of Niagara Falls, Ontario. "*The ancient serpent spirit was once revered by the indigenous inhabitants of the region, but was eventually cast into a negative legacy by the conquering Iroquois nation, falling into obscurity for generations.*"[396] Attaching their name, devotion, lore and music to this rejuvenated entity, the *Dragon Ritual Drummers* have achieved unprecedented acclaim for their musical genius worldwide, and attribute much of their success to their reciprocal relationship with this ancient dragon-serpent spirit.

The opposite of animism is the "cult of the individual" so celebrated in modern society, and the loss of the animist worldview is at the root of our spiritual disconnect and looming ecological crisis. In the time of ancient Greece, Plato identified this overall interconnection as *Anima Mundi*, or "world soul" - "*a living being endowed with a soul and intelligence.....a single visible living entity containing all other living entities, which by their nature are all related.*"[397] Human beings are just one strand woven into the complex systems of *Earth Community*, and the animistic perspective is fundamental to the paradigm shift and the recovery of our IK/EIK. By choosing to embrace our emotional, physical and spiritual bonds to the land, we are living as part of nature, and by immersing our children in the natural world we provide the opportunity for the next generation to become ecologically grounded as well. Self-identifying as an Animist means that one's moral code is guided by the desire to realize the pre-eminence of the other-than-human world, and to become an ongoing advocate for earth protection, environmental sustainability and spiritual ecology. As we focus on the heart of nature as our cultural and spiritual practice our auto-ecology will thrive, and by sharing these old/new ways of living with others, the false values and synthetic programming of Empire will diminish in meaning. Our reawakening to Animism, arising from our collective ancient past, will naturally move us forward to a positive future of ecocentric ethics and reciprocity with the *Circle of All Life*.

"*Everything in nature is alive and speaking. Our spiritual practice is about opening our eyes, ears and hearts to hear, understand, and communicate back. The elements, the Ancestors and the spirit beings that surround us want us to communicate with them. They want to work with us to protect and heal the Earth, but they need our invitation.*"[398] (Starhawk)

---

394. For a glimpse into how communication and co-creation with nature intelligences has been done on a large scale, projects such as the Findhorn Garden community in the UK or Perelandra in the USA provide fascinating guideposts. For more on *The Findhorn Community* see (www.findhorn.org) and on the nature-spirit communication work of Machaelle Small Wright see (www.perelandra-ltd.com).
395. Dorothy MacLean, *To Honor the Earth: Reflections on Living in Harmony with Nature,* HarperCollins, 1991.
396. For *Dragon Ritual Drummers* information, downloads and tour schedule visit their website at (http://dragonritualdrummers.com).
397. Plato, *Timaeus,* 29/30, 4th century B.C.
398. Starhawk, "A Pagan Response to Katrina," *Starhawk's Tangled Web: Goddess and Pagan Resources,* September 14, 2005. (www.starhawk.org)

EARTH FIRST ~ *Ecomysticism & Nature Spirituality*

*"May all things move and be moved in me
and know and be known in me,
may all creation dance for joy within me."* [399]
(Chinook Psalter)

Ecomysticism, or *Nature Spirituality,* is the reclaiming of wild nature as central to our appreciation of the Great Mystery, and is embodied in our reverence and love for the Earth and the more-than-human world. By seeing the wonders of nature close-up and having primal experiences in the wild we develop a spiritual bond to the plants, elements and creatures, and realize a powerful kinship with all life. Embracing nature as our spiritual guide gives our reality depth and meaning far beyond the mundane ideology offered by the superficial and materialistic values of urban life. By experiencing the "wild within" of our own ecology and that of *Earth Community,* we find that we need no intermediaries, special philosophies or religions to realize that the Earth is sacred. It can be said that for millennia, ecomysticism was the governing force in Indigenous earth-connected cultures that lived in balance and harmony with the land. As Carl Jung explains, modern man remains archaic in his deepest psyche, and *"the archetypal endowment with which each of us is born prepares us for the natural life cycle of our species, in the natural world in which we evolved."*[400] It is our birthright as human beings to have a reciprocal, active relationship with the cycles of nature, and we have an intrinsic need to respect the Earth not just as an experience but as a living breathing presence, a being to whom we owe our existence and our joy.

When we are in the wild, we are affected by the blessings of nature whether we are aware of it or not. Our senses are heightened, we find ourselves more focused and in tune with our bodies, and we feel more at peace - happy, blissful even. Many of our mystical experiences in connection with nature occur in solitude, far away from the technology and distractions of modern life. As a child I was blessed with the expansion experience well-known to many mystics, whereby everything in the green space of my backyard - the plants, flowers, birds, insects, gentle breeze and bright sun - all of a sudden became hyper-alive, glowing and luminous. Vibrating with an immense joy that filled my being with a multi-faceted peace and light, this divine radiance connected me for all time to the *Great Mystery* inherent in nature and the cosmos. I have experienced countless times of ecstasy and epiphany in the deep forest, walking along the river, ambling beside farmer's fields, floating in the lake, hiking the trail and descending the rocky hillside. For me, nature is the lens through which myth, magic and mystery appear, and these euphoric moments are the treasures, like beads on a string, that I lovingly preserve from my memories of sojourns in wild places. My definition of transcendence, the heart of my own spiritual journey and contemporary practice, has always either originated from, or led back to, the natural world.

A mystical experience is the feeling that leaves us speechless and awed, knowing that some great power has touched our lives. As Carl von Essen tells us, *"these feelings are ineffable, indescribable; noetic, true; transient, brief; and passive, unexpected."*[401] Touched by a great vision, manifestation of divinity, awakening or epiphany (akin to the "kundalini rising" experience in Eastern wisdom traditions), numinous experiences can lead to great feats of physical endurance, sublime creativity in works of art, unforgettable memories and even a complete change in one's life. As an Ecomystic, there are many benefits to having these kind of peak experiences in nature, such as extraordinary perceptions and miraculous, magical events that defy explanation. Practicing nature spirituality activates the deep psychic abilities inherent within us all, enabling us to experience the world(s) of hidden things. Entering gateways or portals into other realms, we form a deeper understanding of ourselves, our life purpose and our trans-personal connection to the life-giving forces of the *Great Mystery*, or alternatively said "Anima Mundi," the Infinite, the Creator, the Divine, or Great Mother Goddess.

"To commune with nature is an essential aspect of the spiritual journey. By going back to nature we are in a sense returning to the garden, to

399. Chinook Psalter, "The Daily Round," *Earth Prayers From Around the World: 365 Prayers, Poems, and Invocations for Honoring the Earth,* Elizabeth Roberts and Elias Amidon (editors), Harper Collins Publishers, 1991.

400. Carl Jung quoted in *Evolutionary Psychiatry: A New Beginning,* by Anthony Stevens and John Price, Taylor and Francis Inc., 2000.

401. Carl von Essen, *Ecomysticism: The Profound Experience of Nature as Spiritual Guide,* Bear & Company, 2010.

*the place where we were contained within nature's wholeness, where
we were not separated from the Divine, from whence our visions and
calls emanate."*[402] (Bell Hooks)

Examples abound from those having transcendent experiences in
nature (or even in cities and urban places) at the formative time of
childhood or later in life. These ecstatic moments of rapture remain
deeply embedded in our psyches, and can inform our experiences,
creativity and goals as we mature and grow. In the western tradition,
well-known ecomystic Henry David Thoreau embraced "wildness" with
his whole being, and became a *"transcendentalist of simplicity and
roughness."*[403] (Emerson) His spiritual unity with nature went far
beyond physical proximity, and his marvellous writings express *"the
poetry of nature, which uplifts the spirit within us and opens to our
imagination a world of spiritual beauty and holiness."*[404] (John Ruskin)
The Irish writer, mystic, theosophist and clairvoyant George Russell
received dazzling insights into the *"memory of the Earth"*[405] which he
"tuned into" at will on the hillsides outside of Dublin and at sand dunes
by the sea. At these liminal sites, revelations of the *"most ancient
places and peoples, and landscapes lovely as lost Eden"* [406] were made
known to him. Nobel prize-winner Rabindranath Tagore also believed
in the earth-based unity of spiritual truth, and spent his life observing
and writing about the human experience and its relation to the Divine.
His explorations and spiritual enlightenment began in childhood when
he entered a realm of cosmic consciousness in close proximity to the
natural fairyland of trees and gardens in his own backyard. *"I had been
blessed with that sense of wonder which gives a child his right to enter
the treasure-house of mystery in the heart of existence."*[407]

Emma Restall Orr attributes the early beginnings of her life-long
spiritual quest to the transcendence of a childhood awakening to
divinity, wholeness and peace. *"My first religious experiences came
to me both in wild and human places. Lying on a warm stone in
rural Spanish sunshine, alone, my eyes closed, my soul infused with
the scents of cistus and thyme, listening to the sound of goat bells
above the tumbling rush of the river, I knew - with that subjective
certainty which so thoroughly imbues such moments - that time did*

402. Bell Hooks, "Mind, Body and Soul," *11th Annual Women of Color Conference
Keynote,* University of Oregon, March 5, 2008. (www.youtube.com)
403. Emerson on Thoreau quoted in *Ecomysticism: The Profound Experience of Nature
as Spiritual Guide,* by Carl von Essen, Bear & Company, 2010.
404. John Ruskin, "A Sacred Place," *Earth Prayers From Around the World: 365
Prayers, Poems, and Invocations for Honoring the Earth,* Elizabeth Roberts and Elias
Amidon (editors), Harper Collins Publishers, 1991.
405. George William Russell, *The Candle of Vision,* New Hyde Park, University Books,
1965.
406. Ibid.
407. Amiya Chakravarty (editor), *A Tagore Reader,* Macmillan Company, 1961.

not exist, and that everything around me was the wholeness of all that had ever happened in that ancient valley. At eight years old, it was an experience of being completely held in peace and security, to the extent that I recognise my spiritual journey to be in some measure a seeking to re-create that exceptional feeling."[408] Teri Degler examines both creativity and spiritual experience as linked to the cosmic feminine force in her book *The Divine Feminine Fire*, and finds that the classic kundalini-rising experience can be prompted by many things – trauma, seeking, great yearning, and being in nature. One of her own experiences with deep ecology and the divine energies in nature culminated in feelings of limitless love and connectivity. "*With the blue-green waves washing onto the shore and my bare feet digging into the cold, damp sand, I began to move slowly through a set of exercises. As I focused my eyes on the horizon, something in my perception shifted. The line separating sky and water began to dissolve. Sky and water became one, water became one with the sand, and slowly all boundaries, all lines of demarcation dissolved. Suddenly I could see, actually physically see, that all edges were an illusion. Everything that had once appeared to be separate to me was in fact one vast, limitless expanse of pulsating life energy. Intense sensations began to rush through my body, and my heart exploded with love.*" [409] As we can see from these examples, nature worship and spiritual ecology can give us ecstatic experiences and the ability to see into the heart of the things that really matter.

The cosmic consciousness of *Nature Spirituality* places us in a position of great humbleness and humility before the immensity and grandeur of creation. Surrendering to the cycles of time, the forces of nature, and the diverse patterns of weather – gentle or turbulent – means being in alignment with our ancestral knowledge, and rejecting the model of human-centric domination. It is not simplistic to suggest a return to nature, and many are embracing *Ecomysticism* as an important spiritual path in response to the current global eco-crisis, and to sanctify one's relationship to the natural world. Our connection to our essential eco-self has withered over the generations, but there is an ancestral memory in all of us that, if given the opportunity, can renew our kinship to the circle of all life. "*The idea of a completely profane world, the wholly desacralized cosmos, is a recent discovery in the history of the human spirit.*"[410] (Mircea Eliade) Re-awakening ancient memories from our primeval past allows our consciousness and conscience to unite again in harmony with Mother Earth. Evoking our biophilia, reclaiming nature as a mystical mirror of ourselves, having spiritual adventures and experiences in green spaces - these are the blessings of ecomystic practice that can assist us in the rewilding of our souls. And finally, as a powerful expression of the sacred balance, *Ecomysticism* can renew humanity's spiritual connection to nature and support true environmental healing.

408. Emma Restall Orr, "Pagan Ecology: On Our Perception of Nature, Ancestry, and Home," *The Wanton Green: Contemporary Pagan Writings on Place*, Mandrake, 2012.
409. Teri Degler, *The Divine Feminine Fire: Creativity and Your Yearning to Express Your Self*, Dreamriver Press, 2009.
410. Mircea Eliade, *Patterns in Comparative Religion*, New American Library, 1974.

EARTH FIRST ~ *Ecopsychology*

"It is Theodore Rosack who emphasized that we are on the verge of discovering that the deep unconscious is not sexual (Freud), or spiritual (Jung), but related to the ecosystem in which we live. And in that regard we must understand how Western people have diverged very far indeed from their unconscious in a destructive way. The destruction of the environment goes hand in hand with the destruction of our relationship to the unconscious, which is at its very depth our natural habitat and indigenous culture. The recovery of this relatedness of all things can be accomplished as individuals, simply, genuinely and honestly without external trappings or borrowed traditions."[411] (Helene E. Hagan)

As the urbanization of the world continues to interfere with our awareness of nature, we are being denied our connection to the Earth as our primary source of healing, growth and mystic inspiration. Removing humankind from the sacred crucible of the natural environment has had devastating consequences, some masked by denial and societal distractions, and others highly obvious in the manifestation of psychopathic behavior. Industrial and urban spaces affect us physically, mentally and spiritually, and modern ills such as environmental sensitivities or allergies, frenzied highs and lethargic lows, delusions, and the lack of focus, purpose or spiritual meaning are all endemic of a disconnect from the natural world. In response to the modern dysfunction of "nature deficit disorder"[412] as fully examined by Richard Louv and others, the mainstream promotion of spending more time in nature for mood enhancement, health benefits, better concentration and an overall re-enchantment with life is on the rise. As part of the re-balancing that is occurring in western society, the new field of ecopsychology (alternatively framed as "terrapsychology," "ecotherapy," "Gaia psychology" or "nature relatedness") focuses on methods for breaking the stranglehold of industrial society. A blend of ecology, sociology, philosophy and environmental science, eco-psychology explores the psychological benefits associated with nature, as well as introducing practices that ultimately reconnect us to our "ecological unconscious." Compared to the eons that human beings have spent embedded in the primal matrix and in close kinship with the other-than-human world, our current malaise of modernity is the result of quite recent domestication, and ecopsychology reminds us of familiar strategies for overcoming the emotional trauma of our alienation from the Earth.

"This was a great joy – to be out in the air....a pure and intense joy, a blessing, to feel the sun on my face and the wind in my hair, to hear birds, to see, touch and fondle the living plants. Some essential connection and communion with nature was re-established after the horrible isolation and alienation I had known. Some part of me came alive when I was taken into the garden."[413]   (Oliver Sacks)

Being drawn to places that enliven us, appreciating the beauty of green space, interacting with animals and participating in nature firsthand are fundamental human needs that ecopsychology addresses. For decades now scholars, social and natural scientists, humanists, practitioners and eco-therapists have advanced the practice and theory of ecopsychology into the public sphere. Ecotherapy rituals and exercises bring us into direct contact with the knowledge that our lives are deeply entwined with the natural world, and deepen our spiritual experience of the timeless human/nature/cosmos relationship. Cultivating awe and wonder in the face of the *Earth Mysteries*, developing conscious intention, using guided imagery, and re-centering ourselves in the grounding of our own sensate bodies are all ways to promote the healing of self, family and community. A wide range of natural places like our own backyards, wildlife preserves, urban parks, or remote wilderness places can speak to us of our membership in biotic community, and offer us the benefits of enhanced mental, emotional, physical and spiritual well-being.

> *As dreams are the healing songs*
> *from the wilderness*
> *of our unconscious —*
> *So wild animals, wild plants, wild landscapes*
> *are the healing dreams*
> *from the deep singing mind of the earth.*[414]   (Dale Pendell)

It terms of western scientific studies, data has shown that the brain-wave patterns of those in urbanized, busy areas are frustrated and aroused, while the brain-wave readings of those in woodlands and parks tend to be meditative and focused. Studies have shown time after time that people prefer green space over cities and urban sprawl - which is not surprising, since human beings are hardwired to position our

411. Helene E. Hagan, "The Plastic Medicine People Circle," *Institute of Archetypal Ethnology Newsletter,* September l992.
412. Richard Louv, *Last Child in the Woods: Saving Our Children from Nature-Deficit Disorder*, Algonquin Books of Chapel Hill, 2005. Nature deficit disorder (NDD) is defined as living in an urban environment without contact to nature, with a wide range of symptoms and physical or emotional illnesses appearing as mood disorders, childhood obesity, diminished use of the senses, myopia and attention difficulties.
413. Oliver Sacks, *A Leg to Stand On,* Touchstone, 1998.
414. Dale Pendell, *Living With Barbarians: A Few Plant Poems*, Wild Ginger Press, 1999.

relationship to nature at the core of our psychology. The sights and sensations of a vast expanse of water, green landscapes and panoramic views are a basic human necessity. It is also our eternal nature to interpret the connections between phenomena in the natural world and ourselves in a holistic loop, or back-and-forth dynamic. Our minds possess an amazing ability to translate outer events into inner ones through symbols and motifs that heal and inspire us, and make us happy and productive. A flowering shrub can easily become a metaphor for our own blossoming, a tree in winter translates into a symbol for strength and resilience, a turtle outlines our own steadfastness and self-protection, and an otter becomes a representation of playfulness and spontaneity. For millennia human beings have acknowledged the land, elements and creatures as living beings deeply implicated in our psychological life, and we know that encounters in nature are healing both to the psyche and the body. The practices of ecopsychology today are intent on reclaiming this enchantment with the world, returning to the wild for our "ensouling," uncovering authentic truths and ancient origins, and re-establishing the connection to nature that is so vital to our well-being.

"Humans have long recognized the healing power of nature, the peace of wild places, and the more than physical craving for clean water and space, all of which are no more than a recognition of the human need to be in harmony with the natural world."[415]   (Ian Mills)

To enhance our biophilia and self-realization through "re-earthing" we need to go wild (!) by walking in the woods, hiking, canoeing, camping, wilderness trekking, survival training, climbing trees, wildcrafting, bird watching, going on retreat, meditating in nature, journaling, or having a beacon bonfire - all activities that put us in "the flow" and generate vitality and happiness. Other direct pathways to *"re-inhabiting what was taken away – our spirituality, our imaginative resources and our unity with nature"*[416] (Lorenna Bousquet-Kacera) are found through ritual dance and primordial movement, or by exploring the powerful tools of imagery and eco-art therapy for self-discovery and healing. The sights and scents of the green world uplift, de-stress and open our hearts, and we can find healing in the garden too, as our mental well-being is definitely enhanced by "horticultural therapy." Being near the calm profound life of trees in the forest (and tree hugging!) has been scientifically validated to improve many health issues such as attention deficit hyperactivity disorder (ADHD), concentration levels,

---

415. Ian Mills (editor), *A Sound of Thunder: A Green Anthology*, Addison-Wesley Publishers, 1993.
416. Permaculture educator, gardener and eco-creativity guide Lorenna Bousquet-Kacera is the founder of the *Living Centre and Living Arts Institute* in London, Ontario, and she offers open circles, ritual dance, primordial movement and workshops such as "Reclaiming Ourselves in the Age of Nature," "WomanEarth: Living in the Heart of Gaia" and "Spiritual Ecology." (www.thelivingcentre.com)

reaction times, depression, and illnesses such as headaches and arthritis. The vibrational properties of trees, plants, and green space can slow us down, quiet our nervous system, release endorphins, lower blood pressure, restore our ability to concentrate, and generate feelings of calm, tranquility and transcendence. The contemporary practice of "forest bathing" ("shinrin-yoki" in Japan) allows us to soak up the scents, sights, sounds and atmosphere of the forest for protective and healthful effects on the human body, mind and heart. Walking or spending time in the forest boosts immunity, relieves stress and promotes energy, and studies have found a high level of anti-cancer cells in blood samples after forest bathing. Similar to the benefits of aromatherapy, the natural essential oils of the forest that we breathe in have antioxidant, anti-inflammatory and anti-microbial effects, and enhance our overall mood and outlook on life. Without question, our capacity for healing, happiness, insight, emotional catharsis and ecomystic experience blossom with our immersion in deep forests and wilderness places.

> *"Primal natural forests are temples of magnificent peace.*
> *Saturated in Earth's ancient stillness,*
> *sanctuary for the human soul.*
> *Focusing our profound affinity with Nature.*
> *In deep, sleeping dreamtime, as in a trance,*
> *we rediscover lost, forgotten dreams,*
> *recharging passion and following our hearts*
> *to health and harmony."*[417]   (Mark Berry)

Experiencing the "earth matrix"[418] firsthand is especially important for children and youth, who may be deprived of meaningful nature connection in this extreme era of monolithic technology, artificial environments, über-consumerism and eco-fascism. Instead of the "nature deficit disorder" that results from the emphasis on human-centric activities in simulated spaces, children and youth who are offered opportunities to interact with the natural world exhibit heightened creativity, enhanced cognitive abilities, emotional mastery, and improved health and well-being. Nothing could be more important than to teach the adults of tomorrow the spiritual, emotional, physical and mental benefits of interacting with nature, not to mention that bonding deeply to place encourages the love of the land that can lead to activism and environmental protection. Placing our relationship with nature as central to our existence reconnects us to our own personal mythology, the timeless realm of spirit, the eternal cycles, and the ongoing progression of life itself. The more deeply we embrace nature as a healing force, the more balanced we will become as true human beings. Overall, adopting the theory and practice of ecopsychology reminds us of our value as essential to the whole, and gives our lives deeper meaning and sacred purpose.

417. Poetry by Mark Berry, *Gaia: Journey into Vanishing Worlds,* by Paige Deponte, Global Art in Action, 1999.
418. Richard Louv, *Last Child in the Woods: Saving Our Children from Nature-Deficit Disorder*, Algonquin Books of Chapel Hill, 2005.

EARTH FIRST ~ *Earth Story*

"When the stories a society shares are out of tune with its circumstances, they can become self-limiting, even a threat to survival. This is our current situation."[419] (David Korten)

"Our Ancestors experienced life in terms of imagination and intuition, and this mythic worldview has value for us today. A new interest is awakening in primal mind, fantasies and dreams. We have the need to relate back to a deeper level of life which is more direct and full of feeling, with a natural grace and wisdom that is more appealing than all the dazzling accomplishments of the intellectual ego. Myth has once again become important."[420] (Tom Chetwynd)

The technologies, conveniences, mobility, communication devices and television bombardment of our fast-paced modern lifestyle give us the illusion that human beings are the centre of the universe. What spell have we been under? The addiction to entertainment and diversion, the ongoing incestuous interaction with our human inventions and emotional dramas to the exclusion of all other life on Earth, is narcissistic, dysfunctional and immoral. Thinking that human endeavors and humancentric concerns are the only ones that matter keep us trapped in the sinkhole of modernism, contribute to the "old story" of Empire, and do nothing to return us to right relationship with the land. Creating, believing and experiencing new narratives that honour and celebrate the natural world and our place within it, are urgently needed to bend the curve. We need to tell new stories about ourselves, new myths to guide us forward, and new manifestos that celebrate our integration with the natural world. Our archaic spirit needs to rise again in a weaving of timeless myths and stories of growth, regeneration, rites of passage, motion, energy, illumination, magic, decay, and all the Earth's processes that dwell both in us and the more-than-human world.

In the last days of Empire, the imperialist corporatist agenda of religion, economic hegemony, politics and science is dissolving, falling apart under the weight of unsustainability, and countless awake and aware people are moving away from these delusional and insane systems. The paradigm of humanity as lord and master of Mother Earth has run its course, and it is becoming harder and harder to believe in the myth of a mechanical universe and our separation from the natural world. *"We are living at a time in which the old story of domination and control has lost its power, and we are in a liminal, in-between time, still searching for a new story."*[421] (Charles Eisenstein) The narrative of industrial civilization we are labouring under was marginally acceptable when it first began, when the materials to build mighty technological empires seemed endless and plentiful, and a palatial lifestyle could easily be shaped by the ongoing extraction of "resources." That the "colonial dream" would have been adopted by everyone on the planet was perhaps something the early "meme spreaders"[422] did not foresee, but the Earth clearly cannot sustain billions of people living at the height of civilizational benefit and luxury. *"Unless you believe infinite growth is possible on a finite planet"*[423] (Charles Eisenstein) it is time to redefine our values and adopt a different paradigm for self, community and the world, and a return to the beauty of interconnection and a respect for natural law.

Mirroring the "new myth" in full interaction with others as both a spiritual and political act will disrupt the business-as-usual of Empire in ways we can only imagine. So, what is myth? Numerous and diverse, myths and creation stories across the world are the tales of our most sacred origins, holding the central beliefs, cultural meanings, values and destinies specific to each society. Origin stories, or accounts of how a particular social order came into being, along with explanations and exemplars, are human attempts to answer the most fundamental questions of existence, and form the building blocks of our collective reality. Arising from both the intellect and the imagination, narrative epics, mythic stories and parables are "lessons for living" that offer us guidance for navigating both the inner and outer worlds. Myths, keystone stories and important events in history are transferred from generation to generation, and are integrated into rituals and ceremonies that include the bardic arts, music, song, call-and-response, poetry, dance and drumming. Throughout history, Indigenous peoples have relied on the storykeepers to maintain the tribal records, and to further the richness of history, culture and identity. Storytellers can reach back through time to ancestral knowledge, convey important teachings, and validate the prestige and responsibilities of tribal members, each presenting a unique piece of the IK/EIK puzzle. In this way, the oral transmission of collective memory becomes a living worldview that keeps the cultural traditions of the group alive.

---

419. David C. Korten, *The Great Turning: From Empire to Earth Community*, Berrett-Koehler/Kumarian Press, 2006.
420. Tom Chetwynd, *The Age of Myth,* Mandala, 1991.
421. Charles Eisenstein, *Sacred Economics: Money, Gift and Society in the Age of Transition,* Evolver Editions, 2011.
422. Daniel Quinn calls the foundational worldviews of culture "memes." Daniel Quinn, *Beyond Civilization: Humanity's Next Great Adventure*, Broadway, 2000.
423. Charles Eisenstein, *A New Story of the People*, TEDxWhitechapel, February 13, 2013. (www.youtube.com)

Focused on our interactions and soul connections with *Earth Community*, our collective stories can outline our rapport with other beings, interspecies communication, and the realm of the shapeshifters. The natural world is the entry point to the "dreamtime" - a place where our access to ensouled expressions and personal mythology merge. *"Stories and their ceremonies weave our world together: the story of corn maiden and mother, of salmon's death and rebirth, of bear's human wife, of coyote's foul tricks and lynx's loneliness. These stories of ecological conscience are a council where the voices of all species may be heard. It is through these stories that the Earth can be restored, for these eco-narratives are an 'ilbal', a 'seeing instrument'. Looking through the eyes of others as their stories are told, we may hear and understand the voices of our relatives."*[424] (Joan Halifax)

An important purpose for oral history is to record the ongoing interactions and lived experiences that arise from our essential bond to the other-than-human world, and to recount the stories that are held within geographical locations on the land. Whether at key points like sacred sites or more humble personal places, the storied landscape brings our lore to life - the earth deities or sages we honour, the possibilities we dream about, and the paradoxes we cannot explain. Unfortunately, the dynamic that cultural narratives and lifeways arise from the land itself is something the early Settler Society did not understand. *"Edward Chamberlin described one of the first encounters between Gitksan people and the Canadian government. When surveyors informed them that the government owned their land, the Gitksan replied by asking: 'If this is your land, where are your stories?' "*[425] (Derek Rasmussen)

For a powerful example of the oral tradition as a living worldview we can look to the great Okanagan storyteller and orator Harry Robinson, who was wholly immersed in the natural world in every waking moment. During the transcribing of his priceless story-cycles, scholar Wendy Wickwire tells us that *"Harry travelled to Vancouver to undergo medical treatment under the care of an elderly Chinese herbalist. Only then did the depth of Harry's mythological world become truly apparent to me. As we passed through downtown Vancouver on his visits to the doctor, I realized that all the traffic lights and cars meant nothing to Harry. They were almost an abstraction, an interesting but fleeting diversion from the timeless real world of Coyote, Fox and Owl."*[426] (Wendy Wickwire) In our own work to reject the failed experiment of industrial civilization, connect deeply to the land and embody the beautiful archeomythology of our own IK/EIK, can we also have no doubt that entering urban space is an illusion and an aberration, an insult to ourselves, the Earth and Her many creatures and elements? Can we too walk among the ruins of Empire and see it as an abstraction, a fleeting diversion that for a long and unmerciful time tried to demonize Gaia and separate us from our one true home?

To re-indigenize ourselves means to reinhabit place, and return to the various features and creatures in our landbase that inform and inspire our own mythic worldview. Developing eco-literacy means unlearning the consensual rational worldview of Empire in favor of older ways to see the world, to think and feel our way into an ecological perspective with storytelling, eco-poetics, ceremonies, intuitive workings and sacred art. Our creative, mystic, and poetic selves blossom when we dwell in a sense of oneness with the natural world, and we gain new knowledge and wisdom when we are living as part of (rather than apart from) the web of all life. A keen knowledge of the surrounding ecosystem is fundamental to our deep sense of interconnection and imperative to a sustainable future, as we need the visions and stories of an earth-friendly paradigm to counteract Empire's mandate to devour the Earth's resources and spirit. Communicating this eco-literacy to others, especially children, is the most important task we face.

"Stories nurture our connection to place and to each other. They show us where we have been and where we can go. They remind us of how to be human, and how to live alongside the other lives that animate this planet."[427] (Susan J. Tweit)

So, what is the new *Earth Story*?

These thoughts, explorations and "chapters" may be a good beginning ~

- To reorient our body, mind, heart and soul toward a more integral relationship with the Earth,
- to return to our indigenity knowing we are all children of Earth, and that our place is within, not above, the circle of creation,
- to look to nature as a knowledgeable and inspiring teacher, as Gaia herself provides us with the stories for a new era,
- to place the stories we tell about the unique geoforms, landmarks, processes, species, quirks and cycles of the land around us - our local ecosystem - at the heart of our lives,
- to revive and embrace the natural law of species diversity in a multiplicity of belief systems, partnerships, unique societies, ethnicities and Earth communities,
- to address ecological solutions that maintain and improve the health of natural systems and the diversity of all life,
- to revalue our bodies, the dignity of materiality, and working with our hands,
- to live each day as a sacred act,
- to love the land as central to our most cherished dreams and memories, to care for and restore the Earth, and
- to take a stand for ecological defence.

"The urgency is such that no longer can we isolate any part of creation from any other, and in our new personal and active storytelling, narratives that inter-relationship with the natural world, and our shared destiny awaken to the powers of mystery again. We need to discover a new way of seeing and living in the world."[428]   (James Conlon)

In this time of transition, sharing and collaborating with our kindred spirits on the new *Earth Story* is an integral part of reclaiming a collective worldview and practice. We need a new story in these times of cataclysmic return - and it is the same one already in place that humanity has had for millennia, embedded in Indigenous worldview(s) that respect the human place within the circle of creation, and express our love for *Earth Community*. As we re-examine our own life story within the context of Empire-building, we need to relinquish the experiences that do not serve us, and reclaim the kinship model of our relationship to the wild. Deconstructing, reframing, and rewriting our own mythology within the context of nature (instead of the technoculture) will enlarge our transformation to knowing that we belong to the Earth, and evoke the stories that honour each other, all beings, and the earth as *Sacred*.

The human mind is as much a part of nature as a boreal forest, and the imaginal states of dreaming, imagining, wandering in nature, making magic and creating stories are intrinsic to our being. A return to this "mythic mode of consciousness" can bring us the profound experiences and insights that are missing from the modern worldview, and promote the healing of our separation from the *Circle of All Life*. A collective myth or meaningful framework stressing interexistence and earth ethics is needed now more than ever, and it is time to adopt a natural place either physically or metaphorically, dig in with all our might, and incorporate the new *Earth Story* into our lives!

"Having a place means that you know what a place means in a storied sense of myth, character and presence, but also in an ecological sense......integrating native consciousness with mythic consciousness."[429]   (Gary Snyder)

---

424. Joan Halifax, *The Fruitful Darkness: Reconnecting with the Body of the Earth*, Harper Collins, 1993.

425. Derek Rasmussen, "Assimilating Canadians into the wisdom of Indigenous ancestors," *Rabble*, April 23, 2013. (http://rabble.ca)

426. Harry Robinson and Wendy Wickwire (editor), *Write it on Your Heart: The Epic World of an Okanagan Storyteller*, Talonbooks, 1989. From the first of three volumes, the stories of Harry Robinson (Interior Salish, Lower Similkameen Band, B.C.) as collected by Wendy Wickwire. Working on her doctoral thesis, Wendy Wickwire recognized in Harry Robinson what Thomas King would describe as "*the most powerful storytelling voice in North America.*"

427. Susan J. Tweit, *Walking Nature Home: A Life's Journey*, University of Texas Press, 2009.
428. James Conlon, *Lyrics for Re-Creation: Language for the Music of the Universe*, Continuum Publishing, 1997.
429. "Quotes by Gary Snyder," *Goodreads*, 2014. (www.goodreads.com)

EARTH FIRST ~ *Sacred Sites*

"Sacred places are the foundation of all other beliefs and practices because they represent the presence of the sacred in our lives. They properly inform us that we are not larger then nature, and that we have responsibilities to the rest of the natural world that transcend our own personal desires and wishes."[430] (Vine Deloria Jr.)

"With the loss of our ancestral wisdom teachings, we are fortunate to be able to reconnect with ancient memory through our relationship with the Earth, most vividly with sacred places."[431] (Leila Castle)

Sacred sites worldwide, like Stonehenge, Iona ("the isle of Druids"), Camino de Santiago de Compostela, Machu Picchu, the Great Serpent Mound in Ohio and Kinomagewapkong (Peterborough Petroglyphs), are special "high energy vortex" places that hold deep meaning and spiritual power. As earth-connected peoples have for millennia, we continue to gravitate toward unique locations in the landscape such as hilltops, rock formations, ancient forests and natural springs that evoke a timeless mystery. Even today we can feel the vibrancy and mystic possibilities when we interact with the animated presence, "numina" or "genius loci" of a highly-charged ecotone. Each sacred site has a distinct geo-magnetic energy or vibration that can be experienced as calming or grounding, or inspire us with epiphanies, visions or deep healing - and all give us the great joy of bonding with the natural energies of the land.

In traditional earth-centered societies, the keystone origin stories, myths, folklore and other person/place resonances are anchored to ancient landmarks in the beloved landscapes of home. Like sacred texts embedded in the land and waters, narratives describing how the human, natural and spiritual worlds intertwine are transferred from generation to generation through storytelling and the oral tradition. Incredibly detailed information gathered from the natural world culminates over time and is held in tribal memory, and each sacred location gives rise to teachings on ethical behavior and interaction with the nonhuman world. Like a mythic geography or "psychogeography," events and experiences in time and place all over the world continue to inform the cultural continuity of the collective. Ancestral records hold "songlines" and maps for travelling through the landscape, and offer guideposts to the dwellings of mysterious spirits, sacred forces and legendary beings.

Unique human creations such as megalithic stone circles, mounds, petroforms, petroglyphs, medicine wheels, spirit roads, labyrinths, earthworks, shrines and temples mark the presence of the living numina in the land, and can function as portals to the spirit world.

"The old seers knew that the earth is a sentient being. In the past, certain places on the planet were sanctified because of their high magnetic density; they were places of cultural renewal, where one could study the stars or approach the gods."[432] (Suzi Gablik)

Sacred sites are powerful, evocative and magical places that can lift our spirits, and inspire us to uphold the fragile balance of nature with earth-honouring prayer, song, ceremony and celebration. In an animist universe, the intelligent beings that we acknowledge and revere - the entities, elements, faeries, elves, wights, orbs or deities connected to place - have the power to provoke, inform and guide our lives. For those who can see them, mysterious faces, shapeshifters and unusual creatures animate the clouds, are visible in the patterns of ice, rocks and sand, arrangements of leaves and branches, and seashells in the water; and are known in movements of light, shade and wind. The ability to recognize and evoke zoomorphic and anthropomorphic forms in the natural world is a tradition going back thousands of years, and affirms that all things are alive with consciousness and spirit. Forms in nature can echo our humanity, as mountains may resemble human bodies, craggy cliffs or hillsides show us wise faces, and the womblike shapes of deep crevices, caves and dolmens can symbolize feminine fertility and evoke the eternal cycle of life, death and rebirth. Mystical places have been sites of worship for millennia, and the lore of hallowed hills, mysterious mountains, holy islands, vast lakes, underground springs, wishing wells, rushing rivers and sacred groves remain deep in our hearts and souls, ready to be activated at any time. Our yearning for something deeper, more transformative and more reflective is fulfilled by visiting sites of antiquity, or by discovering new places, diverse in natural wonder and spiritual significance. As an extension of biophilia, "topophilia" refers to our affinity for the "spirit of place," and our geomantic ability to hear the magical call of sacred sites and sacred land.

"Sacred places are landscapes of the holy, centers of inspiration where human consciousness is temporarily set free. The experience of a sacred place and thus sacredness itself is a re-entry into a state of wholeness, and an introduction to your true origins."[433] (T.C. McLuhan)

---

430. Vine Deloria Jr., *God Is Red: A Native View of Religion*, Fulcrum Publishing, 2003.
431. Leila Castle, "Dragon Priestesses of the Earth," *Earthwalking Sky Dancers: Women's Pilgrimages to Sacred Places*, Frog Ltd. Books, 1996.
432. Suzi Gablik, *The Reenchantment of Art*, Thames & Hudson, 1995.
433. T.C. McLuhan, *Cathedrals of the Spirit: The Message of Sacred Places*, Thorsons, 1996.

Since ancient times, the tradition of pilgrimage and travel to magical destinations has connected spiritual seekers to lands and places rich in metaphor and meaning. Following specific pilgrimage routes or wandering intuitively in the wild returns us to our inherent belonging within creation, and functions as a rite of passage that links us deeply to our own soul and the soul of the land. Throughout human history, the interaction between place and society has given rise to our most important guiding spirits, faith traditions and cultural expressions, and provides essential links between the divine, the sacred universe, natural law and *Earth Community*. As both an inner and outer journey, pilgrimage is a mysterious and magical process that returns us to our authentic self, and provides inspiration, vision and new energy.

Outside of linear time and the demands of modernity, our days "wandering in the wilderness" with travel to ancestral sites, geomantic temples or historic markers heightens our senses, shifts our everyday consciousness, and enriches our connectivity. No longer an obscure activity, the pilgrimage tradition has become increasingly popular, and geomythic adventures resonate with the human need to celebrate the winding road to self-discovery. Well-travelled historic pilgrimage routes are found worldwide, such as tracing St Patrick's footsteps in Northern Ireland, the "Pilgrim's Way" from Hampshire to Canterbury, England, or Spain's Camino de Santiago. And at sacred sites such as Stonehenge, Glastonbury Tor, Chalice Well, the Avebury Complex, the springs of Sulis at Bath, Newgrange, Callanish, Neolithic Orkney, the oracular Temple of the Pythia at Delphi in Greece or the Lasceaux Caves in France, we can feel the ancient energies of the world come alive.

Sacred Landscape, Sacred Site

sanctuary
earth temple
majestic ruins
primeval garden
mighty sculptures
otherworldly monolith
astronomical observatory
shrine for saint or earth spirit
home of oracle, goddess or god
cryptic earthwork on a massive scale
liminal space for vision quest or initiation

As we set out to trace the footsteps of the founders of ancient wisdom traditions, deities or saints, or simply visit a local shrine or special place in nature, arriving in a receptive frame of mind is key to perceiving the resident spirit, or aura of sanctity. To approach the unknown is to feel truly alive and in the "now," and *"how one travels to a sacred place is as important as reaching one's destination, or rather, it is the journeying, guided by the spirits, that decides what the experience will actually be at the sacred site. One has to be open for the unexpected and have no preconceived notions, and one has to approach with love, awe and respect."*[434] (Monica Sjoo) In the same spirit as the ancients who roamed the mountains making personal pilgrimages and honoring cherished cultural markers, travel to holy sites and sacred architecture today can be demanding but inspiring, and the journey a profound act of reverence, contemplation, healing and spiritual renewal. In the Americas, to commune with the numina at sites sacred to Turtle Island First Nations, such as the mesas of Arizona, Chaco Canyon, Cahokia, the Black Hills, the medicine wheels of the Great Plains, the stone road spirit lines of ancient Mesoamerica, or the magnificence of Machu Picchu, is to mark the points of our epiphanies with both inner and outer shrines that bond us to the beauty of the Earth, and those who live in deep connection to Her. Sacred sites are transformational gateways that evoke ancient memory, restore the healing power of the *Earth Mysteries*, and reconnect us to our own wisdom nature and the wisdom of the land.

"I envision a world where all cultures are based on the ecstatic experience, creative expression, exploration and protection of the interconnectedness of all life embodied within Gaia. It is possible to create a realized world but we must return to our primordial nature. That is the pilgrimage we are on, and the sacred place from which all sacred places are born."[435] (Leila Castle)

Many sacred sites are places of burial for the *Beloved Dead* of earth-centered societies, and these structures uphold the significance of cyclical worldviews, provide affirmation for the enigma of regeneration, and maintain continuity between the Ancestors and the living. Resting places marked by standing stones, passage tombs, long barrows, funerary cairns, burial mounds, rock-hewn temples, holy caves, mortuary platforms, earthwork burials, corpse roads, symbolic carvings, kists (stone boxes in the ground), or beautiful locations in the landscape set aside to hold the bones of the dead are all sacred sites of memory and reverence. As a reflection of their beliefs, values and IK/EIK, all societies create sacred space to honour the dead, and as significant spiritual habitats, burial grounds are places of power, myth, ritual and ceremonial magic. Somber, reflective, vibrant or joyful, these otherworldly landscapes hold the collective soul (and souls) of the group, and the memories and keystones of the culture.

---

434. Monica Sjoo, "Well Worship: The Cult of the Sacred Waters," *Earthwalking Sky Dancers: Women's Pilgrimages to Sacred Places*, edited by Leila Castle, Frog Ltd. Books, 1996.
435. Leila Castle, "Serpent Tales," Earthwalking Sky Dancers: Women's Pilgrimages to Sacred Places, Frog Ltd. Books, 1996.

"The swirl of the cycle holds ~ within its wheel ~ the rhythm of life. ~ We build our graves ~ and bury our dead ~ in stones ~ fashioned to last ~ and shaped to hold ~ our hope of rebirth."[437] (J.J. Lafferty)

"The megalithic tomb played a duel role. Inside, it was a memorial for the departed. Outside, it was a place of worship where, once the tomb chamber had been sealed off, the people continued, generation after generation, to honour the memory of the Ancestors still present through their bones, which had now become relics."[436] (Jean-Pierre Mohen)

Found worldwide, petroglyphs and pictographs painted or carved on cliffs, stone outcroppings or cave walls are sacred narratives inscribed on living rock that tell ancient tales of clan and tribe. Other types of rock art such as petroforms and geoglyphs are designs, patterns and formations created in the landscape from rock, stones, wood or earth. As messages to us across the centuries from our remotest ancestors, the visual literacy and meaning of these enigmatic images, constructions and sites are obscure, but the mystery remains. To encounter them anywhere in the world as an invited guest, or to participate in active IK/EIK teachings, ceremony or sacred space with Elders and wisdom keepers, is to take part in a mythologized conversation with the soul of the world. As with many of my own peers, living in close proximity to *Kinomagewapkong,* an ancient petroglygh site in the Kawarthas region of Ontario, continues to contribute in a monumental way to our connectivity with local First Nations and *Earth Community.*

The Peterborough Petroglyphs, a sacred site of global importance, is the largest known concentration of Indigenous rock carvings in Canada. Over a thousand years ago the Algonquian-speaking societies that travelled widely throughout the rich landscape of the Canadian Shield established *Kinomagewapkong (The Teaching Rocks)*[438] on a worldwide meridian of earth energy, or ley line. With the creation of a vast visual library - animals, human figures, spirit beings, shapeshifters and other evocative symbols were depicted on a monumental ridge of crystalline limestone. Red ochre, an igneous pigment used for illustration purposes and to consecrate sacred space throughout the Americas, was applied to the carvings. It is thought that the visual literacy encoded in the petroglyphs communicated tribal myth and memory, individual dreams and visions, cultural teachings and guidance to the First Nations who traversed great distances to this pristine and magical wilderness place. It was also a sacred site for ceremonies, petition, prayer and healing, as confirmed by the present-day First Nations who claim cultural meaning and stewardship of the *Peterborough Petroglyphs,* now an important location for spiritual resurgence and cultural reclamation. Ceremonies, vision quests and other events are held regularly at the site, which continues to be a place of pilgrimage for Indigenous and earth-connected peoples from all over the world.

 One of the few rock art sites in Canada to be designated a *National Historic Site*, the First Nations cosmology and spiritual belief system is depicted with images of turtles, birds, snakes, plant life, items of material culture such as tools and boats, men's and women's fertility, sacred geometry, and characters important to the oral tradition. The audible flow of water under the sloping rock indicates this outcropping to be the home of animate water spirits in-situ, and the naturally-occurring fissures in the rock are thought to have been revered as the entrance to the underground springs and lower worlds. Many of these fissures have been enhanced with petroglyph carvings and red ochre, such as that of a woman's womb, breasts and body. To the ancient ones it was obvious that women, with their regenerative cycles, performed the same function as the Earth, which was the source of all nourishment, protection and procreative power. The large figures on the rock that depict clans or human/animal fusion, the recurring themes of turtle and snake, the importance of the fertility symbols and the relationship of the images to each other truly come alive through interpretive narratives by contemporary Anishnaabe or Haudenosaunee scholars and wisdom keepers. Stunning in their immediacy and evocative expression, these petroglyph master-works speak directly to us across time and space. *Kinomagewapkong* is a mystical place that has deep significance to us today as we renew our connection to the Earth, and as allies to First Nations, recognize their foundational claims to the land.

Sacred sites are powerful places where the veils between our world and the spirit world are thin enough to observe the luminous whole of nature, to feel unusual forces, and to experience the giving and receiving of messages in direct communion with the residing ancestors or earth spirits. In Celtic mythology, sites of beauty and thresholds of magic are called "thin places" where the visible and invisible worlds come into close contiguity, and our task as spiritual beings has always been to seek them out for our deepest inquiries, epiphanies, healing, and soul connections. Today, coming home to our unity in nature is essential, and hearing the call of the old places and spending time at sacred sites is a powerful way to receive the blessings of *Earth Community*. Wilderness sojourns, fasting, vision-seeking, dreamwork and introspection are all ecomystic and aesthetic practices that can be

436. Jean-Pierre Mohen, *Megaliths: Stones of Memory*, Harry N. Abrams, 1999.
437. J.J. Lafferty, *Seeking the Stones*, ©2000 J.J. Lafferty, Vogon Publishing, SOCAN, All rights reserved. (www.jjlafferty.ca)
438. For *Petroglyph Provincial Park* hours, facilities, directions and other information see (www.ontarioparks.com/english/petr.html).

enhanced by visiting sacred sites. Leaving behind the gadgets, distractions and psychic noise of modern life, our deeply experiential time at special places or sacred sites can be enriched by these ideas, evocations and recommendations.

- In a spirit of reverence, approach the special place or sacred site as a conscious being, or a collection of living entities.
- Embrace the solitude and silence.
- See how the site, park or monument fits into the wider ecotone of *Earth Community.*
- Remind yourself of any teachings or IK/EIK that you may know about this place as you explore the site and environs.
- Open your total sensory awareness to the site – what do you see? What can you smell? What can you touch (if possible)? What do you feel? What do you sense?
- Stroll around or sit in place, and just "be" - sink your roots deep and let the atmosphere, beauty and feeling of the site wash over you.
- Be in the "now" - release the linear left brain world of modernity, calm your mind, and embrace a relaxed state of cyclical thought and being.
- Focus on entering the "timeless time" of archaic IK/EIK - open your "mythic mind" by imagining how this place was important or symbolic to the ancients, and try to see and feel what they would have seen and felt, and what was most meaningful to them.
- Evoke your gratitude, love and respect for the earth spirits of this sacred place, and the ancestors and their living descendants who may be sharing their wisdom teachings and cultural knowledge with all visitors.
- After a time, you may be visited by answers to direct questions or unstated inquiries, distinct messages felt or known, other associations, insights, impressions, epiphanies, songs, dreams, visions or synchronicities.
- Psychic experiences or visionary states are possible in proximity to concentrated earth energies, and inexplicable events may occur, like unusual sightings of animals or other creatures, otherworldly sounds, flickering lights, orbs or other phenomena.
- Respond to the magnetic pull of the Earth and allow your intuitive self to expand into the terrain that surrounds you, training yourself to feel and sense direction, time and space in a new way, opening up to interactions and directions meaningful to your personal mythology.
- Spend time in contemplation and meditation, or by journaling and drawing create a written and visual record of your experience, insights and dreams.
- Sacred sites can be places of spontaneous ritual or rites of passage – trust and embody these impulses as much as the site allows.
- Let the site inspire you to discover earth-centered practices such as oracular work, dowsing, plant-spirit medicine, rewilding, and charting the bounty of the land.

- Feel the joy of being grounded in the natural processes of the Earth, and be aware of the excellent progress you have made in shifting to your eco-self and finding your true place in *Earth Community*.
- If possible, collect a small stone, piece of bark, leaf, greenery, pinch of earth or other natural found object(s) to take home, and keep them safe in a special box or container.
- With gratitude and reverence, establish the bond in your heart to this special place, as it will be a sacred relationship that will sustain you, and to which you can return spiritually and in the material world.

Once we have fully experienced the energy and enlivenment of a sacred site and the resident numina, the sacred bond never leaves us. To deepen our geomantic connection and the miracles we have encountered, spending time with the natural objects we have collected can evoke sacred space and the memories that we hold. Our "nature found" memorabilia allows us to re-visit the experience and continue to interact with the spirits of place in the dreamtime, such as receiving further messages or visions that add to our empowerment and overall purpose in life. In my own connectivity with wild nature and sacred sites I have had countless mystical experiences, and have recorded these events in visual art, journals and other writings. In 2005, on a beautiful cloudless summer day I visited the sacred geography of *Serpent Mounds Park*[439] on the north shore of Rice Lake, Ontario. I remember feeling overwhelmed by the beauty of a site that seemed to exist outside of space and time, and being full of gratitude for the ancient peoples who constructed the mounds.

Walking the site, I "dowsed" with my body until I found the perfect place to "be," a section of the curving *Green Serpent* that felt right and true. Sitting in silent contemplation I turned my attention to surveying the scene, listening to the birds and opening my senses, and I imagined what the activity would have been like millennia ago. Then, strongly feeling or sensing a presence (or presences) was uncanny, but similar to other experiences I have had at places when the spirit world is near. After a timeless time when I was ready to continue my explorations, I looked down and found a small green pen in the long grass, a few inches from where I was sitting. I was stunned to find that from the shape and colour of the pen, my instantaneous association was with a poem I adore, *"the force that through the green fuse drives the flower"* by Dylan Thomas. As I walked away from the mound holding the pen in wonder, I received loud and clear the message *"write on behalf of Earth Community!"*

---

439. *Serpent Mounds Park* on Rice Lake, Ontario owned by *Hiawatha First Nation*, contains the only serpent-shaped "effigy" mound built by ancient peoples in Canada (dated 60 BCE). The largest mound, sinuous like a snake, is surrounded by smaller circular mounds (the serpent's eggs?). Archaeological excavations have uncovered burials and artifacts from the mounds and surrounding area that offer clues to the mysterious *Mound-Builder Culture*, both in Canada and the Ohio Valley. (www.hiawathafirstnation.com)

Deeply ensouled by this encounter, and pretty much feeling that I had interacted with a numinous spirit (or spirits), I collected some natural objects and greenery, and left the park. Now of course the material explanation is that someone left their pen in the grass (!) but still, what if? The shape and the colour of the pen was so incredibly significant to me, and whether an ancestral presence or the spirits of place were telling me I had writing abilities, *or* just to go write (!) I really don't know, but either way in the following years I expanded my writing practice far beyond what I ever would have imagined. And without a doubt, the fact that the pen was green will forever be associated (in my mind) with writing on behalf of Mother Earth, and all those who live in deep connection to Her. My affinity with snakes, serpent energy and sacred sites also continues to grow, and my story may serve as a quirky reminder of how our deep bonds and mythic relationship to place can be formed. The process to re-awaken our geomantic consciousness and embrace the *Earth Mysteries* is one of personal transformation, and in the course of these explorations we may also find a renewed desire to become an eco-warrior, and protect all sacred sites and sacred lands.

My treasure collection from *Serpent Mounds* ~ plant material, feathers and the *Green Pen.* Preserving the essence of that wonderful day!

As well as visiting major sacred sites, there is a movement flourishing to build brand-new sites as markers of *The Sacred* in the landscape, such as integrated earthworks, temples, cairns, sculptures, standing stones, stone circles, spirals and labyrinths. Using the principles of sacred geometry, dowsing tools, and other magical and sensory processes of geomancy, the "megalithic revival" is well underway all over the world. Creating and building new sacred destinations in local ecotones can benefit our earth-emergent practice, that of our kinship group and community, and the land itself. There are different ways to locate places for new sites, such as assessing the key points or crossings of the ley lines, "dragon pathways," or serpentine energy patterns of electrical "telluric" currents that flow beneath our feet in response to the earth's magnetic field. From local legend or intuitive process, a living presence in the land, water or geoform can be identified such as a local goddess, "genius loci," ancestor, earth spirit or deva, and with the building of new earth architecture, an ongoing relationship with the sacred numina of place is established. On a less elaborate scale, even creating a simple circle with branches or small stones can delineate a sanctuary or sacred zone for contemplation, and the "axis mundi" experience of being at the center, attuning to the four directions, and feeling the different atmospheres and aspects at the points and rotations of the sphere. In regard to the ideas, evocations and recommendations mentioned for travel to sacred sites, the same experiential benefits also apply to the sacred site or earthwork that you have built or created. Small rituals, cyclical offerings, and deep listening are all ways to open communications with the sacred site and its luminous living presence, as we continue to be informed of best practices to honour and celebrate place with devotionals, song, poetry and seasonal rites. Integrating the sacred into our daily lives is a powerful affirmation of the blessings that are both given and received in *Earth Community*.

A powerful and minimalist way to create sacred space and honour the land is to install a labyrinth with grass, bark or stone pathways. An ancient tool for non-dual awareness and self-knowledge, walking the winding path of the labyrinth is a journey home to one's true nature, an external journey that reflects the journey within. The first labyrinths were depicted in Neolithic times, with carved petroglyphs on rock, similar to the "Classic" or "Cretan" designs later adapted by the Greeks and other cultures from roots in *Old Europe*. The original meaning of these ancient labyrinths is unclear, but hunting magic has been suggested, or that they were a symbolic reference to the universal human journey through birth, life, death and rebirth. For the Hopi and other tribes of the Southwest, the labyrinth is an oral tradition and visual literacy tool for their origin stories, mythic worldviews and journeys of ancestral deities. On the other side of the world, the famous myth of the Minotaur, imprisoned in a labyrinth by King Minos and eventually freed by Ariadne's red thread, derives from a 300 BCE Goddess-worshipping matriarchal culture on the island of Crete. From Egypt to the Roman Empire, Africa to Norway, the near East to medieval fortresses, Chartres Cathedral in France to Turtle Island (and all the far-flung outposts in between), the sacred geometry of the labyrinth has an important function for a wide diversity of societies and cosmologies within the global ethnosphere.

Sacred space is the place where two worlds flow into each other, the visible with the invisible. The finite world touches the infinite. In sacred space we can let down our guard and remember who we are. The rational mind may be released. In sacred space we walk from chromos time to kairos time, as we allow our intuitive self to emerge.[440] (Lauren Artress)

Walking the labyrinth and engaging with these teachings and symbols today is like an ancient form of body prayer, and a sacred way to connect directly with the ley lines, serpentine patterns and energizing properties of the land. The labyrinth offers a "unicursal" path with a clear entry and exit point, and can be a symbolic form of pilgrimage, or a practice of self-integration that emulates the spiraling journey of life. As a powerful tool for movement, meditation, healing, and a deeper knowledge of the self, walking the labyrinth connects our hearts and minds in a journey that is both physical and spiritual. Letting go, being in the "now" and focusing on specific questions are just a few of the many unique ways to use the labyrinth. The elder who makes the labyrinth a daily part of their exercise regime, the spiritual seeker who wishes to uncover deep mysteries, the earth-connected animist who is working to reclaim their traditional European IK, or the rewilder who enjoys the grounded connection to nature are all valid approaches to labyrinth practice. As a multi-purpose space, labyrinths are also perfect for community events, festivals, storytelling, weddings, sacred ceremonies such as solstice celebrations, and children's games or races. From ancient societies to contemporary times, labyrinths continue to be a powerful tool for insight and spiritual growth, and can facilitate the journey into the otherworldly realm of our own intuitive nature. Over time, our labyrinth practice can deepen into a communion with *Earth Wisdom*, and a profound love for Gaia and the beauty and spirit of wild nature. By walking the labyrinth we contemplate the wonders of the universe, receive wisdom and guidance, and move to the music of the soul.

"We need sacred places where we go with veneration rather than to seek resources or opportunity,"[441] (David Suzuki)

Sacred sites are calling us to remember them, to attune to the timeless energies, re-discover the sacred maps and honour *Earth Community* once again. The landscape is full of sacred places, rivers, waterfalls, sand dunes, woodland trails and forests, each with spiritual significance and cultural potential, and we can re-invent and recover these mythic pathways close to home, or even in our own backyard. Our integration with beloved and familiar landscapes, or journeys along archaic tracks to great stone circles, ancient crossroads, "betwixt and between" locations, or "vortexes" of numinous presence and power, are all places where we make contact with eternity. Tuning into the land and our inner essence creates a heightened state of awareness and èmpathy, and by interacting with sacred sites we *"develop a sense of the rapture and fragility of nature, coming gradually to accept our rightful place within it. We are after all, part of the ecosystem."*[442] (Tilda Truchan) We are the earth, and at places of geomantic power we honour the other-than-human-world, and experience the transcendent union of body, mind, heart and soul. Our sublime encounters with spirits or elemental forces enlarges our framework for expression that stems from these experiences, such as ritual, ceremony, earth art, eco-poetry or song. And encountering the ancient knowledge that is encoded in the landscape teaches us that we can listen to the voices of the Earth for guidance in every human endeavor, which is essential for delving into the secrets of our ancestral past. Re-landing ourselves at sacred sites evokes memories of our original culture and place of origin, and as we renew our ancient lifeways and the landscapes that nurture them, we revitalize the importance of mythic geography to our collective human journey.

"There are no sacred and unsacred places, there are only sacred and desecrated places."[443] (Wendell Berry)

440. Lauren Artress, *Walking a Sacred Path: Rediscovering the Labyrinth as a Spiritual Tool*, Riverhead Books, 2006.
441. David Suzuki, *The Legacy: An Elder's Vision for Our Sustainable Future*, Greystone Books, 2010.
442. Tilda Truchan, "The Vision," *A Resource Guide for Green and Alternative Enterprises in the Haliburton Highlands Bioregion*, Haliburton County Community Co-operative, 2000.
443. "Wendell Berry: Poet & Prophet," interview with Bill Moyers, *Moyers & Company*, September 4, 2013. (http://billmoyers.com)

EARTH FIRST ~ *Earth Love*

"The ecological crisis is deepening our love for the Earth. We are being called to love more fully, and to express our love in more powerful, visionary and effective ways."[444] (Drew Dellinger)

"The holiest words I've ever read or thought or sung or prayed
Were praises, praises for the world
And if I die tomorrow may the last words that I know
Be praises, praises for the world"[445] (Jennifer Berezan)

In these times of massive change, the task of the re-indigenist is to bond with the land, to revere nature again as our Ancestors did, and to see ourselves as part of this thin and fragile biosphere, *Our Earth*, the source of all life and our spiritual home. The love of the land has always been central to our most cherished dreams and memories, and if we delve far enough below the surface of the modern mechanistic overlay, we find that Gaia has been patiently waiting for us to return. *"We miss the world and the world misses us."*[446] (Frances Weller) By interacting with the Earth through our human senses and eco-mind, our hearts naturally open to a space of unconditional love full of gratitude for nature's abundance, and the gift of life itself. When we experience the sights, sounds, smells, tastes and textures that are nature's enchantment and joy, we realign with the fascination and magic of 'naturans," our luxuriant green world, the kingdom of the plant spirits, and the intrinsic harmony of natural law.

Of course, in a humancentric society, there is a huge lack of knowledge about the natural world, and the human/nature separation is painfully extreme, leading to callous attitudes and misguided fears. *"We cannot win this battle to save species and environments without forging an emotional bond between ourselves and nature - for we will not fight to save what we do not love."*[447] (Stephen Jay Gould) Educating ourselves about the landforms, plants, trees, creatures and seasonal patterns in our local ecosystem is a life-long undertaking, and in the meantime, there is so much to love in the natural spaces that surround us. Graceful horizon lines, stalwart trees, soft breezes shaking the seed pods, animal tracks, sinewy snake tracings, endless variations in leaf and stone, patterns in sprout and decay, feathered shade and bird song all speak to the senses, and we know the charm and delight of the creatures endlessly calling their names. Are we listening? What are they telling us? When we hear the voices of *Earth Community*, we are transfixed by the many distinct expressions of beauty, spirit and practicality, and we also learn that Mother Earth is suffering from our disregard and disrespect. If we hold the ethics of caring for all life, the best way to restore balance and peace with the Earth is to feel her, know her, listen to her, be open to her gifts, and ultimately, to love Her. Entering the "timeless time" of indigenous mind is a way to bond with nature, revere nature, and with love, express the earth-honoring ceremonies that align us with *The Sacred* that dwells in ourselves, all beings and the natural world.

"The earth is boundless love, a profound source of joy – the earth is humankind's great educator." (Daisetz Suzuki)

If we don't experience nature fully, how are we going to love nature, and if we don't love nature how are we going to respect and protect Her? Love the land! Go out to the natural places, transmit your love to Mother Earth and all the different spirits, elements and creatures, and practice gentleness with yourself and the land. Both the macrocosm and microcosm of Gaia are sentient in countless unique ways, and Her response to your biophilia, reverence and positive energy may surprise you. As re-earthing, ecomystic and animist practices confirm, nature spirituality can give rise to ecstatic experiences, and the ability to see into the heart of things that matter. We are but a humble part of *Earth Community*, and if human beings started to worship the trees, plants, animals, birds, insects and elements as the "supreme divine beings" of the universe, industrial civilization would probably collapse overnight! To revere the elements, creatures and landforms of nature as sacred and inviolable divinities might be just the turnaround this monotheistic patriarchal system requires.

A wonderful practice to adopt is "Earth Blessing" - the recognition that spirit flows through the land, elements and all beings, that the entire *Earth Community* is sacred, and that each moment is a gift of vitality and joy. The essence of love is found everywhere in nature, and love is the ultimate vibratory field for the plant kingdom, the kinship of the creatures, the nurturing power of the feminine, and elements such as the water. Blessing and being blessed, expressing our wonder and gratitude for nature and the regenerative life force with song, chant, drumming, prayer and reflection creates an atmosphere of celebration and love between us and the nonhuman world. By evoking the spiritual realms, and acknowledging the sacred in ourselves and the land, we are expressing the powerful force of unconditional love that empowers all of our partnerships in *Earth Community.*

"Elders, poets and philosophers in all cultures, including our own, have expressed a similar sense of brotherhood or sisterhood, of mutual compassion and common interest with the rest of the living world - a relationship that can only be described as love. Its source is 'fellow-feeling' - the knowledge that we are, like all other forms of life, Children of the Earth and members of the same family."[448] (David Suzuki)

Our search for belonging and all things external is the result of our rift from nature. Yes we have the capacity to heal from this disconnect, to "be love" and express a daily appreciation for life, for the food that nourishes us, and for the ecotones where we live. The Earth is part of us, linked to us body and soul, and by spending time in nature we become re-rooted in place, and actively keep this timeless bond, or spiritual ecology, at the forefront of our lives. Loving the earth means to cherish wild nature above all, and to honour the sacred elements of earth, water, air and fire. And to embrace the *Great Heart* in nature is to locate an indigenist worldview immersed in the land just waiting to be rekindled, and to be enveloped in *The Sacred* during the seasonal cycles and daily round of our lives. Nurturing our own hope and positivity is essential, as we return to right relationship with the earth's sacred body (of which we are a part).

Loving the Earth with a fierce devotion may mean that we view the damage being done to nature as attacks on our own family and kinship group. The despair and rage we feel as witnesses to terracide, animal exploitation and the everyday callous disregard for the land can be channelled into creating awareness, resistance efforts, the earth rights movement, and by rejecting the numbing and destructive values of Empire. *"Fighting for our survival in the 21st century is less about defeating the aggression of an external enemy than it is about finding new ways to love the land."*[449] (Taiaiake Alfred) By opening our hearts to the Earth in our thoughts, words, actions and cultural life we find sacred purpose in the co-creation of an earth-honoring society, and restore much-needed balance. Our re-enchantment with the natural world is essential for devoting ourselves to eco-activism, environmental healing, earth restoration and rewilding, and the future rests with us!

"To the woman in the earth,
Who is my first and ever beloved.
Whose smiles and rages and storms and weepings
And tremblings and lashings and eruptions
And ripenings and witherings and musings
Are my life, my terror,
My thought, my wild joy
And all of beauty I ever want to know.
Who takes me into her after every journeying,
Who is my source, my end, and my obsession."
(Paula Gunn Allen)

444. Drew Dellinger, "Study Guide," *Occupy Love: Revolution of the Heart*, Dir. Velcrow Ripper, Fierce Love Films, 2013. (www.occupylove.org)
445. Jennifer Berezan, *Praises for the World Song and Chant*, © SOCAN/ASCAP, Edge of Wonder Records, 2002. (www.edgeofwonder.com)
446. Francis Weller, "Five Gates of Grief," *Robert Bly's Minnesota Men's Conference*, November 4, 2013. (www.youtube.com)
447. Stephen Jay Gould, *Eight Little Piggies: Reflections in Natural History*, W. W. Norton & Company, 2010.
448. David Suzuki, *The Sacred Balance: Rediscovering Our Place in Nature*, Greystone Books, 2007.
449. Taiaiake Alfred, "Opening Words," *Lighting the Eighth Fire: The Liberation, Resurgence and Protection of Indigenous Nations*, Leanne Simpson (editor), Arbeiter Ring Publishing, 2008.

EARTH FIRST ~ *Rewilding*

"We have been wounded by a dominating culture that has feared and hated the natural world, has not listened to the voice of the land, has not believed in the inner worlds of human dreaming and intuition - all things that have guided Indigenous people since time stood up in the east and walked this world into existence. Many of us in this time have lost the inner substance of our lives and have forgotten to give praise and remember the sacredness of all life. But in spite of this forgetting, there is still a part of us that is deep and intimate with the world. We remember it by feel, we experience it as a murmur in the night, a longing and restlessness we can't name, a yearning that tugs at us. For it is only recently, in earth time, that the severing of the connections between people and land have taken place. Something in our human blood is still searching for it, still listening, still remembering. There is a longing place inside us that seeks to be whole and connected with the earth. This, too, is a place of beginning, the source of our living."[450] (Linda Hogan)

As a part of *Earth Community*, it is our responsibility to protect Mother Earth from the onslaught of industrial civilization, and to reintegrate the wild back into our lives and communities. In response to this societal shift the "rewilding" movement has emerged with a dual purpose - both to restore the health of ecosystems, and to reject the values of Empire in our personal lives by adopting earth-connected philosophies and traditional skills (often in fusion with localized culture). To take action through rewilding means to acknowledge that wilderness and green space are essential to humanity and all life, and that the presence of vibrant natural areas close to home inspires our ecocentric focus to live sustainably as an intra-connected part of the whole. By giving us an opportunity to reverse the destruction of the natural world, rewilding is an exciting new model for ecological renewal, and allows us to open our hearts to the ethics of care for the *Seven Generations* to come.

As part of a worldwide rewilding environmental campaign, scientists, wildlife biologists, conservationists, nature lovers, grassroots activists and visionaries are utilizing research and imagination to create realistic strategies for securing our green commons and eco-heritage. In many cases, rewilding programs include restoration of habitat to save existing species, as well as reintroducing "new" species that align with the original biodiversity of ancient ecotones, such as the vestiges of old-growth forest that can still be found in the Algonquin Highlands of the Canadian shield. Designating new lands for wildlife sanctuaries is key, as well as reviving ancient migration corridors, and creating new green passages connecting one wildlife refuge to another. This is exactly what is needed for free-ranging herds and large predators such as elk, bison, bears and wolves, who require much more space than the lands currently designated for wildlife preserves. Existing wilderness areas, national parks and reclaimed agricultural lands also fit into the rewilding model, but incorporating "buffer" zones and other human-occupied areas will require more creative solutions. To make wildlife corridors a functioning reality, we also need to move away from the humancentric capitalist economy that destroys vast chunks of land in the "resource" extraction process, and return to the values of peaceful co-existence between all species in *Earth Community.*

Successful rewilding projects that are friendly to nature[451] are already taking place in North America, such as the *Yellowstone to Yukon Conservation Initiative* (Y2Y), a vast network of partners and collaborators including grassroots groups, local communities, First Nations, government agencies, businesses, funders (both institutional and individual), NGO's, scientists, researchers and environmental org-anizations. Securing private lands as well as working with existing wildlife refuges, wilderness areas, and state or provincial parks, the Y2Y conservation strategy promotes a healthy future for lands, waters, wildlife and human communities. Although the area covered is incredibly diverse in ecosystems and human infrastructure, the Y2Y initiatives have already led to the expansion of protected territory, green corridors and underpasses, and an increase in mountain lion and bear populations.

In Olympic National Park, Washington, the *Elwha River Restoration* and dam removal is excellent news for the largest unmanaged herd of elk in the world, and the project will restore natural watersheds to a vast acreage of mountains, forests, rivers, lakes and coastlines. The traditional culture, sacred sites and IK of the *Lower Elwha Klallam Tribe* (who have lived in the area for millennia) have been revived, and the salmon are returning upstream for the first time in a hundred years. Over the next five years, 350,000 native seedlings and 5,000 pounds of seed are to be planted at the sites of former dams and reservoirs. Following the precept that nature is fully capable of taking care of itself, *Rewilding Europe* is an equally ambitious project that seeks to rewild an astounding one million hectares in six countries by introducing keystone species, restoring the ecological role of native herbivores, protecting natural areas, and showcasing these wilderness lands to the rest of Europe.

With a passion for environmental justice and rewilding, there is much that we can do to restore damaged and contaminated sites in our own communities, as well as partner with the landscape to grow and gather healthy food and medicine. "Bioremediation skills" are the various techniques used for working with living ecosystems, such as biological interventions with plants, fungus or bacteria to detox and regenerate the health of contaminated lands and waters. Grassroots bio-remediation offers simple methods and valuable tools for reversing the legacy of environmental pollution left behind by industrial civilization. Learning to use sustainable strategies and our living plant allies to detox and restore degraded soil and water are excellent skills to have should an environmental disaster such as an oil spill (or worse) occur. In the uncolonization of self and community, green sanctuary work, bioremediation and rewilding offer us a wealth of knowledge for the care and healing of precious natural environments.

The rewilding movement has extended its reach into cities and urban areas as well, with new organizations and projects[452] greening the cities with neighbourhood connectivity, eco-zones, urban watershed restoration, massive planting efforts and reforestation. Urban sustainability has a unique set of issues, and innovative non-profits such as *Evergreen*

---

450. Linda Hogan, *Dwellings: A Spiritual History of the Living World*, Touchstone Books, 1995.
451. Elwha River Restoration (www.nps.gov) Yellowstone to Yukon Conservation Initiative/Y2Y (http://y2y.net) ; and Rewilding Europe (www.rewildingeurope.com)
452. Evergreen/ Evergreen Brick Works (www.evergreen.ca);
City Repair (http://cityrepair.org);
Save Princess Vlei (www.princessvlei.org); and
Homegrown National Park (https://homegrown.projexity.com)
(www.facebook.com/HomegrownNationalPark).

in Toronto, Ontario with their vision of "Green Cities, Healthy Planet," and *City Repair* in Portland, Oregon with their "placemaking" model are leading the way to resilient green cities. Rewilding school playgrounds, supporting local farms, food sharing, community gardens, reintroducing native plants, improving bike lanes, and promoting recycling centres are all ventures that create urban eco-resiliency.

Save Princess Vlei in Cape Town, South Africa, is a successful collaboration to rehabilitate and protect a massive wetland system that filters thousands of acres flowing to the sea. They describe the importance of place and their objectives as collective memory, heritage, identity, spiritual significance, building future community, promoting equity for all, and conserving nature for nature's sake. A model for rewilding projects everywhere, *Save Princess Vlei* stresses that to sustain biodiversity, new building development has to acknowledge the natural limits and boundaries of important ecosystems. *"We cannot remove ourselves from ecologies, and the new understanding is to live side by side with ecology."*[453] (Dressing the Princess) Wildlife and bird populations are on the rise, marginalized communities are active and empowered by *Save Princess Vlei*, and the future initiatives of this amazing action include transforming the land around the wetland into an urban nature park that will honour its natural and cultural heritage. In Toronto, the world's first *Homegrown National Park* initiative led by the David Suzuki Foundation will establish a green corridor through the heart of the city along the former route of Garrison Creek. With crowd-sourcing and collaboration between local residents, businesses, partner groups and networks of volunteers, the project seeks to rewild the commons with trees, shrubs, gardens and flowers in streets alleys, rooftops, yards, parks and green spaces throughout the corridor.

Rewilding projects have the potential to "bring nature back home," and momentum is building to address the challenges and opportunities as related to urban sustainability, and to create green cities all over the world. Being aware of ecosystem complexity and the many factors involved in maintaining balance is the only way to live on the Earth, and rewilding presents the most realistic strategies for saving and conserving the rapidly diminishing nonhuman world. Nature will respond when we stop trying to control Her, and rewilding practices in partnership with natural growth and vitality offer unlimited hope for a richer, wilder future. In this age of overwhelming loss, we need to cooperate with the fertility of the "green fuse," and the regenerative principle that more biodiversity equals more thriving ecosystems, and more life.

"We know ourselves to be made from this earth. We know this earth is made from our bodies. For we see ourselves. And we are nature. We are nature seeing nature. We are nature with a concept of nature. Nature weeping. Nature speaking of nature to nature."[454]
(Susan Griffin)

In our personal lives, rewilding means rejecting the domestication we have adopted from the techno-industrial world in favor of earth-wise skills, and learning how to be "true human beings" once again. Rewilding challenges the disconnected physical, emotional and mental habits of modernity, as we seek to uncolonize ourselves and return to the rich matrix of indigenous mind. Embracing the traditional knowledge and *Old Ways* of our ancestors through cultural recovery and reconstruction empowers us to engage with family, village and tribe. Our animist relationships with the *Circle of Life*, and learning how preconquest First Nation communities interacted with the bio-region, will give us our deep roots and a dedication to the land. And, by resisting the colonial urge to "keep moving," hopefully our values will shift to a simple life in harmony with the seasons and the daily round, more ethical partnerships with nature, and gratitude for our blessings - lifeways that have worked for millennia all over the world.

Rewilding crosses every spectrum of our lives, and by either taking it slowly or making abrupt life changes, there is much we can do to live sustainably and engage with *Earth Community.* In terms of personal care, aspects of rewilding the self may include adopting a paleo diet, walking barefoot on the earth, wearing loose clothing made from natural fibres, drinking spring water, exercise, dance or primal movement that grounds us in the body, performing strength training for better endurance, and detoxing with whole foods, herbs or sauna bath (hot springs would be ideal!). For our homes and the domestic sphere, going off the grid, moving to a sustainable dwelling such as a yurt, earthship or Celtic roundhouse, sourcing alternative and clean energy such as wood, wind, passive solar, geothermal or water wheel for light, heat and water, and other practical living skills are all part of the rewilding process. Many "new" practices such as integrated system design, neighborhood bee yards, or harvesting rainwater to restore local watersheds are *Old Ways* shaped from common sense methods already in place from a slower time of pastoral living and the time-tested *Original Instructions* from our ancient IK/EIK. Our "green living" or "intentional living" activities can also include taking on meaningful work in the areas of community building, eco-ventures, the healing arts, animal rescue, and environmental restoration.

To develop strong bonds of community based on indigenist principles and earth connectivity, creating sustainable eco-villages allows everyone to share skills, knowledge, resources, creative solutions, food, healing, storytelling, music, the arts, rites of passage, rituals and spiritual life.

---

453. *Dressing the Princess,* Dir. Carlos Francisco, A Steps/Sanbi Production, 2013, *CareTakers - Sustaining South Africa's Rich Biodiversity.* (www.caretakers.co.za)
454. Susan Griffin, *Woman and Nature: The Roaring Inside Her*, Harper & Row, 1978.

As we continue to replace external colonial authority with uncolonized alternatives, co-housing partnerships and intentional community will also become extremely important. Not only is social interaction key to a happy fulfilled life, strong social relationships are just as important as overall physical health for increasing our longevity, and as we see in traditional Indigenous societies, belonging to tribe is crucial for the protection and survival of the entire collective. Enveloped in the larger purpose of our kinship group in *Earth Community*, another keystone for happiness are the practices of generosity, selfless giving, mentoring, and helping others. Collaborative leadership skills, circle support networks, community teach-ins, social enterprises and creative alliances in the arts all contribute to the patchwork of a life-sustaining society. Yet these alone are not enough, and new structures will not survive or take root unless we also hold the deeply ingrained values of love for the Earth. It is only by nurturing our eco-self that we form the wellspring of care and compassion for all beings at the core of our consciousness.

Developing strong cooperative relationships with the farmers in our area is vital, as well as getting our own hands into the soil with permaculture, bio-dynamic farming, co-creative gardening and companion planting. Learning First Nations stories and knowledge as related to nature's gifts, and foraging the local foodshed can become collaborative ventures that benefit all involved. The land offers an abundance of native fruits, berries, nuts, seeds, vegetables, leaves, flowers, shoots, roots, herbs, barks, sap, grain, wild rice, insects, fish, eggs, and other wild foods and medicine sources that contribute to our healing, health and well-being. First Nations were tending, cultivating and caring for a wide diversity of plant communities long before the Settler Society arrived, and with their guidance, these established practices can continue to enhance both human and ecosystem health. It is important that we ask permission and express our gratitude for any element we harvest from the natural world, whether it is water, animals, plants or medicine, and that our wildcrafting practices are gentle acts of reverence and respect. A rule that has worked for millennia is to not over-harvest, but leave a section of the plant colony to propagate itself and nourish other species. As we become more adept at rewilding, restoring the heirloom or foundational varieties and well-adapted native plants that were part of a region's biodiversity before Empire will stabilize the soil, provide food and shelter for native wild animals, and offer incredible beauty. Age-old methods for preserving and storing our own food such as drying, canning, culturing or creating root cellars will become essential, as will our commitment to the dynamic choices of "reduce, reuse and recycle."

Rewilding is a hands-on undertaking, and by embracing experiences and sharing skills with others, we gain the awareness and confidence that it is possible to live on the land. Taking an outdoor survival class is an investment in your own future, and you can discover what is truly essential to life. Unlearning the habits of civilization with skills and technologies such as starting a fire with a wooden bow-drill, building wilderness shelters, tracking animals or tool-making based on the success of ancient designs, will lead to deep change and self-sufficiency. For ongoing learning and companionship on the rewilding journey, you can access the many "Rewilding," "Primitivism," "Anarcho-Primitivism," "Future Primitive," "Paleo Community," "Feralculture," "Feral Subculture," "Nature Immersion," "Wilderness Schools," "Survival Training" and "Traditional Skills" forums, books, websites, courses and conferences, each with their own root philosophies, belief systems and methodologies. With the advent of social media, joining groups and the forming of intentional communities online before moving to a landbase are exciting new movements toward eco-resiliency. When you are drawn more and more to natural materials to provide for your needs – bone/awl, reed/basket, clay/pottery, shell/ornament, hide/blanket or stone/hearth, and fire comes alive again under your hands, you will remember what it is to have beauty and balance. *"The age of H. sapiens domesticfragilis is drawing to its close just as the age of H. sapiens neoaboriginalis - the 'new aboriginal' - is finally dawning!"*[455] (Daniel Vitalis)

---

455. Daniel Vitalis, "The Intrinsic Taboo," *ReWild Yourself Magazine: Dispatch 1*, 2014. (www.danielvitalis.com)

EARTH FIRST ~ *Earth Rights*

"Geo-Justice weaves together the global, local and psychosocial components as we fashion language and images for our common work. We awaken from the dream of separateness, relate to our own bioregion, and remember our relationship to the land. We discover that the way to the sacred is through the place of our dwelling, and we come to understand Earth's oppression as our own."[456] (James Conlon)

"Wilderness is necessary to our spiritual and psychological well-being, yet it is a container of far more, of mystery, of a life apart from ours. It is not only where we go to escape who we have become, but it is also part of the natural laws, the workings of a world of beauty and depth we do not yet understand. It is something beyond us, something that does not need our hand in it. There are laws beyond our human laws, and ways above ours."[457] (Linda Hogan)

"There is nothing more important than the land – that is the fight."[458] (Leanne Betasamosake Simpson)

Human beings are hard-wired for a greater passion, which is to sustain and care for the earth's ecosystems and the diversity of all life in accordance with Gaia's laws. We are an interconnected part of the whole, and we have our place within the natural world, just like every other species. When we do not overstep these boundaries (such as a culture based on resource exploitation) we are fulfilling our true role as earth-connected tribal peoples. *"I did not believe - had never believed - that humans were the center of the world, that the Earth was their playground, and that they had the right to do what they liked."*459 (Paul Kingsnorth) We are dependent on the gifts of the green and natural world, and we need to treat the Earth with care and respect. The rise of earth-connected community, reclaiming a sense of ourselves as "ecocentric," and the resurgence of Indigenous nations is a sign of the return to balance and wisdom for both people and planet.

*"The Earth is not just here for human consumption. All species have a right to exist for their own sake, and humans must learn to live in balance with the needs of nature instead of trying to mold nature to fit the needs of humans."*460 (the definition of "biocentrism")

An incredibly exciting movement is happening today to assign "earth rights" and legal protection to all aspects of the natural world, and global initiatives are underway to recognize that ecosystems, landscapes, trees and animals have intrinsic rights equal to human rights. As members of the planetary family, our highest duty is to care for the Earth, and the environmental justice movement is working to create fundamental change in our legal practices. The objective is for the ecosystem itself to be named as a rights-bearing subject with standing in a court of law, and to install the legal authority and responsibility to enforce these rights on behalf of living ecosystems everywhere. As Robert Lovelace reminds us, *"the only fundamental human right is to live in harmony with the Earth,"*461 and by extension earth rights also become human rights as they flow from the intrinsic rights of Gaia - the right to a healthy and safe environment, the right to basic needs like nourishing food and clean water, the right to a bio-

---

456. James Conlon, *Lyrics for Re-Creation: Language for the Music of the Universe,* Continuum Publishing, 1997.

457. Linda Hogan, *Dwellings: A Spiritual History of the Living World,* Touchstone Books, 1995.

458. Leanne Betasamosake Simpson (Michi Saagiig Nishnaabeg), *Amnesty International Keynote,* Fundraising Dinner, Amnesty International Peterborough Group 46, March 3, 2013, Peterborough, ON.

459. Paul Kingsnorth, "Confessions of a Recovering Environmentalist," *Orion Magazine,* January/February 2012. (www.orionmagazine.org)

460. "Biocentrism" is an ethical point of view that extends inherent value to all living things. Advocates of biocentrism promote the preservation of biodiversity, animal rights and environmental protection, and the term has also been employed by advocates of "left biocentrism," which combines deep ecology with an "anti-industrial and anti-capitalist" position.

461. Robert Lovelace (Tslagi/Algonquin), *The Architecture of a Decolonized Society: Reindigenizing the Self, Community and Environment,* presentation, Kawartha World Issues Centre (KWIC), Trent University, Peterborough, ON, 01/18/13.

diversity of seeds, and the right to the commons, including the oceans, rivers, shorelines, urban green spaces, parks and community forests. Aptly-named "Earth Democracy" by Vandana Shiva, *"the new paradigm of Earth Community and respect for the rights of Mother Earth as a living democracy is based on the intrinsic worth of all species, all people, and all cultures; a just and equal sharing of the earth's vital resources; and sharing decisions about the use of the earth's resources."*[462]

On Earth Day 2010 in Cochabamba, Bolivia, a process was started to address the dynamic that without earth rights there can be no human rights, and to adopt a *Universal Declaration of the Rights of Mother Earth.*[463] This powerful and timely document, written by "the peoples and nations of Earth" makes a series of excellent points including:

- *We are all part of Mother Earth, a living community of interdependent beings with a common destiny,*
- *we are grateful to Mother Earth as the source of all life, nourishment and learning,*
- *the capitalist system has caused great destruction to Mother Earth putting life as we know it at risk,*
- *to guarantee human rights it is necessary to recognize and defend the rights of Mother Earth, and there are practices and laws in place to do so, and*
- *we can take decisive, collective action to transform the structures and systems that cause climate change and other threats to Mother Earth.*

The Declaration goes on in wonderful detail to outline the many definitions of Mother Earth, and the intrinsic rights held by Mother Earth and all beings:

- *Mother Earth is a living being,*
- *Mother Earth and all beings are entitled inherent rights for all species including organic and inorganic beings,*
- *Mother Earth and all beings have the right to exist, be respected, regenerate, maintain identity and integrity,*
- *Mother Earth and all beings have rights to water, clean air and health free of contamination,*
- *Mother Earth and all beings have the right to live freely without abuse from human beings,*
- *Mother Earth and all beings are entitled to full and prompt restoration from any violation caused by human activity, and*
- *each being has the right to a place and to fulfill its role in Mother Earth for her harmonious functioning.*

The Declaration finishes with a section outlining the obligations of human beings to Mother Earth:

- *Every human being is responsible for respecting and living in harmony with Mother Earth,*
- *to establish and apply effective norms and laws for the defence and conservation of the rights of Mother Earth,*
- *to respect and protect the vital ecological cycles, processes and balances of Mother Earth,*
- *to guarantee that the damages caused by human violations of the inherent rights of Mother Earth are rectified and that those responsible are held accountable for restoring the integrity and health of Mother Earth,*
- *to empower human beings and institutions to defend the rights of Mother Earth,*
- *to establish precautionary and restrictive measures to prevent human activities from causing species extinction, the destruction of ecosystems or the disruption of ecological cycles, and*
- *to promote and support practices of respect for Mother Earth and all beings, in accordance with their own cultures, traditions and customs.*

Of course, for Indigenous nations around the world, recognizing the inherent rights of Mother Earth is consistent with deeply-held traditions of living in balance with the principles of natural law. Moving away from the destructive memes of Empire toward a new paradigm that honors the *Original Instructions*, a growing number of communities worldwide are now basing their environmental protection systems on the premise that nature has inalienable rights apart from human beings and human structures. Determining whether human behavior is damaging or beneficial to *Earth Community* **by law** is a welcome new development, and the earth jurisprudence framework is a radical departure from the assumption that nature and natural systems are considered property under the law. With powerhouse environmental attorneys and activists[464] at the helm, the "earth rights," "animal rights," "wild law," "eco-justice," "geo-justice" and "rights of nature" movements are flourishing, with campaigns, conferences, ethics tribunals and working groups intersecting with other social movements and global issues. Countries are beginning to recognize the rights of nature in their constitutions, and trail-blazing Bolivia has developed a historic *Mother Earth Law* that gives rights to nature, which in turn supports a radical ecological transition of both economy and society. Bolivia continues to push for the universal adoption and recognition of the *Rights of Mother Earth* at both the United Nations and worldwide. Ecuador included a "rights for nature" chapter in their 2008 Constitution, articling that nature and all life forms have the right to exist, maintain and regenerate their vital cycles, and legal authority has been granted to enforce these rights on behalf of the ecosystems. Under this new legal mandate, the ecosystem itself can be named as a defendant!

"Nature's worth does not accrue from how useful it is proved to be to humankind. Nor is it sentiment, aesthetics or some other human judgement that confers value on nature. As a whole and in its every part, as every creature and every fragment, nature has inherent value."[465] (Emma Restall Orr)

Working hard to legislate an international law to end ecocide by 2020 and change the course of history, earth justice activists, associates, partnerships and organizations are focusing on the adoption of "Ecocide Law," the primary "law for life" that puts people and the planet first. Rejecting any further mass destruction or damage to Mother Earth, ecocide law places the *"health of all beings both now and in the future at the forefront of our decision-making. Ecocide Law affirms humanity's right to life, nature's right to life and future generation's right to life."*[466] It is obvious that humanity cannot go on destroying our planetary habitat, and imposing Ecocide Law at the very top by amending the Rome Statute will mean that countries worldwide can adopt the Ecocide Act into their national legislations. In addition to making ecocide an offense, a legal model known as "duty of care" (or applied trusteeship) refers to the sanctity of the relationship between trustee and beneficiary, and evokes duties and responsibilities that have nothing to do with assigning a dollar value to resources or the commodification of ecosystems. *"No amount of money will bring back the land, the community, or the sense of what was once home for those who lived there."*[467] (Polly Higgins) Tightly interwoven with Indigenous rights, Ecocide Law upholds environmental protection orders, issues prohibition and enforcement notices, addresses the unlawful use of land, holds perpetrators responsible for the costs of injury or loss, and offers a process of restorative justice to repair and heal both communities and the ecosystems affected by ecocide.

---

462. Vandana Shiva, "Earth Democracy and the Rights of Mother Earth," *Tikkun Magazine,* December 12, 2011. (www.tikkun.org)

463. "Universal Declaration of Rights of Mother Earth," *World People's Conference on Climate Change and the Rights of Mother Earth*, Cochabamba, Bolivia, April 22, Earth Day 2010. (http://therightsofnature.org/universal-declaration)

464. Earth Rights organizations include *Eradicating Ecocide: Global Initiative*, planetary citizen's initiative founded by Barrister and author Polly Higgins, "end ecocide by 2020," (http://eradicatingecocide.com); "The Ecocide Project" and *The Human Rights Consortium, School of Advanced Study, University of London,* (www.sas.ac.uk/ hrc/projects/ecocide-project); *Global Alliance for the Rights of Nature,* Maude Barlow, Cormac Cullinan, Natalia Greene, Bill Twist, Vandana Shiva, Michelle Maloney and Liz Rivers, a worldwide movement creating human communities that respect and defend the rights of nature, (http://therightsofnature.org); *End Ecocide in Europe*, "Crimes against nature are crimes against peace and humanity" (www.endecocide.eu).

465. Emma Restall Orr, *The Wakeful World: Animism, the Mind and the Self in Nature.* Moon Books, 2011.

466. Polly Higgins, "One Law for All," *Eradicating Ecocide: Global Initiative*, 2012-14. (http://eradicatingecocide.com)

The international thrust of Ecocide Law is at the heart of an emerging body of law called "Earth Law" that ensures the well-being of the entire *Earth Community* by acknowledging the natural boundaries and limits of the Earth. There are Earth Law movements at the local level as well, such as the *Community Bill of Rights* created in the U.S. by the *Community Environmental Legal Defence Fund* (CELDF)[468] that elevates the rights of communities and nature **above** the rights of corporations involved in fracking, extraction, mining, water privatization, factory farming and genetically modified seeds. This "bottom up" legal structure gives community members self-governance and the right to decide what happens on their own landbase, and empowers their actions to put people and planet first. By addressing sustainable food systems, fundamental rights to water, and affordable renewable energy, legalized self-government is the perfect structure for decolonization, and integration with the land at the community level. In the same way as Ecocide Law, the *Community Bill of Rights* also states that nature has intrinsic value, and cannot be defined solely as "property" or as a source of profit. With the objective to halt crimes against Mother Earth that impact the *Seven Generations* by legal means and methods, The *Community Bill of Rights* complements and supports Ecocide Law at the international level. Assisting with grassroots organizing, research, public education and the legislative drafting of new laws that change the status of ecosystems from property or commerce to rights-bearing entities, CELDF offers excellent services and models for communities every-where who are embracing the paradigm shift to ecological civilization.

"We must go beyond the arrogance of human rights. We must go beyond the ignorance of civil rights. We must step into the reality of natural rights because all of the natural world has a right to existence and we are only a small part of it. There can be no trade-off."[469]
(John Trudell)

As we return to experiencing our lives as members of *Earth Community*, there is nothing more important to establishing our own humanity and moral code than the way we treat animals. Not only do animals have intrinsic rights to regenerate, maintain their integrity and contribute to the ecosystem in their own specialized ways, they have their own consciousness, sentience, awareness, identity, kinship systems, cultures, emotional life and spiritual presence. There is no such thing as a "superior species," and the dominance over the animal world with humancentric science, genetic engineering, factory farming, sport hunting or fishing, captivity, exotic pet marketing and other exploitations

467. Polly Higgins, "Overview: Earth Law," *Eradicating Ecocide: Global Initiative,* 2012-14. (http://eradicatingecocide.com)
468. *Community Environmental Legal Defense Fund* (CELDF), Mercersburg, PA. (www.celdf.org)
469. John Trudell and Paola Igliori (editor), *Stickman: Poems, Lyrics, Talks,* Inanout Press, 1994.

are acts of the deepest injustice and barbarism. The fact that animals can experience the same pain and suffering as humans must impact our ethics in the treatment of them, and we become morally obligated to acknowledge the same fundamental principles of compassion and care that we extend to other humans. In our uncolonization process we need to reject the idea that animals are "lesser than," or exist to serve the human world as "property," "commodities," or "natural resources." Today the ethical treatment of animals and animal rights are an international concern, and the expanding "animal justice," "animal welfare" and "abolitionist (vegan)" movements[470] first and foremost recognize that each animal and creature has independent value, and are deserving of our respect and protection.

> "When the animals come to us,
> asking for our help,
> will we know what they are saying?
>
> When the plants speak to us
> in their delicate, beautiful language,
> will we be able to answer them?
>
> When the planet herself
> sings to us in our dreams,
> will we be able to wake ourselves, and act?"[471]
> (Gary Lawless)

Not having the ability to speak for themselves, it is our responsibility to speak up and use our voice to protect the other-than-human world. The philosophy of animal rights requires a commitment to serve the animals who are weak, vulnerable and in many cases unable to defend themselves from human greed and callousness, not because it is in our self-interest to do so, but because it is the right thing to do. The animal rights movement instills in us the same empathy as the human rights movement, as all our kindred are deserving of our defense and care. "No one has a right to benefit as a result of violating another's rights, whether that 'other' is a human being or some other animal."[472] (Tom Regan) It is not reform that is required, but the complete elimination of speciesism and all the systems that exploit and destroy animals, both in the human-built world and the wild, especially the practices of hunting and trapping for pleasure or profit. Working toward "peace in the world" today implies a nonviolent attitude toward all sentient beings, and by performing our duty to respect the rights of animals, we also practice non-violence to ourselves and Mother Earth. To truly stand for peace and the shift to ecological civilization is to eliminate speciesism in our cultural mores, power structures, laws and economic systems, and to embrace a philosophy of Earth Rights that extends far beyond the boundaries of humanity.

"We don't have a right to ask whether we're going to succeed or not. The only question we have a right to ask is what's the right thing to do? What does this earth require of us?"[473] (Wendell Berry)

470. Animal rights organizations online include *Animal Justice Canada* (www.animaljustice.ca); *Animal Welfare Institute* (AWI) (https://awionline.org); *Animal Rights: The Abolitionist Approach* (www.abolitionistapproach.com); *People for the Ethical Treatment of Animals* (PETA) (www.peta.org); *Cetacean Rights: Fostering Moral and Legal Change* (www.cetaceanrights.org); *Compassion in World Farming*, "the world's leading farm animal welfare organization" (www.ciwf.org.uk); *Culture & Animals Foundation* (CAF) "advancing animal advocacy through intellectual & artistic expression" (www.cultureandanimals.org); and *Center for Biological Diversity* (www.biologicaldiversity.org).
471. Gary Lawless, "The Passion of the Earth," *Earth Prayers From Around the World: 365 Prayers, Poems, and Invocations for Honoring the Earth*, Elizabeth Roberts and Elias Amidon (editors), Harper Collins Publishers, 1991.
472. Tom Regan, "The Philosophy of Animal Rights," *Culture and Animals Foundation*, Raleigh NC., 2015. (www.cultureandanimals.org)
473. "Wendell Berry: Poet & Prophet," interview with Bill Moyers, *Moyers & Company*, September 4, 2013. (http://billmoyers.com)

So far, our *Ancient Spirit Rising* journey has taken us along a collection of diverse paths, both ancient in origin and modern in voice that place the *Earth First*. Now fully grounded in place, let us turn to tracing our ancestry, locating our indigenous roots, honoring our Ancestors, and reviving the *Old Ways*!

23. Tracing Euro-Indigenous Knowledge (EIK)

"Spend time getting to know who you really are. Return to the Old Ways, know who your ancestors are, know who your tribes are, understand your place with the land you live on, understand who and what you are. Hear stories of your ancestors before you were born - your family constellation that was grounded in one place, at one with their surroundings. They knew who they were. Their ways led to a confidence in self, faith in self, knowledge of self and a responsibility to the land."[474] (Krow Fischer)

Those of us in the Settler Society can hold James Dumont's epic anti-appropriation statement *"everyone needs to get back to their own IK"* as our manifesto, yet the multiracial blending of bloodlines is so common in the Americas it may be difficult to have easy-to identify ethnicity or ancestry. Assuming that the antithesis of James Dumont's statement is *"that everyone needs to stay away from Turtle Island First Nations IK,"* we are definitely challenged in these perilous times to reconstruct the details of our own heritage and authentic indigenous wisdom, by all means and methods available. Researching our ancient DNA origins; tracing our family tree(s) that chart the many pathways of our ethnicity; researching our cultural traditions through literature and the archaeological record; recovering and listening to the oral tradition and folklore of our families; delving into metaphysical recoveries such as dream archaeology and consulting with the Ancestors;

and encouraging our intuitions, visions and UPG (unverified personal gnosis) are the journeys we need to make in the physical, historical, imaginal and/or dream worlds. As UPG is not particularly reliable without the checks and balances that an embedded cultural group provides, it may be better to stand tall in our own ethnic rootedness, that is, the DNA and biological building blocks that comprise our physical being. Being in alignment with our ethnicity can give us access to complete EIK/IK systems as treasures just waiting to be discovered.

"We all need to connect with who we are and where we come from, before we can successfully move forward."[475] (Zainab Amadahy)

To literally re-indigenize ourselves and our communities, we must reach back hundreds of years, to a time that predates the impulse to build civilization, and the misguided need to dominate others and the land. The diverse scholarship of archaeologists and academics place the dawn of civilization in various ages and epochs, yet defining our pre-colonial "EIK - Euro-Indigenous Knowledge" as a set of principles that respect the boundaries of natural law must be an important criteria. Hierarchy, class stratification, exploitation, commerce, resource extraction and capitalism have been around a long, long time, and we need to be mindful that we don't replicate the dominator models of colonization in our cultural recovery. It is also useful to take a realistic look at the challenges we face before we enter into the work of cultural reconstruction. There is so much in the way, so much hegemony and reliance on technology, that it may be impossible to recover a complete earth-wise worldview. The barriers of time, place, diaspora and Empire-building confront us, and at the end of it all, the severing of our roots that has compelled us to create and re-create our identities over and over again. Up against the reality of forced compliance with capitalism, conforming with economic systems to earn a living, dependence on CO_2-emitting vehicles for transport (because towns and cities are built that way) plus religious and educational brainwashing, our identities have become completely interwoven with the machinations of Empire. But as much as modernity has been normalized in our hearts, minds and bodies, and irrespective of outward circumstance, the wild still lives in our souls. Our agency and imagination are still free, and actualizing the timeless archetypes that dwell both in nature and deep within our psyches is an excellent starting point indeed. As we engage with the ongoing process to uncolonize ourselves and recover our ancestral EIK, we must be aware of the effects of modernization, and how our identities have been subsumed and repressed in the building of Empire.

---

474. Krow Fischer, *Weavers of Light: A Channelled Book of Knowledge for Our Changing Times,* Here On Earth, 2008.
475. Zainab Amadahy, "Why Indigenous and Racialized Struggles will Always be Appendixed by the Left," *Unsettling Settlers: Where We Talk about Unsettling Our Settler Selves,* August 1, 2012. (http://unsettlingsettlers.wordpress.com)

"In the case of the North Americans who came and went, there was no simple reason for their arrival or departure. It was the opinion of Don Enrique that in coming to Amapolas they had moved too far from the dwellings and graves of their own ancestors. 'One must not discard the legacy of one generation to the next, and their roots are too shallow from frequent transplanting,' he said."[476] (Harriet Doerr)

The severing of the Settler Society from our roots, places of origin, cultural traditions, languages, foods, music, games, rituals and spiritual expressions in mass movements and diasporas (either voluntarily or by forced assimilation), was reframed as a positive value in the Empire-building process. This monumental loss, masked by illusory trade-offs and benefits, is the dysfunction at the heart of the colonial experience. Indigenous scholar Paula Gunn Allen examines this phenomena, and compares the nationalistic values of the colonizer to First Nations epistemology.

"The immigrants to America were eager to cast off cultural ties, often seeing their antecedents as backward, restrictive, and even shameful. Rejection of tradition constitutes one of the major features of American life, an attitude that reaches far back into American colonial history, and now validated by virtually every cultural institution in the country. The American idea that the best and the brightest should willingly reject and repudiate their origins leads to an allied idea - that history is of little value, and should be forgotten as quickly as possible. This causes us to reinvent the wheel continually, and we find ourselves discovering our collective pasts over and over, having to retake ground already covered in the preceding decades and centuries. The Native American view, which values continuity with one's cultural origins and the maintenance of traditional customs, might result in slower societal change and less social upheaval, but has the advantage of providing a solid sense of identity and lowered levels of psychological and interpersonal conflict. In short, Native Americans think it is important to remember, while Americans believe it is important to forget."[477]

In one short generation, the echoes of village life, clan affiliations and the "ancien régime" societies of Europe, based on history and common origins (the deepest sources of human affection and commitment) were left behind. Outside of religious sects such as the Amish, Mennonites, Pennsylvania Dutch or the Doukhobors, and culturally cohesive traditions such as Appalachian Folk Wisdom, Gaelic Cape Breton, Nova Scotia or the Acadie of Moncton, New Brunswick, the homogenous populations of the Americas are still off-the-rails as distinct

476. Harriet Doerr, *Consider This, Señora*, Harcourt, 1993.
477. Paula Gunn Allen, "Red Roots of White Feminism," *The Sacred Hoop: Recovering the Feminine in American Indian Traditions*, Beacon Press, 1992.

cultural groups connected to ethnicity, thanks to imperialism and "melting pot" immigration policies. In the absence of a collective identity based on ethnic memory, the colonized mind is characterized by a sense of continuous change, novelty, mobility and rootlessness. With AngloEmpire as the default, hyperindividualized white people put autonomy first, and consider the "other" or the "minorities" as the only groups that have a distinct culture.

Capitalist hegemony has become the great leveller and agent of ethnocide as well. Instead of responding with force when groups gained too much freedom or human rights during the growth of Empire, nation-states devised a propaganda and public relations machine to fabricate consumerism as a system of control. Concentrating our attention on the superficial things, our true attitudes, ideas and beliefs (including our EIK) were controlled and repressed in favor of capitalist domination. *"We now belong to the Church of the Holy Dollar which swallows people alive, their souls sipped up in the form of consumerism. But we are greater than the product of our whole - we have our spirit, soul and mind, and the Church of the Holy Dollar doesn't cater to our spirit and our mind, the arenas of compassion that humankind is greatly endowed with."*[478] (Diana Beresford-Kroeger) The other consideration is that unlike Europe, countries in the Americas are too young to have developed distinct societies, and become perfect storms of erased diversity and homogeneity, with wage economy, consumerism and accumulation as the only "culture" left. Having nothing in the way of a true culture to identify with except the toys and distractions of Empire, it is no easy task to build earth-centered cultural identity from the ground up, but that is exactly our challenge.

In the Americas, nation-states are artificial colonial constructs that have managed people's affairs and decimated the beautiful ecosystems of Turtle Island since their Euro-patriarchal inception. "Canada" and "USA" are white supremacist capitalist fantasies that have nothing to do with earth-connection, and in turn, have created a populace that has stronger ties to regional or national identity than to the land itself. As we work with land-emergent traditions and spiritualities, we come to understand that human beings do much better in small localized earth-based cultures, not monolithic nationalistic bureaucracies. We also begin to see that spiritual practice is entwined with ethnicity all over the world, but the capitalist societies of the Americas seem to have erased this essential fact. For those of us descended from European groups, our EIK has to be re-created using references that are in some cases over 2,000 years old (!), but this archeomythology is at the root of who we

---

478. Silver Donald Cameron, "Interview with Diana Beresford-Kroeger," *The Green Interview*, Mount Saint Vincent University, March 26, 2011. (http://www.youtube.com) (www.thegreeninterview.com)

are as i.e. Gaelic, Baltic or Nordic people. If we are truly sincere about authenticity, we can look to these ancient traditions as our valid spiritual path. All peoples originated from an Indigenous culture, and we must recover the land-based knowledge, traditions and lifeways of our own cultural group. And even though many of the Indigenous cultures of Europe were wiped out long ago, and we have internalized a colonial and diasporic identity, reclaiming *Earth Community* and a positive Settler presence on the land is essential. White privilege and entitlement has given us the erroneous idea that we can choose any path we want from any part of the world, and the attraction to our own ancestral roots is not particularly strong. We need to sit down and have a spiritual conversation with our DNA! Not only is cultural recovery a powerful act of renaissance and reawakening, we also have the responsibility to embrace eco-activism, and do the hard work of caring for and protecting the land.

"To acknowledge our Ancestors means we are aware that we did not make ourselves, that the line stretches all the way back, perhaps, to the Gods. We remember the Ancestors because it is an easy thing to forget: that we are not the first to suffer, rebel, fight, love and die. The grace with which we embrace life, in spite of the pain and the sorrows, is always a measure of what has gone before."[479] (Alice Walker)

What is Your Ancestry?

The discovery of ancestral connections is both a joy and a pleasure, and as genealogical research is extremely popular today, there are many exciting opportunities and methods available for finding our ancestors. Tracing the bloodline of your mother or father (or both) begins with a family exchange, by asking parents, grandparents, aunts, and uncles for as much information as they can recall – names of relatives or ancestors, places of residence, family stories and other information they may remember. It is possible that a relative or someone in your family circle has already initiated genealogical research and charted your family tree (or parts thereof), which is lucky indeed! The next step would be to access the internet by visiting sites such as **www.ancestry.com** and **www.familysearch.org**, which are both highly sophisticated services providing worldwide access to millions of records. The incredibly exciting part begins when you are able to match the names, dates and places you find with birth, death and census records in the Americas or Europe. Many of the original records are on file, and contain details on our forebears such as addresses, dates of marriage, occupations, countries of origin and specifics on immigration. *Ancestry.com* and other genealogical search engines put seekers in touch with those who are researching the same ancestors, and this "branching of the family

---

479. Alice Walker, *Revolutionary Petunias & Other Poems,* Harcourt Brace Jovanovich, 1973.

tree" may connect you to numerous relatives you have never known. When you begin connecting with your extended clan, they may be aware of other narratives and stories that can be collected to enlarge the overall family history.

Locating an ancestor in a specific time and place through an immigration date and location (for example) allows you to consult the historical record to discover what was going on at the time, the reason for the emigration, migration, relocation, or diaspora, what groups of people were affected, and the outcome in the Americas. Discovering an antebellum address for an ancestor in a major city, and then accessing the historical record plus the arts and literature of the time, may allow you to flesh out a picture of who your ancestor was. Sometimes it takes persistence and detective work to trace your ancestral origins through family stories or the family tree. For example, when my maternal ancestors arrived to build the village of Orillia, Ontario from Belfast, Ireland in 1832 it was naturally assumed they were Irish, but by consulting family research[480] I discovered that Robert Bailey, Ann Linton and their newborn baby Eliza Emily were of Scottish descent. Taking this fascinating fact to the historical record, I then discovered that many Scottish people were forced to relocate to Ireland in a series of religious wars, which I am still investigating. Also, many names were changed in the trans-oceanic immigration process, such as the anglicization of hard-to-pronounce surnames at Ellis Island, or the imperialist anti-Irish bias as held by Dr. Barnado and his associates that "authorized" them to change Irish-sounding names among the influx of British Home Children for a new life in a new land.

"I saw the leaves (of www.ancestry.com) in my sleep, curling and waving, beckoning coquettishly on the periphery of my dreams, my Ancestors calling, COME FIND ME, across the generations."[481] (Leslie Larson)

Connecting the events of history to your own life, even the tragic ones, can be incredibly exciting and illuminating. It is both strange and comforting to think that our own ancestors inhabited many of the same places and territories that we are familiar with today. The trail is cold, but it may still be possible to walk in their footsteps, to see the same landscapes and landmarks they would have seen, and to feel their lives as powerful parts of ourselves. Also showing up in the historical record may be the colonial practices of lands either bequeathed, given away, stolen, purchased or acquired by fraudulent "treaty," starkly outlining the normalization of the imperialist agenda by the Settler Society in their rush to populate the Americas. Visiting local, regional, provincial

480. Jane Eyers, *History and Analysis of the Family from Early 19th Century to Present Day*, unpublished paper, University of Guelph, March 26, 1981.
481. Leslie Larson, "Up a (Family) Tree: the Exhilarating Search for My Ancestors," *O: The Oprah Magazine*, August, 2012. (www.oprah.com)

or state archives can uncover documents such as birth certificates, marriage certificates, death certificates, war service records, church records or newspaper clippings, and old telephone books, maps, street plans and photographs all provide incredibly detailed information. Local or regional archives are experts in the preservation of fonds and document collections from civic or private records, and can offer excellent tools through microform digitization, online databases, research consultation services, research retrieval and reprographic services. The most thrilling part of genealogy is to locate the specific names and birthplaces of our ancestors, and then to place their lives within the greater context of history. An excellent example of this process is the popular television series *Who Do You Think You Are?* which features the genealogical quests of well-known individuals throughout the world.

 "It's the blood of the ancients that flows through our veins, and the forms pass, but the circle of life remains."[482] (Charlie Murphy)

There is also a wealth of information available from specific countries of origin, i.e. if you have Scottish heritage there are internet tools and accessible documents in the *National Records of Scotland*, with vast archives of recorded data on births, marriages, addresses, census records, taxation lists, legal disputes, deaths, wills, behests and other genealogy as related to family history. Networks of data exist through newspapers, universities, colleges, cemeteries, military service, parishes and churches, as records have been kept going back for centuries. Scotland has the best-maintained facilities of any country in the world for undertaking family research, and in a major new development the *National Archives of Scotland* in Edinburgh merged with the Registrar General's office, bringing a monumental collection of documents together under one roof in the *National Records of Scotland*.[483] There are countless other Celtic genealogy tools online, in Facebook groups and around the blogosphere, including the Irish government-supported site that offers research into past generations of Irish family history (www.irishgenealogy.ie) with an emphasis on church records, census returns and civil registers; the *British Isles Family History Society - U.S.A.* (BIFHS-USA) at (www.rootsweb. ancestry.com/~bifhsusa), a membership site with support, study groups, genealogy research tools and much more for those with ancestors from England, Ireland, Scotland, Wales, the Isle of Man and the Channel Islands; and from a Canadian perspective, John D. Reid offers *Canada's Anglo-Celtic Connections* at (http://anglo-celtic-connections.blogspot.ca), a comprehensive blog with a vast amount of information on all aspects of genealogy studies, family history resources, and new developments in ancestral research methods and genetic genealogy.

"If you look deeply into the palm of your hand, you will see your parents and all generations of your Ancestors. All of them are alive in this moment. Each is present in your body. You are the continuation of each of these people."[484] (Thich Nhat Hanh)

We can revel in the contemporary abundance of information and assistance available to trace our specific ancestry leading to the recovery of our Euro-Indigenous Knowledge (EIK). For examples of other origins, *PolishRoots: The Polish Genealogy Source* at (http://www.polish roots.org) is a guide to Polish history, culture, genealogy research, immigration, recommended reading and other resources; and *PolishOrigins: Uncovering Your Roots in Old Poland* at (http:// polishorigins.com) offers services, tools, videos, databases, historic tours, resources for finding forefathers or living relatives, and forums for shared interests in Polish origins, genealogy and culture.

A great guide to Norwegian ancestry, heritage and culture, *Norwegian Ancestry: Find Your Norwegian Roots* at (http://norwegianancestry. com) is a blog maintained by genealogist Liv Marit Haakenstad. Also the author of *A Taste of Norwegian Ancestry,* Liv offers ancestral research, courses and lectures in Norwegian genealogy, internet genealogy research, transmigration (Norway-England-US) and emigration from Norway in general. Another extensive set of resources can be found at *How to Trace your Ancestors in Norway* at (http://digitalarkivet.uib.no/sab/howto.html) which offers an intro-duction to accessing the central public archives in Norway, as well as itemizing all the different sources available for genealogy such as parish registers, census returns, military records and emigrant lists.

"Whichever road I follow,
I walk in the land
of many gods,
and they love
and eat one another.

Suddenly
all my Ancestors
are behind me.
Be still, they say.
Watch and listen.
You are the result
of the love of thousands."[485]
(Linda Hogan)

If your ancestry is unknown, or you are having difficulty finding your ancestors, or you simply want more connectivity to the past generations in your family tree, the rapidly expanding DNA science of individual genetic tracing is incredibly enlightening and empowering. DNA testing[486] is easily done with a saliva sample, and the maternal line (mitochondrial DNA, or "mtDNA") can be mapped; or the paternal line (Y-chromosome, or "Y-DNA"); or the entire genome, which is both our maternal and paternal lineage. Our own unique DNA sequences exhibit the evolution of our ethnicity over time, and are also the keys to new genetic discoveries about ourselves and/or the validation of our family tree. Geneticists have compared DNA sequences with the archaeological record and the present-day descendants of groups worldwide to determine geological distribution, which tells us where our ancestors originated from, and even more miraculously, places us squarely into the roots of our ancient culture(s). For example, through *Oxford Ancestors*, I discovered that I am a member of the largest and most resilient Celtic group, the mtDNA-based Helena Clan (world clans descended from "Mitochondrial Eve" as traced by Bryan Sykes in *The Seven Daughters of Eve*). This knowledge, combined with Scotland being the country of my deepest known matriline ancestry, means that I can eliminate Danish Viking, Norse Viking or Norman from my lineage, making me wholly of Celtic origin. How empowering to know that I can now fully access and embrace the treasures, language, beauty and traditions of Celtic/Gael culture! Also, using the DNA test results in combination with genealogy searches can widen your present-day family circle considerably, and these new connections offer the potential for warm relationships, family reunions and an enhanced sense of clan and cultural continuity.

---

482. Charlie Murphy, "Blood of the Ancients," *Chants and Lyrics from Rituals, Circles and Witch Camp*, Reclaiming & Friends, 1996.

483. Resources for Scottish ancestors and genealogy include the *National Records of Scotland* (www.nrscotland.gov.uk), *ScotlandsPeople: The Official Scottish Genealogy Resource* (www.Scotlandspeople.gov.uk) and the historical records database *ScotlandsPlaces*. (www.Scotlandsplaces.gov.uk).

484. Thich Nhat Hanh, *Teachings on Love*, Parallax Press, 1997.

485. Linda Hogan, *Dwellings: A Spiritual History of the Living World*, Touchstone Books, 1995.

486. There is nothing more thrilling than pinpointing your DNA signature and genetic homeland. Among others, *23andMe* (www.23andme.com) is a personalized DNA service offering information on lineage, ancestry and health, and other benefits and tools for exploring your DNA; *Oxford Ancestors* (www.oxfordancestors.com) offers mitochondrial DNA testing (mtDNA) for personal research into ancient ancestry; *Irish Origenes* (www.irishorigenes.com) offers the matching of Y-chromosome DNA (Y-DNA) to Irish heritage, with surnames factored in to establish common ancestry and ancestral links to clans and territories; and *Ancestry.com* (http://dna.ancestry.com) now provides DNA testing (*AncestryDNA*) that surveys a person's entire genome, offering an ethnicity map that encompasses both the maternal and paternal lines. *AncestryDNA* is fully integrated with *Ancestry.com*, "*the world's largest online family history resource, with billions of historical records, stories and family trees.*"

What are Your Own Ancestral Traditions?

"You must learn to touch the earth. Sink the roots of your being into the earth. The power that is handed down to you from the Ancestors comes to you when you become one with the earth. Look deep within yourself and you will be at peace. You will reach the sky with joy, knowing that you will never be blown away in the wind."[487]
(Barbara Smith)

Going back in time, we can recover and revitalize elements of our EIK based on our own unique genetic heritage, which can arise from a single source or group, or be based on multiple cultures. If the range of EIK in our entwined ancestry is too complex, we can make choices by delving into the histories and re-creations that are the most meaningful to us. There are challenges we must face in this process, as our ancestral roots and cultural identities were originally embedded in European lands, and recovering our connectivity with *Earth Community* means creating new psychogeographies and bonding with the natural world in the places we are now living. Also, the majority of the Settler Society lacks access to their own Elders or keepers of oral tradition and spiritual knowledge, in contrast to Turtle Island First Nations (for example) who still have access to their IK holders, living cultures, rejuvenated traditions and ancestral lands (in many cases). Beginning with research into sociology, anthropology, mythology, folklore and archaeology, reclaiming our EIK is a learning curve that involves both theory and practice, and for some, deconstructing the overlay of Christianity is also important to cultural recovery. A powerful bond can be formed with our ancestral-sourced IK by travelling to the homelands of our ancestors or significant sites in their immigration experience, and intuitive connections, soul awakening and powerful healing can arise from these sacred pilgrimages. Our journeys through place-based and historic worlds may function as a gateway to remembering our homelands and traditional ways of knowing, which is the very essence of indigenous mind.

"All peoples have indigenous roots that may matter more at this historical juncture than even the various postmodern strands are able to see, or are willing to admit."[488]
(Jürgen Werner Kremer and R Jackson-Paton)

Taking our cues from primal pre-colonial culture, ancestral recovery can be a guided or independent process that spirals us back to a sense of deep belonging and reciprocity with our ancient origins. New texts, tools, workshops and courses for ancestral reclamation work are flourishing, such as the wonderful set of self-directed ethnobiography

487. Barbara Smith, *Sara's Gift*, QuickBooks, 2011.
488. Jürgen Werner Kremer and R Jackson-Paton, *Ethnoautobiography: Stories and Practices for Unlearning Whiteness, Decolonization, Uncovering Ethnicities*, ReVision Publishing, 2013.

practices as offered by Jürgen Werner Kremer and R Jackson-Paton in *Ethnoautobiography: Stories and Practices for Unlearning Whiteness, Decolonization, Uncovering Ethnicities*. Using as much (or as little) that we know from our ethnic heritage as a starting point, we can elaborate on our sense of self, connect with the identity markers that are available, and place our own experiences and those of our ancestors within the recent and more antiquated histories of our cultural group(s). Our own unique ethnoautobiography is a valuable narrative that we can continue to enlarge by delving into community, caring for our ancestors, creating works of the imagination, connecting our personal mythology to landscapes both near and far, and meta-physical experiences such as ecomysticism and dreamwork. New discoveries from the past, and the ongoing journey to reconnect with our IK/EIK may re-activate cultural traits that lie dormant within, and soul recollections or deep memories may arise spontaneously from literature, folklore or art. Creating new self-narratives rich in nature spirituality, poetry and myth can re-awaken our ancestral traditions, and another powerful entry point into igniting the *Old Ways* is our specific creation or emergence story, honoring how our ancient ancestors came to be, and tracing our heritage(s) through time to the present day. When we allow the sacred stories and ancient mythology of our cultural group to fill our consciousness and inform our lives, we are inhabiting the same space that our ancestors held. This kind of cultural ecopsychology is a process that heals our relationship with the Earth, and evokes new ways of seeing and being in the world, grounded in the reclamation of our origins and indigenous consciousness. Remembering our traditional languages, simple living, tending the gardens, following the pagan seasons and cycles, rituals, ceremonies, rites of passage, festivals, music and traditional foods are all powerful practices for cultural recovery.

"If we re-experience the stories which tell our histories, our creation stories, our personal and cultural narratives in the original language embodying the worldview and traditional tribal knowing of our Ancestors, perhaps we would, could, might understand ourselves in a genuine, authentic, more loving and honoring way."[489] (Illana Berger)

For both native and non-native people who have been enveloped in modernity and/or are seeking to revive their connection to tribal roots and ancestral lands through formal study, the *Indigenous Mind* program at *Wisdom University*[490] offers course work and intensives focused on the cultural recovery of our own unique indigenity. Developed by Apela Colorado, scholar and knowledge holder in the field of indigenous mind, the program was founded on the wisdom and heart-knowing of earth-based IK/EIK, and is guided by the mandate that Indigenous consciousness can be recovered for all people, even after generations of loss and separation. The program is both experiential and scholarly, and *"guides students to the threshold of their own Indigenous ancestry, homeland, and traditional ways of knowing - to the remembrance of Indigenous Mind. This involves a profound shift in consciousness, in ways of knowing and living, and requires a clear-minded commitment to biophilia - a love of life.*"[491] Students from all backgrounds focus on engaging deeply with their ancestors, homelands and cultural narratives, and work with healing the Cartesian mind-body split (dissociation between human and nature) that is endemic to the western tradition. Guided by Native Elders, the personalized learning process of the *Indigenous Mind* program is akin to being part of a sacred circle, and scholarship is grounded in the historical, archaeological, mythological and anthropological literature of one's own culture, including a journey to the ancestral homeland. By researching and understanding TEK and the environment from an Indigenous perspective, students shift their basic assumptions and perceptions, and recover a way of thinking and being that promotes interdependence and sustainability. An incredibly unique and valuable course of study, *Indigenous Mind* allows students to realize their interconnectedness to the web of all life through their own unique indigenous wisdom traditions, and "*traditional ways of knowing help us ground ourselves in who we are, and in our responsibilities to future generations. Students bring healing first to themselves and then to their families, their ancestors, and ultimately to the earth. Embracing IK means to stand in the mindset of our tribal ancestors, and to keep hold of that vantage point in today's time.*"[492]

Alternatively found in direct experience, methodology, research and psychogeography, all forms of preserving and practicing ancestral knowledge are valid in this time of deep decolonization, re-indigenization and tribal recovery. There is nothing more thrilling than the warmth and connectivity that comes from feeling the strength of our ancestors, knowing that generations upon generations have gone

---

489. Illana Berger, PhD, *Remembering the Indigenous Mind: A Journey of Healing and Transformation*, Scribd, Apr 18, 2013.
490. Indigenous Mind, Masters and PhD Programs are offered at *The Wisdom School of Graduate Studies at Ubiquity University*, Mill Valley, CA (www.wisdomuniversity.org) "*Recovery of indigenous mind involves an honest examination of the historical process that has split the Western mind. It means grieving the genocidal patterns of colonialism and confronting patterns of internalized oppression. It requires ending one's personal and cultural addiction to 'progress.' It calls for honoring spirits that have been neglected for centuries. It means facing the discomfort of uncertainty - a recognition that our knowledge of community, healing, and nature is incomplete. We invite people who seek authentically to recover an authentic indigenous mind and life. The program is for those who see the importance of preserving and passing on traditional worldviews, and for those who long to recover and re-establish the lifeways and values of their indigenous ancestors - lifeways that teach responsibility for reversing the destruction of the planet.*"
491. Ibid.
492. Indigenous Mind, Masters and PhD Programs are offered at *The Wisdom School of Graduate Studies at Ubiquity University*, Mill Valley, CA. (http://www.wisdomuniversity.org)

before to culminate in our own life, and that their resilence and love is part of who we are. The tools and ideas we are tempted to borrow from other cultures pale in comparison, and we must reject the appropriation impulse in favor of cultural expressions that joyfully match our own personal heritage(s). It is still possible to live in harmony with the earth as we have for millennia, and as we express what the past calls forth in us, our root culture has the potential to re-shape itself. We can continue to acquire knowledge and experience directly from nature, and formulate the wisdom of our vibrant IK/EIK into the mental, physical and spiritual maps that will benefit our communities. However, we cannot underestimate the challenge of this process, and ultimately we need to have great compassion and respect for each other in the work of uncovering ethnicity and cultural reclamation. In the face of all the monumental ways Empire now dictates our lives, it may seem like a titanic struggle to take back our ancestral culture, but we must fight for our ecocultural identity, and that of our communities and kinship groups. As we become adept with building our ancestral house through deep genealogy and practices that align with our tradition, we can in turn help other people reconnect with their ethnic and cultural rootedness as well. Experiencing the riches of our ancestral heritage can be pure delight, as we honour the customs and beliefs of those who came before, and preserve them for all who will follow. We are all *Children of the Earth*, and to embody the elements of our ancestral traditions that sing to our souls, is to experience the joy that comes from authentic living.

24. Ethnic Memory & Connecting with the Ancestors

"May we turn inwards and stumble upon our true roots. May nourishment and power pulse through those roots."[493] (John Seed)

> *"I felt the presence*
> *of ancient beings*
> *all around me.*
> *They left us magic*
> *in everything*
> *the beautiful way*
> *in everything."*[494]
> (Philip Kevin Paul)

A vital aspect of our uncolonization work in rejecting the hyper-rationality of Empire is to restore the spiritual, non-material and so-called "invisible" realms to their appropriate place of power in our re-indigenized lives and communities. Non-linear modalities and metaphysical experiences can be a source of indelible knowing and wisdom in our cultural retrieval work, as we delve into dream archaeology, meeting and consulting with the Ancestors, visions, intuitions and other journeys in the imaginal worlds of ecomysticism and nature spirituality. Mystical experience is common to all people, and familiar feelings like "I know this place" or "I have done this before" can reverberate in our entire being as déjà vu, visions, dreams, or everyday moments of spontaneous recall. These sudden leaps of understanding transcend time and place, and may stem from our ancestral line - epigenetic realizations or epiphanies that arise from the cellular memories we hold in our DNA. The history of our ancestors lives on in our bodies, and from a deep inner place where all eras and timelines meet and mingle, our DNA contains *"a set of genetic instructions from the past that are given to us in the present with the intention of creating a future."*[495] (Raven Grimassi) Tapping into our ancestral heritage by awakening the memories that reside in our physical essence can affirm the vitality of unseen worlds, and the creative fire of the life force that dwells in our hearts and souls. The gifts of ancestral wisdom are waiting for us when we look within, and these inner practices are just as effective as using experiences and resources in the outer world to reconfigure the beliefs of our pre-colonial traditions. We inhabit a sacred universe that is open to all participants, and when we remember who we are, we open a liminal space where the Ancestors can guide us toward our ancient spiritual lineage and unique EIK.

"As living human beings, we exist within a body of light. Long after we have returned to dust, our light lives on in our progeny, both in memory and in the flesh, as our Ancestors inhabit our present bodies. It is their blood and their DNA that formed us, and our bodies are the living memories of our ancient Ancestors."[496] (Moke Kupihea)

"The golden light of wisdom that shines deep within the cave of the heart ignites the spark of divine life that is buried deep in the soul. The knowledge of the Ancestors sleeps within our memory. We journey into the cavern of darkness where we may retrieve the treasures of insight and new understanding."[497] (Isha Lerner)

In addition to the traits of heredity that spiral through the family tree to form our physical being, new scientific inquiry has found compelling evidence for the biological transmission of memories, emotions and other knowledge. Research continues to determine how this kind of

493. John Seed, Joanna Macy and Pat Fleming, *Thinking Like a Mountain: Toward a Council of All Beings,* New Catalyst Books, 2007.
494. Philip Kevin Paul, *Taking the Names Down From the Hill*, Nightwood, 2003.
495. Raven Grimassi, *The Cauldron of Memory: Retrieving Ancestral Knowledge & Wisdom*, Llewelyn Publications, 2009.
496. Moke Kupihea, *The Seven Dawns of the Aumakua: The Ancestral Spirit Tradition of Hawaii,* Inner Traditions, 2004.
497. Isha Lerner, *The Triple Goddess Tarot*, Bear & Company, 2002.

ephemeral information is stored in the DNA material in the first place, and how experiences are transferred from the brain into the genome, allowing them to be passed on to later generations. It has been established with epigenetics that life memories and experiences create chemical changes associated with the DNA, and influence both the structure and function of the nervous system in subsequent generations. The substance of our ancestor's lives is handed down to us, and they continue to shape and strengthen us both in body, mind and soul. Another new field of study known as "morphogenetics" explores how the natural instincts carried by all species, such as the migratory patterns of birds, are also inherited memories residing in the DNA. Information is gathered and imprinted from the natural environment and passed on intergenerationally through energetic patterns or fields of "morphic resonance," showing up in our behavior and bodily maps. In addition to these emotional and environmental residues, we may also carry memories that are spiritual and mystical in nature, and it is likely that the collective consciousness (or subconscious) of our ancestors can also be retained in the DNA. Miraculous communications are being transferred through an inner web of interconnected energy patterns where the past, present and future exist simultaneously, and entire cosmologies (the inner traditions and worldviews of our ancestors) are closer than we know. After all, "*an inner tradition is a system based on an agreement of consciousness between members of that tradition. Inner tradition exists and functions within the group mind of the people that sustain it.*"[498] (Raven Grimassi) After a long occupation by Empire, can it be our destiny in this era of renewed nature connection to realize and further the spiritual legacy of the Ancestors in our own lives?

"*Our Ancestors – going all the way back through the bloodlines, perhaps – and the Ancestors of the land where we live, often appear in spontaneous sleep dreams. Sometimes they come looking for us. As dream journeyers, we may choose to go looking for them. We may even develop the skills to become dream archaeologists.*"[499] (Robert Moss)

Another energetic field of "morphic resonance" is our shared dreamspace, and we can develop skills to access the endless possibilities within this "timeless time" that holds the consciousness of our ancestors, and even meet them face-to-face. Interaction with the ancestors and connecting to significant places in the realm of dreams can provide healing and closure, and add to the ongoing discovery of our beloved homelands, cultural traditions and ancient EIK. At certain times in our lives, our ancestors may have already reached out to us, or appeared to us in spontaneous dreams, and seeking them intentionally

498. Raven Grimassi, *The Cauldron of Memory: Retrieving Ancestral Knowledge & Wisdom*, Llewelyn Publications, 2009.
499. Robert Moss, *Dreaming the Soul Back Home*, New World Library, 2012.

through conscious dream travel can transcend the fixity of time and space to make more of these meetings possible. Planting an intention in your mind as you fall asleep, focusing on an attitude of love and gratitude, and making offerings to the ancestral spirits are all ways to create the conditions for ancestral encounters to unfold in random or lucid dreamtime. The ancestors have the ability to guide, protect, and watch over us, and receiving messages from the past through dreamwork is an excellent process, as Apela Colorado explains. *"When you have been disconnected from your cultural, spiritual heritage and power for hundreds of years, how are those Ancestors going to connect with us? We don't have an intact tribal community to contain it, to hold it, to support and protect us. How is it going to happen with integrity and safety? One of the main ways is through dreams."*[500] Keeping a dream journal, and comparing our dreams with research on the people, places and stories in our family heritage can lead to exciting discoveries. As Robert Moss found after meeting *Island Woman* in the shared dreamspace (see *Note 13*, Page 25), substantiating dream material with language experts, folklore and the historical record can provide links to a living continuum of ancestral and cultural recovery, rich in personal meaning and archeomythology. Deliberately creating the conditions for the Ancestors to meet us in the dreamtime, returning to the exact same dream for more information, and doing extensive research to validate the symbols, messages, and direct communications we receive are all part of the "dream archaeology"[501] process. In addition to paying attention to our dreams, guided meditations, visualization and pathworking are other kinds of spiritual modalities that can bring us closer to the spiritual realm of the Ancestors.

"Dream archaeology is a discipline that enables us to access the living past, to enter into direct communication with the keepers of ancestral wisdom and heal the collective and cultural soul loss that is a feature of our age. The practice of dream archaeology involves reclaiming authentic knowledge of ancestral traditions - including those that may have been buried or suppressed in the course of history - through a combination of careful research and experiential journeying across time and between dimensions."[502] (Robert Moss)

In most Indigenous societies and earth-connected religions, maintaining connectivity to the ancestors is a vital part of life, yet in the western

---

500. Apela Colorado, PhD as cited in "Dreaming in the Indigenous Mind, Part 1 of 2" by Atava Garcia Swiecicki, June 13, 2011. (www.thedreamtribe.com)
501. Author and dreamwork facilitator Robert Moss coined the term "dream archaeology" to describe the empowering practice of establishing direct and authentic communication with the ancestors and refocusing collective memory through dreamwork, lucid dreaming and the authentication of dream material with scholarly research, oral histories, pilgrimage and other methods. (www.mossdreams.com)
502. Robert Moss, *Dreaming the Soul Back Home,* New World Library, 2012.

world these practices have been diminished by the hyper-rationality of scientific reductionism and cultural hegemony. *"Western culture has worked very hard to erase Indigenous cosmologies that call on the past and the future to interrogate present-day actions, with long-dead ancestors always present, alongside the generations yet to come."*[503] (Naomi Klein) We have lost our own ability to care for our ancestors and beloved dead properly, and this flattening of the human spiritual experience negates the blessings from the ancestral circle that should be flowing naturally to us. As the only culture that does not embrace the traditions of ancestor veneration, it is time to renew our respect for the Ancestors, reconnect with their energy, and receive their gifts, support and spiritual guidance. As we revive our animist worldview in a universe populated by a multiplicity of spiritual forces, it becomes clear that all spiritual beings, our *Beloved Dead* included, are part of this inner and outer ecology. Working with the ancestors and reviving the magic of ancestral veneration is vital to the re-enchantment of our cultural stories and landscapes, and is an organic part of the recovery process for all reconstruction movements and earth-rooted societies. By honoring our ancestors and all the souls that have gone before, we acknowledge that these "wise mentors," "special messengers," "spirit elders" and "loving spirit guides" are there to help the living. As they shaped us, and passed on the gift of life with their intentions, sacrifices and achievements, thanking the ancestors is an extension of gratitude for the entire *Earth Community.*

"We call upon those who have lived on this earth, our Ancestors, who dreamed the best for the future generations, and upon whose lives our lives are built. With gratitude we call upon them to teach us and show us the way." (Chinook Blessing)

Indigenous societies and earth-connected religions have universally practiced "ancestor worship" for millennia with sacred earthworks, elaborate grave sites, temples, altars and ceremonies, and ancestral veneration opens a valuable channel of knowledge from the ancestors to ourselves. Honoring the ancestors and keeping them close creates a powerful link between the past and the present, and can bring us great joy, peace and good fortune. We can keep our inner traditions alive by invoking the memory of the ancestors on a daily basis, with prayer and gratitude, making offerings, and politely asking for assistance and guidance. Contact with the ancestral realm brings rewards of empowerment, resilience and strength, and we may even find that our EIK cultural recovery is meaningless without the recognition of the ancestral spirits. The best way to revive the magical potency of ancestral connection and receive their blessings and wisdom is to give them an

---

503. Naomi Klein, *This Changes Everything: Capitalism vs. The Climate*, Knopf Canada, 2014.

honored place in our hearts and homes. Designing ancestor altars with special objects such as photography, artwork, poetry or heirlooms that represent our *Beloved Dead*, creates a vibrant channel or "portal" between the living and the dead. According to specific cultural traditions, there are days set aside when the veil is thinner between the material and spiritual worlds, and candles, flowers, incense, fragrance, and offerings of food and drink are arranged to honour and welcome the spirits back home. "Portable altars" are great for travel, pilgrimage, offerings, outdoor installations, creating sacred space and visiting grave sites, and also function as containers for our grief, respect and honour.

"In many non-western cultures, the Ancestors have an intimate and absolutely vital connection with the world of the living. They are always available to guide, to teach and to nurture. They embody guidelines for what is most valuable about life."[504]
(Malidoma Somé)

Ancestor-honoring ceremonies and celebrations that encourage cultural preservation and connectivity with our *Beloved Dead* are found worldwide. With deep roots in the Indigenous traditions of what is now Mexico, *Dia de los Muertos/Day of the Dead* is a private and public 3-day celebration in many Latin American countries honoring and welcoming the deceased with processions, masks, costumes, music, dance, storytelling, elaborate altars called ofrendas, pan de muerto ("bread of the dead"), skeleton sculptures, tissue paper decorations, and pilgrimages to graves with offerings of sugar skulls, marigolds, and the favorite foods and beverages of the departed. With deep pre-Christian roots, the Celtic festival of Samhain (an old Gaelic word meaning "harvest at summer's end") celebrates the beginning of the pagan year in many traditions, and marks a liminal time when the *Wheel of the Year* turns from light to dark and winter is coming. In Celtic Reconstructionism, Celtic Spirituality, Avalonian, Druidic and Pagan traditions today, Samhain or "All Souls Day" has been revived as an important solitary ritual or "gathering of the tribes," with practices emulated the ancient traditions and rituals of lighting the sacred fire, divination, masquerades and costumes, feasting, dances, songs, storytelling and practical jokes. At Samhain, when the veil between the worlds is at its thinnest point, spirits, deities, fairies (the Fair Folk or "aos sí"), or souls of the dead may choose to visit, and with offerings, rites or libations, much can be accomplished in communing with our Ancestors or interacting with the gods, goddesses and spirit beings. The borderline time of Samhain is excellent for remembering our *Beloved Dead*, receiving their wisdom and guidance, and acknowledging the cycle of life, death and rebirth according to our own specific ancestral traditions.

---

504. Malidoma Somé, *Of Water and the Spirit: Ritual, Magic and Initiation in the Life of an African Shaman,* Penguin Books, 1995.

"With prayer, you may be offered help by those who have crossed over into Spirit. Many cultures make invoking the wisdom and assistance of the Ancestors a part of their daily spiritual practice. The spirits of the Ancestors live on and can connect to us, and they are there to help us everyday."[505] (Sonia Choquette)

We are forever entangled with our ancestors, and the past generations in our family tree are standing side-by-side supporting us and each other, giving us a sense of stability and rooted strength. At times we may feel their memories and wisdom, or experience health issues we carry in our DNA, and our ancestral line can also influence our emotions, loyalties and energy levels. The knowing of the ancestors is a sacred continuum in which all may participate, and with various modes for petitioning our descendants, i.e. with deeply-felt love, forgiveness or praise, it is possible to heal ancestral patterns. The Dagara people of Burkina Faso have a beautiful process of "ancestralization" that addresses grief, inherited trauma and other issues that may still impact the living, and by healing ancestral lines going back in time, balance is restored to self, family and the kinship group. Over a number of consecutive days, the elaborate ceremony assists the *Beloved Dead* to make the transition to the spirit realms, aids the living to release unfinished business with meaningful containers or symbols, and brings a sense of closure and completion. These beautiful Dagara rituals transform the dead (who are finally at home in the spirit world) into powerful allies for the living, and the ancestors can now guide and help their descendants to fulfill their purpose in life. There are also emerging methods for healing the ancestral line in western traditions such as *Constellation Work*, a modality that acknowledges the transfer of energetic patterns from the Ancestors to us, and that transgenerational responses can be addressed and healed.

"Down those old ancient streets,
Down those old ancient roads,
Baby there together we must go
Till we get the healing done."[506]
(Van Morrison)

The entire spectrum of human emotion forms the rich humus at the roots of our being, and acknowledging the experiences of our ancestors through self-discovery, transformation and healing can enrich our lives. We are a product of history, and identifying our entanglements or "bequests" from the collective experiences of the family soul, allows us to face and move beyond ancient or more recent traumas that may

505. Sonia Choquette, *Trust Your Vibes: Secret Tools for Six-Sensory Living,* Hay House, 2004.
506. Van Morrison, "Till We Get The Healing Done," *Too Long In Exile,* © Universal Music Publishing Group, Polydor Records, 1993.

manifest as unresolved issues or be held in the unconscious. Systemic constellation work[507] is a model for an intuitive group process that looks at our origins, roots and foundational families, and addresses collective issues from the perspective of the soul. With the guidance of a trained facilitator, the experiential and energy-based constellation process is offered in a gentle, safe and supportive environment, and recognizes ancestral patterns that can impact our health and happiness. Group movement, expression and ritual allow us to reconnect with hidden memories and loyalties in the family line, which are in turn clarified and resolved. As we come to understand how family dynamics continue to inform our well-being and belief systems, the constellation approach offers deep soul-level integration, healing, and profound peace. The experiences and stories of our relations do not need to hold us back, as we can transform our family legacy and grow into our best selves with inner work and other modalities such as meditation, therapy, journaling, poetry, expressive arts and dance. As we become more attuned with our heritage, both our own life stories and the memories we hold from the family soul can become a rich source of guidance and strength. Any healing work that we do in our lives heals our ancestors as well, as they continue to send us their blessings, and cheer us on!

"If upon summoning the Ancestors, tears of healing come, it is a collective grief that has remained unacknowledged for years. Releasing the sorrow from the lives of our foremothers lifts the weight of their legacies from our shoulders. We become free to remember and develop the many gifts & talents that we have inherited from them."[508] (Christiane Northrup)

As we become more comfortable with interacting in the continuum of nonmaterial reality and honoring the "Council of Ancestors" - politely engaging their help with visualization, prayer, song, offerings and ceremony - we are participating in the ancestral veneration that is at the heart of all Indigenous societies. Connecting with our ancestral lineage expands our entelechy (our true purpose), and family and cultural continuity has the ability to ground us amidst the challenges of life and the cycles of birth, death, and regeneration. Hearing the call of the Ancestors means becoming deeply enmeshed in the multidimensional world(s), paying attention to warnings and advice, learning and practicing our shared traditions, and teaching our EIK to others.

---

507. The *Systemic Constellation Process* is a trans-generational modality with roots in family systems therapy based on the work of Bert Hellinger, and offered by thousands of licensed practitioners worldwide. An experiential process that addresses our issues from a soul perspective through the use of movement, expression and ritual, constellation work can assist with the transformation of consciousness in relation to our ancestral lineage. (http://www2.hellinger.com/en/home) (www.systemicconstellations.com) (www.constellationapproach.com)   (www.caretakingthesoul.com)

508. Christiane Northrup, "Welcoming the Grandmothers," *Mother-Daughter Wisdom: Understanding the Crucial Link between Mothers, Daughters, and Health*, Bantam, 2006.

For, *"when we honour the ancestors - the ones that walked before, the ones that sat in circles and prayed that their children and their grandchildren would follow in their path - we honour ourselves."*[509] (Lillian Pitawanakwat) Mapping our return to earth-wise community in an epoch of massive change may mean acknowledging that we are the Ancestors of the future, as we continue to pass on the spark of life. In the expansive narrative of time suggested by the ancestral role, we have a responsibility toward future generations to care for our inner traditions, and for Mother Earth who nurtures us all.

"Our post-modern culture finds itself in a desperate need for Ancestors right now. The greatest threat today is the unraveling of the Web which connects us to one another. Tracing the stories of our Ancestors allows us to reach beyond our cultural borders to worlds and times not our own. The future may try to monopolize our attention, but some of our most fruitful lessons may come from connecting to our past. May your journeys to the Ancestors yield both wisdom & compassion, which are their truest gifts to us."[510] (Anne Newkirk Niven)

In the process of reawakening ethnic memory our committment to the land is renewed, analogous to the symbiotic relationship with nature and the sacred that our Deep Ancestors experienced. As in life, the Earth remains the dwelling place of the dead, and the perpetual ancestral spirits can inhabit any feature, element, green growth, or creature in the living landscapes we call home. Wild nature provides the containers, vessels, crucibles and cauldrons for our spirits, and *"our souls live in the earth and the earth lives in our souls."*[511] To survive as beings of spirit, we must acknowledge that we are kindred to all the elements and creatures, and embrace this reciprocity in our true human role as stewards of *Earth Community*. With the paradigm shift to biophilia, localization and small-scale communities, we can begin to live in a way that will make our Ancestors proud.

"Because we are made up of the earth - our common ground, so to speak - we are all the descendants of tribes. We have genetic memories. Inside of our genetic memories, the power connection exists to our ancestral past. Each and every one of us is a descendant of a tribe."[512] (John Trudell)

Using our skills in dream archaeology, exciting discoveries can unfold as we uncover the correspondences between our dreams, genetic memories, ancestry, genealogy and the historical record. Focusing and meditating on images of places, symbols and artifacts from our root culture(s) can evoke or awaken our sense of belonging, and access deep regions of ancestral wisdom within. The more we research, visit, and resonate with the sacred sites of our ancestry in real time, the more our root culture will come alive for us and manifest in our daily lives.

When we find our own culturally-specific healing ceremonies, rituals, symbols, music, bardic arts, literature, poetry and chant, we will feel that our soul has finally "come home." Exploring traditional foods, creating new forms of art or writing, offering rites of passage, and becoming a mentor to others are all ways to actualize our newly-found ethnocultural and spiritual life. Unpacking the truth about our ancestors' lives and the challenges they faced is yet another way to uncolonize, and finding the joy in their lives with gratitude and healing is part of reclaiming our own authenticity. We can be comforted by the fact that going back in time, our ancestral line would have existed and enjoyed life long before the rise of Empire, when we depended on our tribal group and our interconnectivity with Gaia for our happiness, health and well-being. We have flourished without the oppression, amenities and toxicity of civilization, and by co-existing peacefully with the Earth and our kindred spirits, we can thrive again.

Do you remember?

"Prayer to the Ancestors
The earth on which we stand,
The slate on which we write,
The roots and rhythm of our race,
The pattern behind our lives.

You who have lived in the time before us,
who laid down the path upon which we walk,
who established the traditions that guide us,
whose blood flows within us,
whose genes have engendered us:

A gift for you – a small one in return
for the great ones you have given us.
Even the greatest, life itself, is your gift to us.
A gift then – from the living to the dead."[513]
(Ceisiwr Serith)

509. Lillian Pitawanakwat, "Ojibwe/ Powawatomi (Anishinabe) Teaching," *Four Directions Teachings/4D Interactive Inc.,* 2006. (www.fourdirectionsteachings.com)
510. Anne Newkirk Niven, "Living the Dream: Letter from the Editor," *SageWoman: Celebrating the Goddess in Every Woman,* Issue 43, "Ancestors "Autumn 1998.
511. See *Chapter 21,* "Eco-Soul" on Page 220.
512. John Trudell, *John Trudell Speaks at Judi Bari Memorial,* Martin Luther King Jr. School, Berkeley CA, April 26, 1997.
513. Ceisiwr Serith, *A Book of Pagan Prayer,* Weiser Books, 2002.

hands in earth, green growing
cavern sweet with flowers and leaves
(diving deep)
earth that is her body
ten thousand things rise and fall

Ancestors!
Ancestors!

the deepest sound is silence
next to hard rock she can remember

listening ~
not with the ear with the spirit

Ancestors!
Ancestors!

the trail is cold
the cave walls echo

•••••••••••

voices of earth, archaic whispers
guided, protected and inspired
rhythmic drums and sacred songs
summoning blissful hallowing
homelands etched on the heart

Ancestors!
Ancestors!

diving deep
earth that is her body

rising up to meet the light
(wings to fly)

Ancient Pictish art from the *Knowe of Burrian* stone,
collection of Orkney Museum, Scotland

25. Ancient Spirit Rising ~ Practices

"Those of European heritage need an authentic place to stand. The perception is that there is nothing in our past but Christianity, and this is just not true. There are deep philosophies, and positive spiritual traditions that predate Christianity and hierarchal church structures. We have our own ancient wisdom and Indigenous Folk Traditions."[514] (Max Dashu)

"The Ancestors have been waiting for years and years for the songs to come back, for our feet to touch the earth again. Dancing in the sacred circle we are people of the earth, filled with joy to reconnect with our selves and the ancient spirits again."[515] (Mi'kmaq Elder)

The resurgence of spiritual life outside the confines of organized religion in recent decades has been amazing, but we need to move through all we have collected at the spiritual feast and reclaim the riches beyond measure in our own European traditions. But where do we start? First and foremost we need to stop jumping from idea to idea, from IK to IK, from fabricated system to syncretic combination that is not based on our own cultural tradition(s). Depending on what we have discovered from exploring our ancestry and tracing the family tree(s) that chart the pathways of our ethnicity, the methodology for our EIK recovery may be narrow or broad-based. From the singular or multiple ethnicities that comprise our being, we can select a specific heritage, or claim ownership of them all. If our ancestry is unknown or undetermined, based on the little we know we can go back in time with DNA testing and/or the historical record to our probable cultural origins. In many cases, the recovery of our EIK and cultural practice may be extremely hard and frustrating work, but the way has already been forged for us with contemporary movements such as Ethnic Reconstructionism in Europe, Celtic Reconstructionism (CR), Celtic Polytheism, Sinnsreachd, and Ásatrú or Heathenry in the Americas. Reclaiming the cultural belief systems that dwell in our EIK, and our own spiritualities that are bursting with earth-connected beauty, wisdom and power, requires commitment, time, energy and focus. Beginning with where we find ourselves in place, and the resources available in community, texts and online, the reclaiming process can be either a solitary experience or initiated in a group. And as we come to realize that our EIK traditions are living traditions, we will recognize that other Indigenous cultures are also alive and thriving, and although it is good to be knowledgeable in the keystone stories of other cultures, the ones that will have the most impact and meaning to us will be our own.

---

514. Max Dashu, "The Fates in Your Journey," *Embrace the Goddess Telesummit,* Kim Wilborn, The Guardian Gateway, May 6-18, 2013. (http://guardiangateway.com)
515. Mi'kmaq Elder, "The Dance," *The Sharing Circle, Season 15,* Century Street Distribution, Winnipeg, ON, 2007.

Essential to thriving in alignment with our heritage and beliefs is to bond with the land, to approach the more-than-human world as sacred, and to find expressions of these values in our daily life. In ways that are realistic for us, we can connect with our ancestral tribal group, make the *Old Ways* new, and express our reverence for nature in our material culture, music, art, rituals, sacred activism, and expressions of daily living.

Central to our *Ancient Spirit Rising* is a "risky conversation" about deity, the Gods and Goddesses such as Cernunnos or Epona (Celtic), Dažbog or Vesna (Polish), and Óðinn or Freyja (Norwegian) that live at the heart of our EIK traditions. Do the divine powers and spirit beings specific to our tradition follow us from place to place? Or are the animist "gods" or the Anishnaabe Manitous (for example) already in-situ from the original Earthkeepers of the land? Do the "ancient ones" arise from the landscape itself and inform us all, whatever our ethnic origin? Or do we hold these timeless and sacred images and archetypes within, ready to be activated at any time? These are all valid questions and not easily answered, either through a colonized or uncolonized lens. If Marian visitations and miraculous sightings can occur in the Americas as the Madonna follows her faithful from place to place, this phenomenon points to the hopeful possibility of cuttings from the towering tree of European IK rooting in American soil as well. Many mythological heroes, deities and symbols have made it intact to the Americas from the UK and Nordic lands, as the flourishing of Celtic Polytheism, Brigid worship, devotional Heathernry, the Faery Faith and the *Green Man* movement can attest. A growing body of evidence suggests that many European gods, goddesses, spirits and archtypes made the transition to the Americas with the early Settlers. Although the indwelling "genius loci" of certain landscapes were not overly welcoming to those of Celtic or Nordic descent, in other places our Celtic or Nordic ancestral spirits were able to make a home, and there is no doubt that creating sacred space in the Americas can be reinforced by spiritual practices within specific bioregions that are reminiscent of earth-based European culture(s), such as taiga, rivers, hedgerows, deer-fed pools and beacon-fire hilltops.

When Settlers learn about or intuit the names and personalities of the earth spirits, mythic beings and Ancestors in places that belong to the Indigenous cultures of these lands, how do we honour those presences? These are not our traditions or our Ancestors, and we are not entitled to either worship or appropriate them in our metaphysical work. I would suggest that as guests on Turtle Island, we are obligated to be polite, deferential and respectful at all times. This may manifest in various ways, such as acknowledging the land ownership of First Nations and their cultural bonds prior to any of our own proclamations or activities. Letting go of the colonial need to dominate, and being gentle with ourselves and those that came before, will bring about a natural harmony.

All cultures have fluid and open boundaries to some extent, and as syncretization often occurs, some of our practices may resonate with what Indigenous people did in that same place for decades, if not centuries. Our ecocultural identity can be influenced by what the environment allows, but we need to honour the original Earthkeepers while sustaining our own practices and deities. Beyond the unresolved burdens of history and the cultural baggage we all carry, the land itself is waiting to tell us what to do, as Pagan activist-leader Starhawk and her kinship group discovered. *"Our fire ritual and our rain return ritual are relatively young – we created them less than ten years ago. They don't correspond to the equinoxes, or the major Celtic feasts, or the indigenous Pomo ceremonies of the land. Yet in some ways they represent the most ancient tradition of ritual and ceremony there is - they are the rituals the land told us to do."*[516] (Starhawk) As it has done for millennia, the land around us will shape our beliefs, and opening to the earth spirits, voices and features of our own bio-region can create a unique spiritual practice and thriving local culture.

Our directive is to build a bridge between our own Ancestors, place, and ourselves, to create strong connections to our traditions and the living land itself. The defining factor in this polemic is how ancestral presence on the land is established over time, as for all earth-connected societies (either imported or original to Turtle Island), the Ancestors continue to be our guiding lights. When our *Beloved Dead* inhabit features in our home landscape, we instantly become bonded to that place, and as superbeings in the landscape, our Ancestors become guardian spirits to the living. As with all sentient forces in wild nature, we can be open to receiving their messages, guidance and protection with respect, wonder and awe. Similar to the concentrated spiritual power at sacred sites that is well-known to Indigenous people, our heart and soul memories can also be traced on the land, and the ongoing relationship with our Ancestors as protectors, allies and good companions on the journey is the best way to define homeland and sacred space. It bears repeating that if we acknowledge the mistakes made by the Settler Society, and the ultimate sacrifices and monumental gifts given by First Nations to build Empire, we are engaged with the work of uncolonization and deconstructing whiteness. By learning about local First Nations without leaning in, contributing to social justice through solidarity and allyship, rejecting racism and the values of the dominant society, and embodying the models of peaceful co-existence, we are well on our way to becoming honorable citizens of Turtle Island.

aoibhneas!

"Everyone, no matter what their cultural background, has a right to discover the sacred in nature; to heal and be redeemed spiritually by nature; and to revere the Ancestors. We are all haunted and saved by our memories."[517]
(Martha Brooks)

With the exciting resurgence and *Ancient Apirit Rising* of cultural recovery happening in recent times, EIK is being recovered and transformed into living lifeways and communities all over the world. Challenging the toxic ideologies and hegemonies of Empire, the return to ancestral ways and tribal religions, or "reconstructionism" as it has come to be known, has never been more popular. EIK recovery in any form brings us full circle to our primal selves, our embeddedness in the natural world, and our hope for an ecocentric future. Ethnic Reconstructionism is flourishing in every European country, and countless ancient cultures, even those thought to be extinct are being revived in both theory and practice. In Iceland, Norway, Finland, Sweden, Denmark, Armenia, Bulgaria, the Czech Republic, Hungary, Latvia, Lithuania, Poland, Romania, Russia, Slovenia and Ukraine, reconstructionism has been adopted by disillusioned modern folk with the desire to develop a religious and cultural practice more in line with their pre-Christian traditions. Based on existing records and in-depth research from literature, history, theology, anthropology, archaeology and sociology, a multi-disciplinary approach is being used to recreate the culture, lifeways and art of the past, and the portals are opening wide to the worship and honour of the ancient deities once again. Both as a methodology and a religious/cultural practice, new interpretations of folklore and sacred expressions make European Ethnic Reconstructionism a revival that encompasses the full spectrum of life - the experiential, scholarly, spiritual and ceremonial aspects – in turn forming a living culture that becomes relevant to both the mainstream and subculture(s) of the entire collective.

In marked contrast to the self-actualization impulse found in New Age Spirituality, Reconstructionism and the revival of the *Old Ways* in both Europe and the Americas hold values of cohesive community, and embrace "hard polytheism," which is a firm belief in the gods and goddesses as individual entities with agency in the material world. Reconstructionists are devoted to the pantheon specific to their own heritage, and strive to cultivate a thorough knowledge of the deities past and present, often putting the needs of the Gods or Goddesses ahead of their own. The priority to love and honour the deities properly is accomplished with abundant and beautiful expressions of ritual, praise, worship and offering, and devotional Polytheist and Reconstructionist Pagans also model the importance of these values to others. A personal relationship to deity, studies in contemporary and historical paganism, religious expressions based on ancient knowledge, the revival of sacred objects and ceremonies, and the reclamation of ecocentric worldviews are all facets of the return to *Ancestral Ways*.

---

516. Starhawk, *The Earth Path: Grounding Your Spirit in the Rhythms of Nature*, HarperOne, 2013.
517. Martha Brooks, *Bone Dance*, Groundwood Books, 2005.

Different manifestations of the pagan sacred days, *Wheel of the Year*, rites of passage and seasonal celebrations are found in each tradition, as well as unique methods for spiritual practice such as oracular work and ancestor veneration. Overall, Reconstructionists are engaged with redesigning their traditions to the best of their ability, and by recreating their culture from the historical record, to better understand the original environment within which their beliefs were practiced. There is no attempt to create a pan-European paganism, as the emphasis is on respecting the diverse practices of every tradition, and to redesign one's specific EIK as authentically as possible.

A revival growing simultaneously in Europe, the Americas and elsewhere in the world, the vast array of Reconstructionist traditions are to be celebrated, each heritage a reclaimed and cherished part of the global ethnosphere. Transcending the "cultureless" and uprooted paradigm of the modern nation-state, the resurgence of EIK challenges the inner and outer framework of the colonial mandate, and embraces the beautiful epistomologies of the past to create a better future. The most exciting and empowering part of these movements is that cultures do not have to be created anew, but can rely heavily on all that remains from the past in history, myth and archaeological discovery. In some cases, there are living Elders that still hold elements of ancient EIK practices today, if we can slow down, locate them, and learn from their guidance and wisdom. Even if centuries separate us from our goal, knowing where we came from and acknowledging what was taken away allows us to free ourselves from the tyranny of Empire. We are all indigenous to the Earth, and models exist in our own traditions to reclaim tribal societies and revive our ancestral folk traditions. In the grand scheme of things, it is our responsibility to liberate both ourselves and the land, and for those of us in the European diaspora, it is even more vital for us to work on the positive transformation of our identities and reconnect to our ancestral roots, to stand tall and proud with what we have accomplished. Cultural continuity will take time, but re-rooting ourselves is a goal we can achieve, and one that can lead to peaceful co-existence with the original Earthkeepers of Turtle Island, as we join together in the *Circle of All Life*.

European Ethnic Reconstruction

The reconstruction of many European ethnicities and cultures in their places of origin is flourishing, as are their counterpoints around the world. For certain EIK traditions in the Americas, actualizing the potential of cultural recovery is at the beginning stages, making it an exciting time to get involved. Organizations for each tradition have been established both in Europe and the Americas, and in addition to the practice of Celtic Reconstructionism (CR)[518] covered in detail, here is a sampling of the other major reconstructionist groups.

Hellenic Polytheistic Reconstructionism (Hellenismos) is a revival of ancient Greek religious and cultural practices focused on humanism and ethics.

Kemetic Reconstruction (Kemeticism/Ancient Egyptian religion) is a movement ranging from eclectic to reconstructionist practice focused on Egyptian deities, mythology and religion.

Religio Romana (Roman Paganism/Nova Roma) is an international movement, dedicated to the revival and reconstruction of ancient Roman culture, religion and beliefs.

Romuva (Baltic Reconstructionist Polytheism/Baltic Pagan Tradition) is based in Lithuania and practice pre-Christian Baltic religion reconstructed from mythological texts and folklore; the **Latvian Dievturiba ("Keeping God")** movement in Latvia has been reconstructed from ancient proto-indo-European songs, customs, beliefs, archetypes and language; and **Taaralased** and **Maausk** are pagan movements in Estonia.

Slavic Reconstructionalism (Rodnovery) paganism or "native faith" is a contemporary revival of the old Slavic tradition focused on mythology, folklore, a pantheist and polytheist theology, and the worship of Slavic deities in Russia, Ukraine, Slovenia, Czech Republic, Poland, Bosnia and Herzegovina. With many aspects of nature-based spirituality, *Rodnovery* is based on indigenous values and earth-connected symbols, tools and practices, with an emphasis on scholarly research, cultural preservation and promotion to the wider community. **Rodzimowierstwo or "Native Faith"** is a slowly growing revival of Polish indigenous identity recovered from ancient pre-Christian beliefs, narratives, folklore and archaeology. They reject the labels of "pagan" or "neo-pagan'" as not specific to Slavic ethnicity.

European Congress of Ethnic Religions

A great starting point for beginning our journey in search of the *Old Ways* of our ancestors is the organization *European Congress of Ethnic Religions* at (http://ecer-org.eu). Charting the cultural recovery of European ethnic and indigenous religions[519] and traditions since 1998, ECER is an international collective that assists with the expression of European earth-connected traditions, and brings together diverse

---

518. I regret focusing on Celtic Reconstructionism to the exclusion of the other beautiful traditions, but my reasons for this survey are threefold (1) considerations of space (2) a focus on my own Celtic heritage, ancestry and cultural group that has informed my positionality, and (3) the fact that many New Age practitioners originate from Celtic Nations. To delve into a wider range of cultural treasures, please refer to the "European Reconstructionism" section of *Resources*, Page 401. Other ancient or syncretic cultures reconstructed in Europe or the Americas such as the Roma of Eastern Europe, Cornish or Basque Witchcraft, Italian Stregoneria, Appalachian Folk Wisdom, New Orleans Vodoun, or African American Folk Spirituality/Hoodoo/Rootwork are beyond the scope of this study.

ethnic and religious groups for common causes. ECER provides a newsfeed, resources, education, new scholarship, project funding, a directory of member groups and organizations, advocacy to oppose racism and discrimination, and an annual gathering at the *World Congress of Ethnic Religions*. The European cultural recovery movement is growing steadily, and representatives meet at the congress held each year in different European countries, with over 100 delegates from Denmark, Norway, Germany, France, Greece, Lithuania, Latvia, Portugal, Czech Republic, Poland, Ukraine and Russia. The ECER is based in Vilnius, Lithuania, and also co-hosts an annual *International Conference and Gathering of the Elders* with themes such as the 2015 "Universal Well-Being: Sustaining Nature, Culture and Communities" event happening in Mysore, India. Delegates continue to gather at the conference from over 50 countries worldwide, representing over 100 ancient cultures and traditions.

From the first collective declaration at the 1998 *World Congress of Ethnic Religions*, a gathering to express solidarity for the ethnic, indigenous, native and/or traditional religions of Europe and other regions of the world, the document states that *"all cultures as well as native religions and faiths should be equally valued and respected. Each region and each people have their distinctive local traditions (native faith, world outlook, mythology, folklore etc.) which articulate their love of the land and history, and cultivate a regard for the sacredness of all life and the divinity of Nature. Just as Nature survives through a wide variety of species, so can humanity be allowed to develop freely and without interference along a wide variety of cultural expressions. According to our ancient traditional ethics, the Earth and all creation must be valued and protected. We as human beings must find our place within the web of all life, not outside or separate from the whole of creation. We believe that the dawn of a new era of individual and intellectual freedom and global exchange of views and information gives us an apportunity to start again to return to our own native spiritual roots in order to re-claim our religious heritage. We are worshippers of Nature just as most of mankind has been for the greater part of human history. We have established the 'World Congress of Ethnic Religions' (WCER) to help all ethnic religions groups survive and cooperate with each other. Our motto is 'Unity in Diversity.'"*[520]

To fast-forward to the 2014 Congress, the ECER outlines in their 3rd collaborative declaration a renewed commitment to worldwide cultural recovery, ancestral connection, and care for Earth Community. *"We are members of diverse European indigenous ethnic cultures who seek to revitalize and reclaim our ancestral religious and spiritual traditions. We honor those who went before us, who gave us our life and our heritage. We are bound to the lands of our ancestors, to the soil that holds their bones, to the waters from which they drank, to the roads that they once walked. And we seek to pass that heritage on to those who come after us, whose ancestors we are in the process of becoming – our children, our grandchildren, and the many generations yet to be born. We send solidarity and support to the other indigenous nations, races and religions who are also engaged in the struggle to preserve their own ancestral heritages. Our ethnic religions are the product of the history of this continent; they are the living expressions, in the present, of our most ancient traditions and identities. At a time when the world is precariously balanced on the edge of environmental and economic upheaval, largely as the result of imbalanced individualism and rampant greed, our religions promote very different models of spiritual and social values: living in harmony, balance and moderation with the Earth; the importance of family and cooperative community; and respect and honor for all forms of life."*[521]

As a reference to what is possible in resisting Empire and engaging with non-colonial cultural recovery, the encouraging and empowering work of the ECER exemplifies the importance of embracing our own European ancestral traditions.

---

519. The ECER clearly states that the definition of *Ethnic Religion* is religion, spirituality and cosmology firmly grounded in a particular people's traditions, NOT including modern occult or ariosophic theories/ideologies, or syncretic neo-religions.

520. *ECER: Declaration*, Vilnius, Lithuania, June 23, 1998. You can view the full declaration at ⟨http://ecer-org.eu/about/declaration⟩.

521. *ECER: 3rd Declaration*, Vilnius, Lithuania, July 9, 2014. You can view the full declaration at ⟨http://ecer-org.eu/about/declaration⟩.

Nordic Paganism

With a focus on the ancestral traditions and EIK from Iceland, Germany, Norway, Sweden, Denmark and Finland, the first reconstructionist revival began in Iceland in the early 1970's, followed by the rapid growth of various *Nordic Paganism* groups both in Europe and the Americas. By 1973, the modern Ásatrú faith was granted official recognition in Iceland, and the *Ásatrú Free Assembly* was founded in the United States. The various subcultures such as as Norse Heathenism, Heathenry, Forn Siðr, Vor Siðr, Odinism, Theodism, Trolldom (Norse Folk Magic) Old Norse Traditions, Urglaawe, Germanic Neo-Paganism, Germanic Reconstructionism, Germanic Heathenism, Kith of Yggdrasil, the Elder Troth, or the "Old Way" all share a focus on polytheistic reconstructionism, and have diverse syncretic, animist, esoteric or mystic approaches. Sourced in modern times from Scandanavian or Norse mythology, history and folklore, the origins of Ásatrú pre-date the "big three" monotheistic religions of Christianity, Islam and Buddhism, and the heart and soul of *Old Europe* can be found in Ásatrú cultural practices and spiritual expressions.

Many of the ancient Nordic societies and tribes worshipped the same pantheons of Gods and Goddesses, known in Old Norse as the Æsir and Vanir - living entities who were involved in all aspects of human life. As they are reclaimed and worshiped today, The Æsir are the Gods of clan or tribe that represent kingship and craftsmanship, and the Vanir are the forces of nature that represent the fertility of the Earth. In contemporary practice, the deities are not distant and aloof to daily interaction, but are regarded as wise relatives and caring Elders, familial and approachable as guides and protectors. Well-loved Goddesses and Gods of the Æsir include Freyja, leader of the Valkyries and earth goddess of love, self-empowerment and beauty; Frigg, Odin's wife, goddess of fertility, motherhood and oracular power; Skadi, goddess of strength, hunting and the mysteries of death; Ostara, fertility goddess of the Spring Equinox; Thor the Thunder God, warrior, protector, healer and philosopher who wielded Mjölnir, the divine Hammer; Odin the warrior, magician, poet and keeper of the Elder Futhark, or runes; and Freyr, god of kingship, fertility, peace, prosperity and successful harvests.

The central tenets of Ásatrú involve rituals and ceremonies to interact with the deities, the "blot" or offering, which is the ritual exchange of gifts with the Gods and Kindred, relationship-building rituals or celebrations known as sumbels, and living in accordance with the *Nine Virtues*. Ásatrú holds an animistic understanding of the world, a respect for the ancestral spirits, and a belief that human beings have an interdependent relationship with an unknowable divine energy or essence, expressed in the diverse forms of the Gods and Goddesses and the wisdom they offer. Related to the elves, dwarfs, brownies, etins (giants) and trolls in Northern European folklore, practitioners of Heathenry and Germanic Neo-Paganism communicate with protective earth spirits called landvaettir or "wights" who inhabit mountains, streams, forests, fields, stones, trees and other topographies in the landscape. Highly sentient, capricious and full of personality, these shapeshifter beings can bring both benefit and harm to human beings, and live in the wild (the landwights), in close proximity to people, or even in human dwellings (the housewights). The *Disir* are feminine ancestral spirits attached to an individual, family or tribe, and the *Norns* are a triad of female entities who weave the web of Wyrd, the pragmatic code of luck, fate and determinism, and the ethical framework of personal ørlög (or wyrd).

A group known as the *Kindred* forms the structure for Ásatrú both in Europe and elsewhere, a community of believers who live in the same area and gather regularily to conduct ritual, take part in blots or sumbels, honour the Holy Days and worship the Æsir and Vanir. Within Heathen groups and organizations such as the UK-based *Kith of Yggdrasil*, local collectives or *Hearths* are the foundation of spiritual life and cultural practice. The beliefs, rites, festivals, study circles, organizations, alliances and special interest groups within Ásatrú are widely divergent, but overall, Ásatrúar promote standards of harmonious behavior consistent with their EIK and spirituality, and are open to sincere newcomers who wish to initiate a learning curve and join a *Kindred* or *Hearth*. In the contemporary recovery of ancient Nordic knowledge, an astounding body of new scholarship has been created, and both as a movement and religious community Ásatrú and Heathenry is thriving. The focus of Ásatrú is to maintain the practices of ancient Norse EIK as accurately as possible, and the emphasis is on reviving ancient narratives, poetry, music, language skills, arts, crafts, dance, cuisine, sports and other lifeways. Ásatrú is NOT connected to any Judeo-Christian religion, New Age Spirituality, Wicca or Neo-Pagan belief system, and many practitioners in the movement object to being included under the umbrella of Paganism or Neo-Paganism.

Unfortunately, since the 1970's individuals and groups within the Ásatrú revival have assumed the position of white supremacy and promote the pathology of racism, and the ideology of a "white master race" continues to appear in certain organizations and activities (see "Ancestral Origins & Cultural Recovery" on Page 137). Employing a great deal of discernment and research before aligning with any Ásatrú group is key, and fortunately the movement as a whole is aware of the problem, with vigilant anti-racism activists working hard within Ásatrú and Heathenry to call out racists wherever they are found, and to educate spiritual seekers in general.

In terms of shared EIK, there is much crossover between Nordic Paganism and Celtic Reconstructionism (CR), and combinations such as Gaelic-German Heathenry, Gaelic Heathenry and Heathen-Anglos are common for those who self-identify as both Celtic and Norse. As a belief system based on nature connection and spirituality, Ásatrú is especially concerned with conservation, deep ecology, rewilding and environmental protection. Bringing the strong Ásatrú qualities of independence, freedom and self-reliance to the struggle, Ásatrúar and Heathens have much to contribute to the paradigm shift and recovery of *Earth Community*. In Ásatrú cosmology, the Earth, or *Midgar* (as personified by the Goddess Nerthus) is the Creatrix (or womb) for both human and nonhuman life, the source of all procreative power, and Her health, well-being, natural cycles and magnificent beauty must be protected and preserved for the generations yet to come.

Celtic Reconstructionism (CR)

"Celtic Reconstructionist Paganism (CR) is a polytheistic, animistic, religious and cultural movement. It is an effort to reconstruct aspects of ancient Celtic religions with scholarship and by relying on our own iomas and aisling - our inspiration and our visionary practices - to

*help us find ways to integrate old practices into a new time and setting. We are nurturing what still lives and helping the polytheistic Celtic traditions grow strong and whole again."*522 (CR FAQ)

In the quest to follow James Dumont's directive, that *"everyone needs to get back to their own IK,"* our ultimate task as Celtic people is to base our cultural recovery on the *Old Ways* of our ancestors, and make them relevant to our lives today. Contributing to the potential for revived theory and practice individually and through our clan and kinship circles is the explosion in Celtic Studies, with new scholarship in history, literature, myth, folklore, philosophy, linguistic studies, sacred sites, psychogeography and archaeology being added everyday. By accessing this new material in addition to the abundant wealth of classical texts, we can unify the spiritual-religious and cultural worlds of our ancestors (as they would have done), to remount a holistic living worldview. We are also indebted to the first visionaries who emphasized the cultural cohesiveness of Celtic traditions back in the early days of Neo-Paganism, leading to the newly-named CR movement and its full manifestation by 1990. Part of a living, growing tradition, the CR communities that are flourishing today are leading by example, and we can look to them for inspiration and models for our own local resurgence, and during the learning curve, to join in the conversation online.523

With a sharp focus on reviving specific historic cultures in their entirety (and except for the shared use of the term "pagan") CR has little in common with the other syncretic, eclectic or generalist practices found in Neo-Paganism. Celtic Reconstruction is based on **actual** cultural and spiritual practices that vary according to the source tradition, and unlike Neo-Paganism, CR does not rely on reinterpretations or appropriations, nor adhere to a universalist, pan-Celtic paganism (or "Celtic monoculture"). As an example of this specificity, the framework of ritual so popular in Neo-Pagan and Wicca eclectism (casting the circle, calling the quarters, invoking the elements and raising energy) has no place in CR practice.

Otherwise known as Celtic Reconstructionism Paganism, Celtic Restorationist Reconstructionism, Celtic Reconstructionist Polytheism, Celtic Polytheism, Celtic Traditionalism, Gaelic Traditionalism, Gaelic Reconstructionist Polytheism and Gaelic Polytheism, CR has also expanded over the years to include the different lanes of Celtic Re-creationism, Celtic/Irish Reconstructionism, Irish Reconstructionism, Welsh Reconstructionism, Scottish Reconstructionism, Gaulish Polytheistic Reconstructionism, Celtic Reconstructionist Druidry, the Avalonian Tradition and Scottish Paganism (among others). Diverse Celtic root cultures are sourced in these recoveries, with a primary focus on the regional, ethnic, linguistic and clan groups of the *Six Celtic Nations* (Brittany, Cornwall, Wales, Scotland, Ireland and the Isle of Man), plus Celtic, German and Iberian societies from antiquity such as the Picts, Brigantes, Gauls (continental Celts), the Gaels (Irish and Scottish) and tribes who were living in close contact with the Roman Empire.

There is a wealth of indigenous lifeways to discover in our Celtic heritage, and much to be proud of in our unique character, as Herbert O'Driscott explains. *"The Celt's nearness to nature, their use of nature for healing, their connectedness to God, their abundance of sacred places, their rich storytelling tradition, their understanding that life is a constantly changing journey, and a willingness to venture into the unknown can be useful today as we move out of the era of Enlightenment."*[524] A key purpose of reconstruction is to revitalize the lost beliefs of our polytheistic traditions, and to reclaim the magico-religious elements of our EIK such as animism, worship of deity and healing practices that were kept alive over the centuries, both in Celtic lands and the colonial diaspora. Even during the rise of Empire, a remarkable amount of Celtic IK was maintained in families, groups, clans, communities and wider cultural regions, and the Scots Gaelic term "gàidhealtachdan" refers to areas where Gaelic languages and cultures continue to flourish, such as the Western Isles of Scotland (*Na h-Eileanan Siar*) or Cape Breton in Nova Scotia. In a feat of amazing continuity, the Gaelic oral tradition holds virtually the same narratives as those found in ancient book fragments and manuscripts, and for some practitioners, a pagan-derived layer of early Celtic Christianity adds an additional richness to these cultural expressions and practices of deep mysticism. The links that Celtic scholars have found between pre-Christian deities, local land spirits, deified ancestors and the early Celtic saints have contributed to closing the gap between ancient and contemporary EIK. In our own family circles, there may be fragments of surviving "fairy faith" practices, folklore, herblore, music or other Celtic lifeways that have always been on the periphery of our lives, and this EIK can be confirmed and expanded with family memoir, research, or by visiting our root communities in the

---

522. NicDhàna, Kathryn Price, Erynn Rowan Laurie, C. Lee Vermeers and Kym Lambert ní Dhoireann, *The CR FAQ: An Introduction to Celtic Reconstructionist Paganism,* River House Publishing, 2007. To date, the CR FAQ remains the guideline for CR in the Americas, and can be found online for free at (www.paganachd.com).

523. The principles of building local community work best, and chances are there is a wealth of Celtic folks in your city, town, or territory interested in engaging with cultural recovery and CR. Online communities and resources include *Pàganachd / Págánacht: A Celtic Reconstructionist Gateway* with articles, message board and the CR FAQ at (www.paganachd.com); *An Chuallacht Ghaol Naofa,* an established Gaelic Polytheism community with online options and resources such as the Ghaol Faofa FAQ at (www.gaolnaofa.org); *Imbas,* online archive of articles promoting *Senistrognata,* the ancestral customs of the Celtic peoples at (www.imbas.org/imbas/index.html); *The Preserving Shrine,* blog by Erynn Rowan Laurie, one of the founders of the CR movement at (www.seanet.com/~inisglas); and *Amhran nam Bandia,* domain and blog by Kathryn Price NicDhàna, one of the founders of the CR movement at (www.bandia.net).

524. Herbert O'Driscott as cited in *Worldview Skills: Transforming Conflict from the Inside Out,* by Jessie Sutherland, Worldview Strategies, 2005.

"old country." For the lucky ones, having access to the elements of a living tradition, either in your own clan or by visiting relatives overseas, can make a huge difference in the reconstruction process. With or without family ties, kindred spirits or community, there is still much we can accomplish with independent study, meditation, ritual, interacting with deities and going on sacred pilgrimage to our original homelands. However we source our time-tested traditional beliefs, lore or cultural tools, our collective efforts contribute to the firm footing of CR today, and the ongoing preservation of culture and language is of prime importance to the CR movement.

Above all, Celtic Reconstructionist Pagans value historical accuracy, cultural legitimacy and a coherent basis in the beliefs of the polytheistic Celts, through visionary practice by individuals or small groups, and seasonal celebrations and cultural rituals that reflect the same mythology as our pre-Christian ancestors. As we delve into our traditional ways we soon discover that the Celtic Gods are very real and very much alive, and this is the first point in the nine excellent guidelines for following a Celtic path by Erynn Rowan Laurie, one of the founders of the CR movement.

"What elements are required to make a path true to the Celtic spirit?[525]

- *A reverence for Celtic deities.*
- *A connection with the ancestors and land spirits. Ancestor worship and reverence for land spirits happens in most old Pagan cultures. We can carry it forward into a modern Celtic spirit by having a general love and reverence for the earth and its creatures.*
- *Poetry as intrinsic to the structure of magick, also the respect for poetry as a social mechanism, and the importance of both reading and writing poetry.*
- *A connection with the past. The Celts had a reverence for history, and that reverence is a part of the Celtic spirit. This connection comes through physical ancestry, study of history, connecting with the feeling of the myths, or in other ways.*
- *A sense of early Celtic cosmology, i.e. doing things in terms of the three realms rather than the classical Greek four elements, using Celtic symbols like triskeles and spirals rather than pentagrams, celebrating Celtic holidays rather than (or more deeply than) the holidays of other religions, threes and nines as ritually important, and use of the sacred/cosmic tree and well combination. Cosmology has had to be painstakingly reconstructed from fragmentary hints, and it goes back again to the argument that historical research is important to learning about and preserving the Celtic spirit."*

In terms of the second point, a connection to the Earth and a love for nature is integral to the Celtic worldview. The central tenets of CR revive the worlds of animism, IK and interexistence that our tribal ancestors inhabited. Historic records, poetry and myth cycles that survive tell us that for the Celts, the beloved Earth and her abundant diversity gave rise to their entire spiritual continuum, and they regarded the Earth and their embeddedness in the natural world as sacred, both in their everyday deeds and elaborate rituals. Mother Earth was the source of all, and her *Cycle Of Life* encompassed the birth, growth, decay and fallowness common to all beings. The Celts venerated features in the landscape such as natural springs, rolling hills, rivers, caverns and groves as the abodes of otherworldly beings, gods, goddesses, ancestral spirits or the Áes Sídhe ("the folk," faeries, Fay or "people of the mounds"). Calling on these beings and dieties for advice, assistance and creative inspiration was a natural and normal part of life, as was extending the human skills of protection, praise, cooperation, and cultural continuity in return. The ancient Celtic tradition of making offerings to the local land spirits, trees, deities and ancestors with food, drink, sacred waters or other meaningful objects is still important to CR practice today. In addition to our prayers, poetry, symbols and artistic expressions, these offerings are made as part of our personal and collective rituals, and in the continuum of time "*leave our own traces in the weave of the pattern.*"[526] (Erynn Rowan Laurie)

"*Some people are born with the 'second sight' which in Scots Gaelic is called an da shealleadh, literally meaning the 'two seeings.' Those in possession of the second sight perceive not only the physical semblance of a person or an event, but also its spiritual aspect.*"[527] (Caitlin Matthews)

For the Celts who were spiritually awake and "waeccan," they were able to perceive and interact with the sacred "anima loci," or spirits of place, the devas, faeries, elements and powerful natural forces that inhabited specific sites or entire landscapes. From Celtic mythology we know that rivers, lakes, groves, hilltops and mountains were especially luminous, the "thin places" at the intersection of the visible and invisible realms that offered intense epiphanies and spiritual experiences. Trained seers had expertise in the "geomantic arts" and the heightened sensory ability to turn to the land for messages, prophecy and divination, to root themselves deeply in place, and to "read" natural locations for much-needed information that contributed to the welfare of individuals and

525. Erynn Rowan Laurie, "Following a Celtic Path," *The Preserving Shrine*, 2010. (www.seanet.com/~inisglas/followingcelticpath.html)

526. Erynn Rowan Laurie, "Creideamh Sí and Celtic Reconstruction," *Book of Leaves: Notes of a Professional Madwoman* (blog), April 17, 2005. (http://erynn999.livejournal.com)

527. Caitlin Matthews, *Celtic Visions: Seership, Omens and Dreams of the Otherworld*, Watkins Publishing, 2012.

the tribe. As visionaries, dreamers, descendants of the Túatha Dé Danann ("the fae") or just generally speaking, many Celtic people have a pronounced skill with telepathy, clairvoyance, intuitive sensitivities, seeing with the mind's eye, and the "sixth sense" or "second sight."[528] Dwelling in an interconnected appreciation for the land and grounded in the everyday sacred, the ancient Celts did not value an ascensionist or vertical spirituality, but found the extraordinary in the ordinary maps of their lives. If the goddesses or elementals were seeking to visit across the Sidhe, they could reach them in the "here and now" of everyday life, the ordinary earth-bound time and space that was at the same time luminous and holy.

"A Celtic worldview expresses the enchanted quality of the world via a complex of beliefs concerning spirits and other beings that haunt the wild woods and fields of life. Ancient Celts lived in a world that was alive with numinous presence."[529] (Montague Whitsel)

Before the rise of Empire, it was unthinkable for the Celts to overstep the boundaries of natural law or ravage the land, and clan, kinship and family groups could live in one place for centuries (if not millennia). They were aware that the energies and emanations of the Earth were the source of all truth, beauty and power, and their mystical expressions in visions, healing, poetry and song arose from these locations, especially from sacred sites. A profound blood-tie to place, and a deep heart-mind connectivity to tribal territory, was evident in their exemplary stewardship of the land. In the Avalon, Gaelic and British bard tradition, rituals and song cycles were performed to support the health and wholeness of the land, and the guardianship of the environment was a major theme for Druids, Avalon priestesses and diverse Celtic seers. In the animist universe that the ancient Celts inhabited, the "green world" held the prevailing archtypes - the Sídhe, faeries, gods, goddesses, creatures and Ancestors – and their sacred vow of love and protection was required. Without over-romanticizing the UK lands as places of myth and mystery, those of us in the diaspora can certainly emulate the ancient Celts today, and experience their same bonded relationship to the land, love of nature and sense of belonging to the beautiful landscapes we call home. The *Celtic Soul* may have embraced rootlessness and mobility, but returning to our ancient heritage means respecting the earth, and honoring the earth spirits and other-than-human creatures that dwell in the land with songs, stories, prayers, offerings and sacred intention. In accordance with Celtic traditions,

---

528. According to Canadian author Patricia Pearson, her extensive research has shown that people from Norway and the Scottish Highlands have the most pronounced "sixth sense" ability, and she suggests it may be through genetic inheritance. Patricia Pearson, *Opening Heaven's Door: Investigating Stories of Life, Death, and What Comes After*, Atria Books, 2014.
529. Montague Whitsel, *Wellsprings of the Deer: A Contemporary Celtic Spirituality*, 1stBooks, 2002.

caring for the land as the repository of sacred deities and our *Beloved Dead* needs to be our focus again as we engage with earth protection. Polytheistic and earthen temples or shrines were kept in families for generations, and the ongoing preservation of this archaeology, plus the many monoliths, landmarks and sacred sites in Celtic lands is vitally important to our culture.

The first step in our our quest to revive our ancestral traditions is to turn to the richness of Celtic Studies, to find surveys on the historical Celts and their symbols, mythology, art, religion, laws, customs, and all the details of daily living. Each person or collective will have their own methodology or creative approach to this process, and sharing with the greater CR community benefits the entire movement. The Celts ranged over much of central/northwest Europe for more than 2700 years, and tracing their origins and full history can be a complex undertaking. Celtic social organization included a leadership group of druids, bards (and a sacred king), a warrior group, and a farmer group - and the *Sacred King* in symbolic marriage with the *Goddess of the Land*. For centuries, these kinship groups with village life at the centre formed the basis of the Celtic Soul. Strong bonds to the mythic geography of the surrounding coast, forest, fen or mountain landscapes influenced their food and costume choices, building of dwellings, and cultural practices. Ancient lore is filled with references to the *Three Realms Cosmology* of land, sea and sky, with the "fire of inspiration" as the central force. These sacred keystones are found at the heart of Celtic ritual structure, and were the triad of realms, the *An Thríbhís Mhòr* (the great triple spiral) considered magically binding for the "taking of oaths."

Hundreds of deities are found in the wide range of Celtic societies, some localized to a family or tribe, while others are renowned across barriers of landscape, tradition and language. Variously portrayed in the origin stories and timeless mythic story-cycles of each Celtic group, the Gods and Goddesses were associated with natural features in the land, sacred sites and the elements; or relevant dreams, visions, events and visitations from the spirit world. For example, the Goddess Sulis (Briton) was associated with sacred springs; Coventina (Briton) with holy wells; Boann (Irish), Sequana (Gaul), Sabrina (Welsh) and the Morrigan (Irish) with rivers; and the Gods Taranis (Celt) and Lugh (Irish) with storms and lightning. The deities had other attributes and skills, i.e. Cernunnos (Celt) and Epona (Gaul) with fertility; Belenus (Gaul) and Sirona (Gaul) with healing; Lugus (Proto-Indo-European) with learning; Arianrhod (Welsh) with transformation; Macha (Irish) with war and sovereignty; Scáthach (Scottish) with martial arts; and Cailleach (Irish, Scottish and Manx) with the wilderness. Often a deity will have multiple attributes and meanings such as Brigid, the Irish goddess of wisdom, medicine, poetry, arts, crafts, home, hearth, blacksmithing, sacred wells, serpents (in Scotland), the blessing of cattle and other livestock, and harbinger for the arrival of early spring.

Being chosen by the deities, learning their intricacies and mysteries, and creating respectful relationships with them is the work of a lifetime. Offerings are presented to the deities, spirits, and Ancestors throughout the year in many Celtic traditions, and in the round of daily life, home rituals of gratitude, healing, protection and purification are practiced. Altars and shrines honoring our own patron deities and spirits can be created as focal points in the home, or placed outdoors at sacred locations such as natural springs or beside beloved trees. The ongoing discovery of prayers and songs from traditional sources such as folklore and ancient poetry is a joyful process, and collective rituals can take place for healing, rites of passage, initiation, vigils and divination (with the permission of the spirits of course). The *Celtic Calendar* is followed with a beautiful round of cultural practices, including community celebrations, festivals, music, dances and feasting for Samhain (October 31), Imbolc (February 1), Beltane (May 1), and Lúghnasadh (August 1). With full immersion in our cultural recovery, we may soon be drawn to the mystic space of more formal or elaborate rituals to interact with the otherworldly realms, and more easily enter the world of Celtic divination practices such as Ogham, or find omens from signs in nature like forms in clouds or the behavior of birds. Resonating with the rich symbols and mythologies of Celtic culture over space, time and ancestral lines, can feed our waking dreams, poetry and artistic creations. In my own life, I have always been dazzled by Celtic stories, and the metaphor of cauldrons, wells, natural springs and stone circles, not knowing until well into my adult life how sacred places and spiritual landscapes such as Newgrange, Callanish, the Rings of Brodgar, Neolithic Orkney, Galloway's Forests, Iona, the Avebury Complex, the Waters of Sulis (Bath), Glastonbury Tor and Chalice Well already lived deeply in my soul. How empowering it is to renew and reclaim that sacred fire!

"When you create a ritual, think of the Ancestors, and wonder how they would have created it. They would not have written it out to be read aloud. They would have known it down to their bones, lived it through every organ of their bodies, and radiated it from their hearts. We should do nothing less."[530] (R.J. Stewart)

In this exciting time of Celtic renewal, an abundance of historic and contemporary resources can be accessed, as well as the use of rich mythological themes in fiction and pop culture. There is something calling us, something we need to discover regarding our overwhelming attraction to standing stones, ancient forests, ocean spray on jagged coastlines and the mysterious parting mists, and numerous portals await to spark our understanding. The shift to *Earth Community* requires us to remember ourselves as we existed before modern civilization, and Celtic Reconstructionism connects us directly to our ancient Celtic roots, language, myths and folklore through historical accuracy and poetic inspiration. By studying the spiritual traditions of your own tribal group you will be able to enact these practices yourself, and with commitment, time and dedication, proclaim yourself when you are ready, go on life-changing pilgrimages within and without, celebrate your root culture, practice solidarity with the different branches of CR, and inform others on the importance of ancestral alignment. You can contribute to the flourishing CR network and spiritual community by celebrating your renewed EIK at conferences and gatherings, or the modern connectivity of online groups promoting mutual sharing, discourse and learning. Akin to the centuries-old practice of "gathering at the hearth" - the Irish cultural tradition of sharing in the community house each evening - I wish you blessings, as we exchange our songs, stories, laughter, respect for each other and the land, and balance our inner and outer lives with rituals to heal "an chroi," the Celtic heart.

---

530. R.J. Stewart, source unknown, from his work on the Celtic Underworld. Among others, his books include *Power Within the Land: The Roots of Celtic and Underworld Traditions, Awakening the Sleepers and Regenerating the Earth*, Mercury Publishing, 1998; and *The Underworld Initiation: A Journey towards Psychic Transformation*, Mercury Publishing, 1998.

Druidry

"We share a common love for learning, a reverence for the earth and the knowledge that the Mighty Kindreds, the Spirits of Nature, the Ancestors, and the Gods and Goddesses are all around us and will interact with us on a daily basis when we learn to slow down and listen."[531] (Robert Lee Ellison)

Of the many exciting Celtic Reconstructions of heritage and spirituality now available to us, we can be indebted to the excellence of diverse contemporary practitioners and scholars for the revival of Druidry in our time. With ancient indigenous roots in Britain and Ireland, Druidry specifically grounds us in our Celtic origins and ancestry, and offers a path of wisdom based on the sacredness of nature and inter-connectivity with *Earth Community*. From the surviving remnants and records of history, a full picture has been formed of the authentic culture, traditions and people of early Druidic societies. The fictional treatment of Druids popularized in recent years with various "Merlin the Magician" themes promotes the "solitary mystic" stereotype, yet *"not only did druids have a religious function as priests and priestesses, the caste also consisted of philosophers, judges, teachers, historians, poets, musicians, physicians, astronomers, prophets and political advisors or counsellors. Druids could sometimes be kings or chieftains, but not all kings were necessarily druids."*[532] (Peter Berresford Ellis) Through archaeology, existing folklore, linguistic studies and the translations of ancient texts, pre-Christian Druidic knowledge has been expanded to create a flourishing modern practice and thriving worldwide community.

Members of the original Druid societies were profound observers of nature, and they practiced their own forms of animism and nature mysticism. Their primary focus was to attend to the "Mighty Kindreds" or *Three Realms Cosmology* of land, sea and sky, to interact with these indwelling spirits, and to receive their wisdom, energy and guidance. Deeply rooted in the forest, the trees provided for the emotional, physical and mental needs of the collective, and tree worship, tree language, tree protocol, tree teachings and tree culture are at the heart of Druid cosmology. Over millennia, outdoor meeting places in ceremonial temples or "nemetons" (sacred groves) and their Wisdom Keepers became an integral part of Druidic epistemology, as well as taboos that functioned as environmental protection for the trees and other natural spaces. In Druidic lore, the other-than-human world and the powers of nature are considered to be sacred, with their own inherent purpose and rights, and understanding the deep patterns in creation is an ongoing exploration in philosophy, storytelling, lore-keeping, poetry, the bardic arts and music. The interconnectivity of nature, the true essence of all beings, and the divine inspiration we receive from the timeless energy of the sacred life force are all aspects of "Awen" (/|\), the guiding principle of Druidry. Discovering otherworldly realms, transforming consciousness, "peaceful abiding," "touching the earth," "parting the mists," oracular work, calendar observation, rites focused on the sun through the cycle of the seasons, the holy days, and Ogham studies are all aspects of mastery within the *Druid Way.*

The diversity of contemporary Druidic and Neo-Druidic practices allows for the reverence of a wide range of deities, from the power of natural forces such as the sun, earth or thunder; to the animist spirits of place such as lakes, rivers, votive pools, wetlands, meadows, forests or hilltops; and to divine guides from the Celtic pantheon such as Brighid, Cernnunos (the Green Man), Taliesin, the Morrigan, Danu or Epona. Mutual respect and peaceful co-existence within Druidry are part of the essential nature of the tradition, and Druidic practice is also based on listening to the voices of the Ancestors, who are honored, considered sacred, and included in ceremony. *"In its personal expression, modern Druidry is the spiritual interaction between an individual and the spirits of nature, including those of landscape and ancestry, together with the continuities of spiritual, literary and cultural heritage."*[533] (The Druid Network) Localization and the reinhabitation of place are extremely important in contemporary Druidry as well, as re-establishing a deep connection to the ecological diversity of our home landscape gives rise to the psychogeography that makes the links between mythology, history, ancestry and heritage possible. Whether you initiate your practice as a Solitary Druid or as a member of a Grove, Order, Branch or Henge, ceremonies marking the seasonal festivals celebrated with public ritual are usually open and free to all. At the foundation of

Druidry is a deep reverence and respect for the Earth, the in-dwelling spirits of place and the sacred relationships between all beings, and the ethics of responsibility for environmental protection and social justice is becoming an increasingly important part of the tradition. Joining the Druid community would be a fantastic place for those seeking to connect with the indigenity, traditions and mysticism of their Celtic heritage. Flowing from the resilience of Celtic languages, myths, stories, laws and intellectual prowess, the renaissance of Druidry meets the challenge today to maintain our connection to the *Old Ways*, and to pass on this living spirituality to the generations that follow.

The Druid Network: Informing, Inspiring and Facilitating (UK)
(http://druidnetwork.org)

OBOD: The Order of Bards, Ovates and Druids (UK)   (www.druidry.org)

Ancient Order of Druids in America   (www.aoda.org)

ADF: Ár nDraíocht Féin: A Druid Fellowship (International)
(www.adf.org)

531. Robert Lee Ellison, *The Solitary Druid: Walking the Path of Wisdom and Spirit*, Citadel Press, 2005.
532. Peter Berresford Ellis, *The Druids*, Wm. B. Eerdmans Publishing, 1994.
533. The Druid Network, *The Definition of Druidry and its Practice as Used By The Druid Network,* 2014. (http://druidnetwork.org)

The Avalon Tradition

*"It is important to begin with study – to learn, experience and understand Avalon through history and literature, art and archaeology, myth and folklore. We can seek out the patterns, uncover the symbols, and learn to reveal the way toward true understanding. Only the path of the inner quest will reveal the whereabouts of the Grail, and once found, we can drink deeply of the same draught our foremothers tasted. And then, what changes will occur in our lives?"*534
(Jhenah Telyndru)

The lore of Celtic Britain is rich in diverse cultures, oral traditions, legends and sacred landscapes, and the mysterious pull from the ancient Isle of Avalon cannot be denied. Seemingly lost to the mists of time, the strands of Avalonian mythos found in texts, poetry, art and music has led to a contemporary and vibrant revival of the *Avalon Tradition*. Based on narratives describing a hidden island that is home to Druidic Priestesses adept at intellectual leadership, oracular wisdom, magic, healing and earth geomancy, the Avalon heritage has remained dormant in hearts and souls for centuries, just waiting to be reborn. The mythic cycles of the Tales of Arthur, the Quest for the Grail, Merlin, Taliesin, Morgen Le Fay, the Nine Morgens, the Lady of the Lake, the Isle of Women (the "Apple Island"), Goddess Brigid/St Brigid, the Holy Thorn, the Mystic Rose, the Faerie Kingdom and the Code of Chivalry are all keystones in Avalon resurgence, and continue to be extremely popular in Celtic scholarship, fiction, pop culture, psychology and other revitalized spiritual practices such as Wicca and Paganism. Through study, research, pathworking, dream archaeology and cultural soul recovery, the sacred essences of ancient priestesses, archetypal goddesses, oracles, healers, warriors, ancient practices and mythic traditions are all waiting to be reclaimed on the Avalon path.

A wonderful example of following a very cold trail and rejuvenating the ancient Avalon wisdom tradition is the *Sisterhood of Avalon (SOA)*, a Celtic women's mysteries organization founded in 1995 by Jhenah Telyndru, author of the foundational text *Avalon Within: A Sacred Journey of Myth, Mystery and Inner Wisdom*. A true sisterhood that continues to welcome all women who hear the Avalonian call, the SOA provide a community focused on reclaiming the myriad functions of a circle of priestesses in today's world. Rooted in the mythology of the Welsh Mabinogion, the SOA revere both the Goddess principle and the individual Welsh goddesses, and embrace spiritual practices such as herbcraft, music, healing, oracles and ceremonies, with a dedication to supporting each other and being of service to others. A blend of scholastic achievement, western esoteric beliefs, sacred geography and goddess spirituality, the work of the SOA is also related to the literature, folklore and traditions of Welsh Druidism. To remember the *Old Ways*, to understand the *Illumination of Awen* (/|\) and the landscape of Avalon both within and without, to reclaim the mythologies and bardic traditions, and to renew and practice the spiritual traditions, is to come home to the shores of Avalon.

The most exciting part about the *Avalon Revival* is that the sacred sites and natural formations that informed every aspect of the Druidic worldview still exist in the landscapes of the British Isles, and can be accessed and experienced today. Ancient people created roads, temples and monuments to interact with the sacred geometry, ley lines, and "high energy vortex" locations in the land, and to pay tribute to the in-dwelling earth energies and spirits of place. Ancient fragments from the realms of Avalonian lore and wisdom are still present within the living landscapes of Glastonbury, the Tor Valley Complex, the Five Hills, Bride's Mound and the Chalice Well. One can walk the mythic paths of the *Isle of Avalon* on spiritual, metaphorical or actual pilgrimages, and honour and connect with these holy places, both as inner and outer experiences. As a gateway between the worlds, Avalon is considered a liminal space of transition that is accessible with great intent and dedication. Climbing the Tor's spiraled path allows us to recall our own heritage, gain new insights and wisdom, and renew our devotion to the

---

534. Jhenah Telyndru, *Avalon Within: A Sacred Journey of Myth, Mystery and Inner Wisdom*, Llewellyn Publications, 2010.

Goddess and all that is sacred to the Earth. Our natural affinity for Arthurian material or metaphors, and the symbology and myths of Celtic spirituality, can re-awaken our connection to our ancestral roots and realize our potential for self-discovery, empowerment, healing and magical practice. All over the world where the seeds of the *Avalon Tradition* have taken root, practitioners follow the lunar cycles and mark the holy days of Samhain, Imbolc, Beltane and Lughnasadh, and celebrate festivals and solstices with both kindred spirits and the wider community.

 For those who are seeking a spiritual home, the "ancient spirit rising" of the *Avalon Tradition* offers sanctuary, the quest for wholeness, the blessings of the Lady, and great sovereignty and joy. With a new-found connectivity to the *Celtic Earth Mysteries* shaped by exploring the unique heritage of Avalonia and communion with The Lady, the Ancestors must be well pleased! As the legend goes, at the end of his life the "Once and Future" King Arthur sailed on a mysterious barge to Avalon's shores, was received into the caring arms of an enclave of Priestesses, and has spent the ensuing centuries waiting to re-emerge in an era of greatest need. The return to the *Old Ways* of Avalon in our time, a major force in the exciting shift to ecological civilization and the spiritual values of the Sacred Feminine, must be the long-awaited fulfillment of that prophecy.

Jhenah Telyndru, The Sisterhood of Avalon,
Remembering, Reclaiming and Renewing
The SOA offers study through the *Avalonian Theological Seminary* online; training intensives; spiritual pilgrimages to Wales, Glastonbury and other Celtic sacred sites; a member's barter program, and a vast networking web. The SOA publishes the member newsletter, *The Barge*, and the e-zine, *The Tor Stone: A Quarterly Journal for Women's Mysteries*. "*May we take our place within a circle of powerful sisters, and may the three foundations - hearth as altar, work as worship and service as sacrament - be our guide and inspiration.*" (www.sisterhoodofavalon.org)

Mara Freeman, The Avalon Mystery School,
Sacred Magic from the Celtic and British Mystery Tradition
Author of *Grail Alchemy: Initiation in the Celtic Mystery Tradition* and founder of *The Avalon Mystery School*, Mara Freeman offers courses in different practices, symbols and archetypes from the Avalonia tradition. "*Avalon is the Inner Temple of the Celtic and British Mysteries, a landscape of the soul, a country of the heart. Avalon does not exist in the dimensions of time and space. It lies within the Otherworld, a place in Celtic teachings that exists now and for all time.*" (www.avalonmysteryschool.net)   (www.chalicecentre.net)

Kathy Jones, Glastonbury Goddess Temple

From time immemorial, Glastonbury, the site of the magical *Isle of Avalon*, has been home to an ancient and powerful Goddess known as the Lady of Avalon. *Priestess of Avalon* Kathy Jones has spent the last thirty years living in Glastonbury learning the ways of the Goddess in this ancient and sacred place. Focusing on the intuitive and lyrical aspects of Avalon, she is the co-founder of the *Glastonbury Goddess Temple*, organizer of the *Glastonbury Goddess Conference*, and author of *Priestess of Avalon, Priestess of the Goddess*. With Erin McCauliff she offers a three-year training to become a Priestess of Avalon, described as "*one who devotes her/himself to the service of the Lady of Avalon, to Her sacred land, and to Her people.*" (www.kathyjones.co.uk)

Druids of Avalon, The Avalon Druid Order

The Avalon Druid Order is based on the indigenous pre-Celtic peoples of Britain referred to as "Faery" and the wisdom passed down through Celtic lore. "*Teaching the keys for spiritual self-empowerment and community through contemplation, communion and conscious resanctification of the natural world, ADO offers guidance in reclaiming our spiritual birthright. We strive to live our lives in balance and dialogue with Nature, and those with the courage to change and adapt will find a template for harmonious living that is desperately needed today.*" For membership requirements, forum, information on gatherings, publications, resources and training see (www.avalondruidorder.org).

Cultural Recovery Beyond the Designations of "Pagan" and "CR"

In recent years a critical debate has developed over the meaning and use of the term "pagan" in Pagan/Neo-Pagan/Wicca/Druidic and Reconstruction circles, and many have stepped away from using "pagan" to self-identify, or as an umbrella term for their cultural practice. Countless interpretations and reinvented meanings for "pagan" have occurred since the first movements, each to suit a specific cultural practice or direction. Today, detractors vary in their positionality i.e. those in the polytheistic camp may discard "Pagan" as a label, as they associate it with self-focused or generic types of Wicca. At the other end of the continuum, earth-connected animists may reject "Pagan" as a label because it is linked to deity-centered polytheism. What I have noticed is that "pagan" is used to describe such an endless array of ideologies, practices, paradigms, movements and markers in history, that this universal scope has rendered it practically meaningless. We also need to take into account that "Pagan" was originally a derogatory term, a fabricated classification used by Greeks, Romans and the early Christians to lump together, dominate, oppress and convert indigenous societies, "the superstitious folk of the countryside." On that basis alone, we can either reclaim the term to give it new life in a positive way, or reject it completely for its associations with Empire and the "triumph of civilization." Also, as a device of western knowledge dominance, "Pagan" continues to be used today to describe any Indigenous culture, and this offensive habit completely ignores the self-identifying titles that cultures such as the Yanõmami or Lakȟóta may have for themselves. As the category of "pagan" is now referenced in contemporary spirituality, *New Age Capitalism* and woo-woo occult studies, the term is misleading. Why should "paganism," which contains the essence of our diverse cultural identities as displaced Europeans, be reduced to a category or "genre," one out of a vast supermarket of choices in spiritual and cultural life? Instead of the "Pagan" label, returning to the tribal names that our ancestors used may be one honorable direction.

Practitioners engaged with Celtic Reconstructionism for a long time, or those new to cultural recovery, may have trouble seeing how the term "pagan" fits, or may find the precepts of CR as a modern movement limiting. They may not want to identify with the neo-pagan community that gave rise to CR, or they may feel that CR is over-complicated, or restrictive, or too deity-focused, or find that their cultural recovery is outside of the *CR FAQ* and "rules and regulations." Perhaps they are finding that CR is not specific enough, or they do not want to identity with a "modern movement," or they want to bypass modernity altogether and resonate with their root culture, which cannot be defined by modern concepts or language. In some cases, there is a perception that CR perpetuates a western worldview, or is a portable religion, rather than having a direct connection to a specific ancestral spiritual worldview and tradition. Others may see that CR functions as a religion rather than a culture (or a blending of both), and question the accuracy or usefulness of the CR umbrella. As a way to deal with these limitations and frustrations, many individuals and groups have decided to bypass CR and go directly to source, in their own practice and for building community.

At the heart of the Celtic mythos, the Faery Faith, Faery Seership or *Creideamh Sí*, is a living breathing tradition that preserves the cultural values and ancestral ways of alignment with the earth spirits and the *Celtic Otherworld*. Learning the prayers, songs, blessings, customs and beliefs of this rich heritage by accessing Celtic and Gaelic resources on our own, as well as interacting with the gods, goddesses, Sídhe and ancestors, is incredibly empowering and rewarding. As a Celtic-Gaelic path for individual or community exploration, the study and practice of *Creideamh Sí* arises directly from source, and there can be great power in the self-definition of naming a tradition directly, rather than using the all-encompassing term of "Celtic Reconstructionist."

Also forming largely outside of the CR designation, *Sinnsreachd*, or *Gaelic Polytheistic Tribalism*, is a flourishing movement that blends

Irish/Scottish polytheistic folk religion and the Faery Faith for those with Gaelic ancestry, their extended families, kin-groups and kindred spirits. A revival of sacred pre-Christian traditions combined with modern restorations of culture and religion, "Sinnsreachd" is a Gàidhlig (Scots-Gaelic) term meaning "customs of the ancestors." United by core values, common beliefs and lifeways, families and households known as hearths or teaghlachs may come together in septs, with the larger clans, organizations, communities or pobal comprising a Túath, or tribe, whose members may (or may not) live together on shared land. The *Sinsearaithe* believe that the recovery and practice of indigenous Gaelic knowledge and lifeways are needed in today's world, and the overall goal is to eventually form a Gaelic Polytheistic network of regional tribes, or Túatha. The most important Sinnsreachd principles, ethics and wisdom teachings are based on belonging to tribe and the bonds of the collective, not on the individual, and this alignment with tribalism as a social arrangement corresponds to the uncolonization and re-indigenization movement that is currently underway on Turtle Island.

Taking a stand on ancestral continuity, some Sinsearaithe communities have initiated gentle policies emphasizing that the faith may have the most meaning to those of Gaelic descent, without marginalizing extended family or those who may be attracted to Sinnsreachd. Through our "unity in diversity," the Sinsearaithe truly believe that all people should celebrate the beauty of their unique heritage(s), and that non-Gaels may find the recovery of their own sovereignty and the honoring of their own gods and ancestors to be the most empowering and rewarding practice. As with all cultural recovery work, ongoing study by developing linguistic skills and learning the lore is incredibly important, as so much of the original EIK is embedded in the original language. In cultural, spiritual and community life, the mandate of Sinnsreachd is to rejuvenate what was lost in the building of Empire, to reject the global monoculture, to adhere to Irish/Scottish ancestral practices and beliefs, to honour the teachings of the Gods and Goddesses, to restore deep connections to the land, and to take pride in the sacred worldview of Túatha once again. With passion and great dedication to these beautiful traditions, is is hoped that the cultural paradigm of Sinnsreachd can be recovered, guided toward the future, and preserved for the generations yet to come. As a starting point to explore the "ancient spirit rising" of Sinnsreachd, websites for localized Túath can be found online.

Túath na Ciarraide: The Ciarraí People

A Túath, or tribe of the Sinnsreachd faith, the members of *Túath na Ciarraide* are *Gael Meiriceánach* in diaspora in America who have preserved and reclaimed their native culture and beliefs. *Túath na Ciarraide* descends from the Ó Ciarraí family from Ciarraí (County Kerry) in Éire (Ireland). (http://ciarraide.org)

Túath na Gaoth Aneas: A Sinsearacht Tuath
Founded by three families in 2006 who share a passion for Irish culture, *Tuath na Gaoth Aneas* is an *Éireannach Sinsearacht Túath* located in Kansas. Based on the importance of lore, language, music and agriculture, *Túath na Gaoth Aneas* reveres the collectivity of the tribe over self-interest, and embraces the rejuvenation of Gaelic heritage. Living the *Sinnsreachd* values and lifeways fully, and passing them on to the next generation is essential to the tradition, as well as making the ancestors proud of their achievements in cultural reclamation. (http://tuathnagaothaneas.awardspace.com)

Sinnsreachd - Gaelic Polytheistic Tribalism
A Facebook group and general forum for members of the *Sinnsreachd* faith and all those interested in learning about the *Sinnsreachd* way of life. (www.facebook.com/groups/sinnsreachd)

For the ultimate inspiration on how to recover and embody our ancient *European Indigenous Wisdom* directly, we can look to the work of Nigel Shaw and Carolyn Hillyer in fine art, music, ceremony, material culture and daily life that sings to the Celtic heart and sets our souls on fire. Deeply embedded in the English landscape, *Seventh Wave Music* offers texts, poetry, music, artwork and musical instruments from richly-reconstructed indigenous traditions affirming the Celtic, Nordic and Northern tribes of Europe. Nigel Shaw and Carolyn Hillyer *"live and work on a thousand-year-old farm in the heart of Dartmoor, a mist-veiled landscape of wild hills and moors, and the inspiration for their work is drawn from the raw beauty, hidden spirit and ancient memory of this deep ancestral land."*[535] Music has the powerful ability to bring us back to our originating culture, and with hand-crafted drums, flutes, rattles and other musical instruments using locally-sourced wood, stone and other materials, the soundscape journeys and primordial rhythms of *Seventh Wave Music* restore us to the spirit of the wild landscape and the gifts of the land.

 *"What is the story of our forgotten people? It is a story of return. It is a story of hearthstones and home; of amber from oceans and copper from earth; of men who soar with buzzards and women who weave heron feathers into their hair. It is also, however, the story of ourselves; in a landscape where time spirals rather than runs ahead of us in rigid lines, we look to our forgotten people to remember something about our own lives. Remembering our people, those who are connected to us by blood or clan or land or any other bond that serves to entwine hearts and souls, is part of rooting ourselves in our landscape and shaping the road along which we chose to travel. We learn from our ancestors in order to understand the ancestors we might become."*[536] (Carolyn Hillyer)

With a foot in both worlds, Nigel Shaw and Carolyn Hillyer are immersed in the *Old Ways*, and have manifested ancient EIK on their Dartmoor land by building a Neolithic-style roundhouse using granite, oak and rye grass thatch, for ceremony and to evoke sacred space. Like a miracle from a dream or the answer to a yearning we never knew we had, hearing their music or reading Carolyn's words transports us directly to our ancestral roots, reconnecting our hearts to the heartbeat of the Earth and the glowing hearth, to stone, bone, willow, reed, antler, feather, copper, and to the warp and weft of stories that are woven in the land.

"we will build our dwelling from the bones of the earth
we are wed to the body of the earth
we will kindle our fire from the heart of the wood
we are wed to the soul of the land
now that the first hearth is set on the ground
to the spirit of this place we are bound......"[537] (Carolyn Hillyer)

The astonishing creative output of *Seventh Wave Music* and their hosted gatherings take us along ancient paths where we can reconnect with the energies of the earth, experience deep animist interactions with the nonhuman world, and feel the echoes of ancient forests, Atlantic coasts and stone circles once again. For over 20 years Carolyn has been offering workshop journeys for women, weaving together shared songs, chants, poetry, stories, ancient mythology, sacred symbols, hearth circles, ritual drumming, ceremony, oracle work, magical ways, rites of passage, wildcrafting, earth shrines, vigil, wayfaring, and interaction with the sacred wild sanctuaries of the land. Viewing her mixed-media art (*"life-size images of archetypal spirit women, the ancient landscape in human form"*[538]), and learning from the sacred prose and poetry of her mystic teachings can ignite our own deep well of remembrance and indigenous talents as seer, bard, story-teller, hearthkeeper, healer, wanderer, hunter, gatherer, shapeshifter and lover of the land.

"Ancient shadows of women spiralling/
through the coils of time
we are part of those women spiralling
with the song of the land
and the dance of the moon inside."[539] (Carolyn Hillyer)

The work of reviving an ancestral paradigm can arise from different motivations, methodologies, groups or inspirations, and diverse sources can guide our passage back to the ancient clanmothers while evoking the vibrancy of our Celtic sensibility in the modern era. With their rich tapestry of music, performance, poetry, story, ceremony and hearthfire, the works of Nigel Shaw and Carolyn Hillyer give form and song to our personal journeys of cultural resurgence, and show us the way home to our EIK.

535. Carolyn Hillyer, *Sacred House: Where Women Weave Words into the Earth*, Seventh Wave Books, 2010.
536. Nigel Shaw and Carolyn Hillyer, "About Seventh Wave Music: Words from the Wild Hills...," *Seventh Wave Music*, 2014. For information on music CDs, books, prints, hand-crafted instruments, concerts, events, *Rivenstone, Festival of Bones, Thirteen Moons Women's Festival 2015* and *Workshop Journeys for Women: Hearth, Trail or Threshold Weekends*, see (www.seventhwavemusic.co.uk).
537. Carolyn Hillyer, *Sacred House: Where Women Weave Words into the Earth*, Seventh Wave Books, 2010.
538. Carolyn Hillyer, "Books and Prints," *Seventh Wave Music*, 2014. (www.seventhwavemusic.co.uk)
539. Carolyn Hillyer, *Sacred House: Where Women Weave Words into the Earth*, Seventh Wave Books, 2010.

A Call for EIK Leadership

Celebrating the *Old Ways* and building a movement to reconnect with earth-emergent wisdom means reaching out to other spiritually-bereft diasporans who are also seeking alternatives to Empire. Brilliant leaders, authors, ceremonialists and seers in Celtic Reconstruction, Ásatrú, Norse Heathenry, Sinnsreachd, the Faery Faith, Druidry, or others who have been on the path for decades, are perfectly positioned to mentor and promote EIK to the culturally-deprived, as we participate in the collective journey to authenticity. With the beautiful renaissance of EIK happening today, we need to "go wide" with our learning and sharing, and reach out in our community-building. There is a model from ancient times to follow, whereby religious and community leaders would offer up their powerful talents, knowledge, guidance and mysticism for the greater good, and this dynamic needs to be stepped-up in today's world. Going beyond the Christian notion of prosteletizing, becoming proactive in informing those with shared heritage that a thriving movement of cultural reclamation is possible and achievable, is exciting and fulfilling work. Paradoxically, it is our advantages and privileges that have given us the leisure to recover our EIK in the first place, and these same entitlements may induce us to cling to the knowledge we have so painstakingly collected. Yet if we can bypass our internalized conditioning in regard to cultural insularism, intellectual detachment or spiritual materialism, we can naturally and organically help to build and restore ancestral-sourced community. People are starved for EIK, and letting go of the tendency to over-protect knowledge means learning from one another, sharing our gifts, and connecting with kindred spirits as we return to our *Sacred Ways*. Reconstructionists and Traditionalists who are adept with EIK after years of immersion have the unique opportunity right now to assume major leadership roles, and by declaring themselves fully representative of their pre-colonial ancestral culture, speak for those of European identity at conferences, symposia, and even gatherings of Indigenous peoples. As those of European descent become more adept at declaring themselves part of the worldwide circle of diversity, their appearance at tribal gatherings will not be as host, or financier, or apologizer, or journalist, or scholar, or anthropologist, or collaborator, or spectator, or as a wannabee aligned with the lifeways of a tradition not their own, but as an equal and full participant, secure in their own ancestral knowledge. If those of European heritage have also done their uncolonizing work by rejecting the memes of Euro-domination, and are clear about holding a position in solidarity with all those decimated and oppressed by Empire, this will naturally form the circle Mother Earth in Her infinite wisdom has been waiting for, as we express our mutual love in *Earth Community.*

26. Ancient Spirit Rising – Directions

"The tracks of our Ancestors have been wiped away by the Great Forgetting. It's not up to us to replant their exact footprints, but to make our own, equally original tracks."[540] (Carl Cole)

"Attuning ourselves to the long-forgotten tides of moon and season, sun and sea, of land and circling stars - our connections with the cog wheels of creation have deep roots in antiquity and are our oldest inheritance."[541] (Marian Green)

The *Ancient Spirit Rising* survey of traditional, reconstructionist and restorationist EIK practices is continually changing and evolving, and these revitalized paths can lead to authentic identities and renewed regard from other Indigenous nations. In our re-indigenization and cultural recovery processes, aligning with our pre-colonial ethnicity and kinship group(s) is difficult work, and many barriers stand in the way. For those who find the access to accurate history across a long timeline too daunting, or have not heard the call of their specific ancestral group, there are more generic contemporary movements that also contain elements of older, earth-based lifeways and spirituality. Rooted in elements of our original European indigenous identities that were transplanted to the Americas, reconfigurations of the *Old Ways* have been rejuvenated by the descendants of the original Settler Society as Paganism, Neo-Paganism, Wicca and Goddess Spirituality, and it is possible to re-frame these contemporary movements and practices as reflective of the much-needed re-indigenization and shift to ecological civilization that is underway in western society.

Paganism/Neo-Paganism

"Pagans have always felt a oneness, a respect, a connection to all things. We are never alone - all beings are with us and we are one with all beings. Solitary work allows a stronger connection with the gods and spirit allies to develop. I do what my spirit remembers, what I hear inside myself, the answers that come from within. That is the path of Ancient Memory."[542] (Cedarmoon)

Since the mid-20th century, the amazing movement to reconnect with earth-rooted traditions and ancestral lifeways has led to an eclectic diversity of practices, and Paganism has grown into the fastest-growing religion in the Americas. Under the "Big Tent" of Paganism there are a wide range of possibilities and faiths, including (and not limited to) Eclectic Paganism, Humanistic Paganism, Jungian Neo-Paganism, Naturalistic Paganism, Eco-Paganism, Earth-Centered Paganism, Pagan Animism, "Pagan Shamanism," Ceremonial Magic, Natural Magic, "Dirt Worship," Celtic Paganism, Wicca, Feminist Witchcraft, Eclectic Wicca, Goddess Spirituality and New Age syncretism. The terms "Pagan" and Neo-Pagan" are often used interchangeably, but technically "Pagan" refers to the root religions, EIK, or classic ideologies from ancient cultures that have informed the reconstructionist movements (who adhere as much as possible to the *Old Ways*), whereas "Neo-Pagan" may refer to modern ideologies blended with practices revived from ancient sources. There is a consensus that both "Pagan" and "Neo-Pagan" are inspired by ancient knowledge, and both are part of the movement toward "green religion," "nature religion," ecological awareness and earth-based spirituality. As there are no rules within Paganism outlining the precise meanings of the different sub-categories (the subject of ongoing debate), self-identification is highly-individualized, with interpretations and combinations having personal significance to the practitioner.

Contemporary Paganism is "deity-centered," with the belief in a pantheon of gods and goddesses such as Thor, Odin and Freya from Norse religion, or Isis and Osiris from Egypt, and these Polytheistic practices can vary from "soft" polytheism, the eclectic worship of multiple deities, to "hard" polytheism, which honors each deity as separate. Influenced by the universal "monomyth" or generic approach of Joseph Campbell (see Page 74-75), "soft" polytheists regard deities as psychological archetypes common to all cultures, and that embracing a multiplicity of ethnic origins for their deities is perfectly acceptable. "Hard" polytheism (or "devotional polytheism") rejects the idea that "all gods are one god" ("monism") or that the gods are psychological archetypes ("psychologism"), as they believe that the deities are separate, distinct and real divine beings. In both the neo-pagan and revivalist communities, polytheistic expressions can vary from eclectic worship, ritual, libations or offerings, to direct experiences with deity and the spirit world that authenticates the bond with the ancient peoples who worshipped the same gods. These wide-ranging practices make for an active exchange within the Pagan community, and the pluriform monotheist-versus-polytheist debate continues to be a lively one.

---

540. Carl Cole, as cited in *Beyond Civilization: Humanity's Next Great Adventure by* Daniel Quinn, Three Rivers Press, 1999.
541. Marian Green, *The Elements of Natural Magic*, Element Books, 1989.

One of the early founders of Neo-Paganism in the Americas, Isaac Bonewits claims that the core Neo-Pagan beliefs include *"(1) a multiplicity of deities of all genders, (2) a perception of those deities as both immanent and transcendent, (3) a commitment to environmental awareness, and (4) a willingness to perform magical as well as spiritual rituals to help both ourselves and others."*[543] As both a movement and a spiritual impulse, the reawakening of Paganism/Neo-Paganism in our time has nourished the roots of diverse cultural traditions, and has recovered space for a much-needed sense of earth-connected community. A brand-new religion has been created, one that is tolerant of difference and diversity, open to unique perspectives, and honoring of individual paths and practices. Pagans embrace the idea of infinite interpretations on the nature of the Divine, and are willing to have dialogue, learn from each other, and cooperate for common causes. As a useful reference, the following features relate to the overall contemporary "Pagan Impulse" and "Pagan Movement."

The Pagan/Neo-Pagan Impulse

- The need for a spiritual life.
- The need for kindred spirits and community.
- The impulse to re-enchant the world.
- Rebellion against the mechanistic imperialism of western society, rigid religiosities and Christian dominance.
- Love of nature and the natural world (even in urban places), evoking natural processes such as earth wisdom, working with earth energies, gardening, herbcraft and green lore.
- Embracing animism, pantheism, elementalism, ecomysticism, spiritual ecology, sacred sites, *European Indigenous Knowledge*, nature spirituality, and other nature-based philosophies and lifeways.
- Strong belief in unseen dimensions, the spirit realms, inner guides and the ancestors, an affinity with oracular tools, readings and revelatory messages.
- Strong experiences of intuition, synchronicities, dreams, sleeping or wakeful visions, magical happenings, prophecy, spirit work and soul journeys.
- Interested in the workings of intent, magic and/or spells for transformation, using the magical arts to change self and circumstances and/or heal the self and the world.
- Strong belief in the healing arts with natural methods and alternative modalities.
- Willing to learn the folkways of one's chosen tradition and practice the *Old Ways*.
- Reconnecting with the seasons and cycles of life, celebrating the ceremonial *Wheel of the Year*, cross-quarters (greater sabbats), solstices, equinoxes and other rites of passage.

- Embracing the Gods and Goddesses as part of life - honoring, evoking and petitioning the deities, elementals and spirits.
- Creating identity, experimenting with different spiritual paths, roles and combinations thereof.
- Acquiring and enjoying the pagan "style" with jewellery, outfits and magical tools.
- Highly creative world of self-generating "wisdom" in art, craft, fashion, music, entertainment, fantasy, literature, storytelling, ecology, solitary practice and group ritual.
- Personal expression based on Pagan experiences, insights, visions, UPG, transformation and magic.
- Modern interpretations of traditional EIK as a synthesis of the old and the new.
- Casual or formal learning, self-discovery, sharing knowledge between teachers, students, mentors and leaders.
- Personal autonomous highly-individualistic syncretic or eclectic belief system self-created from diverse resources, texts, theologies, oracles, rituals, workshops, classes and retail stores.
- Embracing Pagan family, tribe, circle, group, coven, temple or grove; coming home to community; mentoring, teaching and sharing with children and youth.
- Nourishing the roots of Pagan/Neo-Pagan community for future generations.

The Pagan/Neo-Pagan Movement

- A thriving culture with an endless variety of subcultures, paths and modalities.
- Flourishing Pagan groups, circles, covens, groves, kindreds, hearths, communities; gathering spaces and temples with staff, paid clergy, libraries or other facilities.
- Very active convention circuit, ritual gatherings, seasonal celebrations, workshops, retreats, themed festivals i.e. Faeryworlds, witch-camps in the Reclaiming tradition, other transformational gatherings, music soundscape scene, hedonistic revelries, imaginative play.
- Excellent scholarship outlining historical veracity, myth, folklore, cultural origins, cultural practices, EIK, ethnography, philosophy, religion, metaphysics, psychology, literature, poetry cycles, occultism, symbolism, western mystery traditions, Pagan ethics, creeds, tenets, "dogma," social issues, analysis and critique.
- Ongoing conferences for *Pagan Studies* with academics, scholars, authors, activists, practitioners, visionaries and cultural creatives.
- Flourishing communications and publishing industry in the Pagan/Neo-Pagan genre with books, magazines, events, online forums and blogs.

- A long tradition in Paganism with social justice, anti-racism and environmental activism[544] engaging deeply with social problems and political realities; creating public awareness to challenge stereotypes and misinformation about Paganism and Wicca as held by the dominant society; working to end defamation, discrimination and religious persecution in society and the workplace through lobbying, education, legal counsel and representation; ideological and legal advancements recognizing the unique belief systems of Pagans in the military and other sectors of modern life; securing rights as legally recognized religion(s) under the *Freedom of Religion* laws or *Earth Religion*; sustaining rights and respon-sibilities with education and full participation in the interfaith community; ongoing assertion of religious freedom, religious tolerance, religious liberties and the separation of church and state (politics and religion/spirituality); building bridges of under-standing between all religions, spiritualities and faith traditions.

- A large communications and cooperation network linking activists, organizations, legislators, educational institutions, the media, and pagan groups fighting religious discrimination.

- A wonderful tradition of embracing a path of service.

- A growing awareness and critique on serious issues in the Neo-Pagan and Wicca world such as racism, discrimination, stereotypes, knowledge domination, cultural appropriation, diversity issues, syncretism, eclecticism, universalism, the spiritual marketplace mentality, and superficial understandings such as the "fluff bunny"[545] Wiccan youth phenomenon.

- The commonalities in contemporary Paganism are shared language, a ritual calendar, respect for tradition, love for Mother Earth, general knowledge of shared belief systems, awareness of the principal leaders and authors, and tolerance for diversity and dialogue.

The overall movement to reject monotheistic religion in favor of European polytheistic traditions, or older earth-based forms of spirituality, is an excellent trend. Yet, contemporary Neo-Paganism shares a huge overlap with *New Age Spirituality*, and the practices of

---

542. Cedarmoon, as cited in *Exploring the Pagan Path: Wisdom From the Elders* by Kristin Madden, Starhawk, Raven Grimassi and others, New Page Books, 2005.

543. Isaac Bonewits as cited in "Defining Paganism and Neopaganism" by John Halstead, *The Allergic Pagan*, Patheos: The Pagan Channel, 19/09/2012. (www.patheos.com)

544. The *Earth Religions Legal Assistance Network (ERLAN)* is a service organization operating in the U.S. and Canada that helps *Earth Religion Rights* activists communicate so they can help people with legal problems associated with religious discrimination (www.erlan.org). An internet search will yield scores of resources for *Pagan Activism*.

545. *"Fluffy Bunnies, Insta-witches, McWiccans, One-Book Witches, Wicclets, Whitelighters and Wanna Blessed Be's are those people who, most broadly categorized, give the rest of us a bad name, not by doing bad or objectionable things but instead being unserious, sophomoric, or just plain wrong."* Catherine Noble Beyer, "Fluffy Bunnies," *Wicca for the Rest of Us*, (blog), 2011. (http://wicca.cnbeyer.com)

cultural appropriation from First Nations are very much in evidence. As with all members of the dominant Euro-society, white spiritual seekers attracted to Neo-Paganism come from a white supremacist society, have lost the links to their own ancestral traditions, and benefit from the oppressor/oppressed power imbalance on Turtle Island. Placing one's own needs first is a benefit of having unearned white privilege, and this egoic self-absorption is evident with the Neo-Pagans who feel entitled to pick-and-choose between different cultures, faiths, IK systems and disenfranchised minorities. Like New Agers, Neo-Pagans shop openly in the spiritual marketplace for tools and the "stuff" of material culture without any notion of consistency or awareness regarding cultural theft. Eclecticism in the contemporary Neo-Pagan world is worn like a badge of honour, but this "feel-good" self-centered free-for-all can disrespect the original Indigenous Knowledge keepers (as with the "shamanism" phenomenon), or the appropriated Gods and Goddesses of the various *Old Ways*. As the following passage indicates, an awareness is growing in Pagan community that syncretism is not as effective as a more focused worldview, but the critique does not oppose the practice completely. How can we truly put the brakes on things like spiritual materialism or eclecticism, which are just so much fun? *"If we would be responsibly eclectic, if we would add meaning and substance to our religious practices and ceremonies, let us look to other cultures to gain inspiration to create our own rites and rituals. Let us educate ourselves about the spiritualities of other people not so that we can pilfer their practices, but so that we can look deeper into our own heritages and enrich our own myths with actions sacred to and meaningful to us. Let us forge a relationship with our own histo-ries, our own myth and culture, that we might enliven it, enrich it, and carry it forward for the betterment of the future generations of our own people and communities"*[546] (Amber Simmons) The conversation about cultural appropriation is truly the gigantic "elephant in the room" that needs to be fully discussed in New Age and Neo-Pagan circles, yet the monumental resistance to this taboo subject is truly baffling. As the impulse for those on a New Age or Neo-Pagan path seems to be a yearning for authentic spiritual connection, raising awareness, tolerance for diversity, and human equality for all, it must be high time that the paradox in the ideology - the blind spots of white privilege and cultural appropriation - are fully addressed and resolved, with healthy political and cultural dialogue.

There are other dilemmas to be found within contemporary Paganism and Neo-Paganism. Some groups do not reclaim their traditions from a time prior to Christianity, and their ideologies can practice patriarchal behaviors, replicate the status quo of colonialism, and be complicit with the paradigm of dominating the earth for profit. To truly ignite our love for Mother Earth and environmental activism in our time, we need to reach further back, to the tenets of our animistic European indigenities that embrace all of *Earth Community* as sacred. Another contentious issue in the Pagan world is the new "ethnic racism," or "white on white racism" that is happening without any POC present, as discussed in "Ancestral Origins & Cultural Recovery" on Page 137. The misguided "universalist" approach maintains that it is a racist act to align with one's own ethnicity, and under the misnomer of "cultural exchange" promotes the free and uninhibited connectivity with ancestral traditions from any time, any place, or any culture in the world. Another irony is that for the most part, Paganism and Neo-Paganism are modern urban movements situating squarely in the complexity and amenities of city life, and it is an incongruity that Pagans can uphold colonial thinking while at the same time paying lip service to pastoral living. As the original meaning of the term "pagan" is "dweller in the countryside," it is puzzling that those who profess to be earth-connected would not want to live that way, or fight as environmental activists for geo-justice and the protection of Mother Earth to a far greater extent than they are currently doing.

Even though there have been attempts at rules, "etiquette," ethics and dogma in many cases, there is no central focus in contemporary Paganism, and this lack of structure can impact Pagan theory, practice and community cohesion in negative ways. The white liberal "me me me" world of self-actualization stresses the fabrication of a personal path to meet one's personal needs, and the eclectic collection of Pagan practices is infinite indeed. Yet, instead of a quick-fix fantasy driven by synthetic egoism, honestly addressing the lack of ethnic or spiritual roots may lead to the study of a fuller tradition, EIK or heritage, requiring a deeper commitment to discipline and the lifetime it will take to master. Neo-Pagans are already halfway there, and with the re-indigenization that is becoming necessary as time goes on, hopefully the Pagan community will move forward to more cohesive expressions of self, "tribe" and community. One of the founders of the *Reclaiming Collective*, prominent Wiccan M. Macha NightMare speaks to the reality of this disconnect. *"We Pagans often speak of ourselves as belonging to a tribe, and in the broadest sense I feel that way, too. But Pagan groupings are not like the clans of the Celts or the tribes along the Rhine; not like the villagers in Tuscany or Malta. We lack a common familial ethnicity, mores, lore, culture, food, songs. We contemporary Pagans do, of course, share lore, music, customs and a language, but not nearly to the degree that indigenous tribes did and do. We are seeking connection in a rapidly modernizing, culturally diverse, and frequently socially-fragmented world. In essence, we sought a tribal identity and we found it – only the state in which our tribes find themselves is inchoate, rudimentary, immature, not fully formed. We lack the cohesion of a tribe."*[547] As Ethnic Reconstructionism shows us, going deeper into our own ancestral wisdom can resolve the ambivalence of identity confusion by reconnecting us to our authentic selves. Whether we are informed by history or choose the creativity of modern trends in our reclamation of localized earth-rooted community, we must realize that we are subject to the boundaries of natural law, and become grounded in the *Circle of All Life* by shifting from an egocentric to an ecocentric perspective.

---

546. Amber Simmons, *Cultural Appropriation and Responsible Eclecticism*, PaganSpace.net, March 2, 2010. (www.paganspace.net)
547. M. Macha NightMare, "A Witch at Large," *Witches & Pagans: Earthwise Spirituality for Today*, Issue 25, BBI Media Inc., 2012.

Wicca

"The tradition we call Wicca arose from people who were indigenous to their own lands. In England, even until recent times, certain families passed on the tradition of 'earth-walking,' of knowing their own area intimately, understanding the mythological and practical significance of every hill and stream and valley, knowing the uses of the herbs and the medicinal properties of the trees and shrubs, and being responsible for the land's spiritual and ecological health."[548] (Starhawk)

Reviving Wicca and Witchcraft from the remnants of suppressed pagan traditions in the modern era has been a welcome resistance to the long history of religious fanaticism, cultural hegemony and scientific empiricism directed at European people, particularly women and those grounded in earth-based cosmologies. From the ashes of the holocaust known as the "Burning Times," beautiful folk traditions, EIK and healing practices that honour both women and the Earth have been traced by practitioners and scholars,[549] and reconstructed into different traditions with contemporary elements, themes and praxes. Indigenous European folk traditions have been so dispersed, oppressed, margin-alized and lost to time, that the mysterious origins of the modern Wicca revival remain obscure, and the subject of much debate among Pagan scholars. We cannot say for sure that Wicca stems from an unbroken line of pagan traditions, but it is definitely a living, evolving religion based on pre-Christian rites and rituals found in the British Isles and elsewhere in Europe. With ancient roots in Old English and Germanic language, the term "waeccan" may be the root for "wicca" or "witch," and the terms *Wiccan* and *Wicca* as synonymous with *Witch* and *Witchcraft* began to achieve widespread acceptance in the 1960s. As with Paganism in general, there are no centralized tenets in Wicca, and the various traditions have their own organizations and structures. Hereditary witches, or the "cunning folk" are still found as connected to place and ancestry in Cornwall, Yorkshire, or Italy, and modern lineages are established by strict degrees of initiation within traditions such as Gardnerian (Saxon) and Alexandrian (*British Traditional Wicca, or BTW*). BTW seems to have the most influence on modern Wicca, but other movements such as Dianic and Goddess-centered

(Feminist Wicca), Italian (Stregheria), Ceremonial, Minoan, Kemetic, Judeo-Paganism ("jewitchery"), Hedgewitchery and Eclectic are all thriving, as well as the ecofeminist *Reclaiming Witchcraft* tradition based on the craft of Anderson Faery/Feri.

In terms of the prevailing Wicca theology, two deities are honored through a pantheist framework, the *Horned God* who is associated with nature, wilderness and hunting (alternatively known as Cernunnos, Pan or the Green Man), and the *Moon Goddess*, or archetypal triple goddess of *Maiden, Mother and Crone* associated with enchantment, fertility and wisdom. Various mother goddesses and horned gods were worshipped in the British Isles prior to Christianity and during the early medieval period, and this duotheism can be viewed as facets of the *Divine Feminine* and *Divine Masculine*. However, the complementary opposites of the gender polarity model are not embraced by Dianic Wiccans, who regard Goddess as sole deity, both immanent and transcendent - Gaia the Earth Mother and Tribal Goddess of the witch community. Atheist or agnostic Wiccans may view the deities alternatively as principles of life and nature, metaphors, or psychological archetypes of the human mind, instead of Gods or Goddesses with literal personalities, real agency and embodied power. As well as duotheism, many Wiccans adhere to the "all gods are one god" monism of "soft polytheism," and revere a wide range of deities and spiritual forces, while those in the "hard polytheism" camp consider their specific deities to be distinct and real divine beings.

The witches' path may be solitary, such as that of a "kitchen witch," or be part of a circle, coven, community or organization. Across the wide range of beliefs and practices in Wicca commonalities can be found, such as the animistic belief that the entire cosmos is sacred, sentient and alive; the belief in the five classic elements or "sacred things" of earth, water, air, fire and spirit; the belief in the Wiccan rede or golden rule *"an it harm none, do as you will"* as an expression of ethics; the aspiration to the eight virtues of mirth, reverence, honour, humility, strength, beauty, power and compassion from Doreen Valiente's *Charge of the Goddess*; and the alignment with the natural cycles of sun and moon, the *Wheel of the Year*, equinox and solstice celebrations (Yule, Ostara, Litha and Mabon), and the Sabbat festivals of Samhain, Imbolc, Beltane and Lughnasadh. Many Wicca practitioners believe in

548. Starhawk, *The Earth Path: Grounding Your Spirit in the Rhythms of Nature*, HarperOne, 2013.
549. Referencing the writings of Charles Godfrey Leland, Robert Graves and Margaret Murray, the modern Wiccan revival since 1945 is due to the amazing efforts of Gerald Gardner, Dion Fortune, Alexander and Maxine Sanders (Alexandrian Wicca), Raymond Buckland, the "Mother of Wicca" Doreen Valiente, Sybil Leek, Janet and Stewart Farrar, Laurie Cabot, Aiden A. Kelly, Margot Adler, Gavin and Yvonne Frost, Scott Cunningham, Z Budapest, Starhawk and Raven Grimassi (among others) who tirelessly researched long-forgotten aspects, created new approaches, and continue with deconstructing the negative stereotypes of Wicca and Witchcraft as held by the dominant society.

magic (or "magick") as a supernal force intrinsic to natural law that can be aligned with, or manipulated to bring about change, healing and protection, and solitary workings and collective rituals involve casting or conscrating the magic circle, calling the quarters and/or their guardians, invoking the elements and raising energy to a "cone of power." Ceremonies of self-initiation are encouraged in Wicca to actualize a dedicated practice, and other rites of passage are popular such as "wiccaning" for infants, the exchange of marriage vows with hand-fasting, and nature-based condolence practices that celebrate the crossing over of the soul into the Summerland.

The practices of Wicca, or the "Craft of the Wise," range from those influenced by EIK and folk magic, to more elaborate and complex rites, and magical tools include the athame, wand, pentacle, chalice, besom (broomstick), cauldron, candles and incense. Many Wiccans create beautiful temporary and permanent altars for delinating space within the sacred circle, honoring deity, expressing seasonal celebrations, and for individual purposes such as healing and spellcraft. Similar to the grimoires of ceremonial magicians, most Wiccans keep a *Book of Shadows,* or BOS, a personal and unique hand-crafted book of observances, spellwork, important texts, recipes, ceremonies, rituals, rites of passage, myths, stories, images, magic, poetry, chants and songs. Continuing to hone their psychic abilities, Wiccans work with inner guides or guardians, prophecy, divination, oracles, focused intent, spellcraft, charms, candle magic, dreamwork, herbcraft and healing. As opposed to a strict theology, Wicca is highly-individualized and aligned with expressive rituals and practices that emphasize beautiful and memorable experiences of the Divine in a magical blend of fantasy, beauty, dreams, myth, dance, music, pageantry and visionary art. Looking at the many creative variations within contemporary Wicca, there is also a component that attracts lifestyle "dabblers" and "fluff bunnies" more concerned with style, the "hipness factor," rebellion, alternative identities, social events, pop culture and entertainment than with the substance or responsibility of regular practice. Also, the syncretic "eclectic Wicca" path (often referred to as "Shopping Cart Wicca") has been critiqued for mixing and matching deities, rituals, and elements from other times and places. As with Neo-Paganism and *New Age Capitalism,* adopting and reinventing beliefs from various earth religions or ancient cultures such as Egypt, Rome, Greece, Asia, Polynesia or Turtle Island can be seen through the lens of white privilege, as knowledge domination and cultural appropriation.

"Nearly all kinds of Neo-Paganism respect Nature's laws and cycles. We see ourselves as part of Nature, part of the interwoven, interdependent Web of Life, and we commit ourselves to care for this common trust and treasure. In my personal spiritual practice, I seek to remain attuned to Nature's forces, the ebbing and flowing of the

tides, the waning and waxing of the Moon and Sun, the migrations of birds, and the seasons of birth and death."[550] (M. Macha NightMare)

At its heart Wicca is a gentle religion that embraces nature and our kinship bonds to the nonhuman world, the trees, plants, animals, earth spirits and wild green places. Knowing the land as sacred and being deeply connected to place is fundamental to the European Indigenous Paradigm, and experiencing the wonders of nature firsthand is intrinsic to Wiccan practice. Also important is a direct interaction with the devic realm, the energies of Gaia and the larger cosmos. There is a long tradition of environmental activism in the Wicca community, and participation in the movements for ecological justice reflect a deep love and commitment to the land. *"Wicca promotes a way of life that does not conflict with nature, and witches feel it is their personal obligation to protect the earth."*[551] (Bruce K. Wilborn) Valuing the reciprocity between humanity and the green world, Wiccans also have a deep appreciation for the Ancestors and the spirit world, and are open to connections from the past and advice from the *Beloved Dead*. For those who hear the Ancestors speaking, or remember their pre-Christian practices and rituals from a deep well of EIK, Wicca may be the path to recovering the roots of *Earth Wisdom*, and knowing nature as the wellspring of all creation.

---

550. M. Macha NightMare, "A Witch at Large," *Witches & Pagans: Earthwise Spirituality for Today*, Issue 25, BBI Media Inc., 2012.
551. Bruce K. Wilborn, *Witches' Craft: A Multidenominational Wicca Bible*, Skyhorse Publishing, 2011.

Goddess Spirituality

"The women's movement has evolved because the crisis of the eternal world is calling for the rise of the Goddess to restore the balance of nature. All the evidence indicates that the feminine archtype is returning. This is perhaps the most important event of the last 5000 years, and its consequences may well have an immense, unimaginable effect on our cultural and ecological evolution."[552] (Jean Houston)

With roots in contemporary feminism and closely linked to Pagan, Neo-Pagan and Wiccan practice, *Goddess Spirituality* has evolved in synthesis with the rise of women's empowerment, and is one of the fastest-growing spiritual traditions today. Goddess worshippers exhibit a highly individualized set of beliefs and practices, yet all agree on the primacy of the *Divine Feminine* energy that manifests in different forms as individual Goddesses all over the world. With a concise foundational myth, a distinct set of tenets reclaimed from ancient European indigenous identity, and core principles of nature reverence and ecological sustainability, *Goddess Spirituality* is the most exciting matriarchal spiritual movement in western history! And, in terms of challenging the structures of monotheistic religions, the most liberating concept to come along in the 2000 years of patriarchal domination so hostile to women, has got to be the concept of a *Female Deity*.

A surprising and wonderful thing happened over 40 years ago in the early days of the feminist revolution. Drawing on obscure texts, *The First Sex* (Elizabeth Gould Davis, 1971) and *When God Was a Woman* (Merlin Stone, 1976) described ancient matriarchal societies that revered the balance of nature and the power of the *Divine Feminine* in their Goddesses, priestesses and cultural leaders. These peaceful egalitarian societies were eventually overthrown by violent male-dominated warrior-clans that developed into the monotheistic patriarchies we have today, who control the social order by military rule, organized religion and profit-driven economies. *The Civilization of the Goddess* (Marija Gimbutas, 1991) outlined the archeological record of *Old Europe* and the history of matriarchal societies, and is considered to be a milestone of feminist scholarly research. This sacred history, or foundational myth, underpins the political and religious tenets of *Goddess Spirituality* today.

As an alternative to the patriarchal worldview of Empire that has excluded, alienated and persecuted women for centuries, these new versions of history are incredibly empowering, and women everywhere continue to rediscover and develop the language that speaks to their own experience. New versions of womancentric mythologies and history have been unearthed, and more are coming to light all the time. As many talented scholars have discovered, such as Starhawk and Hilary Valentine with *The Twelve Wild Swans: A Journey to the Realm of Magic, Healing, and Action*, the values of European indigenous identity (including those of ancient matriarchies) have been kept alive through the centuries in the oral tradition, storytelling, parables, fairy tales and folklore. Building on years of scholarship, there is a plethora of academic conferences and books being published every year, and Matriarchal Studies (or Goddess Studies) is now considered an official discipline within academia. An interest in the *Divine Feminine* has also been steadily growing among historians, archaeologists, anthropologists, thealogians, Jungian psychoanalysts, community leaders, environmentalists, holistic practitioners, artists, writers, visionaries, social activists, eco-feminists and cultural creatives everywhere.

 *The symbolism of the Goddess is not parallel to the symbolism of God the Father. The Goddess does not rule the world. She IS the world. Manifest in each of us, She can be known internally by every individual, in all of her magnificent diversity.*[553]
(Starhawk)

Goddess Spirituality continues to grow as more and more women are drawn to an alternative view of the Divine. Believing in both the one Goddess and her diverse manifestations worldwide, practitioners define Her as the "One and the Many." She is both immanent and transcendent at the same time, and monotheism is avoided by the animist awareness that the different Goddesses evoke similar cosmic principles of universal love, fertility and abundance, and the upholding of balance and truth. By identifying with the Goddess(es) specific to one's own life experience, the *Divine Feminine* becomes an individualized path of exploration, inner knowing, self-care and regeneration. Oracular work, sacred music and dance, dreamwork, *Earth Love*, recovering IK, rituals, ceremonies and creative expression can all be aspects of *Goddess Spirituality*. Whatever form it takes, *Goddess Worship* is extremely empowering for women. By healing our body/mind/spirit and reclaiming our personal sovereignty, we are the first generation in millennia to recover from the patriarchal damage perpetuated on ourselves, our mother's generation and our ancestral motherlines.

Viewing ancient matriarchal carvings, symbols and Paleolithic goddesses in texts such as Lucy Lippard's *Overlay: Contemporary Art and the Art of Prehistory* or Marija Gimbutas' *The Living Goddesses* for the first time, can open the door to a new version of history, a woman-empowered archaeomythology, a feminine view of Deity - and a model for feminine power. The Goddess has been there all along, waiting to embrace us again, and in turn we can embrace Her with our body, mind and soul! Those on the *Goddess Path* see themselves as part of the interconnected web of life, revere the *Divine Feminine* principle, and speak of the Earth as the body of the Goddess Herself. Spending time in nature, it becomes abundantly clear that the divine presence emanating from, and animating the natural world and indeed, the entire universe, is **feminine** - abundant, fertile, yin, cyclic, ever-renewing, forgiving, and above all, loving and nurturing. All things are born and nurtured by a mother, and this love and nurture is the great cosmic principle of all life. It is so obvious, yet our civilization, based on 2000-plus years of patriarchal rule, has tried very hard to conceal this great and beautiful feminine truth. It is time to realign ourselves, men and women, with the Great Mother, to bring the principles of the *Divine Feminine* back into our lives, to recover what has been lost, and to bring a much-needed balance to the world. For practitioners today, *Goddess Spirituality* merges spirituality and politics, and makes for a strong involvement in environmental and social justice issues as part of a holistic way of life. "*The study of ancient matriarchal cultures that honoured the primal power of the feminine reminds us of the eternal rhythms of nature and all life. Honouring the Goddess is a wisdom path of reverence for the earth, sacredness and interconnectedness. As a species we do not stand apart from nature. Listen to the echoes of the Ancestors. The tradition we keep alive is wholeness.*"[554] (Donna Read)

Core Beliefs and Values of Goddess Spirituality

The Goddess movement is not universal, however, there are common beliefs and values:

- *The basic tenet of Goddess Spirituality is a reverence, love and respect for all life. This is also the basic tenet of all Indigenous Knowledge (IK).*
- *To hold a reverence for the Goddess and the awareness that the Divine Feminine is the ultimate creative power in the Universe.*
- *To hold that the Earth is the Sacred Mother of All, the source of all life and joy.*
- *To honour Our Blessed Gaia and support the interconnected web of life that sustains us all.*
- *To know that the Goddess manifests in diverse forms worldwide, and to focus on the matriarchal values of respect and nurture in self, culture and the natural world.*
- *To realize that the animals, plants, elements and humanity are all kindred spirits, and our common destinies are linked together.*
- *To reclaim all that has been defiled, to resacralize our bodies and all beings as part of Earth Community, and to reenchant our cultures and our lives.*
- *To emphasize a personal relationship with the Sacred through prayer, intuition or creative ritual, without intermediaries or dogma.*
- *To support the integration of heart and mind characteristic of a true human being, placing equal value on both the intuitive-magical and intellectual abilities.*
- *To uphold freedom of belief and respect for each individual's experience of the Sacred.*
- *To work for the empowerment of women worldwide, and to contribute to the work of freeing all beings and the Earth Mother from the dominance of a patriarchal system.*

Goddess Spirituality offers us the components of an EIK system that we can align with, to recover the wise beliefs and practices that our ancestors were forced to give up so long ago. The EIK tenets of Goddess Spirituality hold all life as sacred, connect us to the Earth, give us a holistic view of *Earth Community*, and affirm the divine principle of "as above so below," which is the feminine macrocosm and microcosm within ourselves. Embracing and embodying the Goddess and working with *Divine Feminine* energies allows women to reclaim their feminine power and realize the sacredness of their own bodies, minds, voices and spirits. The resurgence of the Goddess in our time can give us the wisdom, strength, courage and joy that is deeply needed to revitalize ourselves, our communities and the world.

Supporting the empowerment of all women as the resurgence of the *Divine Feminine* in today's society, is a true revolution for all humanity. Women everywhere are rediscovering their love for Mother Earth and the feminine aspect, the Creatrix, that is the cosmic principle generating all life. The fading of the patriarchy that is happening, and the rebalancing of the feminine and masculine are two aspects of the same reality, reconnecting **all** people with the nurture and care that defines a re-indigenized relationship to *Earth Community*. The renewed interest in strong historical feminine deities, philosophers, intellectuals and role models in recent times has been amazing, and the rise of women in leadership roles worldwide is an integral part of the paradigm shift to egalitarian societies. The challenge for women coming into their power is to bring the feminine values of nurture and care to governance, instead of internalizing the patriarchy or assuming the agenda of Empire. If matriarchal cultures were reinstated with their tribal philosophies of interconnectedness and sacred knowing, all people would benefit in wondrous ways. The evolution of our species may depend on the shift toward the feminine values of balance, reciprocity, grassroots democracy, negotiation, non-violence, peace-making, equity, unconditional love, intuition and nature connection.

On a cautionary note, with roots in early feminism, eco-feminism, Neo-Pagan and Wicca practice, Goddess Spirituality has also flourished within the canon of *New Age Capitalism*, and the many texts and tools in this corner of the self-help marketplace reflect a pervasive commodification and appropriation of Indigenous Knowledge (IK) to create consumer products. The modern Goddess Spirituality movement encourages women to work with any Goddess deity, Goddess metaphor or Goddess "energy" from any cultural tradition they choose, and rituals, petitions and pathworking can remove the deity from the originating culture or epistemology in newly-created narratives. By taking the particular Goddess out of context, and revising or fabricating the traditions and IK of the "other" for the monetary gain of selling books and conducting workshops, Goddessians are dominating the knowledge of specific cultures and practising cultural appropriation. As members of the privileged white society, the same ethical considerations apply to all spiritual seekers, who may simply be unaware that they are furthering the racist and destructive practices of colonialism. It may be best to resonate with the Goddesses of your own ethnicity, or if you must reference the Goddesses of Turtle Island First Nations or other Indigenous communities, be sure to cite genuine mythologies from authentic Indigenous scholars and storytellers themselves, and be discerning that these narratives are not Neo-Pagan or New Age versions that have been absorbed, whitewashed, "painted-up" or reflected back (which can happen). For *Goddess Studies* scholars and activists who are aligned with the principles of uncolonization, engaged with deconstructing whiteness, and in the process of reclaiming their own ethnoautobiography, the work they present to the feminist or *Goddess Spirituality* public could easily be prefaced with *"you really need to focus on honoring the Goddesses of your own ancestral tradition(s)."*

552. Jean Houston, *Women of Wisdom: Empowering the Dreams and Spirit of Women*, edited by Kris Steinnes, Wise Woman Publishing, 2008.
553. Starhawk, *The Spiral Dance: A Rebirth of the Ancient Religion of the Great Goddess*, HarperCollins, 1999.
554. *Women & Spirituality: Goddess Remembered*, Dir. Donna Read, Studio D, National Film Board of Canada, Direct Cinema Limited, 1989.

Other Earth-Centered Movements

Primitivism

In fierce resistance to Empire and its values of linear, reductionistic and hegemonic thinking, modern anarcho-primitivists advocate rewilding and the return to a "feral," paleolithic hunter-gatherer or eco-village existence that predates the rise of civilization. Contrary to prevailing narratives, primitivists are convinced that hierarchy, monoculture, technology, progress, industrialization, materialism, population growth and institutional life have had deleterious affects on both humanity and the Earth. Domesticated by civilization and surrounded by the restrictive controls and authoritarian rules of the techno-capitalist nation-state, it is clear that human beings have relinquished their basic freedoms, and are deeply alienated from each other and the land. The resource extraction model that fuels Empire continues to destroy wild nature, and the worldview of patriarchal dominance furthers the engineered agenda of civilization, with its toxic ethics of speciesism, ecocide, racism, slavery, forced labour, the subjugation of women and the genocide of Indigenous people.

Primitivists are engaged with understanding the many layers of domestication in our social patterns, and work with eco-healing, deep ecology, ecopsychology, and rewilding focused on self-sufficiency, sustainability, wilderness survival skills and a deep connectivity to the plants, animals and elements of our local bioregions. By embracing both wild nature and our own "wild mind," the goal of primitivists is to re-inhabit our bodies, senses and human animality, and to recover the associated benefits of positive health and holism. Excellent scholarship[555] in the genres of *Primitivism* and *Anarcho-Primitivism* present powerful ideas relevant to *Rejecting Empire* and the paradigm shift to Earth Community, and anarcho-primitivists are active in the contemporary decivilization, anti-globalization, anti-capitalism and animal liberation movements.

From its early roots in cultural anthropology, archaeology, and the "anarchist naturism" philosophy of the late 19th century, the term "primitivism" can be perceived to be representative of Eurocentric superiority, as "primitive" has been used as demeaning code for "less-than" and "savage." There are many in the primitivism movement who find the associations with this racist colonial attitude problematic, and self-identify as "green anarchists" or "primal anarchists" instead, whereas other primitivists continue using it as a way to reclaim the etymology, and consciously challenge the imperialist origins of the term. Considering that there are green anarchists who are not anarcho-primitivists, a good substitute for "primitivism" might be "anarcho-naturism" - the original idiom used to define anti-civilization ideology and practice. However it is framed, the primitivist impulse to resist and reject civilization by returning to the gift economy & forest gardening of true egaligarian tribal communities, expresses an ultimate connectivity and peaceful co-existence with all of our relatives in *Earth Community*.

555. Ecologism, anti-civilization ideology and anarcho-primitivism scholarship can be traced in the Americas to Henry David Thoreau, followed by the writings of John Zerzan and Kevin Tucker, with Bob Black, John Bodley, Bob Brubaker, Stanley Diamond, Brian Fagan, John Filiss, Chellis Glendinning, John Gowdy, Richard Heinberg, William H. Kotke, Lewis Mumford, Fredy Perlman, Karl Polanyi, Marshall Sahlins, Paul Shepard, David Watson and George Woodcock.

Neotribalism/Tribal Revival

There is no stopping the paradigm shift to re-indigenization, and each generation continues to find new ways to define and practice the renewal and celebration of tribal life. Human beings are designed to live in earth-connected communities, not monolithic bureaucracies, and in the nomadic hunter-gatherer, village life, or "gathering of the clans" aspects, contemporary neotribalism draws close to fulfilling these archaic and essential needs. Developing organically without a centralized movement or theme, so far neotribalism has been defined by a thriving festival scene, and related statements in the genres of urban fantasy, fashion, alternative subculture(s), sacred art, New Age expressions, rewilding and creative nativization. Coming together in self-selected family groups, urban tribes or temporary gatherings, neotribalists are determined to experience personal transformation, promote the spiritual revolution, and be part of the shift to a world that practices connectivity, sustainability, the gift economy and environmental justice. Hugely popular festivals like *Burning Man*, *Faerieworlds, Shambhala, Evolvefest, Lucidity, Moontribe, Firefly Gathering, Lightning in a Bottle* and *Wanderlust* have a carnival atmosphere, and offer electronic dance music, a wild and colourful kaleidoscope of magical identities, eclectic cultural crossings, incredible sculptural creations, collaborations in visual art, and built environments such as modernistic shapeshifters, neoteric temples, futuristic geometry, and other elaborate crucibles for transformation.

Drawing from a wide spectrum of cultural influences such as the radical philosophies of the early counterculture movement, anti-consumerism, green anarchism, alternative lifestyles, deep ecology, expansive spirituality and IK/EIK, the new *Tribal Revival,* or transformational culture, draws seekers from the diverse worlds of streampunk, faerie, Neo-Paganism, performance art, urban circus, the rise of the *Divine Feminine*, and the world beat, techno and hip hop music scenes. Neotribal artists, pagans, free spirits, eco-warriors and modern-day hippies gather together on the festival circuit to party, dance, form community, hold ritual, create art, offer healing modalities, explore new ways of learning, and experience sacred play. Leaving the ordinary linear world of conformity and categorization behind, festival-goers enter the liminal space of another realm. Ecstatic celebrations and rituals can last for days, with the communal ethos resembling many elements of ancient tribal life. Alternating between the sacred and the profane, neotribal festivals and gatherings can be zones of liberation, adventure, exultation, collective magic, positive energy, culture shock, astonishment, and genuine happiness and love. Coming together to hold sacred space, delve into new art forms, share innovative technologies, explore imaginative fantasy, embody tribal identity, experience wellness, and participate in the gift economy, the new *Tribal Revival* continues to celebrate our capacity for wild mysticism and our interconnectivity with nature and the *Earth Mysteries*.

However, in the mad rush to find community and embrace tribal identity, neotribal folk seem to be oblivious to the issues and oppressions faced by genuine Indigenous peoples, which is the face of white perspectivism and cultural arrogance. Neotribal interaction with Turtle Island First Nations has incurred disrespect on native lands, cultural appropriation, and exclusionist practices under the guise of so-called "diversity." Perpetuating inequality and social hierarchy is a continuation of colonialism, and neotribal participation in the "Indigenous Industry" is also an issue, with the tokenism of Turtle Island wisdom keepers and the datamining of IK happening without moral considerations. Also troubling is the new trend to expand the festival circuit and create temporary alternative tribal universes in exotic locations. Setting up a "festy" on a tropical beach has a negative impact on the local ecosystem, perpetuates the privilege of the affluent class, promotes the toxic carbon footprint of luxury travel, and disregards the movement toward local re-inhabitation. Fortunately, awareness is growing in the neotribal sphere to exhibit the proper respect for cultural boundaries, and to interact with Indigenous people in a positive way by applying the correct methodologies of allyship, solidarity and alliance-building. The first priority is to eschew the white entitlement of pan-Indian or "tribal fusion" fantasies such as stereotypical costumes, and to avoid the theft of culturally-significant spiritual and IK tools. Owning white privilege, taking responsibility, acknowledging local First Nations, considering the impact on the land, building relationships, and becoming grounded in one's own ancestral traditions are all ways to work toward mutual decolonization, build genuine community and form true "unity in diversity." By emulating ancient tribal organization and village life, the changemakers, cultural creatives, festivals and urban collectives of the *Tribal Revival Movement* have a role to play in creating sustainability and environmental justice, and neotribal gatherings hold great value for the resurgence of localized bonds of community and the restoration of EIK. Shifting from humancentric concerns to the ecocentric perspectives of placing *Earth First*, the reliance on kindred spirits and care for *Earth Community* are neotribal patterns and maps for what is possible. Returning to ancestral roots and recovering traditional tribal ethics can transport us to the deep archaic pulse of ancient lifeways that have been patiently waiting. By transforming identity and culture, and modelling this re-indigenization to the wider society, transformational culture and neotribalism have the potential to make permanent change in the world.

Ancient Spirit Rising – Common Directions

Grounded in ancient European cultures and polytheistic religions, the *Old Ways* are flourishing once again in the worlds of Paganism, Neo-Paganism, Wicca, Goddess Spirituality, Primitivism and Neotribalism, and these movements share many perennial elements of our original European IK and identity. With the flourishing of contemporary earth-honouring epistemologies our primal needs are being met, such as marking the wheel of life with rites of passage for birth, adolescence, marriage, croning, funerary rites or ancestor veneration, as well as connectivity to community through feasting, art, performance and music. Whether we are engaged in the full cultural recovery and re-membering of our ancestral earth-connected path or not, it is important to honour the cycles in our lives by reclaiming ritual, social engagement and communal life. Joining or creating like-minded community gives us an important sense of routine and structure, collective values, shared laughter, creative resiliency, a fundamental sense of security and the fulfillment of belonging. The possibilities for group activity are as boundless as the imagination, and celebrating holy days creates living links to ancient patterns and constellations. Following the great *Cycle of the Year* with ceremonies and circles based on the rhythms of sun and moon, the movements of the stars and the annual solstices, equinoxes and cross-quarters, can evoke our mystic sense of wonder and sacred awe. Members of the Neo-Paganism, Wicca, Goddess Spirituality, Primitivism and Neotribal communities all have a part to play in re-enchanting the world, by reconnecting us to the metaphysical realms, facilitating healing and well-being, and bringing respect for natural law and the care of *Earth Community* back to front and center. How blessed we are to celebrate our lives, grounded in place and immersed in a sacred universe, knowing that the Earth is alive, all beings are vibrating with love and positive energy, magic is at hand and joy is our natural expression!

"Let us seek ways to center a celebratory life in this world, that is without the need to somehow ground it upon beliefs about another realm. This world is awesome enough. Let us "ground" ourselves in the actual ground. We may begin to imagine a spiritual life centered **here***, on this Earth, in this Cosmos - and therefore, one might hope, far easier to embrace and to share."*
(Anthony Weston, *Mobilizing the Green Imagination: An Exuberant Manifesto,* New Society Publishers, 2012)

27. Entwining Heart and Mind

Gatekeepers
When I speak to the wilderness
with my heart more than my mind,
the world responds in kind.
The Ancient Ones whisper my name
from the forested ridge,
their breath in rhythm with mine.
Love fills my life,
as I immerse myself
within the patterns of Nature
and flow, unfettered,
sublime.[556]
(Myra Dutton)

As diverse spiritual traditions and Turtle Island First Nations remind us, true knowledge is gained by thinking with both the head and the heart - a journey of emotion as informed by the mind. The heart-knowing, intuitive and magical faculties of our right brain are just as important as the intellectual, critical thinking and analytical masteries of our left brain. To utilize the powerful gifts of both heart and mind, we are constantly processing our feelings and thoughts back and forth in a necessary weaving. Both dynamics are required - the theory we obtain from deep reflection, research and analysis, as well as the agency to act on this information in sync with our creativity and intuition. The figure-8 or infinity symbol, a mathematical and philosophical construct developed in the ancient worlds of India and Greece, is a great illustration of this process. If the infinity symbol is placed vertically and assigned to the human form, the bottom half represents the energy of the earth (the physical), the top half represents the energy of the cosmos (the spiritual), and both meet in the middle, which is the human heart. Balancing both aspects of mind and heart can mean recognizing that many of our thoughts are illusionary tricksters, and conversely, that indulging in emotional entanglement may not allow for the critical thinking process that can actually propel one forward. Empowerment and true knowledge come about when the radiant intelligences of our hearts, minds, bodies and spirits are entwined and work together, and *"the essence of being human is taking the divine and the earthly aspects of ourselves and integrating them through love."*[557] (Marci Shimoff)

Reclaiming and co-creating ecological civilization today means rejecting and moving away from the over-emphasis on linear thinking which is the toxic legacy of Empire. The meme-carriers of western empiricism opined that *"the birthright of our intelligence is calculation, not sensitivity,"*[558] and this patriarchal ideology has perpetuated the rule of all that is mechanistic, disembodied, material and subject to control. Empire has taught us to ignore the holistic connections, to sort things into the appropriate categories, and to divide and conquer our own reality. The logic of domination views the land, elements and creatures in *Earth Community* as objects to be owned instead of kindred spirits, and the classification system of binary dualism has enabled conquest and ecocide all over the world. The misguided anthropocentric worldview of "man as ruler and pinnacle of creation" places human beings and their acquisitions at the center of the world, and renounces all care or responsibility to nature, natural processes or the other beings in *Earth Community*. In our time, challenging the insatiable entitlement and narcissism that this worldview has generated means including our hearts in the conversation, with a renewed focus on all that is intuitive and empathic. Becoming compassionate, loving and grounded, both in our physical bodies and the Earth, is a large part of our mutual re-indigenization process, and the emergence of holistic thinking in our time is a necessary rebalancing that is required after centuries of fractured, separatist patriarchal thinking.

"The Yup'ik elders in southwest Alaska call western society the reverse society, because we reverse the laws for living. The heart used to tell the mind what to do, and now the mind tells the heart what to do. These and many other kinds of reversals have put the life support systems of the planet on the brink."[559] (Larry Merculieff)

"You've got to look at things with the eye in your heart, not the eye in your head."[560] (Lame Deer)

Concurrent with the millions of hearts welcoming the paradigm shift to the values of love, unity and care, there also continues to be an appalling lack of critical thinking in spiritual practice today (as noted in *Chapter 11,* "New Age Thinking" on Page 81), which is endemic of a capitalist society having the wealth, privilege and entitlement to apply the principles of "fast food" consumerism to both our spiritual and intellectual lives. In these chaotic times, a multitude of strange ideologies and belief systems are being promoted, and the values of kindness, gentleness and love must be tempered by discernment, healthy scepticism and critique. In an alarming tendency toward intellectual laziness and/or anti-intellectual bias, Empire has created an entire demographic that has no desire to read texts or expand their worldview, and prefer to obtain their information second-hand or from urban legends and the media. In the interest of promoting the timeless values of intellectual discourse and good scholarship, my "Entwining Heart and Mind" chart outlines the heart knowledge and critical thinking processes, both beneficial and indispensable, both complementary to the other, and both equally important. We have an intellect for a reason, so why not use it? That is true mastery.

Ultimately, to gain true knowledge and wisdom-in-action is to weave our scholarship with our own insights, experiences and unique promptings of the heart. Without referring to both spheres simultaneously, and embracing the balance of our knowledge and experience equally, errors and misconceptions can occur. We understand with our mind (theory), but what we come to value and how we respond to important ethical matters (practice) comes from the heart. We can achieve spiritual wisdom from a confluence of sources, but connecting the intelligence of the heart to the intelligence of the mind is how we grow fully into our own lives. As we learn from animism, rewilding, voluntary simplicity and our own ancestral practice, leaving the buzz of civilization behind and immersing ourselves in nature easily and effortlessly puts us into the intuitive knowing of indigenous mind. Opening to the natural world with interaction and appreciation, and stilling our inner dialogue enables the mysterious unfolding of our hearts. Simply from being in nature we can see the world through the lens of love, and come to know that the "Great Heart" is the connective force in all creation. Filtered through the harmonious and beautiful space of love, our thoughts become allied with *Earth Community*. Clarity replaces confusion, and our thinking becomes a joyful series of inspirations in service to furthering the goals of Gaia, which are to flourish and thrive. Trusting in the balance, the wondrous gifts of the human heart and the human mind revolve as required, for nurturing and sustaining a good life for ourselves and all beings. Instead of identifying with the separatist and mechanistic worldview of industrial civilization in body, mind or soul, we find that we are at home again in the *Sacred Circle* of the heart. And in fact, we have never left.

556. Trish Tuley and Myra Dutton, *Healing Ground: A Visionary Union of Earth and Spirit*, Celestial Arts, 2003.
557. Marci Shimoff, *Love for No Reason: 7 Steps to Creating a Life of Unconditional Love*, Free Press/Simon & Schuster, 2010.
558. Philip Shepherd, *New Self New World: Recovering Our Senses in the 21st Century*, North Atlantic Books, 2010.
559. Larry Merculieff, "Native Knowing," *TEDx Talks, TEDxHomer: Heart Matters*, November 9, 2011. (www.youtube.com)
560. Lame Deer, *Lakota Woman* by Mary Crow Dog and Richard Edroes, Harper Perennial, 1991.

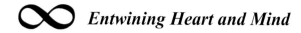 *Entwining Heart and Mind*

Intellectual/Critical Thinking

Access to knowledge is preserved through lineages of written texts, visual literacy such as scrolls, artworks, petroglyphs and earthworks, and recorded or living oral narratives that enliven specific cultural traditions.

Access to western knowledge has been preserved in libraries protected through eras of war and oppression, collections of texts built over millennia and drawn from global sources.

The intellectual process is grounded in the knowledge that has gone before, from the oral tradition, story cycles, reading and research.

Exposure to new perspectives, different ideas and opinions is important, as new knowledge leads to new understandings and positive change.

Learning is necessary to combat ignorance.

Scholarship can provoke, awaken reasoning and rational processes, and encourage critical thinking.

The critical thinker must continue to research facts, test validity, and question scholarly claims for truth and accuracy.

False arguments can be identified, as authors can be in error, fabricate information, or indulge in delusional thinking promoted as truth.

Scholarship can function as a springboard to greater discoveries of truth, wisdom, empowerment and freedom.

Scholarship is an opening, a key, a portal that can evoke great resonances and epiphanies within.

Scholarly research can find the history and backstory that sets the imagination free.

Learning from fictional stories and poetry can expand our empathy and humanity.

An over-emphasis on intellectual prowess can lead to egoic missteps that dominate, over-judge, gain advantage, initiate conflict with others, and control culture and the environment.

The western intellectual paradigm has limitations, as Eurocentric thinking is more binary than holistic, and tends to invalidate local experience and IK.

Heart Knowledge/ Imagination

More than just an emotion, pure unconditional love is the highest vibration shared by all beings in *Earth Community.*

An open heart is the portal to the ocean of love that is the essence of the universe, and gives rise to our aliveness, inner peace and joy.

The ability to reason and analyze is enhanced by the ability to find connection and harmony in the world.

Heart knowledge sees the world through the eyes of kindness and love, beyond brainpower to the higher intelligence of spiritual wisdom.

Over-thinking and critique is balanced with intuition and by accessing one's inner compass.

Non-linear experiences cannot be explained or understood by the intellect, only felt by the heart.

The heart has its own memory, magnetic power, intelligence and neural net.

Heart knowledge is our deep connection to all life, a belief in magic, and a desire to re-enchant the world.

Finding the place of stillness one listens to the heart, which is the source of all wisdom and enlightenment.

Heart knowledge understands inner guidance as the voice of the soul that continues to send us valuable information.

Heart knowledge accepts the flow of emotions as natural.

Heart knowledge follows the creative impulse and produces works of the imagination that bring great passion and joy.

Heart knowledge models courage, gentleness and heart-focused spirituality to the world.

The greatest mysteries are much more than book knowledge!

Too much scholarship may mean relying on the knowledge of others instead of your own experience – be true to yourself.

It does not matter how educated you are.......it matters how your heart uses it.

Heart knowledge is derived from nature and natural law, which is expressed in a wide diversity of cultural and spiritual practices.

28. *Ancient Spirit, Modern Voice*

"If you don't go back to your own IK,
your mind won't be able to read your soul."[561]
Onaubinisay (Walks Above the Ground) / James Dumont, Anishnaabe Elder
and Traditional Teacher, 5th Degree - Three Fires Midewiwin Lodge

It may be hard work to recover, practice and declare our authentic
IK/EIK, but we owe it to ourselves and our kinship groups to join the
worldwide circle of *Earth Community*, and the integrity of our
commitment will earn the full respect of other traditional, Indigenous
and re-indigenized cultures. By returning to *Ancient Spirit* in our own
unique way, we come to understand the monumental efforts of all
oppressed and marginalized groups who are engaged in decolonization
and the recovery from Empire. Whatever our positionality or starting
point (with or without privilege), and without using our whiteness to
center, dominate, mediate or overwhelm, we have the opportunity to
move through great change and turmoil to a time of "unity in diversity"
as we align ourselves and our communities with a holistic paradigm
once again. Embracing earth-wise traditional knowledge will *"help us
learn to lovingly and patiently attune our hands to the heartbeat of the
land, teaching us anew the Ancient Ways. Beckoning us onward is the
reenchantment of Earth."*[562] (Kenny Ausubel) It may be difficult for us
to reclaim earth-rooted identity after centuries of being told that
western civilization is the only way to live, or that we cannot exist
without the cultural treasures, benefits and amenities of the Eurocentric
world. And it may be a daunting task to "read our own souls" as
ecocentric beings dwelling in an animistic universe once again, but the
outcome is clear that by *Rejecting Empire* in principle, thought and
deed, we naturally align with the sacredness of the Earth, and reaffirm
a deep love and respect for nature at the heart of our worldview(s).

*"Some would call it a reawakening to the spiritual wisdom of our
ancient past. Others might liken it to the sense of awe at the wonder
and beauty of life that follows a near-death experience. However we
choose to characterize it, the Great Turning is opening the way for an
evolutionary leap to a new level of human, social, intellectual and
spiritual possibility. A unique and epic opportunity is presently at
hand."*[563] (David Korten)

Knowing the Earth to be the source of spiritual wisdom allows
indigenous mind to unfold, and to perceive that there are a million
ways that the living magic and primal matrix of *The Sacred* is trying to
come back into the world. Tribal sounds fading in and out, the shapes
of things, the ancient shadows, the hidden meanings......the eternal
archtypes that weave natural law into human life continue to arise,
even within the frivolities of consumer culture - fashion, décor, popular
tastes in literature - and show up in profound expressions of mythic

storytelling, reconstructed music and open-air earth art installations that translate the ancient patterns and organic forms. The mystic symbols of the archaic force arise again and again whether they are recognized or not. Beyond the toxicity of the rectangular-steel flatline, concrete-girded industrial world modern man has created for himself, the truth of the tribal human soul and the touch of the tribal human hand continue to manifest, and the guiding forces are already in place for the collective recovery of our *Ancient Spirit* and return to eco-sanity. We have eternal access to a deep well of ancestral knowing, the divine pattern lives on in the DNA, and Gaia's matrix and the *Web of Life* sustain all beings with an everlasting restoration of healing and new growth. And even though urbanized humanity seems to be able to live with the illusion of separation from the natural world, and it may appear that we have given up on the Earth, the harmonic intelligence and *Great Heart* in nature is waiting, and the Earth has not given up on us.

"The ordered wisdom of nature inside the global forest still stands tall. It is the majesty that beckons us to keep still and behold a beating heart in a feathered breast. The forest forecasts our future in every breath it takes and every seed it releases into the leaf mold of the forest floor. This wisdom is the universal voice of life, seeping in silence in search of our souls."[564]
(Diana Beresford-Kroeger)

The essence of Natura, the Green Goddess, or "veriditas"[565] is the irreducible principle that all things rise again in perennial growth, and that the green soul of the entire *Earth Community* is blessed with renewal and rebirth. Remaining in place as a timeless, thriving and ever-rejuvenating mystery, the power of life itself is eloquently described by Dylan Thomas as *"the force that through the green fuse drives the flower, drives my green age."*[566] The unfailing themes of abundant life and green growth on Earth continue to manifest, even as we move into an unpredictable future. As the era of Empire ends after centuries of misdirection, our journey comes full circle in a surprising paradox, with our primal return, or re-indigenization, becoming the "future primitive" wave of the future. The beauty and timelessness of ancestral wisdom is an unstoppable force, as rewilding and recovering indigenous mind become the goal for all people. And even though we have ancient models to follow, with the shift to ecocultural identity we are entering new ground, and it is simplistic to suggest that we can renounce ourselves completely as modern people. In our uncolonization process we also need to avoid the stereotypical or Eurocentric theories of "indigene" and "primitive" taken from anthropological thought and western knowledge systems. It may be more helpful to identify the foremost components of modern mind, and then set out to reclaim the opposite in whatever shape and form that takes, keeping in mind that our rational, critical thinking and analytical skills continue to be powerful gifts we can apply as informed and enlightened human beings.

The following visual aid is not comprehensive as a universal human study, but sets out certain aspects of western mind that we may want to revise or discard, and elements of indigenous mind that we may want to encourage or embrace. Looking at how children instinctually feel the magic in nature, have a natural affinity for the sacredness of the earth, and spontaneously create, play and live in the moment gives us great hope for the future, and further inspiration for our eco-journey.

―――――――――――――

Modern Thinking/ Western Mind

Human separate from nature.
Bounded by the ego, set apart from others.
Self-absorbed.
Material and having a sense of linear time.
Linear thinking "gets the job done" but linearity interferes with the natural ability to experience life and emotions in a holistic way.
Over-rational, over-analytical, over-verbal.
Subject-object relations, seeks utility.
Dualistic "either/or" and fragmented thinking.
The emphasis on reductionism, over-thinking and verbal aquity can limit freedom and authentic reflection or exploration.
Learning is forced through curriculum, supervision, instruction and discipline.
Sense of self is socially-conditioned.
Restless mind, living in the past and future.
Focused on facts, figures and explanations.
Eager to control and acquire.
With an egocentric bias, western society produces minds that are dysfunctional, immoral and immature.
The belief that intelligence only comes from logic and linear thinking.

Ancestral Thinking/ Indigenous Mind

Human as part of nature.
Connected, empathic, resonating with others.
Physically grounded and embodied.
In the now, time is perceived spirally.
Cyclical thinking based on spirit connectivity, natural processes, creativity and peace, rather than singularity, ownership or dominance.
Nonverbal, cogent, integrated, transcendent.
Ancestral mind evoked when in nature.
Non-dualistic holistic thinking.
Words are limiting, behaviors speak louder than words, one is connected to creation through the heart, the intuition and intelligence of the senses.
Learning is purely experiential, one is empowered to acquire knowledge at own pace in own way.
Identity is based on experience and self-reflection.
Restless mind suspended, spiral and cyclical thought.
Vibrant and present in the field of mindfulness and awareness.
Sense of the mystery, wonder, awe.
With an ecocentric foundation, indigenous societies integrate self-discovery, soul, wisdom and responsibility.
All intelligences are combined, and our holistic potential as a "true human being" is fulfilled.

Recovering ancestral thinking and entwining heart and mind continues to be key as "*all humans are indigenous to planet Earth and every one of us has the ability to awaken indigenous mind, which is the innate ability to become aware of the Earth at an intimate and dynamic level and respond to messages and stimuli from all beings and life in the moment. Accessing indigenous mind means a commitment to slowing down, remembering and re-conceiving on a smaller scale, to reclaim intimacy with nature and its layers of species as an aspect of our own essential nature.*"[567] (Kaylynn Sullivan TwoTrees)

In the re-indigenization process, as we unhinge our being from the constraints of time to take the "long view," or consider the "eternities," we have to question why we were born at this particular time and in this particular place. In our overwhelming love for the Earth and all natural things, we cannot imagine a mindset that would seek to destroy even the smallest element nurtured by the interwoven perfection of nature. Our hearts ache with the poignant implication of any potential harm to the land, and we face a cascade of unanswered questions. What did destiny or the *Great Mystery* have in mind for us, and why did our spirit chose to be part of this momentous era, when humanity is at a crossroads? When the sheer weight of human infrastructure and technology is crushing the natural ecosystems that give life to all beings? When human beings have lost their care for the natural world and the creatures of Mother Earth? When human beings have lost their gratitude for nature's gifts on which we are dependent for our very lives? Why are we here? Is it to further the goals of urbanized humanity, which does not seem to have any regard for the planet? Or is it to be a warrior on behalf of the Earth, to honour the Earth in all we think, say and do? Is it to mourn, to serve, to witness, to be part of the solution instead of the problem? Is it to stop supporting the hegemony of an unsustainable economy by our silence, to stop lusting after money and superiority, to stop idolizing machines and their makers, to stop indulging in consumerism, to stop worshipping our wardrobes and toys, to stop escaping into the disposable commodities of entertainment, to stop consuming junk that erodes our life force, to stop our complicity in a civilization that enticingly offers us great benefits while at the same time destroying the only things that matter? Why are you here?

Perhaps the answers lie in the embodiment of our own root culture, and the principle that all Indigenous cultures share, which is to be deeply bonded to the more-than-human world. As we acknowledge all beings as our relatives, our brothers, sisters and kindred spirits in the dance, we become devoted to the balance and harmony of the entire *Earth Community*. The gentleness, love, respect and care we feel means that we are incapable of using or abusing nature past the carrying capacity of the land, and in the end, these are the mindful qualities that will translate into sustainable societies and well-being for all.

"Each of us is put here in this time and this place to personally decide the future of humankind. Did you think the Creator would create unnecessary people in a time of such terrible danger? Know that you yourself are essential to this World."[568]   (Chief Arvol Looking Horse)

"Don't sit this one out. Do something. You are by accident of fate alive at an absolutely critical moment in the history of our planet."
(Carl Sagan)

We are the ancestors of the future, and this is how ancestors live. Learn the *Old Ways* of your people and find or adopt a piece of land to love with all your heart. Re-embrace your true home and become empowered to hold space for uncolonizing community to arise. Carve out a natural lifestyle, listen to what the earth is telling you, and your ecodigenity will naturally follow. This is after all, how human beings have acquired IK since the beginning of time. Love the land, respect all beings and creatures on the land, live in harmonious and sustainable ways on the land, celebrate and honour the land, and praise the land. Create the ceremonies, rituals, artistic expressions, crafts, songs, feasts, sacred sites, altars and dances that convey your interaction with the spirits of the land you love. Practice the sacred activities that dovetail with the cycles and the *Great Wheel of the Year* on the land. Plant when it is time, harvest when it is time, rest when it is time, and respect the living things - the plants and animals that have given their lives for your existence. Practice reciprocity and honour all beings, write and tell the stories when it is time, and prepare the soil when it is time. Root your heart to the earth where it can stay strong, stay your face to the moon, your skin to the sun, your hands to the soil, your eyes to the beauty of nature, your heart to the creatures, your gratitude to the *Green Fuse*, your wonder to the interconnectivity of it all, your mind in service to the Mother, and your soul anchored in the deep dreaming of the land that will hold you in loving embrace throughout your long revolutions of birthing, living, dying and being born to live again.

"The elders remind us of the importance of the long view when they say 'pin peyeh obe' – look to the mountain. They use this phrase to remind us that we need to look at things as if we are looking out from the top of a mountain, seeing things in the much broader perspective of the generations that are yet to come."[569] (Gregory Cajete)

"Connectedness with Ancestors and future generations lifts us out of the microplots of 'business as usual' and places us in a truer and more expansive story. In life's epic journey, every one of our Ancestors lived long enough to pass on the spark of life. This ancestry extends back in time far beyond the reaches of our human past. With the shift in identity to our ecological self, we discover that the entire span of recorded history is just a fraction of a page in a more extensive volume."[570] (Joanna Macy)

561. James Dumont, "Biimaadiziwin," *Elders and Traditional Peoples Gathering*, Trent University, Peterborough, Ontario, February 12-14, 2010.
562. Kenny Ausubel, *Dreaming the Future: Reimagining Civilization in the Age of Nature*, Chelsea Green Publishing, 2012.
563. David C. Korten, *The Great Turning: From Empire to Earth Community*, Berrett-Koehler Publishers/Kumarian Press, 2006.
564. Diana Beresford-Kroeger, *The Global Forest*, Viking Penguin, 2010.
565. "Veriditas" is the spiritual term coined by German Abbess, composer, herbalist and mystic Hildegard von Bingen (1098 –1179), to describe her vision of the green power of nature and the unity of all creation.
566. Dylan Thomas, "The force that through the green fuse drives the flower," *The Collected Poems of Dylan Thomas*, J.M. Dent & Sons, 1957.
567. Kaylynn Sullivan TwoTrees, "Indigenous Mind," *Hope Beneath Our Feet: Restoring Our Place in the Natural World* North Atlantic Press, 2010.
568. Chief Arvol Looking Horse (Lakota), Keeper of the Sacred White Buffalo Calf Pipe, *Native American Encyclopedia on Facebook*, May 24, 2012.
569. Gregory Cajete, PhD (Tewa), *Words of Power: Voices from Indian America*, edited by Norbert S. Hill Jr., Fulcrum Publishing, 1999.
570. Joanna Macy and Chris Johnstone, *Active Hope: How to Face the Mess We're In Without Going Crazy*, New World Library, 2012.

29. Peaceful Co-existence

"Reconciliation is ultimately a paradigm shift from staunch individualism to one that fosters interdependence between humans and all of creation. There are four dimensions to reconciliation embedded in many traditions and cultures – reconciliation with the spiritual realm, reconciliation with one's self, reconciliation with others, and reconciliation with nature. These dimensions are not linear processes but a series of highly interrelated relationships that flow one into another."[571] (Hizkias Assefa)

"We need a radical re-alignment! I am suggesting reconciliation as a theory of change to help nurture the genesis of a new era that is more in alignment with our current understanding of the universe, and how best to organize human affairs accordingly."[572] (Jessie Sutherland)

Reclaiming our eco-identity, authentic cultural and indigenist practices - either independently, within a small group, or in community - and doing the work of *Rejecting Empire* (uncolonization) allows us to fulfill the promise of respecting all religions and IK/EIK traditions, while lifting up the sacredness and interconnectivity of all life. As the People of the Earth (formerly known as the Kogi) assure us, *"our unity in ancestral norms and our collective return to the Original Instructions will bring about change."*[573] Having shared values in our mutual love for the land, coming together with the original Earthkeepers of Turtle Island for common causes and issues of environmental protection will do much to heal the First Nation/Settler divide. Yet peaceful cohabitation on Turtle Island will not occur automatically, until our process of "unsettling the settler" has acknowledged the original treaties that set out terms for peaceful co-existence on much of the land now occupied by the Settler State. As agreements set up between sovereign nations, treaties guide the rights, actions and obligations of both First Nations and Settlers, and the phrase "we are all treaty people" is not just a metaphor. On lands that are governed by treaties, our white identity needs to be reframed by our responsibility to our own community, First Nations and to the land itself. We also need to acknowledge that the basic premise of the treaties was flawed, as the Settler understanding of the treaty process was based on money and land acquisition, whereas the understanding of First Nations was based on a shared responsibility to the land, and the other-than-human world.

"Any parallel, peaceful coexistence is plainly impossible if one party is irrevocably altering and poisoning that shared land." [574] (Naomi Klein)

The Kawarthas where I live in Southern Ontario are subject to the Williams Treaties (1923), *"the worst First Nations treaties ever implemented in Canadian history,"*[575] with the original signing currently under legal challenge from the seven First Nations involved. With a massive outlay of finances, time and resources, the Chippewas of Beausoleil First Nation, Georgina Island First Nation, Rama First Nation, the Mississaugas of Alderville First Nation, Curve Lake First Nation, Hiawatha First Nation, and Scugog Island First Nation are pursuing parallel processes in both negotiation and litigation. Facing delays and challenges from the pervasive colonial apparatus, they continue to seek recovery of their basic rights to fish, hunt, and trap for food in their traditional territories, gather wild plants and herbs, and have access to the land for social and ceremonial purposes - all activities that are keystones to their history, culture and identity. The inherent right of a cultural group to determine their own destiny and govern their own people in their own traditional homeland does not have a dollar value, but this basic fact seems to escape the "grand organizers"[576] of Empire. Intrinsic rights to land-embedded culture were negotiated in the original treaties to empower all people to live

---

571. Hizkias Assefa, *Peace and Reconciliation as A Paradigm: A Philosophy of Peace and Its Implications on Conflict, Governance and Economic Growth*, ACIS Press, 2007.

572. Jessie Sutherland, *Worldview Skills: Transforming Conflict from the Inside Out*, Worldview Strategies, 2005.

573. José Dingula Moscote & Luntana Dingula Nacogi, People of the Earth, La Sierra Nevada de Santa Marta, Colombia (formerly the Kogi), "Sacred Water Circle Gathering," *Gchi-Nbi Sacred Water Circle*, Peter Gzowski College, Trent University, May 2-4, 2014. (www.sacredwatercircle.ca)

574. Naomi Klein, *This Changes Everything: Capitalism vs. The Climate*, Knopf Canada, 2014.

575. Maurice Switzer, "Williams Treaty: Crown Concedes some Hunting Rights," *Anishinabek News*, Volume 24, Issue 10, December, 2012. (http://anishinabeknews.ca/wp-content/uploads/2013/04/2012-12.pdf)

576. *"The Colonizers saw themselves as 'grand organizers.' "* *Tortured People: The Politics of Colonization* by Howard Adams, PhD, (Métis), Theytus Books, 1999.

peacefully on the land, and the directives for mutual First Nations/Settler co-existence are still in place today. What better model to follow than the treaties, as the paradigm shifts to localized peak-oil communities and we challenge the imperialist worldview, both for First Nations and ourselves? As the engine of Empire continues to be fueled by the oil, water, trees, and minerals extracted from beleaguered ecosystems, it may come to pass that the *"only protection may be located in the small First Nation communities spread across the country, that still have the interests of the land in mind, and the legal power to govern those lands."*[577] (Tara Williamson) Placing our trust in First Nations community instead of Empire, and giving them our support to restore the treaties in our shared territories would seem the logical thing to do.

Against all odds, First Nations continue to remind us of our shared responsibility as treaty people, and continue to welcome us into a future that would manifest the original visions of mutuality and respectful relationship that their Ancestors held. With honesty and respect, we can share the ethics of this journey right now, as we move back and forth between the processes of allyship, activism, reconciliation and finally, retribution. It is also our responsibility to educate the overculture on these issues, for *"as long as Canadians see a wilderness extending beyond their cities and towns, they do not belong to the land and will continue to view aboriginal peoples ambivalently, with envy and sometimes disgust. Before Canadians can feel comfortable with themselves and their territory, and cast away their obsessions with identity and goodness, Canada needs a rite of passage, a cathartic experience, through which non-aboriginal Canadians earn aboriginal peoples' respect. I am not referring to 'truth and reconciliation' – reconciliation is more than a confession or apology, it must include some form of restitution. Beneficiaries of injustice must be willing to share their wealth and privileges with the victims; they must believe that by sharing, they too gain something - trust and a shared country."*[578] (Russel Lawrence Barsh) As for the reconciliation process, this has been happening in Canada with the participation of Settler individuals, small-scale groups and church communities nation-wide. By taking the high moral ground **first** in the oppressor/oppressed relationship, First Nations motivated the Canadian government to establish the *Truth & Reconciliation Commission* (TRC),[579] to focus on

---

577. Tara Williamson, "We are All Treaty People," *Decolonization: Indigeneity, Education & Society*, December 24, 2012. (http://decolonization.wordpress.com)

578. Russel Lawrence Barsh, "Aboriginal Peoples and Canada's Conscience," *Hidden in Plain Sight: Contributions of Aboriginal Peoples to Canadian Identity and Culture*, edited by David R. Newhouse, Cora J. Voyageur and Dan Beavon, University of Toronto Press, 2005.

579. The *Truth and Reconciliation Commission of Canada* website features events, projects, resources and ways to get involved. *"The truth of our common experiences will help set our spirits free and pave the way to reconciliation."* (www.trc.ca)

the seven generations of First Nations children who were incarcerated by the Indian Residential School (IRS) system from 1831-1998.

The creation of the TRC in 2008 set a historic precedent, with the mandate to promote awareness and education to all Canadians regarding the IRS system and its impacts; to provide space for survivors and thrivers to tell their stories; for their testimony to be heard and acknowledged by participants from the dominant society; to collect applicable records and formulate as complete a historical record as possible; and to submit a full report with recommendations for action to the Canadian government. Breaking up First Nations families and forcing the children into residential schools was a genocidal agenda devised by the Euro-Colonizers to destroy Indigenous culture, and assimilate the "primitives" into the "superior society." As part of the TRC process, the shocking and horrific stories told by survivors will ensure that these heart-breaking narratives are held within the collective memory forever. Framed within the larger context of First Nations resilience, the truth-telling has culminated in a healing experience for some survivors. Those from the dominant society who are willing to participate in TRC sessions need to hear the residential school stories without denial or a "paternalization" mindset, and then to recognize their shared history with First Nations. Overall, the journey of the progressive Settler in the TRC process has been to acknowledge the essential humanity of the "other," form compassionate bonds, take ownership of their responsibility to "repair the breach,"[580] become empowered to make a difference, and contribute to the overall renewal of justice and hopeful reconciliation between colonizer and colonized.

"I'm grateful for the acknowledgment and solidarity that many churches and organizations are extending today - sometimes the reconciliation road feels so overwhelmingly daunting, but I hold faith that all of us who call Turtle Island our home will walk together in peace, friendship and mutual respect one day."[581]
(Georgie Horton Baptiste)

An ongoing process for many years, by the time the TRC mandate comes to completion in June 2015 it is doubtful that full reconciliation will be accomplished, as many in the Settler mainstream continue to perpetuate racism, and to ignore and resist our common heritage with First Nations. Also, the Canadian government has continued to be hostile to Indigenous people during the entire TRC process. They failed to cooperate with the TRC by refusing to release important documents as originally agreed, and continued to enact colonial and genocidal legislation against First Nations both at the community and national

---

580. "Conclusion," *From Truth to Reconciliation: Transforming the Legacy of Residential Schools* by Marlene Brant Castellano, Linda Archibald and Mike DeGagné (editors), Aboriginal Healing Foundation, 2008.
581. G. Horton Baptiste (Saulteaux Anishinaabe), Facebook comment, 2014.

level. The epic fail of the Canadian government and the whitestream disavows the path of true reconciliation, which is a much more extensive process than simply having the oppressed explain their side of the story. The oppressor must also claim full responsibility with the truthful acknowledgement of history, and offer a genuine and meaningful apology instead of a vacuous expression of regret or a tokenistic gesture. Until Indigenous human rights, land claims and treaties are addressed and honored, it is not true reconciliation and healing cannot begin, let alone the wealth-sharing and restitution that Russel Lawrence Barsh speaks of. In the meantime, what can those of us in the dominant society do, who wish to repair the First Nations/Settler relationship? First we need to acknowledge the truth of history, then educate others, learn about allyship, listen to First Nations, and work as anti-racism activists to support the restoration of treaty agreements, seeking new ways to build non-colonial relationships with Indigenous peoples and their lands. We must shift our own worldview toward peaceful co-existence and motivate others to do the same, as *"in the end, reconciliation is a spiritual process, which requires more than just a legal framework. It has to happen in the hearts and minds of the people."*[582] (Nelson Mandela)

We are the generation that must voluntarily (or under duress) abandon Empire, and reject the old relationships that are based on the oppression and destruction of both human beings and the land. Can we offer restitution, turn the page and move forward to a new paradigm? We need to prove the sceptics wrong, such as Taiaike Alfred who asks the valid question. *"What if the Settlers chose not to change their ways? It is becoming more and more apparent each day, as capitalism and materialism grow into ever more powerful and arrogant forces and continue to roll over landscapes and cultures with impunity, that restoring a regime of peaceful co-existence with Settler Society and believing in the Settler potential for friendship and enlightenment is impossible."*[583] (Taiaike Alfred) What if we don't change our ways? There is much at stake, and each according to our capabilities, our resistance efforts must fly in the face of the dominant hegemony and the divisive colonial arrangements of exploitation and control. Nation-states such as the USA and Canada serve the oligarchy while *"maintaining a neo-liberal system of economic and social apartheid,"*[584] and it is time to replace them with grassroots initiatives, localized governance and community cohesion. If all parties are willing,

582. Nelson Mandela, *Annual Methodist Church Conference*, Mthatha, South Africa, September 18, 1994.
583. Taiaiake Alfred, "Opening Words," *Lighting the Eighth Fire: The Liberation, Resurgence and Protection of Indigenous Nations*, Leanne Simpson (editor), Arbeiter Ring Publishing, 2008.
584. Nora Butler Burke, "Building a "Canadian" Decolonization Movement: Fighting the Occupation at Home," *The Anarchist Library*, August 20, 2004. (http://theanarchistlibrary.org)

Decolonial Bioregionalism gives us the best opportunity to transform our relationships with First Nations in whose territories we are living, to one that is *"mutually negotiated, and premised on a core respect for autonomy and freedom."*[585] (Nora Butler Burke) With the collective vision of a sustainable future as our beacon, true reconciliation is possible with active grassroots leadership, divestment from fossil fuels, advances in environmental protection, and the restructuring of major institutions that will lead to a fundamental shift in society.

There is no holding back the overall shift in public perception, or the move to indigenous values for all people, and there is much to celebrate in the many recent successes and collaborative ventures between Settlers and First Nations. For the first time ever in June 2014, the Supreme Court of Canada granted declaration of aboriginal title to more than 1,700 square kilometres of land in British Columbia to the Tsilhqot'in First Nation, much to the joy of Indigenous people and their allies. Also in June 2014, making history with proper recognition after centuries of denial, Vancouver formally acknowledged that the city is situated on the unceded traditional territory of the Musqueam, Squamish and Tsleil-Waututh First Nations, and that there has never been a colonial treaty. So far, this Vancouver action is mostly a symbolic gesture, but streets and parks in the city are to be renamed after First Nations history and place markers in future, and aboriginal protocol is to be followed when "welcoming people to the territory" or when Indigenous blessings are given in city hall, city council, city events and public spaces. As a much-needed action to deconstruct Euro-imperialism, and following the same decolonizing initiatives as Minneapolis and Berkeley, in July of 2014 the Seattle Human Rights Commission passed a resolution declaring that in the future *Columbus Day* will be recognized as "Indigenous Peoples Day." And in another positive act of solidarity and accord, Don Iveson, the Mayor of Edmonton, proclaimed March 2014 to March 2015 the "Year of Reconciliation," with the mandate to educate 11,000 city staff on the history and impact of the residential school system, involve aboriginal youth in civic programs, and create public spaces in the city for Indigenous ceremony and cultural programming.

Other alliances are flourishing, and in a progressive coming together for common causes, the Haudenosaunee Six Nations and the City of Hamilton founded the *Joint Stewardship Board* in 2002, committed to the environmental restoration and guardianship of the Red Hill Valley for future generations. Combining their diverse knowledge and resources into a collaborative framework, the *Joint Stewardship Board* is guided by a set of agreements touching on Indigenous burial sites; archaeology; hunting, fishing, trapping and wild foods; nurturing and gathering medicine plants; economic opportunity; and protecting the human heritage of their shared territory. As a model for communities everywhere, details, highlights and updates on the *Joint Stewardship Board: Respect, Trust, Friendship* can be viewed at (http://joint stewardshipboard.com). More recently, the *Occupy* movement followed by *Idle No More* acted as a catalyst for renewed Settler solidarity with the social justice mobilization of First Nations, and a groundswell of awareness, discourse and action are continuing in regard to allyship, reconciliation and mutual decolonization. An excellent example of these initiatives is Occupy Victoria's *Statement of Intent and Action for Decolonizing Victoria & Memorandum of Solidarity and Support with Indigenous Peoples*[586] dated November 7, 2011, that acknowledged Indigenous communities in the territory as sovereign nations; that the presence of Settlers on unceded Lekwungen land is illegal; and that the wealth of Empire has been derived from the ongoing theft of Indigenous lands and resources. Realizing that the colonial terminology of "Occupy Victoria" may be alienating to Indigenous peoples, the group renamed themselves *The Peoples' Assembly of Victoria* and included other resolutions such as taking greater responsibility to learn about Indigenous history, the colonial process and the treaties; and to work to undo both contemporary and historic injustice through the development of political and social relationships with Indigenous community.

More than a mere courtesy or obligation, an intercultural dialogue with mutual recognition, openness and sharing is a vital human need, and the potential lies within all of us to enlarge our abilities for reconciliation and our tolerance for diversity. *"Reconciliation is about relationship, and it will be determined by all parties through conversation and engagement. It is about becoming good neighbours and healing the relationship so that there is respect for each other and respect for our history."*[587] (Viola Robinson) We are all treaty people, and it is possible to have a respectful, cooperative vision of *Earth Community*, to peacefully co-exist, and to build ecological resilience for the future through our shared spiritual connection to the land. It has become increasingly clear that both native and non-native people are opposed to the unsustainable exploitation of the Earth, and are open to potential forms of alliances in our mutual desire for localized subsistence and ecologically-balanced living. An exciting and hopeful turn of events are the many decolonizing groups and communities, both native and non-native, who are taking up the threads of wampum diplomacy.

---

585. Nora Butler Burke, "Building a "Canadian" Decolonization Movement: Fighting the Occupation at Home," *The Anarchist Library*, August 20, 2004.

586. People's Assembly of Victoria, *Statement of Intent and Action for Decolonizing Victoria & Memorandum of Solidarity and Support with Indigenous Peoples*, November 7, 2011. (http://occupyvictoria.ca)

587. Viola Robinson (Mi'kmaq), "Conclusion," *From Truth to Reconciliation: Transforming the Legacy of Residential Schools* by Marlene Brant Castellano, Linda Archibald and Mike DeGagné (editors), Aboriginal Healing Foundation, 2008.

Established between the Haudenosaunee (Iroquois) Nations and Dutch Settlers at the time of contact, the *Two-Row Wampum* are excellent agreements for friendship, respect, and peaceful co-existence between sovereign nations unified in their reverence and care for Mother Earth. The wampum belts are created with patterned rows of purple quahog clam shell beads denoting the movement of both a Haudenosaunee canoe and a European ship, set on a background of white whelk shell beads signifying peace and friendship. The symbolism of the belt represents two vessels travelling together down the river of life, parallel but not touching, both with equal roles and responsibilities, neither one superior to the other. The two-row wampum principles are referenced in the original Haudenosaunee reply to a Dutch treaty proposal which has been kept in the historical record. *"Our treaties symbolize two paths or two vessels, travelling down the same river together. One, a birch bark canoe, will be for the Indian People, their laws, their customs and their ways. The other, a ship, will be for the white people and their laws, their customs and their ways. We shall each travel the river together, side by side, but in our own boat. Neither of us will make compulsory laws nor interfere with the internal affairs of the other. Neither of us will try to steer the other's vessel."*[588] (Tehanetorens) Among other initiatives, the *Two Row Wampum Renewal Campaign,*[589] a partnership between the *Onondaga Nation* and *Neighbors of the Onondaga Nation,* was established in 2013 to expand the alliance between the Haudenosaunee and their allies, both locally and around the world. Their educational campaign and advocacy seeks to renew the chain of friendship established by the *Two Row* between the Haudenosaunee and the Dutch, extending the same values to France, Britain and America, with an emphasis on environmental protection and restoration. Haudenosaunee politics, diplomacy and philosophy continue to inform and guide all settlers, as the *Two-Row Wampum* principles of peace, respect and friendship offer a moral compass for living on the land. We are living on Turtle Island, and isn't it time we started acting that way?

As we fully embrace the model of the *Two-Row Wampum*, our mindset naturally extends to all of nature, and the other-than-human-world. As Winona LaDuke reminds us, *"natural law is the highest law, higher than the law made by nations, states, municipalities or the World Bank, and one would do well to live in accordance with natural laws, with those of our Mother, and in respect for all our relations."*[590] Reclaiming peaceful co-existence with the natural world may include a radical shift to "habitecture,"[591] which is the integration of natural biomes into existing and new human infrastructure so that native plants, animals, birds and other creatures are not excluded, marginalized or displaced. Many species have already wonderfully adapted to the human-built world, but many have not, and the design principles for cohabitation, co-existence, rewilding, ecosystem restoration and biophilic architecture are not all that difficult.

"We need to live among wild habitats and creatures even more than they need to live among us, yet the idea of putting out the welcome mat to other species remains a curiously radical concept, so much so that it is artists, not architects or city planners, who are leading the way."[592] (J.B. MacKinnon) With symbiotic earth art in both wilderness and urban spaces, the creations and statements by artists and artisans are powerful reminders of the biodiversity and life cycles of *Earth Community*, but we need to do much better. We need to make ecosystem co-habitation and land restoration the "new normal," for when we rewild our precious green world Gaia, we are also restoring the human heart and soul.

By caring for one other and living interdependently with one other and the land, our harmonious relationship with the natural world rests on a foundation of non-violence. This dynamic is outlined by Satish Kumar as the trinity of soil, soul and society, as *"soil represents the natural world, soul signifies the spiritual world, and society stands for the human world."*[593] Beneath the fabricated overlay of division, violence and conflict as promoted by Empire, our natural resting place is in a field of deep compassion, and achieving understanding through non-violent communication is the best way to return to heart-intelligence and mutual kindness for all. The anger we all feel in varying degrees is an excellent tool for opposition and change, but instead of allowing it to become a way of being, we can also decide on the alternative, which is to direct our anger at the social injustice and manipulations of Empire instead of at the "other." Compassion is inherent to all of us and just needs to be activated, as *"there is nothing we human beings like better than contributing to each other's well-being."*[594] (Marshall Rosenberg) Becoming peacemakers for ourselves, our community, the wider society and Mother Earth herself means living with an open heart, and this love and compassion is essential to the survival of both the human and more-than-human world.

Both the practical and the mystical can be blended into an everyday knowing that all life is sacred, which fills our lives with transcendent well-being and peace. *"When we are filled with reverence and respect for all life, not just human life but animal and plant life, water life, and the life of the earth, then the qualities of compassion and love blossom in us, which in turn makes us more creative, imaginative, and even happy."*[595] (Satish Kumar) Many cultural creatives, visionaries, and

588. Tehanetorens (Ray Fadden), *Wampum Belts of the Iroquois*, Native Voices, 1999.
589. *Two Row Wampum Renewal Campaign.* (http://honorthetworow.org)
590. Winona LaDuke (Anishnaabe), *The Winona LaDuke Reader: A Collection of Essential Writings*, Voyageur Press, 2002.
591./592. J.B. MacKinnon, *The Once and Future World: Nature as it Was, as it Is, as it Could Be*, Random House Canada 2013.
593. Satish Kumar, *Nonviolence and Quality of Life: Soil, Soul and Society - A Workshop with Satish Kumar*, California State Polytechnic University, Pomona, CA, April 30, 2006.

Indigenous leaders share and promote diverse prophecies that claim we are entering a new era of peace. This is a very real contemporary movement based on the collaborative values of forgiveness and peace, and we are being offered the opportunity to learn how to live with one another, respect one another's diversity, and create a new future grounded in reciprocity. *"We don't have to say 'deep down you're just like me' in order to get along with other people or a different culture. We don't have to assume they're seeking the same things in different ways. We just have to respect their inherent dignity and worth and trust they'll do the same for us."*[596] (John Beckett)

As we have seen, one way that diversity can exist in a context of harmony is by recognizing and defining common ground, and forming cultures of resistance together, as in our "co-existence through co-resistance."[597] Our passion for justice, our collective care for each other, and our mutual communion with nature must be at the heart of any successful cultural revival, healing of *Earth Community*, or peaceful and sustainable future.

"True enduring peace – between countries, within a country, within a community, within a family – requires real reconciliation between former enemies based on forgiveness to restore good relations. The wholeness of relationships is what we need in this world that is polarized, and fragmented – only restoration can heal us and make us whole. And only forgiveness enables us to restore trust and compassion to our relationships. If peace is our goal, there can be no future without forgiveness."[598] (Archbishop Desmond Tutu)

The incredible diversity in ecotones, species, human ethnicity and cultural practices on Earth needs to be valued and celebrated as a great gift, not something to deny or homogenize. According to Anishnaabe epistemology, the four colours of human beings – yellow, black, red and white – all have wondrous gifts to share, each contributing their unique skills, each with an important role to play, and each having sacred truths that are integral to the whole. These attributes, principles or "four covenants" of humanity are found in different IK systems and

---

594. Michael Mendizza, "A Conversation with Marshall B. Rosenberg," *Puddle Dancer Press*, Center for Nonviolent Communication, April, 2000. (www.nonviolentcommunication.com)
595. *Nonviolence and Quality of Life: Soil, Soul and Society - A Workshop with Satish Kumar,* California State Polytechnic University, Pomona, CA, April 30, 2006.
596. John Beckett, "Unfortunate Effects of Joseph Campbell," *Under the Ancient Oaks: Musings of a Pagan, Druid and Unitarian Universalist* (blog), March 2, 2014. (www.patheos.com/blogs)
597. Stephanie Irlbacher-Fox, "#IdleNoMore: Settler Responsibility for Relationship," *Decolonization: Indigeneity, Education & Society,* December 27, 2012. (http://decolonization.wordpress.com)
598. Archbishop Desmond Tutu, "Truth and Reconciliation," *Greater Good*, University of California, Berkley, September 1, 2004. (http://greatergood.berkeley.edu)

cosmologies worldwide, such as this teaching from Floyd Looks for Buffalo Hand (Lakota). *"Yellow people from the east have the covenant of looking after the water, which is the blood of our body. The whites are responsible for keeping the air, what we need to breathe. The covenant of the blacks is the fire, the energy force, the heart and electricity that keeps the world turning, and the red people have the covenant of the earth, which is our flesh."*[599] Indigenous peoples have never forgotten that all human beings belong within the circle of creation, and it is our directive to return to this sacred place, renewed and empowered by our own spiritual roots and cultural traditions.

As the timeless wisdom of Elder and Wisdom Keeper James Dumont has guided this book from the beginning, once again we can turn to his good counsel, teachings and inspiration. *"It is a core value stemming from the Anishnaabe creation story that the aboriginal self and the white Other are so inextricably intertwined that they are almost the same, connected by the spirit, and of the same mother, the Earth. Moreover, it is a relationship that needs ongoing attention and care as it changes over time, in perpetuity."*[600] The kind-hearted traditions of Indigenous hospitality and benevolence have always been found on Turtle Island, and the time has come for Settlers to demonstrate the same goodwill, and to be better house-guests this time around. In spite of the ravages of Empire and the shared history between colonizer and colonized, First Nations remind us of our responsibilities as "true human beings," to honour the sacred relationships we have with each other and all life, and to respect our bond with the *Original Earthkeepers* with whom we share Turtle Island. Great leaders are modelling the values of peaceful co-existence to us all, and at this point in history, an incredibly radical act would be to make deep change in our hearts and minds, expanding our lives to find ways to be genuinely empathic and loving to others and our entire *Earth Community.*

The great hope is that the millions of heartfelt inititives, the current paradigm shift to *Occupy Love*,[601] and the "thousand points of light"

---

599. Floyd Looks for Buffalo Hand (Lakota) as cited in "Selling the Sacred: Get Your Master's in Native American Shamanism?" by Christina Rose, *Indian Country Today: Media Network*, November 5, 2014. (http://indiancountrytodaymedianetwork.com)

600. James Dumont quoted by Kevin Fitzmaurice, PhD., "Are White People Obsolete? Indigenous Knowledge and the Colonizing Ally in Canada," *Alliances: Re/Envisioning Indigenous-non-Indigenous Relationships*, edited by Lynne Davis, University of Toronto Press, 2010.

601. Arising from the recent Occupy Movement, *Occupy Love* is a feature documentary by acclaimed director Velcrow Ripper chronicling the revolution of worldwide heart-awakening that is happening all over the world. *Occupy Love* explores the *"growing realization that the dominant system of power is failing to provide us with health, happiness or meaning. The old paradigm that concentrates wealth founded on the greed of the few, is causing economic and ecological collapse. The resulting crisis has become the catalyst for a profound awakening, millions of people are deciding that enough is enough, and the time has come to create a new world, a world that works for all life."* (http://occupylove.org)

will lead to an overturning of the old order, and manifest as post-racial and post-capitalist societies. We can create local communities that say *"please recover your root tribe and your ancestral knowledge, as we need you to uncolonize and recover your original place in the Sacred Circle!"* A tolerance for diversity is the key principle that allows all cultures and subcultures the same rights, each according to their own unique systems of self-governance, organization and economics. We have the ability to re-imagine a future world where multiple cultures can exist side-by-side with both individual and shared values, and the stability of soul-oriented community is promoted for all. By tending our relationships with care and generosity, we can learn from one another and share cultural traditions together, such as earth remediation, offerings to the local spirits, and celebrating our sacred lands and seasonal cycles. The most authentic definition of "earth citizenship" must be our mutualism in earth-centered culture and earth-based democracy, and *"through respect for the cultures and religions of each nation, human diversity is upheld, celebrated, sustained, and included in the future vision of the world."*[602] (Duane Champagne) To realize this remarkable vision will take a groundswell from every demographic and ethnic background, from activists and the general public alike, uncolonizing and reinstating the most nourishing and meaningful aspects of life - the natural world, the spiritual realm, our ancient wisdom traditions, close-knit community, and our sense of belonging.

As we continue to build resilient communities and shape a future in reciprocity with *Earth Community*, it may be helpful to engage once again with the opening directive *"everyone needs to get back to their own IK."* Both on a personal and a collective level, we have explored how the reclamation of our IK/EIK and ancestor veneration is integral to earth restoration, and that ancient knowledge and earth-based cosmologies can reunite humanity in the *Sacred Circle*. Diane Longboat (Kahontakwas Mohawk) confirms the vital importance of this task when she says that *"indigenous wisdom is now called forth in the world to guide all sectors of human development to restore balance in the world, so that human beings can live by Sacred Spiritual Law and the Natural Laws of Mother Earth. The hoop of humanity is a great circle of seats for every human being."*[603] Also in agreement with the principles of this directive are The People of the Earth (formerly known as the Kogi), who are telling us that *"when we reconnect with our origins we will find the ways to help restore the Earth, to rejuvenate and recover, and the Mother takes care of us all."*[604]

602. Duane Champagne, "Can Indigenous Beliefs Save the Contemporary World?" *Indian Country Today: Media Network*, September 14, 2013.
(https://indiancountrytodaymedianetwork.com)
603. Diane Longboat (Kahontakwas (Mohawk), "Indigenous Wisdom and Prophecies Are Helping Humanity Shift to New Paradigms," *Global Indigenous Wisdom Summit*, The Shift Network, November 18-20, 2014.

As well as localization, re-landing and reinhabitation of place, the re-centering of First Nations values and indigenism is a movement that needs to happen in every society worldwide, as it is *"about re-indigenizing the peoples of the planet to the planet."*[605] (John Mohawk) And lastly, the fusion of our ethnoautobiography with the natural places we call home to define our nativization is addressed by Melissa K. Nelson. *"We come from our DNA, our ancestors and our descendants – the strands of spiraling heritage that give us our roots and the threads to the future. Revitalizing indigenity means reclaiming the personal and ecological watersheds we come from, as part of our eco-cultural identity."*[606] Our pursuit of true eco-centric values and EIK cultural expressions can only come from a strong, grounded connection to a specific place and love of the land, in combination with our ancestral spiritual practices and Euro-indigenous roots.

Sifting through the many themes of cultural recovery, we have discovered that our IK/EIK is **NOT** found in:

- Whitewashed "painted up and handed back" pan-Indian IK-tinged commodities or products,
- the identity confusion and cultural appropriation practices of non-native pseudo-shamans,
- the indulgent, privileged, flavour-of-the-moment spirituality of the capitalist New Age or Neo-Pagan supermarket and workshop circuit,
- the "we are all one" neotribal monomyth fantasies or generic memes of universalism,
- any creative or cultural practice that lifts IK without giving back in a concrete way to the original holders of that IK,
- or in the eclectic, free-for-all, high-consumption, high-carbon, high-mobility modernist lifestyle.

In stark contrast to this panoply of synthetic modernism, our authentic IK/EIK **IS** located in:

- Specificity, ethnicity, and our root tradition(s) beyond the monoglot memes of Empire,
- accessing the land as the source of our individual and collective identity, well-being, mythic narratives and spiritual life,
- being grounded in an ecocentric worldview that places the localized stewardship of the earth first,
- and, revolving around caring for our basic needs in reciprocity and harmony with all diverse species and ethnocultures in *Earth Community.*

We have learned that there better ways to show respect to each other than cultural appropriation and exploitation, and that if we genuinely love and value First Nations culture(s), we will relinquish our privilege and find ways to act in solidarity with them as allies. We have learned that our understanding of our own identity is powerfully transformed when we reconnect with our ancestors before they became colonizers and beneficiaries of white privilege. We have learned that cultivating a tolerance for diversity and peaceful co-existence is key, not an imaginary "we are all one" scenario that reinforces homogeneity and white perspectivism. We can clearly see what colonization has stolen from both Settlers and First Nations, that we have all been wounded by Empire, and that we can inspire and support each over in our cultural recovery. *"As westerners retrieve the memory of their earliest ancestors, they begin to grieve their lost connection to the Earth as well as becoming invigorated to lead more meaningful and authentic lives. As both indigenous and Western peoples tap into their own wellspring of losses, they also come together to grieve."*[607] (Herbert O'Driscott) We have discovered that all cultures share a social ecology of earth-based reverence and spiritual luminosity, and that the path to reconciliation and egalitarian co-existence means rejecting the construct of "whiteness" and white supremacy that continues to dominate others and oppress the land. We have learned that the natural world offers us intuitive access to aliveness and mythical modes, and that our relationship to the *Creator* or *Great Mystery* fills our hearts with gratitude, kindness and generosity of spirit.

As the *Ancestors of the Future*, we have learned that our humility and the ability to make the most of our journey in preparation for the next is what gives meaning to our lives. Rejecting the alienation of the dominant hegemony, we see the value in furthering the work of re-enchanting the world, and recognizing the sacred in every activity with words, relationships and creative expressions that express our essential eco-self and our bond to our sacred Mother Earth. We see that fully becoming a part of *Earth Community* will open our hearts to wonder and delight, and that in the place of our deepest knowing, we can embrace the wilderness both within and without to restore magic to our world. We have also come to know that our land-based healing, rewilding and self-indigenization is deeply entwined with the restoration of geo-justice, inherent rights for nature and earth remediation, and the reclamation of the Indigenous commons.

And lastly, we have learned that presenting ourselves to the world, grounded and strong in our own cultural identity, language, oral tradition, music and spiritual expressions, will give us a place in the circle of unconditional love, with all the support, consensus and community-building that our flourishing "Unity in Diversity" will offer.

"We are all made in the image of the Creator, and there is no contest, no competition - we are all unique and we each have so much to offer, and we need to treasure each other."[608]
(Melissa K. Nelson)

604. José Dingula Moscote & Luntana Dingula Nacogi, People of the Earth, La Sierra Nevada de Santa Marta, Colombia (formerly the Kogi), "Sacred Water Circle Gathering," *Gchi-Nbi Sacred Water Circle*, Peter Gzowski College, Trent University, May 2-4, 2014. (www.sacredwatercircle.ca)
605. John Mohawk (Seneca), "Re-Indigenization Defined," *Original Instructions: Indigenous Teachings for a Sustainable Future*, edited by Melissa K. Nelson, Bear & Company, 2008.
606. Melissa K. Nelson, "Revitalizing Indigeneity," *Bioneers Conference 2011*, January 26, 2015. (www.bioneers.org) (www.youtube.com)
607. Herbert O'Driscott as cited in *Worldview Skills: Transforming Conflict from the Inside Out*, by Jessie Sutherland, Worldview Strategies, 2005.

In Closing

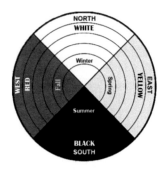

*Let's have a back-and-forth sharing, a meta-circle where we all take turns! Starting in the **East** with an ancient Shinto prayer of welcome and blessing for the new day dawning, we give thanks for the sacred waters from every corner of the globe, bringing in the fresh breezes of spring, the peeping of the frogs, the crickets chirping and the flight of the majestic herons overhead. Led by an ancient Malay poetry cycle of mystic and animist wonders, we channel **South** to receive more messages and mark the mighty thrust of a pod of baleen whales as they break the surface of the ocean next to the lands of the Ngāti Porou, Māori iwi in New Zealand. Then, accompanied by Sanskrit chants we spiral across Mother Africa to the flourish of Oyo-Yorùbá dundun drums in an Orisha-devoted Nigerian dance of cleansing fire, all humanity arising from the same sacred source and reunited again. We circle in equality side-by-side in the highland heat, each one of us a spark of gratitude, radiance, creativity and joy, then holding the wisdom of Bonobo, Crocodile, Elephant, Lion, Meercat, Rhinoceros and Wildebeest gently in our hearts, we move past the blazing of an infinity of council fires. Shifting to a Sufi prayer for spiritual healing and reciprocity we grow relationships of deep listening, and circle **West** to the people of the Americas, grounding ourselves in the rich embrace of earth restoration as the tupelo branches fill with honey bees, the chittering racoons and the howling of the wolves making their presence known. As the beloved creatures pass the staff to the*

*Seminole we are offered traditional songs honoring the plant spirits for their nurturing healing power, followed by a Lakota blessing for Mother Earth and the Horse Nation, an Oji-Cree sacred pipe ceremony for the bonding of all people, and in the leaf-strewn meadow, we join a lively Métis dance and fiddle jig that celebrates the abundant harvest from orchard, field and fen. As we read the glyphs on stone and revere the red insignas of earth ochre, we raise our voices in an honour song for the passing of the Beothuk of Newfoundland, whose ancestral spirits hover on the margins of the circle. Then, crossing the great shell of Turtle Island we give space to the Hawaiian Earth Keepers to lead us in the Hoponopono chant, as we offer sacred blessings to our brothers and sisters, the more-than-human-world, and the entire Earth Community. "I am sorry. Please forgive me. I thank you. I love you."[609] Then, blown to the **North** by a hurricane force gale, we hear the beauty of Greek prayers, the strains of Romani music and Hungarian folk songs rising on the wintery wind, followed by a Basque petition to the Goddess Mari to return to Her mountain cave, and a Gaelic Blessing that calms the breeze and offers kindness, compassion, love and devotion. United again with the sacred flora and fauna found in the folktales of Old Europe, an ancient Slavic Kolo round dance moves us deosil as night falls and we complete the circle, and take our transformative expressions of Unity in Diversity back to our beloved landscapes of home.*

People of the Earth! *Sacred as the Earth is sacred, our interexistence with all beings is our greatest joy, and we form the unbreakable bonds of Earth Community. Rooted deeply in our love for the Earth, we know that our physical, emotional, mental and spiritual well-being is dependent on the health of the land, and our fate is bound to the fate of Gaia. Strong as the Earth is strong, we go forth as warriors for Her protection and care. Let the beacon bonfires blaze out, the sparks leaping from coast to coast and mountain to mountain, as we pass the torch from hand to hand in acceptance of this sacred trust and responsibility.* **May we forever bless the Earth, and may She bless us in return.**

---

608. Melissa K. Nelson, "Revitalizing Indigeneity," *Bioneers Conference 2011*, January 26, 2015. (www.bioneers.org) (www.youtube.com)

609. Ho'oponopono is an ancient Hawaiian practice for reconciliation and forgiveness. With elaborate variations found throughout the island cultures of Polynesia, Ho'oponopono beautifully and powerfully corrects, restores and maintains good relationships between the human, spiritual and natural realms, with processes of prayer, reflection and a "letting go" that can transcend time and place. The IK of Ho'oponopono has been adapted to modern life through practices of restorative justice, and has been communicated worldwide by healing priests (Kahunas) and others. Briefly, "I am sorry" means accepting one's own actions and taking responsibility; "please forgive me" means asking for acceptance and engaging the other in the understanding and energy of forgiveness; "I thank you" means acknowledging what one has gained from the situation; and "I love you" means untangling the conflict entirely and returning to love, the source of all creation.

30. Poetics: Last Words

The Civilian

In the vessel of fifteen centuries,
blown into afternoon, feeling
for the fringe of India.....he
stumbled over half a world
he had not known was there.

Finding the place inhabited
he hurried to inhabit it;
Welcomed with hospitality he
fetched his guns ashore.

Finding generosity he set up a market.
Finding health he brought disease.
Finding freedom he brought slavery.

Offered trust he returned betrayal.

Standing in the forest he saw lumber.
Looking out over Eden he saw real estate.
Fed by the hand of god he bit the hand.
Free to use all he needed he took all there was.

Finding a learned people he built schools.
Finding god let loose and laughing in the forests
he brought his tortured god from home and
chained him in a thousand new-world churches.

Finding America he imported Europe.

Now.......finding that Europe is not in America
that freedom is not in rectangles,
that beauty is not in boxes,
that peace is not in power,
nor learning in schools,
nor god in churches

........his blindness mocks him.

But his children may yet learn to see.

This compelling poem by D.G. (Ted) Poole appears in *For Every North American Indian Who Begins to Disappear I Also Begin to Disappear: Being a Collection of Essays Concerned with the Quality of Human Relations Between the Red and White Peoples of This Continent,* by Wilfred Pelletier, Neewin Publishing, 1971. As a beautiful and productive example of native/non-native alliances, D.G. (Ted) Poole and First Nations academic Wilfred Pelletier (Anishnaabe) were friends and collaborators in life, letters and decolonial activism.

SOURCES CONSULTED

Abram, David. Becoming Animal: An Earthly Cosmology. Vintage Books, 2011

Abram, David. *The Spell of the Sensuous: Perception and Language in a More-Than-Human World.* Vintage Books, 1997

Adams, Howard. *Tortured People: The Politics of Colonization.* Theytus Books, 1999

Agger, Helen. *Nimishoomis: The Trout Lake History of Dedibaayaanimanook Sarah Keesick Olsen.* Theytus Books, 2008

Aikenhead, Glen and Herman Michell. *Bridging Cultures: Indigenous Ways and Scientific Ways of Knowing Nature.* Pearson Canada, 2011

Arosio, Paola and Diego Meozzi. *Stone Pages.* Online reference for news, forum, links, information on the archaeology of megalithic Europe, including Stonehenge, stone circles, dolmens, ancient standing stones, cairns, barrows and hillforts. (http://stonepages.com)

Artress, Lauren. *Walking a Sacred Path: Rediscovering the Labyrinth as a Spiritual Practice.* Penguin Books, 2006

Ausubel, Kenny. *Dreaming the Future: Reimagining Civilization in the Age of Nature.* Chelsea Green Publishing, 2012

Ausubel, Kenny and J.P. Harpignies (editors). *Nature's Operating Instructions: The True Biotechnologies.* Sierra Club Books, 2004

Benton-Banai, Edward. *The Mishomis Book: The Voice of the Ojibway.* University of Minnesota Press, 2010

Beresford-Kroeger, Diana. *The Global Forest.* Viking Penguin, 2010

Castle, Leila (editor). *Earthwalking Sky Dancers: Women's Pilgrimages to Sacred Places.* Frog Ltd. Books, 1996

Chomsky, Noam. *Power Systems: Conversations on Global Democratic Uprisings and the New Challenges to U.S. Empire.* Metropolitan Books, 2013

Clifton, Chas S. *Her Hidden Children: The Rise of Wicca and Paganism in Americ*a. AltaMira Press, 2006

Conlon, James. *Lyrics for Re-Creation: Language for the Music of the Universe.* Continuum Publishing, 1997

Davis, Lynne, PhD (editor). *Alliances: Re/Envisioning Indigenous-non-Indigenous Relationships.* University of Toronto Press, 2010

Davis, Wade. *The Wayfinders: Why Ancient Wisdom Matters in the Modern World.* House of Anansi Press, 2009

Davis, Wade. *Light at the Edge of the World: A Journey through the Realm of Vanishing Cultures.* Douglas & McIntyre, 2001

de Botton, Alain. *Religion for Atheists: A Non-believer's Guide to the Uses of Religion.* Pantheon, 2012

Degler, Teri. *The Divine Feminine Fire: Creativity and Your Yearning to Express Your Self.* Dreamriver Press, 2009

Devereux, Paul. *Spirit Roads: An Exploration of Otherworldly Routes.* Collins & Brown, 2003

Devereux, Paul. *Earth Mysteries.* Piatkus Publishers, 1999

Devereux, Paul. *Places of Power: Measuring the Secret Energy of Ancient Sites.* Blandford, 1999

Devereux, Paul. *Revisioning the Earth: A Guide to Opening the Healing Channels Between Mind and Nature.* Simon & Schuster, 1996

D'Souza, Dinesh. *The End of Racism: Principles for a Multiracial Society.* The Free Press, 1995

Eisler, Riane. *The Chalice and the Blade: Our History, Our Future.* HarperCollins, 1988

Elgin, Duane. *Voluntary Simplicity: Toward a Way of Life that is Outwardly Simple, Inwardly Rich.* Quill, 1981

Esteva, Gustavo and Madhu Suri Prakash. *Grassroots Post-Modernism: Remaking the Soil of Cultures.* Zed Books, 1998

Francis, Daniel. *National Dreams: Myth, Memory, and Canadian History.* Arsenal Pulp Press, 2002

Francis, Daniel. *The Imaginary Indian: The Image of the Indian in Canadian Culture.* Arsenal Pulp Press, 1992

Freeman, Victoria. *Distant Relations: How My Ancestors Colonized North America.* McLelland & Stewart, 2000

Glendinning, Chellis. *My Name is Chellis and I'm in Recovery from Western Civilization.* Shambhala, 1994

Glendinning, Chellis. "Notes Toward a Neo-Luddite Manifesto." *Utne Reader,* March/April, 1990

Goettner-Abendroth, Heide. *Societies of Peace: Matriarchies Past, Present and Future.* Inanna Publications, 2009

Halifax, Joan. *The Fruitful Darkness: Reconnecting with the Body of the Earth.* HarperCollins, 1993

Hillyer, Carolyn. *Sacred House: Where Women Weave Words into the Earth.* Seventh Wave Books, 2010

Hood, Robert. *Labyrinth Creations.* Offering labyrinth design, labyrinth art, custom installation and guided labyrinth experiences, 2015 (www.labyrinthcreations.com)

Hogan, Linda. *Dwellings: A Spiritual History of the Living World.* Touchstone Books, 1995

Hopman, Ellen Evert and Lawrence Bond. *Being a Pagan: Druids, Wiccans, and Witches Today.* Destiny Books, 2012

Huhndorf, Shari M. *Going Native: Indians in the American Cultural Imagination.* Cornell University Press, 2010

Hunter, James. *Scottish Exodus: Travels Among a Worldwide Clan.* Mainstream Publishing, 2007

Hutton, Ronald. *The Triumph of the Moon: A History of Modern Pagan Witchcraft.* Oxford, 1999

Jensen, Derrick, Aric McBay and Lierre Keith. *Deep Green Resistance: Strategy to Save the Planet.* Seven Stories Press, 2011

Jensen, Robert. *We Are All Apocalyptic Now: Moral Responsibilities in Crisis Times.* KDP, 2013

Jensen, Robert. *The Heart of Whiteness: Confronting Race, Racism and White Privilege*. City Lights Publishers, 2005

Johnston, Basil. *The Manitous: The Supernatural World of the Ojibway*. Key Porter Books, 1995

Kalaga, Wojciech and Marzena Kubisz (editors). *Multicultural Dilemmas: Identity, Difference, Otherness*. Peter Lang International Academic Publishers, 2008

Kanehsatake: 270 Years of Resistance. Dir. Alanis Obomsawin. The National Film Board of Canada, 1993

Kaulins, Andis. *Stars, Stones and Scholars: The Decipherment of the Megaliths as an Ancient Survey of the Earth by Astronomy*. Trafford Publishing, 2006

King, Thomas. *The Inconvenient Indian: A Curious Account of Native People in North America*. Doubleday Canada, 2012

Korten, David C. *The Great Turning: From Empire to Earth Community*. Berrett-Koehler Publishers/Kumarian Press, 2006

Kupihea, Moke. *The Seven Dawns of the Aumakua: The Ancestral Spirit Tradition of Hawaii*. Inner Traditions, 2004

The Labyrinth Society. Organization for labyrinth enthusiasts who create, maintain and use labyrinths, serving the global community by providing education, networking and opportunities for labyrinth practice and experience. (www.labyrinthsociety.org)

LaDuke, Winona. *The Winona LaDuke Reader: A Collection of Essential Writings*. Voyageur Press, 2002

LaDuke, Winona. *All Our Relations: Native Struggles for Land and Life*. South End Press, 1999

Lippard, Lucy R. *Overlay: Contemporary Art and the Art of Prehistory*. The New Press, 1983

Loendorf, Lawrence L., Christopher Chippindale and David S. Whitley (editors). *Discovering North American Rock Art*. University of Arizona Press, 2006

Long, David and Olive Patricia Dickason (editors). *Visions of the Heart: Canadian Aboriginal Issues, 2nd Ed*. Thomson-Nelson, 1998

Louv, Richard. *The Nature Principle: Human Restoration and the End of Nature-Deficit Disorder*. Algonquin Books, 2012

Louv, Richard. *Last Child in the Woods: Saving Our Children from Nature-Deficit Disorder*. Algonquin Books of Chapel Hill, 2005

Magliocco, Sabina. *Witching Culture: Folklore and Neo-Paganism in America*. University of Pennsylvania Press, 2004

Marsh, Jason, Rodolfo Mendoza-Denton and Jeremy Adam Smith (editors). *Are We Born Racist? New Insights from Neuroscience and Positive Psychology*. Beacon Press Books, 2010

McIntosh, Alastair. *Soil and Soul: People Versus Corporate Power*. Aurum Press, 2004

McLuhan, T.C. *Cathedrals of the Spirit: The Message of Sacred Places*. Thorsons, 1996

The Megalithic Portal. Online community focused on ancient sites worldwide with databases, photos, prehistoric archaeology, news and resources. (www.megalithic.co.uk)

Merchant, Carolyn. *Earthcare: Women and the Environment*. Routledge, 1995

Meyer, Carter Jones and Diana Royer (editors). *Selling the Indian: Commercializing and Appropriating American Indian Cultures*. University of Arizona Press, 2001

Milloy, John S. *A National Crime: The Canadian Government and the Residential School System, 1879 to 1986*. University of Manitoba Press, 1999

Mohen, Jean Pierre. *Megaliths: Stones of Memory*. Harry N. Abrams, 1999

Molyneaux, Brian Leigh and Piers Vitebsky. *Sacred Earth Sacred Stones: Spiritual Sites and Landscapes, Ancient Alignments, Earth's Energy Lines*. Laurel Glen Publishing, 2001

Monaghan, Patricia. *Magical Gardens: Cultivating Soil and Spirit*. Llewellyn Worldwide, 2012

Moss, Robert. *Dreaming the Soul Back Home*. New World Library, 2012

Moss, Robert. *Dreamways of the Iroquois: Honoring the Secret Wishes of the Soul*. Destiny Books. 2005

Nabhan, Gary Paul and Stephen Trimble. *The Geography of Childhood: Why Children Need Wild Places*. Beacon Press, 1994

Nabokov, Peter. *Where the Lightning Strikes: The Lives of American Indian Sacred Places*. Viking Penguin, 2006

National Geographic Society. *Sacred Places of a Lifetime: 500 of the World's Most Peaceful and Powerful Destinations*. Toucan Books, 2008

Nelson, Melissa K. (editor). *Original Instructions: Indigenous Teachings for a Sustainable Future*. Bear & Company, 2008

Newhouse, David R., Cora J. Voyageur and Dan Beavon (editors). *Hidden in Plain Sight: Contributions of Aboriginal Peoples to Canadian Identity and Culture*. University of Toronto Press, 2005

Ober, Clinton, Stephen T. Sinatra and Martin Zucker. *Earthing: The Most Important Health Discovery Ever?* Basic Health Publications, 2010

Orr, Emma Restall. *The Wakeful World: Animism, the Mind and the Self in Nature*. Moon Books, 2011

Painter, Nell Irvin. *The History of White People*. W.W. Norton & Company, 2010.

Palmer, Martin and Nigel Palmer. *Sacred Britain: A Guide to the Sacred Sites and Pilgrim Routes of England, Scotland and Wales*. Piatkus Publishers, 1997

Paul, Daniel N. *We Were Not the Savages: First Nations History - Collision Between European and Native American Civilizations*. Fernwood Publishing, 2007

Plotkin, Bill. *Soulcraft: Crossing into the Mysteries of Nature and Psyche*. New World Library, 2010

Plotkin, Bill. *Nature and the Human Soul: Cultivating Wholeness and Community in a Fragmented World*. New World Library, 2008

Prinz, Jesse. *Beyond Human Nature: How Culture and Experience Shape Our Lives*. Allen Lane/Penguin Group, 2012

Quinn, Daniel. *Beyond Civilization: Humanity's Next Great Adventure*. Broadway, 2000

Quinn, Daniel. *The Story of B: An Adventure of the Mind and Spirit*. Bantam, 1997

Quinn, Daniel. *Ishmael: An Adventure of the Mind and Spirit*. Bantam, 1995

Rajnovich, Grace. *Reading Rock Art: Interpreting the Indian Rock Paintings of the Canadian Shield*. Dundurn, 2009

Rebick, Judy. *Transforming Power: From the Personal to the Political.* Penguin Canada, 2009

Regan, Paulette. *Unsettling the Settler Within: Indian Residential Schools, Truth Telling and Reconciliation in Canada.* UBC Press, 2010

Richmond, Randy. *The Orillia Spirit: An Illustrated History of Orillia.* Dundurn Press, 1996

Roberts, Elizabeth and Elias Amidon. *Earth Prayers From Around the World: 365 Prayers, Poems, and Invocations for Honoring the Earth.* HarperCollins, 1991

Robinson, Harry and Wendy Wickwire (editor). *Write it On Your Heart: The Epic World of an Okanagan Storyteller.* Talonbooks, 1989

Roy, Rob. *Stone Circles: A Modern Builder's Guide to the Megalithic Revival.* Chelsea Green, 1999

The Sacred Natural Sites Initiative. Collaborations between custodians, traditional knowledge holders, conservationists, academics and others in support of the conservation and revitalisation of sacred natural sites and territories. (http://sacrednaturalsites.org)

Schultz, Emily and Robert Lavenda. *Cultural Anthropology: A Perspective on the Human Condition, 5th Ed.* Mayfield Publishing, 2001

Semali, Ladislaus M. and Joe L. Kincheloe. *What is Indigenous Knowledge? Voices from the Academy.* Routledge, 1999

Shepherd, Philip. *New Self New World: Recovering Our Senses in the 21st Century.* North Atlantic Books, 2010

Sherman, Paula. *Dishonour of the Crown: The Ontario Resource Regime in the Valley of the Kiji Sibi.* Arbeiter Ring Publishing, 2008

Simpson, Leanne. *Dancing on our Turtle's Back: Stories of Nishnaabeg Re-Creation, Resurgence, and a New Emergence.* Arbeiter Ring Publishing, 2011

Simpson, Leanne and Kiera L. Ladner (editors). *This is an Honour Song: Twenty Years Since the Blockades.* Arbeiter Ring Publishing, 2010

Simpson, Leanne (editor). *Lighting the Eighth Fire: The Liberation, Resurgence, and Protection of Indigenous Nations.* Arbeiter Ring Publishing, 2008

Spielmann, Roger. *Anishnaabe World: A Survival Guide for Building Bridges Between Canada and First Nations.* Your Scrivener Press, 2009

Starhawk. *The Empowerment Manual: A Guide for Collaborative Groups.* New Society Publishers, 2011

Starhawk. *The Earth Path: Grounding Your Spirit in the Rhythms of Nature.* HarperCollins, 2004

Starhawk and Hilary Valentine. *The Twelve Wild Swans: A Journey to the Realm of Magic, Healing and Action.* HarperCollins, 2000

Sutherland, Jessie. *Worldview Skills: Transforming Conflict from the Inside Out.* Worldview Strategies, 2005

Suzuki, David. *The Legacy: An Elder's Vision for Our Sustainable Future.* Greystone Books, 2010

Suzuki, David. *The Sacred Balance: Rediscovering Our Place in Nature.* Greystone Books, 2007

Sykes, Bryan. *The Seven Daughters of Eve: The Science that Reveals Our Genetic Ancestry.* W. W. Norton & Company, 2010

Tedlock, Barbara (editor). *Dreaming: Anthropological and Psychological Interpretations*. SAR Press, 1992

Tilley, Christopher. *Body and Image: Explorations in Landscape Phenomenology*. Left Coast Press, 2008

Tuley, Trish, and Myra Dutton. *Healing Ground: A Visionary Union of Earth and Spirit*. Celestial Arts, 2003

Veriditas: Inspiring Transformation through the Labyrinth Experience. Training and support of labyrinth facilitators worldwide, and events that promote understanding of the labyrinth as a tool for personal and community transformation. (www.veriditas.net)

Verschuuren, Bas, Jeffrey McNeely, Gonzalo Oviedo and Robert Wild (editors). *Sacred Natural Sites: Conserving Nature and Culture*. Routledge, 2012

Von Essen, Carl. *Ecomysticism: The Profound Experience of Nature as Spiritual Guide*. Bear & Company, 2010

Walker, Alice. *We Are the Ones We Have Been Waiting For: Inner Light in a Time of Darkness*. The New Press, 2006

Westwood Creative Artists. *Passages: Welcome Home to Canada*. Doubleday Canada, 2002

Whitsel, Montague. *Wellsprings of the Deer: A Contemporary Celtic Spirituality*. 1stBooks, 2002

The Wild Hunt: A Modern Pagan Perspective. Online media focused on perspectives, commentary, social justice, current events, scholarship, history, archives, links and posts by Pagan authors, scholars and cultural creatives. (http://wildhunt.org)

Wise, Tim. *White Like Me: Reflections on Race from a Privileged Son*. Soft Scull Press, 2011

Zimmerman, Larry. *The Sacred Wisdom of the American Indians*. Watkins Publishing, 2011

Zinn, Howard. *A People's History of the United States*. Harper Perennial, 2010

RESOURCES

Cultural Appropriation

Aldred, Lisa. "Plastic Shamans and Astroturf Sun Dances: New Age Commercialization of Native American Spirituality." *The American Indian Quarterly,* University of Nebraska, 2001

Battiste, Marie and James Youngblood Henderson. *Protecting Indigenous Knowledge and Heritage: A Global Challenge*. Purich Publishing, 2000

Bell, Diane. *Some Readings on Cultural Appropriations, Native America, and the New Age*. Holy Cross College, 1996 (www.hanksville.org)

Berkhofer, Robert F. *The White Man's Indian: Images of the American Indian from Columbus to the Present*. Vintage, 1979

Bird, S. Elizabeth (editor). *Dressing in Feathers: The Construction of the Indian in American Popular Culture*. Westview Press, 1996

Brant, Beth. "Anodynes and Amulets." *Writing as Witness: Essay and Talk*. Three O'Clock Press, 1995

Brascoupe, Simon and Howard Mann, PhD. *A Community Guide to Protecting Indigenous Knowledge.* Indian and Northern Affairs Canada, June 2001 (www.publications.gc.ca)

Brown, Michael F. *Who Owns Native Culture?* Harvard University Press, 2004 Also, online resource for debates on the legal status of Indigenous art, music, folklore, biological knowledge and sacred sites. (http://web.williams.edu)

Carroll, Al. "Tribe of Many Colors or Tribe of Many Dollars?" *Racial Justice, IMC Network,* January 11, 2011 (www.indybay.org)

Champagne, Duane (editor). *Contemporary Native American Cultural Issues.* AltaMira Press, 2013

Cook-Lynn, Elizabeth. "Who Gets to Tell the Stories?" *Wicazo Sa Review: Native American Literature on the Edge of a New Century,* Volume 9, Number 1, 1993

Dashú, Max. "Respect and Responsibility." *La Gazette,* Santa Cruz, October 1994 (www.suppressedhistories.net)

Declaration of War Against Exploiters of Lakota Spirituality. 500 representatives from 40 different tribes and bands unanimously passed this declaration at the Lakota Summit V, a gathering of Lakota, Dakota and Nakota Nations from the U.S.A. and Canada, June 10, 1993. (www.aics.org)

Deloria, Philip J. *Playing Indian.* Yale University Press, 1999

Donaldson, Laura E. "On Medicine Women and White Shame-ans: New Age Native Americanism and Commodity Fetishism as Pop Culture Feminism." *Signa: Journal of Women in Culture and Society,* 1999

Doxtator, Deborah. *Fluffs and Feathers: An Exhibit on the Symbols of Indianness.* Woodland Cultural Centre, Brantford, ON, 1992

Egan, Timothy. *Short Nights of the Shadow Catcher: The Epic Life and Immoral Photographs of Edward Curtis.* Houghton Mifflin Harcourt, 2012

Eyers, Pegi. "Beyond the Pale: Lifting IK and Inventing Identity." *Bringing Race to the Table: An Exploration of Racism in the Pagan Community.* Brandy Williams, Taylor Ellwood and Crystal Blanton (editors), Megalithica Books, 2015

F.A.I.R. MEDIA (For Accurate Indigenous Representation). "Indigenous Peoples reserve the right to define how and where we are represented in popular culture. F.A.I.R. provides a safe, secure venue by and for Indigenous Peoples to confront stereotypes, while at the same time promoting accurate representations in popular culture." (www.facebook.com)

Francis, Daniel. *The Imaginary Indian: The Image of the Indian in Canadian Culture.* Arsenal Pulp Press, 1992

Geismar, Haidy. *Treasured Possessions: Indigenous Interventions into Cultural and Intellectual Property.* Duke University Press Books, 2013

Graber, Christoph Beat and Mira Burri-Nenova (editors). *Intellectual Property and Traditional Cultural Expressions in a Digital Environment.* Edward Elgar Publishers, 2008

Green, Rayna. "The Tribe Called Wannabee: Playing Indian in America and Europe." *Folklore* 99, No. 1, 1988

Hagan, Helene E. "The Plastic Medicine People Circle," *Institute of Archetypal Ethnology Newsletter,* September, 1992

Harney, Corbin. "Spiritual Phonies." *The Way It Is: One Water, One Air, One Mother Earth.* Blue Dolphin Publishing, 2009

Hemachandra, Ray A. "Selling the Sacred? American Indians and the New Age." *New Age Retailer,* November/December 2003

Hobson, Geary. "The Rise of the White Shaman as a New Version of Cultural Imperialism." *The Remembered Earth: An Anthology of Contemporary Native American Literature.* Geary Hobson (editor), University of New Mexico Press, 1981

Huhndorf, Shari M. *Going Native: Indians in the American Cultural Imagination.* Cornell University Press, 2010

IPinCH: Intellectual Property Issues in Cultural Heritage - Theory, Practice, Policy, Ethics. International collaboration of archaeologists, Indigenous organizations, lawyers, anthropologists, ethicists, policy makers and others concerned with the theoretical, ethical, and practical implications of commodification, appropriation, and other flows of knowledge about the past, and how these affect communities, researchers and other stakeholders. Simon Fraser University (www.sfu.ca/ipinch)

Jean, Terri. "Selling Native Spirituality." *Blue Corn Comics: New Age Mystics, Healers and Ceremonies,* 2007 (www.bluecorncomics.com/newage.htm)

Jenkins, Philip. *Dream Catchers: How Mainstream America Discovered Native Spirituality.* Oxford University Press, 2004

Johnson, Myke. "Wanting To Be Indian: When Spiritual Searching Turns into Cultural Theft." *Unsettling America: Decolonization in Theory & Practice,* September 20, 2011. (http://unsettlingamerica.wordpress.com)

Keene, Adrienne. *Native Appropriations: Examining Representations of Indigenous Peoples.* Online resources and blog focusing on issues of cultural appropriation and stereotyping. (http://nativeappropriations.com)

Kehoe, Alice. *Shamans and Religion: An Anthropological Exploration in Critical Thinking.* Waveland Press, 2000

Lischke, Ute and David T. McNab (editors). *Walking a Tightrope: Aboriginal People and Their Representations.* Wilfrid Laurier University Press, 2005

Meyer, Carter Jones and Diana Royer (editors). *Selling the Indian: Commercializing and Appropriating American Indian Cultures.* University of Arizona Press, 2001

NAFPS (New Age Frauds and Plastic Shamans). Anti-racism forum, resource and watchdog site for investigating, outing and warning the public about impostors, exploiters, cultural appropriators and pseudo-shamans. Maintained by First Nations scholars, activists, and their allies. (www.newagefraud.org)

Our Red Earth. *Death Among Us: Observations On Internet Exploiters Of American Indian Spirituality.* Our Red Earth, 2000 (www.oocities.com/ourredearth/index.html)

Owen, Suzanne. *Appropriation of Native American Spirituality.* Continuum, 2011

Root, Deborah. *Cannibal Culture: Art, Appropriation & the Commodification of Difference.* Westview Press, 1996

Rose, Wendy. "The Great Pretenders: Further Reflections on White Shamanism." *The State of Native America: Genocide, Colonisation and Resistance.* M. Annette Jaimes (editor), South End Press, 1999

Scafidi, Susan. *Who Owns Culture? Appropriation and Authenticity in American Law.* Rutgers University Press, 2005

Shanley, Kathryn W. "The Indians America Loves to Love and Read: American Indian Identity and Cultural Appropriation." *American Indian Quarterly,* Vol 21, Number 4, 1997

Specktor, Mordecai. "Shamans or Charlatans? Do Some Teachers of Native American Spirituality Distort Indians' Culture?" *Utne Reader,* July/August 1989

Strom, Karen M. *A Line in the Sand.* Online resource for cultural appropriation, cultural property issues, stereotypes and cultural sovereignty. (www.hanksville.org/sand)

Strong, Pauline Turner. *American Indians and the American Imaginary: Cultural Representation Across the Centuries.* Paradigm Publishers, 2013

Sunder, Madhavi. *From Goods to a Good Life: Intellectual Property and Global Justice.* Yale University Press, 2012

United Nations. *Declaration on the Rights of Indigenous Peoples.* Adopted by the General Assembly September 13, 2007. View or download the full declaration at the *United Nations Permanent Forum on Indigenous Issues* website. (http://undesadspd.org /IndigenousPeoples/DeclarationontheRightsofIndigenousPeoples.aspx)

Waegner, Cathy Covell (editor). *Mediating Indianness.* Michigan State University Press, 2015

Wallis, Robert J. *Shamans/Neo-Shamans: Ecstasies, Alternative Archaeologies and Contemporary Pagans.* Routledge, 2003

Wernitznig, Dagmar. *Going Native or Going Naive? White Shamanism and the Neo-Noble Savage.* University Press of America, 2003

Win, Wambli Sina (Lakota), "The Red Road is Not For Sale," *The Native Times*, March 2011.

York, Michael. "New Age Commodification and Appropriation of Spirituality." *Journal of Contemporary Religion*, Vol. 16, No. 3, 2001

Young, James O. and Conrad G. Brunk (editors). *The Ethics of Cultural Appropriation.* Wiley-Blackwell, 2012

Ziff, Bruce and Pratima V. Rao (editors). *Borrowed Power: Essays on Cultural Appropriation.* Rutgers University Press, 1997

Unpacking New Age Spirituality

Caplan, Mariana. *Eyes Wide Open: Cultivating Discernment on the Spiritual Path.* Sounds True, 2009

Caplan, Mariana. *Halfway Up the Mountain: the Error of Premature Claims to Enlightenment.* Hohm Press, 1999

Carrette, Jeremy and Richard King. *Selling Spirituality: The Silent Takeover of Religion.* Routledge, 2004

Ehrenreich, Barbara. *Bright-sided: How the Relentless Promotion of Positive Thinking Has Undermined America.* Metropolitan Books, 2009

Heath, Joseph and Andrew Potter. *Nation of Rebels: Why Counterculture Became Consumer Culture.* HarperBusiness, 2004

Keith, Lierre. "Culture of Resistance." *Deep Green Resistance: Strategy to Save the Planet.* Derrick Jensen, Aric McBay and Lierre Keith, Seven Stories Press, 2011

Lau, Kimberly J. *New Age Capitalism: Making Money East of Eden.* University of Pennsylvania Press, 2000

Masters, Robert Augustus. *Spiritual Bypassing: When Spirituality Disconnects Us from What Really Matters.* North Atlantic Books, 2010

McCutcheon, Russell T. *Critics Not Caretakers: Redescribing the Public Study of Religion.* State University of New York Press, 2001

Parenti, Michael. "The New Age Mythology." *Land of Idols: Political Mythology in America.* St. Martin's Press, 1994

Pike, Sarah M. *New Age and Neopagan Religions in America.* Columbia University Press, 2006

Roof, Wade Clark. *Spiritual Marketplace: Baby Boomers and the Remaking of American Religion.* Princeton University Press, 2001

Rothstein, Mikael (editor). *New Age Religion and Globalization.* Aarhus University Press, 2002

Schmidt, Leigh Eric. *Restless Souls: The Making of American Spirituality.* University of California Press, 2012

Sobe, Eliezer. *Why I Am Not Enlightened.* Reality Sandwich Singles, 2012

Trungpa, Chogyam. *Cutting Through Spiritual Materialism.* Shambhala Publications, 2010

Walker, Julian. *Devil in the Details: 3 Keys to Thinking More Clearly About Spirituality.* KDP, 2012

Webster, David. *Dispirited: How Contemporary Spirituality Makes Us Stupid, Selfish and Unhappy.* Zero Books, 2012

Turtle Island First Nations

Alfred, Taiaiake. *Peace, Power, Righteousness: An Indigenous Manifesto.* Oxford University Press, 2009

Alfred, Taiaiake. *Wasáse: Indigenous Pathways of Action and Freedom.* University of Toronto Press, 2005

Blair. Peggy J. *Lament for a First Nation: the Williams Treaties of Southern Ontario.* UBC Press, 2008 (www.ubcpress.ca/books/pdf/chapters/2008/lamentforafirstnation.pdf)

Cajete, Gregory. *A People's Ecology: Explorations in Sustainable Living.* Clear Light Publishing, 2003

Coulthard, Glen. *Red Skin, White Masks: Rejecting the Colonial Politics of Recognition.* University of Minnesota Press, 2014

Cultural Survival. Advocates for Indigenous peoples' rights, and supports the self-determination, cultures and political resilience of Indigenous communities. (www.culturalsurvival.org)

CWIS/Centre for World Indigenous Studies. Non-profit research and education dedicated to wider understanding and appreciation of the ideas and knowledge of Indigenous peoples and the social, economic and political realities of Indigenous nations. (http://cwis.org) Also publisher of *Intercontinental Cry/IC Magazine.* (https://intercontinentalcry.org)

Decolonization: Indigeneity, Education & Society. Undisciplinary, peer-reviewed, online open access journal committed to decolonization within education as part of the larger project of decolonization in society. (http://decolonization.org)

Deloria, Vine Jr. *Red Earth, White Lies: Native Americans and the Myth of Scientific Fact.* Fulcrum Publishing, 1997

Dunbar-Ortiz, Roxanne. *An Indigenous Peoples' History of the United States.* Beacon Press, 2014

Ellingson, Ter. *The Myth of the Noble Savage.* University of California Press, 2001

Four Arrows (Don Trent Jacobs). *Unlearning the Language of Conquest: Scholars Expose Anti-Indianism in America.* University of Texas Press, 2010

Green, Joyce (editor). *Indivisible: Indigenous Human Rights*. Fernwood Publishing, 2014

Indigenous Environmental Network: Working for the Rights of Indigenous Peoples and for Environmental and Economic Justice. Grassroots organization created to address environmental and economic justice issues, build the capacity of Indigenous communities to protect sacred sites, land, water, air, natural resources, health of the people and all living things, and to build economically sustainable communities. (www.ienearth.org)

Jaimes, M. Annette (editor*). The State of Native America: Genocide, Colonization and Resistance.* South End Press, 1999

Wall Kimmerer, Robin. *Braiding Sweetgrass: Indigenous Wisdom, Scientific Knowledge and the Teachings of Plants.* Milkweed Editions, 2015

Kino-nda-niimi Collective. *The Winter We Danced: Voices From the Past, the Future, and the Idle No More Movement.* Arbeiter Ring Publishing, 2014

Kovach, Margaret. *Indigenous Methodologies: Characteristics, Conversations, and Contexts.* University of Toronto Press, 2010

Kulchyski, Peter. *Aboriginal Rights Are Not Human Rights: In Defense of Indigenous Struggles.* Arbeiter Ring Publishing, 2012

LaRocque, Emma. *When the Other is Me: Native Resistance Discourse 1850-1990.* University of Manitoba Press, 2011

Maldonado, Julie Koppel, Benedict Colombi and Rajul Pandya (editors). *Climate Change and Indigenous Peoples in the United States: Impacts, Experiences and Actions.* Springer, 2014

Mander, Jerry and Victoria Tauli-Corpuz (editors). *Paradigm Wars: Indigenous Peoples' Resistance to Globalization.* Sierra Club Books, 2006

Switzer, Maurice (editor). *Nation to Nation: A Resource on Treaties in Ontario.* Union of Ontario Indians, 2013

Switzer, Maurice. *We Are All Treaty People.* Union of Ontario Indians, 2011

Tehanetorens (Ray Fadden). *Wampum Belts of the Iroquois.* Native Voices, 1999

Wagner, Sally Roesch. *Sisters in Spirit: Haudenosaunee (Iroquois) Influence on Early Feminists.* Native Voices, 2011

Weatherford, Jack. *Indian Givers: How Native Americans Transformed the World.* Broadway, 2010

Wildcat, Daniel R. *Red Alert! Saving the Planet with Indigenous Knowledge.* Fulcrum Publishing, 2009

Settler Re-indigenization & Indigenous Mind

Aikenhead, Glen and Herman Michell. *Bridging Cultures: Indigenous Ways and Scientific Ways of Knowing Nature.* Pearson Canada, 2011

Antieau, Kim. *The Salmon Mysteries: A Guidebook to a Reimagining of the Eleusinian Mysteries.* Ruby Rose's Fairy Tale Emporium, 2010

Ana Oihan Ametsa (Naomi Archer). *Awakening the Horse People – Ancestral Recovery, Re-Indigenization, & Unsettling Whiteness Resources for People of European Heritage.* Acclaimed work on white studies, Settler uncolonization, re-indigenization and authentic cultural recovery. (http://awakeningthehorse.wordpress.com)

Beck, Diane B. and Roger Spielmann. "Comparing Stories: Embracing the Circle of Life." *The Canadian Journal of Native Studies,* Vol. XXVI, 2006

Berger, Illana, PhD. *The Snake and the Four Winds, Nachash v' Arba Ruchot: Jewish Entrances into the Indigenous Mind, A Journey of Memory and Healing.* KDP, 2010

Bioneers Indigeneity Program. "Bioneers Indigeneity Set." Compilation of 12 plenary sessions by renowned native authors, activists and wisdom-keepers highlighting the most pressing issues in Indian Country. (www.bioneers.org)

Chalquist, Craig. *The Tears of Llorona: A Californian Odyssey of Place, Myth, and Homecoming.* World Soul Books, 2009

Corban-Arthen, Andras and associates. *EarthSpirit Web.* Pagan organization dedicated to the preservation and development of Earth-centered spirituality, culture and community, focused on the Indigenous traditions of pre-Christian Europe. (www.earthspirit.com/index.html)

Crowe, Raine. *The Village Mystery School.* Facilitator and cultural visionary focused on serving the interdependence of life, supporting the resilience and imagination of diverse communities rooted in re-membered and relational practices of the ancestors. (https://callingourselveshome.weebly.com)

Davis, Erik. *Tribal Revival: West Coast Festival Culture.* Lovelution Press, 2009

Durant, John. *The Paleo Manifesto: Ancient Wisdom for Lifelong Health.* Harmony, 2013

Elpel, Thomas J. *Primitive Living Skills.* Educational programs, resources, articles, journal, links and directory of wilderness survival, primitive living and nature awareness schools in North America. (www.hollowtop.com) Also, *Thomas J. Elpel's Web World Portal: Connecting the Dots from Wilderness Survival to Sustainable Living.*

Fina, Fabio. *Culture Seed: Center for Ecopsychology, Social Justice and Indigenous Wisdom.* Decolonization, healing, rewilding, rituals, healing walks, earth rights and restorative justice. *"To cultivate seeds of cultural hope in a time of great transition."* (http://greenfabiofina.wix.com/culturalseed)

Forward Alliance. "Festival Culture, Indigenous Peoples and Collective Liberation." *Reality Sandwich/Evolver*, September 24, 2013   (http://realitysandwich.com)

Gedgaudas, Nora T. *Primal Body, Primal Mind: Beyond the Paleo Diet for Total Health and a Longer Life.* Healing Arts Press, 2011

Godesky, Jason. *The Fifth World.* Role-playing game based on a neotribal, ecotopian future with participants maintaining the traditions of the ancestors and web of relationships, both human and other-than-human. (http://thefifthworld.com)

Gould, Rebecca Kneale. *At Home in Nature: Modern Homesteading and Spiritual Practice in America.* University of California Press, 2005

Griffin, Wendy (editor). *Sacred Lands and Spiritual Landscapes.* ADF Publishing, 2014. Readings from a Pagan Studies symposium and gathering of scholars serving the communities of Pagan and Earth-based religions.

Herman, Louis G. *Future Primal: How Our Wilderness Origins Show Us the Way Forward.* New World Library, 2013

Hillyer, Carolyn. *Sacred House: Where Women Weave Words into the Earth.* Seventh Wave Books. 2010   (www.seventhwavemusic.co.uk)

Hillyer, Carolyn. *Nameless Drum: Song Words and Other Voices.* Seventh Wave Music, 2004

Jenkinson, Stephen. *Orphan Wisdom/Orphan Wisdom School.* Teaching and learning for skills of deep living and making human culture, rooted in knowing history, being claimed by ancestry, and working for a time yet to come. (http://orphanwisdom.com)

Kremer, Jürgen Werner and R Jackson-Paton. *Ethnoautobiography: Stories and Practices for Unlearning Whiteness, Decolonization, Uncovering Ethnicities.* ReVision Publishing, 2013 (http://ethnoautobiography.net)

Larsen, Willem. *The College of Mythic Cartography: Every Place a Riddle, Every Riddle a Poem, Every Poem a Spirit, Every Spirit a Place.* Blogs on animism, rewilding, uncolonization and storyjamming published as a book. (www.lulu.com)

Lily. "We Were All Indigenous, and Can Again Become." *Unsettling America: Decolonization in Theory & Practice,* May 26, 2011 and *Green Anarchy #19,* Spring, 2005 (https://unsettlingamerica.wordpress.com)

Meredith, Jane. *Rituals of Celebration: Honoring the Seasons of Life through the Wheel of the Year.* Llewellyn, 2013

Plotkin, Bill. *Wild Mind: A Field Guide to the Human Psyche.* New World Library, 2013

Plotkin, Bill. *Soulcraft: Crossing into the Mysteries of Nature and Psyche.* New World Library, 2010

Plotkin, Bill. *Nature and the Human Soul: Cultivating Wholeness and Community in a Fragmented World.* New World Library, 2008

Prechtel, Martin. *The Unlikely Peace at Cuchumaquic: The Parallel Lives of People as Plants, Keeping the Seeds Alive.* North Atlantic Books, 2012

Robinson, Walter. *Primal Way and the Pathology of Civilization.* iUniverse, 2012

Seruntine, Cliff. *Seasons of the Sacred Earth: Following the Old Ways on an Enchanted Homestead.* Llewellyn Publications, 2013

Shepard, Paul. *Coming Home to the Pleistocene.* Island Press, 1998

Sisson, Mark. *The Primal Connection: Follow Your Genetic Blueprint to Health and Happiness.* Primal Nutrition, 2013

Tucker, Kevin. *Roots: A Field Guide to Anarcho-Primitivism.* Black and Green Press, 2014 (www.blackandgreenpress.org)

Tucker, Kevin. *For Wildness and Anarchy.* Black and Green Press, 2010

Walla, Nala. "The Farmer and the Witch: Reclaiming the Seeds of Indigeneity." *Ecosomatica: Integrative Arts and Ecology* (blog), May 20, 2013 (http://ecosomatica.wordpress.com/tag/neoindigenous)

Yaotl, Tlalli (Recovering Wasi'chu/Wetiko). "Decolonizing Our Hearts & Minds: Part I: Preliminary Thoughts & Explorations." Article on Settler re-indigenization. *Unsettling America: Decolonization in Theory & Practice,* January 7, 2011 (http://unsettlingamerica.wordpress.com)

Zerzan, John. *Future Primitive Revisited.* Feral House, 2012

Zerzan, John. *Origins: A John Zerzan Reader.* Black and Green Press, 2010

Tracing Ancestral Roots, Ancestral Healing

Baxter, Angus. *In Search of Your British & Irish Roots: A Complete Guide to Tracing Your English, Welsh, Scottish and Irish Ancestors.* Genealogical Publishing Company, 2000

Boring, Francesca Mason. *Connecting to Our Ancestral Past: Healing through Family Constellations, Ceremony and Ritual.* North Atlantic Books, 2012

Clarke, Tristram. *Tracing Your Scottish Ancestors: The Official Guide.* The National Records of Scotland and Birlinn, 2011

Flèche, Christian. *The Biogenealogy Sourcebook: Healing the Body by Resolving Traumas of the Past.* Healing Arts Press, 2008

Foor, Daniel. *Ancestral Medicine: Rituals for Personal and Family Healing.* Inner Traditions, 2017

Franke, Ursula. *The River Never Looks Back: Historical and Practical Foundations of Bert Hellinger's Family Constellations.* Carl Auer International, 2003

Grimassi, Raven. *The Cauldron of Memory: Retrieving Ancestral Knowledge & Wisdom.* Llewellyn Publications, 2009

Haakenstad, Liv Marit. *A Taste of Norwegian Ancestry.* Genit AS, 2013

Irish Roots Magazine. Accessing Irish genealogy and ancestor networks, resources, databases, Irish and Celtic history, book reviews, historical societies and pictorials for the worldwide Irish diaspora. (www.irishrootsmagazine.com)

Lewis-Williams, David and David Pearce. *Inside the Neolithic Mind: Consciousness, Cosmos, and the Realm of the Gods.* Thames & Hudson, 2005

Manne, Joy, Ph.D. *Family Constellations: A Practical Guide to Uncovering the Origins of Family Conflict.* North Atlantic Books, 2009

Moffat, Alistair. *The British: A Genetic Journey.* Birlinn Ltd., 2013

Moffat, Alistair. *The Scots: A Genetic Journey.* Birlinn Ltd., 2012

Moss, Robert. *Dreaming the Soul Back Home.* New World Library, 2012

Moss, Robert. *Dreamways of the Iroquois: Honoring the Secret Wishes of the Soul.* Destiny Books. 2005

Payne, John L. *The Language of the Soul: Trans-Generational Healing & Family Constellations.* Findhorn Press, 2006

Schneider, Jakob Robert. *Family Constellations: Basic Principles and Procedures.* Carl Auer International, 2007

Schutzenberger, Anne Ancelin. *The Ancestor Syndrome: Transgenerational Psychotherapy and the Hidden Links in the Family Tree.* Routledge, 1998

Serith, Ceisiwr. *Deep Ancestors: Practicing the Religion of the Proto-Indo-Europeans.* ADF Publishing, 2009

Swiecicki, Atava Garcia. *Journey Into My Polish Indigenous Mind.* Naropa University, December 2003. Also *Ancestral Apothacary* (blog). (www.ancestralapothecary.com)

Sykes, Bryan. *The Seven Daughters of Eve: The Science that Reveals Our Genetic Ancestry.* W. W. Norton & Company, 2010

Sykes, Bryan. *Saxons, Vikings, and Celts: The Genetic Roots of Britain and Ireland.* W. W. Norton & Company, 2007

Thomas, Ariann. *Healing Family Patterns: Ancestral Lineage Clearing for Personal Growth.* Ancestral Wisdom Press, 2011

van der Kolk, Bessel. *The Body Keeps the Score: Brain, Mind, and Body in the Healing of Trauma.* Penguin Books, 2014

Van Kampenhout, Daan. *The Tears of the Ancestors: Victims and Perpetrators in the Tribal Soul.* Zeig, Tucker & Theisen, 2008

Wells, Spencer. *Deep Ancestry: The Landmark DNA Quest to Decipher Our Distant Past.* National Geographic, 2007

Ravages of Empire

AbdelRahim, Layla. *Wild Children - Domesticated Dreams: Civilization and the Birth of Education.* Fernwood Books, 2014

Bagnell, Kenneth. *The Little Immigrants: The Orphans Who Came to Canada.* Dundurn, 2001

Berger, Thomas R. *A Long and Terrible Shadow: White Values, Native Rights in the Americas Since 1492.* Douglas & McIntyre, 1999

Brown. Douglas M. *Insatiable Is Not Sustainable.* Praeger, 2001

Chomsky, Noam. *Year 501: The Conquest Continues.* South End Press, 1999

Costa, Rebecca. *The Watchman's Rattle: A Radical New Theory of Collapse.* Vanguard Press, 2012

Daschuk, James. *Clearing the Plains: Disease, Politics of Starvation, and the Loss of Aboriginal Life.* University of Regina Press, 2013

Dawkins, Richard. *The God Delusion.* Mariner Books, 2011

de Graaf, John, David Wann and Thomas H. Naylor. *Affluenza: How Overconsumption Is Killing Us - and How to Fight Back.* Berrett-Koehler Publishers, 2014

Drinnon, Richard. *Facing West: The Metaphysics of Indian-Hating and Empire-Building.* University of Oklahoma Press, 1997

Fanon, Frantz. *The Wretched of the Earth.* Grove Press, 1963

Ferguson, Niall. *The Great Degeneration: How Institutions Decay and Economies Die.* Penguin Press, 2013

Forbes, Jack D. *Columbus and Other Cannibals: The Wetiko Disease of Exploitation, Imperialism, and Terrorism.* Seven Stories Press, 2011

Glendinning, Chellis. *Off the Map: An Expedition Deep into Empire and the Global Economy.* New Society Publishers, 1999

Glendinning, Chellis. *When Technology Wounds: The Human Consequences of Progress.* William Morrow & Company, 1990

Gordillo, Gastón R. *Rubble: The Afterlife of Destruction.* Duke University Press Books, 2014

Gray, Kevin, JoAnn Wypijewski and Jeffrey St. Clair (editors). *Killing Trayvons: An Anthology of American Violence.* Counterpunch, 2014

Griffin, Susan. *A Chorus of Stones: The Private Life of War.* Doubleday, 1992

Hall, Anthony J. *Earth into Property: Colonization, Decolonization, and Capitalism.* McGill Queens University Press, 2010

Hall, Anthony J. *The American Empire and the Fourth World.* Carleton University Press, 2005

Hamilton, Clive. *Requiem for a Species: Why We Resist the Truth About Climate Change.* Routledge, 2010

Hansen, James. *Storms of My Grandchildren: The Truth about the Coming Climate Catastrophe and Our Last Chance to Save Humanity.* Bloomsbury USA, 2009

Harvey, David. *Seventeen Contradictions and the End of Capitalism.* Oxford University Press, 2014

Harvey, David. *A Brief History of Neoliberalism*. Oxford University Press, 2007

Hedges, Christopher. *The World As It Is: Dispatches on the Myth of Human Progress*. Nation Books, 2011

Hesse, Barnor. *UN/Settled Multiculturalisms: Diasporas, Entanglement, Transruptions*. Zed Books, 2001

Hilary, John. *The Poverty of Capitalism: Economic Meltdown and the Struggle for What Comes Next*. Pluto Press, 2013

Hill, Michael Ortiz. *Dreaming the End of the World: Apocalypse as a Rite of Passage*. Spring Publications, 2004

Jensen, Derrick. *The Culture of Make Believe*. Chelsea Green Publishing, 2011

Jensen, Derrick. *Endgame, Volume 1: The Problem of Civilization*. Seven Stories Press, 2011

Jensen, Derrick. *Endgame, Vol. 2: Resistance*. Seven Stories Press, 2006

Kivel, Paul. *Living in the Shadow of the Cross: Understanding and Resisting the Power and Privilege of Christian Hegemony*. New Society Publishers, 2013

Klein, Naomi. *This Changes Everything: Capitalism vs. the Climate*. Knopf Canada, 2014

Kolbert, Elizabeth. *The Sixth Extinction: An Unnatural History*. Henry Holt, 2014

Kolbert, Elizabeth. *Field Notes from a Catastrophe: Man, Nature, and Climate Change*. Bloomsbury USA, 2010

Kotke, William. *The Final Empire: The Collapse of Civilization and the Seed of the Future*. Arrow Point Press, 1993

Kunstler, James Howard. *The Long Emergency: Surviving the End of Oil, Climate Change, and Other Converging Catastrophes of the Twenty-First Century*. Grove Press, 2006

Lymbery, Philip. *Farmageddon: The True Cost of Cheap Meat*. Bloomsbury Publishing, 2014

Lynas, Mark. *Six Degrees: Our Future on a Hotter Planet*. National Geographic, 2008

Magdoff, Fred and John Bellamy Foster. *What Every Environmentalist Needs to Know About Capitalism*. Monthly Review Press, 2011

Mander, Jerry. *The Capitalism Papers: Fatal Flaws of an Obsolete System*. Counterpoint, 2013

Marsden, William. *Stupid to the Last Drop: How Alberta Is Bringing Environmental Armageddon to Canada (And Doesn't Seem to Care)*. Vintage Canada, 2010

Marshall, George. *Don't Even Think About It: Why Our Brains are Wired to Ignore Climate Change*. Bloomsbury USA, 2014

McIntosh, Alastair. *Hell and High Water: Climate Change, Hope and the Human Condition*. Birlinn, 2008

McPherson, Guy R. *Killing the Natives: Has the American Dream Become a Nightmare?* Whitmore Publishing, 2009

Merchant, Carolyn. *The Death of Nature: Women, Ecology, and the Scientific Revolution*. HarperOne, 1990

Miller, J.R. *Compact, Contract, Covenant: Aboriginal Treaty Making in Canada*. University of Toronto Press, 2009

Milloy, John S. *A National Crime: The Canadian Government and the Residential School System, 1879 to 1986.* University of Manitoba Press, 1999

Mohawk, John C. *Utopian Legacies: A History of Conquest and Oppression in the Western World.* Clear Light Publishers, 2000

Monbiot, George. *Bring on the Apocalypse: Essays on Self-Destruction.* Anchor Canada, 2008

Monbiot, George. *Heat: How to Stop the Planet from Burning.* Doubleday Canada, 2006

Morgan, Robin. *The Demon Lover: The Roots of Terrorism.* Washington Square Press, 2001

Nikiforuk, Andrew. *The Energy of Slaves: Oil and the New Servitude.* Greystone Books, 2012

Oreskes, Naomi and Erik M. Conway. *The Collapse of Western Civilization: A View from the Future.* Columbia University Press, 2014

Orr, David W. *Down to the Wire: Confronting Climate Collapse.* Oxford University Press, 2009

Richardson, Boyce. *People of Terra Nullius: Betrayal and Rebirth in Aboriginal Canada.* Douglas & McIntyre, 1993

Roy, Arundhati. *The Cost of Living.* Modern Library, 1999

Sandel, Michael J. *What Money Can't Buy: The Moral Limits of Markets.* Farrar, Straus and Giroux, 2012

Schmookler, Andrew Bard. *Illusion of Choice: How the Market Economy Shapes Our Destiny.* State University of New York Press, 1993

Schor, Juliet B. *Born to Buy: The Commercialized Child and the New Consumer Culture.* Scribner, 2005

Smil, Vaclav. *Harvesting the Biosphere: What We Have Taken from Nature.* The MIT Press, 2012

Smithers, Gregory D. and Brooke N. Newman (editors). *Native Diasporas: Indigenous Identities and Settler Colonialism in the Americas.* University of Nebraska Press, 2014

Solnit, Rebecca. *Savage Dreams: A Journey into the Landscape Wars of the American West.* University of California Press, 2000

Stannard, David E. *American Holocaust: The Conquest of the New World.* Oxford University Press, 1993

Stolzenburg, William. *Where the Wild Things Were: Life, Death, and Ecological Wreckage in a Land of Vanishing Predators.* Bloomsbury USA, 2011

Terreblanche, Sampie. *Western Empires, Christianity and the Inequalities between the West and the Rest.* Penguin, 2014

Weisman, Alan. *The World Without Us.* T homas Dunne Books, 2007

Wilkerson, Isabel. *The Warmth of Other Suns: The Epic Story of America's Great Migration.* Vintage, 2010

Williams Robert A. *Savage Anxieties: The Invention of Western Civilization.* Palgrave MacMillan, 2012

Wise, Tim. *Culture of Cruelty: How America's Elite Demonize the Poor, Valorize the Rich and Jeopardize the Future.* City Lights Publishers, 2014

Woolford, Andrew. *Colonial Genocide and Indigenous North America.* Duke University Press, 2014

Wright, Ronald. *Stolen Continents: 500 Years of Conquest and Resistance in the Americas.* Mariner Books, 2005

Zerzan, John. *Twilight of the Machines.* Feral House, 2008

Zerzan, John. *Against Civilization: Readings and Reflections.* Feral House, 1998

Zinn, Howard. *A People's History of the United States.* Harper Perennial Modern Classics, 2010

Racism, White Privilege, White Studies

Alcoff. Linda Martin. "What Should White People Do?" *History is a Weapon - From Resistance to Revolution.* (www.historyisaweapon.com)

Alexander, Michelle. *The New Jim Crow: Mass Incarceration in the Age of Colorblindness.* New Press, 2012

Allen, Theodore W. *The Invention of the White Race: Racial Oppression and Social Control, the Origin of Racial Oppression in Anglo-America.* Verso, 2012

Baldwin, Andrew, Laura Cameron and Audrey Kobayashi (editors). *Rethinking the Great White North: Race, Nature, and the Historical Geographies of Whiteness in Canada.* UBC Press, 2012

Baum, Bruce. *The Rise and Fall of the Caucasian Race: A Political History of Racial Identity.* NYU Press, 2006

Benjamin, Rich. *Searching for Whitopia: An Improbable Journey to the Heart of White America.* Hyperion, 2009

Bonilla-Silva, Eduardo. *Racism without Racists: Color-Blind Racism and the Persistence of Racial Inequality in America.* Rowman & Littlefield Publishers, 2009

Bradley, Michael. *The Iceman Inheritance: Prehistoric Sources of Western Man's Racism, Sexism and Aggression.* Kayode Publications, 1991

Clark, Kendall. "The Global Privileges of Whiteness." *Colours of Resistance Archive,* courtesy of the Monkeyfist Collective. (www.coloursofresistance.org)

The Colour of Fear. Dir. Lee Mun Wah. StirFry Seminars & Consulting, 1994. Acclaimed film on race relations in America, now considered a classic for diversity training and cross-cultural management seminars around the world. (www.diversitytrainingfilms.com)

Crenshaw, Kimberle, Neil Gotanda, Gary Peller and Kendall Thomas (editors). *Critical Race Theory: The Key Writings That Formed the Movement.* The New Press, 1996

DiAngelo, Robin. *What Does it Mean to Be White? Developing White Racial Literacy.* Peter Lang, 2012

DiAngelo, Robin. *White Fragility: Why It's So Hard for White People to Talk about Racism.* Beacon Press, 2018

Doane, Ashley W. and Eduardo Bonilla-Silva (editors). *White Out: The Continuing Significance of Racism.* Routledge, 2003

DuBois, W.E.B. *The Souls of Black Folks.* Eucalyptus Press, 2013

Dyer, Richard. *White: Essays on Race and Culture.* Routledge, 2013

Freire, Paulo. *Pedagogy of the Oppressed.* Bloomsbury Academic, 2000

Hughey, Matthew. *White Bound: Nationalists, Antiracists, and the Shared Meanings of Race*. Stanford University Press, 2012

Ignatiev, Noel. *How the Irish Became White*. Routledge, 2012

Jealous, Ann Todd and Caroline T. Haskell. *Combined Destinies: Whites Sharing Grief about Racism*. Potomac Books, 2013

Jensen, Robert. *The Heart of Whiteness: Confronting Race, Racism and White Privilege*. City Lights Publishers, 2005

Johnson, Allan G. *Privilege, Power, and Difference*. McGraw-Hill, 2005

Johnson, Genevieve Fuji and Randy Enomoto. *Race, Racialization and Antiracism in Canada and Beyond*. University of Toronto Press, 2013

Kivel, Paul. *Uprooting Racism: How White People Can Work for Racial Justice*. New Society Publishers, 2011

Lipsitz, George. *The Possessive Investment in Whiteness: How White People Profit from Identity Politics*. Temple University Press, 2006

Mansur, Salim. *Delectable Lie: a Liberal Repudiation of Multiculturalism*. Mantua Books, 2011

Marsh, Jason, Rodolfo Mendoza-Denton and Jeremy Adam Smith (editors). *Are We Born Racist? New Insights from Neuroscience and Positive Psychology*. Beacon Press Books, 2010

Memmi, Albert. *The Colonizer and the Colonized*. Plunkett Lake Press, 2013

Menakem, Resmaa. *My Grandmother's Hands: Racialized Trauma and the Pathway to Mending Our Hearts and Bodies*. Central Recovery Press, 2017

Painter, Nell Irvin. *The History of White People*. W.W. Norton & Company, 2010

Race: the Power of an Illusion. Producer/Dir. Larry Adelman. ITVS, 2003. Acclaimed 3-part documentary on race in society, science and history. (www.pbs.org)

Razack, Sherene. *Race, Space, and the Law: Unmapping a White Settler Society*. Between the Lines, 2002

Roithmayr, Daria. *Reproducing Racism: How Everyday Choices Lock in White Advantage*. NYU Press, 2014

Rothenberg, Paula S. *White Privilege: Essential Readings on the Other Side of Racism*. Worth Publishers, 2011

Takaki, Ronald. *A Different Mirror: A History of Multicultural America*. Back Bay Books, 2008

Veracini, Lorenzo. *Settler Colonialism: A Theoretical Overview*. Palgrave MacMillan, 2010

Weekes, Karen. *Privilege and Prejudice: Twenty Years with the Invisible Knapsack*. Cambridge Scholars Publishing, 2009

Welsing Frances Cress. *The Isis Papers: The Keys to the Colors*. Third World Press, 1991 A collection of 25 essays examining the pathology of white supremacy.

Wise, Tim. *Dear White America: Letter to a New Minority*. City Lights Publishers, 2012

Wise, Tim. *White Like Me: Reflections on Race from a Privileged Son*. Soft Scull Press, 2011

Wise, Tim. *Colorblind: The Rise of Post-Racial Politics and the Retreat from Racial Equity*. City Lights Publishers, 2010

Activism and Anti-Racism

America Healing. *Racial Equity Resource Guide*. Raising awareness on unconscious biases and inequities, a comprehensive and interactive guide with resources, articles, books, media strategies and curricula aimed at helping organizations and individuals working to achieve racial healing and equity. W.K. Kellogg Foundation. (www.racialequityresourceguide.org)

Best, Steven and Anthony J. Nocella II (editors). *Igniting a Revolution: Voices in Defense of the Earth*. AK Press, 2006

Bowser, Jeriah. *Elements of Resistance: Violence, Nonviolence, and the State*. Hampton Institute Press, 2014

Boyd, Andrew and Dave Oswald Mitchell (editors). *Beautiful Trouble: A Toolbox for Revolution*. OR Books, 2012

Brown, Cynthia Stokes. *Refusing Racism: White Allies and the Struggle for Civil Rights*. Teachers College Press, 2002

Choudry, Aziz, Jill Hanley and Eric Shragge (editors). *Organize! Building from the Local for Global Justice*. PM Press, 2012

Colours of Resistance Archive. Archive of articles, resources, analysis and tools from the COR collective for organizing and building anti-authoritarian movements against global capitalism; anti-racist, anti-imperialist, feminist, multiracial politics within an anti-oppression framework. (www.coloursofresistance.org)

Crass, Chris. *Towards Collective Liberation: Anti-Racist Organizing, Feminist Praxis, and Movement Building Strategy*. PM Press, 2013 (www.chriscrass.org)

D'Arcy, Stephen. *Languages of the Unheard: Why Militant Protest is Good for Democracy*. Zed Books, 2014

Earth First! *Direct Action Manual*. The Gloo Factory, 2015

Gelderloos, Peter. *The Failure of Nonviolence*. Left Bank Books, 2013

Hooks, Bell. *Killing Rage: Ending Racism*. Henry Holt and Company, 1995

Jensen, Derrick, Aric McBay and Lierre Keith. *Deep Green Resistance: Strategy to Save the Planet*. Seven Stories Press, 2011

Jensen, Robert. *Arguing for Our Lives: A User's Guide to Constructive Dialogue*. City Lights, 2013

jones, pattrice. *Aftershock: Confronting Trauma in a Violent World, a Guide for Activists and Their Allies*. Lantern Books, 2007

Katz, Judith. *White Awareness: Handbook for Anti-Racism Training*. University of Oklahoma Press, 2003

Kingsnorth, Paul. *One No, Many Yeses: A Journey to the Heart of the Global Resistance Movement*. Simon & Schuster, 2012

Kumar, Satish. *Small World Big Ideas: There's an Activist in All of Us and You Don't Have to Shout to be Heard*. Ivy Press, 2014

Lakey, Berit and George Lakey. *Grassroots and Nonprofit Leadership: A Guide for Organizations in Changing Times*. New Society Publishers, 1998

McMillan, Stephanie. *Capitalism Must Die! A basic introduction to capitalism: what it is, why it sucks, and how to crush it*. INIP, 2014

McMillan, Stephanie. *The Minimum Security Chronicles: Resistance to Ecocide*. Seven Stories Press, 2013

Nieto, Leticia with Margot F. Boyer. *Beyond Inclusion, Beyond Empowerment: A Developmental Strategy to Liberate Everyone.* Cuetzpalin, 2010

O'Brien, Eileen. *Whites Confront Racism: Antiracists and their Paths to Action.* Rowman & Littlefield, 2001

Potter, Will. *Green is the New Red: An Insider's Account of a Social Movement Under Siege.* City Lights Publishers, 2011

powell, john a. *Racing to Justice: Transforming Our Conceptions of Self and Other to Build an Inclusive Society.* Indiana University Press, 2012

Reddy, Maureen T. (editor). *Everyday Acts Against Racism: Raising Children in a Multiracial World.* Seal Press, 1996

Rettig, Hillary. *The Lifelong Activist: How to Change the World without Losing Your Way.* Lantern Books, 2006

Sullivan, Shannon. *Good White People: the Problem with White, Middle-Class Anti-Racism.* SUNY Press, 2014

White, Micah, PhD. *The End of Protest: A New Playbook for Revolution.* Knopf Canada, 2016

Alliances, Allyship, Reconciliation and Peace Work

The Arbinger Institute. *The Anatomy of Peace: Resolving the Heart of Conflict.* Berrett-Koehler Publishers, 2008

Assefa, Hizkias. *Peace and Reconciliation as A Paradigm: A Philosophy of Peace and its Implications on Conflict, Governance and Economic Growth.* ACIS Press, 2007

Azcona, Maria Cristina. *About Peace and Peacemaking.* Cook Communication, 2014

Bishop, Anne. *Becoming an Ally: Breaking the Cycle of Oppression in People.* Zed Books, 2002

Bowers, Christopher. "10 Ways to be an Ally." *White Privilege* (blog), February 3, 2010 (www.whitepriv.blogspot.com)

Castellano, Marlene Brant, Linda Archibald and Mike DeGagné (editors). *From Truth to Reconciliation: Transforming the Legacy of Residential Schools.* Aboriginal Healing Foundation, 2008

Council for a Parliament of the World's Religions. Created to cultivate harmony among the world's religious and spiritual communities and foster their engagement with the world and its guiding institutions in order to achieve a just, peaceful and sustainable world. (www.parliamentofreligions.org)

Davis, Lynne, PhD, Brodie Ferguson, Cherylanne James, Kristen Lloyd, Tessa Nasca, Sara Taylor and Julian Tennent-Riddell. *Transforming Relations: A Collaborative Collection.* A progressive collection of over 150 native/non-native partnerships, coalitions and bridgebuilding initiatives in Canada. (http://transformingrelations.wordpress.com)

Davis, Lynne, PhD (editor). *Alliances: Re/Envisioning Indigenous-non-Indigenous Relationships.* University of Toronto Press, 2010

Heinrichs, Steve (editor). *Buffalo Shout, Salmon Cry: Conversations on Creation, Land Justice, and Life Together.* Herald Press, 2013

Indigenous Action Media: Action, Art, Strategic Communications, Workshops & Support. *Accomplices Not Allies: Abolishing the Ally Industrial Complex*, May 4, 2014 (www.indigenousaction.org)

Krznaric, Roman. *Empathy: Why It Matters, and How to Get It.* Perigee Books, 2014

Occupy Love. Dir. Velcrow Ripper. SuperChannel and the Canada Media Fund. Gravitas Ventures, 2013 (http://occupylove.org)

Oelrich, Inger Lise. *The New Story: Storytelling as a Pathway to Peace*. Troubador Publishing, 2014

Regan, Paulette. *Unsettling the Settler Within: Indian Residential Schools, Truth Telling and Reconciliation in Canada*. UBC Press, 2010

Rollo, Tobold. "Ethos of the Ally: Deference, Dialogue, and Distance." *Toby Rollo* (blog), July 7, 2013 (www.toboldrollo.com)

Rosenberg, Marshall. *Nonviolent Communication: A Language of Life - Life-Changing Tools for Healthy Relationships*. Puddledancer Press, 2008. (www.nonviolent communication.com) *Center for Nonviolent Communication* (www.cnvc.org)

Schulman, Sarah. *Conflict Is Not Abuse: Overstating Harm, Community Responsibility, and the Duty of Repair*. Arsenal Pulp Press, 2016

Sharp, Gene. *Waging Nonviolent Struggle: 20th Century Practice and 21st Century Potential*. Porter Sargent Publishers, 2005. Founder of the *Albert Einstein Institution: Advancing Freedom through Non-Violent Action*, a non-profit organization advancing the use of strategic nonviolent action in conflicts around the world, free downloadable books, films and other resources. (www.aeinstein.org)

Tutu, Desmond. *No Future Without Forgiveness*. Image, 2009

Two-Eyed Seeing/Etuaptmumk. Mi'kmaw concept of learning to see from one eye with IK and ways of knowing, and the other with Western knowledge and ways of knowing, using both together for the benefit of all. Developed by Mi'kmaw Elder Albert Marshall. *The Institute for Integrative Science & Health* (archived), Unama'ki College and Cape Breton University. (www.integrativescience.ca/Principles/TwoEyedSeeing)

Wallace, Rick. *Merging Fires: Grassroots Peacebuilding Between Indigenous and Non-Indigenous Peoples*. Fernwood Publishing, 2013

Worldwide Indigenous Science Network (WISN). Educational organization working locally, nationally and internationally to create an interface between western and Indigenous cultures. (www.wisn.org)

Younging, Gregory, Jonathan Dewar and Mike DeGagné (editors). *Response, Responsibility and Renewal: Canada's Truth and Reconciliation Journey*. Aboriginal Healing Foundation, 2009

Zehr, Howard. *The Little Book of Restorative Justice*. Good Books, 2002

Rejecting Empire (Uncolonization)

Alexander, Samuel. *Entropia: Life Beyond Industrial Civilisation*. Simplicity Institute Publishing, 2013

Ausubel, Kenny. *Dreaming the Future: Reimagining Civilization in the Age of Nature*. Chelsea Green Publishing, 2012

Baker, Carolyn, PhD. *Sacred Demise: Walking the Spiritual Path of Industrial Civilization's Collapse*. iUniverse, 2009

Berman, Morris. *The Reenchantment of the World*. Cornell University Press, 1981

Berry, Thomas. *The Great Work: Our Way into the Future*. Crown, 2011

Brown, Lester R. *World on the Edge: How to Prevent Environmental and Economic Collapse*. W. W. Norton & Company, 2011

D'Alisa, Giacomo, Federico Demaria and Giorgos Kallis (editors). *Degrowth: A Vocabulary for a New Era*. Routledge, 2014

Eisenstein, Zillah. *Against Empire: Feminisms, Racism and the West*. Zed Books, 2013

Esteva, Gustavo and Madhu Suri Prakash. *Grassroots Post-Modernism: Remaking the Soil of Cultures*. Zed Books, 1998

Farnish, Keith. *Time's Up! An Uncivilized Solution to a Global Crisis*. UIT Cambridge, 2009

Foster, John. *After Sustainability: Denial, Hope, Retrieval*. Routledge, 2014

Greer, John Michael. *The Long Descent: A User's Guide to the End of the Industrial Age*. New Society Publishers, 2008

Harris, Malcolm and Neal Gorenflo (editors). *Share or Die: Voices of the Get Lost Generation in the Age of Crisis*. New Society Publishers, 2012

Heinberg, Richard. *Afterburn: Society Beyond Fossil Fuels*. New Society Publishers, 2015

Heinberg, Richard. *Peak Everything: Waking Up to the Century of Declines*. New Society Publishers, 2010

Horgan, John. *The End of War*. McSweeney's, 2014

Jensen, Derrick. *Truths Among Us: Conversations on Building a New Culture*. PM Press, 2011

Jensen, Robert. *We Are All Apocalyptic Now: Moral Responsibilities in Crisis Times*. KDP, 2013

Kaufman, Cynthia. *Getting Past Capitalism: History, Vision, Hope*. Lexington Books, 2013

LaConte, Ellen. *Life Rules: Nature's Blueprint for Surviving Economic and Environmental Collapse*. New Society Publishers, 2012

Lopez, Barry. *The Rediscovery of North America*. Vintage, 1992

Macy, Joanna, Peter Reason and Melanie Newman (editors). *Stories of the Great Turning*. Vala Publishing Cooperative, 2013

McKibben, Bill. *Eaarth: Making a Life on a Tough New Planet*. Knopf Canada, 2010

McPherson, Guy R. *Walking Away from Empire: A Personal Journey*. PublishAmerica, 2011

Moore, Kathleen Dean and Michael P. Nelson. *Moral Ground: Ethical Action for a Planet in Peril*. Trinity University Press, 2011

Ross, Alexander Reid (editor). *Grabbing Back: Essays against the Global Land Grab*. AK Press, 2014

Rubin, Jeff. *The End of Growth*. Random House Canada, 2012

Sahn, Jennifer (editor). *Thirty-Year Plan: Thirty Writers on What We Need to Build a Better Future*. Orion Books, 2012

Sale, Kirkpatrick. *Rebels Against the Future - the Luddites and their War on the Industrial Revolution: Lessons for the Computer Age*. Basic Books, 1996

Shiva, Vandana. *Making Peace with the Earth*. Pluto Press, 2013

Spretnak, Charlene. *The Resurgence of the Real: Body, Nature, and Place in a Hypermodern World*. Routledge, 2012

Stein, Matthew. *When Technology Fails: A Manual for Self-Reliance, Sustainability, and Surviving the Long Emergency.* Chelsea Green Publishing, 2009

Unsettling America: Decolonization in Theory & Practice. Network dedicated to mental and territorial decolonization throughout Turtle Island, documenting spiritual and psychological decolonization and liberation, and seeking true sovereignty and self-determination for all people. Essays, articles, art, poetry, resources, allyship guidelines, solidarity projects, events, actions and recommended reading. (http://unsettlingamerica.wordpress.com)

Unsettling Minnesota Collective. *Unsettling Ourselves: Reflections and Resources for Deconstructing Colonial Mentality.* Sourcebook compiled by the Unsettling Minnesota Collective, 2009. E-book download at (http://unsettlingminnesota.org).

European Reconstructionism

Acker, Paul and Carolyne Larrington (editors). *Revisiting the Poetic Edda: Essays on Old Norse Heroic Legend.* Routledge, 2013

Aitamurto, Kaarina and Scott Simpson (editors). *Modern Pagan and Native Faith Movements in Central and Eastern Europe.* Acumen Publishing, 2013

Ásatrúarfélagið. Official Ásatrú organisation in Iceland. (http://asatru.is)

Bauschatz, Paul. *The Well and the Tree: World and Time in Early Germanic Culture.* University of Massachusetts Press, 1982

Crowell, Casper Odinson and Linda Crowell. *Vor Forn Sidr: (Our Ancient Religion).* Vinland Kindred Publishing, 2012

Davidson, H.R. Ellis. *Myths and Symbols in Pagan Europe: Early Scandinavian and Celtic Religions.* Syracuse University Press, 1989

European Congress of Ethnic Religions. International collective that assists with the expression of European earth-connected traditions, and brings together diverse ethnic and religious groups for common causes. (http://ecer-org.eu)

Frazier, J.G. *The Golden Bough: A Study in Magic and Religion.* MacMillan, 1974

Gundarsson, Kveldulf. *Our Troth: History and Lore Volumes I/II.* BookSurge Publishing, 2006

Het Rad. Official site for the Dutch Ásatrú tradition and network. (www.hetrad.nl)

Jones, Prudence and Nigel Pennick. *A History of Pagan Europe.* Routledge, 1997

Kaldera, Raven. *Northern-Tradition Paganism.* Reconstructionist-derived polytheistic religious tradition based on ancient northern Eurasian practice and personal gnosis, not affiliated with Ásatrú or Heathenry. (www.northernpaganism.org)

Krasskova, Galina. *Exploring The Northern Tradition: A Guide To The Gods, Lore, Rites And Celebrations From The Norse, German And Anglo-Saxon Traditions.* New Page Books, 2005

Kvilhaug, Maria Christina. *The Seed of Yggdrasill: Deciphering the Hidden Messages in Old Norse Myths.* Whyte Tracks, 2013 (https://bladehoner.wordpress.com/author)

Lindow, John. *Norse Mythology: A Guide to the Gods, Heroes, Rituals and Beliefs.* Oxford University Press, 2002

Metzner, Ralph. *The Well of Remembrance: Rediscovering the Earth Wisdom Myths of Northern Europe.* Shambhala, 1994

Mountfort, Paul Rhys. *Nordic Runes: Understanding, Casting, and Interpreting the Ancient Viking Oracle.* Destiny Books, 2011

Paxson, Diana L. *Essential Asatru: Walking the Path of Norse Paganism*. Citadel, 2006

Price, Neil S. *The Viking Way: Religion and War in Late Iron Age Scandinavia*. Oxbow Books, 2013

Puryear, Mark. *The Nature of Asatru: An Overview of the Ideals and Philosophy of the Indigenous Religion of Northern Europe*. iUniverse, 2006

Simek, Rudolf. *Dictionary of Northern Mythology*. BOYE6, 2008

Strmiska, Michael (editor). *Modern Paganism in World Cultures: Comparative Perspectives*. ABC-CLIO, 2005

Swedish Forn Sed Assembly. Official Pagan organization and nature religion based in Sweden, inspired by pre-Christian Norse and Germanic tradition and myth adapted to contemporary times. (www.samfundetfornsed.se)

Thorsson, Edred. *Futhark: A Handbook of Rune Magic*. Weiser Books, 2012

Turville-Petre, Edward O.G. *Myth and Religion of the North: The Religion of Ancient Scandinavia*. Praeger, 1975

Wells Peter S. *Beyond Celts, Germans, and Scythians: Archaeology and Identity in Iron Age Europe*. Bristol Classical Press, 2001

Celtic Studies, Polytheism, Folklore, Druidry

Air n-Aithesc: A Celtic Reconstructionist Peer-Reviewed Magazine. Online material for Celtic Reconstructionists and others, who value both the academic and spiritual in their practice. (http://ciannai2.wix.com/air-n-aithesc)

An Chuallacht Ghaol Naofa. An organization and established community committed to the practice and advancement of Gaelic Polytheism, preserving the Gaelic earth-based, pre-Christian cultural traditions through scholarship and collaboration, and reviving and reconstructing polytheistic Gaelic spiritual ways. Action points include education, community, restoration, practice and preservation, with online resources such as the *Ghaol Naofa FAQ*. (www.gaolnaofa.org)

An Comunn Gàidhealach Ameireaganach (ACGA: American Scottish Gaelic Society). "Striving to promote and preserve the Gaelic language and culture by supporting Gaelic language study and interest in Gaelic literature, song, music, art and history in North America and the world." (www.acgamerica.org)

Basford, Kathleen. *The Green Man*. D. S. Brewer, 1998

Black, Ronald. *The Gaelic Otherworld*. Birlinn, 2012

Bonewits, Isaac. *Bonewit's Essential Guide to Druidism*. Kensington Publishing, 2006

Borsje, Jacqueline, Ann Dooley, Seamus Mac Mathuna and Gregory Toner (editors). *Celtic Cosmology: Perspectives from Ireland and Scotland*. PIMS, 2014

Bradley, Ian. *The Celtic Way*. Darton Longman & Todd, 2004

Branston, Brian. *The Lost Gods of England*. Thames & Hudson, 1984

Briggs, Katherine. *The Vanishing People: Fairy Lore and Legends*. Pantheon, 1978

Brown, Nimue. *Druidry and the Ancestors: Finding our Place in our Own History*. John Hunt Publishing, 2012

Brunaux, Jean-Louis. *The Celtic Gauls: Gods, Rites and Sanctuaries*. Routledge, 1987

Burne, Charlotte Sophia. *The Handbook of Folklore*. HardPress Publishing, 2013

Burl, Aubrey. *A Guide to the Stone Circles of Britain, Ireland and Brittany.* Yale University Press, 2006

Carmicheal, Alexander. *Carmina Gadelica, Vol. I & II.* KDP, 2012

Carmina Gadelica. Online collection of Scottish prayers, charms, incantations, blessings, folklore, poems, songs, nature writing and history. (www.smo.uhi.ac.uk/gaidhlig/corpus/Carmina)

Carr-Gomm, Philip and Richard Heygate. *The Book of English Magic.* Overlook Press, 2012

Carr-Gomm, Philip. *Druid Mysteries: Ancient Wisdom for the 21st Century.* Random House, 2003   (www.philipcarr-gomm.com)

CELT: Corpus of Electronic Texts. Extensive online collection of translated texts in Celtic studies, literature, mythology and history. (www.ucc.ie/celt/transpage.html)

Clarke, David. *A Guide to Britain's Pagan Heritage.* Robert Hale, 1995

Clarke, David and Andy Roberts. *Twilight of the Celtic Gods: An Exploration of Britain's Hidden Pagan Traditions.* Blandford, 1996

Condren, Mary. *The Serpent and the Goddess: Women, Religion and Power in Celtic Ireland.* Harper San Francisco, 1989

Corrigan, Ian. *Sacred Fire, Holy Well: A Druid's Grimoire.* ADF Publishing, 2014

Croker, Thomas Crofton. *Fairy Legends and Traditions of the South of Ireland.* Ulan Press, 2012

Cunliffe, Barry. *The Ancient Celts.* Penguin Books, 2000

Curran, Bob. *Walking With the Green Man.* New Page Books, 2007

Daimler, Morgan. *Fairy Witchcraft: A Neopagan's Guide to the Celtic Fairy Faith.* Moon Books, 2014

Dames, Michael. *Mythic Ireland.* Thames & Hudson, 1996

Danaher, Kevin. *Irish Customs and Beliefs.* Mercier Press, 2012

Ellis, Peter Berresford. *A Brief History of the Celts.* Constable & Robinson, 2003

Ellis, Peter Berresford. *The Druids.* Wm. B. Eerdmans Publishing, 1994

Ellison, Robert Lee. *The Solitary Druid: Walking the Path of Wisdom and Spirit.* Citadel Press, 2005

Evans-Wentz, W. Y. *The Fairy-Faith in Celtic Countries.* Forgotten Books, 2007

The Fairy Faith. Dir. John Walker. John Walker Productions, National Film Board of Canada (NFB).   Wellspring Media, August 21, 2001   (www.youtube.com)

Freeman, Philip. *The Philosopher and the Druids: A Journey Among the Ancient Celts.* Simon & Schuster, 2006

Gaeltacht Bhaile na hÉireann (the North American Gaeltacht). A designated Irish-speaking area in Tamworth, Ontario, where Irish language, culture and traditions are alive and thriving. Emphasizing the link with Ireland, the *North American Gaeltacht* was created as a permanent meeting place for Irish speakers from North America and beyond. (www.gaeilge.ca)

Gibson, Marion, Shelley Trower and Garry Tregidga (editors). *Mysticism, Myth and Celtic Identity.* Routledge, 2012

Glassie, Henry (editor). *Irish Folktales.* Pantheon, 2012

Green, Miranda J. *The World of the Druids*. Irish Books & Media, 1997

Green, Miranda J. *Celtic Goddesses: Warriors, Virgins and Mothers*. George Braziller, 1996

Greer, John Michael. *The Druidry Handbook: Spiritual Practice Rooted in the Living Earth*. Weiser Books, 2006

Guyonvarc'h, Christian J. *The Making of a Druid*. Inner Traditions, 2001

Henderson, Lizanne. *Scottish Fairy Belief: A History*. John Donald, 2007

Hopman, Ellen Evert. *A Druid's Herbal for the Sacred Earth Year*. Destiny Books, 2014

Hopman, Ellen Evert. *Scottish Herbs and Fairy Lore*. Pendraig Publishing, 2011

Hutton, Ronald. *Pagan Britain*. Yale University Press, 2014

Hutton, Ronald. *Blood and Mistletoe: The History of the Druids in Britain*. Yale University Press, 2011

Hutton, Ronald. *The Pagan Religions of the Ancient British Isles: Their Nature and Legacy*. Wiley Blackwell, 1993

Kondratiev, Alexei. *The Apple Branch: A Path to Celtic Ritual*. Citadel, 2003

Laurie, Erynn Rowan. *A Circle of Stones: Journeys and Meditations for Modern Celts*. Megalithica Books, 2012

Laurie, Erynn Rowan. *Ogam: Weaving Word Wisdom*. Megalithica Books, 2007

Laurie, Erynn Rowan. "Following a Celtic Path." *The Preserving Shrine: Articulating the Unspeakable Since 1961* (blog). Erynn Rowan Laurie is one of the founders of the Celtic Reconstructionist movement. (www.seanet.com/~inisglas)

Lenihan, Eddie with Carolyn Eve Green. *Meeting the Other Crowd: The Fairy Stories of Hidden Ireland*. Gill & MacMillan, 2010

Loughlin, Annie (Seren). *Tairis*. Online resources on Gaelic Polytheism. (http://tairis.co.uk) *Tairis: A Gaelic Polytheist Blog* (http://tairis-cr.blogspot.ca)

MacKillop, James. *The Oxford Dictionary of Celtic Mythology*. Oxford University Press, 2000

MacLean, Fitzroy. *Scotland: A Concise History*. Thames & Hudson, 2012

Mann, Nicholas R. *The Isle of Avalon: Sacred Mysteries of Arthur and Glastonbury*. Green Magic, 2001

Markale, Jean. *The Druids: Celtic Priests of Nature*. Inner Traditions, 1999

Matthews, Caitlin. *Celtic Visions: Seership, Omens and Dreams of the Otherworld*. Watkins Publishing, 2012

Matthews, Caitlin. *Celtic Wisdom: Celebrating the Seasons*. Thunder Bay Press, 2008

Matthews, Caitlin and John Matthews. *The Encyclopedia of Celtic Wisdom*. Element Books, 1994

McCaffrey, Carmel. *In Search of Ancient Ireland: The Origins of the Irish from Neolithic Times to the Coming of the English*. Ivan R. Dee, 2012

McNeill, F. Marian. *The Silver Bough*. Birlinn, 2001

Moffat, Alistair. *The Faded Map: Lost Kingdoms of Scotland*. Birlinn, 2011

Newton, Michael. *A Handbook of the Scottish Gaelic World*. Four Courts Press, 2000

NicDhàna, Kathryn Price, Erynn Rowan Laurie, C. Lee Vermeers and Kym Lambert ní Dhoireann. *The CR FAQ: An Introduction to Celtic Reconstructionist Paganism.* River House Publishing, 2007. Also an extensive bibliography on Celtic Reconstructionism and Celtic Studies is found in *The CR FAQ: An Introduction to Celtic Reconstructionist Paganism - the Ever-Popular Reading Lists.* (www.paganachd.com/faq/readinglist.html)

Nichols, Ross. *The Book of Druidry.* The Aquarian Press/Harper Collins, 1992

O'Brien, Lora. *A Practical Guide to Irish Spirituality: Sli Aon Dhraoi.* Wolfpack Publishers, 2012

Ó Crualaoich, Gearóid. *The Book of the Cailleach: Stories of the Wise Woman Healer.* Cork University Press, 2006

O'Donohue, John. *Anam Cara: A Book of Celtic Wisdom.* Harper, 1998

O'Driscoll, Robert (editor). *Celtic Consciousness.* George Braziller, 1985

O Duinn, Sean. *In Search of the Awesome Mystery: Lore of Megalithic, Celtic and Christian Ireland.* Columba Press, 2012

O Duinn, Sean. *Where Three Streams Meet: Celtic Spirituality.* Columba Press, 2000

O'Hogain, Dáithí. *The Sacred Isle: Pre-Christian Religions in Ireland.* BOYE6, 1999

O'Kelly, Michael J. *Early Ireland: An Introduction to Irish Prehistory.* Cambridge University Press, 1989

Oliver, Neil. *A History of Ancient Britain.* Weidenfeld & Nicolson, 2012

Oliver, Neil. *A History of Scotland.* Phoenix, 2011

Orr, Emma Restall. *Living Druidry: Magical Spirituality for the Wild Soul.* Piatkus Books, 2004

Owen, Trefor M. *Welsh Folk Customs.* Gomer Press, 1987

Palmer, Martin and Nigel Palmer. *Sacred Britain: A Guide to the Sacred Sites and Pilgrim Routes of England, Scotland and Wales.* Piatkus, 1997

Paper, Jordan. *The Deities Are Many: A Polytheistic Theology.* State University of New York Press, 2005

Patterson, Nerys T. *Cattle Lords and Clansmen: The Social Structure of Early Ireland.* University of Notre Dame Press, 1994

Pemberton, Cintra. *Soulfaring: Celtic Pilgrimages Then and Now.* Morehouse Publishing, 1999

Pennick, Nigel. *Celtic Sacred Landscapes.* Thames & Hudson, 2000

Rees, Alwyn and Brinley Rees. *Celtic Heritage: Ancient Tradition in Ireland and Wales.* Thames & Hudson, 1989

Robb, Graham. *The Ancient Paths: Discovering the Lost Map of Celtic Europe.* Picador, 2013

Ross, Anne. *The Folklore of the Scottish Highlands.* Barnes & Noble, 1993

Rowan, Arthur. *The Lore of the Bard: A Guide to the Celtic & Druid Mysteries.* Llewellyn, 2003

Ryder, Lisabeth, PhD. DRUID. Facebook group for information and community. "*Druidry has become a vital and dynamic nature-based spirituality that is flourishing all over the world, and that unites our love of the Earth with our love of creativity and the arts. And flowing through all the exciting new developments in modern Druidism is the power of an ancient tradition: the love of land, sea and sky - the love of the Earth, our home.*" (www.facebook.com)

Stewart, R. J. *Power Within the Land: The Roots of Celtic and Underworld Traditions, Awakening the Sleepers and Regenerating the Earth.* Mercury Publishing, 1998

Stewart, R. J. *Earth Light: The Ancient Path to Transformation, Rediscovering the Wisdom of Celtic and Fairy Lore.* Element Books, 1992

Talboys, Graeme K. *Way of the Druid: The Renaissance of a Celtic Religion and its Relevance for Today.* O Books, 2005

Telyndru, Jhenah. *Avalon Within: A Sacred Journey of Myth, Mystery and Inner Wisdom.* Llewellyn Publications, 2010

Waddell, John. *Archaeology and Celtic Myth: An Exploration.* Four Courts Press, 2014

Walsh, Brian. *The Secret Commonwealth and the Fairy Belief Complex.* Xlibris Corporation, 2002

Westwood, Jennifer and Sophia Kingshill. *The Lore of Scotland: A Guide to Scottish Legends.* Random House UK, 2011

Whitsel, Montague. *Wellsprings of the Deer: A Contemporary Celtic Spirituality.* 1stBooks, 2002

Wright, Brian. *Brigid: Goddess, Druidess and Saint.* The History Press, 2009

Yeats, W. B. *The Celtic Twilight: Faerie and Folklore.* Dover Publications, 2011

Ecofeminism, Goddess Spirituality, Matriarchal Studies

Adovasio , J. M., Olga Soffer and Jake Page. *The Invisible Sex: Uncovering the True Roles of Women in Prehistory.* Left Coast Press, 2009

Anderson, Danica Borkovic. *Blood & Honey Icons: Biosemiotics & Bioculinary.* Kolo Press, 2012

Archer, Leonie, Sarah Fischler and Maria Wyke (editors). *Women in Ancient Societies.* Routledge, 1994

The Association for the Study of Women & Mythology (ASWM). Goddess Spirituality and Matriarchal Studies, art, resources, blog and symposia. (http://womenandmyth.org)

Birnbaum, Lucia Chiavola. *The Future Has an Ancient Heart: Legacy of Caring, Sharing, Healing and Vision from the Primordial African Mediterranean to Occupy Everywhere.* iUniverse, 2012

Budapest, Zsuzsanna E. *The Holy Book of Women's Mysteries.* Red Wheel/Weiser, 2007

Daly, Mary. *Beyond God the Father: Toward a Philosophy of Women's Liberation.* Beacon Press, 1993

Dashu, Max. *Women's Power* (DVD). Suppressed Histories Archives, 2008

Eyers, Pegi. "The Tenets of Goddess Spirituality (and a Cautionary Tale)." *She Rises: Why Goddess Feminism, Activism, or Spirituality? The Collective Writing Series.* Mago Books, 2015

Eyers, Pegi. "Our Struggles Are Not the Same: Inspired Solidarity with Turtle Island First Nations Women." *Whatever Works: Feminists of Faith Speak.* Trista Hendren and Patricia Kendall (editors), Girl God Books, 2015

Federici, Silvia. *Caliban and the Witch: Women, the Body and Primitive Accumulation.* Autonomedia, 2004

Foster, Judy and Marlene Derlet. *Invisible Women of Prehistory: Three Million Years of Peace, Six Thousand Years of War.* Spinifex Press, 2013

Gadon, Elinor W. *The Once & Future Goddess: A Symbol for Our Time*. HarperCollins, 1989

Gimbutas, Marija. *The Language of the Goddess*. Thames & Hudson, 2001

Gimbutas, Marija. *The Civilization of the Goddess: The World of Old Europe*. HarperCollins, 1992

Goettner-Abendroth, Heide. *Matriarchal Societies: Studies on Indigenous Cultures across the Globe*. Peter Lang International Academic Publishers, 2013

Goettner-Abendroth, Heide (editor). *Societies of Peace: Matriarchies Past, Present and Future*. Inanna Publications, 2009

Griffin, Susan. *Woman and Nature: The Roaring Inside Her*. Harper & Row, 1978

Hogan, Linda and Brenda Peterson (editors). *The Sweet Breathing of Plants: Women Writing on the Green World*. North Point Press, 2001

Merchant, Carolyn. *Earthcare: Women and the Environment*. Routledge, 1995

Pollack, Rachel. *The Body of the Goddess: Sacred Wisdom in Myth, Landscape and Culture*. Element Books, 2003

Sjöö, Monica and Barbara Mor. *The Great Cosmic Mother: Rediscovering the Religion of the Earth*. HarperCollins, 1991

Starhawk. *The Spiral Dance: A Rebirth of the Ancient Religion of the Great Goddess*. HarperCollins, 1999   (http://starhawk.org)

Stuckley, Johanna H.   *Women's Spirituality: Contemporary Feminist Approaches to Judaism, Christianity, Islam and Goddess Worship*. Inanna Publications, 2010

Tate, Karen. *Walking an Ancient Path: Rebirthing Goddess on Planet Earth*. O Books/ John Hunt Publishing, 2008

Warren, Karen J. *Ecofeminist Philosophy*. Rowman & Littlefield Publishers, 2000

Earth Justice and Eco-Ethics

Burdon, Peter. *Earth Jurisprudence: Private Property and the Environment*. Routledge, 2014

Burdon, Peter (editor). *Exploring Wild Law: The Philosophy of Earth Jurisprudence*. Wakefield Press, 2012

Cormac Cullinan. *Wild Law: A Manifesto for Earth Justice*. Chelsea Green Publishing, 2012

DesJardins, Joseph R. Ph.D. *Environmental Ethics: An Introduction to Environmental Philosophy*. Cengage Learning, 2012

Earth Law Alliance. Collaborative platform for multi-disciplinary sharing of ideas and successes in developing and using law to protect all life. Sowing new seeds in the development of *Earth Law* globally, and accelerating the implementation of governance systems that recognize the interconnectedness of all life. (http://earthlawyers.org)

Francione, Gary L. and Anna Charlton. *Eat Like You Care: An Examination of the Morality of Eating Animals*. Exempla Press, 2013

Global Alliance for the Rights of Nature. Worldwide movement building human communities that respect and defend the rights of nature; resources, news, activism, scholarship, membership, the *Rights of Nature Ethics Tribunal* and the *Global Rights of Nature Summit*. (http://therightsofnature.org)

Global Exchange, the Council of Canadians, The Pachamama Alliance and Fundacion Pachamama. *The Rights of Nature, The Case for a Universal Declaration on the Rights of Mother Earth.* The Global Exchange, 2011

Hawthorne, Mark. *Striking at the Roots: A Practical Guide to Animal Activism.* Changemakers Books, 2007

Higgins, Polly. *Earth is Our Business: Changing the Rules of the Game.* Shepheard-Walwyn, 2011

Higgins, Polly. *Eradicating Ecocide: Laws and Governance to Stop the Destruction of the Planet.* Shepheard-Walwyn, 2010

jones, pattrice. *The Oxen at the Intersection: A Collision.* Lantern Books, 2014

Maloney, Michelle and Peter Burdon (editors). *Wild Law in Practice.* Routledge, 2014

Nash, Roderick Frazier. *The Rights of Nature: A History of Environmental Ethics.* University of Wisconsin Press, 1989

Newkirk, Ingrid. *The PETA Practical Guide to Animal Rights: Simple Acts of Kindness to Help Animals in Trouble.* St. Martin's Griffin, 2010

Regan, Tom. *Empty Cages: Facing the Challenge of Animal Rights.* Rowman & Littlefield Publishers, 2013

Shiva, Vandana. *Earth Democracy: Justice, Sustainability and Peace.* South End Press, 2005

Singer, Peter. *Animal Liberation: The Definitive Classic of the Animal Movement.* Harper Perennial Modern Classics, 2009

Stone, Christopher D. *Should Trees Have Standing? Law, Morality, and the Environment.* Oxford University Press, 2010

"The Earth Charter," *The Earth Charter Initiative: Values and Principles to Foster a Sustainable Future.* (www.earthcharterinaction.org)

Wood, Mary Christina. *Nature's Trust: Environmental Law for a New Ecological Age.* Cambridge University Press, 2013

Gaia, Ecology, Animism, Ecomysticism, Ecopsychology

Anderlini-D'Onofrio, Serena. *Gaia and the New Politics of Love: Notes for a Poly Planet.* North Atlantic Books, 2009

Ausubel, Kenny and J.P. Harpignies (editors). *Nature's Operating Instructions: The True Biotechnologies.* Sierra Club Books, 2004

Ausubel, Kenny. *The Bioneers: Declarations of Interdependence.* Chelsea Green Publishing, 2001

Beresford-Kroeger, Diana. *The Global Forest: Forty Ways Trees Can Save Us.* Particular Books, 2011

Berry, Thomas. *The Dream of the Earth.* Counterpoint, 2006

Boring, Francesca Mason and Kenneth Edwin Sloan (editors). *Returning to Membership in Earth Community: Systemic Constellations with Nature.* Stream of Experience Productions, 2013

Buzzell, Linda and Craig Chalquist (editors). *Ecotherapy: Healing with Nature in Mind.* Sierra Club Books, 2009

Carson, Rachel. *The Sense of Wonder.* Open Road Media, 2011

Center for Ecozoic Societies: Seeking Well-being in all Life Communities. The mission of CES is to advance new ideas and ways of living for an ecological-cultural (ecozoic) age through publications, education, events, arts and action. *The Ecozoic Journal: Reflections on Life in an Ecological-Cultural Age.* (www.ecozoicsocieties.org)

Chalquist, Craig. *Rebearths: Conversations with a World Ensouled.* World Soul Books, 2010

Chalquist, Craig. *Terrapsychology: Reengaging the Soul of Place.* Spring Journal, 2007

Crombie, Robert Ogilvie. *Gentleman and the Faun: Encounters with Pan and the Elemental Kingdom.* Findhorn Press, 2009

Devereux, Paul. *Revisioning the Earth: A Guide to Opening the Healing Channels Between Mind and Nature.* Simon & Schuster, 1996.

Eisenberg, Evan. *The Ecology of Eden.* Knopf, 1998

The Findhorn Community. *The Findhorn Garden Story.* Findhorn Press, 2008

Graves, Julia. *The Language of Plants: A Guide to the Doctrine of Signatures.* Lindisfarne Books, 2012

Harvey, Graham. *Animism: Respecting the Living World.* Columbia University Press, 2005

Hückstädt, Bernd. *Gradido: Natural Economy of Life.* Lulu, 2013

Jensen, Derrick. *Listening to the Land: Conversations about Nature, Culture and Eros.* Chelsea Green Publishing, 2010

Kaza, Stephanie. *Mindfully Green: A Personal and Spiritual Guide to Whole Earth Thinking.* Shambhala, 2008

Kellert, Stephen R. *Birthright: People and Nature in the Modern World.* Yale University Press, 2012

Kumar, Satish. *Soil Soul Society: A New Trinity for Our Time.* Ivy Press, 2013

Lake, Osprey Orielle. *Uprisings for the Earth: Reconnecting Culture with Nature.* White Cloud Press, 2010

MacGregor, Catriona. *Partnering with Nature: The Wild Path to Reconnecting with the Earth.* Atria Books/Beyond Words, 2010

MacLean, Dorothy. *To Honor the Earth: Reflections on Living in Harmony with Nature.* HarperCollins, 1991

Maitland, Sara. *Gossip from the Forest.* Granta Books, 2012

Marley, Christopher. *Biophilia.* Harry N. Abrams, 2015

McCallum, Ian. *Ecological Intelligence: Rediscovering Ourselves in Nature.* Fulcrum Publishing, 2009

Merchant, Carolyn. *Radical Ecology: The Search for a Livable World.* Routledge, 2005

Orion Reader. *Wonder and Other Survival Skills: A Selection of Essays from Orion Magazine.* The Orion Society, 2012

Orr, David W., Michael K. Stone and Zenobia Barlow (editors). *Ecological Literacy: Educating Our Children for a Sustainable World.* Sierra Club Books, 2012

Pilgrim, Sarah and Jules N. Pretty (editors). *Nature and Culture: Rebuilding Lost Connections.* Routledge, 2013

Pipher, Mary. *The Green Boat: Reviving Ourselves in Our Capsized Culture.* Riverhead, 2013

Pogacnik, Marko. *Nature Spirits & Elemental Beings: Working with the Intelligence in Nature.* Findhorn Press, 2010

Princen, Thomas. *Treading Softly: Paths to Ecological Order.* The MIT Press, 2010

Resurgence & Ecologist Magazine. Promoting ecological sustainability, social justice and spiritual values. Founder Satish Kumar, also online home of *The Resurgence Trust.* (www.resurgence.org)

Rivers, Dennis. *The Cooperative University of the Great Turning: Resources for Imagining and Building a Green and Compassionate Civilization.* Scholar-activists, curriculum developers and mutual learners engaged with cultivating and nurturing compassion and wisdom, while working to protect the integrity of life on Earth. (www.univ-great-turning.org)

Roszak, Theodore. *The Voice of the Earth: An Exploration of Ecopsychology.* Phanes Press, 2001

Roszak, Theodore, Mary E. Gomes and Allen D. Kanner (editors). *Ecopsychology: Restoring the Earth, Healing the Mind.* Sierra Club Books, 1995

Sampson, Scott D. *How to Raise a Wild Child: The Art and Science of Falling in Love with Nature.* Houghton Mifflin Harcourt, 2015

Sanders, Scott Russell. *A Conservationist Manifesto.* Indiana University Press, 2009

Seed, John, Joanna Macy and Pat Fleming. *Thinking Like a Mountain: Toward a Council of All Beings.* New Catalyst Books, 2007

Selhub, Eva M. and Alan C. Logan. *Your Brain on Nature: The Science of Nature's Influence on Your Health, Happiness and Vitality.* Collins, 2013

Shaw, Martin. *A Branch from the Lightning Tree: Ecstatic Myth and the Grace of Wildness.* White Cloud Press, 2011

Shaw, Martin. *Scatterlings: Getting Claimed in the Age of Amnesia.* White Cloud Press, 2016

Small-Wright, Machaelle. *Perelandra Garden Workbook: A Complete Guide to Gardening with Nature Intelligences.* Perelandra, 1993

Snyder, Gary. *The Practice of the Wild.* Counterpoint, 2010

Sponsel, Leslie E. *Spiritual Ecology: A Quiet Revolution.* Praeger, 2012.

Taylor, Bron. *Dark Green Religion: Nature Spirituality and the Planetary Future.* University of California Press, 2009

Tracey, David. *The Earth Manifesto: Saving Nature with Engaged Ecology.* Rocky Mountain Books, 2013

Tweit, Susan J. *Walking Nature Home: A Life's Journey.* University of Texas Press, 2009

Uhl, Christopher. *Developing Ecological Consciousness: The End of Separation.* Rowman & Littlefield Publishers, 2013

Van Eyk McCain, Marian (editor). *GreenSpirit: Path to a New Consciousness.* Earth Books, 2010

Weston, Anthony. *Mobilizing the Green Imagination: An Exuberant Manifesto.* New Society Publishers, 2012

Wilson, Edward O. *Biophilia.* Harvard University Press, 1984

Worthy, Kenneth. *Invisible Nature: Healing the Destructive Divide Between People and the Environment.* Prometheus Books, 2013.

Earth Remediation, Re-landing, Rewilding

Chamberlin, J. Edward. *If This is Your Land, Where Are Your Stories? Re-Imagining Home and Sacred Space.* Pilgrim Press, 2004

Cohen, Michael J. *Reconnecting with Nature: Finding Wellness through Rebuilding Your Bond with the Earth.* Ecopress, 1997

Darwish, Leila. *Earth Repair: A Grassroots Guide to Healing Toxic and Damaged Landscapes.* New Society Publishers, 2013

Durning, Alan Thein. *This Place on Earth: Home and the Practice of Permanence.* Sasquatch Books, 1996

Foreman, Dave. *Rewilding North America: A Vision for Conservation in the 21st Century.* Island Press, 2013

Elpel, Thomas J. *Participating in Nature: Wilderness Survival and Primitive Living Skills.* HOPS Press, 2009

Fraser, Caroline. *Rewilding the World: Dispatches from the Conservation Revolution.* Metropolitan Books, 2014

Glotfelty, Cheryll and Eve Quesnel (editors). *The Biosphere and the Bioregion: Essential Writings of Peter Berg.* Routledge, 2014

Hopkins, Alix W. *Groundswell: Stories of Saving Places, Finding Community.* Trust for Public Land, 2005

Jackson, Wes. *Becoming Native to This Place.* Schumacher Center for a New Economics, 1993

Lerner, Rebecca. *Dandelion Hunter: Foraging the Urban Wilderness.* Lyons Press, 2013

MacFarlane, Robert. *The Wild Places.* Penguin Books, 2007

Monbiot, George. *Feral: Searching for Enchantment on the Frontiers of Rewilding.* Penguin Books, 2013

Mudge, Ken and Steve Gabriel. *Farming the Woods: An Integrated Permaculture Approach to Growing Food and Medicinals in Temperate Forests.* Chelsea Green Publishing, 2014

Ohlson, Kristin. *The Soil Will Save Us: How Scientists, Farmers, and Foodies Are Healing the Soil to Save the Planet.* Rodale, 2014

Olson, Miles. *Unlearn, Rewild: Earth Skills, Ideas and Inspiration for the Future Primitive.* New Society Publishers, 2012

Rewild.com: Creating New Cultures Inspired by Ancestral Lifeways. Resources and interactive forum for building rewilding community. (http://rewild.com)

Rewilding Europe: Making Europe a Wilder Place. Working to make Europe a wilder place, a continent that allows for more space for wildlife, wilderness and natural processes, because this is good for man and nature alike. (www.rewildingeurope.com)

The Rewilding Institute. Developing and promoting ideas and strategies to advance continental-scale conservation in North America, particularly the need for large carnivores and permeable landscape for their movement, and to offer a bold, practically achievable, and hopeful vision for the future of wild Nature and human civilization in North America. (http://rewilding.org)

Rezendes, Paul. *The Wild Within: Adventures in Nature and Animal Teachings.* Jeremy P. Tarcher/Putnam, 1998

Sale, Kirkpatrick. *Dwellers in the Land: The Bioregional Vision.* University of Georgia Press, 2000

Suzuki, David. *The Sacred Balance: Rediscovering Our Place in Nature.* Greystone Books, 2007

Thompson, Mary Reynolds. *Reclaiming the Wild Soul: How Earth's Landscapes Restore Us to Wholeness.* White Cloud Press, 2014

Wescott, David. *Primitive Technology: A Book of Earth Skills.* Gibbs Smith, 2001

Wild Abundance: Teaching Practical Skills for Living Closer To the Earth. Educational programming, workshops and apprenticeships for eco-homesteading, self-sufficiency, organic gardening, wild food and medicine, natural building, permaculture, living off-grid, survival adventures, primitive skills and annual Firefly Gathering. *"We believe that it is possible for humans to live in balance with the web of life."* (www.wildabundance.net)

Young, Jon, Evan McGown and Ellen Haas. *Coyote's Guide to Connecting with Nature.* Owlink Media, 2010

Permaculture, Localvore, Sustainable Community

Ackerman-Leist, Philip. *Rebuilding the Foodshed: How to Create Local, Sustainable and Secure Food Systems.* Chelsea Green Publishing, 2013

Ausubel. Kenny. *Seeds of Change, The Living Treasure: The Passionate Story of the Growing Movement to Restore Biodiversity and Revolutionize the Way We Think About Food.* Harper San Francisco, 1994

Bollier, David. *Think Like a Commoner: A Short Introduction to the Life of the Commons.* New Society Publishers, 2014

Brown, Doug. *Being Is Enough: Collective Self-Help for a Sustainable World.* University Press of America, 2005

Chamberlin, Shaun. *The Transition Timeline: For a Local, Resilient Future.* Chelsea Green Publishing, 2009

Christian, Diana Leafe. *Finding Community: How to Join an Ecovillage or Intentional Community.* New Society Publishers, 2007

Clark, Susan. *Slow Democracy: Rediscovering Community, Bringing Decision Making Back Home.* Chelsea Green Publishing, 2012

Commons Transition: Policy Proposals and Ideas to Implement a Social Knowledge Economy. An environmentally-grounded mode of societal organization based on the commons, and the collaborative stewardship of shared resources. Peer-to-peer dynamics, property and governance address the needs of civil society and the environment to create an egalitarian, just and environmentally stable society. (http://commonstransition.org)

Danaher, Kevin and Alisa Gravitz. *Green Festival Reader: Fresh Ideas from Agents of Change.* Paradigm Publishers, 2008

Elgin, Duane. *Voluntary Simplicity: Toward a Way of Life that is Outwardly Simple, Inwardly Rich.* Quill, 1981

Fosket, Jennifer and Laura Mamo. *Living Green: Communities that Sustain.* New Society Publishers, 2009

Global Peace Initiative of Women/GPIW (editors). *Sacred Seed: a Collection of Essays.* The Golden Sufi Center, 2014

Greer, John Michael. *Green Wizardry: Conservation, Solar Power, Organic Gardening, and other Hands-on Skills from the Appropriate Tech Toolkit.* New Society Publishers, 2013

Hoelting, Kurt. *The Circumference of Home: One Man's Yearlong Quest for a Radically Local Life.* Da Capo Press, 2010

Holmgren, David. *Permaculture: Principles and Pathways Beyond Sustainability.* Holmgren Design Services, 2002

Hopkins, Rob. *The Transition Handbook: From Oil Dependency to Local Resilience.* UIT Cambridge, 2008

Jackson, Hildur and Karen Svensson. *Ecovillage Living: Restoring the Earth and Her People.* UIT Cambridge, 2002

Litfin, Karen T. *Ecovillages: Lessons for Sustainable Community.* Polity, 2014

Menzies, Heather. *Reclaiming the Commons for the Common Good.* New Society Publishers, 2014

Miller, Daphne. *Farmacology: Total Health from the Ground Up.* William Morrow, 2013

Mollison, Bill. *Permaculture: a Designers Manual.* Tagari Publications, 1988

Permaculture: Practical Solutions for Self Reliance. Resources, news, reviews, books, tools, webinars, courses and *Permaculture Magazine.* (www.permaculture.co.uk)

Ray, Janisse. *The Seed Underground: A Growing Revolution to Save Food.* Chelsea Green Publishing, 2012

Resilience: Building a World of Resilient Communities. Information source and network of action-oriented groups, scholarship, articles and practical skills for the world transition away from fossil fuels toward sustainable, resilient communities. Post Carbon Institute. (www.resilience.org)

Reynolds, Richard. *On Guerilla Gardening.* Bloomsbury USA, 2008

Shein, Christopher with Julie Thompson. *The Vegetable Gardener's Guide to Permaculture: Creating an Edible Ecosystem.* Timber Press, 2013

Shiva, Vandana (editor). *Manifestos on the Future of Food and Seed.* South End Press, 2007

Soler, Ivette. *The Edible Front Yard: the Mow-Less, Grow-More Plan for a Beautiful, Bountiful Garden.* Timber Press, 2011

Wittman, Hannah Kay, Annette Aurelie Desmarais and Nettie Wiebe (editors). *Food Sovereignty: Reconnecting Food, Nature and Community.* Food First Books, 2010

New Economy

Alperovitz, Gar. *America Beyond Capitalism: Reclaiming Our Wealth, Our Liberty, and Our Democracy.* Democracy Collaborative Press, 2011

Botsman, Rachel and Roo Rogers. *What's Mine Is Yours: The Rise of Collaborative Consumption.* HarperBusiness, 2010 (www.collaborativeconsumption.com)

Boyle, Mark. *The Moneyless Man: A Year of Freeconomic Living.* Oneworld Publications, 2010

Community Exchange System. Online global network and community-based registry for exchanging and sharing goods and services to create a healthy, sustainable world. (www.community-exchange.org)

Cunningham, Storm. *The Restoration Economy: The Greatest New Growth Frontier.*
Berrett-Koehler Publishers, 2002

Daly, Herman E. and Kenneth N. Townsend (editors). *Valuing the Earth: Economics,*
Ecology, Ethics. MIT Press, 1993

Eisler, Riane. *The Real Wealth of Nations: Creating a Caring Economics.*
Berrett-Koehler, 2007

Estill, Lyle. *Small is Possible: Life in a Local Economy.* New Society Publishers, 2008

FairCoop: the Earth Cooperative for a Fair Economy. Open global cooperative to reduce
economic and social inequality and contribute to the commons of a new global economic
system. (https://fair.coop)

Ivanko, John and Lisa Kivirist. *Ecopreneuring: Putting Purpose and the Planet before*
Profits. New Society Publishers, 2008

Luna, Mira. "How to Start a Community Currency." *Utne Reader – Utne Blogs – Politics,*
October 17, 2012 (www.utne.com)

Matofska, Benita. *The People Who Share.* UK-based non-profit to mainstream the
Sharing Economy with a global campaign to raise awareness, initiate action and host
an annual Global Sharing Day.   (www.thepeoplewhoshare.com)

McDonough, William and Michael Braungart. *The Upcycle: Beyond Sustainability--*
Designing for Abundance.   North Point Press, 2013

McKibben, Bill.   *Deep Economy: The Wealth of Communities and the Durable Future.*
Henry Holt and Company, 2007

Mommaerts, Marissa and Ken White. *Weaving the Community Resilience and New*
Economy Movement: Voices and Reflections from the Field. Post Carbon Institute, 2014

New Economy Coalition. We support a just transition to a new economy that enables
both thriving communities and ecological health. (www.neweconomy.net)

North, Peter. *Local Money: How to Make It Happen in Your Community.* UIT
Cambridge, 2010

The Pollinator Project: Seeding Projects that Change the World. Providing seed grants
to social change visionaries and changemakers. (https://thepollinationproject.org)

Research & Degrowth (R&D). Academic association dedicated to research, training,
awareness-raising and events related to *Degrowth.*   (www.degrowth.org)

Rowe, Jonathan with Bill McKibben, Peter Barnes and David Bollier. *Our Common*
Wealth: The Hidden Economy That Makes Everything Else Work. Berrett-Koehler
Publishers, 2013

Rustrum, Chelsea, Gabriel Stempinski and Alexandra Liss. *It's a Shareable Life: A*
Practical Guide on Sharing. Shareable Life, 2014

Sharable. Online news, articles and connection hub for the common good, community
resilience and the transformation to the Sharing Economy. (www.shareable.net)

Shuman, Michael H. *Going Local: Creating Self-Reliant Communities in a Global Age.*
The Free Press, 1998

Slow Money: A Local and Global Gathering on Food, Investing and Culture. Social
change, food security, sustainability and philanthropy. (https://slowmoney.org)

Vaughan, Genevieve. *Women and the Gift Economy: A Radically Different Worldview*
is Possible. Inanna Publications, 2007 (http://gift-economy.com)

Wann, David.   *Simple Prosperity: Finding Real Wealth in a Sustainable Lifestyle.*
St. Martin's Griffin, 2007